Contents

About this book

In the three years since the 12th edition of this book was published a spate of new and amending legislation, heralded by the Government's *Fairness at Work* White Paper and a number of EU Directives, has expanded the right of employees (and workers) and the duties and responsibilities of employers in a variety of areas.

As might be expected, this millennium edition of *Waud's Employment Law* has been updated to include new and amending legislation relating to • human rights • trade union recognition • part-time workers • gender reassignment • parental leave • protection for 'whistleblowers' • the payment of tax credits by employers • fixed term contracts • posted workers • data protection • time off for dependants • European Works Councils • dismissal during 'protected industrial action' • enhanced maternity rights • accompaniment at disciplinary and grievance hearings • increased compensation for unfair dismissal • the 48-hour week • the national minimum wage • paid annual holidays • time off for study or training • rest breaks and rest periods • a reduction in the qualifying period for unfair dismissal and additional maternity leave • workplace protection for children and young persons; and so on.

Those readers who deal frequently with employment-related issues should first read Chapter 1, and then glance through the other chapters to acquire a cursory knowledge of points for further reference. The book is fully cross-referenced throughout and there is a comprehensive index. Points of law are illustrated by decided cases, while abbreviations (see below) are used to identify relevant legislation.

Gender bias in the English language

Author's Note: Gender-bias in the English language has been the subject of debate for many years and is likely to be so for many years to come. Efforts to eliminate that bias have been largely unsuccessful as successive governments and their departments have long since acknowledged when drafting legislation and producing guidance notes and associated codes of practice.

The fact that our language has no common-sex personal pronoun in the singular does not, in my view, excuse the ungrammatical use of *their* in contexts (as Fowler* put it) that call logically for *his* or *his or her*. I am likewise unconvinced that the pronoun *it* is appropriate when referring to an *employer* already mentioned. Overuse of *he or she* (or *his or hers*), especially in paragraphs in which the nouns *employee* and *employer* compete for space is not only clumsy, but irritating and confusing, as is the practice, preferred by some authors, of repeating the nouns *employer* and *employee* in the same sentence or paragraph, seemingly to avoid the tedium of having to select a pronoun at all.

My solution (with apologies to those who do not share my views) is to use the masculine singular pronoun throughout the book when alluding to an *employer* and the phrases *he (or she)* or *his (or hers)* (once, and once only) in each paragraph in which the noun *employee* first appears. My intention in using these less than satisfactory devices is (a) to produce a readable text; (b) to reassure readers that I am not unaware of the problems associated with gender bias in the English language; and (c) to remind them, as if they needed reminding, that employment legislation applies equally to men and to women.

* *Fowler's Modern English Usage*, 2nd Edition (*Oxford University Press*)

Statutes, Regulations and Orders

Statutes, Regulations and Orders referred to only occasionally in this book (eg the Tax Credits Act 1999, or the Part-time Workers (Prevention of Less Favourable Treatment) Regulations 2000) are given their full titles in the accompanying text. The more dominant statutes and Regulations (such as the Employment Rights Act 1996) – which feature in almost every chapter of the book – are accorded the following abbreviations:

DDA 1995	Disability Discrimination Act 1995
EPA 1970	Equal Pay Act 1970
ERA 1996	Employment Rights Act 1996
ERA 1999	Employment Relations Act 1999
ETA 1996	Employment Tribunals Act 1996
ETCRP Regs	Employment Tribunals (Constitution & Rules of Procedure) Regulations 1993
HASAWA 1974	Health & Safety at Work etc Act 1974
HRA 1998	Human Rights Act 1998
ROOA 1974	Rehabilitation of Offenders Act 1974
RRA 1976	Race Relations Act 1976
SDA 1975	Sex Discrimination Act 1975
TICER 1999	Transnational Information & Consultation of Employees Regulations 1999

| TULRA 1992 | Trade Union & Labour Relations (Consolidation) Act 1992 |
| TUPE Regs | Transfer of Undertakings (Protection of Employment) Regulations 1981 |

Other abbreviations

The abbreviations used in this book (notably in cited cases) have the meanings given in the right-hand column below:

Courts

HL	House of Lords
PC	Privy Council
CA	Court of Appeal
CS	Court of Session (Scotland)
ChD	Chancery Division of High Court
QB	Queen's Bench Division of High Court
QBD	*ditto*
DC	Divisional Court of High Court
EAT	Employment Appeal Tribunal
NIRC	National Industrial Relations Court
ECJ	European Court of Justice
ECHR	European Court of Human Rights
ET	Employment Tribunal

Law Reports

AC	Appeal Cases
AER	All England Reports
ChD	Law Reports, Chancery Division
CMLR	Common Market Law Reports
ECR	European Court Reports
ER	English Reports
ICR	Industrial Cases Reports
IRLR	Industrial Relations Law Reports
ITR	Industrial Tribunal Reports
LGR	Local Government Reports
TLR	Times Law Reports
QB/QBD	Law Reports, Queen's Bench Division
WLR	Weekly Law Reports

1

The law at work

GENERAL INFORMATION

1.1
The law governing the rights and duties of employers and employees is derived from three sources: the 'common law', UK legislation (mostly statutes and subordinate legislation introduced since 1963), and European Community Law. It is also influenced by the European Convention on Human Rights, recently given further effect in the UK by the Human Rights Act 1998 which came into force on 2 October 2000 (as to which, please see para 1.31 below and Chapter 26).

1.2
This subject has become extremely complicated, not least because of the flood of decisions flowing from UK courts, the European Court of Justice (ECJ) and (to a lesser extent) from the European Court of Human Rights. Faced with this array of law, some of it highly technical, what is the ordinary employer or worker to do when faced with an employment problem? He (or she) may not want to incur the expense or go to the trouble of consulting a solicitor. And yet, if the wrong decision is made, the consequences can be very costly.

1.3
The purpose of this book is to explain the law in simple terms. It cannot hope to be more than a guide for employers in what is becoming an increasingly complex area of the law. Where the law is derived from Acts (or statutes), the intentions of Parliament are explained, as well as the principles to be applied. Included also are summaries of the decisions of the tribunals and courts. New legislation – supplementing, revoking or amending earlier statutes, regulations and orders – is appearing with almost undignified frequency. The reader will be familiar with (or, at the very least, be aware of) the National Minimum Wage Regulations 1998, the

Maternity & Parental Leave, etc Regulations 1999, the Public Interest Disclosure Act 1998, and of the many provisions of the Employment Relations Act 1999 (most of which are now in force). The 'Posted Workers' Directive (unfamiliar to many, as there was no need for UK implementing legislation) came into force on 16 December 1999; the Transnational Information & Consultation of Employees Regulations 1999, on 1 February 2000 ('European Works Councils'); and the Data Protection Act 1998, on 1 March 2000 – the implications of which are summarised elsewhere in this book.

1.4
The impetus is likely to be maintained as even more European Union (EU) legislation appears. Lord Denning MR saw the problem in this way: '[W]hen we come to matters with a European element, the Treaty is like an incoming tide. It flows into the estuaries and up the rivers. It cannot be held back. Parliament has decreed that the Treaty is henceforward to form part of our law. It is equal in force to any statute. The draftsmen of our statutes have striven to express themselves with the utmost exactness. They have tried to foresee all possible consequences and provide for them. They have foregone brevity. How different is this Treaty! It lays down general principles. It expresses its aims and purposes. All in sentences of moderate length and commendable style. But it lacks precision... All the way through the Treaty there are gaps and lacunae. They have to be filled in by the judges, or by Regulations or directives. It is the European way' (*H P Bulmer Ltd v J Bollinger SA* [1974] Ch 401, CA).

PRESENT POSITION

1.5
Employment law up to 1963 was almost exclusively derived from the 'common law' – that is to say, the law made by judges over the centuries (see Chapter 8). It developed under the somewhat arcane heading of 'master and servant' and, in most respects, was clearly unsuited to the needs of the second half of the 20th century.

1.6
Parliament first introduced statutory employment rights over 35 years ago, when it passed the Contracts of Employment Act 1963. Under

that Act, employees were entitled to be given written particulars of the terms and conditions of their employment. They were entitled also to receive (and were required to give) a minimum period of notice to terminate their contracts of employment. Both these requirements are currently to be found in the Employment Rights Act 1996. Since 1963, there has been a deluge of legislation (much of it flowing from EC directives) covering almost every aspect of the relationship between employer and employee – from dismissal, redundancy, sex discrimination, equal pay, etc to the right of employees to be allowed paid time off work in prescribed circumstances. There is almost no aspect of the employment relationship that is not now affected by one Act of Parliament or another.

1.7
Some of the law relating to the older common law claims, such as 'wrongful dismissal' (see Chapter 8), which were formerly the exclusive province of the civil courts, can now be heard in the tribunals. Although common law claims have fallen away dramatically in recent years, not all are covered by statute law (*Source*: Employment Tribunals Extension of Jurisdiction [England & Wales] Order 1994, and the Employment Tribunals Extension of Jurisdiction [Scotland] Order 1994).

TRIBUNALS OR COURTS – WHICH COURSE TO FOLLOW?

1.8
Nowadays, most complaints arising out of an employer's failure to acknowledge the statutory rights of employees are brought before the employment tribunals, where the proceedings are faster and less cumbersome. An employee may have little to gain by pursuing his (or her) claim before the civil courts, unless the compensation or damages sought are much higher than the tribunals are empowered to award; or unless there is some other aspect of the contractual relationship (eg breach of a restrictive covenant) which the tribunals are not yet empowered to deal with. The reader will note the reference to 'employment tribunals' rather than 'industrial tribunals'. The change of name was effected on 1 August 1998 by section 1 of the Employment Rights (Dispute Resolution) Act 1998, per Commencement No. 1 Order 1998 (SI 1998/1658).

Merits of each case

1.9

It should be borne in mind at this early stage that employment tribunals are not bound by their own decisions. The decision of a tribunal in a similar case elsewhere may appear to contradict a ruling by another tribunal in the same or a different location on almost identical facts (although the circumstances and dynamics of each case will never be identical). A tribunal comprises a legally qualified chairman and two lay members representing both sides of industry and having identifiable skills and experience in one or more aspects of the employer–employee relationship (such as race relations). There is inevitably a 'grey area' in which one tribunal or court will take one view, and another, the opposite. Badly drafted legislation has been responsible for many seemingly strange decisions.

1.10

Whereas one witness may impress, another giving identical evidence may not. This problem alone can (and has been known to) affect the outcome of a tribunal hearing.

RELATIONSHIP BETWEEN COMMON AND STATUTE LAW

1.11

When ascertaining the contractual rights and obligations of employers and employees, a tribunal will consider the 'common law' aspects of the relationship and the statutory provisions that apply to the particular facts. A lorry driver may, for instance, complain to an employment tribunal that he had been unfairly dismissed for refusing to drive on the Continent, contending that (under his contract of employment) he was only required to drive within the UK. Before determining the fairness or otherwise of the dismissal itself, the tribunal will look to the express and any implied terms in the driver's contract to establish whether he might on occasion (or as a matter of course) have been legitimately required to drive outside the UK. In other words, the ordinary common law canons of construction would be used to determine the extent of the driver's duties.

1.12

Some terms in a contract of employment will be *express*; others will be implied. The express terms will not generally cause any difficulty, so long as they are clear and unequivocal. The *implied* terms may be more difficult to establish. It is in this latter area that many disputes and differences of opinion will arise. Where there *is* ambiguity in a 'contract of employment' or in any accompanying or associated document (works handbook, collective agreement, policy document, etc) the general rule is that the ambiguity will be construed against the party seeking to rely on it. For instance, an employer facing a complaint of unfair dismissal brought by an employee who was sacked for refusing to transfer from one branch of the company to another, relying on a mobility clause in the employment contract which is not wholly clear, is likely to find that the lack of clarity will not work to his advantage (*Litster v Fram Gerrard Ltd* [1973] IRLR 302, NIRC).

Effects of difference

1.13

Under the common law, an employee has no legal redress if he (or she) is summarily dismissed for gross misconduct (or serious insubordination). An employee who repudiates his employment contract thereby forfeits any and all rights under that contract. However, under the Employment Rights Act 1996, such a fundamental breach of contract would be one of the factors (albeit an important factor) which a tribunal will take into account when determining the fairness or otherwise of an employee's dismissal. A failure by an employer to follow the correct procedure (eg by not investigating the relevant circumstances fully, or by refusing to allow an employee to explain) could lead to a finding of unfair dismissal, although any award of compensation is likely to be reduced to the extent that the employee had contributed to his (or her) own dismissal (see Chapter 5, paras 5.147 to 5.155).

Interpretation of words and phrases

1.14

Employment (and other) statutes, regulations and orders contain many words and phrases that have particular meanings under the common law. The *Interpretation Provisions* in a statute will sometimes, but not always, give the very same meanings to those words and phrases. For example, the word 'employee' might well be defined in different ways in different statutes, but the same common law tests will be applied to determine the true nature of the employment relationship. Is a person an 'employee' or a 'self-employed' person? (see Chapter 2, paras 2.1 to 2.15).

Common law concepts

1.15

Some common law concepts have been imported into the statutes. For example, the Employment Rights Act 1996 acknowledges the common law right of an employee to resign (with or without notice) if the employer's conduct is so gross as to amount to fundamental breach of the employment contract. One example of this would be an employer's unilateral decision to make a substantial cut in an employee's rate of pay. Under the 1996 Act, an employee left with no option but to quit in such circumstances may complain to an employment tribunal that he (or she) had been unfairly and 'constructively dismissed'. When examining the rights and wrongs of the situation, the tribunal would apply the normal common law rules to determine whether the employer's conduct was indeed tantamount to a fundamental breach of contract (going to the very root of the employment relationship) sufficient to justify the employee's decision to leave (see Chapter 8, paras 8.11 to 8.15).

1.16

Some common law rules will apply in other situations. Under both the common law and the statutory provisions, an employee who has been dismissed (or forced to resign) is nonetheless required to 'mitigate any loss' (see Chapter 2, paras 2.61 to 2.68) resulting from that dismissal or resignation; and the same tests would be applied in each case (*Gallear v J F Watson & Son Ltd* [1979] IRLR 306, EAT) (*Source*: ERA 1996, s. 123(4)).

1.17

However, the common law and statute law *do* part company in some situations. Under the common law a purported dismissal, which is in breach of contract, is void and ineffective unless the employer's repudiation is accepted by the innocent party (see Chapter 8, para 8.23). However, because the right to receive remuneration and the obligation to render services are mutually dependent, it is rare that the contract can remain alive except for very limited purposes (*Gunton v Richmond-upon-Thames BC* [1980] ICR 755, CA). Under statute law, a dismissal takes effect on the date specified by the employer. However, under the 'deeming provisions' of the Employment Rights Act 1996, the 'effective date of termination' of an employee's contract of employment may, for certain purposes, be deemed to occur on a date later than that on the employment actually ended (see Chapter 3, paras 3.15 to 3.26). The result is that there may be one date for dismissal under the common law and quite another under the 1996 Act (*Robert Cort & Son Ltd v Charman* [1981] ICR 816, EAT and *R v East Berkshire Health Authority, ex parte Walsh* [1984] ICR 743, CA). The common law rule, that ambiguous terms in a contract or document will be construed against the party seeking to rely on them, also applies in tribunal proceedings. The wording in a contract must be sufficiently precise before the term will be enforceable (*Litster v Fram Gerard Ltd* [1973] IRLR 302, NIRC).

LEGISLATION – HOW AFFECTED

Parliament

1.18
The primary source of employment legislation is to be found in statutes such as the Trade Union & Labour Relations (Consolidation) Act 1992, the Employment Rights Act 1996, the Equal Pay Act 1970 (and a variety of others), and in their subordinate regulations and orders. Other substantial changes in UK domestic legislation will be prompted in the main by relevant EC directives (under the European Communities Act 1972).

Laws made under the Treaty of Rome

1.19
Articles in the Treaty of Rome and EC regulations are binding and directly enforceable in the tribunals and courts of the United Kingdom. They have primacy over UK domestic legislation. If there

is any conflict or inconsistency, Community law takes precedence (*Shields v E Coombes (Holdings) Ltd* [1978] ITR 473, CA) (*Source*: European Communities Act 1972, s. 2(1))

1.20
If the UK refuses fails to import Treaty Articles into its domestic legislation an individual adversely affected by the omission can rely directly on an Article (in the Treaty) in the UK's national courts and, ultimately, before the European Court of Justice (ECJ). If the relevant Treaty Article relates to employment law, it can be enforced in an employment tribunal even though the tribunals have no express or statutory authority to do so (*Pickstone & Others v Freemans plc* [1987] ICR 867, CA – upheld on appeal by the House of Lords on other grounds). When this occurs, the tribunals must adopt procedural rules that are not less favourable than similar provisions in UK domestic law. Further, they must not be so unreasonable as to render it virtually impossible to exercise rights conferred by Community law (see para 1. 22 below) (*Livingstone v Hepworth Refractories Ltd* [1992] ICR 287, EAT).

1.21
The Council of the European Communities issues so-called 'directives' to Member States – after considering (i) proposals from the Commission, (ii) the opinion of the European Parliament and (iii) the views of the Economic and Social Committee. The Member States must integrate those directives into their domestic laws within the time limits (usually one or two years) prescribed by the directives themselves. Several such directives have already been incorporated into UK law, mostly in the form of statutory regulations and orders.

1.22
If a Member State fails to import an EC directive into its domestic legislation, any person employed by an 'organ (or 'emanation') of the State' can rely directly on that directive before the UK courts (which may include a reference to the ECJ) – provided it is sufficiently clear, precise and unconditional. Furthermore, any time limits imposed by the general law for pursuing a complaint or claim before a tribunal or court do not apply until such time as the Member State has implemented that directive (*vide Marshall v Southampton & SW Hampshire Area Health Authority (Teaching)* [1986] ICR 335, ECJ and *Emmott v Minister for Social Welfare & Another* [1991] IRLR 387, ECJ).

1.23

The European Court of Justice has ruled that the term 'organ of the State' applies to any organisation or body, whatever its legal form, which (a) is responsible for providing a public service under the control of the State, (b) has special powers for that purpose, and (c) is not available to the ordinary employer (*Foster & Others v British Gas plc* [1991] ICR 84, ECJ, [1991] ICR 463, HL). Before privatisation, British Gas was held to be an 'organ of the State' (a) because its monopoly powers were conferred by Parliament, (b) because its role was to provide a public service, (c) because it was generally controlled by the State, and (d) because the Government were entitled to its surplus revenues (*Foster & Others v British Gas plc* [1991] ICR 463, HL). Rolls-Royce, on the other hand, was held *not* to be an organ of the state even though Crown nominees held 100 per cent of the company's shares and its trading links with the State were important to the defence of the realm (*Doughty v Rolls-Royce plc* [1992] IRLR 126, CA).

1.24

Private sector employees can rely only on UK domestic law. They may be able to achieve the same result as persons employed by an organ of the State, but the route is more circuitous. In short, they would need to persuade the UK courts to refer a case to the European Court for a declaration as to whether the obligations emanate from the Treaty. If there *is* a ruling in their favour, the UK courts will enforce it (see Chapter 28, paras 28.41 to 28.43) (*Worringham v Lloyds Bank plc* [1982] ICR 299, CA).

1.25

The European Court has ruled that where a Member State fails to implement a directive:

- which confers rights on individuals;

- whose contents are clearly identifiable; and

there is a causal link between the Member State's failure to implement the directive and the damage suffered by the person affected, the State in question will be liable for the loss. In short, an individual can sue the government of a Member State for the damages he or she has sustained as a direct consequence of the Member State's failure to implement a directive by importing it into its domestic legislation. Procedures for recovering that loss must not be more onerous than those relating to any similar action for damages under the national law (*Francovich & Others v Italian Republic* [1992] IRLR 84, ECJ).

1.26
Some directives are promulgated to facilitate the practical application of duties imposed by the Articles of the Treaty of Rome. As such, they may be relied upon directly in actions against employers (*Duke v GEC Reliance Ltd* [1988] ICR 339, HL). The European Court tends to adopt a generous approach to the interpretation of the Treaty and directives, especially where it may result in remedying an obvious injustice. But where rights are conferred, they must be clear and precise (not conditional or qualified) before they can be relied upon. In recent times, UK courts and tribunals have adopted a similar approach when interpreting the very general phrases found in the Treaty. But, if there is a direct conflict between UK domestic legislation and any EC directive which requires legislation before it becomes effective, a private sector employee cannot rely on that directive. However, the courts and tribunals are not permitted to distort the meaning of a statute so as to enforce a directive which is incompatible with it (*Duke v GEC Reliance Ltd* [1988] ICR 339, HL).

1.27
If UK legislation is sufficiently widely drawn to be capable of two (or more) interpretations, then that which accords with European Community law must be followed (*Pickstone & Others v Freemans plc* [1988] ICR 697, HL). This means that words and phrases have 'to be construed, if they are reasonably capable of bearing such a meaning, as intended, to carry out the obligation and not be inconsistent with it' (per Lord Diplock in *Garland v British Rail Engineering Ltd* [1982] ICR 434, HL). Consequently, it is always necessary to consider the European law in many employment problems (*Von Colson & Kamann v Nordrhein Westphphalia, The Times*, 25 April 1984, ECJ).

1.28
The present position is still uncertain because the European Court has ruled that, where an EC directive has direct effect on a national

of a Member State, then the national court is obliged to interpret national law so as to comply with that directive (*Verholen & Others v Sociale Verzekeringsbank Amsterdam* [1992] IRLR 39, ECJ). This duty goes further than what had been said in an earlier decision, namely '... in applying the national law... the national court called on to interpret it is obliged to do so wherever possible in the light of the text and of the [purpose] of the directive in order to achieve the result envisaged' (*Marleasing SA v La Comercial Internacional de Alimentacion SA* [1990] ECR 4153, ECJ). Further a court, *of its own motion*, should apply it.

1.29

It has been stated by the European Court of Justice that national rules should not be interpreted in such a way as to hamper the purpose of the European law. So where an English court had decided that, under English law, an interim injunction could not be ordered against the State, the European Court decreed that the rule should be abandoned (*R v Secretary of State for Transport ex parte Factortame Ltd & Others* [1990] 3 CMLR 375, ECJ).

1.30

An important consequence of a party being able to bring a claim directly under Community law is that there may be no time limits for doing so. Judicial pronouncements have pointed out the desirability of bringing time limits into line. The European Court of Justice has stated that so far as its rulings are concerned, it alone may decide on any time limitation (*Stevens & Others v Bexley Health Authority* [1989] ICR 224, EAT and *Burra & Others v Belgium State & City of Liege, The Times*, 4 April 1988, ECJ).

European Convention for the Protection of Human Rights & Fundamental Freedoms

1.31

In 1953, the United Kingdom ratified the *European Convention for the Protection of Human Rights and Fundamental Freedoms*. Since 1959, when the European Court of Human Rights (ECHR) was established, the UK has submitted to the court's jurisdiction. The Government has since given 'further effect' to the rights and freedoms guaranteed under that Convention with the enactment of the Human Rights Act 1998, which came into force on 2 October 2000. Under the 1998 Act, UK 'public authorities' are duty-bound to act in a way that is compatible with a Convention right. The tribunals and courts, for their part, must read and give effect to existing UK legislation in a way that is compatible with the Convention rights – 'so far as it is possible to do so'. For further particulars, please refer to Chapter 26.

DIVISION OF WORK

Employment tribunals

1.32
The jurisdiction of the employment tribunals is limited to those cases where jurisdiction is conferred on it by statute (but see para 1.20 above). Most of the tribunals' workload relates to unfair dismissal and redundancy claims and complaints brought under (or by virtue of):

- the Equal Pay Act 1970;

- the Sex Discrimination Act 1975;

- the Race Relations Act 1976;

- the Transfer of Undertakings (Protection of Employment) Regulations 1981;

- the Trade Union & Labour Relations (Consolidation) Act 1992;

- the Disability Discrimination Act 1995;

- the Employment Tribunals Act 1996 ;

- the Employment Rights Act 1996;

- the National Minimum Wage Act 1998;

- the Tax Credits Act 1999;

- the Working Time Regulations 1998;

- the Part-time Workers (Prevention of Less Favourable Treatment) Regulations 2000;

as well as certain appeals under the Health and Safety at Work etc Act 1974, and appeals in respect of training levies, awards of compensation for loss of office, and so on.

1.33
There are, for the most part, statutory limits on the amount of compensation that the tribunals can award. For example, for 2001/02, the maximum statutory redundancy payment that can be awarded is £7,200. The maximum basic award of compensation for unfair dismissal (calculated in much the same way as the statutory redundancy payment) is likewise – £7,200; the maximum compensatory award is £51,700; and so on. However, in equal pay, unlawful discrimination, health and safety, and 'protected disclosure' cases, there is *no* upper limit on the amount of compensation that may be awarded. (See also paras 5.171, 11.98, 11.99 and 12.43).

1.34
The tribunals are empowered to order an employer to reinstate or re-engage a dismissed employee. Indeed, on a finding of unfair or unlawful dismissal, it is the first duty of an employment tribunal to determine the wishes of the employee (balanced by those of the employer) in relation to the practicability of reinstatement or re-engagement. If an employer refuses to comply (or to comply fully) with an order for reinstatement or re-engagement, he (or she) will be ordered to pay the employee an additional amount of compensation of between 26 and 52 weeks' pay (*Source*: ERA 1996, ss 113 to 117).

Common law jurisdiction

1.35
On 12 July 1994, the jurisdiction of the employment tribunals was extended to include certain common law claims for damages at the suit of employees (eg wrongful dismissal, and other breach of contract claims) provided they are outstanding or arose on the termination of the claimant's employment. However, the tribunals are not empowered to 'entertain' claims for damages for personal injuries; breach of contract claims relating to restrictive covenants, confidentiality clauses, terms relating to intellectual property (copyright, trademarks etc), or claims concerning living

accommodation. Nor can they award damages in a breach of employment contract claim for an amount exceeding £25,000. Such claims will continue to be the province of the civil courts. (*Source*: Employment Tribunals Extension of Jurisdiction (England & Wales) Order 1994 and the Employment Tribunals Extension of Jurisdiction (Scotland) Order 1994).

1.36

Claims for damages arising out of a breach of contract (including 'wrongful dismissal' claims) must be 'presented' to the Secretary to the Tribunals within three months of the effective date of termination of the complainant's contract of employment (see Chapter 3, paras 3.15 to 3.26), or within three months of the date of an employer's failure to comply with a relevant statutory duty (eg the right of an employee to a 'guarantee payment in respect of a workless day'). Where that is not reasonably practicable, the complaint must be presented within such further period as the tribunal considers reasonable in the circumstances (see Chapter 3, paras 3.68 to 3.78) – although acceptance of complaints presented 'out of time' is rare nowadays. An employer must submit his or her claim (or counter-claim) within 21 days of receiving Form IT3 from the Secretary to the Tribunals, accompanied by a copy of the employee's Originating Application (Form IT1) (see Chapter 27, paras 27.10 to 27.16).

Representation

1.37

When the tribunals were first given jurisdiction to deal with complaints arising out of an employee's statutory employment rights, the intention was that they should 'provide a quick and cheap remedy for what it had decided were injustices in the employment sphere. The procedure was to be such that both employers and employees could present their cases without having to go to lawyers for help' (per Lawton LJ in *Clay Cross Ltd v Fletcher* [1979] ICR 1, CA). There is a duty on both sides to ensure that a case is dealt with swiftly. An employee who 'lets sleeping dogs lie' for too long, risks having his (or her) claim dismissed on the grounds of want of prosecution (but see Chapter 27, paras 27.40 to 27.41) (*Credit Aid Ltd v Russell-Taylor*, 28 February 1983, EAT).

1.38

Unfortunately, some aspects of employment legislation have become so complicated that even the judiciary has difficulty in understanding them. Browne-Wilkinson J (as he then was) described the provisions relating to maternity leave and pay as being 'of inordinate complexity exceeding the worst excesses of a taxing statute' and as a 'legislative jungle'. Further legislation, he said, has not helped (*Lavery v Plessey Telecommunications Ltd* [1982] ICR 373, EAT).

Using the services of lawyers

1.39

Over the years, there has been a notable tendency (particularly amongst respondent employers) to employ lawyers to represent their interests at tribunal hearings, especially where the subject matter is complicated and where losing a case could have a serious and costly 'knock-on' effect throughout the employer's business. Procedure also plays an increasingly important role. A failure to comply with time limits and orders may result in a good claim being lost or a valid defence being debarred (see Chapter 3, paras 3.68 to 3.83).

1.40

The applicant employee (the complainant) at a tribunal hearing is entitled to appear on his or her own behalf, or alternatively, to be represented by a lawyer, a trade union, an industrial relations specialist (or consultant), or by a friend, relative or anyone else (*Source*: ETA 1996, s. 6). The risk associated with using the services of an unqualified person, or of one unfamiliar with employment law and procedure, is that the person in question may make a mess of it. This could also result in the applicant being ordered to pay costs (see Chapter 27, paras 27.80 & 27.81). In *Martin v British Railways Board* [1989] ICR 24, EAT, Wood J emphasised that 'it is important that advisers of all kinds, not only lawyers, but those who seek to put themselves forward as advisers or advocates before tribunals and this court, should appreciate that they are expected to know the law and the procedure. It is perhaps only when those acting in person need guidance', he added, 'that a more lenient approach is justifiable'.

1.41

Legal aid is available for advice *before*, but not representation *at*, an employment tribunal hearing. The Citizens Advice Bureaux and Legal Advice Centres will provide advice (as will the Equal Opportunities Commission or the Commission for Racial Equality) and very often will either appear for a party or, alternatively, arrange the free services of a legal practitioner. Trade associations or unions will often advise their members and will also appear on their behalf.

County court

1.42

The County court has power (now shared with the employment tribunals) to deal with all common law breaches of contract, such as wrongful dismissal, non-payment of monies owing to an employee (eg accrued holiday pay, etc) (see Chapter 8).

1.43

Claims up to £50,000 are now commenced in the county court, but some may be transferred to the High Court in accordance with statutory requirements or practice directions. A new procedure has been introduced and it will have to be seen how it works. The court has no power to adjudicate on employment legislation (which is the preserve of the employment tribunals).

Representation

1.44

In any proceedings, the following people only have the right to address the court:

- any party to the proceedings;
- a barrister, instructed by a solicitor;
- a solicitor;
- any other person allowed by leave to appear instead of that litigant;
- an officer of the local authority concerning property relating to the authority where the proceedings are adjudicated upon by the District Judge.

Legislation is expected that will extend the list of persons who may represent their firms or clients in court, eg accountants, surveyors and other professional persons. Legal aid is available where a person is represented by a solicitor (with or without counsel).

Employment Appeal Tribunal (EAT)

1.45
Appeals from employment tribunals lie to the EAT, except those relating to health and safety at work. The composition and powers of the EAT are reviewed in Chapter 28, paras 28.1 to 28.30 (*Source*: ETA 1996, Part II).

Representation

1.46
The same rules about representation apply as in the tribunals. The proceedings are much more informal than in the High Court, but it does require some expertise to be able to argue a case before it. Appeals from the EAT are heard by the Court of Appeal. Legal aid is available and should be used wherever possible.

The High Court

1.47
The High Court generally adjudicates in all common law claims where the anticipated damages or award exceed £50,000. It may also deal with smaller claims where important points of principle are involved. Generally the court is limited to making an award of damages for breach of contract but it cannot order reinstatement or re-engagement (see Chapter 5, paras 5.158 to 5.165). But if there has been no loss of confidence and there exists a good working relationship between the parties, it can make an order for 'specific performance'. Such an order directs the employer to take the employee back into employment, usually for a limited time (*Hill v C A Parsons & Co Ltd* [1971] 3 AER 1345, CA and *Powell v London Borough of Brent* [1988] ICR 176, CA). But, an injunction cannot be obtained, even when the employee's contract has not finally ended, if that would have the effect of forcing an employer to retain him in

employment where there has been a loss of confidence (*Alexander & Others v Standard Telephones & Cables plc* [1990] ICR 291, CD.

Judicial Review

1.48
The court, under powers conferred on it when constituted as a 'Divisional Court', also hears appeals, under a procedure known as 'judicial review'. It considers cases brought under the Health and Safety at Work etc Act 1974 from the tribunals. It also adjudicates on appeals from the Certification Officer (see paras 1.77 to 1.82 below). Although the High Court has jurisdiction to rule on allegations of misbehaviour by a tribunal, these are invariably dealt with by the EAT.

1.49
The High Court's appellate powers are also exercised under the same procedure to hear cases where any person or body exercises a statutory power that affects the rights or legitimate expectations of citizens and is of a kind that the law requires to be exercised judicially. The Court may review decisions of public bodies and thereby control the misuse of administrative powers through the making of *certiorari*, *mandamus* and *prohibition* orders. It can also make a declaration or grant an injunction (*R v Deputy Governor of Parkhurst Prison, ex parte Leech, The Times*, 5 February 1988, HL).

1.50
Before a claim can go ahead, leave must be obtained from a High Court judge, who has to be satisfied that there is an arguable case. Furthermore, except where there has been an abuse of natural justice or action has been taken by a body in excess of its jurisdiction (*ultra vires*), it is normally only available where all other remedies or avenues of appeal have been exhausted. A claim for judicial review must be brought within three months of the matter about which the complaint is made (*Calveley & Others v Merseyside Police* [1986] IRLR 177, CA; *McLaren v Home Office* [1990] IRLR 338, CA; and *R v Durham City Council, ex parte Robinson, The Times*, 31 January 1992, DC).

1.51
The High Court has no jurisdiction to entertain an application for judicial review unless there is a sufficient element of public law present.

Private disputes have to proceed by an ordinary county court action. Thus it was held that the relationship between the Crown as employer and a prosecutor as employee was ordinarily of a private law nature. Judicial review would only be appropriate where the prosecutor's independence in the performance of his duties had been impugned (*R v Crown Prosecution Service, ex parte Hogg, The Times,* 14 April 1994, CA).

1.52

Where Parliament has conferred powers on a body but made no provision for an appeal, the judicial review procedure cannot be used where there has been a mistake of fact or law. Only if there was some illegality, irrationality or procedural impropriety (*per incuriam*) can the decision of such a body be open to judicial review (see Chapter 3, para 3.100) (*R v Independent Television Commission, ex parte TSW Broadcasting Ltd, The Times,* 30 March 1992, HL).

1.53

A union had legitimately expected to be consulted about proposed redundancies, but not under any enforceable agreement. The employers failure to consult was a breach of UK law and of EC Directive 75/129/EEC (see Chapter 4, paras 4.41 to 4.47). It was held that there was a procedural irregularity that gave the trade union a right to apply to the High Court for judicial review. The failure to consult was also held to be irrational (*R v British Coal Corporation ex parte Vardy & Others* [1993] ICR 720, Div Ct).

1.54

Decisions of public bodies are subject to review in respect of failures under three main heads. First, the body must have understood its decision-making power and applied it correctly. Second, in coming to its decision, it must have taken into account relevant factors and disregarded immaterial ones, so that it did not come to a decision that no reasonable and right-minded body could have reached. Lastly, it must have adopted a fair procedure (*R v Secretary of State for Foreign and Commonwealth Affairs ex parte Council of Civil Service Unions & Others* [1985] IRLR 28, HL).

1.55

Where a statute specifically provides a quick and easy means of appealing against an order made against an aggrieved party (concerning some matter that is alleged to have serious consequences if allowed to continue), that appeal procedure must be followed. This is so even though there might have been grave procedural improprieties in the way in which the order came to be made (*R v Birmingham City Council ex parte Ferrero Ltd, The Times*, 30 May 1991, CA).

1.56

In employment cases, the judicial review procedure may generally be used if a public sector employee's contract is underpinned by statutory provisions. The High Court may intervene where an employer is circumscribed in the manner in which the employee can be disciplined or dismissed, and there has been a breach of those requirements (*Ridge v Baldwin* [1964] AC 40, HL and *R v Lord Chancellor's Department ex parte Nangle* [1991] ICR 743, DC). Even where an aggrieved party is able to show a *prima facie* breach of statutory procedure in the interviewing process, leave to proceed may nonetheless be refused on the grounds that there has been no injustice (*R v Birmingham City Council, ex parte McKenna, The Times*, 16 May 1991, DC).

1.57

A woman prison officer was able to invoke the procedure. She had been suspended without pay and without the matter having been referred to the Home Secretary. This was held to be in breach of the disciplinary code. It was held that there was a sufficient public law element. In the event the Secretary of State had residuary powers to act as he did, and the claim was dismissed (*R v Secretary of State for the Home Department, ex parte Attard, The Times*, 29 June 1989, DC).

1.58

The issuing of a Non-discrimination Notice by the Commission of Racial Equality (or, for that matter, by the Equal Opportunities Commission) comes within this jurisdiction, but not the dismissal of a nursing officer. In the latter case the breach of contract of employment was not a matter of public law (*R v CRE ex parte Westminster CC* [1985] IRLR 426, CA and *R v East Berkshire HA ex parte Walsh* [1984] ICR 743, CA).

1.59

On the other hand, where a doctor complained that the Family Practitioners' Committee had reduced his allowances, payable pursuant to an Act of Parliament, it was held that he could use the process of judicial review if the Committee had (wrongly) refused to include him on their list. Once there, his only remedy for breach of any of his rights lay under private law, eg a claim for breach of contract by way of an civil action for damages (*Roy v Kensington Chelsea & Westminster Family Practitioners' Committee* [1992] IRLR 233, HL).

1.60

The High Court's power to intervene can also be exercised where proceedings are commenced by ordinary writ for a 'declaration' and an injunction (to prevent someone from doing something). This could arise if an employer's discretionary power to terminate employment is conditional upon certain procedural steps, and the employer fails to follow those steps. The court may declare a purported dismissal to be void, with the consequence that the employment continues until it is validly ended (*Jones v Lee & Another* [1980] ICR 310, CA). There is also a discretionary power to halt a domestic hearing if criminal proceedings are taking place against an employee at the same time. But there must be a real danger of a miscarriage of justice occurring in those criminal proceedings as a result (*R v BBC ex parte Lavell* [1982] IRLR 404, DC).

1.61

In determining whether there has been a default by an official body under an agreement, the Court applies the strict contractual test. The Secretary of State for Health refused to consider representations made to him by a medical consultant over the latter's summary dismissal on the ground that he lacked the necessary jurisdiction. The court held that the Minister had acted correctly. The conditions of service only gave him power to intervene where the dismissal was 'on notice' (*R v Secretary of State for Health & Another, ex parte Guirguis* [1990] IRLR 30, CA).

1.62

The judicial review procedure was used when a secretary was dismissed for refusing to obey an instruction to type a letter relating to abortions. She had a conscientious objection to abortions and a statutory right of refusal to act. But her action failed because there was not sufficient proximity between her duties and the exception granted by the legislation (*R v Salford Area Health Authority, ex parte Janaway, The Times*, 2 December 1998, HL).

Representation

1.63
Litigants are entitled to represent themselves before the High Court, but should be wary of doing so, as considerable expertise is required. There are very strict rules of procedure. Legal aid is available and should be used where possible. Companies *must* be represented by counsel (instructed by solicitors). If litigants wish to be represented, they can only appear through counsel.

The Court of Appeal

1.64
The Court of Appeal hears appeals from the EAT and the High Court. Apart from litigants-in-person, everyone has to be represented by counsel instructed by solicitors. See also Chapter 28, paras 28.33 to 28.37.

The House of Lords

1.65
Appeals from the Court of Appeal go to the House of Lords, although there is a procedure, in very special circumstances, where the High Court can 'leapfrog' the Court of Appeal and appeal directly to the House of Lords. Apart from litigants in person (see Chapter 28, paras 28.38 to 28.40), all parties appearing before the House of Lords must be represented by counsel instructed by solicitors.

The European Court of Justice (ECJ)

1.66
The European Court of Justice (ECJ) was established under the Treaty of Rome and sits in Luxembourg. It has power to deal with all

employment law laid down in the Treaty, and with Regulations and directives made under that Treaty. The ECJ can give a decision in favour either of an individual who has petitioned it, or of the European Commission set up under the Treaty. The Commission may take proceedings before the ECJ against any Member State (of its own initiative or at the suit of another Member State) that has failed to implement Community law by importing it into its domestic legislation. In recent times, the Commission has had occasion to warn the UK of proceedings unless the latter acted swiftly to import the 'Working Time Directive' (93/104/EEC) into domestic legislation. This, of course, has now been attended to.

1.67

The UK courts are responsible for giving effect to decisions of the European Court. The latter tries to ensure that there is uniform interpretation of the Treaty and that there is no divergence between the case laws of the Community and those of the national courts (*Dzodzi v Belgium, The Times*, 7 January 1991, ECJ).

Representation

1.68

Litigating parties before the ECJ must be represented by a lawyer entitled to practise before a court in the relevant Member State. The lawyer must submit credentials from the Bar Council or the Law Society. Member States and Community institutions may be represented by an agent, who may be helped by an adviser or a duly accredited lawyer. The agent is not required to be legally qualified. Thus, a government minister could appear if he or she so wishes.

The European Court of Human Rights (ECHR)

1.69

The European Court of Human Rights sits at Strasbourg. The Court can only pronounce judgment against the United Kingdom (or against any other signatory country) on a complaint by another country signatory to the Treaty, or on the petition of a person who alleges that the country in question is in breach of the European Convention on Human Rights (see paras 1.31 above). There is no machinery for enforcing a decision of the Court, although in practice a signatory to the Convention will usually comply with any such decision. The UK has, of course, now imported the Convention into UK legislation with the enactment of the Human Rights Act 1998, although, at the time of writing, the latter had not yet been brought into force.

Representation

1.70

A litigant may present his (or her) case in person before the court although it is highly desirable that he be assisted or represented by a barrister, a solicitor, or some other lawyer. The person appearing must be approved by the court.

ACAS AND THE CENTRAL ARBITRATION COMMITTEE

Advisory, Conciliation and Arbitration Service (ACAS)

1.71

ACAS is a statutory body created in 1975 whose general duty is 'to promote the improvement of industrial relations (*Source*: TULRA 1992, ss 209 & 210). Where there is a dispute, or one is apprehended, ACAS may offer its services to try to effect a settlement (if approached by a party or by an interested person) (*Source*: ETA, ss 18 & 19). One of the Service's tasks is to seek to settle any dispute between an employee and his (or her) employer (or former employer). Any advice given by ACAS is confidential and cannot be disclosed in any subsequent proceedings (see Chapter 2, paras 2.45 to 2.47).

1.72

ACAS has considerable experience in assessing the likely outcome of proceedings. It will give the parties its views so as to enhance industrial relations, but it does not give legal advice as such. In performing its duty, it is able to settle nearly two-thirds of cases brought before the tribunals. Not all result in a cash settlement – a number are withdrawn, either because of a technicality, eg the employee is out of time, or has not completed the qualifying period of continuous employment, or because his (or her) claim lacks merit. The Service may also refer a matter in dispute to arbitration or to the Central Arbitration Committee (the CAC), provided it has the consent of the parties, and they have exhausted all their agreed procedures, or there are some special reasons to justify arbitration (*Source*: TULRA 1992, s. 212).

1.73
ACAS may issue codes of practice containing such practical guidance as it thinks fit for the purpose of promoting the improvement of industrial relations. To date, ACAS has produced three such codes, titled:

- *Disciplinary and Grievance Procedures* (COP1);

- *Disclosure of Information to Trade Unions for Collective Bargaining Purposes* (COP2);

- *Time Off for Trade Union Duties & Activities* (COP3).

For further particulars, please turn to Chapter 3, paras 3.111 and 3.112 (*Source*: TULRA 1992, ss 199 to 202).

1.74
ACAS may, on request or otherwise, give employers, employers' associations, workers and trade unions such advice as it thinks appropriate on matters concerned with, or affecting or likely to affect, industrial relations. It may also publish general advice on matters concerned with (or affecting, or likely to affect), industrial relations (*Source*: TULRA 1992, s. 213).

Note: Under the Employment Rights (Dispute Resolution) Act 1998, section 7 of which came into force on 1 August 1998, ACAS is empowered to develop a 'voluntary arbitration scheme' under which disputes between employers and employees may be resolved by arbitration. Any resultant agreement (or settlement) will be legally binding on both parties to the dispute (in much the same way as 'COT 3' and 'compromise' agreements). The new scheme is expected to be 'up and running' in Summer, 2001.

Central Arbitration Committee (CAC)

1.75
The CAC was also created in 1975 and inherited the duties formerly exercised by arbitration boards and other similar bodies. The CAC arbitrates on disputes referred to it by ACAS. For example, a trade union may complain to the CAC that an employer had refused or failed to disclose information needed by the trade union for the purposes of collective bargaining with that employer (*Source*: TULRA, ss 183 & 259 to 265). Since June 2000, the CAC has been actively involved in 'trade union recognition disputes'.

1.76
However, it cannot force an employer to give information about groups of employees (sufficient to enable those employees to be identified) or information about issues in respect of which the union has no negotiating or bargaining rights. Even where it is, the information is privileged where it relates to individuals who have not given their consent to disclosure (*ACTSS v Chloride Legg Ltd*, CAC Award 84/15).

CERTIFICATION OFFICER

1.77
The Certification Officer, is appointed by the Secretary of State for Education & Employment and is responsible for 'overseeing' the activities of trade unions, including their:

- observance of statutory procedures governing the setting up and operation of political funds and dealing with members' complaints concerning breaches of fund rules (TULRA 1992, ss 71 to 73, 82 & 135);

- compliance with statutory procedures for mergers and transfers of engagements, and complaints about the conduct of merger ballots (TULRA 1992, ss. 21, 44, 46, 59 & 61).

The Certification Officer also:

- maintains a list of unions and employers' associations ensuring that they keep proper accounts and that superannuation schemes conform to requirements for actuarial examination (TULRA 1992, ss 2 to 4, 9, and 123 to 126);

- reimburses unions for certain expenditures incurred in the conduct of secret postal ballots (TULRA 1992, ss 115 & 254); and

- scrutinises and approves the balloting rules of any union wishing to continue spending money on political objectives, and deals with complaints that unions have not held secret ballots for elections to certain offices (*Source*: TULRA 1992, ss 46, 59, 61, 74, 84 & 94, and 254 to 258).

1.78

The Certification Officer must exercise some discretion when asked to reimburse a trade union for expenditure incurred in the conduct of postal ballots. In one case, a trade union had adhered strictly to its own rules when it reasonably disallowed a candidate who had won the highest votes, because the area in question was over-represented. It was held that the union was nevertheless entitled to recover the costs of the ballot. Only weighted voting, block voting or voting through an elected college would entitle the Certification Officer to withhold such a payment lawfully (*R v Certification Officer, ex parte Electrical Power Engineers' Association* [1990] ICR 682, HL).

1.79

The Royal College of Nursing (RCN) held a ballot seeking the views of its members about amending the rule book so as to permit strikes and other forms of industrial action. Under the College's then existing rules, only a committee could decide whether the rules could be altered. A court held that attention should be paid to the purpose behind the regulations. Too narrow a construction should not be applied. Even though balloting costs are normally refundable only when a ballot asks for votes for and against a strike or other form of industrial action, the RCN were nonetheless held entitled to be reimbursed (*R v The Certification Officer, ex parte Royal College of Nursing of the United Kingdom* [1991] IRLR 258, DC).

1.80

A union, whose name is on a list maintained by the Certification

Officer, may apply for a certificate that it is independent. The Certification Officer will issue a certificate of independence if satisfied that the union is not under the domination or control of an employer, and is not liable to interference by that employer (*Government Communications Staff Federation v Certification Officer & Another, The Times,* 16 December 1992, EAT) (*Source:* TULRA 1992, s. 6).

1.81

If the Certification Officer refuses to issue a certificate of independence to a particular trade union, the latter may appeal against that refusal to the EAT (see Chapter 28, paras 28.1 to 28.30). If satisfied that a certificate should have been issued, the EAT will make a declaration to that effect and will give the appropriate directions (*Source:* TULRA 1992, s. 9(2) & (3)).

1.82

The Government Communications Staff Federation, which was the only union which staff at GCHQ were allowed to join, applied to the Certification Officer for a certificate of independence. The application was refused on the grounds that it was vulnerable to interference. The EAT held that the Certification Office had acted correctly in finding that the union was *not* independent (*Government Communications Staff Federation v Certification Officer & Another* [1993] ICR 163, EAT). (*Note:* That decision has since been overturned.)

Matters of mutual concern to common law and statute law

EMPLOYEE OR SELF-EMPLOYED?

2.1

In the context of an employee's common law and statutory employment rights, it is important to understand the distinction between an *employee* and a *self-employed person*. While an employer owes a great many duties and responsibilities to his employees (and is vicariously liable for any wrongdoing committed by employees in the course of their employment), his relationship with self-employed persons is different.

2.2

A self-employed person is a person engaged under a *contract for services*. Such a person is in business on his (or her) own account and (unlike the employee engaged under a *contract of service* or under a *contract of employment* as it is more commonly styled) is directly accountable to the Inland Revenue for the payment of tax and national insurance contributions. The self-employed person will submit an invoice for services rendered; must, where appropriate, be VAT-registered with HM Customs & Excise; must prepare and submit annual accounts for scrutiny by the Inland Revenue; and so on. The duties owed by an employer to his employees under both the common law and contemporary employment law do not extend to independent contractors and other self-employed persons working on an employer's premises. But, as the occupier of business premises, an employer must comply with the requirements of the Occupiers' Liability Acts 1957 & 1984, and with his duties under health and safety legislation.

2.3

Some Acts of Parliament (and their subordinate legislation) provide a definition of the word 'employee'. Except for those cases where the word is specifically stated to include a restricted class of independent contractor, as in the Race Relations Act 1976, the ordinary common law tests apply.

2.4
In deciding whether a person is an *employee*, the courts will look at a number of factors, notably the following:

- Is there some measure of control indicative of an employer/ employee relationship?

- Is the person carrying out the work for and on behalf of the employer or in business on his (or her) own account?

- Is the person free to accept or refuse work at will?

- Is the person supplied with a uniform and equipment?

- Is the person subject to disciplinary or grievance procedures?

- Must the person take holidays when and as directed?

- Is the person paid regularly either weekly or monthly? And are wages or salary paid gross or net of tax?

- What has been agreed with the Inland Revenue?

(*O'Kelly v Trusthouse Forte plc* [1983] ICR 708, CA.)

2.5
No one test is decisive but the 'most important' criterion for determining the relationship is the extent to which the person is under the direction and control of the other party with regard to the manner in which he does his work (*Narich Pty Ltd v Commission of Payroll Tax* [1984] ICR 286, PC).

2.6
Lack of mutuality may not be fatal. Where a person has worked as an outworker on a full-time basis for several years, there comes a stage when the relationship is likely to be translated into that of employer/employee (*Nethermere (St Neots) Ltd v Gardiner & Another* [1984] ICR 612, CA).

2.7

So too a person working in the construction industry was held to be an employee where he did not provide his own equipment, did not hire helpers, carried no financial risk, and was paid piece work according to the employer's tariff (*Lee Ting Sang v Chung Chi-Keung & Others* [1990] ICR 409, PC). An impression of a person's work activity has to be gained from an accumulation of detail, each of which will be of varying importance. In coming to a decision, the 'traditional contrast between a servant and an independent contractor' is the test that should be applied (*Hall (HM Inspector of Taxes) v Lorimer* [1994] ICR 218, CA).

2.8

If the relationship between the parties 'is in doubt or... is ambiguous, so that it can be brought under the one relationship or the other, it is open to the parties by agreement to stipulate what the legal situation between them shall be' (per Lord Denning MR in *Massey v Crown Insurance Co Ltd* [1978] ITR 5, CA).

2.9

It is not possible for the parties to change the true relationship between them by putting the wrong label on it. A young woman had an agreement with an employment agency under which she was employed under a 'contract of service' but worked as a 'temp' for various client firms. It was held that she was not an 'employee'. There was a minimum of control over her, there were no mutual obligations to provide or accept work, there was no continuity, and the arrangement did not resemble any contract of service. So too were 'casual' waiters in a restaurant who could refuse or accept work when they wished (*Wicken v Champion Employment* [1984] ICR 365, EAT and *O'Kelly v Trusthouse Forte plc* [1983] ICR 708, CA).

2.10

Problems can sometimes arise over the true status of agency-supplied workers. Are they employed by the agency, the client firm for whom they are working, or are they self-employed? If they are unable to bring their status under one of these headings, they will be classified as being on a contract of *sui generis* (a contract 'of its own kind') (*Ironmonger v Movefield Ltd t/a Deering Appointments* [1988] IRLR 461, EAT and *Construction Industry Training Board v Labour Force Ltd* [1970] 3 AER 220, DC).

2.11

A Youth Opportunities Programme trainee was held not to be an 'employee' as there was no contract between her and the firm which provided her with work experience. She was paid a training allowance and had to comply with instructions given to her as a trainee. But her attendance was optional (*Daley v Allied Suppliers Ltd* [1983] ICR 90, EAT). On the other hand, a person engaged in carrying out such a scheme was held to be an 'employee' because he fell within all the tests. So, too, was a person who participated in a Community Programme because he was paid a 'wage' and was otherwise treated as an 'employee' (*City of Glasgow DC v McNullity*, 29 November 1983, EAT and *Dyson v Pontefract & DC CVS CP Scheme*, 13 January 1988, EAT).

2.12

There are several occupations where the relationship between the parties might suggest the existence of a contract of employment, although no such contract exists in law, eg prison officers. But where there is power to enter into a contract of employment, and the parties do so, then they are bound by the terms agreed. Office-holders such as magistrates are not generally regarded as employees as their rights and duties are derived from the office they hold and not from a contract of employment. Crown servants are in a special category, but many are protected by statutory provisions (*McLaren v Home Office* [1990] IRLR 338, CA).

2.13

Sometimes the nature of the relationship precludes a person from being an employee. Equity partners, for example, who, under the statutory definition, 'carry on business in common with a view to profit', do not have any employment relationship with each other (Parliament Act 1890, s. 1). Nor is there normally a contract of employment between a minister of religion and a church, which is true also of priests in a Sikh temple (*Cowell v Quilter Goodison & Co Ltd & Another* [1989] IRLR 392, CA and *Santokh Singh v Guru Nanak Gurdwara* [1990] ICR 309, CA).

2.14

A working director of a company is normally an employee, provided he (or she) is paid a salary as distinct from fees, and satisfies the other tests, eg holidays are fixed, he works only for that company, and is not free to work for others. In some cases it has been held that it does not matter that the person is the sole director and employee of the company. Even if for tax reasons he (or she) draws no salary for a period, but carries on working normally, he does not lose his status of being an 'employee' (*Albert J Parsons & Son Ltd v Parsons* [1979] IRLR 117, CA and *Europanel Processing Co Ltd v Nimmo* 24 April 1992, EAT).

2.15

An employee who has deliberately put a false label on his relationship to obtain fiscal advantages may find himself debarred from obtaining other statutory advantages. 'He gets the benefits of it by avoiding tax deductions and getting his pension contributions returned. I do not see that he can come along afterwards and say it is something else... Having made his bed as being 'self-employed', he must lie on it' (per Lord Denning MR in *Massey v Crown Insurance Co Ltd* [1978] ITR 5, CA).

BURDEN OF PROOF

2.16

Different Acts of Parliament often refer to one party or the other having to 'prove' some fact or to 'satisfy' the tribunal on a particular matter. Irrespective of the actual wording used, the standard of the burden of proof is always the same, namely, that of 'a balance of probabilities'. This means that a tribunal will decide a point based on which allegation is more probable in the circumstances. The members of the tribunal must consider the evidence put before them, assess the reliability of witnesses, and apply their experience in life and common sense. This has some practical importance, because sometimes the burden is on one party at one point and then switches to the other for the next. A failure somewhere along the line might result in an otherwise sound case failing (*The Financial Times Ltd v Byrne & Others*, 7 January 1992, EAT).

2.17

Thus, if an employee proves that he (or she) has been discriminated against (or victimised) by a fellow employee, the employer will normally be held to be vicariously liable. To escape liability, the employer will need to show that he (or she) took all reasonably practicable steps to prevent any such discrimination occurring (see Chapter 11, para 11.86 and Chapter 12, para 12.24) (*Sources*: Sex Discrimination Act 1975 (s. 41), Race Relations Act 1976 (s. 32), and Disability Discrimination Act 1995 (s. 58)).

Note: When Council Directive 97/80/EEC of 15 December 1997, 'on the burden of proof in cases of discrimination based on sex' is imported into UK domestic legislation – as it must be by 27 July 2001 – the burden of proof in such cases will shift from employees to employers.

2.18

In (direct) discrimination cases, the burden does not pass to the employer to prove that he (or she) has not discriminated, except where the 'circumstances [are] consistent with the treatment being based on grounds of sex or race [when] the employment tribunal should be prepared to draw the inference that the discrimination was on such grounds unless the alleged discriminator can satisfy the tribunal that there was some other innocent explanation' (per Neill, LJ, *London Borough of Barking & Dagenham v Camara* [1988] ICR 865, EAT and *Baker v Cornwall County Council* [1990] ICR 432, CA). But see again the *Note* at the end of the previous paragraph.

2.19

Where a party relies on inferences to be made from primary facts to prove discrimination, there generally must be some hint of prejudice on racial or sexual grounds before a tribunal can hold that a person has been treated less favourably on either ground in comparison to others. If the explanation given for the treatment is unsatisfactory then a tribunal may infer discrimination (*Quereshi v London Borough of Newham* [1991] IRLR 264, CA and *King v Great Britain China Centre* [1992] ICR 516, CA).

2.20

Where an allegation of failure to mitigate damages is raised, the tribunal has to assess whether there has been adequate mitigation by an employee. The onus still remains on the employer to prove it (see para 2.62 below) (*Bessenden Properties Ltd v Corness* [1974] IRLR 338, CA).

OBLIGATION TO PROVIDE WORK

2.21

It is now settled law that it is an implied term in every contract of employment that an employee has the right not only to be paid the agreed wage or salary but also to be given the opportunity to do his (or her) work when it is available (*Langston v Amalgamated Union of Engineering Workers* [1974] IRLR 15, CA). Unless a contract of employment *specifically* allows an employer to lay off an employee without pay, any attempt to do so would amount to a fundamental breach of contract. That would entitle the employee to leave (with or without notice) and to claim compensation on the grounds that he or she had been unfairly (constructively) dismissed (see Chapter 3, paras 3.47 to 3.60). Alternatively, the employee could remain in employment but claim damages equivalent to wages lost as a result of the breach (*R H & D T Edwards Ltd v Evans & Walters* 16 July 1985, EAT and *Miller v Hamworthy Engineering Ltd* [1986] ICR 846, CA).

2.22

Even if a contract of employment does allow an employer to lay off without pay, he (or she) may do so for a reasonable time only. If the lay-off or period of supension without pay goes beyond what is 'reasonable', the employee may leave and pursue a claim for compensation. But if the contract provides that the employee may be laid off indefinitely, the length of the lay-off period would be irrelevant (*A Dakri & Co Ltd v Tiffen* [1981] ICR 256, EAT and *Kenneth MacRae & Co Ltd v Dawson* [1984] IRLR 5, EAT).

2.23

Where an employee's income is (mainly) dependent on the employer providing work, eg he (or she) is paid at an hourly rate without there being a minimum number of hours, or, on a nominal basic salary plus commission, there would be an implied term that the employer would supply that employee with a reasonable amount of work (*Devonald v Rosser & Sons* [1906] 2 KB 726, CA). Sales plummetted when a sales director employed on a commission basis fell ill. This led to a substantial drop in his earnings. It was held that the man's employers had breached their implied contractual duty to take steps to maintain sales during his absence – thereby depriving him of a major portion of his income. He was entitled to resign and present a complaint of unfair 'constructive dismissal' (see para 2.21 above) (*McClelland Fergusson & Partners v Fergusson*, 1 January 1985 EAT).

2.24

In some professions, such as acting, where publicity is an important part of the contract, there is an implied right to work. A person is entitled to enhance his or her reputation, which can only be done by advertising and appearing in a play or on film. An actor playing a leading part in a play was wrongly prevented from acting. It was held that he was entitled to recover damages flowing from that breach. It did not extend to any injury to his existing reputation or feelings (*Withers v General Theatre Corporation* [1933] 2 KB 536, CA).

ILLEGAL CONTRACTS

2.25

If both parties enter into a contract which is wholly or partly illegal, the employee is not generally entitled to invoke the benefits of employment legislation. This applies even if, for instance, his (or her) dismissal was manifestly unfair. It matters not whether the point has been raised by one or other of the parties to the contract (*Napier v National Business Agency Ltd* [1951] 2 AER 264, CA and *Tomlinson v Dick Evans U Drive Ltd* [1978] IRLR 77, EAT). Once a tribunal or court (including an appeal court) learns of an illegal contract (or suspects such a contract), it has a duty to investigate. Before giving a ruling, each party must be given the opportunity to call any evidence and/or make submissions to support or refute the point (*Cohen v Sandhu*, 7 May 1981, EAT).

2.26
Illegal contracts generally fall into two groups:

• those that are illegal from the start; and

• those that are *prima facie* legal, but become illegal because of the mode of carrying them out.

The latter generally involve defrauding a third party, usually the Inland Revenue. It does not extend to dishonest conduct by an employee against his employer (*Broaders v Kallare Property Maintenance Ltd* [1990] IRLR 421, EAT).

2.27
A contract of employment that is illegal at inception can never be enforced, whether or not the employee in question is aware of the illegal nature of the contract. The law treats the contract as though it had never been made. They are not restricted to pure criminal acts (*Miller v Karlinski* [1945] 62 TLR 85, CA). Browne-Wilkinson, J (as he then was) said that contracts would not be enforced where they are 'entered into for purposes which are... (although not forbidden by the general law)... immoral... The word 'immoral' connotes only sexual immorality... Illegal contracts... include not only contracts to do criminal acts but also contracts to achieve an immoral purpose' (*Coral Leisure Group v Barnett* [1981] ICR 503, EAT). The fact that a person has, during his (or her) employment, committed an unlawful or immoral act will not necessarily, of itself, prevent him from enforcing his rights, unless the contract was entered into for one of those purposes. So the lorry driver who knowingly and frequently uses an overweight vehicle, or the doorman of a hotel who procures prostitutes for guests, can pursue a claim. Whether such a claim will succeed on its merits may be a different matter.

2.28
An agreement that part of an employee's pay should not go 'through the books', and would be paid free of tax, would be illegal. The employee would not be able to enforce his (or her) common law or statutory rights. But the employee would not be debarred from making a claim if he was unaware that his employer had been acting illegally, eg by deducting the equivalent of PAYE tax from the employee's wages but not passing on the tax to the Inland Revenue. The test to be applied is not *ought* the employee have known, but *did* he know, of the illegality? (*Corby v Morrison t/a the Card Shop* [1980] ICR 564, EAT and *Newland v Simon & Willer (Hairdressers) Ltd* [1981] ICR 521, EAT).

2.29
After an illegality ceases, an employee can pursue his (or her) statutory rights (eg the right to a guarantee payment, statutory maternity pay, or not to be unfairly dismissed) if he has the

necessary qualifying period of employment; but that period would only start to run from the date on which the illegal practice ended (*Hyland v J H Barker (North West) Ltd* [1985] ICR 861, EAT). If an employee helps an employer to defraud a third party from which the employee derives no benefit, public policy may not preclude him from bringing a claim. This is especially so where the contract of employment was not illegal at inception (*Hewcastle Catering Ltd v Ahmed & Elkamark* [1991] IRLR 473, CA).

2.30
This has been held to be so where:

- an employee derived no benefit from a fraud;

- had been instructed to participate in it;

- had subsequently cooperated with the authorities in bringing the fraud to an end; and where

- the employer's conduct had been 'so reprehensible in comparison with that of the [employee] that it would be wrong to allow the [employer] to rely on it [to resist the claim]'.

(*Euro-Diam Ltd v Bathurst* [1988] 2 WLR 517, CA.)

2.31
Two waiters were instructed to provide cash customers with separate bills to enable their employers to avoid having to account for VAT to HM Customs & Excise. It was held that the waiters were not precluded from bringing a claim. Their dismissals, which resulted from their helping the authorities to prosecute, were declared unfair. Public policy decreed that employees should be encouraged to disclose frauds on Customs & Excise (*Hewcastle Catering Ltd v Ahmed & Elkamark* [1991] IRLR 473, CA).

Note: Under the Public Interest Disclosure Act 1998 (known as *the Whistleblower's Act*) a worker (whether 'employee' or otherwise) who makes a so-called 'protected disclosure' (see **Index**) cannot lawfully be dismissed or subjected to any other detriment for doing so. There is no upper limit on the amount of compensation that can be awarded in such cases (see Chapter 23).

FRUSTRATION OF CONTRACT

2.32

Frustration occurs where the main provisions of a contract cannot be performed because of unforseen circumstances beyond the control of either party that were not provided for in the contract. Thus, where there is an agreement to rent a chalet, but it is burnt down beforehand, that event effectively brings the contract to an end without any action by either party (*Davis Contractors Ltd v Fareham UDC* [1956] AC 696, HL).

2.33

The doctrine of frustration, which is usually to be found in commercial contracts, does not depend on an opinion, or intention, or even knowledge of any of the parties, but on the occurrence of an event that renders the performance of the contract radically different from that which was agreed. In the absence of any terms to the contrary, the liabilities of each party under the contract cease.

2.34

It has now been settled in the House of Lords that all contracts (including contracts of employment) are subject to the doctrine of frustration. In the employment field, it usually applies in sickness and imprisonment cases. However, not all reported cases can be reconciled (*National Carriers Ltd v Penelpina (Northern) Ltd* [1981] I AER 161, QB).

2.35

The significance of the doctrine of frustration in employment cases is that an employee whose contract has been frustrated will not have been 'dismissed' within the accepted meaning of the word and would, accordingly, forfeit many of his (or her) statutory rights. Some 'common law' rights would also be forfeit. The general rule is that self-induced frustration does not bring the doctrine into operation. So if a singer, for instance, were to lose her voice intentionally by walking coatless and hatless in the winter rain, she would not be able to respond to a civil action for damages by claiming that her contract to sing at a concert had been frustrated by laryngitis. In imprisonment cases, although the view is by no means unanimous, the weight of judicial pronouncements is that an employment contract is frustrated by the employee's being unavailable for work, *not* by his having been sent to prison. The employee could obviously have avoided committing the offence which he must have known would very likely result in his being deprived of his liberty (*Chakki v The United Yeast Co Ltd* [1982] ICR 140, EAT). It follows that a relatively short term in prison (eg three weeks for non-payment of maintenance) would not be long enough to constitute a frustrating event, bearing in mind that employees are routinely absent from work for similar periods – annual holidays, sick leave, approved leave of absence without pay, etc – without running the risk of losing their jobs. A sentence of 12 months' imprisonment *would*, on the other hand, be a frustrating event. A minimum absence of some months (assuming the earliest release) would make the carrying out of the contract radically different from that contemplated when it was made (*Harrington v Kent CC* [1980] IRLR 353, EAT).

2.36

Even where there was a special procedure for dismissing apprentices for absences (for any reason), it has been held that the concept of frustration still applies. There was no dismissal when a youth was sent to Borstal training, because the contract had been frustrated (*F C Shepherd & Co Ltd v Jerrom* [1986] ICR 802, CA).

2.37

Sickness or serious injury can also be a frustrating event. If a tyre fitter is knocked down by a car and confined to a wheelchair for the rest of his (or her) life (unable to do any work), the contract would be frustrated. The same would be true of the contract of a violin player who loses a hand. For less serious matters, it can be difficult to determine the point when frustration occurs and when it does not (*Egg Stores (Stamford Hill) Ltd v Leibovici* [1977] ICR 260, EAT). The general considerations applied are:

- the length of the previous employment and (if relevant) how long it would have been expected to continue;

- the type of work, and the employer's need for the work to be done and/or find a replacement;

- the nature of the illness or disabling event, and the prospects for recovery;

- whether a reasonable employer could be expected to wait any longer;
- any contractual terms relating to sickness and sick pay.

(*Williams v Watsons Luxury Coaches Ltd* [1990] ICR 536, EAT.)

2.38
Where the circumstances are appropriate, the doctrine of frustration also applies to contracts that can be ended at short notice. An employee with 26 years' service suffered a coronary. This prevented him from working again. It was held that the illness had automatically frustrated the contract. The employer did not need to take any further action (*Notcutt v Universal Equipment Co (London) Ltd* [1986] ICR 414, CA). The margin between whether there has been frustration or not is necessarily blurred. An employer should be wary of assuming that a contract of employment has ended. If he (or she) takes any action inconsistent with the continuance of a contract, he runs the risk of being held to have dismissed the employee. It may turn out to have been unfair on procedural grounds (see Chapter 5, paras 5.94 to 5.100). In a doubtful case, the best advice to an employer would perhaps be to treat the situation as a dismissal on grounds of ill-health (see Chapter 5, paras 5.128 to 5.134) (*Lawton v Bowden International Ltd*, 13 December 1990, EAT).

2.39
If a sick employee is absent from work for an extended period (perhaps on a nominal rate of pay), the subsequent termination of his or her contract (because the employee is incapable of work) will be deemed to be a 'dismissal' in law. In short, it would be unwise of an employer in a similar situation to assume that the employee's contract had become frustrated. The law allows that continuity of employment is preserved if an employee dismissed on grounds of ill health or injury is re-engaged by the same or an associated employer within the next 26 weeks. But if not re-engaged until after 26 weeks have elapsed, continuity is automatically broken and the employee will have forfeited all statutory rights earned up to the time of his (or her) dismissal (see Chapter 3, paras 3.27 to 3.37). This does not apply, of course, to statutory rights that do not depend on a qualifying period of

continuous employment (*Glenboig Union Fireclay Co Ltd v Stewart* [1971] ITR 14, CS) (*Source*: ERA 1996, s. 212).

REPUDIATORY OR FUNDAMENTAL BREACH

2.40
Where an employer (or employee) does, or omits to do, something, which amounts to a repudiatory breach of the employment contract, it is open to the other party either to accept the repudiation and consider the contract to be at an end, or to 'affirm' the contract by continuing to work or by allowing the other party to do so (see Chapter 3, para 3.58). An employee who took an extended holiday to the West Indies, in defiance of his employer's instructions, was held to have repudiated his contract of employment by deliberately making himself unavailable for work. When his employer accepted the repudiation, the contract of employment ended (*London Transport Executive v Clarke* [1980] ICR 532, CA). It is not necessary for an act of repudiation to amount to industrial misconduct. The test is an objective one. During an employee's absence on sick leave his employer closed down the premises where the employee worked. The EAT held that '... the closing of the works [constituted] a dismissal by way of repudiation, even though the employee at that particular time [was] unfit for work. [The] repudiation was accepted by [the employee] when he asked for redundancy payments' (per Browne-Wilkinson J, *Northgate Laundries Ltd v Jenner*, 5 February 1982, EAT).

2.41
A fundamental breach generally occurs when one of the parties to a contract of employment commits a breach so serious that it goes to the very root of the contract. An example of a fundamental breach of contract is that of the employer who unilaterally halves the salary of one of his employees. In some situations, a sequence of less serious breaches might well add up to a fundamental breach (but see Chapter 3, para 3.50). When there has been a fundamental breach, either party can withdraw from the contract. An employee may resign and seek redress by complaining to a tribunal that he (or she) had been 'constructively dismissed' (see Chapter 3, para 3.38). But speed is of the essence. An employee might well be deemed to have waived his rights by 'affirming' the contract. Furthermore there must

be some overt acceptance of the repudiation communicated to the employer. The contract does not automatically end by a wish of a party that it should do so (*Western Excavating (EEC) Ltd v Sharp* [1978] ITR 132, CA and *Rigby v Ferodo* Ltd [1988] ICR 29, HL).

2.42
If an employer informs an employee that he (or she) (the employer) intends to take some unlawful action in the future (an 'anticipatory breach'), the employee need not wait for that breach to occur. If, on the other hand, the employer retracts and notifies the employee accordingly, *before* the employee resigns, the right to act on the anticipated breach is lost (*Norwest Holst Group Administration Ltd v Harrison* [1985] ICR 668, CA).

2.43
An employer's behaviour can be taken into account, along with other breaches, to determine whether, cumulatively, it and they amount to repudiatory conduct. If, on the other hand, there is a continuing series of the same breaches (eg repeated non-payment of commission), each of which would entitle an employee to resign, the employee would not forfeit his (or her) right to rely on any subsequent breach simply because he had failed to react when the first breach occurred (*Lewis v Motorworld Garages Ltd* [1986] ICR 157, CA; and *Reid v Camphill Engravers* [1990] ICR 435, EAT).

2.44
Many constructive dismissal cases arise where it is alleged that there has been a breach of the implied term of mutual trust and confidence (as to which, see Chapter 5, paras 5.85 to 5.91).

'OUT OF COURT' SETTLEMENTS

2.45
Many parties to proceedings will do their best to settle their dispute 'out of court'; that is to say, without going to the expense of a court or tribunal hearing. In tribunal cases, the Advisory, Conciliation & Arbitration Service (ACAS) is duty-bound to attempt to resolve disputes between employers and employees (see Chapter 1, paras 1.71 to 1.74) (*Source*: ETA 1996, ss 18 & 19).

2.46

Any contract of employment that purports to override an employee's statutory rights, including his (or her) right to bring proceedings before an employment tribunal, is *prima facie* void and unenforceable. But that right can be overriden if a dispute or difference of opinion between an employer and one of his employees is settled by means of a 'COT 3' agreement (following the intervention of an ACAS conciliation officer). The same is true of a 'compromise agreement', and of an agreement made under the yet to be introduced ACAS-developed arbitration scheme (prescribed by section 7 of the Employment Rights Dispute Resolution Act 1998). An employee who signs such an agreement thereby waives his right to have his complaint resolved before an employment tribunal. In other words, he cannot then change his mind. The *quid pro quo* will be an agreed amount of compensation or the employer's agreement to make restitution by other means, including reinstatement or re-engagement.

'COT 3' agreements

2.47

When an originating application (Form IT1) is sent to the Secretary to the Tribunals, an ACAS Conciliation Officer may be invited to intervene to bring about a settlement. If a settlement is reached and terms agreed, both parties to the dispute or disagreement will be invited to put their signatures to Form COT 3. Once this is done, the agreement is legally binding on both parties (*Source*: ERA 1996, s. 203(2)(e); ETA 1996, s. 18).

'Compromise' agreements

2.48

A 'compromise agreement' (properly concluded) is also legally binding on both parties. An employee who believes that his (or her) employer has breached one or other of his statutory rights under:

- the Sex Discrimination Act 1975;
- the Race Relations Act 1976;
- the Trade Union & Labour Relations (Consolidation) Act 1992;

- the Disability Discrimination Act 1995;

- the Employment Rights Act 1996;

- the Working Time Regulations 1998; or

- the National Minimum Wage Act 1998;

may agree to 'sign away' his right to bring (or continue with) proceedings in return for a mutually acceptable 'out of court' payment or other form of settlement. To be valid and legally binding:

- a compromise agreement must be in writing and must relate to the particular dispute (liable to give rise to tribunal proceedings) between the conflicting parties;

- the employee must have received legal advice from a 'relevant independent adviser' (see next paragraph) – named in the agreement – as to the terms and effect of the proposed agreement and, in particular, its effect on his (or her) ability to pursue his rights before an employment tribunal;

- there must be in force, when the *relevant independent adviser* gives his (or her) advice, a contract of insurance (or an indemnity provided for members of a profession or professional body) covering the risk of a claim by the employee in respect any loss arising in consequence of his having acted on that advice; and

- it must state that the agreement satisfies the conditions regulating compromise agreements under one or other of the Sex Discrimination Act 1975 (s. 77(4A)), the Race Relations Act 1976 (s. 72(4A)), the Trade Union & Labour Relations (Consolidation) Act 1992 (s. 288(2B)); the Disability Discrimination Act 1995 (s. 9(2)(b)); the Employment Rights Act 1996 (s. 203(2)(f) & (3)); the Working Time Regulations 1998 (reg 35); and the National Minimum Wage Act 1998 (s. 49).

2.49
A person is a *relevant independent adviser* if he (or she) is:

- a qualified lawyer – that is to say, a barrister, advocate, a solicitor who holds a practising certificate, or (as respects England and

Wales) a person other than a barrister or solicitor who is an authorised advocate or authorised litigator (within the meaning of the Courts & Legal Services Act 1990).

Since 1 August 1998, when s. 9(1) of the Employment Rights (Dispute Resolution) Act 1998 came into force, a person is also a *relevant independent adviser* if he (or she):

- is an officer, official, employee or member of an independent trade union who has been certified in writing by the trade union as competent to give advice and as authorisied to do so on behalf of the trade union; or

- works at an advice centre (whether as an employee or a volunteer) and has been certified in writing by the centre as competent to give advice and as authorised to do so on behalf of the centre; or

- is a person of a description specified in an order made by the Secretary of State.

A person is *not* a *relevant independent adviser* to one of the parties to a dispute if he (or she) is in any way connected with (or employed by) the other party; or if (in the case of advice given by a person working for an advice centre) there is any fee charged for such advice (*Sources*: SDA 1975 (s. 77(4A)(d); RRA 1976 (s. 72(4A)(c)); TULRA 1992 (s. 288(2B)(c)); DDA 1995 (s. 9(3)(a)); ERA 1996 (s. 203(3)(c)), WTR 1998 (reg 35(5)), and NMWA (s. 49(6)).

'Arbitration' agreements

2.50
On 1 August 1998, when section 7 of the Employment Rights (Dispute Resolution) Act 1998 came into force, a new section 212A was inserted in the Trade Union & Labour Relations (Consolidation) Act 1992 to empower ACAS to prepare and promulgate a scheme providing for arbitration in the case of disputes that involve (or could involve) complaints to an employment tribunal under Part X of the Employment Rights Act 1996 (*Unfair Dismissal*), or complaints under any enactment specified in an order made by the Secretary of

State. Once the new scheme is promulgated (Summer, 2001), the resolution of any dispute or complaint under that scheme will be legally binding on both parties.

'WITHOUT PREJUDICE'

2.51

Frequently, a party feels that there is justice in his (or her) claim or defence. No amount of persuasion will make him change his mind, even if it comes from an independent and objective source. Any negotiations that take place through ACAS are privileged. Nothing can be revealed as to what has been said or as to the outcome or that would indicate a view taken by ACAS (*Source*: ETA 1996, s. 18(7); TULRA 1992, s. 290).

2.52

So-called 'without prejudice' correspondence – which usually arises when one party to a dispute writes (on one or more occasions) to the other party offering to compromise or to settle 'out of court' – is not admissible in evidence before a court or tribunal unless both parties agree. Verbal discussions can also be conducted 'without prejudice'. But if there is a dispute over whether such discussions *were* 'without prejudice', some or all of what was said during those discussions may have to be revealed to the court or tribunal to enable the question to be resolved. By that time, the damage will already have been done. If letters or memoranda are marked 'without prejudice', the question brooks of no argument. But no privilege will be accorded to a 'without prejudice' letter if there was no dispute between the parties (or if no negotiations had begun or taken place) at the time the letter was written (Re *Daintrey, ex parte Holt* [1893] 2 QB 116, QBD).

2.53

When a party to a dispute makes an offer to settle (or reach a compromise), it tends to suggest an admission of some liability – leaving only the question of the amount to be decided. The actions of an employer (or other respondent) in attempting to reach a settlement might be viewed as trying either to rid himself (or herself) of a troublesome dispute, or to save money. For that reason, it is usually felt better that the adjudicating body does *not* know what has gone on before the case is heard. Indeed in the High Court, and County Court, the judge is not allowed to know about an offer to settle or about any 'payment into court' (see Chapter 27, paras 27.93 & 27.94) until the case is concluded and liability has been established. Once correspondence is marked 'without prejudice', it is said to be 'privileged'. It can only be produced in proceedings if both sides agree (*Walker v Wiltshire* [1889] 23 QBD 355, QB). A consequence of this is that a party cannot rely on a 'without prejudice' letter purporting to 'accept' repudiatory conduct (see paras 2.40 to 2.44 above), and so bring the contract to an end, because the letter is ineffective. In any event, it cannot be shown to the court (except by agreement) (*Norwest Holst Group Administration Ltd v Harrison* [1985] ICR 668, CA).

2.54

Where there is a claim for something other than a monetary one, for instance, for a declaration about some matter, and one party put forward proposals 'without prejudice' to settle the action, the letter containing those proposals can be produced after liability has been determined. The court can then decide what order for costs is appropriate. Notice of an intention to take this course of action should be given to the other side (*Cutts v Head & Another* [1984] 1 AER 597, CA). A similar procedure can be adopted in the tribunals where there is no procedure for making a 'payment into court'. An employer might offer a former employee the sum of £500 'without prejudice' in settlement of his (or her) claim. If the applicant employee fails to obtain an award above that figure, then the tribunal can be shown the letter and asked to make an order for costs against the employee – on the basis that the proceedings have been carried on unreasonably (*Source*: Employment Tribunals (Constitution & Rules of Procedure) Regulations 1993, Sch 1, Rule 12(1)).

'IN HONOUR ONLY'

2.55

Usually, a union that has concluded a collective agreement with an employer (or association of employers), will not wish to be exposed to a claim for damages in the event of a breach of contract. The union is protected under TULRA 1992, which provides that a collective agreement 'shall be conclusively presumed not to have been intended by the parties to be a legally enforceable contract – unless the agreement is in writing and contains a provision that (however expressed) states that the parties intend that the agreement *shall* be a legally enforceable contract'. The same applies if the parties to the agreement intend that certain clauses in the agreement are intended to be legally enforceable, and the remainder, not (*Source:* TULRA 1992, ss 179 & 180).

2.56

If some of the terms in a collective agreement between an employer and a union are incorporated into a contract of employment, and include the words: 'This agreement is binding in honour only...', it has been held that this clause did not prevent an employee from relying on the terms that formed part of his (or her) own contract. The exclusion clause had not been incorporated into the employee's contract of employment (*Marley v Forward Trust Group* [1986] ICR 891, CA and *Robertson v British Gas Corporation* [1983] ICR 351, CA). Only those terms that were apt to be enforced were included, eg those fixing terms of pay, hours of work, disciplinary proceedings etc. Those relating to procedures designed to resolve disputes between employers' and employees' representatives were excluded (*National Coal Board v NUM & Others* [1986] ICR 736. ChD).

2.57

If there is a redundancy clause in a collective agreement, an employee seeking to rely on that clause can do so in two ways. Either he (or she) can show that the clause has been expressly incorporated into his contract of employment or, if unable to do so, may be able to establish an implied incorporation by showing an intent that is apparent within the contract. The wording must be sufficiently clear to show that it was intended to be contractually binding (*Alexander & Others v Standard Telephones & Cables plc* [1990] ICR 291, ChD).

'EX GRATIA' PAYMENTS

2.58

The essence of an award of damages or compensation is that the injured party should be placed in the same position he (or she) would have been in but for the breach of contract (or breach of a statutory duty, or any other wrongdoing). In short, the employee should be compensated, so far as is possible, for the loss and damage he has suffered.

2.59

An employer will make an *ex gratia* payment to a former employee for a variety of reasons. He (or she) may want to 'buy off' a prospective tribunal hearing or court case. He may be uncertain about the extent of his own liability, or he may merely want to be generous. An *ex gratia* payment, paid to an employee in purported settlement of a possible future claim, can be offset against an award of compensation ordered by an employment tribunal. In short, the loss to the employee will have been mitigated to the extent of that *ex gratia* payment (*Chelsea Football Club v Heath* [1981] ICR 323, EAT and *Rushton v Harcros Timber & Building Supplies Ltd, The Times*, 17 December 1992, EAT). Difficulties sometimes arise when an *ex gratia* payment has been made, but the employee is held to have been partly responsible for his or her own dismissal (as to which, see also Chapter 5, paras 5.147 to 5.153).

2.60

At the time of his dismissal, an employee received an *ex gratia* payment of £2,000 from his former employer. At the subsequent tribunal hearing, the employee is awarded a total of £5,000 as compensation for unfair dismissal. But the tribunal decides that the employee was 25 per cent to blame for his dismissal. The question is this: should the tribunal deduct the 25 per cent from the full award of £5,000, or should they deduct that 25 per cent from the net amount now due to the employee (that is to say, £5,000 less the £2,000 already paid)? There is a difference of judicial views; however, on general principles it would seem that the latter approach is the right one (*Parker & Farr v Shelvey* [1979] ICR 896, EAT and *Clement-Clarke International Ltd v Manley* [1979] ICR 74, EAT). The *ex gratia* payment will have to be taken off the gross amount of the loss and not from the statutory limit placed on an award. Thus an employee who has suffered an actual loss of £20,000, and who has received an *ex gratia* payment of £6,000, will still be entitled to £11,500, that is to say, the (then) current maximum 'compensatory' award (*McCarthy v British Insulated Cables plc* [1985] IRLR 94, EAT). For further information about awards of compensation, please turn to Chapter 5 (or the Index to this book).

'MITIGATION OF LOSS'

2.61

It is a cardinal principle of law, and a statutory requirement in unfair dismissal claims, that a person who suffers damage as a result of the wrongful act of another must attempt to 'mitigate' his (or her) loss by making all reasonable efforts to reduce the extent of the damage (*Gallear v J F Watson & Son Ltd* [1979] IRLR 306, EAT and *A G Bracey Ltd v Iles [1973] IRLR 210, NIRC*). That duty will usually be discharged where it can be said that he has acted 'as a reasonable person would do if he had no hope of seeking compensation from his previous employer' (*Archbold Freightage Ltd v Wilson* [1974] IRLR 10, NIRC) (*Source*: ERA 1996, s. 123(4)).

2.62

The onus of proving failure to mitigate, both under the common law and statute law, lies on the employer. The test applied is whether the employee has acted reasonably. All the surrounding circumstances including any relating to his (or her) personal situation have to be considered. This does not mean that any whim or fancy will justify a refusal to take a suitable job (*Bessenden Properties Ltd v Corness* [1974] IRLR 338, CA and *Johnson v Hobart Manufacturing Co Ltd*, 20 July 1990, EAT).

A 55-year-old employee with a bad back, who was nonetheless able to perform his work satisfactorily, was held to have been unfairly dismissed. He was rejected for other jobs on health grounds, and so 'signed on sick' with the Department of Social Security (DSS) to get additional benefits. This had the effect of taking him off the work register. After a while, he reverted to his unemployed status. It was held that he had acted reasonably and was entitled to compensation based on his age and likelihood of obtaining other work. It was not limited to the time up to when he signed on sick (*Wilson v Glenrose (Fish Merchants) Ltd & Another*, 21 July 1992, EAT).

2.63

The local economic climate is also important. In difficult times, an employee will generally be expected to accept lower-paid or lower-level employment, or travel further afield. Furthermore, he (or she) must take energetic steps to secure another job. Becoming self-employed, or seeking retraining, may amount to mitigation in appropriate circumstances (*Daley v Dorsett (Alma Dolls) Ltd* [1981] IRLR 385, EAT and *Gardiner-Hill v Roland Berger Technics Ltd* [1982] IRLR 498, EAT).

2.64

Under the common law, when a dismissal is wrongful (Chapter 8, paras 8.21 to 8.25), a contract of employment can subsist in special circumstances. As an employee is only entitled to be paid for work that he (or she) actually performs, he is bound to seek alternative employment and thus 'mitigate' his loss (*Gunton v Richmond-upon-Thames BC* [1980] ICR 755, CA).

2.65

Under statute law, a repudiatory act by an employer immediately brings the contract of employment to an end. Consequently, the employee should look for alternative work, unless he (or she) intends to seek reinstatement or re-engagement (as to which, see Chapter 5, paras 5.158 to 5.165). In such a case, he must pursue his claim before an employment tribunal as soon as possible (*Robert Cort & Sons Ltd v Charman* [1981] ICR 816, EAT). A dismissed employee's unreasonable refusal to accept an offer of reinstatement or re-engagement by his former employer will ordinarily be treated as having failed to mitigate his loss. However, if the employee had been treated in a humiliating manner while in employment, or if the terms of an offer to re-engage would result in a substantial drop in earnings (and / or a loss of benefits), the employee will usually be entitled to decline that offer (*Fyfe v Scientific Furnishings Ltd* [1989] ICR 648, EAT) (*Source:* ERA 1996, s. 117(8)).

2.66

The rules relating to mitigation do not apply to a redundancy payment (see Chapter 4), except as set out in Chapter 5, paras 5.168 to 5.170. Such payments are treated as payments for past service. Nor do they usually apply to the notice period (see Chapter 3, para 3.9). Any earnings during that time must normally be disregarded when computing the employee's loss (see Chapter 5, paras 5.171 to 5.175) (*TBA Industrial Products Ltd v Locke* [1984] ICR 228, EAT, *Addison v Babcock Fata Ltd* [1987] ICR 805, CA, and *Isleworth Studios Ltd v Richard* [1988] ICR 432, EAT).

2.67

There is conflicting authority over whether a failure to use an internal appeal procedure can amount to a breach of duty to mitigate. The better view is that it might do so in appropriate circumstances. However, where an employee does pursue an appeal, his (or her) failure to seek alternative employment before the hearing does not amount to a failure to mitigate loss (*Hoover v Forde* [1980] ICR 239, EAT, *W Muir Ltd v Lamb* [1985] IRLR 95, EAT, and *Williams v Loyds Retailers Ltd* [1973] IRLR 262, IT).

2.68

Neither do the rules apply to the sum payable to an employee for the period between dismissal and an order for reinstatement or re-engagement (see Chapter 5, para 5.164) even though the employee delayed instituting proceedings. But if an employer fails to comply with such an order, then the tribunal will bear in mind any failure by the employee to mitigate when it decides at what point within the relevant period (see Chapter 5, paras 5.176 to 5.178) to assess any *additional* award of compensation (*City & Hackney Health Authority v Crisp* [1990] ICR 95, EAT).

AGENTS AND REPRESENTATIVES

2.69

Under the ordinary law of contract, the act of a person (an 'agent') who is employed on behalf of another will bind that other (the 'principal') if he (or she) acts within his actual or ostensible authority. Thus, employers will be held liable for the consequences when one of their managers unfairly sacks a worker. The extent of this principle is questionable when applied to a member of a union, where the union has been consulted by the employers over proposed redundancies. One division of the EAT thought that no reasonable employer was entitled to infer that individual employees were privy to the content of discussions between him and the union. Another division doubted the correctness of that decision (*Huddersfield Parcels Ltd v Sykes* [1981] IRLR 115, EAT and *McClafferty v Tesco Stores Ltd*, 20 February 1985, EAT). A distinction is drawn between the powers of a union representative to act for an employee in general matters and his powers in a specific context. Although a union may negotiate wage rates for its members, it cannot, in the absence of express authorisation, accept a notice of dismissal on behalf of one of its members (*Ramalheira & Others v Bloomsbury Health Authority*, 15 December 1988, EAT).

2.70

A union formally agreed with an employer that being at work under the influence of alcohol was so serious a misdemeanour as to warrant summary dismissal of the offender. The EAT held that the employers were 'entitled to assume that all employees who are members of the union know of and are bound by its provisions. There could be no stability in industrial relations if this were not so' (per Lord McDonald in *Gray Dunn & Co Ltd v Edwards* [1980] IRLR 23, EAT).

2.71

Where a liquidator is appointed, his (or her) acts bind the company, as he is acting as an agent for an insolvent company (*Re Hartlebury Printers Ltd & Others (in liquidation)* [1992] ICR 559, Ch.D).

ACTS OF SOLICITORS AND OTHER SKILLED ADVISERS

2.72

Solicitors and other persons (or bodies) holding themselves out as skilled advisers are agent for the parties for whom they act. Consequently, if a litigant leaves the conduct of his (or her) case in the hands of a solicitor, a legal advice centre, or the Citizens' Advice Bureau, and through an error, no Originating Application (see Chapter 27, paras 27.10 to 27.16) was 'presented' to the Secretary to the Tribunals in time, then that failure will be deemed to be the fault of the litigant. Although the litigant may then be unable to prosecute his claim, he would have a right of action for negligence or breach of contract against the adviser (*Allen v Hammett* [1982] ICR 227, EAT). Where a solicitor or other skilled adviser fails to take action in time because of an erroneous view of the law, and the court or tribunal has discretion to allow the omission to be put right, then the principle that is applied is whether 'there was good cause or sufficient reason' for the error. Salmon, LJ, put it this way: 'That was in my judgment a wrong view of the rules. Was it, however, a view which any trained lawyer could reasonably take? I think undoubtedly it was. For one thing, a very experienced practice master who, when asked the question, rather late, obviously took the same view. It would be difficult for this court to say that the solicitor could not reasonably take the view which had been adopted by the practice master: and it must be remembered that until this case there had been no authority at all upon the construction of [the rule]'. (*Jones v Jones* [1980] 2 QB 577, CA).

2.73

Where there is some question mark over which of two dates is correct, a prudent lawyer or adviser should generally play safe. He (or she) should assume that the action should be taken on the earlier date. The same principles (regarding the exercise of discretion by a court or tribunal) apply where a person consults a solicitor or other skilled adviser and is given advice that turns out to be incorrect. Was there 'good cause or sufficient reason' for it? (See Chapter 3, para 3.75) (*Riley v Tesco Stores* [1980], ICR 323, CA). The term 'skilled adviser' means anyone who holds himself out as an expert in a particular field, either expressly or by implication. Rather like motor car drivers, there is no differentiation made over the standard of skill. Skilled advisers are all expected to be of a minimum standard, whatever their experience.

2.74

Under both statutory and common law, a solicitor or other representative who negligently fails to take action in time, resulting in a claim being lost, will be exposed to an action for damages in the ordinary civil courts. But, if it is shown that the proposed claim in the tribunal would have failed because, for instance, the evidence called in the civil court established that it would have been within the reasonable response of a reasonable employer to dismiss, and the particular employer would have sacked him (or her), he will recover nothing from the solicitor or representative. He would have suffered no loss (*Siraj-Eldin v Campbell Middleton Burness & Dickson* [1989] IRLR 208, Ct.S).

2.75

A solicitor or other skilled adviser, instructed to act for a litigant, has 'ostensible authority' to settle a case through ACAS. The resultant agreement (a 'COT 3' agreement) is binding on the parties and it matters not that the litigant had given instructions that the case was not to be compromised, unless the other side knew of the restriction on the solicitor or adviser's authority to act. Further, the settlement can include other potential claims arising out of the employment relationship (*Freeman v Sovereign Chicken Ltd* [1991] ICR 853, EAT). Although the general rule in litigation is that a person is bound by the acts of his (or her) representative, there are circumstances where a court or tribunal can go behind an agreement or concession (*Harber v North London Polytechnic* [1990] IRLR 198, CA). Under the common law, the ostensible authority is limited to those issues that are raised in the pleadings. Counsel or solicitors cannot bind a litigant on other matters unless expressly instructed to do so.

3

Statutory employment rights (general)

RIGHTS OF EMPLOYEES NOT TO BE OVERRIDDEN

3.1
As we have seen, employees nowadays have a great many statutory rights. Employers, for their part, have a parallel duty to respect those rights and an implied responsibility to ensure that employees are not kept in ignorance of those rights. The penalties for infringement of an employee's statutory right can be very harsh indeed. Any term in a contract of employment (or other agreement) that purports to exclude or limit the operation of the relevant provisions of the Employment Rights Act 1996, the Trade Union & Labour Relations (Consolidation) Act 1992, or of any related employment legislation (Equal Pay Act 1970, Sex Discrimination Act 1975, etc), is void and unenforceable.

3.2
Any agreement that purports to override an employee's statutory rights, notably the right of an employee to bring proceedings before an employment tribunal, will *not* be legally binding *unless* it is:

- a so-called 'COT 3' agreement (concluded with the intervention of an ACAS conciliation officer);

- a 'compromise' agreement (which satisfies the conditions regulating compromise agreements; or

- an agreement under a yet-to-be-promulgated ACAS-inspired 'arbitration scheme' (which complies with sections 7 and 8 of the Employment Rights [Dispute Resolution] Act 1998).

(*Sources*: SDA 1975, s. 77(4)(aa); RRA 1976, s. 72(4)(aa); DDA 1995, s. 9(2)(b); TULRA 1992, s. 288(2A); ETA 1996, s. 18; ERA 1996, s. 203(2)(f); ER(DR)A 1998, ss 7 & 8.)

'COT 3' agreements

3.3

The Employment Tribunals Act 1996 (at s. 18) requires an ACAS conciliation officer to attempt to promote the reinstatement or re-engagement of a dismissed employee on equitable terms. If the employee has no wish to be re-employed or such a solution would be impracticable from the point of view of either or both the employer and the employee, the role of a conciliation officer would be confined to promoting an 'out of court' settlement and recording the agreed terms on Form COT 3. However, it is not a conciliation officer's role to express a view about the rights and wrongs of a particular dispute or to propose an appropriate settlement figure. Indeed, anything said by a conciliation officer to the parties in dispute is inadmissible in any subsequent tribunal hearing. Before the parties put their signatures to a 'COT 3 agreement', the conciliation officer will explain the legally binding nature of such an agreement Once the terms are genuinely agreed, they are binding on both parties (*Gilbert v Kembridge Pictures Ltd* [1984] ICR 188, EAT and *Slack v Greenham (Plant Hire) Ltd* [1983] IRLR 271, EAT).

3.4

It should be pointed out that an employee who claims that his (or her) employer has infringed one or other of his statutory rights (eg the right of a pregnant employee to paid time off work for ante natal care) has no need to resign in order to refer his complaint to an employment tribunal. Indeed, if the employee is dismissed for doing so (or for threatening to do so) the employer will be liable to pay a substantial award of compensation. Once an employee's originating application (Form IT1) has been received by the Secretary to the Tribunals, copies will be sent both to the employer and to ACAS. In such cases, a conciliation officer will intervene only if *both* parties agree. But, if the employee has not yet initiated proceedings, a conciliation officer may intervene at the request of *either* party to the dispute. An employee's agreement not to press ahead with proceedings before a tribunal will be valid so long as a conciliation officer has intervened in the manner described in the previous paragraph.

3.5

In *Trafford Carpets Ltd v Barker (Case A)*, 13 November 1990, EAT, the EAT held that the terms set out in what purported to be a COT 3 agreement were merely a device to enable an employee to gain a benefit under a Government Enterprise Scheme. In *Livingstone v Hepworth Refractories plc* [1992] ICR 287, EAT, an ACAS conciliation officer intervened to promote a settlement in a dispute about an employee's dismissal. The resultant COT 3 agreement stated that the terms agreed were 'in full and final settlement of *all* claims which the [employee] may have against the [employer] arising out of his employment'. The EAT held that the agreement was not all embracing and did not debar the employee from instituting further proceedings against his employer alleging unlawful discrimination.

'Compromise' agreements

3.6
A so-called 'compromise agreement' (concluded without the intervention of ACAS) is a form of 'out of court' settlement which is binding on the parties if it:

- is in writing;
- relates to the particular complaint and no other;
- was concluded after the employee has received independent advice from a *relevant independent adviser*
- identifies the adviser;
- states that conditions regulating compromise agreements have been satisfied.

(For further particulars, please turn to Chapter 2, paras 2.48 & 2.49.)

3.7
Even if a tribunal has held a dismissal to have been unfair and has sent the parties away to agree (and they do agree) an acceptable amount of compensation, an employee can still contest that agreed amount before a tribunal. Only if the agreement is a 'COT 3' or 'compromise' agreement will a party be prevented from bringing further proceedings (*Courage Take Home Trade Ltd v Keys* [1986] ICR 874, EAT).

'Arbitration' agreements

3.8
From 1 August 1998, when section 7 of the Employment Rights
(Dispute Resolution) Act 1998 came into force, an agreement under a
yet to be promulgated ACAS-inspired 'arbitration scheme' will also
be legally binding on the parties to a dispute; as to which, see
Chapter 2, para 2.50.

STATUTORY NOTICE PERIODS

3.9
Under the Employment Rights Act 1996, an employee who has
worked for his (or her) employer for one month or more is entitled
to:

- a minimum of one week's notice to terminate his or her contract
  of employment; rising to

- two weeks' notice, on completion of two years' service; plus

- an additional week's notice for each further year of service up to
  a maximum of 12 weeks' notice for 12 and more years' service.

(*Source*: ERA 1996, ss 86 to 91.)

Section 86(2) of the 1996 Act states that an employee who has been
continuously employed for one month or more is not required to
give more than one week's to terminate his (or her) contract of
employment – unless the contract requires the employee to give
more than that statutory minimum amount.

Note: In computing when the notice period begins and ends, the day on which notice
was actually given must be disregarded (*West v Kneels Ltd* [1987] ICR 146, EAT; and
Misset v Council of the European Communities, *The Times*, 23 March 1987, ECJ.

3.10
At 'common law' (see Chapter 8) the notice period is either that
specified in the contract of employment, or if nothing is said, then
that which is implied by law. The length of an implied period is that
which is reasonable in the circumstances. This will depend on the
nature of the employment, the seniority of the employee, the general
custom in that type of occupation, and perhaps also on the period

over which pay is calculated. An employee's 'common law' right to notice can vary considerably – with a senior manager being entitled to more than six months' notice in the appropriate circumstances. In one case, the director of a small company was held to be entitled to three months' notice. In another, the Court of Appeal held that the correct period of notice for a person in charge of several cinemas was six months (*Hill v C A Parsons & Co Ltd* [1971] 3 AER 1345, CA; and *Brindle v H W Smith (Cabinets) Ltd* [1973] ITR 69, CA).

Employee's rights during notice

3.11
An employee must be paid his (or her) normal wages or salary during the notice period (net of any payment of sick pay, statutory sick pay, maternity pay, statutory maternity pay, holiday pay, or otherwise, in respect of that same period of notice). That same rule applies (subject to the *Qualification* below) whether or not it was the employer or the employee who gave notice, if, during the notice period:

- the employee is ready and willing to work but no work is provided for him to do; or

- the employee is incapable of work because of sickness or injury; or

- the employee is absent from work wholly or partly because of pregnancy or childbirth; or

- the employee is absent from work in accordance with the terms of his employment relating to holidays.

Qualification: However, that right arises *if, but only if,* the period of notice required to be given *by the employer* is the same or not more than one week more generous than the notice required to be given in accordance with s. 86(1) of the 1996 Act. For example, an employee with two years' service has the statutory right to be given two weeks' notice to terminate his (or her) contract of employment. But his contract states that he is entitled to one month's notice. As his contractual right to one month's notice is more than one week more generous than his statutory right to be given two week's notice, he has no right to be paid during the notice period (unless, of course, his contract states otherwise).

Information about notice to be included in the written statement of employment particulars

3.12

The written statement of terms of employment, which an employer is required to give to each of his employees (within two months of the date on which employment began), *must* specify 'the length of notice which an employee is obliged to give and entitled to receive to terminate his (or her) contract of employment'. An employer's refusal or failure to include this information in the written statement will very likely lead to a reference to an employment tribunal and the imposition of legally binding provisions relating to notice with which the employer will have no choice but to comply (*Source*: ERA 1996, ss 1(4)(e), 11 & 12).

Notice and the 'effective date of termination'

3.13

The Employment Rights Act 1996 points out that, unless dismissed for an inadmissible or unlawful reason, an employee does not qualify to present a complaint of unfair dismissal if he (or she) had not been continuously employed for at least two years ending with the 'effective date of termination' of his contract of employment.

3.14

Furthermore, a tribunal will not normally consider a complaint of unfair dismissal unless it is presented before the end of the period of three months beginning with that 'effective date of termination' (see below). See also *Time Limits For Complaints* (paras 3.68 to 3.83).

'EFFECTIVE DATE OF TERMINATION'

3.15

The expression 'effective date of termination' referred to in paras 3.13 and 3.14 above (and elsewhere in this book) has two different meanings. It means one thing when calculating an employee's length of continuous service on the termination of his (or her) employment, and quite another when reckoning the 'time limits' for presenting a complaint to an industrial tribunal.

Definition 1: Had the employee been continuously employed for the requisite period?

3.16

To determine whether an employee had been continuously employed for the prescribed minimum period of one year ending with the 'effective date of termination' of his (or her) employment, that effective date is the date on which the statutory period of notice (if longer than the actual or contractual period of notice) *would have expired* had it been duly given on the date on which notice of termination was given by the employer. Otherwise, it is the date on which the notice actually given by the employer expired. If no notice was given, it is the date on which the statutory minimum period of notice would have expired had it duly been given by the employer on the date on which the employment was terminated. The same 'deeming' rules apply even when an employee has agreed to be paid money in lieu of notice or to accept a shorter period of notice (*Secretary of State for Employment v Staffordshire CC* [1989] IRLR 360, CA). (*Source*: ERA 1996, s. 97(2).)

3.17

If it was the employee who gave notice (in circumstances in which he or she was entitled to do so, with or without notice, by virtue of the employer's conduct, ie in a 'constructive dismissal' situation), the 'effective date of termination' is the date on which the *employer's* notice (as required by s. 86 of the 1996 Act) would have expired had it been the employer who gave notice to terminate and not the employee. If the employee resigned without notice (in the same 'constructive dismissal' situation), it is the date on which the employer's s. 86 notice would have expired had it been given on the date on which the employee left (*ibid* s. 97(4)).

3.18

For instance, a man who has been continuously employed by his employer for eleven months and twenty-five days has the statutory right to be given one week's notice by his employer to terminate his contract of employment. If he is dismissed without notice, his employment will nonetheless be deemed to have continued for a further week – which means that on the 'effective date of termination' of his employment he will have completed the prescribed minimum one year's continuous service – sufficient to qualify him to pursue a complaint of unfair dismissal before an employment tribunal.

Note: A dismissal without notice or with less notice than is prescribed either by statute or, if longer, or by an employee's contract of employment, is *prima facie* a 'wrongful dismissal' (not to be confused with the expression 'unfair dismissal'). An employee who has been 'wrongfully dismissed' can apply to a tribunal or court for damages arising out of his (or her) employer's failure to pay wages in respect of the 'missing' notice period. Although an employee forfeits his entitlement to notice when summarily dismissed for gross misconduct, the 'effective date of termination' (for the purposes of determining whether he or she had been continuously employed for the requisite one year) will be the date on which the statutory period of notice would have expired had it been duly given on the date the dismissal took place.

3.19

The 'effective date of termination' (as defined in paras 3.16 and 3.17 above) will also be used to determine an employee's entitlement or otherwise to a statutory redundancy payment (and the amount of any such payment). Furthermore, that same method of calculation (wth minor modifications) is used by an employment tribunal to calculate the basic award of compensation for unfair dismissal.

Definition 2: Complaint to be presented within three months of the 'effective date of termination'

3.20

For the purposes of para 3.14 above – time limits for presenting a complaint of unfair dismissal – the 'effective date of termination' of an employee's contract of employment is the date on which the employment actually ended (in common parlance, the date on which the employee 'cleared out his [or her] locker or desk' and left, or was escorted from, the premises). If the employee was dismissed with notice, it is the date on which that period of notice expired (regardless of whether the correct amount of notice was given). If the employee was dismissed without notice, it is the date on which the dismissal took place.

3.21

If it was the employee who resigned *with notice*, it is the date on which that notice expired. If the employee resigned *without notice*, it is the date on which the employee actually quit his (or her) job. It follows that an employee minded to present a complaint of unfair or wrongful dismissal to an employment tribunal must do so within three months beginning with the date on which his employment actually came to an end (*Source*: ERA 1996, s. 97(1)).

Summary dismissal – dismissal without notice

3.22

An employee guilty of conduct, which is tantamount to a repudiation of the contract of employment, thereby forfeits his (or her) right to notice and may be dismissed summarily (that is to say, 'on the spot'). In practice, an employer should not dismiss summarily without first investigating the circumstances and giving the employee an opportunity to present his 'side of the story'. While the facts are being investigated, the employee should be suspended on full pay (*Source*: ERA 1996, s. 86(6)).

3.23

To establish whether an employee who has been summarily dismissed has the right to present a complaint of unfair dismissal (in other words: had he (or she) been continuously employed for at least one year ending with the 'effective date of termination'?) the formula described in para 3.16 above must be applied. To determine the time limits within which such a complaint should be presented, the formula to be used is that described in para 3.20.

3.24

A newspaper's chief sports writer was annoyed at restrictions placed on his activities. He gave vent to his feelings at a press conference. His summary dismissal on the grounds that his damaging public attack had undermined the trust and confidence that must exist between a journalist and his employers was held to have been fair. What had to be considered was whether his conduct was 'insulting and insubordinate to such a degree as to be incompatible with the continuance of the relation of master and servant' (per Edmund Davies LJ in *Sanderson v Mirror Group of Newspapers Ltd*, 22 May 1986, EAT). See also *Wilson v Racher* [1974] ICR 428, CA.

3.25

Disobeying a lawful order will often be so serious a breach of an employee's contractual obligations as to warrant summary dismissal. However, it has to be established that the repudiation was intentional. An employee was given contradictory instructions by two senior line managers. Uncertain as to which to follow, she chose to comply with those given by her immediate superior. She was then sacked by the more senior of the two managers. It was held that her summary dismissal was unlawful (*Laws v London Chronicle (Indicator Newspapers) Ltd* [1959] 1 WLR 698, CA).

3.26

An employee, who was a shop steward, deliberately made use of an unauthorised password to gain access to sensitive information stored in his employer's computer. The EAT held that the employee's conduct *prima facie* warranted summary dismissal. The only 'escape' open to the employee would be to show that there were exceptional circumstances which justified his conduct (*Denco Ltd v Joinson* [1991] ICR 172, EAT).

'CONTINUITY OF EMPLOYMENT'

3.27

The concept of 'continuous employment' – first introduced by the (long since repealed) Contracts of Employment Act 1963 – is now to be found in Part XIV, Chapter I of the Employment Rights Act 1996. Many of an employee's statutory rights in employment depend on him (or her) having been 'continuously employed' for a prescribed period. For instance, to qualify for *paid* maternity leave, a pregnant employee must have average weekly earnings of £72 or more (2001/2002) and must have been continuously employed for 26 weeks or more at the beginning of the 14th week before the expected week of childbirth. Likewise, an employee's right to a guarantee payment in respect of a 'workless day' does not arise unless he had been continuously employed for a period of not less than one month ending with the date immediately preceding the relevant 'workless day'; and so on.

3.28

At a tribunal hearing, a person's employment during any period will be presumed to have been continuous, unless the employer presents clear evidence to the contrary. But where there has been a change of employer, it will for the employee to prove that continuity has not been broken. This can be shown by establishing that there was no real change in the employment apart from the name of the employer (*Secretary of State for Employment v Cohen & Another* [1987] ICR 570, EAT; and *Cannell v Council of the City of Newcastle upon Tyne*, 8 October 1993, EAT) (*Source*: ERA 1996, s. 210(5)).

3.29

An employee's period of employment begins on the day he (or she) started work under the relevant contract of employment – even if not actually at work on that day – and ends on the effective date of termination of that contract of employment (which, as was demonstrated earlier – see paras 3.16 to 3.21) may fall on a date later than that on which termination actually occurred (*General of the Salvation Army v Dewsbury* [1984] ICR 498, EAT). But the continuity of a period of employment will be broken by any week which does not count in computing a period of continuous employment.

3.30

So long as there is a contract of employment, an employee's period of employment under that contract will be deemed to be 'continuous' (unless the employer provides evidence to the contrary). This rule applies to every employee, part-time as well as full-time. Indeed, there are situations in which the interval between an employee's resignation or dismissal and his (or her) subsequent re-employment by the same or an associated employer will nonetheless count as part of an employee's total period of continuous employment. Thus:

(a) Continuity of employment is preserved if an employee resigns or is dismissed on grounds of ill health or injury and is re-employed by the same or an 'associated' employer within 26 weeks of the effective date of termination of his (or her) previous contract of employment. In other words, the intervening period counts as part of the employee's total period of continuous employment.

   Case Law: An employee resigned because the work he was doing became too onerous. He obtained employment elsewhere but, after five weeks, was fit enough to return to his old job. His former employers took him back. It was held that the change to lighter work for health reasons was to bridge the gap in his employment; consequently continuity was preserved (*Donnelly v Kelvin International Services* [1992] IRLR 496, EAT).

(b) Continuity of employment is also preserved if an employee is dismissed because of a temporary cessation of work (as often happens with seasonal workers) and is subsequently re-employed by the same or an associated employer when work once again becomes available. Once again, the intervening period counts as part of the employee's total period of continuous employment (regardless of how long that interval is).

Case Law: A teacher was employed over an eight-year period under a series of fixed-term contracts. It was held that it was necessary to find out the reason for the non-renewal of her contracts on each occasion. Continuity was preserved, as each 'temporary cessation of work' was of a 'transient' nature. The court applied a mathematical approach, because the pattern was regular, eg time at work compared to being away (*Ford v Warwickshire CC* [1983] ICR 273, HL; and *Sillars v Charrington Fuels Ltd* [1989] ICR 475, CA).

Where the pattern of work is irregular, a broad approach should be adopted, reviewing the entire previous period of employment. It is necessary to consider, not whether a temporary absence of work was caused by a cessation of work, but whether the absence from work was caused by a temporary cessation of work (*Fitzgerald v Hall, Russell & Co Ltd* [1970] AC 984, HL; and *Flack & Others v Kodak Ltd* [1986] ICR 775, CA).

If a person is employed by two associated employers (see paras 3.108 to 3.110 below), it is necessary to look at the history with each separately. If there is continuity in both, then the effect of the change from one company to the other has to be considered. If the break was short and the employee carried on with the same type of work, continuity for the whole period is likely to be preserved (*Corkhill v North Sea Ferries*, 10 November 1992, EAT).

Continuity is lost where there is a break, caused not by a general diminution of work, but because the employer spreads the work amongst others in the same pool of casual labour as the employee (*Byrne v Birmingham DC* [1987] ICR 519, CA).

A break was caused by lack of funds, during which an employee was not paid. It was held that the employee's enforced absence did not break the continuity of his employment (*University of Aston in Birmingham v Malik* [1984] ICR 492, EAT).

(c)   Continuity is preserved if an employee is absent from work (for whatever length of time) in circumstances in which, by arrangement or custom, he (or she) is regarded as continuing in his employer's employment for any purpose.

Case Law: A trawler skipper had worked on and off for the same employer for more than 35 years, signing off at the end of one voyage and signing on again at the beginning of another voyage. Whenever work was short, the employer would inform the skipper that he would be re-hired as soon as another vessel became available. On one occasion, the skipper had heard nothing for several months and decided to bring proceedings. The EAT held that custom and practice in the relationship between the skipper and the employer over the years resulted in continuity of employment being preserved, even though the final break had lasted nine months (*Boyd Line Ltd v Pitts*, 11 November 1985, EAT; and *Murphy v A Birrell & Son Ltd* [1978] IRLR 458, EAT).

In another case, continuity was *not* preserved when an employee was told, before he left to start up his own business, that he could return to his old job if his venture was not successful. The business failed and he returned to work with his former employer after an interval of five months. An agreement was made that continuity would be preserved during that five-month period of absence. It was held that, because the agreement was retrospective, it was not enforceable under the statute (*Secretary of State for Employment v Davis*, 19 July 1985, EAT).

An employer cannot confer statutory rights simply by agreeing that an employee's service with one employer will be treated as 'continuous' with his service with a second employer – the more so if the second employer is not an associated employer of (or a successor employer to) the first employer. An employer who breaks such an agreement can be sued for breach of contract under the common law but not under the (now) Employment Rights Act 1996 (*MSA (Britain) Ltd v Docherty*, 18 August 1982).

3.31
The same applies:

(d)   If the employee is on strike, whether official or unofficial, but returns to work once the strike is over. Although a strike does not break the continuity of a period of continuous employment, the period of absence on strike (measured in days) does not count in computing an employee's total period of continuous employment. In practice, the date on which the employee's period of continuous employment began will be treated as having been postponed by the number of days (during the period of employment) when the employee was on strike (*Source*: ERA 1996, ss 211 & 216).

It matters not whether a worker is sacked during the dispute provided the employer does not replace him (or her) permanently or the employee does not take another permanent job (*Bloomfield & Others v Springfield Honey Finishing Co Ltd* [1972] ICR 91, NIRC).

(e)   If the employee was absent from work as a result of a 'lock-out' by the employer (although the number of days lost because of the lockout will not count in computing the employee's total period of continuous employment (as to which, see (f) above). The test to be applied is whether the employers had instituted a 'lock-out' with a view to compelling employees to comply with the old or accept new terms of employment – which may or may not have involved a breach of contract (*Express & Star Ltd v Bundy & Others* [1987] ICR 379, CA).

(f)   If the employee was engaged wholly or mainly in work outside Great Britain *and* was not, during that period, an employed earner for the purposes of the Social Security Contributions & Benefits Act 1992 in respect of whom secondary Class I National Insurance contributions were payable under that Act (Source: ERA 1996, s. 215).

Note: Although continuity of employment is not broken in the circumstances described above, any week during the whole or part of which the employee in question worked outside Great Britain will *not* count in computing his (or her) total period of continuous employment with his employer.

(g)   If an employee is reinstated or re-engaged with the same or an associated employer, or by a successor to that employer, in consequence of a successful complaint of unfair or unlawful dismissal or where there is the potential for such a complaint (whether or not an originating application had been forwarded to the Secretary to the Tribunals) but ACAS has successfully intervened and, or a relevant 'compromise' or 'arbitration' agreement (or contract) has been entered into (*Source*: ERA 1996, s. 219).

3.32
Changing a lawful contract into an illegal contract at any stage – eg by agreeing that part of an employee's income would not be declared to the Inland Revenue – will result in a break in continuity. The qualifying period of continuous employment would not begin to run again until the illegality has been rectified.

Continuity and the transfer of a business or undertaking

3.33
If a trade, business or undertaking is transferred from one person to another, the transferee 'inherits' the contracts of employment of the persons employed in that trade or business at the time of the transfer and continuity of employment is preserved (*Source*: ERA 1996, s. 218). Related provisions are to be found in the Transfer of Undertakings (Protection of Employment) Regulations 1981 (usually referred to as the TUPE Regulations), implementing European Council Directive 77/187/EEC . The two provisions overlap in some respects and this can cause complications. As the EAT remarked in *Green-Wheeler v Onyst (UK) Ltd*, 30 July 1993, it may be necessary to proceed down each route separately, rather than switch from one to the other to try and enhance an employee's statutory rights. Most actions are now brought under the TUPE Regulations, as they are generally more favourable to the employee. For further particulars, please turn to Chapter 17.

3.34
Under s. 218 of the Employment Rights Act 1996, continuity is preserved if an employee is employed in a 'trade, or a business or an undertaking' or in an identifiable part of it that is sold. The business must have been purchased as a 'going concern' and this will usually include the goodwill, know-how, benefits of existing contracts, etc (*Melon v Hector Power Ltd* [1981] ICR 43, HL). Use of the term 'part of a business' does not mean that the part in question was previously carried on as a separate or self-contained entity. Suffice that it is capable of being run as a business by the new owner, whether or not he (or she) chooses to do so (*Kenmir Ltd v Frizzell* [1968] ITR 159, DC).

It is wrong to look at the transactions from the point of view of the employee. The correct test is whether the purchaser had become the owner of the business in succession to the vendor. If it is a different business after the transfer, continuity is broken (*Woodhouse v Peter Brotherhood Ltd* [1972] ICR 186, CA; and *Crook & Others v H Faiman Ltd*, 10 October 1989, CA).

Case Law: After his employer's business was sold, an employee stayed on with the transferor company for two weeks to deal with normal problems associated with business transfers. He then joined the transferee company. It was held that he was protected by the 1996 Act (*A & G Tuck Ltd v Bartlett & Another* [1994] IRLR 162, EAT).

3.35
Continuity is not lost:

(a) when an employee transfers from one firm to another, where that other is an 'associated employer' (see paras 3.108 to 3.110 below); or

(b) where there is a change of partners. There is some doubt whether this applies where there is a transfer from one person (a 'sole partner') to several partners, or from several partners to a single person. Usually the employee's position is protected by section 218(5) of the Employment Rights Act 1996 (*Wynne v Hair Control* [1978) ITR 401, EAT; *Jeetle v Elster* [1985] ICR 389, EAT; and *Allen & Son v Coventry* [1980] ICR 870, EAT).

3.36
As was indicated earlier, Council Directive 77/187/EEC (the 'Acquired Rights' directive) was imported into UK legislation by the TUPE Regulations 1981. They make provision for the continuance of an employee's employment by the purchaser of the business (the transferee) upon the acquisition of a business. The Regulations have been dubbed a 'Pandora's box of ambiguities'.

3.37
Continuity of employment is maintained where there is a 'relevant transfer' of 'any trade or business' and the employee was employed in that trade or business 'immediately before the transfer'. It does not matter that no property had been transferred (*Dr Sophie Redmond Stichting v Bartol & Others* [1992] IRLR 366). An earlier provision in

the Regulations that the relevant trade or business had to be a 'commercial venture' has since been revoked. There never was any such requirement in the 'Acquired Rights' directive. Regulation 5(1) states that '... a relevant transfer shall not operate so as to terminate the contract of employment of any person employed by the transferor in the undertaking or part transferred; but any such contract which would otherwise have been terminated by the transfer shall have effect after the transfer as if originally made between the person so employed and the transferee'. Regulation 5(2) adds that 'on completion of a... transfer... all the transferor's rights, powers, duties and liabilities under or in connection with any such contract shall be transferred... to the transferee; and anything done before the transfer is completed by or in relation to the transferor in respect of that contract or a person employed in that undertaking or part shall be deemed to have been done by the transferee'.

The phrase 'immediately before the transfer' is given a wide interpretation. It covers any person in the employ of the vendor who is dismissed in anticipation of a proposed sale, whether or not negotiations for the sale had yet been completed or a buyer identified (see Chapter 5, para. 5.17). It could apply where a liquidator trims his workforce to make his business more attractive to would-be purchasers, but will not apply if the order book is empty and there is a genuine redundancy situation (*P Bork International A/S v Foreningen af Arbejdsledere i Danmark* [1989] IRLR 41, ECJ; *Litster v Forth Estuary Engineering Ltd* [1989] ICR 341, HL; and *Wendleboe v L J Music Aps* [1985] ECR 457, ECJ).

For a further examination of the TUPE Regulations 1981, please turn to Chapter 17.

DISMISSAL

3.38
To claim a redundancy payment or compensation for unfair dismissal, an employee must, of course, have been dismissed. Section 95 of the Employment Rights Act 1996 states that an employee will be treated as having been dismissed by his (or her) employer if:

- the contract under which that person is employed is terminated by the employer (with or without notice);

- the person is employed under a contract for a fixed term and that term expires without being renewed under the same contract;

- the employee terminates the contract of employment (with or without notice) in circumstances in which he is entitled to do so – without notice – by reason of the employer's conduct (commonly referred to as a 'constructive dismissal') (*Western Excavating (EEC) Ltd v Sharp* [1978] ITR 132, CA); or

- the employer gives notice to the employee to terminate his contract of employment, to which the employee responds by resigning with notice which expires on a date earlier than the date on which the employer's notice to terminate is due to expire – in which event, the reason for the dismissal will be taken to be the reason for which the employer gave notice.

(*Source*: ERA 1996, s. 95.)

Employer's dismissal

3.39
There will be occasions when an overwrought and angry employee will tell his (or her) employer that he 'wants his cards'. If the employee and the employer both know that the employee has no intention of leaving but is merely giving vent to his anger, the employer's acceptance of the employee's words 'at face value' would constitute a dismissal, not a resignation. In one case, an employee resigned when he was told that 'You might as well put your jacket on' after having been twice reassured that he was not about to be dismissed for failing to carry out his duties. The circumstances surrounding the incident suggested that the employee had not been dismissed, even though the employer's true intentions were unclear (*Tanner v D T Kean* [1978] IRLR 110, EAT; and *Norrie v Munro's Transport (Aberdeen) Ltd*, 7 December 1988, EAT).

3.40
But, if (as happened in *Sothern v Franks Charlesly & Co* [1981] IRLR 278, CA) an employee states in unambiguous terms and perfectly normally that she is resigning, her resignation must stand. It does not matter that she did not intend her employer to accept her words at face value. The criterion is: what is the legal effect of what she said? See also *Walmsley v C & R Ferguson Ltd* [1989] IRLR 112, CS. The position may be different where the circumstances should have led

the reasonable employer to doubt the employee's intentions, especially if the situation is somewhat unusual. By failing to seek clarification, the employer runs the risk of being informed by a tribunal that he had wrongly interpreted the facts (*Goodwill Inc (Glasgow) Ltd v Ferrier*, 8 August 1989, EAT; and *Kwik-Fit (GB) Ltd v Lineham* [1992] ICR 183, EAT).

3.41

Following a heated meeting with her manager, a woman tendered her resignation which was accepted. When she later sought to retract it, the employer responded by giving her one month's notice. It was held to be an *employer's dismissal*. Although a resignation, once submitted, cannot unilaterally be withdrawn, it was implicit in the manager's reaction that he had accepted that withdrawal. But he then chose to give her a month's notice of dismissal (*Senews Ltd v Baker*, 11 February 1988, EAT).

3.42

Even if an employee has agreed that his (or her) contract of employment will end if he fails to report for work on a pre-agreed date (eg following an extended and reluctantly approved holiday abroad) his failure to turn in for work on the due date would not bring about an automatic termination without a proper investigation. The 'reasonableness' test would still apply. Any agreement purporting 'to exclude or limit' the operation of the 1996 Act is void and unenforceable (see paras 3.1 & 3.2 above) (*Igbo v Johnson Matthey Chemicals Ltd* [1986] ICR 505, CA).

3.43

The fact that a particular manager had no contractual right to dismiss an employee does not necessarily mean that his (or her) dismissal of an employee was invalid – so long as neither party was aware that the manager had exceeded the limits of his authority and that the termination could have been ignored. However, there is nothing to prevent an employee who is aware of the true position from applying to the civil court to have the dismissal nullified. If successful, his employment would continue (*Warnes & Another v Trustees of Cheriton Oddfellows Social Club* [1993] IRLR 58, EAT).

Expiry and non-renewal of a fixed-term contract

3.44
With the coming into force on 25 October 1999 of section 18 of the Employment Relations Act 1999 (amending section 197 of the Employment Rights Act 1996), a waiver clause in a fixed-term contract of one year or more (which purports to exclude an employee's statutory right to pursue a complaint of unfair dismissal on the expiry and non-renewal of that contract) no longer has any legal effect.

However, a waiver clause in a fixed-term contract of two years or more *is* enforceable, if the employee has agreed (in writing) to waive his (or her) right to a statutory redundancy payment in respect of the expiry and non-renewal of that contract. If such a contract *is* renewed, a fresh waiver clause must be inserted (ERA 1996, s. 197(3), (4) & (5)).

3.45
A worker was employed under a two-year fixed-term contract. She had signed a 'waiver of statutory rights' clause which prevented her from claiming a redundancy payment upon the expiry and non-renewal of her contract. At the end of the two-year period, she was offered an extension of four months, which she accepted. It was held that this was not a re-engagement under a new fixed-term contract but a continuation of her original contract. The waiver clause still applied (*Mulvine v University of Ulster* [1993] IRLR 545, CA [Northern Ireland]).

3.46
Because of the special nature of their contracts, apprentices who have completed a three-year apprenticeship will not normally qualify for redundancy payments at the end of those three years – unless their employer had previously given an undertaking to employ them on a permanent basis when their training finished. Although technically a 'dismissal', the non-renewal of their contracts would normally be held to be fair (*North East Coast Ship-Repairers v Secretary of State for Employment* [1978] IRLR 149, EAT).

Constructive dismissal

3.47

An employee has the right to resign and present a complaint of unfair 'constructive dismissal' if the employer's breach of a fundamental term of the employment contract is so serious as to destroy the very basis of the contractual relationship. There must be a contractual breach, not merely a failure on the employer's part to act 'reasonably' (*Wadham Stringer Commercials (London) Ltd & Another v Brown* [1983] IRLR 46, EAT).

3.48

The test to be applied to an alleged 'constructive dismissal' is objective. The fact that an employee erroneously felt that his employers were in breach of the implied term of mutual trust and confidence was held not to be good enough. But an employee was held to have been 'constructively' dismissed when his employer stopped paying him in the genuine but mistaken belief that he had resigned (*Pressurefast Ltd v Turner*, 20 January 1994, EAT; and *Brown v JBD Engineering Ltd* [1993] IRLR 568, EAT).

3.49

A mobility clause in his contract of employment operated harshly against a particular employee who felt that he had been left with no choice but to resign. The EAT held that it was of no consequence that the employer had acted unreasonably in enforcing the mobility clause. The test was: had there been a fundamental breach of contract? (*Rank Xerox Ltd v Churchill & Others* [1988] IRLR 280, EAT). In a not dissimilar case, a junior bank employee with a sick wife and two children was given just six days in which to settle his affairs and move from Leeds to another branch of the bank in Birmingham. He resigned when his pleas for more time went unheard. Although there was a clearly stated mobility clause in the employee's contract of employment, the EAT, which upheld his complaint of unfair constructive dismissal, remarked that 'in our view, [a mobility clause in a contract] includes, as a necessary implication, first, the requirement to give reasonable notice and, secondly, the requirement so to exercise the discretion to give relocation or other expenses, in such a way as not to make performance of the employee's duties impossible' (*United Bank Limited v Akhtar* [1989] IRLR 507).

3.50

Further, an employee who resigns in response to one of several breaches of contract by his (or her) employer (having waived his rights under the others) will normally lose his entitlement to claim constructive dismissal if that one breach does not amount to a fundamental breach of the employment contract (but see Chapter 2, paras 2.40 to 2.44) (*Watson v Bedford Bakery Ltd*, 20 January 1988, EAT). An employer does not have to have acted maliciously. A serious breach of contract can occur quite unintentionally. This happened when an employee lost his job when a partnership comprising two solicitors was dissolved. At the time, the employee was working under a fixed-term contract that had not run its full term. The dissolution of the partnership meant that the employee's contract had been repudiated. Once the employee accepted that repudiation, the contract was brought to an end. Furthermore, the repudiation meant that the employee was no longer bound to comply with the restrictive covenants in that contract (see Chapter 10) (*Briggs v Oates* [1990] ICR 473, Ch D).

3.51

A manager's contract of employment contained a clause to the effect that he could be demoted if he did not attain a satisfactory level of performance. Following a series of warnings relating to administrative errors, including a failure to keep up with his paperwork, the manager was indeed demoted. He resigned and claimed unfair constructive dismissal. The EAT held that the employers had acted correctly within the terms of the contract (*Halstead v Marshall of Wisbech Ltd*, 5 October 1989, EAT).

3.52

When pursuing a complaint of unfair constructive dismissal, an employee must show that he (or she) resigned because of his employer's breach of contract. If he would have left anyway, his complaint would not be upheld (*Walker v Josiah Wedgwood & Sons Ltd* [1978] ICR 744, EAT). Furthermore, an employee minded to resign, because of his employer's breach of contract, must act reasonably promptly. If he delays making a decision, he could be deemed to have 'affirmed' the contract and would lose his right to resign and pursue a complaint of unfair 'constructive' dismissal (*W E Cox Toner (International) Ltd v Crook* [1981] ICR 823, EAT). Once an employee has tendered his resignation, it cannot be withdrawn without the employer's express agreement. The same applies if an employer has served unconditional notice of dismissal on an employee. If the employee is happy to have his job back, well and good. If not, the dismissal stands (*Tanner v D T Kean* [1978] IRLR 110, EAT).

3.53

If an employee tenders his (or her) resignation (with notice), and his employer responds by dismissing him within the notice period, the general rule is that the employee will be treated as having been dismissed. But if the employer exercises a contractual right to waive the notice period and pay money in lieu of notice, the employee will be treated as having resigned (*British Midlands Airways Ltd v Lewis* [1978] ICR 782, EAT; and *Marshall (Cambridge) Ltd v Hamblin* [1994] IRLR 260, EAT).

3.54

An employee threatened with dismissal unless he (or she) resigns will be treated in law as having been dismissed by the employer, even if the employee resigns in consequence of such a threat. This is because the employer's behaviour is tantamount to a breach of the duty of 'mutual trust and confidence' implicit in every contract of employment (*Allders International Ltd v Parkins* [1981] IRLR 68, EAT). The same rule applies if an employee is given false information by his employer and is effectively tricked into resigning (*Caledonian Mining Co Ltd v Bassett & Steel* [1987] ICR 425, EAT).

3.55

Advance notification that a factory is likely to close at some unspecified time in the future does not give an employee the right to resign and claim that he (or she) had been (constructively) dismissed. If the closure date is fixed, and the employee quits before that date, having forewarned his employer that he would do so, his resignation would (generally) be held to be a 'dismissal' (*Haseltine Lake & Co v Dowler* [1981] ICR 222, EAT; *Ready Case Ltd v Jackson* [1981] IRLR 312, EAT) Whether or not such a dismissal would be characterised as 'unfair' is quite another matter.

3.56

There would, on the other hand, be no dismissal in a law if an employee resigns with a mutually agreed severance package after being told that his (or her) employer would prefer that he left. The same would apply if an employee faced with disciplinary proceedings is given the *option* to quit and does so – when the outcome of the proceedings is by no means certain (*Sheffield v Oxford Controls Co Ltd* [1979] ICR 396, EAT; *Birch & Humber v University of Liverpool* [1985] ICR 470, CA; and *Martin v MBS Fastening* [1983] IRLR 198, CA). The test usually applied when an employee alleges unfair dismissal, on the grounds that he was given no choice but to resign, is: 'Who really terminated the employment?' or 'Who was it made the final decision for a particular employee?'. A subjective approach is generally appropriate in such circumstances (*Bickerton v Inver House Distillers Ltd*, 20 April 1992, EAT).

3.57

If a contract of employment is terminated by mutual agreement, there is no 'dismissal'. But mere acquiescence by two directors in their own redundancies, forced upon them by their company's deteriorating financial position, does not mean that they have not been dismissed, regardless of the fact that they had voted for their own dismissals. When they took that decision, they were 'wearing their directors' hats' (*Birch & Humber v University of Liverpool* [1985] ICR 470, CA; and *Morley v C T Morley Ltd* [1985] ICR 499, EAT).

3.58

A 'dismissal' can also occur if an employee is guilty of gross misconduct that amounts to a repudiation of his (or her) contract of employment (see Chapter 2, paras 2.40 to 2.44). The dismissal takes place when the employer 'accepts' that repudiation. There is conflicting authority as to when such a dismissal becomes effective. The better view is that it occurs when the employee is notified of that fact, either expressly or impliedly (*London Transport Executive v Clarke* [1980] ICR 532, CA; and *Hindle Gears Ltd v McGinty* [1985] ICR 111, EAT). The acceptance of repudiatory conduct (either by the employer or the employee) must be clear and unambiguous before it becomes effective. Continued acceptance by an employee of a reduced rate of pay, in clear breach of his contractual right to a higher rate of pay, could be construed as an 'affirmation' of contract – unless the acceptance is accompanied by protests or is on a 'without prejudice' basis (see Chapter 2, paras 2.51 to 2.54) (*Vose v South Sefton Health Authority*, 15 October 1985, EAT; and *Bliss v SE Thames Regional Health Authority* [1987] ICR 700, CA).

3.59

An employee's obligations under his (or her) contract of employment may also be discharged by performance, eg when a person engaged to carry out a specific task completes that task. In such a case there *is* no 'dismissal' – so long as the employee has been given to understand that his employment would end when he had done what he had been employed to do (*Wiltshire CC v Natfhe* [1980] ICR 455, CA).

3.60
But there *is* a 'dismissal' when a compulsory winding-up order of a company is made. The contracts of all staff are automatically ended, except for those kept on by the liquidator.

Frustration of contract

3.61
Contracts of employment can end in many ways without there being a 'dismissal'. There could be a termination if the employer dies, or a termination brought about by frustration of contract if an employee is sent to prison for a lengthy period or is permanently disabled and unable to carry on working in any capacity (see Chapter 2, paras 2.32 to 2.39) (*Notcutt v Universal Equipment Co (London) Ltd* [1986] ICR 414, CA).

Failure to permit return to work after childbirth – treated as a dismissal in law

3.62
Denying a woman her statutory right to return to work after childbirth (in the job in which she was employed at the beginning of her ordinary maternity leave period) is a dismissal in law and automatically unfair – unless justifiable on grounds that have nothing whatsoever to do with her having been pregnant, or given birth, or having availed herself of her statutory maternity rights.

3.63
With the coming into force on 15 December 1999 of the Maternity & Parental Leave etc Regulations 1999, there have been a number of changes to the rules relating to the rights of pregnant employees and new mothers. For further particulars, please turn to Chapter 14.

Other considerations

3.64

When (as often happens) an employee is not required to work out his (or her) notice period, it is not clear whether the employment ended on the day the employee stopped work or whether termination occurred on the day on which the period of notice expired. In *Stapp v Shaftesbury Society* [1982] IRLR 326, CA, it was held that employment ends on the date on which the employee stops work – unless there are indications to the contrary, eg tax deducted from the money given in lieu of notice, retention of a company car during the notice period, or some prior indication by the employer that the employee would be treated as remaining 'on the books' until the period of notice expired.

3.65

If no notice of dismissal was given, the general rule is that the employment ended on the day on which the employment ended. This rule applies even though the dismissal itself is in breach of contract. It may also apply where the employee appeals against the dismissal and is suspended pending the hearing, provided the decision to dismiss is subsequently upheld on appeal. If an employee's appeal against dismissal is successful, the notice of dismissal would be cancelled with retrospective effect (*Batchelor v British Railways Board* [1987] IRLR 136, CA; *J Sainsbury Ltd v Savage* [1981] ICR 1, CA).

Time of dismissal

3.66

A summary dismissal (that is to say, a dismissal without notice), arising out of gross misconduct by an employee, generally brings the employment to an end immediately. It is of no consequence that the employee had been paid until the end of the relevant working day or had been paid for the time spent travelling to and from the final disciplinary hearing (*Octavius Atkinson & Sons Ltd v Morris* [1989] IRLR 158, CA).

3.67

Where an employer sends a notice of dismissal by post, it is only effective from the date when it is received, or is deemed to have been received, and *not* when it is posted (*Brown v Southall & Knight* [1980] ICR 617, EAT). But where an employee wishes to 'accept' his (or her) employer's repudiatory conduct and terminate the employment (see Chapter 2, paras 2.40 to 2.44), the contract only ends when he has adequately communicated his intention to his employer. This may be done indirectly. For instance, if the employer has been informed by the Department of Employment that the employee had applied for a Jobseeker's Allowance or equivalent benefits, this would be effective notice. The Department is obliged to obtain confirmation that the person is no longer in the employer's employ (*Norwest Holst Group Administration Ltd v Harrison* [1985] ICR 668, EAT; and *Wight v Blackstone Franks Smith & Co*, 2 April 1988, EAT).

TIME LIMITS FOR COMPLAINTS

3.68
Employment legislation lays down that a complaint to an employment tribunal must be presented within three months (or, in some situations, within six months) of the 'effective date of termination' of an employee's contract of employment. Unless the originating application – consisting either of Form IT1 or a simple letter that includes the appropriate information – is 'presented' to the Secretary to the Tribunals before midnight on the last day, it will be 'out of time'. As the Court of Appeal pointed out in *Hetton Victory Club Ltd v Swainston* [1983] ICR 341, there is a letter box outside most regional tribunal offices. If the last day for presenting a complaint to a tribunal falls on a bank holiday, that day does not count. Technically, a bank or public holiday is a *dies non* (a non-day), and the time limit is extended by one day (*Ford v Stakis Hotels & Inns Ltd* [1987] ICR 943, EAT).

3.69
In considering time limits, the precise words used are important. In tribunal rules, the phrase 'before the date of the hearing' will be found. This means that where notices have to be given or where documents have to be served within a fixed number of days those days must be clear days in order for service to be valid. The words 'beginning with' mean that the day in question is included in the period (*Derrybaa Ltd v Castro-Blanco* [1986] ICR 546, EAT). If there is no corresponding date in a future month, eg in February of a leap year, the last date of that month will the last date for presenting a complaint to a tribunal (*University of Cambridge v Murray* [1993] ICR 460, EAT).

3.70

A complaint presented 'out of time' will not normally be heard unless a tribunal is satisfied that it was 'not reasonably practicable' for the complaint to have been presented within the prescribed time limits, but only if the tribunal considers it 'just and equitable' to do so. The various Acts of Parliament lay down which test has to be applied (dealt with elsewhere in this handbook under the appropriate heads of claim) (*Source*: ERA 1996, ss 111 & 164).

3.71

The expression 'not reasonably practicable' means that there must have been some physical or other cogent reason to explain a complainant's failure to present his (or her) complaint on time (eg illness or injury, absence overseas, inability to attend to one's affairs, etc). Perhaps the relevant documents were sent off in good time but were inexplicably held up in the post (*Palmer & Saunders v Southend-on-Sea BC* [1984] IRLR 119, CA).

3.72

Following *Practice Direction (QBD: Postal Service)* [1985] 1 WLR 489, documents despatched by first-class post would be expected to be delivered to the addressee, in the ordinary course of events, on the second working day after posting. For second-class post the time lapse is the fourth working day after posting (*St Basil's Centre Ltd v McCrosson* [1992] ICR 140, EAT). If there is a postal strike or other reason for believing that documents will not be delivered in time, allowance should be made for that. If necessary other means of delivery should be arranged (*Beanstalk Shelving Ltd v Horn* [1980] ICR 273, EAT).

3.73

Ignorantia iuris non excusat. To claim ignorance of the law is now generally not good enough. Employees' rights in employment have been well publicised over the years (as have the time limits for presenting complaints to employment tribunals). Putting off presenting a complaint pending the outcome of criminal proceedings (or domestic appeals) is likewise unacceptable (*Porter v Banbridge Ltd* [1978] IRLR 271, EAT; and *United Cooperatives Ltd v Mansfield*, 27 July 1988, EAT).

Ignorantia facti excusat. But there might be a different outcome where the ignorance relates to the factual basis of a claim which was fundamental to bringing it. For example, discretion to extend the time limits for presenting a complaint might well be exercised if the facts show that an allegedly redundant employee was for some time unaware that someone else had been recruited to fill his (or her) old job immediately after his dismissal. However, a complainant must act reasonably quickly once he has learnt of the true state of affairs. In considering such a time lapse, the circumstances that led to the further delay must be considered (*Machine Tool Industry Research Association v Simpson* [1988] ICR 558, CA; *Grampian Health Board v Taylor*, 27 June 1991, EAT; and *Marley (UK) Ltd & Another v Anderson* [1994] IRLR 152, EAT).

3.74

The onus lies on the employee (the putative complainant) to show that it was not 'reasonably practicable' for him (or her) to have presented his complaint on time (see Chapter 2, paras 2.16 to 2.20) and that could be difficult. In one instance, the burden was discharged when dismissed employees were able to prove that their former employers had misled them into believing that they would be re-employed after a short break. They delayed submitting their claims until the firm went into liquidation (*James W Cook & Co (Wivenhoe) Ltd v Tipper & Others* [1990] ICR 716, CA).

3.75

A claim may also be lost if a person is given advice by a solicitor, or by any other skilled adviser such as the Citizens' Advice Bureaux or a trade union, and there is a failure to take action in time, or the wrong advice is given (*Riley v Tesco Stores Ltd* [1980] ICR 323, CA). It has been succinctly put this way: '... the sins of the negligent or incorrect adviser do have to be visited on the applicant for the purposes of considering... what was reasonably practicable' (per Garland J in *Trusthouse Forte (UK) Ltd v Halstead*, 10 June 1986). Confusion between a litigant and his (or her) appointed adviser is no excuse. So where an employee had either failed to ask his union to act for him, or the union had been so instructed but failed to act in time, it was held that the applicant could not rely on the escape clause (*Dowty Aerospace Gloucester Ltd v Ballinger*, *The Times*, 5 March 1993, EAT). But where an employee presented her claim 'out of time' because she had received erroneous advice from a member of staff at an office of the employment tribunals, the EAT held that she was entitled to rely on that advice. Consequently, she had satisfied the burden of proof by showing that it was 'not reasonably practicable' for her to have presented her claim in time (*Rybak v Jean Sorelle Ltd* [1991] ICR 127, EAT). The same principle applies even when a person has been given erroneous advice from a solicitor and seeks verification of it from a tribunal office where the advice given by a clerk again is wrong (*London International College Ltd v Sen* [1993] IRLR 333, CA).

3.76
There is an onus on a professional adviser to ensure that an originating application (Form IT1) sent by ordinary post has not gone astray. If he (or she) receives no acknowledgement from the Secretary to the Tribunals, he should get in touch with the Central Office of Tribunals (see Chapter 27, para 27.10) to check the position. Better still, he should send the application by recorded delivery or by fax. Unfortunately, it is the prospective complainant (or applicant) who must accept responsibility for a default by his professional adviser (*Capital Foods Retail Ltd v Corrigan* [1993] IRLR 430 EAT).

3.77
'Just and equitable' is a less stringent test. A tribunal is entitled to 'take into account anything which it judges to be relevant... to say how far it thinks it necessary to look at the circumstances of the matter complained of. No doubt it will want to know what it is all about; it may want to form some fairly rough idea as to whether it is a strong complaint or a weak complaint, and so on' (per Phillips J in *Hutchinson v Westward Television Ltd* [1977] ITR 125, EAT). If a case is put into the hands of a solicitor who fails to commence proceedings in time, it is doubtful whether a plea that it would be 'just and equitable' to extend the time limits will succeed (*Gloucester Working Men's Club & Institute v James* [1986] ICR 603, EAT) (although there is nothing to prevent the applicant from pursuing a claim for damages arising out of the solicitor's negligence).

3.78
Where a person suspects that he (or she) has been discriminated against but only acquires proof of that discrimination after the time limit for presenting a complaint has expired, then provided the period of elapsed time is not excessive and he acts promptly, leave to proceed will normally be granted (*Clarke v Hampshire Electro-Plating Co Ltd* [1992] ICR 312, EAT).

Amending an Originating Application to include other claims

3.79

Where an amendment is sought 'out of time' to add or substitute a new claim to an Originating Application, the test to be applied is different. A tribunal would have to consider the relative hardship and injustice that both parties would suffer if the amendment was permitted. If reference in the facts was impliedly made to such a claim, it would normally be allowed. But the ordinary tests would apply where there was a change in the identity of the respondent (*British Newspapers Printing Corporation (North) Ltd v Kelly & Others* [1989] IRLR 222, CA; and *Ketteman & Others v Hansel Properties Ltd* [1987] 2 WLR 312, HL).

Relying on the Treaty of Rome and EC Directives

3.80

Where there is no statutory limit for bringing a claim based (solely) on the Treaty of Rome or an EC Directive, the appropriate approach might well be to follow the time limits applicable to an analogous claim under domestic legislation. For instance, a claim in respect of an unlawful deduction from a redundancy payment paid to a woman approaching 60 must be brought within six months of the deduction. But time would only start to run when it is reasonable to expect a party to know of the right to make such a claim (*Cannon v Barnsley Metropolitan Borough Council* [1992] ICR 698, EAT; and *Rankin v British Coal Corporation* [1993] IRLR 69, EAT).

3.81

If a respondent employer is an 'organ or emanation of the State' (eg a Government department, health authority, etc), the time limit for presenting a claim would not begin to run until the UK had incorporated the provisions of an EC directive into its domestic legislation. If the date for implementing a directive has come and gone without having been imported into a Member State's domestic legislation, an person employed by an emanation of the State may rely on one or other of the provisions in that directive before a national court so long as the provision in question is sufficiently precise and unconditional (*Marshall v Southampton Area Health Authority (Case 152184)* [1986] 1 CMLR 688).

3.82

Where on an appeal there has been a declaration that the lower courts had misinterpreted the law, litigants with similar cases who seek to bring claims out of time will have to obtain leave to do so. In each case, a tribunal would have to consider the period involved, and the reason for the lateness of the claim; and, in respect of cases where the 'reasonably practicable' test applies, whether the claim had been lodged within a reasonable time of the change in the law (*Foster v South Glamorgan Health Authority* [1988] ICR 526, EAT).

3.83

In some instances a chairman sitting alone (see Chapter 27, para 27.7) is empowered to extend the time limits, merely by using his (or her) discretion. For instance, the chairman may validate a Notice of Appearance filed 'out of time'. Although discretion is normally exercised because of the importance of trying to arrive at the truth in a case, nevertheless time limits should not be taken too lightly. An adverse decision by a chairman may be difficult to overturn on appeal. However, before an order is made on an employee's application, the employer must be sent a written notice giving him the opportunity to show cause why an extension should not be granted before a decision is made on the application (*147 Snooker Club v Shirley*, 28 April 1988, EAT; and *Aspris & Sons Ltd v Demetriou* [1989] ICR 246, EAT).

WHO 'ORDINARILY WORKS' IN GREAT BRITAIN?

3.84

Before 25 October 1999 (when section 32 of the Employment Relations Act 1999 came into force) employees who ordinarily worked outside Great Britain were, for the most part, excluded from the rights and benefits afforded by the UK's domestic employment legislation. For example, before 25 October 1999, an employee would not qualify for a statutory redundancy payment if he (or she) ordinarily worked outside Great Britain – unless, on the relevant date, he was in Great Britain in accordance with instructions given to him by his employer. Such exclusions no longer apply. Related provisions in the Trade Union & Labour Relations (Consolidation) Act 1992 have also been repealed, as have those in the Sex Discrimination Act 1975, the Race Relations Act 1976, and the Disability Discrimination Act 1995 (per the Equal Opportunities

(Employment Legislation) (Territorial Limits) Regulations 1999, which latter came into force on 16 December 1999).

Note: Mariners who are ordinarily resident in the UK will continue to qualify for certain rights under the Employment Rights Act 1996 if, but only if, the ship on which they are employed is registered as belonging to a port in the UK and the work they are employed to do under their contracts of employment is not wholly outside the UK (per s. 199(7), ERA 1996, as inserted by s. 32(4), ERA 1999).

3.85
These repeals facilitate the implementation in the UK of Council Directive 96/71/EC of 16 December 1996 'concerning the posting of workers in the framework of the provision of services'. In future, UK workers sent by their employers to carry out temporary work in another EU Member State must receive no less favourable treatment (in terms of minimum rates of pay, holidays, rest breaks, etc) than the workers who ordinarily live and work in that other Member State. The same rules apply to workers from another EU Member State who are sent to work temporarily in the UK – hence the removal of the restrictive provisions referred to in the previous paragraph.

MEANING OF THE EXPRESSION 'A WEEK'S PAY'

3.86
The amount of a 'week's pay' is relevant when a tribunal is assessing the amount of compensation to be awarded to an employee who has been unfairly dismissed. It is also needed to establish an employee's entitlement to a statutory redundancy payment. This does not present too great a difficulty when an employee is/was paid a fixed wage or salary under his (or her) contract of employment

3.87
If the evidence shows that an employee's gross earnings varied from week to week, or that he (or she) was paid at piece rates or on a 'commission only' basis, the amount of a week's pay will be the average of the employee's gross earnings over the period of 12 weeks ending with the last complete week before the relevant calculation date (or, if the calculation date is the last day of a week, the period of 12 weeks ending with that week). If an employee was duty-bound, under the terms of his contract, to work a certain amount of overtime or to work at hours in respect of which a higher rate of pay applies, the calculation of a week's pay must include those additional

amounts. But if the employee worked overtime on a voluntary basis only or did so at his employer's sole discretion, that must not be included, even though its exclusion has the effect of diluting the employee's average hourly rate of pay (*Tarmac Roadstone Holding Ltd v Peacock* [1973] ICR 273, CA; and *British Coal Corporation v Cheesborough & Another* [1990] ICR 317, HL) (*Source*: ERA 1996, ss 220 to 229).

3.88
A bonus or merit payment or other amount which is regularly made, forms part of the 'week's pay'. Tips are not included unless they emanated from an obligatory service charge paid to the employer who then distributed it in fixed proportions to staff. So too if voluntary payments representing tips were added to a cheque or credit card voucher in settlement of a bill. It becomes the property of the employer and when distributed to staff becomes part of their 'pay' (*Palmanor Ltd v Cedron* [1978] IRLR 303, EAT; and *Nerva & Another v RLOG Ltd*, 9 June 1994, QBD).

Upper limit to the amount of a week's pay

3.89
For the purposes of assessing the amount of a statutory redundancy payment (see Chapter 4, paras 4.33 to 4.37) or the basic or additional award of compensation for unfair dismissal (see Chapter 5, paras 5.168 to 5.170 and 5.176 to 5.178), a 'week's pay' is the employee's average gross weekly pay or £240, whichever is the lesser of those two amounts. £240 is the current (2001/02) upper limit on the amount of a week's pay for these purposes. For the purposes of calculating the amount of the compensatory award in an unfair dismissal case (see Chapter 5, paras 5.171 to 5.175), the net figure is used, subject to a limit of £51,700 (*Source*: ERA 1996, s. 227).

'NORMAL RETIRING AGE'

No redundancy pay for employees aged 65 or over

3.90
Section 156 of the Employment Rights Act 1996 states that an employee does *not* have a right to a redundancy payment if before his (or her) employment ended, he had attained the age of 65 *or*, if there was a 'normal retiring age' of less than 65 for an employee

holding the position which that employee held (which lower retiring age must be same whether the employee holding that position was a man or a woman), that 'normal retiring age'. The age limits described here do not, repeat do not, apply if an employee believes that he (or she) was selected for redundancy for an inadmissible or unlawful reason (as to which, please turn to Chapter 5, paras 5.19 *et seq*.

3.91

An employee aged 65 or over at 'the effective date of termination' of his (or her) contract of employment is likewise debarred from presenting a complaint of unfair dismissal *unless* the 'normal retiring age' for a person occupying the same or an equivalent position was higher (or lower) than 65 and that normal retiring age was the same regardless of the sex of the person occupying that position (*Source*: ERA 1996, s. 109(1)). Again this rule does not apply to an employee who is dismissed (or alleges that he or she has been dismissed) for an inadmissible or unlawful reason (see Chapter 5, paras 5.19 *et seq*). There is a presumption that the 'normal retiring age' is the retiring age specified in the contract of employment. This presumption is open to rebuttal if the evidence shows that, in practice, employees in the same position tend to (and can reasonably expect to) retire at a specific age, in which case that other age applies. If they retire at different ages then the fallback age of 65 applies (*Waite v Government Communications Headquarters* [1983] ICR 653, HL).

3.92

In *Nash v Marsh/Roe Group Limited* [1998] IRLR 168, a 69-year-old warehouse manager was made redundant in 1997 after 25 years' service. He presented a complaint to an employment tribunal alleging, *inter alia*, that sections 109(1) and 156(1) of the Employment Rights Act 1996 were incompatible with Article 119 (now Article 141) of the Treaty of Rome in that the statutory prohibition on redundancy payments to employees aged 65 or over discriminated against men – given that there was ample statistical evidence to show that a higher proportion of men than women remained in employment beyond the age of 65. The tribunal upheld Mr Nash's complaint, concluding that ss 109(1) and 156(1) of the 1996 Act are indeed incompatible with Article 119. As Mr Nash has since died, it is by no means certain that the tribunal's decision will be appealed to the higher courts (or referred to the ECJ).

3.93

The relevant group in which an employee fits must be identified, eg messengers, typists with word-processing skills, clerks at particular grades and so forth. Any term that only deals with retirement and is not linked to another facet of the employment is irrelevant. Nor is it appropriate to consider the history of persons within the group. If persons in a group are basically doing the same job and some retire at one age and the remainder, at another, then there *is* no 'normal retiring age' (*Hughes v Department of Health & Social Security* [1985] ICR 419, HL). In another case, an employer had two groups of employees on different contracts but performing the same job function. He wished to bring both under the same terms, but exempted a number of senior employees who enjoyed more favourable terms and who were nearing retirement age. It was held that this did not offend against (the now) s. 109 of the Employment Rights Act 1996 (*Barber v Thames Television plc* [1992] ICR 661, CA).

3.94

If an employer, as a matter of administrative policy, changes the age at which a group of staff is required to retire, that new age will be the normal retiring age for persons in that group. But where the change was from a retiring age of 65 years to a new retiring age of between 62 and 63 years, the latter band was held to be too imprecise – and so the fall-back position applied (*Swain v Health and Safety Executive* [1986] ICR 498, EAT). Where it is shown that there were abnormal or particular circumstances (of a temporary nature) that necessitated people remaining at work beyond the contractual retiring age, the 'normal retiring age' would nonetheless be the age specified in their contracts of employment. Further it is not permissible to look only at the reasonable expectations of those approaching retirement age: the expectations of everyone in the group have to be taken into account (*Whittle v Manpower Services Commission* [1987] IRLR 441, EAT; and *Brooks & Others v British Telecommunications plc* [1992] ICR 414, CA).

DISCIPLINARY RULES AND PROCEDURES

3.95

Most employers have well-documented procedures for dealing with allegations of misconduct (or whatever) at the workplace. Indeed, the written statement of terms of employment that employers are duty-bound to issue to every employee (in compliance with ss 1 to 7 of the Employment Rights Act 1996) must include a note specifying any disciplinary rules applicable to the employee or referring the employee to a document specifying such rules that is reasonably accessible to the employee. The note must also specify (by description or otherwise) a person (such as a supervisor or manager) to whom the employee can apply if dissatisfied with any disciplinary decision relating to him (or her). If there are further steps consequent on any such application, the note must also explain those steps or refer the employee to a document explaining them which is reasonably accessible to the employee.

However, these requirements do not apply to businesses or organisations in which the total number of people employed – *including* people employed in other branches or offices of the same organisation or by any associated employer – is fewer than 20.

3.96

The approach of tribunals and courts to an employer's internal disciplinary hearings was succinctly put by Lord Denning, MR, thus: 'We must not force these disciplinary bodies to become entrammelled in the nets of legal procedure. So long as they act fairly and justly, their decisions should be supported' (*Ward v Bradfield Corporation* [1971] LGR 27, CA). Domestic disciplinary hearings should not be conducted like a court of law. All an employer has to do is follow certain basic rules, which may need to be adapted to deal with particular problems. It is possible to identify certain areas where employers have been held to be in default.

3.97

The *first* requirement is that there must be openness. An employee accused of misconduct or incompetence must know what he (or she) is alleged to have done or failed to do. Furthermore, the employee must be given the opportunity to state his own case and to repudiate (or challenge) the allegations or complaints made against him (*Khanum v Mid-Glamorgan Health Authority* [1979] ICR 40, EAT). So where an employee was accused by his employers of having started a fight, natural justice required that he not only be given a chance to put his side of the story but that he should also be told in sufficient detail about what was being said against him (*Bentley Engineering Co Ltd v Mistry* [1979] ICR 47, EAT). This can be done either by allowing the employee to listen to what witnesses have to say or by providing him with copies of witness statements. If he is not given a detailed account of the case against him, his dismissal is likely to be adjudged unfair. In the appropriate circumstances, he should be afforded an opportunity to cross-examine his accusers (*Louies v Coventry Hood & Seating Co Ltd* [1990] ICR 54, EAT; and *Shakespeare & Another v British Coal Corporation*, 30 March 1988, CA). A chief constable had received a report from a delegated officer containing assessments on a probationary police officer. The report recommended that the probationer be dismissed. The probationer was not shown a copy of the report. His dismissal, in reliance on the delegated officer's report, which he had not seen, was held to have been a breach of natural justice (*R v Chief Constable of Thames Valley Police, ex parte Stevenson*, *The Times*, 22 April 1987, QBD).

3.98

The *second* matter that should be borne in mind is that an employee attending a disciplinary hearing should be given an opportunity to be represented (or accompanied) either by his (or her) union representative or by a fellow employee of his own choosing. An employee might become inarticulate or confused, or be 'reduced to jelly', when confronted by senior members of management. He might fail to put over his case effectively, which could lead to a dismissal on the basis of erroneous information. Such a dismissal might well be held to have been unfair, even wrongful, the more so if the employee is young, naive or a bit 'simple'. In the absence of an express contractual right (or agreement) to the contrary, an employee has no right to insist on being legally represented at an employer's disciplinary hearing. 'The ordinary realities of everyday industrial relations do not permit of quasi-legal trials on every disciplinary occasion' (per Browne-Wilkinson J in *Sharma v British Gas Corporation*, 27 July 1983, EAT).

Note: Section 10 of the Employment Relations Act 1999 which came into force on 4 September 2000, allows that a worker who is required by his (or her) employer to attend a disciplinary or grievance hearing has the legal right (on request) to be accompanied at that hearing either by a workmate of his own choosing, by a shop steward or works convenor or by a full-time trade union official. An employer who refuses or fails to allow a worker to be so accompanied will be ordered by an employment tribunal to pay compensation to the worker of an amount not exceeding two weeks' pay.

3.99

Thirdly, it may be advisable to allow an employee to meet his (or her) accusers face to face, or at least permit his representative to interview them or call them to a hearing. This is especially so where acts of violence are concerned, or where the issues are complex and there is likely to be some difficulty in arriving at the truth (*British Railways Board v Kugler*, 16 May 1989, EAT; and *Ulsterbus Ltd v Henderson* [1989] IRLR 251, CA (Northern Ireland)). The same principle applies when complaints are made by others against an employee. But where written complaints from several patients about a nurse were produced at the disciplinary hearing, and objection was limited to the panel reading them, but there was no request for the patients to be called, it was held that the dismissal was fair (*Khanum v Mid-Glamorgan Health Authority* [1979] ICR 40, EAT). Problems sometimes arise when an employee gives damaging information about a fellow employee but refuses to be identified for fear of reprisals. Likewise, supplying employees with a copy of an anonymous letter naming them as having engaged in industrial misconduct could unwittingly reveal the identity of the author. What should an employer do in such a case? Every case must depend on its own facts. Provided there has been a full and reasonable investigation of the circumstances, and there is sufficient independent evidence to support the allegations, a disciplinary hearing (and any appeal) may act on the evidence before it without disclosing the source of that information. However, an employer would have to be satisfied that there would be a real risk of danger should the identity of the informants be disclosed or ascertainable (*Barr & Others v Kay Metzeler Ltd*, 5 March 1991, EAT).

3.100

Fourth, there must be good faith and fairness by the adjudicators in the conduct of disciplinary hearings. They must do all that they reasonably can to get at the truth (*Calvin v Carr* [1980] AC 573, PC). Persons conducting a disciplinary hearing must exercise a degree of discretion on what matters it may or may not consider. The decision must be one that a reasonable employer could reach, ie one that is not 'so absurd that no sensible person could have dreamt that it lay within the powers of the authority. [For] example... the red-haired teacher dismissed because she had red hair. It is so unreasonable that it might also be described as being done in bad faith' (per Lord Greene MR in *R v Hertfordshire CC ex parte NUPE & Others* [1985] IRLR 258, CA). See also *Associated Provincial Pictures Ltd v Wednesday Corporation* [1948] 1 KB 223, CA).

3.101

Where police officers were called to a disciplinary inquiry and questioned an employee, a dismissal based on the answers given was held to be unfair. The employee had been 'cautioned' that he need not say anything, and was inhibited from giving his own version of events (*Read v Phoenix Preservation Ltd* [1985] ICR 164, EAT). On the other hand, where an employee was interviewed by police quite separately and had made a written confession, which led to criminal proceedings, it was held that although the judge at the trial ruled the confession 'inadmissible', it did not preclude an employer from acting on its contents provided he had reasonable grounds for believing it was true (*Dhaliwal v British Airways Board* [1985] ICR 513, EAT).

3.102

Fifthly, justice must not only be done in a particular case, it 'must be manifestly seen to be done'. This principle is subject to a degree of flexibility according to the particular circumstances. It is not possible to define precisely where the borderline between a breach and a non-breach lies; but it can usually be recognised (*Peter Simper & Co Ltd v Cooke* [1986] IRLR 19, EAT; and *Wiseman v Borneman* [1971] AC 279, HL). It is generally advisable to place the investigative and disciplinary functions in different hands to avoid any accusation of bias. A failure to do so may be a breach of procedure (for which there may be a remedy in either of the civil courts or the tribunals), but it would not necessarily make a dismissal unfair. It would be one of the factors to be taken into account when determining the reasonableness or otherwise of a dismissal (*Slater v Leicestershire Health Authority* [1989] IRLR 16, CA).

3.103

A chief constable adjourned a disciplinary hearing against a police sergeant in order to confer with a senior officer about other urgent matters. It was that same senior officer who had proffered the complaint against the sergeant. It was held that, in the special circumstances, the sergeant had no valid grievance. There had been no breach of the rules of natural justice (*R v Chief Constable of South Wales, ex parte Thornhill* [1987] IRLR 313, CA). It would, on the other hand, be a serious breach of the rules of natural justice for a person conducting an internal appeal to discuss the case with the person who took the original decision to dismiss or with the person responsible for presenting the employer's case on appeal (*Campion v Hamworthy Engineering Ltd* [1987] ICR 966, CA).

3.104

Sixth, no person should be a judge in his (or her) own cause. What really matters is that the disciplinary body should act fairly and justly (*Haddow & Others v ILEA* [1979] ICR 202, EAT). A person who has presided at a tribunal that heard and rejected an application by an aggrieved employee will not normally be debarred from adjudicating at a later hearing by the same individual concerning other applications (*R v Oxford Regional Mental Health Review Tribunal, ex parte Mackman, The Times,* 2 June 1986, DC). When there are several tiers of appeal, those who make decisions or carry out investigations at a lower level should not sit in judgement at a higher level appeal hearing. A person cannot be expected to be impartial when considering an appeal from his own decision or views formed during investigations. It does not mean that there must not be any contact between people at different levels, but they must all act fairly and justly (*Rowe v Radio Rentals Ltd* [1982] IRLR 177, EAT; and *Byrne v BOC Ltd* [1992] IRLR 505, EAT).

3.105

Lastly, even if an employee has been acquitted of the same offence in a magistrates' court or the Crown Court, that does not undermine an employer's right to take disciplinary action against the same employee always provided that he (or she) has reasonable grounds for believing that the employee committed the offence in question. It could be that the employer had lost confidence in the employee's ability to perform his duties effectively (*Saeed v Greater London Council (ILEA)* [1986] IRLR 23, QBD).

Consequence of a breach

3.106

A breach of the rules of natural justice will not automatically make a dismissal unfair. It depends largely on whether a decision is being reviewed by the ordinary courts or by the tribunals. A tribunal may find that an employer has not acted entirely fairly. But if the facts show that the employer has an overwhelming case against the employee, and that the employee would have been dismissed regardless of the breach in procedure, the dismissal will not normally be unfair (*Polkey v A E Dayton Services Ltd* [1988] ICR 142, HL). If it is alleged that a breach of natural justice occurred when an employee was denied an opportunity to state his (or her) case, the courts apply the following test: 'Would there be any 'real,... sensible,... substantial chance of any further observations on the applicant's part [which would] in any way alter... the final decision?' (*R v Chief Constable of Thames Valley Police, ex parte Cotton* [1990] IRLR 344, CA).

Internal appeals

3.107
If an internal appeal consists of a complete rehearing as opposed to a review of the decision reached at an earlier disciplinary hearing, then any defect at the earlier hearing may be cured provided that '... at the end of the day, there has been a fair result reached by fair methods...' (*Shearlaw v British Aerospace plc*, 17 December 1987, EAT; and *Calvin v Carr* [1980] AC 573, PC).

'ASSOCIATED EMPLOYER'

3.108
The term 'associated employer' appears regularly in the statutes. Section 231 of the Employment Rights Act 1996 states that 'any two employers shall be treated as associated if:

- one is a company of which the other (directly or indirectly) has control, or

- both are companies of which a third person (directly or indirectly) has control;

and "associated employer" shall be construed accordingly'. The 'associated employers' provision applies in several situations. As access to a number of statutory rights is dependent on an employee having been 'continuously employed' for a prescribed minimum period, s. 231 of the 1996 Act must be strictly construed. This has led to some curious results. The word 'company' means a company limited under the Companies Act 1985, or, if it is a foreign firm, then it must, in its essentials, be similar to a British limited company. The US term 'Inc' was held to be similar to 'Ltd' under the Companies

Act 1985 (*Merton London Borough Council v Gardiner* [1981] ICR 186, CA; and *Hancill v Marcon Engineering Ltd* [1990] ICR 103, EAT) (*Source*: Companies Act 1985, s. 735).

3.109

'Control' is restricted to cases where a person is a major shareholder in a company with voting rights attached. That a person operates with *de facto* control is not enough. Nor is it enough if a person has a 50 per cent shareholding and the 'control' consists of an ability to block any resolution (*Wynne v Hair Control* [1978] ITR 401, EAT; *Zarb & Samuels v British & Brazilian Produce Co* [1978] IRLR 78, EAT; and *Hair Consultants Ltd v Mena* [1984] IRLR 386, EAT). It is now established that the 'third person' must have voting control in each of two relevant companies which together are 'associated employers'. Generally, the 'third person' may not consist of two persons who normally act in concert. But when the third party does consist of two or more persons, it must be the same combination of persons in each company. Where a husband has sole control over company A, and joint control with his wife over company B, those two companies are not 'associated employers' (*Strudwick v Iszatt Brothers Ltd* [1988] ICR 796, EAT; *South West Laundrettes v Laidlow* [1986] ICR 455, CA; and *Cardiff Galvanizers (1969) Ltd v Parsons*, 20 October 1989, EAT).

3.110

Where justice demands it, the rules can be stretched on occasion. A person employed by a builder was temporarily transferred to a limited company to carry out a particular job of work. The limited company was owned in equal parts by the builder and his wife. The wife's position was merely nominal in order to comply with relevant requirements of the Companies Acts. It was held that the builder and the limited company were one and the same employer (*Payne v Secretary of State for Employment* [1989] IRLR 352, CA). A young woman worked in a hairdressing business for a sole proprietor. She then moved to another salon that was jointly owned by that same proprietor and a partner. It was held that the two salons were not 'associated employers'. Neither was a limited company. But continuity of employment may be preserved under s. 218 of the 1996 Act (see paras 3.27 to 3.37 above) (*Wynne v Hair Control* [1978] ITR 401, EAT). In a similar case, an employee had worked for four local authorities for more than 12 years doing similar work for each of them. The Court of Appeal held that the authorities in question were not 'associated employers'. None of them was a limited company and no third person had control over them. Nor did one control the other (*Gardiner v London Borough of Merton* [1981] ICR 186, CA).

CODES OF PRACTICE

3.111
In the employment arena, codes of practice may be (and have been) issued by:

- the Advisory, Conciliation & Arbitration Service (ACAS);

- the Secretary of State for Education & Employment;

- the Equal Opportunities Commission (EOC);

- the Commission for Racial Equality (CRE);

- the Health & Safety Commission (HSC); and

- the Disability Discrimination Commission (DDC);

and, as might be expected, provide guidance on areas and activities that include disciplinary and grievance procedures in employment, disclosure of information to trade unions for collective bargaining, time off for trade union duties and activities, picketing, industrial action ballots, equal pay, sex, racial and disability discrimination, equal pay, and a great many issues relating to health and safety at the workplace.

3.112
A failure on the part of any person (employer, trade union official or employee) to observe any provision of an approved code of practice does not of itself render that person liable to proceedings before a court or tribunal. But in proceedings brought, for example, under the Sex Discrimination Act 1975, the failure to observe any relevant provision of an accompanying code of practice is admissible in evidence and will be taken into account in relation to any question that arises during such proceedings.

MEANING TO BE GIVEN TO STATUTES

3.113
The ordinary rules of construction of a statute require that where the

meaning is clear, effect must be given to it. But where it is possible to interpret the words in a statute in two ways, the one that gives effect to the apparent intention of Parliament should be adopted. In determining that intention, the courts are entitled to take into account the background leading to the enactment of the legislation (*Secretary of State for Employment v Cox* [1984] IRLR 437, EAT; and *British Coal Corporation v Cheesborough & Another* [1990] ICR 317, HL). For example, the words 'on racial grounds' that appear in the Race Relations Act 1976 were held to be capable of narrow interpretation or a broad meaning. When holding that the broad meaning should apply, the EAT said: 'It seems to us that Parliament must have intended such an employee to be protected so far as possible from the consequence of doing his lawful duty by refusing to obey such an instruction [to discriminate]' (*Showboat Entertainment Centre Ltd v Owens* [1984] ICR 65, EAT).

3.114

In another case, a claim failed because one of the sections in an Act of Parliament had not 'been aptly drafted to cover the rather exceptional circumstances of [the] case'. It mattered not that it fell 'within the mischief aimed at' by the legislation. Lord Dilhorne put it this way: 'If it ... appear[s] that an Act might have been better drafted, or that amendment to it might be less productive of anomalies, it is not open to the courts to remedy the defect. That must be left to the legislature. The existence of anomalies, if they exist, cannot limit the meaning to be attached to clear language in a statute' (*Stock v Frank Jones (Tipton) Ltd* [1978] ITR 289, HL). The House of Lords has proceeded in a contrary direction in interpreting Orders based on an EC Directive. It added the words, 'as between the woman and the man with whom she claims equality' in an equal pay case to enable a statute to be interpreted in the manner they thought necessary to give effect to an EC Directive (*Pickstone & Others v Freemans plc* [1988] ICR 697, HL; and *Litster & Others v Forth Estuary Engineering Ltd* [1989] ICR 341, HL).

3.115

When seeking out the meaning of an Act, Regulation or Order, it is not normally permissible for a court to look at extraneous sources. What is contained in a White Paper, or what was said in Parliament (and recorded in *Hansard*) may not be considered. An exception lies where a statute is ambiguous or its intention obscure. In that case reference may be made to *Hansard* to ascertain what a responsible minister said in Parliament in order to ascertain the true legislative intent (*Pepper (Inspector of Taxes) v Hart & Others* [1993] IRLR 33, HL). The construction of an Act of Parliament or a statutory instrument (Regulations, Orders, etc) is a matter for the judgment of the courts and tribunals. It is determined in the light of the circumstances prevailing at the time of enactment (*Duke v GEC Reliance Ltd* [1988] ICR 339, HL). Where there are two possible interpretations of a statute, then the one most suited to follow our European obligations should be followed. But if the domestic law is capable of having only one meaning, it cannot be distorted to make it comply with a European Directive that has a different meaning. However, an employee might be able to rely on a Directive (see Chapter 1, paras 1.19 to 1.30) (*Dines & Others v Initial Health Services Ltd & Another* [1994] IRLR 336, CA).

European law

3.116

The European Court of Justice (ECJ) has jurisdiction to give a preliminary ruling on the interpretation of any provision of European law. It is anxious to avoid divergences developing in the courts of the Member States (*Dzodzi v Belgium, The Times*, 7 January 1991, ECJ).

THE PARTIES TO A DISPUTE

3.117

Generally, it is the employer who is the 'respondent' at a tribunal hearing (the employee being the 'applicant' or 'complainant'). It is the 'respondent' who is liable to pay any award of compensation ordered by the tribunal (see also Chapter 5, para 5.166 and Chapter 27, para 27.90).

3.118

An employer, who alleges that a trade union or other person (eg a shop steward) used the threat of industrial action to put pressure on him (or her) to dismiss a particular employee (perhaps because he or she had refused to be or remain a member of the trade union in question), may apply to an employment tribunal for an order directing that the union or person who exercised that pressure be joined (or, in Scotland, sisted) as a party to the subsequent tribunal proceedings. Such a request will be granted if made before the hearing begins, but may be refused if submitted after that time. If the tribunal upholds the dismissed employee's complaint and agrees that the union or other person was wholly or partly responsible for the employee's dismissal, it will order the union or person in question to pay the whole or part of any award of compensation ordered to be paid to the employee (*Source*: TULRA 1992, ss 152 & 160).

3.119
The same applies if an employer takes 'action short of dismissal' against an employee for being or seeking to become a member of an independent trade union, or for refusing to be or remain a member of a particular trade union (or of any trade union), or for taking part in the activities of an independent trade union. If the employer's actions were wholly or partly attributable to pressure brought to bear on him (or her) by a trade union or other person, the union may yet again be joined or sisted as a party to any subsequent tribunal proceedings and may be ordered to pay the whole or part of any compensation awarded to the employee (*Source*: TULRA 1992, ss 146 & 150).

VEXATIOUS LITIGANTS

3.120
There are some (essentially litigious) people who are prone to complain to an employment tribunal for any minor or imagined slight, knowing full well that their complaints have little chance of being upheld. There is very little that a tribunal can do to prevent a case going ahead. The prospect of the applicant being ordered to pay a deposit of up £500 under para 7 of Schedule 1 to the Employment Tribunals (Constitution, etc) Regulations 1993 – to be forfeited if his or complaint is not upheld – is unlikely to faze an applicant or complainant who is living on state benefits. Para 7(5) (*ibid*) requires that a tribunal should not make such an order without first taking reasonable steps to ascertain the ability of an applicant (or respondent) to pay a deposit (see also Chapter 27, para 27.56).

Restriction of vexatious proceedings

3.121
The Attorney General or Lord Advocate may make an application to

the EAT seeking 'a restriction of proceedings order' against an individual. Such an order would prevent that person from bringing, continuing or making an application in any proceedings before the tribunal or the EAT without obtaining leave from EAT. Before an order is made, the EAT has to be satisfied that the litigant has habitually, persistently and without any reasonable grounds either instituted vexatious proceedings or made vexatious applications in such proceedings, whether before the tribunal or the EAT. There is no right of appeal from that decision (*Source*: ETA 1996, s. 33).

Redundancies

GENERAL INFORMATION

4.1
Since 1965, employers have been duty-bound to pay redundancy payments to those of their employees who have been dismissed on grounds of redundancy. Part-time employees nowadays enjoy the same statutory rights as their full-time colleagues, including the right to redundancy payments. The amount payable in each case is determined by the employee's age, length of service and income when their employment ends. But there are conditions.

4.2
To qualify for a statutory redundancy payment, an employee must have been continuously employed for two or more years ending with the 'effective date of termination' of his (or her) contract of employment (excluding any period of employment that began before the employee's 18th birthday). Furthermore, on that effective date, the employee must have been below the 'normal retiring age' for a person occupying the position he held or below 65 (whichever occurs sooner). The 'normal retiring age' for a woman must be the same as that for a man occupying the same position; otherwise the normal retiring age will be deemed to be 65. See also *Excluded Classes of employment* below (*Source*: ERA 1996, ss 155 & 156).

Meaning of 'effective date of termination'

4.3
The 'effective date of termination' (or 'relevant date') referred to in the previous paragraph is the date on which the notice given to a redundant employee expires. But if no notice was given or the notice actually given was less than that required by section 86 of the Employment Rights Act 1996, the effective date of termination will be the date on which that section 86 notice would have expired had

it been duly given on the day that notice *was* given. The same 'deeming' rules apply even when an employee has agreed to be paid money in lieu of notice or to accept a shorter period of notice (*Secretary of State for Employment v Staffordshire CC* [1989] IRLR 360, CA). (*Source*: ERA 1996, s. 97(2)).

4.4

For example: John Smith, a 35-year-old warehouseman, had worked for the same firm for some nine years and 11 months when he was told by his boss at the beginning of the week that he was to be made redundant on the following Friday. John's contract stated (wrongly) that he was entitled to just one month's notice to terminate his contract of employment. Under section 86 of the Employment Rights Act 1996, John is legally entitled to a minimum of nine weeks' notice (one week for each complete year of service). Although John actually finished work on the Friday, his employment is nonetheless 'deemed' to have continued for a period of nine weeks starting with the day following the day on which his boss told him that he had been made redundant. This means also that, by the time John's contract had ended in law, he had completed 10 years' service and was, therefore, entitled to 10 weeks' statutory redundancy pay. The same 'deeming' provisions would apply even if John had been dismissed without notice on the Monday.

4.5

For redundancy payment purposes, there has always been a statutory upper limit on the amount of a week's pay. For 2001/2002 (the figure is reviewed annually), that upper limit is £240. It follows that when calculating an employee's entitlement to a statutory redundancy payment, earnings in excess of £240 must be disregarded. Service in excess of 20 years (reckoned backwards from the 'effective date of termination') must likewise be disregarded. Redundancy payments are payable for complete years of service only; which means that odd months must also be discounted. See 'Calculation of Redundancy Pay' (paras 4.33 to 4.37) below.

4.6

There is nothing in law to prevent an employer 'topping-up' a statutory redundancy payment with a so-called severance payment. The latter might be paid on an 'ex gratia' basis or in accordance with severance terms written into an employee's contract of employment. Redundancy and severance payments are tax-free, so long as the total paid to a redundant employee does not exceed £30,000. An accompanying payment of money in lieu of notice is also tax free unless the employee has a contractual right to such a payment as an alternative to serving out the notice period.

4.7

It should be borne in mind that the purpose of the redundancy payments scheme is to compensate an employee for the loss of his (or her) job. It is *not* intended to provide a redundant employee with sufficient funds to survive a period of unemployment (*Wynes v Southrepps Hall Broiler Farm Ltd* [1968] ITR 407). For that reason, a redundancy payment will not be taken into account by the authorities when assessing an employee's entitlement to a Jobseeker's Allowance or related benefits. A redundancy payment does not have to be repaid, even if the recipient starts work with a new employer within a matter of days. The same applies if he is re-employed by his former employer within a week of his dismissal – as might very well happen if his employer's business expectations are suddenly revived (eg following the receipt of a sizeable order from an unexpected quarter).

4.8

The tribunals are now dealing with a great many cases brought by employees alleging either that there was no genuine redundancy situation at the time of their dismissal, or that they had been unfairly selected contrary to an agreed redundancy procedure, or that their selection had been for an inadmissible or unlawful reason (eg on grounds of sex, race, disability, trade union membership, etc).

4.9

An employee who believes that he (or she) has been unfairly or unlawfully selected for redundancy (or that there was not a genuine redundancy situation) may present a complaint of unfair dismissal before an employment tribunal. If the tribunal upholds his complaint, the employer will be directed to pay compensation comprising a *basic award* (calculated in much the same way as the statutory redundancy payment), a *compensatory award* (current upper limit: £50,000) and, very possibly, an *additional award* (of between 26 and 52 weeks' pay) based on the reasons for the dismissal and the employer's refusal or failure to comply fully with an order for reinstatement or re-engagement. Unlawful selection for redundancy is discussed in Chapter 5 (paragraphs 5.19 to 5.53).

WHO IS ENTITLED TO REDUNDANCY PAY?

4.10
As a general rule (and subject to the provisions explained earlier) every 'employee' (part-time as well as full-time), with two or more years service, is entitled to a redundancy payment if legitimately dismissed on the grounds of redundancy.

Excluded classes of employment

4.11
However, the following are not entitled to redundancy payments:

- persons employed in a public office within the meaning of section 39 of the Superannuation Act 1965;

- persons employed in employment which is (for the purpose of pensions and other superannuation benefits) treated as service in the civil service of the state;

- persons employed in any capacity under the government of an overseas territory;

- persons employed in domestic service in a private household where the employer is the parent (or step-parent), grandparent, child (or stepchild), grandchild or brother or sister (or half-brother or half-sister) of the employee;

- serving members of the naval, military or air forces;

- persons employed as the master, or as a member of the crew, of a fishing vessel where employees are remunerated only by a share in the profits or gross earnings of the vessel (unless the redundancy dismissal consists of a failure to permit an employee to return to work after childbirth).

(*Source*: ERA 1996, ss 159, 160(1), 161, 191(6) & 199(2).)

Employment outside the United Kingdom

4.12

With the coming into force on 25 October 1999 of section 32(1) of the Employment Relations Act 1999 (and the concomitant repeal of section 196 of the Employment Rights Act 1996), employees engaged in work wholly or mainly outside the UK are no longer excluded from the right to be paid redundancy payments on the termination of their employment. This change was introduced in compliance with Council Directive 96/71/EC of 16 December 1996 (the 'Posted Workers' Directive , as to which, please turn to Chapter 22).

Fixed-term contracts

4.13

A person employed under a contract of employment for a fixed-term of two years or more is *not* entitled to a redundancy payment in respect of the expiry of that term without its being renewed if, before the term expires, the employee had agreed in writing to exclude any right to a redundancy payment in that event. The 'waiver clause' may either be in the contract itself or in a separate agreement. If the contract is renewed for a further two or more years, the waiver clause must be renewed with it; otherwise it will cease to have effect (*Source*: ERA 1996, s. 197(3) & (4)).

Offer of suitable alternative employment

4.14

An employee under notice of redundancy is *not* entitled to a redundancy payment if, before the end of his (or her) employment, his employer (including any associated employer):

- offers him suitable alternative employment (on the same or very similar terms) to begin *either* on the first working day following the end of his employment in his present job *or* within the next four weeks,

- but the employee unreasonably refuses that offer. (*Source*: ERA 1996, s. 141) (*Benton v Sanderson Kayser Ltd* [1989] ICR 136, CA; and *McHugh v Hempsall Bulk Transport Ltd*, 1 June 1992, EAT.)

In determining whether the new job offered is suitable and whether the employee had good reason to reject it, the tribunal must consider the personal circumstances of the employee. In appropriate cases, his standards and aspirations should be taken into account provided they are 'reasonable in the round' (*National Carrier Control Services v Urey*, 14 September 1990, EAT).

Trial period in new job (if terms different)

4.15

If an employer (or an associated employer) offers an otherwise redundant employee a job that is less favourable to the employee in terms of pay, location, skills, etc, and that is intended to start either on the first working day after his (or her) present job finishes or within the next four weeks, the employee has the legal right to try out the new job for a period of up to four weeks (or longer, if both parties are agreed and further training is needed). If, at the end of the trial period, the employee decides that the job is unsuitable, he will be treated in law as having been made redundant on the date on which his original job ended (*Source*: ERA 1996, s. 138(2), (3) & (4)).

For the meaning of the expression 'associated employer', please turn to Chapter 3, paras 3.108 to 3.110.

4.16

Two redundant school cleaners declined to accept a new contract on reduced working hours to carry out essentially the same cleaning duties. Even though their employers were prepared to accept lower standards, the cleaners were held not to have acted unreasonably. They were entitled to redundancy pay (*Gloucester CC v Spencer & Another* [1985] ICR 401, CA). The offer of a new job on different terms should specify what the new terms of employment are (pay, working hours, duties, etc), but only to the extent that those terms differ from those otherwise included in the written statement of employment particulars issued in accordance with sections 1 to 7 of the Employment Rights Act 1996 (as to which, see Chapter 9, paras 9.3 *et seq*). To ensure that continuity of employment is preserved, the new job must commence within four weeks of the cessation of the old job (*McKindley v William Hill (Scotland) Ltd* [1985] IRLR 492, EAT and *McHugh v Hempsall Bulk Transport Ltd*, 1 June 1992, EAT).

4.17

An employee who volunteers for redundancy is usually entitled to a redundancy payment (subject to the usual qualifying conditions relating to age and length of service) but only if the employer has appealed for volunteers as part of the pre-redundancy consultation process. However, where an 'early retirement' scheme was put forward and two employees decided to apply for it, it was held that the agreement to retire early did not amount to a 'dismissal'. The employees were debarred from recovering any redundancy pay. The critical question is: what brought the employment to an end? (*Burton, Allton & Johnson Ltd v Peek* [1975] IRLR 87, EAT and *Birch & Humber v University of Liverpool* [1985] ICR 470, CA).

Are 'bumped' employees genuinely redundant?

4.18

The question arises as to whether an employee is truly redundant (and therefore entitled to a redundancy payment) if he (or she) is 'bumped' out of his job in order to make way for a more senior or longer-serving employee whose own job has been made redundant. In *Gimber v Spurrett* (1967) 2 ITR 308 (followed by the EAT in *Elliott Turbomachinery Ltd v Bates* [1981] ICR 218), it was held that an employee dismissed in such circumstances had indeed been dismissed by reason of redundancy.

4.19

But, in a more recent case, that of *Church v West Lancashire NHS Trust* [1998] ICR 423, the EAT ruled otherwise, declaring that although 'bumping' was one way of managing a redundancy situation, the 'bumped' employee's dismissal was not of itself attributable to a diminution in the requirement for employees to do work of the kind done by that employee.

4.20

Although the *Church* decision has been appealed to the Court of Appeal, the 'bumping' issue appears to have been resolved by the decision of the House of Lords in *Murray & Another v Foyle Meats Limited* (8 July 1999). There, the Law Lords held that an employee's dismissal could be due to redundancy even if the work on which he (or she) was engaged was unaffected by a fall in demand or a business setback elsewhere within the employing organisation.

There was no reason, they said, why the dismissal of such an employee should not be attributable to a diminution in the employer's need for employees to do work of a particular kind, although an employer in such a case would nonetheless need to explain the causal connection.

WHEN DOES A REDUNDANCY SITUATION ARISE?

Meaning of 'redundancy'

4.21
Section 139 of the 1996 Act explains that an employee who is dismissed shall be taken to be dismissed by reason of redundancy if the dismissal is wholly or mainly attributable to the fact:

- that the employee's employer has ceased or intends to cease

  (a) to carry on the business for the purposes of which the employee was employed by him (or her); or

  (b) to carry on the business *in the place* where the employee was so employed; or

- that the requirements of that business:

  (c) for employees to carry out work of a particular kind; or

  (d) for employees to carry out work of a particular kind *in the place* where the employee was employed by the employer,

  have ceased or diminished or are expected to cease or diminish.

Sub-paragraphs (a) and (b) envisage a situation in which a business or a major portion of an employer's business either shuts down completely or moves to another part of the country, or to another part of the same city or town. If a business shuts down completely, everyone working in that business will be redundant. The same applies if the business is relocated – unless, of course, some or all of the workforce are prepared to move to the new site on mutually acceptable terms. If an identifiable part of a business shuts down, most but not necessarily all of the employees will be redundant.

Some of them might well be absorbed within the remaining part of the business or be prepared to relocate elsewhere.

Sub-paragraph (c) envisages a situation in which the introduction of new technology, or a major change in working practices, or a near-empty order book, will prompt an employer to streamline the workforce in order to remain competitive or simply 'to stay afloat'. Sub-paragraph (d) envisages a situation in which an employer with several branch offices or outlets may decide to close several of those offices or outlets, or to transfer some of the activities carried on in those outlets to a central location.

4.22

The presumption of redundancy might well be countered by an employer who produces evidence to the effect that a particular employee was dismissed wholly or mainly for a reason other than redundancy eg incompetence or misconduct. An employee's selection for redundancy might likewise be challenged on the grounds that there was no genuine redundancy situation or that his (or her) dismissal had little to do with redundancy but was wholly or mainly for an inadmissible or unlawful reason (eg on grounds of sex, race, trade union membership or non-membership, disability; and so on).

4.23

The fact that the amount of work within a firm remains the same, but increased efficiency or reorganisation, mechanisation or automation, results in an employee being dismissed, will generally not debar that person from claiming a redundancy payment. The Act preserves the employee's rights where there has been a diminution in the requirements of the business for the employee to do the work in the place where he (or she) was engaged (*Halfords v Roche*, 30 January 1989, EAT).

4.24

Furthermore, an employee is not precluded from recovering a redundancy payment:

- where his (or her) employer's business is sold or transferred to another employer and he is dismissed for an 'economic, technical or organisational' (ETO) reason involving changes in the workforce (see Chapter 5, paras 5.14 to 5.18) before or after the sale (*Gorictree v Jenkinson* [1985] ICR 51, EAT); or

- where there is a reallocation of duties following a reorganisation or mechanisation in the business and the employee is dismissed as a result of there being a cessation or diminution of the work previously carried out by him. It matters not that there has been no general reduction in the employers' business (*Sutton v Revlon Overseas Corporation Ltd* [1973] IRLR 173, NIRC and *Murphy v Epsom College* [1985] ICR 80, CA).

The test that must be applied is this: what caused the employer to dismiss the employee? When that question is answered, it then has to be shown that the reason for dismissal matches the statutory definition of redundancy (*Limb Group of Companies v Baxter & Others*, 30 July 1993, EAT).

4.25

To be eligible for a redundancy payment, an employee must bring his (or her) case strictly within the statutory definition. A part-time teacher was displaced by a full-time master who had been transferred from another school that was overstaffed. As there was no diminution of work, the Court of Appeal held that the part-timer was not entitled to redundancy pay upon her dismissal (*Fay v North Yorkshire CC* [1986] ICR 133, CA).

4.26

The contractual position of the parties is important to determine whether there is an entitlement to a redundancy payment. So if an employee can be required, under the terms of a 'mobility clause' in his (or her) contract, to transfer to other work and he unreasonably refuses to do so, he will lose any such entitlement (*Cowen v Haden Ltd* [1983] ICR 1, CA). Mobility clauses can sometimes cause problems. An employer who owned several premises had mobility clauses in the contracts of employment of all his staff. He also specified where they were to work. He closed down an office and offered an employee a position at another location far away from her home. She refused it. It was held that the mobility clause could not defeat her claim to a redundancy payment. Her contract specified her place of work, and the premises had closed down (*Bass Leisure Ltd v Thomas* [1994] IRLR 104, EAT).

4.27

The phrase 'work of a particular kind' may include, in appropriate circumstances, a change from night work to day work. So where employees were not contractually bound to change, but were dismissed for refusing to do so, they could still claim redundancy pay. But a minor adjustment to working hours may not amount to a change in the kind of work that the relevant employees were employed to do (*Macfisheries v Findlay* [1985] ICR 160, EAT; *Johnson v Nottingham Combined Police Authority* [1974] ICR 170, CA; and *Ransomes Sims & Jefferies Ltd v Tatterton*, 14 April 1992, EAT). Difficulties sometimes arise when an employer, who is running out of work for a particular employee to do, tells that employee either to accept other work, on less favourable terms, or leave, and the worker reluctantly accepts that other work for a short time, and then leaves (*Marriott v Oxford & District Co-operative Society Ltd* [1969] ITR 377, CA). If there was not a true agreement by the employee to the variation in the contract, the effect in law will be that this amounts to a dismissal by the employer. The employee will be entitled to a redundancy payment; but if there is too long a delay, he 'will be regarded as having elected to affirm the contract' (*Western Excavating (EEC) Ltd v Sharp* [1978] ITR 132, CA [as explained in *W E Cox Toner (International) Ltd v Crook* [1981] ICR 823, EAT]).

4.28

An HGV driver who was disqualified from driving was given temporary alternative work at a nearby depot while a permanent job was sought for him. When that other site closed and no other position could be found, he was dismissed. It was held that the termination of his contract was mainly attributable to the loss of his driving licence. Accordingly, he was not entitled to a redundancy payment (*Tipper v Roofdec Ltd (No. 2)*, 11 March 1991, EAT).

LAY-OFFS AND SHORT-TIME WORKING

4.29

In the absence of any contractual agreement to the contrary, an employer has no legal right to lay-off his workers or put them on short-time, even if the business is running into difficulties. However, if there is such an agreement or arrangement (understood and accepted by the employees), any employee who is laid-off or kept on short-time will in time be entitled to resign and claim a statutory redundancy payment. The procedure is explained in Chapter III, Part XI of the Employment Rights Act 1996. A person is 'laid-off' for a week if he (or she) is available for work but receives no wages or salary at all in respect of that week. A person is on 'short time' for a week if he receives less than half his contractual entitlement to wages for that week.

An employee, otherwise available for work, who is laid-off by his (or her) employer or kept on short time for four or more consecutive weeks, or for six or more weeks in the aggregate (of which not more than three were consecutive) during a period of 13 consecutive weeks, or a combination of both, is entitled to terminate his employment and apply for a statutory redundancy payment (*Source*: ERA 1996, ss 147 & 148).

4.30

Within four weeks of the end of either of the periods referred to in the preceding paragraph, the employee must serve written notice on the employer that he (or she) intends to claim a redundancy payment (which notice is referred to in the 1996 Act as a 'notice of intention to claim'). The employer can contest his liability to pay a redundancy payment by serving a written counter-notice on the employee within the next seven days reassuring the employee that normal working will resume for a period of at least 13 consecutive weeks, starting within the next four weeks.

If no counter- notice is served, the employee must (within the next four weeks) give at least one week's written notice to terminate his contract of employment. If the employee's contract stipulates a longer period of notice, he must comply with that stipulation. If the employer serves a counter-notice but subsequently withdraws it, the employee must tender his resignation within three weeks of that withdrawal. If an employment tribunal confirms that the employee is entitled to a redundancy payment, the resignation must be tendered within three weeks of the tribunal's decision.

STRIKES AND OTHER INDUSTRIAL ACTION

4.31

Employees who withdraw their labour by going on strike are in breach of contract and (under the common law) have effectively dismissed themselves. All an employer needs to do in such circumstances is accept the repudiation and the termination is automatic (see Chapter 5, paras 5.7 to 5.10). Any employee given notice of dismissal on grounds of redundancy, who responds by going on strike and is 'dismissed' for doing so, thereby forfeits any and all entitlement to a redundancy payment which might otherwise have been paid had the employee continued to work normally. The employer may, on the other hand, write to the employee offering to pay any redundancy payment due so long as the employee agrees to make up for the number of working days lost because of the strike action. In short, the employee would have to return to work after the strike ends and must remain at work until he (or she) has made up for the number of working days lost because of the strike. The employer must explain his reasons for making that offer, and must also make it clear that non-acceptance will result in the forfeiture of any redundancy payment otherwise payable (*Source*: ERA 1996, ss 140(2) and 143).

4.32

A strike does not break the continuity of a period of employment so long as the employee in question returns to work (or is permitted to do so by his (or her) employer) after the strike has ended. But days spent on strike do not count as part of a period of continuous employment. This means that when determining an employee's total period of continuous employment, any days spent on strike must be deducted (by effectively postponing the date on which employment began by the number of days spent on strike) – which may impact on the amount of any redundancy payment subsequently payable to the employee on the termination of his employment (*Source*: ERA 1996, s. 216).

CALCULATION OF REDUNDANCY PAY

4.33

An employee's entitlement to a statutory redundancy payment is calculated by:

(a) determining the period, ending with the effective date of termination (or 'relevant date'), during which the employee has been continuously employed;

(b) reckoning backwards, from the end of that period, the number of years of employment – not exceeding 20 – falling within that period;

(c) allowing the 'appropriate amount' for each of those years of employment.

Redundancy payments are payable in respect of up to 20 complete years of service, reckoned backwards from the effective date of termination, but ignoring any period of employment that began before the employee's 18th birthday. As is illustrated in the next paragraph, an employee's age at the time of his (or her) dismissal is also an important factor.

4.34

A redundant employee under 'normal retiring age' or under the age of 65 (whichever occurs sooner) at the time of his (or her) dismissal, who has been continuously employed for two or more years is entitled to a statutory redundancy payment calculated as follows:

• one-and-a-half weeks' pay for each complete year of service in which the employee was not below the age of 41;

• one week's pay for each complete year of service in which the employee was below the age of 41 but not below the age of 22; and

• a half week's pay for each complete year of service in which the employee was below the age of 22 but not below the age of 18.

It follows that the maximum redundancy payment payable to any redundant employee (given the present 2001/02 upper limit of £240 on the amount of a week's pay) is £7,200 — payable to a employee aged 41 and over, with 20 years' service 'under his belt' and average weekly earnings in excess of £240 (but see next paragraph) (*Source*: ERA 1996, s. 162).

Redundancy pay reduced if employee over the age of 64

4.35

In a situation in which a redundant employee had already reached the age of 64 before the 'effective date of termination' of his (or her) contract of employment, the employer may lawfully reduce the amount of any redundancy payment due to that employee on the termination of that employment by *one-twelfth for each whole month of service beyond that 64th birthday*. Accordingly, a redundant employee aged 64 years and eight months at the effective date of termination of his contract of employment can expect to have his redundancy pay reduced by eight-twelfths (or two-thirds) when the employment ends. However, it should be pointed out that there is nothing in law to prevent an employer ignoring this provision or, indeed, any provision imposing a limit on the amount of redundancy pay payable, always provided that the amount that the employer *does* pay (by way of a severance payment, or whatever) is not less than that to which the employee is lawfully entitled under the 1996 Act (*Source*: ERA 1996, s. 162(4) & (5)).

Offsetting pension payments

4.36

In certain circumstances, an employer may choose to offset pensions and any lump sum payable to an employee under an occupational pension scheme against any statutory redundancy payment otherwise due to be paid to that employee. The amount to be offset in such circumstances will depend on the employee's total period of continuous employment, including service with previous employers – except where the pension (or a lump sum) was being (or had been) paid before the dismissal took effect (*Royal Ordinance plc v Pilkington* [1989] ICR 437, CA). Full details of the statutory provisions relating to reductions on account of pension, and examples showing the method of calculation, are to be found in Department of Employment Leaflet RPL 1 available from local offices of the Department for Education & Employment (*Source*: Redundancy Payments Pension Regulations 1965).

Meaning of 'a week's pay'

4.37
A week's pay in the case of an employee paid monthly (whose salary is invariably expressed as an annual amount) is his (or her) annual salary divided by 52. When an employee's pay varies with the amount of work done, as when pay is partly made up of bonuses or commission, the amount of a week's pay will be the *average of that employee's gross weekly earnings over the 12-week period ending with the last complete week in which he actually worked*. The same rule of thumb applies in the case of hourly-paid employees or people paid on piece-work rates. Overtime payments should not feature in calculations unless the employee's contract requires the employer to provide a specified number of overtime hours each week and requires the employee to work those extra hours. If overtime working is in any way voluntary or discretionary, the premium payments it generates must be disregarded, even if overtime has been a regular feature of the employee's working arrangements for a number of years.

AN EMPLOYER'S REFUSAL OR FAILURE TO PAY

4.38
An employee may complain to an employment tribunal if his (or her) employer has refused (or failed) to pay a redundancy payment to which the employee is lawfully entitled. If the tribunal upholds the employee's complaint, it will make a declaration to that effect and will order the employer to pay the amount due (with interest). However, before presenting such a complaint, the employee must have taken all reasonable steps (short of legal action) to persuade the employer to pay the money owed.

4.39
If the employer is insolvent or in serious financial difficulties, and therefore unable to pay, the employee may apply to the Secretary of State for Education & Employment for a payment out of the National Insurance Fund. If the Department of Employment is satisfied that the employee has little chance of recovering the money from his (or her) employer, it will pay the money due directly to the employee. The Department will then take whatever steps are necessary to

recover the money from the defaulting employer (or, as appropriate, from the relevant liquidator or trustee in bankruptcy) (*Source*: ERA 1996, ss 166 to 169).

4.40

A complaint to an employment tribunal in the circumstances described above must be presented within six months of the employer's refusal or failure to pay. A complaint presented 'out of time' will not normally be heard unless the tribunal is satisfied that is was not reasonably practicable for the complaint to have been presented sooner.

PRE-REDUNDANCY CONSULTATIONS

Collective redundancies

4.41

An employer contemplating making 20 or more employees redundant within a period of 90 days or less is duty-bound to consult with persons who are *appropriate representatives* of any of the employees who may be affected by the proposed dismissals or may be affected by measures taken in connection with those dismissals (*Source*: TULRA 1992, s. 188). The expression *appropriate representatives* means either *trade union representatives* (shop stewards, and the like) appointed by one or more independent trade unions that are recognised by the employer as having bargaining or negotiating rights in respect of some or all of the employees (or description of employees) who are likely candidates for redundancy or, in the absence of trade-union-appointed representatives (or trade union involvement), *employee representatives* (either specifically elected by fellow-workers to consult about their employer's redundancy proposals or previously elected by their colleagues to represent their interests in other matters). In a workplace in which there are both employee-elected and trade union-appointed representatives, the employer must defer to the former (if the would-be redundant employees are of a description in respect of which the union in question is a recognised independent trade union). Otherwise, the employer should consult with both (*Source*: TULRA 1992, s. 188(1B)).

4.42

If the employees in a particular workplace have not yet elected one or more of their colleagues to represent their interests in redundancy consultations, the employer must allow then sufficient time to do so – *before* the consultation process is due to begin (see next paragraph) (*Source*: TULRA 1992, s. 188(7A)).

When must redundancy consultations begin?

4.43

Consultations with the *appropriate employee representatives* must begin at the earliest opportunity, and must in any event begin:

- at least 90 days before the first of the dismissals is due to take place – if 100 or more employees at the same establishment are to be dismissed as redundant within a period of 90 days or less; or

- at least 30 days before the first dismissal takes effect – if 20 or more, but fewer than 100, employees at the same establishment are to be dismissed as redundant within 90 days or less.

An employer is *not* relieved of his (or her) duty to consult if he plans to make fewer than 20 people redundant. Case law suggests that he must consult with *every* such employee on a one-to-one basis to consider any counter-proposals and ensure that the employee is treated reasonably and fairly. See 'Individual consultations', paras 4.50 & 4.51.

4.44

The consultation period is calculated from the time the redundancies are notified until the date when it is *proposed* that the first of the dismissals will take place. It is not when they actually take place. So, if one or more employees leave earlier as a result of negotiation or for other reasons, then there is no breach of the (now) 1992 Act (*TGWU v R A Lister & Co*, 21 May 1986, EAT). It is unlawful and unacceptable for an employer to refuse to enter into consultations with the *appropriate representatives*, or to fail to provide the written particulars listed in paragraph 4.45 below, on the grounds that the decision to make 20 or more employees redundant was taken by a parent company located elsewhere in the UK, or overseas, and that he does not have the authority to explore ways and means of avoiding the redundancies or reducing the number of employees to be dismissed (*Source*: TULRA 1992, s. 188(7)).

Scope of consultations

4.45
For consultation purposes, an employer contemplating 20 or more redundancies must write to the appropriate representative/s:

(a) explaining the reasons for the dismissals;

(b) listing the numbers and descriptions of employees likely to be made redundant;

(c) specifying the total number of employees of any such description who are currently employed at the establishment in which the redundancies are to take place;

(d) outlining the criteria to be used for selecting the employees who may be made redundant;

(e) explaining how and when the dismissals are to take place and over what period; and

(f) explaining what severance payments (if any) are to be make to the redundant employees – in addition to their entitlement (if any) to statutory redundancy pay – and how those severance payments are to be calculated.

The letters or documents containing the information described in (a) to (f) above must either be delivered by hand to each representative or be posted to an address nominated by the representatives. Trade-union-appointed representatives will usually require the letter (or a copy of it) to be sent by post to the union's head office (*Source:* TULRA 1992 s. 188).

4.46
The information referred to in the preceding paragraph must be disclosed before the consultation process begins. Furthermore, the consultations must not be a sham. Their purpose must be to find ways to avoid the redundancy dismissals, reduce the numbers of employees to be dismissed, and mitigate the consequences of the dismissals. In short, they must be undertaken with a view to

reaching an agreement with the representatives concerned (*Source*: TULRA 1992, s. 188(2)).

4.47

If there are special circumstances that render it not reasonably practicable for the employer to comply with any of the requirements listed above, he (or she) must nonetheless take all such steps towards compliance as are reasonably practicable in the circumstances. Where, for example, a sudden disaster strikes a company, making it necessary to close the whole or part of the business, then plainly that would be a matter capable of amounting to a 'special circumstance'. And that would be so whether the disaster was physical or financial. 'If, on the other hand, an employer's insolvency was due merely to a gradual rundown of the company, then those are facts on which the [employment] tribunal can come to the conclusion that the circumstances were *not* special. In other words, to be "special" the event must be something out of the ordinary, something uncommon...' (per Lane LJ, *Clarks of Hove Ltd v The Baker's Union* [1978] IRLR 366, DC). A compulsory winding-up order was made against an insolvent company pursuant to directions given by a judge. This had the effect of terminating the employment of all staff, which was deemed to be on the grounds of redundancy. It was held that this was not a 'special circumstance'. The application for leave to proceed to claim a protective award (see below) was refused because the administrator was not proposing to dismiss for redundancy. There was no duty to consult (in *re Hartlebury Printers Ltd & Others (in liquidation)* [1992] ICR 559, Ch D).

Duty to notify Secretary of State

4.48

When contemplating or proposing 20 or more redundancies at the one establishment, an employer must not only enter into consultations with the *appropriate representatives*, but must also inform the Secretary of State (in practice the nearest office of the Department of Trade & Industry [DTI]) about his plans *before* he puts those plans into effect (*Source*: TULRA 1992, s. 193). The notification must be given in writing (on Form HR1, supplied by the DTI):

- at least 90 days before the first of the dismissals is intended to take place – if 100 or more employees are to be dismissed as redundant within a period of 90 days or less; or

• at least 30 days before the first dismissal is due to take place – if 20 or more (but fewer than 100) employees are to be dismissed as redundant within a period of 90 days or less.

A copy of the completed Form HR1 must also be sent to each of the appointed representatives involved in the consultation process (*Source*: TULRA 1992, s. 193).

4.49

Once the DTI has received formal notification of proposed redundancies, it may approach the employer for further information. Any employer who refuses or neglects to forewarn the DTI about those proposals, or who fails to respond to a request for further information, is guilty of an offence and liable, on summary conviction, to a fine of up to £5,000 (*Source*: TULRA 1996, s. 194).

Individual consultations

4.50

'Redundancy' is one of a number of so-called 'permitted' reasons for dismissal listed in section 98 of the Employment Rights Act 1996 (see Chapter 5, para 5.13). As such, it must be approached in much the same way as a dismissal for any other permitted reason. In short, an employer must not dismiss any employee on grounds of redundancy (or for any other reason) without first discussing the matter with the employee in question and allowing that employee to advance his (or her) own views and (where appropriate) to put forward counter-proposals. Otherwise, the fairness of the dismissal might be successfully challenged before an employment tribunal. In a redundancy context, the employer should at least consider the possibility of finding suitable alternative employee for the employee elsewhere within the business or organisation.

4.51

The importance of consultation at an individual level was emphasised in *Langston v Cranfield University* [1998] IRLR 172. There, a research assistant was made redundant when the last of a series of fixed-term contracts expired without being renewed. He complained to an employment tribunal that he had been unfairly selected for redundancy. The tribunal dismissed his complaint. However, on appeal, the EAT held that by failing to consult the employee about the non-renewal of his contract and by failing to take reasonable steps to find alternative employment for him, the employers had acted unreasonably. In doing so, the EAT referred, *inter alia*, to the House of Lords decision in *Polkey v A E Dayton Services Ltd* [1987] IRLR 503. There Lord Bridges had remarked that 'in the case of redundancy, the employer will normally not act reasonably unless he warns and consults any employees affected..., adopts a fair basis on which to select for redundancy and takes such steps as are reasonable to avoid or minimise redundancy by redeployment within his own organisation'.

PROTECTIVE AWARDS

4.52

A complaint may be presented to an employment tribunal that an employer has refused or failed to comply with his duty to consult the *appropriate representatives* about his redundancy proposals. The complaint may be brought by an employee-elected representative, the relevant trade union or (if there were no representatives) by any of the employees who have been (or may be) dismissed as redundant. Such a complaint must be presented either before the date on which the *last* of the intended dismissals takes effect or within three months beginning with that date, or within such further period as the tribunal considers reasonable in the circumstances (*Source*: TULRA 1992, s. 189). If an employment tribunal upholds such a complaint, it will make a declaration to that effect and may order the employer to pay a protective award to the employees who were (or are about to be) made redundant. A protective award is equivalent in effect to an employee's normal earnings, to be paid by the employer for a 'protected period' of up to 90 days. The rate of remuneration under a protective award is a week's pay for each week of the protected period; and remuneration in respect of a period of less than one week shall be calculated by reducing proportionately the amount of a week's pay (*Source*: TULRA 1992, ss 190 to 192).

4.53

As was indicated earlier, an employer may argue in his defence that there were special circumstances which rendered it not reasonably practicable for him to comply with his statutory duties, or that he took all such steps as were reasonably practicable in the circumstances (*Source*: TULRA 1992, s. 189(6)).

4.54

A protective award made by a tribunal covers all employees of the description specified in the award, whatever their length of service. It requires the employer to pay remuneration for such part of the 'protected' period as the tribunal deems fair and equitable in all the circumstances. The effect of a protective award is to preserve the employment for such period as is stipulated by the tribunal (*Transport & General Workers Union v Ledbury Preserves (1928) Ltd* [1986] ICR 855, EAT).

4.55

An employer, who sold his business, made all of his staff redundant without first consulting the appropriate trade union representatives. It was held that liability for a protective award remained with him and was not transferred across to the purchaser (*Angus Jowett & Co v NUTGW* [1985] ICR 646, EAT). Only an employee can complain to a tribunal if he or she receives no payment under the terms of a protective award. The complaint must be presented within three months of the last date on which payment should have been made or, if that was not reasonably practicable, within such further period as the tribunal considers reasonable (*Source*: TULRA 1992, s. 192(2)).

CASE LAW

Examples of redundancy complaints upheld

4.56

A canteen manageress employed by a firm with a concession at a police station was offered suitable employment elsewhere when the concession ended. She refused to transfer because the company taking over the work led her to believe she would be employed by them, but in the event she was not (*Exec of Everest v Cox* [1980] ICR 415, EAT).

Held: The canteen manageress was entitled to a redundancy payment as her refusal to transfer was not unreasonable at the time she took that decision.

4.57
An expanding firm of builders and decorators decided that it would be more economical to use self-employed staff rather than their own men. Two employees were dismissed and the work was taken over by outside labour (*Bromley & Hoare v Evans* [1972] ITR 76, NIRC).

Held: The need for employees (as such) had diminished; and so the two dismissed employees were entitled to redundancy payments.

4.58
An employee took time off work to have an eye operation. His return to work was delayed when it was decided that he also needed an operation on his other eye. During the whole period of his absence, the employee kept in touch with his employers who agreed he could remain off sick. When he returned to work after an absence of some 10 months, his employers refused to take him back. They argued that his contract had been frustrated through illness (*Hebden v Forsey & Son* [1973] ITR 8, NIRC).

Held: If the employers considered that the employee had been absent from work for too long, they could have given him notice to terminate his employment. But they had not done so. The employee was entitled to a redundancy payment.

4.59
A college lecturer accepted the offer of a job knowing that his workload would ultimately 'slacken-off' because of a reduction in the number of student teachers over a period. This meant that he would eventually lose his job (*Lee v Nottingham County Council* [1980] IRLR 284, CA).

Held: Advance knowledge of a likely redundancy situation did not negate the employee's statutory rights. As the lecturer' s dismissal was wholly or mainly attributable to redundancy, he was entitled to a redundancy payment.

Examples of redundancy complaints dismissed

4.60
A toy manufacturer reorganised the working methods in his factory in order to increase efficiency. Although this led to a reduction in the

amount of overtime available, the amount of work to be done remained the same. Nine employees refused to accept the new working arrangements and left (*Lesney Products & Co Ltd v Nolan & Others* [1977] ITR 6, CA).

Held: As the amount of work had not ceased or diminished, the employees' claim for redundancy payments failed.

4.61

An alleged trouble-maker was sacked for absenting himself from a site when he should have been working. He claimed it was a cover-up for redundancy (*J Stott & Son Ltd v Stokes* [1971] ITR 50, QBD).

Held: As it was proved that the employee had been guilty of gross misconduct, entitling his employers to sack him summarily, the employee was not entitled to redundancy pay, even though there was a genuine redundancy situation at the time of his dismissal.

4.62

Anticipating increased sales, a printing firm expanded its workforce. When the additional work failed to materialise, it reduced the workforce to the original level (*O'Hare v Rotaprint Ltd* [1980] ICR 94, EAT).

Held: As there had been no cessation or diminution in the amount of work to be done, redundancy payments ought not to have been made.

5

Unfair dismissal

GENERAL INFORMATION

5.1
Nowadays, most people employed under contracts of employment have the right not to be unfairly dismissed. Furthermore, that general (if qualified) right extends to part-time employees as well as to their full-time counterparts. The distinction is no longer relevant. The exceptions to this rule and the conditions that apply before an employee can present a complaint of unfair dismissal to an employment tribunal are explained below (*Source*: ERA 1996, Part X).

Qualifying conditions

5.2
Except when dismissed (or allegedly dismissed or selected for redundancy) for an inadmissible or unlawful reason (see paras 5.19 to 5.53 below), an employee does not qualify to present a complaint of unfair dismissal to an employment tribunal unless:

- continuously employed for a minimum period of one year ending with the effective date of termination of his (or her) contract of employment; and

- under 'normal retiring age' at that time.

For the meaning of the expression 'effective date of termination', please turn to Chapter 3, paras 3.15 to 3.21.

The 'normal retiring age' for a person holding down the same or an equivalent job must be the same, regardless of the sex of the person concerned. If there is no 'normal retiring age' for the employment in question or if the retiring age is different for men and women doing the same or equivalent jobs, that normal retiring age will be deemed to be 65 (*Source*: ERA 1996, s. 109(1)).

5.3

However, as was indicated earlier, the qualifying conditions summarised above (based on age and length of service) do *not* apply if the employee in question was (or claims to have been) dismissed (or selected for redundancy) for a so-called inadmissible or unlawful reason (sex, pregnancy, race, disability, trade union membership, etc) – as to which, please see *'Inadmissible & Unlawful Reasons for Dismissal'* (at paras 5.19 to 5.53 below).

Complaints of unfair or unlawful dismissal

5.4

A complaint of unfair or unlawful dismissal must be presented to an employment tribunal within three months of the 'effective date of termination' of the employee's contract of employment (as defined in Chapter 3, paras 3.15 to 3.21). A complaint presented 'out of time' will not normally be entertained unless there is an especially good reason for the delay. (*Note*: That period extends to six months in the circumstances described in paras 5.9, 5.10, 5.10A & 5.12 below) (*Source*: ERA 1996, ss 108(1) & 111).

If any such complaint is upheld, the tribunal will order the employer either to reinstate or re-engage the dismissed employee (although this is not always a practicable proposition) or to pay that employee an award of compensation (discussed later in this Chapter).

EXCLUDED CLASSES (EMPLOYEES NOT PROTECTED)

5.5

The right to present a complaint of unfair or unlawful dismissal is available only to 'employees' (see Chapter 2, paras 2.1 to 2.15 earlier in this handbook). A self-employed person, whose *contract for services* is abruptly terminated must lodge a claim for damages for breach of contract with the civil courts.

5.6

The 'unfair dismissal' provisions of the Employment Rights Act 1996 do not apply to the following classes of employment:

- employment as master, or as a member of the crew, of a fishing vessel where the employee is remunerated only by a share in the profits or gross earnings of the vessel – unless dismissed during her maternity leave period or denied the right to return to work after childbirth (*ibid* s. 199(2) & (3));

- employment under a contract of employment in police service (that is to say, service as a member of a constabulary maintained by virtue of an enactment) (*ibid* s. 200);

Any dismissed employee who has reached an 'out of court' settlement with his (or her) employer – by putting his signature to a 'COT 3' agreement, a 'compromise' agreement, or to an agreement under a yet-to-be-promulgated ACAS-inspired 'arbitration scheme' (which latter features large in the Employment Rights [Dispute Resolution] Act 1998), is thereby precluded from presenting a complaint of unfair dismissal to an employment tribunal. For further particulars, please turn to Chapter 2, paras 2.45 to 2.50.

Employees dismissed for taking unofficial industrial action

5.7
Under the common law, an employee who withdraws his (or her) labour by going on strike has effectively terminated his contract of employment and there is no dismissal. In practice, the employer will notify the employee that his employment has ended (usually on the date on which the strike began). That common law position is reinforced by s. 237(1) of the Trade Union & Labour Relations (Consolidation) Act 1992, which cautions employees that they forfeit their right to complain of unfair dismissal if, at the time of their dismissals, they were taking part in an *unofficial* strike or other form of *unofficial* industrial action (but see the next paragraph).

5.8
Note the use of the word 'unofficial' in the preceding paragraph. An unofficial strike (or other form of unofficial industrial action (eg a 'go slow' or 'work to rule') is one that does not have the support of a ballot in favour of such action and has not been authorised or endorsed by the trade union of which the employee is a member. Trade union officials must repudiate unofficial industrial action as soon as it comes to their notice. The procedure is explained in Chapter 7, paras 7.21 to 7.36. Once the repudiation has been relayed to the striking workers (or to those taking some other form of unofficial action), those workers *must* resume normal working at the

start of the first working day or shift which begins after the end of the next working day following the date on which the notice of repudiation was received. If they do *not* do so, they automatically forfeit their right to complain of unfair dismissal and have effectively dismissed themselves. This same rule applies to workers who are not members of the trade union in question (or of any trade union), but who have nonetheless elected to take part in the strike or other form of industrial action mounted by their trade-union-connected colleagues (*ibid*).

Employees dismissed for taking official industrial action

5.9
Employees taking part in an *official* strike or other form of *official* industrial action are no less liable to dismissal. However, they enjoy a greater measure of protection than is available to those taking part in unofficial action.

To avoid the prospect of having to respond to one or more complaints of unfair dismissal, an employer who dismisses employees taking part in *official* industrial action must dismiss each and every one of those employees. Furthermore, he (or she) must *not* make any positive offer to re-engage any of those employees for at least three months beginning with the date on which the last of their number was dismissed (*Highland Fabricators v McLaughlin* [1985] ICR 183, EAT) (*Source*: TULRA 1992, s 238) – but see para 5.10A below.

5.10
An employee dismissed for taking part in *official* industrial action (other than in the circumsances described in para 5.10A below) retains the right to complain of unfair dismissal if, but only if, it is apparent that one or more of his (or her) striking colleagues had not been dismissed, or that one or more of his colleagues had been offered their jobs back within three months of the date of his own dismissal (but that no such offer had been made to him). Such a complaint must be presented to an employment tribunal within the period of *six* months beginning with the effective date of termination of the employee's contract of employment (or, if that is not reasonably practicable, within such further period as the tribunal considers reasonable in the circumstances (*Source*: TULRA 1992, s 239).

Dismissal during 'protected industrial action'

5.10A
However, there is an exception to the rule relating to the selective dismissal or re-employment of employees who took part in official industrial action.

Sections 238(2B) and 238A of the Trade Union & Labour Relations (Consolidation Act 1992, which came into force on 24 April 2000) caution employers that, notwithstanding section 238(2) of the 1992 Act, dismissing an employee for taking part in an *official* strike (or other form of *official* industrial action) will be treated as unfair if:

(a) the dismissal occurred within the period of eight weeks beginning with the day on which the employee started to take official industrial action; or

(b) the dismissal occurred more than eight weeks after the day on which the employee first took official industrial action, in circumstances in which the employee had returned to work within those first eight weeks; or

(c) the dismissal occurred more than eight weeks after the employee first went on strike (or took some other form of official industrial action), in circumstances in which the employee had not returned to work and his employer had failed to take all reasonable steps to resolving the dispute to which the official industrial action related.

Contrary to the usual qualifying conditions (see para 5.2 above), an employee dismissed in the circumstances described in sub-paragraphs (a), (b) or (c) above (ie, while taking protected industrial action) may complain to an employment tribunal *regardless* of his (or her) age or length of service at the material time (*ibid*. s 239(1)).

Note: Whether or not the employer in (c) above had taken reasonable procedural steps to resolve the industrial dispute will depend in large part on the extent to which either party had complied with (or had been willing to comply with) any previously-agreed 'dispute resolution procedure' (eg, as laid down in a collective agreement), or on the willingness of either of the parties to commence or resume negotiations with a view to bringing the industrial action to an end, or whether an offer of conciliation by ACAS had been made and rejected (and by whom), or whether either or both of the parties had unreasonably refused a request that mediation services be used in relation to procedures to be adopted with a view to ending the dispute.

Case law

5.11

The words 'other industrial action' do not necessarily indicate a breach of contract. It is generally sufficient that the action is concerned with pressure being applied by two or more employees to obtain an advantage in relation to a 'trade dispute' (see Chapter 7, para 7.17). Anything said before and at the time of dismissal will be relevant (*Glenrose (Fish Merchants) Ltd v Chapman & Others*, 11 December 1990, EAT).

Thus a refusal by several employees to work essential overtime, which they were not contractually required to do, was held to be 'industrial action'. Their motives in applying pressure on the employer over pay had to be considered (*Power Packing Casemakers Ltd v Faust* [1983] ICR 292, CA). A concerted refusal to work obligatory overtime, in order to force a concession from the employer, is classified as a strike. The fact that the industrial action lasted just a short time is of no consequence (*Anderson & Others v British Coal Corporation* 28 January 1993 QBD).

A strike generally starts from the moment the workers express their intention to withdraw their labour – not from the time that they are normally expected to be at work. An employer is not bound to wait until the workers are contractually bound to be at work before acting (*Winnett v Scamaska Bros Ltd* [1978] ICR 1240, EAT).

An employer who fails to dismiss every worker taking part in *official* industrial action, or who offers to re-employ one or more but not every such worker, will need to contest any subsequent complaint of unfair dismissal on its merits. Was the complainant dismissed for a reason unconnected with the strike, eg sickness-related absenteeism? The motive is irrelevant. However if an employee resigns or retires at that time, then he (or she) is no longer an 'employee' and consequently his existence may be disregarded (*Manifold Industries Ltd v Sims & Others* [1991] ICR 504 EAT, *Coates & Another v Modern Methods Materials Ltd* [1982] IRLR 318 CA, and *Jenkins v P & O European Ferries (Dover) Ltd* [1991] ICR 652, EAT).

There must have been a positive offer to re-engage an employee dismissed for taking part in official industrial action (see paras 5.9, 5.9A & 5.10 above). Reliance on an advertisement inviting former employees to apply for their previous jobs is not sufficient (*Crossville Wales Ltd v Tracey & Others* [1993] IRLR 60, EAT).

Time can be crucial. A dismissal notice sent by post will not take effect until the letter is delivered (see Chapter 3, para 3.67). Striking workers, who return to work before receiving letters notifying them of their dismissals, are not debarred from bringing proceedings. If workers notify their employers that the strike has been called off, then any dismissals later on the same day may be subject to proceedings (*Heath & Another v J F Longman (Meat Salesmen) Ltd* [1973] ICR 407, NIRC).

The time for determining whether there are any employees remaining who have not been dismissed, when a strike is continuing, is at the conclusion of the tribunal proceedings. It matters not whether it is at a preliminary hearing to consider the point or at the full hearing (see Chapter 27) (*P & O European Ferries (Dover) Ltd v Byrne* [1989] IRLR 254, CA).

An employer will have sufficient time to dismiss the employee, whose name came to light during the proceedings, so as to defeat the employee's claim. In any event, the employee's identity could have been obtained by way of *Further Particulars* before the hearing (see Chapter 27, paras 27.19 to 27.23).

An employer can escape liability for unfair dismissal if a former employee uses subterfuge to obtain reinstatement, eg by giving a false name and address. But a tribunal *can* adjudicate on the issue if the employee's true identity should have been known (*Bigham & Keoch v GKN Kwikform Ltd* [1992] ICR 113, EAT).

It is not necessary for an employee to be offered his (or her) old job back, but only one that is reasonably suitable. The employer is entitled to impose terms, eg by notifying the employee that he is on a final warning and will be dismissed if he again takes industrial action (*Williams & Others v National Theatre Board Ltd* [1982] ICR 715, CA).

Dismissal during a 'lock-out'

5.12

An employee dismissed during an employer's 'lock-out' may complain of unfair dismissal if one or more 'relevant employees' had not been dismissed or if his (or her) (former) employer had made a positive offer to re-engage one or other of those same employees within three months of the effective date of termination of his own contract of employment – but had made no such offer to him. The time limit for presenting a complaint of unfair dismissal to an employment tribunal, in the circumstances described here, is *six* months (or within such further period as the tribunal considers reasonable) (*Source*: TULRA 1992, ss 238 & 239). However, paragraph 5.9 above will also apply to the dismissal of employees locked-out by their employers once sections 238(2B) and 238A of TULRA 1992 come into force.

In a 'lock-out' situation, the 'relevant employees' are those who were directly affected or interested in the dispute at the date of the institution of the lock-out (*H Campey & Sons Ltd v Bellwood* [1987] ICR 311, EAT).

PERMITTED OR LEGITIMATE REASONS FOR DISMISSAL

5.13

Section 98 of the Employment Rights Act 1996 lists seven (7) permitted or legitimate reasons for dismissal. These are dismissal on grounds of:

- incompetence (an employee's inherent inability to carry out the duties of his (or her) job);

- illness or injury (accompanied by unacceptable levels of absenteeism);

- lack of qualifications;

- misconduct;

- redundancy;

- illegality of continued employment (eg forfeiture of driver's licence; no legal right to seek and obtain work in the UK; and so on); or

- 'some other substantial reason' of a kind such as to justify the dismissal of an employee holding the position which that employee held.

Although these may be legitimate reasons for dismissal, it will be for an employment tribunal to deal with the question of 'fairness' (as to which, see paras 5.58 *et seq* below).

TUPE-related dismissals

5.14
Where an undertaking or part of an undertaking is transferred from one person to another the contracts of employment of the persons employed by the transferor (the vendor) are automatically 'inherited' by the transferee (the purchaser). If any such employee is dismissed in consequence of the sale or transfer (other than for an 'economic, technical or organisation' (ETO) reason involving changes in the workforce), that dismissal will be treated in law as having been automatically unfair (*Source*: TUPE Regs 1981, Reg 8). If an ETO dismissal is held to have been fair, it will be treated as having been for 'some other substantial reason', that is to say, for one of the 'permitted' reasons described in the previous paragraph.

Comment: Although the 1981 Regulations clearly state that a dismissal in such circumstances is automatically unfair, a somewhat contradictory amendment introduced, with effect from 26 October 1995, by the Collective Redundancies & Transfer of Undertakings (Protection of Employment) (Amendment) Regulations 1995, means that such an employee would not qualify to present a complaint of unfair dismissal to an employment tribunal unless continuously employed for a minimum period of one year ending with the effective date of termination of the employee's contract of employment. The 'upper age limit' rule referred to in paragraph 5.2 above would also apply.

Case law

5.15

Without any instructions, the liquidator of an insolvent company dismissed the employees one hour before he sold the business to another firm. It was held that the dismissals were unfair as they were for a reason connected with the transfer. The liability of the liquidator to pay the compensation (which he was unable to do) was automatically passed to the purchaser (*Litster & Others v Forth Estuary Engineering Ltd* [1989] ICR 341, HL).

5.16

In another case, the liquidator's liability for redundancy payments was not passed on to the purchaser. The employees had been dismissed by the time of the completion of the sale and there were genuine grounds for their dismissal. Furthermore, where receivers hoped to keep on all staff and sell a business as a going concern, but it became necessary to rationalise costs and minimise trading losses by dismissing some of those staff, it was held that the dismissals were for a reason unconnected with the transfer (*Secretary of State for Employment v Gilbraith & Others*, 10 July 1987, EAT and *Longden & Another v Ferrari Ltd & Another* [1994] IRLR 157, EAT).

5.17

Where administrators of a company unfairly dismissed staff before the possibility of a transfer was little more than a possibility, their liability to those staff was not passed on to the firm that subsequently purchased the company (*Ibex Trading Co. Ltd v Walton & Others*, *The Times*, 29 July 1994, EAT).

5.18

A purchaser of a business dismissed a number of staff when it became clear that its modest turnover was unable to support the number of staff previously employed. The EAT agreed that the dismissals had been for an 'economic, technical or organisational reason' involving changes in the workforce. However, they were unfair because the purchaser had failed in his duty to forewarn the employees and to carry out proper consultations with their representatives (*Trafford v Sharpe & Fisher (Building Supplies) Ltd* [1994] IRLR 325, EAT).

INADMISSIBLE AND UNLAWFUL REASONS FOR DISMISSAL

5.19

The Employment Rights Act 1996 and the Trade Union & Labour Relations (Consolidation) Act 1992 point out that the dismissal (or selection for redundancy) of any employee in the circumstances described in paragraphs 5.20 to 5.53 below is either 'inadmissible' or automatically unfair. What this means is that a complaint may be presented to an employment tribunal by any affected employee regardless of that employee's length of service or age at the time the dismissal took place. Furthermore, the penalties on a finding of unfair dismissal are likely to be considerably higher than those awarded in routine unfair dismissal cases.

Similar provisions are to be found in the Sex Discrimination Act 1975, the Race Relations Act 1976, and the Disability Discrimination Act 1995. Indeed, allegations of unlawful discrimination on grounds of sex, marital status, gender reassignment, race or disability might more profitably be pursued under one or other of those three enactments – given that there is no upper limit on the amount of compensation that may be awarded in such cases.

Dismissal on grounds of pregnancy or maternity, etc

5.20

An employee will be treated in law as having been unfairly dismissed, if the reason (or, if more than one, the principal reason) for her dismissal (or selection for redundancy) was that she:

- was pregnant or any other reason connected with her pregnancy;

- had given birth to a child or any other reason connected with her having given birth to a child;

- had taken (or had availed herself of the benefits of) ordinary maternity leave;

- had taken (or sought to take) additional maternity leave, parental leave or time off for dependants;

- had, on the advice of her doctor (or of an employment medical adviser or 'appointed doctor') been suspended from work on maternity grounds.

Complaints of unfair dismissal (or unfair selection for redundancy) in the circumstances described above may be brought by any employee regardless of her length of service at the material time. Such a complaint must nonetheless be presented within three months of the effective date of termination of the employee's contract of employment, or within such further period as the tribunal considers reasonable in a case where it is satisfied that it was not reasonably practicable for the complaint to be presented before the end of that period of three months (*Source*: ERA 1996, ss 99, 105 & 111).

5.21

An employee who is dismissed during her ordinary or additional maternity leave periods, or at the end of maternity leave, or after she resumes work – either because she had taken maternity leave (or, in the case of ordinary maternity leave) or because she had taken advantage of the terms and conditions of employment available to her during such leave – likewise has the right to pursue a complaint of unfair dismissal on the termination of her employment (*ibid*).

5.22

An employee who is made redundant during either of her ordinary or additional maternity leave periods has the right to be offered 'suitable alternative employment' by her employer to take effect immediately on the termination of her employment under her original contract. It will be for her employer to satisfy an employment tribunal that no such employment was available or that he had made an offer of suitable alternative employment which the employee had accepted or unreasonably refused (*Source*: Regulations 10 & 20, Maternity & Parental Leave, etc Regulations 1999 (SI 1999/3312)).

5.23

An employee will not be treated as having been dismissed if, immediately before the end of her additional maternity leave period (or before her dismissal, if dismissal took place before the end of that period), her employer employed five or fewer employees – so long as the employer (or his successor) can satisfy an employment tribunal that it was not reasonably practicable for him to permit the employee to return to work in the same or an equivalent job (*ibid* Regulation 20(6)).

Note: An employee's rights in pregnancy and maternity (under the Employment Rights Act 1996) are discussed in more detail in Chapter 14.

5.24
A pregnant woman was given notice of the termination of her existing job to take effect when she would have been on maternity leave. At that time, she could have been re-engaged in an alternative post. It was held that her dismissal was for a reason connected with her pregnancy, and was therefore unfair (*Stockton-on-Tees BC v Brown* [1988] ICR 410, HL; and *Intelligent Applications Ltd v Wilson*, 6 October 1992, EAT). It is no defence for an employer to show that special circumstances obliged him (or her) to dismiss an employee who was absent on maternity leave.

5.25
A dentist was held to have fallen foul of the law when he dismissed his dental nurse within a few days of the birth of her child. He had argued that he had found it impossible to recruit a temporary replacement and that he had no choice but to recruit somebody on a permanent basis. At the time of her dismissal the nurse had not yet served notice of her intention to return to work (*Clayton v Vigers* [1989] ICR 713, EAT)

Dismissal on grounds of trade union membership or activities

5.26
An employee's rights in relation to trade-union membership and activities are to be found in Part III of the Trade Union & Labour Relations (Consolidation) Act 1992.

An employee will be treated as having been unfairly dismissed if the reason (or, if more than one, the principal reason) for his (or her) dismissal (or selection for redundancy) was that the employee:

- was, or proposed to become, a member of an independent trade union; or

- had taken part, or proposed to take part, in the activities of an independent trade union – either at a time outside his contractual working hours, or at a time within those working hours at which, in accordance with arrangements agreed with (or consent given by) his employer, it is permissible for him to take part in such activities; or

- was not a member of any trade union, or of a particular trade union, or of one of a number of particular trade unions, or had refused, or proposed to refuse, to become or remain a member; or

- had refused, or proposed to refuse, to make a payment to his (or her) employer, or to agree to have money deducted from his wages or salary as an alternative to trade union membership – regardless of any term to the contrary in his contract of employment.

An employee dismissed in the circumstances described above may complain of unfair dismissal regardless of his age or length of service at the material time. Such a complaint must nonetheless be presented within three months of the effective date of termination of the employee's contract of employment, or within such further period as the tribunal considers reasonable in a case where it is satisfied that it was not reasonably practicable for the complaint to be presented before the end of that three-month period (*Source*: TULRA 1992, ss 152, 153 & 154; ERA 1996, s. 111). See also paras 5.54 to 5.57 below (*Interim relief*).

Collective bargaining: recognition

5.27
Since the coming into force on 6 June 2000 of Section 70A and Schedule A1 to the Trade Union & Labour Relations (Consolidation) Act, it is inadmissible and automatically unfair to dismiss an employee (or to select such an employee for redundancy) for:

- acting with a view to obtaining or preventing recognition of a union;

- indicating support for, or opposition to, trade union recognition;

- acting with a view to securing or preventing the ending of bargaining arrangements;

- indicating support or opposition to the ending of bargaining arrangements;

- influencing or seeking to influence the way in which other workers cast their votes in a ballot for trade union recognition;

- influencing or seeking to influence other workers to vote or to abstain from voting in a ballot for trade union recognition;

- voting in a ballot for trade union recognition;

or for proposing to do, failing to do, or proposing to decline to do, any of the things referred to in the list above. See also paras 5.54 to 5.57 below (*Interim relief*).

Note: Schedule A1 to TULRA 1992 was inserted by s. 1(1) & (3) and Schedule 1 to the Employment Relations Act 1999. Since 6 June 2000, employers with 21 or more workers 'on the payroll' (including workers employed by any associated employer) must respond positively to a valid request for recognition by one or more independent trade unions. If an employer refuses or fails to respond to a request for recognition, the Central Arbitration Committee (CAC) will be asked to intervene. If all else fails, recognition will be accorded if a majority of workers (comprising 40 per cent or more of those entitled to vote), vote in favour of recognition. For a summary of these new provisions, please turn to Chapter 25.

Dismissal in health and safety cases

5.28
Under regulation 7 of the Management of Health & Safety at Work Regulations 1999 (SI 1999/3242), every employer is obliged to appoint one or more 'competent persons' to advise and assist him (or her), and to help him understand and comply with his duties under health and safety legislation. The Health & Safety at Work etc Act 1974 likewise requires an employer to provide facilities and paid time off work for trade union-appointed safety representatives or (where there is no recognised trade union) *representatives of employee safety* (elected by the workforce). There is also provision for the establishment of safety committees.

5.29
It is inadmissible and automatically unfair to dismiss a 'competent person', safety representative, representative of employee safety, member of a safety committee, or any other person designated by the employer to carry out activities in connection with preventing or reducing risks to health and safety (or to select such a person for redundancy), if the reason (or, if more than one, the principal reason) for the dismissal (or selection) was that the employee carried out (or

proposed to carry out) his or her safety-related functions. See also paras 5.54 to 5.57 below (*Interim relief*).

5.30
The same rule applies if an employee is dismissed or selected for redundancy for using reasonable means to draw his (or her) employer's attention to circumstances connected with his work which he reasonably believed to be harmful or potentially harmful to health and safety – although this rule only applies if there were no safety representatives and no safety committee at the employee's place of work, or if it was not reasonably practicable for the employee to raise his concerns by those means.

5.31
It is also *prima facie* unfair to dismiss an employee or select him (or her) for redundancy:

(a)   for leaving (or proposing to leave) his place of work in circumstances of danger – which the employee reasonably believed to be serious and imminent and which he could not reasonably have been expected to avert; or

(b)   for refusing to return to his place of work (or any dangerous part of his place of work) so long as the danger in (a) persisted; or

(c)   for taking (or proposing to take) appropriate steps to protect himself or other persons from that danger.

Whether or not the steps the employee in (c) above took (or proposed to take) were appropriate must be judged by reference to all the circumstances including, in particular, his (or her) knowledge and the facilities and advice available to him at the time. Indeed, the employee will not be treated as having been unfairly dismissed if the employer can satisfy an employment tribunal that it was (or would have been) so negligent for the employee to have taken the steps he took (or proposed to take) that any reasonable employer might have dismissed him for taking (or proposing to take) such steps.

5.32
An employee dismissed in the circumstances described in paras 5.28 to 5.31 above may complain of unfair dismissal regardless of his (or her) age or length of service at the material time. Such a complaint

must nonetheless be presented within three months of the effective date of termination of the employee's contract of employment, or within such further period as the tribunal considers reasonable in a case where it is satisfied that it was not reasonably practicable for the complaint to be presented before the end of that three-month period (*Source*: ERA 1996, ss 100, 105, 108, 109 & 111).

Dismissal for refusing Sunday work

5.33

It is inadmissible and automatically unfair to dismiss a *protected* or *opted-out* shop worker or betting worker (or to select such a person for redundancy) if the reason (or, if more than one, the principal reason) for the dismissal was that the worker in question had refused (or proposed to refuse) to do shop or betting work on Sundays or on a particular Sunday (*Source*: ERA 1996, s. 101).

5.34

It is similarly unfair to dismiss an *opted-out* shop or betting worker, or to select such a person for redundancy, if the reason (or, if more than one, the principal reason) for the dismissal was that the worker gave (or proposed to give) an opting-out notice to his (or her) employer.

5.35

An employee dismissed in the circumstances described in paras 5.33 and 5.34 above may complain of unfair dismissal regardless of his (or her) age or length of service at the material time. Such a complaint must nonetheless be presented within three months of the effective date of termination of the employee's contract of employment, or within such further period as the tribunal considers reasonable in a case where it is satisfied that it was not reasonably practicable for the complaint to be presented before the end of that three-month period (*Source*: ERA 1996, ss 101, 105, 108, 109 & 111).

5.36

Workers employed (or recruited to work) in shops or betting shops must be informed in writing of their statutory rights in relation to Sunday work. A shop worker or betting worker who is happy to work on Sundays will be asked to sign an *opting-in* notice stating that he or she wishes to work on Sundays or does not object to doing so. Both parties (the employer and the employee) will then enter into an express agreement setting out what shop work the employee will undertake, and/or on what Sunday(s). The consent may be withdrawn so long as the employee gives three months' advance written notice, during which time he or she must continue to work on Sundays in accordance with the agreement. If the employer had failed to explain the employee's rights, that notice period is reduced to one month.

Working time cases

5.37
Under the Working Time Regulations 1998, which came into force on 1 October 1998, a worker has the legal right to refuse to work more than an average 48-hour week calculated over a reference period of 17 consecutive weeks. The Regulations also prescribe an average eight-hour limit on night work; health assessments and transfers from night workers to day work in prescribed circumstances (with special provisions for young persons under the age of 18); adequate rest breaks; rest periods of not less than 11 consecutive hours in each 24-hour period (12 hours, in the case of young workers); an uninterrupted rest period of at least 24 hours in each seven-day period (48 hours in the case of workers under 18); a rest break of at least 20 minutes when an employee's daily working time is more than six hours (30 minutes for a young worker working more than four-and-a-half hours a day); and a minimum of four weeks' paid annual holidays in every 'holiday year'. The Regulations also make provision for so-called 'workforce agreements' (a legally-enforceable agreement between the employer and his workers, 'putting flesh on the bare bones' of the Regulations) and for the election of one or more workforce representatives). For further particulars, please turn to Chapter 18.

5.38
Any employee or worker who is dismissed (or selected for redundancy) will be treated, for the purposes of Part X of the Employment Rights Act 1996 (*Unfair Dismissal*) as having been unfairly dismissed if the reason or (if more than one, the principal reason) for the dismissal (or selection) was that he (or she) had:

- refused (or proposed to refuse) to comply with a requirement which the employer imposed (or proposed to impose) in contravention of the employer's obligations under the Working Time Regulations 1998;

- refused (or proposed to refuse) to forgo a right conferred by those Regulations;

- failed to sign a workforce agreement for the purposes of those Regulations, or to enter into, or agree to vary or extend, any other agreement with the employer as provided for in those Regulations; or

- being (i) a representative of members of the workforce for the purposes of Schedule I to those Regulations (*Workforce Agreements*), or a candidate in an election which any person elected will, on being elected, be such a representative, performed (or proposed to perform) any functions or activities as such a representative or candidate.

(*Source*: Employment Rights Act 1996, ss 101A & 104, as inserted or amended by Reg 30(1) & (2) of the 1998 Regulations.)

5.39

Any worker or *workforce representative* (or candidate for election as such a representative) who is dismissed (or selected for redundancy) for pursuing his (or her) rights under the 1998 Regulations or for carrying out or presuming to carry out his functions as such a representative (or candidate) may present a complaint to an employment tribunal regardless of his age or length of service at the material time. The complaint must be presented within three months of the effective date of dismissal or within such further period as the tribunal considers reasonable in the circumstances. If such a complaint is upheld, the worker or representative will be awarded compensation for unfair dismissal (including a minimum basic award [2001/02] of £3,300). See also paras 5.54 to 5.57 below (*Interim relief*).

Dismissal of pension scheme trustees

5.40

An employee who is a trustee of a relevant occupational pension scheme has the legal right to perform his (or her) duties as such a trustee without interference and without fear of being dismissed for doing so. Indeed a pension scheme trustee (duly nominated and elected in accordance with the provisions of the Pensions Act 1995) is entitled to a reasonable amount of paid time off work (during normal working hours) to enable him to carry out such duties.

5.41
A pension scheme trustee who is dismissed (or selected for redundancy) for carrying out his (or her) duties may present a complaint to an employment tribunal regardless of his age or length of service at the material time. In short, his dismissal will be treated as inadmissible and automatically unfair. If the employee's complaint is upheld, he will be awarded compensation for unfair dismissal (including a minimum basic award of £3,300 – which latter is the figure for 2001/02). The complaint must be presented within three months of the effective date of termination of the employee's contract of employment. A complaint presented 'out of time' will not be heard unless there are exceptional reasons for the delay (*Source*: PA 1995, s. 16; ERA 1996, s. 102). See also paras 5.54 to 5.57 below (*Interim relief*).

Dismissal of an 'employee representative'

5.42
An employee who is dismissed will be treated in law as having been unfairly dismissed if the reason (or, if more than one, the principal reason) for his (or her) dismissal (or selection for redundancy) is that the employee, being:

- an *employee representative* for the purposes of Chapter II of Part IV of the Trade Union & Labour Relations (Consolidation) Act 1992 (employer's duty to consult with 'appropriate representatives' concerning proposed collective redundancies) or Regulations 10 & 11 of the Transfer of Undertakings (Protection of Employment) Regulations 1981 (duty to consult with 'appropriate representatives' concerning the proposed sale or transfer of an undertaking);

- a candidate in an election for the role of *employee representative* had performed (or proposed to perform) any functions or activities as such a candidate;

An employee dismissed in the circumstances described may complain to an employment tribunal regardless of his age or length of service at the effective date of termination of his contract of employment. The complaint must be presented within three months of the effective date of termination or within such further period as the tribunal considers reasonable in the circumstances (*Source*: ERA 1996, s. 103). See also paras 5.54 to 5.57 below (*Interim relief*).

Dismissal for making a 'protected disclosure'

5.43

It is inadmissible and automatically unfair to dismiss an employee (or to select such an employee for redundancy) if the reason (or, if more than one, the principal reason) for the dismissal (or selection) is that the employee had made a protected disclosure. For these purposes, a 'protected disclosure' is any disclosure of information (to an employer or other responsible person which, in the reasonable belief of the person making the disclosure tends to show:

- that a criminal offence has been committed, is being committed or is likely to be committed;

- that a person has failed, is failing or is likely to fail to comply with any legal obligation to which he (or she) is subject;

- that a miscarriage of justice has occurred, is occurring or is likely to occur;

- that the health or safety of any individual has been, is being or is likely to be damaged;

- that the environment has been, is being or is likely to be damaged; or

- that information or evidence concerning any of the above matters has been, or is likely to be, deliberately concealed.

There is no upper limit on the amount of compensation that may be awarded to an employee held to have been unfairly dismissed or selected for redundancy for having made a 'protected disclosure'. See also paras 5.54 to 5.57 below (*Interim relief*).

(*Source*: s. 103A, Employment Rights Act 1996, inserted by the Public Interest Disclosure Act 1998, s. 1.)

Dismissal for asserting a statutory right

5.44

It is inadmissible and automatically unfair for an employer to dismiss an employee (or to select such an employee for redundancy) for complaining to a tribunal about an infringement of a 'relevant statutory right' in employment *or* for alleging that his (or her) employer had infringed one or other of those rights. It is of no consequence that the employee's claim to that right (and that it had been infringed) was incorrect – so long as it was made in good faith (*Source*: ERA 1996, s. 104).

5.45

For these purposes, a 'relevant statutory right' is:

- any right conferred by the Employment Rights Act 1996 for which the remedy for its infringement is by way of a complaint (or reference) to an employment tribunal;

- the right of an employee under s. 86 of the 1996 Act to minimum notice to terminate his (or her) contract of employment;

- any right conferred by ss 68, 86, 146, 168, 169 and 170 of the Trade Union & Labour Relations (Consolidation) Act 1992, namely:

  (a) the right of an employee not to have trade union dues deducted from his pay without prior authorisation;

  (b) the right of an employee to opt-out of paying contributions to a trade union's political fund;

  (c) the right of an employee not to have 'action short of dismissal' taken against him because of his membership or non-membership of a trade union, or for taking part at an 'appropriate time' in the activities of an independent trade union;

  (d) the right of a trade union official (eg shop steward or works convenor) to take paid time off work for the purposes of carrying out his duties as such an official;

  (e) the right of an employee, who is a member of a recognised independent trade union, to take unpaid time off during working hours for the purposes of taking part in any activities of that union (either as a member or as a representative of that union), excluding any activities which themselves consist of industrial action;

- any right (the 48-hour week, four weeks' paid annual holidays, rest periods, etc) conferred by the Working Time Regulations 1998 – as to which, please turn to Chapter 18; and

- the right to be paid no less than the appropriate national minimum wage prescribed by the National Minimum Wage Regulations 1999 (as to which, please turn to Chapter 19).

National minimum wage cases

5.46
It is inadmissible and automatically unfair to dismiss an employee (or to select such an employee for redundancy) for enforcing or proposing to enforce his (or her) entitlement to be paid the national minimum wage; or for having been instrumental in prosecuting his employer for an offence under the National Minimum Wage Act 1998; or because the employee qualified (or would or might have qualified) for the national minimum wage (*Source*: Employment Rights Act 1996, sections 104A & 105(7A)).

5.47
Under the National Minimum Wage Regulations 1999 (SI 1999/584), which came into force on 1 April 1999, every worker aged 18 to 21, inclusive, must be paid no less than £3.20 an hour. For workers aged 22 and over (save for those receiving 'accredited training' during their first six months of employment), the appropriate national minimum wage (NMW) is £3.70 per hour. The 1999 Regulations do not prescribe a NMW for workers aged 16 and 17. For more information on the NMW, please turn to Chapter 19.

Tax credit cases

5.48
An employee will be treated in law as having been unfairly dismissed if the reason (or, if more than one, the principal reason) for his (or her) dismissal or selection for redundancy was that he had taken or proposed to take action to enforce (or otherwise secure the

benefit of) a right conferred by regulations made under section 6(2)(a) or (c) of the Tax Credits Act 1999 or that the employer had been penalised for refusing or failing to comply with his obligations under that Act (*ibid* sections 104B & 105(7B)).

5.49
Since 6 April 2000, employers have assumed responsibility (on behalf of the Inland Revenue) for paying working families' tax credits and disabled persons' tax credits directly to the employees concerned. They must also include related information in the itemised pay statements necessarily issued to those employees. An employer who refuses or fails to comply with his obligations under the 1999 Act is guilty of an offence and (depending on the nature of the offence) liable to a fine of up to £3,000.

European Works Council cases

5.50
Since the coming into force on 15 January 2000 of the Transnational Information & Consultation of Employees Regulations 1999 (SI 1999/3323) (the 'TICE Regulations') any large company or organisation employing 1,000 or more employees within the European Economic Area (EEA) (of whom 150 or more work in each of at least two EEA Member States) must respond positively to a valid request from employees for the establishment of a European Works Council (EWC).

Note: The TICE Regulations (sometimes referred to as 'TICER') implement Council Directive 97/74/EC of 15 December 1997 'on the establishment of a European Works Council or a procedure in Community-scale undertakings and Community-scale groups of undertakings for the purposes of informing and consulting employees'. The EEA comprising the 15 EU Member States and the three remaining Contracting Parties of the EEA (Norway, Liechtenstein and Iceland).

5.51
Any employee who is dismissed (or selected for redundancy) for being instrumental in promoting, supporting or enforcing the establishment of an EWC, or for standing as a candidate for election as a member of a 'special negotiating body' (SNB), or for voting in a ballot for the election of employees to an SNB, or for performing (or proposing to perform) his (or her) functions as an elected or appointed member of an SNB or EWC, or as an information and consultation representative, etc, will be treated in law as having been unfairly dismissed – regardless of his or her age or length of service at the

material time. (*Source*: Regulations 28 & 29 of the TICE Regulations 1999 and section 105(7D), Employment Rights Act 1996). For further information, please turn to Chapter 20, paras 20.28 to 20.30).

Part-time workers

5.52
Under the Part-time Workers (Prevention of Less Favourable Treatment) Regulations 2000 (SI 2000/1551), which came into force on 1 July, 2000, part-time workers have the legal right not to treated less favourably than 'comparable full-time workers' as regards the terms of their contracts of employment, or by being subjected to any other detriment (including termination of their contracts) by any act (or deliberate failure to act) by their employers. This means that they have the right to be paid the same hourly rate of pay as comparable full-time workers; to receive the same premium payments for overtime work; to have the same right of access to occupational sick pay, contractual maternity pay and parental leave (*without* having to complete longer qualifying periods of service); and to be subjected to the same redundancy selection criteria as their full-time counterparts. Different treatment of full-time and part-time workers will be lawful if, but only if, justified on objective grounds.

5.53
A part-time worker (who is an 'employee') who is dismissed (or selected for redundancy) for challenging his (or her) employer's failure to comply with the 2000 Regulations, or for bringing proceedings before an employment tribunal or court to enforce his rights under those Regulations, or for refusing (or proposing to refuse) to forgo a right conferred by the Regulations, will be treated as having been unfairly dismissed and may bring proceedings before an employment tribunal regardless of his age or length of service at the material time (*ibid*. Regulation 5 and section 105(7E), Employment Rights Act 1996). For further information, please turn to Chapter 24, paras 24.13 to 24.17.

Interim relief pending determination of complaint

5.54
An employee who has presented a complaint to an employment tribunal that he (or she) has been unfairly dismissed (or unfairly

selected for redundancy) for one or other of the following reasons, that is to say:

- for being or not being (or for refusing to become or remain) a member of an independent trade union (or for taking part in the activities of an independent trade union) (see para 5.26);

- in the circumstances described in para 5.27 above (*Collective bargaining: recognition*)

- for carrying out (or attempting to carry out) his functions as a safety representative or representative of employee safety, or as a 'competent person' or other person designated by his employer to carry out safety-related functions (see para 5.29);

- for carrying out his functions as a workforce representative elected to represent the interests of fellow workers when negotiating a workforce agreement (or as a candidate for election as such a representative) for the purposes of Schedule 1 to the Working Time Regulations 1998 (see para 5.39 above);

- for carrying out (or proposing to carry out) his functions either as a trustee of a relevant occupational pension scheme or as an employee representative when collective redundancies or a TUPE transfer are, or is, mooted (see paras 5. 40 to 5.42 above);

- for having made a *protected disclosure* within the meaning given to that expression by section 43A of the Employment Rights Act 1996 (see Chapter 23);

may apply for interim relief, that is to say, an order for reinstatement or re-engagement pending a full hearing of the employee's complaint (*Source*: ERA 1996, s. 128; TULRA 1992, ss 152 & 161 to 167).

5.55
An application for 'interim relief' must be submitted to the Secretary to the Tribunals within seven days of the *effective date of termination* of the employee's contract of employment (see Chapter 3, paras 3.15 to 3.21). In the case of a dismissal on grounds of trade union membership or activities, the employee's application must be accompanied by a certificate signed by an authorised official of the relevant trade union confirming that there appears to be reasonable grounds for supposing that the employee had indeed been dismissed

for one or other (or both) of those reasons. The hearing of an application for interim relief must take place as quickly as possible – but not before the employer has been sent a copy of the employee's application and has been given at least seven days' advance notification of the date, time and place fixed for the hearing. If the application relates to a dismissal on alleged trade union grounds, the employer will also receive a copy of the trade union certificate referred to in the previous paragraph.

5.56

If an employment tribunal, in considering whether to grant 'interim relief', is satisfied that the claim is 'likely' to succeed at a full hearing, it will make a declaration to that effect. What this means in practice is that a tribunal will grant an application for interim relief if (using the non-legal vernacular) they decide that the complaint has 'a pretty good chance of success' (*Taplin v C Shipham Ltd* [1978] ICR 1068, EAT).

5.57

The employer will be invited to reinstate or re-engage the employee (see paras 5.158 to 5.165 below), on terms that are acceptable to the employee, until such time as the full tribunal hearing takes place. If the employer does not consent or fails to attend the interim hearing, the tribunal will order the continuation of the employee's contract of employment until the proceedings are completed. An employer who refuses to reinstate the employee until the date set for the full tribunal hearing must, nonetheless, continue to pay that employee his (or her) full wages or salary from the date of dismissal until the tribunal hearing *does* take place. The total sum paid by way of wages or salary will not be recoverable even if the employee loses his case at the main hearing. Although there is a duty on the tribunal to ensure a speedy trial, the employer too must take energetic steps to arrange for an early hearing, if only to keep his losses to a minimum (*Initial Textile Services v Rendell*, 23 July 1991, EAT).

DISMISSAL – FAIR OR UNFAIR?

5.58

At a tribunal hearing on a complaint of unfair dismissal (or unfair selection for redundancy), the onus is on the employer (the respondent) to show:

- the reason (or, if more than one, the principal reason) for dismissing the employee; and

- that the reason fell within one of the permitted reasons for dismissal listed in paragraph 5.13 above.

In short the employer will need to satisfy the tribunal that the employee had been dismissed because he (or she) was:

- incompetent;

- incapable of work due to illness or injury;

- unqualified;

- guilty of misconduct;

- redundant; or

- illegally employed.

If none of those reasons apply, the employer will need to demonstrate that the employee was dismissed for 'some other substantial reason' of a kind such as to justify the dismissal of a person holding the position which that employee held.

5.59

Once the (respondent) employer has shown what the reason (or principal reason) for the dismissal was, and has demonstrated that it was for a permitted reason, the determination of the question whether the dismissal was fair or unfair (having regard to the reason shown by the employer) depends on whether, in all the circumstances (including the size and administrative resources of the employer's undertaking), the employer had acted reasonably or unreasonably in treating it as a sufficient reason for dismissing the employee, and the answer to that question shall be determined in accordance with equity and the substantial merits of the case (*Source*: ERA 1996, s. 98).

Dismissal on grounds of incompetence or lack of capability

5.60

These grounds may be relied upon where the employee's 'skill, aptitude, health or any other physical or mental quality' falls below that which is required for the job. The duties on which the worker is engaged must relate to 'work of a kind which he (or she) was employed... to do'.

This will usually include incompetence where it relates to an inherent fault and not just to laziness or negligence (*Sutton & Gates (Luton) Ltd v Boxall* [1979] ICR 67, EAT).

Dismissal on grounds of misconduct

5.61
An employee who is insubordinate, abusive, lazy, aggressive, violent, dishonest, habitually late for work, disdainful of safety rules, etc, is arguably guilty of misconduct. Unless he (or she) responds quickly to advice, counselling and warnings, dismissal is inevitable. In serious case, such an employee is guilty of gross misconduct and can be dismissed 'on the spot'. However, in every case, the employer must be able to demonstrate that he had acted reasonably and fairly before taking the decision to dismiss. An employee might have an answer to the complaints and allegations made against him. He might assert that he was the victim of violence (not the aggressor); or that he misunderstood the rules about claiming expenses, or that he did not intend to be rude when confronted by an angry or violent customer; and so on.

5.62
There is at times a thin dividing line between capability and conduct. For instance, an employee may keep on making mistakes despite being warned of the serious consequences. If he (or she) is dismissed, it may be difficult to determine whether he is wilfully in default or is inherently incapable of doing his work properly. If an employee's competence is at issue, the employer will need to satisfy a tribunal that he made every effort (through guidance, counselling and training) to improve the employee's performance in his job.

Dismissal on grounds of redundancy

5.63
Although redundancy is a permitted reason for dismissal, an employer will still need to satisfy the test of 'reasonableness'. If an employee was selected for redundancy for an inadmissible or

unlawful reason (see paras 5.19 to 5.53 above), or contrary to any agreed selection procedure, the dismissal will be held to have been unfair (or automatically unfair).

Illegally employed?

5.64

There will be occasions when it would be unlawful for an employer to continue employing a particular employee. Such a situation would arise if an HGV driver is banned from driving for a year or if a foreign national's work permit has expired and there is no prospect of its being renewed, or if an employee is an illegal immigrant. Pregnant women and women 'of reproductive capacity' must not be employed in work that exposes them to lead or to ionising radiation; and so on. In every such case, the employer will nonetheless need to demonstrate that he had done all that he reasonably could to resolve the particular problem before taking the decision to dismiss. In the case of a new or expectant mother, the employer would be expected either to offer 'suitable alternative employment' or to suspend the woman on full pay until such time as it is lawful for her to resume her normal duties (as to which, please turn to Chapter 14, para 14.49).

Note: Under the Asylum & Immigration Act 1996 (which came into force on 27 January 1997) an employer is liable to a fine of up to £5,000 if he employs a person subject to immigration control if the person in question has not been granted leave to enter or remain in the UK; if the person's leave to enter or remain is no longer valid and subsisting; or if the leave to enter or remain is subject to a condition precluding him (or her) from taking up employment.

Dismissal for 'some other substantial reason'

5.65

This is a very wide provision. It gives the employer protection where, for instance, he carries out a genuine reorganisation to improve the efficiency and profitability of his business, eg by introducing new working methods or a different pattern of shifts (to accommodate a full order book) or by simply coming to terms with advances in technology. If, when doing so, he has to dismiss one or more employees, they would usually be entitled to a redundancy payment. Lord Denning, MR put it this way: 'It is important that nothing should be done to impair the ability of employers to reorganise their workforce and their terms and conditions of work so as to improve efficiency'. But the terms offered must be reasonable in the circumstances. The issue is not of weighing the advantages to the employer against the disadvantages to the employee, but the interests of each party have to be considered.' (*Lesney Products Ltd v Nolan & Others* [1977] ICR 235, CA); *Robinson v British Island Airways* [1978] ITR 111, EAT; *Elliott Turbomachinery Ltd v Bates* [1981] ICR 218, EAT).

5.66

There must be real negotiations with the employee, or his (or her) representatives, or an attempt made to come to an agreement if the employee is being especially difficult. The position must be fully explained to him. This extends to non-contractual matters and the employer's plans to abolish 'institutionalised' overtime (*Ford v Milthorn Toleman Ltd* [1980] IRLR 30, CA; and *Trebor Bassett Ltd v Saxby & Another*, 3 November 1993, EAT). What has to be examined is the employer's motives. If the changes he has in mind are arbitrary and of little advantage to the business, they will fail the test of 'reasonableness'. But if they are accepted by the union and many employees, then they will probably be held to be reasonable (*Catamaran Cruisers Ltd v Williams & Others* [1994] IRLR 386, EAT).

5.67

An employee who has been hired *specifically* to replace another employee who is absent on maternity leave, or who has been suspended from work on medical or maternity grounds, can lawfully be dismissed when that other employee returns to work – if, but only if, the replacement employee had been informed in writing (before accepting the offer of employment) that his (or her) employment would be terminated as soon as the permanent employee returns to work (see also paras 5.156 & 5.157 below). A dismissal on such grounds will be treated as having been for 'some other substantial reason' and will be held to be fair. However, the outcome might well be different if the replacement employee had been given to understand, rightly or wrongly, that he would be transferred to another job when the permanent employee returned to work (*Webb v EMO Air Cargo (UK) Ltd (No 2)* [1995] IRLR 645) (*Source*: ERA 1996, s. 106).

5.68

Likewise, when a person is recruited on a fixed short-term contract to stand in for a member of staff seconded elsewhere or to provide cover for someone who is absent on long-term sick leave, the termination of his (or her) contract upon that other's return will not normally be unfair. The dismissal will have been for 'some other substantial reason'; and the employee would not qualify for a redundancy payment (*Fay v North Yorkshire CC* [1986] ICR 133, CA).

5.69

When a trade union, a shop steward or some other person brings pressure to bear on an employer to dismiss another employee, the employer's yielding to such pressure would not amount to 'some other substantial reason' for dismissing the employee in question. An employer's fear of industrial action is no defence to a complaint of unfair dismissal (*James Ferries & Co. Ltd v Johnstone*, 30 October 1984, EAT) (*Source*: ERA 1996, s. 107).

5.70

The fact that a man could not get on with his fellow workers would be relevant in considering whether it was 'fair and equitable' to dismiss. But that position would have to be ignored if the threat of industrial action over the person's presence was the real reason for dismissal (*Yusuf v Aberplace Ltd* [1984] ICR 851, EAT).

5.71

Third party pressure to dismiss can, in certain circumstances, entitle an employer to plead 'some other substantial reason'. In order for the plea to be successful, efforts must have been made to find suitable alternative employment for the employee in question. A local authority had a contractual right to approve security staff provided by a contractor at an airport. Friction developed between one of the contractor's employees and an authority manager. The contractor was instructed to remove the man from the site. As there was no alternative work for the man to do, he was dismissed. The dismissal was held to be fair on the grounds of 'some other substantial reason' (*Dobie v Burns International Security Services (UK) Ltd* [1984] ICR 812, CA).

5.72

The 'some other substantial reason' provision is a sweeping-up provision designed to deal with situations that are not covered by one of the other permitted grounds for dismissal. If a husband and wife run a public house together, with accommodation 'thrown in', and one is dismissed, the sacking of the spouse may be justified on that ground. So too where a fixed-term contract comes to an end with no other work being available for the employee. Or where a new recruit is dismissed for misrepresenting his (or her) qualifications at the employment interview and it is found that he could not perform his job properly.

Actual reason for dismissal

5.73
Under normal circumstances, it devolves on the employer to prove reason (or, if more than one, the principal reason) for dismissing an employee and that that reason fell within one of the *permitted* reasons for dismissal discussed earlier. The fact that the employer had put the 'wrong label' on the dismissal is irrelevant – so long as the real (or correct) reason for the dismissal was a *permitted* reason.

5.74
An exception to the 'some other substantial reason' rule arises in *constructive dismissal* cases (see Chapter 2, paras 2.40 to 2.44). If an employee in such a situation states that he (or she) is going to resign, and the employer responds by taking steps to recruit and train a replacement, the subsequent dismissal of the employee who had changed his mind would be labelled as having been for 'some other substantial reason'. The fact that the employee had subsequently sought to retract his declared course of action, or that the employer had misinterpreted the employee's true intentions, did not render the dismissal unfair (*Ely v YKK Fasteners (UK) Ltd* [1993] IRLR 500, CA).

The test of 'reasonableness'

5.75
Bristow, J summarised the principle as follows: '[it] is concerned only with the reasonableness of what you do, not how you do it... Very often... the way in which you do something affects, or may affect, the question: Was it reasonable for you to do it at all? If... you dismiss a senior employee of long standing at a moment's notice with no consultation whatever, you are not simply treating him with discourtesy... you are depriving yourself of the opportunity to explore with him the possibility of finding another slot in which to place him; and, on this basis, it would be open... to find your action in dismissing him in the circumstances to be unreasonable.' (*Abbotts & Standley v Wessex-Glyndwood Steels Ltd* [1982] IRLR 51, EAT).

5.76

The issue of 'reasonableness' has generated a welter of reported cases. It is important to remember that each case is decided on its own peculiar facts. No two cases are exactly alike. The outcome of one case with near identical facts to another could nonetheless lead to a different outcome (*Rentokil Ltd v Mackin & Another* [1989] IRLR 286, EAT).

5.77

In a consolidated appeals hearing, that of *The Post Office v Foley*; *HSBC Bank plc* (formerly the Midland Bank) *v Madden* [31 July 2000], the Court of Appeal effectively reinstated the mantra that a tribunal should not substitute its own views with those of an employer and the 'band of reasonable responses' test enunciated by Court of Appeal in *British Leyland UK Ltd v Smith* [1981] IRLR 91 and reinforced by the EAT (with guidance, subsequently approved by the Court of Appeal) in *British Home Stores v Burchell* [1978] IRLR 379 and *Iceland Frozen Food Ltd v Jones* [1983] ICR 17. In 1999, in *Haddon v Van den Bergh Foods Limited* [1999] IRLR 91, the EAT had characterised the 'band of reasonable responses' test and the mantra as being 'singularly unhelpful. It conjured up, said the EAT, the possibility of extreme views at either end of the band or range, and posed a danger to tribunals testing the fairness of a dismissal by reference to the extreme. We disagree, said the EAT in *Midland Bank plc v Madden* [2000] IRLR 288. Under the doctrine of precedent, it is not for the EAT to outlaw the 'band of reasonable responses' test, thereby presuming to invalidate a decision of the Court of Appeal. Quite so, said the Court of Appeal. The EAT in *Haddon* had been wrong to encourage tribunals to act upon their own subjective views of what they would have done had they been 'in the employer's shoes'. It is sufficient that the employer had a reasonable belief in the employee's guilt and had carried out a reasonable investigation before taking the decision to dismiss. So long as that decision was within the 'band of reasonable responses', it is not open to a tribunal to say: 'We would have done otherwise'.

The employer's duty to consult

5.78

Except in very rare cases, an employee should never dismiss an employee without first consulting that employee and listening to what the employee has to say. Lord Bridge put it thus: 'An employer having *prima facie* grounds to dismiss... will in the great majority of cases not act reasonably... unless and until he has taken steps, conveniently classified... as 'procedural', which are necessary in the circumstances to justify that course of action. Thus, in the case of incapacity, the employer will not normally act reasonably unless he gives the employee fair warning and an opportunity to mend his ways and show that he can do the job; in the case of misconduct, the employer will normally not act reasonably unless he investigates the complaint of misconduct fully and fairly and hears whatever the employee wishes to say in his defence or in explanation or mitigation; in the case of redundancy, the employer will normally not act reasonably unless he warns and consults any employees affected or their representative, adopts a fair basis on which to select for redundancy and takes such steps as may be reasonable to avoid or minimise redundancy by redeployment within his own organisation.'(*Polkey v A E Dayton Services Ltd* [1988] ICR 142, HL.)

5.79
An employee was informed in no uncertain terms that he (or she) – and any other employee – would be dismissed if he brought drugs onto the employer's premises or reported for work in a drugged or intoxicated state. The employers were also entitled to carry out drug-screening tests. The employee in question provided a sample that proved positive on a fail-safe test. It was held that his summary dismissal without a formal hearing was fair. Prior consultation would have served no useful purpose (*Sutherland v Sonat Offshore (UK) Inc.*, 1 July 1993, EAT). An employer does not have to prove that he had made a conscious decision not to consult; only that, on the facts known to him at the time, a reasonable employer would have concluded that consultation would have been useless (*Duffy v Yeomans & Partners Ltd, The Times*, 26 July 1994, CA). An employer's decision to dismiss does not need to have been perverse before an employment tribunal will intervene. Suffice that it is outside the 'band of reasonable responses'. That is to say no reasonable employer could have taken that course (*Cullion v Scottish Midland Co-operative Society Ltd*, 27 September 1989, EAT).

5.80
In some extreme cases where the facts are basically agreed, the answer is obvious. If an employee is sent to prison for five years for setting fire to his (or her) employer's premises, a dismissal on grounds of

misconduct would be patently fair. In any event, the employee's contract would almost certainly be frustrated by the length of the prison sentence (as to which, see Chapter 2, paras 2.32 to 2.39).

5.81
On the other hand, it would probably be unfair to dismiss an employee who has been sent to prison for six weeks for non-payment of his wife's maintenance. What would need to be taken into account in such a situation is whether the employer could reasonably hold the man's job open until his release. But, if this was the tenth time in two years that the employee had lost his liberty, there would come a stage when his employer could lawfully say: 'Enough is enough!'

5.82
It is what happens up to the date of dismissal (or an appeal) that has to be considered and not what occurred afterwards. So, if an employer's failure to dismiss an employee with the notice he (or she) was entitled to be given under his contract resulted in the employer not offering the employee a job that had become unexpectedly vacant after the employee had actually left, that was irrelevant (*BSC Sports & Social Club v Morgan* [1987] IRLR 391, EAT; and *Treganowan v Robert Knee & Co* Ltd [1975] ITR 121, QB). Likewise, if an employer discovers after making an employee redundant that the employee had been stealing, then if no true redundancy existed, the dismissal would be held to have been unfair. But compensation would be reduced to nil on the basis that the employee would only be entitled to an award that is 'just and equitable' in the circumstances (*W Devis & Son Ltd v Atkins* [1977] ICR 662, HL; and *Trico Folberth Ltd v Devonshire* [1989] IRLR 396, CA).

Express and implied terms in the contract

5.83
In deciding whether a dismissal is fair or unfair, a tribunal may have to look to the employee's contract to find out the contractual position of the employee (see Chapter 8, paras 8.3 to 8.7). For instance, was there an express or implied term in the employee's contract that required him (or her) to spend nights away from home? There may be an express clause to that effect. Or such a term may be implied by the very nature of the employee's job. This would be so in the case of a long-distance lorry driver.

In ascertaining whether there is an 'implied term' in a contract, the underlying principle is:

- whether such a term is necessary in order to give the contract 'business efficacy'; that is to say, to make it work in practice, *and*

- whether it would probably have been agreed to by the parties, had they applied their minds to it at the time the employment began, that such a term was not only reasonable but sensible.

(*Jones v Associated Tunnelling Co Ltd* [1981] IRLR 477, EAT; and *Courtaulds Northern Spinning Ltd v Sibson & Another* [1988] ICR 451, CA.)

5.84

If a long-distance lorry driver were to refuse to undertake any long-distance trips that involved spending nights away from home, a dismissal for that reason would probably be fair – so long as there is nothing in the employee's contract to justify the refusal. The test to be applied when an employee has refused to obey a lawful instruction is whether the employer had acted reasonably in the circumstances (*UCATT v Brain* [1981] ICR 542, CA; and *Davies v Jack Troth t/a Richards Transport*, 16 December 1987, EAT).

Mutual trust and confidence

5.85

Some terms are implicit in every contract of employment. There must be mutual trust and confidence (*BBC v Hearn* [1977] IRLR 273, CA). The test is: '[Y]ou have to look at the conduct of the party whose behaviour is being challenged and determine whether it is such that its effect, judged reasonably and sensibly, is to disable the other party from properly carrying out his or her obligations' (per Talbot J in *Post Office v Roberts* [1980] IRLR 347, EAT).

5.86

A female employee complained to her manager that two supervisors had sexually assaulted her. The manager's refusal to act on the complaint undermined not only her own confidence, but that of the other female staff. It was held that the complainant had every right to quite her job and present a complaint to an employment tribunal that she had been constructively dismissed (*Bracebridge Engineering Ltd v Darby* [1990] IRLR 3, EAT).

5.87

A bank sought to exercise its contractual right to transfer a lowly-paid employee from Leeds to Newcastle with just one week's notice and no relocation allowances. With a sick wife and two small children, it was virtually impossible for the employee to comply with his employer's instructions. He resigned in protest, claiming that he had been constructively dismissed and that his dismissal had been unfair. It was held that the employer had been in breach of an overriding implied duty not to behave in a way likely to destroy or seriously damage the relationship of confidence and trust between himself and his employees. There *was* a constructive dismissal and it *was* unfair (*United Bank Ltd v Akhtar* [1989] IRLR 507, EAT).

5.88

On the other hand, where an employer, in the exercise of an unfettered right, transferred an employee to another department and this resulted in a loss of income, it was held that there was no fundamental breach. The employee was not entitled to leave. The 'reasonableness' test could not be imported through the back door (*White v Reflective Roadstuds Ltd* [1991] ICR 733, EAT).

5.89

An employee only gained a very small sum of money from a deliberate fraud. It was held that, whatever the sum, it struck at the fundamental relationship of mutual trust and confidence, entitling the employer to dismiss (*Conlin v United Distillers* [1994] IRLR 169, Ct Sess). When a section leader with 20 years' service in a retail store was dismissed for shoplifting in another shop, his dismissal was held to be fair. The trust necessary in the job had been undermined (*Moore v C & A Modes* [1981] IRLR 71, EAT).

5.90

There is a fundamental obligation on an employer not to treat an employee arbitrarily, capriciously and inequitably in matters of pay. To do so would entitle the employee to leave and claim constructive dismissal. This would be on the basis of a breach of the implied term of mutual trust and confidence (*GEC Avionics Ltd v Sparham*, 12 October 1993, EAT).

5.91

An employee must serve his (or her) employer faithfully. If he secretly sets up a competitive business or passes his employer's secrets to another firm, he may be dismissed without notice. Except on procedural grounds it would be most unlikely that any such dismissal would ever be unfair (see Chapter 10).

Breach of disciplinary rules

5.92
Most employers lay down specific rules of conduct and behaviour. Indeed, in organisations employing 20 or more employees (including persons employed by any associated employer) the 'written statement of terms of employment' issued to every employee must include a note specifying any disciplinary rules applicable to the employee or referring the employee to some other document that specifies such rules. Depending on the nature of the employer's business, some of those rules will be held to be more important than others. Drunkenness by an employee in charge of a high-speed cutting machine or when working in a hospital operating theatre would be infinitely more serious than that by a farm labourer hoeing onions in a distant field. If an employer specifies that breach of a particular rule will lead to summary dismissal, he may need to justify the fairness of the rule itself as well as show that it had been reasonable for him to rely on it (*Ladbroke Racing Ltd v Arnott & Another* [1983] IRLR 154, Ct Sess; and *Leonard v Fergus & Haynes Civil Engineering Ltd* [1979] IRLR 235, Ct Sess).

Introduction of new rules

5.93
As his business grows and expands, so will an employer introduce new rules and working practices. For example, the acquisition of new machinery will lead to the imposition of more stringent health and safety rules. Some rules may affect or clash with the views of members of staff. Provided those rules are appropriate and within the scope of the contract of employment, an employee who leaves in consequence of them, cannot later claim constructive dismissal. An employee, who was a heavy smoker, worked in a hospital theatre. The local Health Board, after extensive consultations with staff and other interested parties, introduced a total smoking ban throughout their premises. The applicant found it impossible to comply with the ban and resigned. It was held there where a rule is introduced for a legitimate purpose, the fact it bears harshly on a particular employee

does not in itself justify an inference that the employer has acted in such a way as to repudiate the employee's contract of employment (*Dryden v Greater Glasgow Health Board* [1992] IRLR 469, EAT).

Procedural defect

5.94

An employer who ignores or fails to follow the grievance or disciplinary procedures set out in his employees' contracts of employment may find that a dismissal in breach of those procedures is castigated as unfair. The way in which procedural breaches can occur is considered in Chapter 3, at paras 3.95 to 3.107 (*Polkey v A E Dayton Services Ltd* [1988] ICR 142, HL). It is of no consequence that, on a balance of probabilities, it would have made no difference to the outcome had the correct procedure been followed or had there been no breach of natural justice. However if there were facts known to the employer at the time, which justified the dismissal, and the breach was technical, the dismissal is likely to be fair.

5.95

There can be a subtle difference between a 'procedural' and 'substantive' default. If a redundancy programme is carried out without any consultation ('procedural') but the basis of the selection is flawed ('substantive'), there would be a substantive unfair dismissal and compensation would be at large (*Stell Stockholders (Birmingham) Ltd v Kirkwood*, 10 August 1993, EAT).

5.96

Minor breaches, provided they are not of fundamental importance when considered 'in the round', will not usually turn a fair dismissal into an unfair one. This applies even where there has been a breach of natural justice. In a marginal case it may be safer to start the disciplinary procedures again. This would be especially so where there has been a flaw that could only be cured on an appeal, but that would be dependent on the employee appealing (see Chapter 3, para 3.107) (*Sartor v P & O European Ferries (Felixstowe) Ltd*, 13 February 1992, CA; *Fuller v Lloyds Bank plc* [1991] IRLR 336, EAT; and *Spink v Express Foods Group Ltd* [1990] IRLR 320, EAT). But where a dismissal is technically unfair, the compensation may be reduced to 'Nil' if the employee would certainly have been dismissed had the proper procedure been followed. If he (or she) might have been dismissed, some compensation should be awarded – the amount being governed by the degree of doubt (*Moore v Sumner Products plc,* 14 June 1988, EAT)

5.97
Where an employer relies on an employee's plea of 'guilty' to a criminal offence to justify a dismissal, he should know the basis upon which the plea was made. Except in rare circumstances, the employee should normally be afforded an opportunity to state his (or her) side of the story. He may have pleaded guilty to avoid publicity or have been badly advised by a lawyer, but still have a cast iron defence to the charge (*McLaren v National Coal Board* [1988] ICR 370, CA). An employee unambiguously admitted that he used a fraudulent parking voucher, and then advanced a variety of explanations for his conduct. It was held that the employer did not need to make an independent investigation to satisfy himself that the employee had forged the document. The dismissal for the forgery was fair (*Rumbelows Ltd v Ellis* 15 June 1988, EAT).

5.98
The words of Sir Robert Megarry, Vice-Chancellor, should be borne in mind: 'When something is obvious' they may say, 'why force everybody to go through the tiresome waste of time involved in framing charges and giving an opportunity to be heard? The result is obvious from the start'. Those who take this view do not, I think, do themselves justice. As everyone who has anything to do with the law knows, the path of law is strewn with examples of "open and shut" cases, which somehow were not; of unanswerable charges which, in the event, were completely answered; of inexplicable conduct which was fully explained; of fixed and unalterable determination that, by discussion, suffered a change. Nor are those with any knowledge of human nature who pause to think for a moment likely to underestimate the feelings of resentment of those who find that a decision against him has been made without their being afforded any opportunity to influence the course of events.' (*John v Rees & Others* [1969] 2 AER 274, CD.)

5.99
This does not always prove to be the case. An employer called in the police when he discovered that a substantial quantity of high grade metal had gone missing from his factory. The police asked him not to disclose their presence while they covertly observed the activities of several employees. After making suitable enquiries, the employer

was satisfied that two of his staff had manipulated samples so as to increase their bonuses. He dismissed them without giving them an opportunity to state their cases. The dismissals were held to be fair in view of the need for secrecy. At the tribunal hearing, the employees were unable to give any satisfactory answer to the allegations made against them (*Pritchett & Dyjasek v J McIntyre Ltd* [1987] ICR 359, CA).

5.100
As a general rule of thumb, an employee who has been dismissed should be given an opportunity to appeal against his (or her) dismissal. But the fact that no such opportunity was given does not, of itself, make a dismissal unfair. In a small business, the decision to dismiss may necessarily be taken by the directors. There may not be anyone more senior with whom to lodge an appeal. Even so, where there is no contractual right of appeal, it may be appropriate or even prudent to hold one (*Sanderson v H K Clarkson & Sons Ltd*, 25 January 1988, EAT; and *Whitbread & Co plc v Mills* [1988] ICR 776, EAT).

Gross misconduct

5.101
The term 'gross misconduct' is imported from the common law. It means conduct of sufficient seriousness to warrant dismissal without notice (see Chapter 3, paras 3.22 to 3.26). The term is often used by employers in their disciplinary rules, which usually include examples of conduct regarded as constituting 'gross misconduct'. In *Hamilton v Argyll & Clyde Health Board*, 18 August 1992, EAT, an employee was dismissed for gross misconduct when she failed to follow instructions given to her by a doctor. However, her employer told her that he would be prepared to re-employ her in another area. She refused the offer and complained to an employment tribunal that her employer's offer to re-engage her in another job was inconsistent with his decision to dismiss her for gross misconduct. It was held that although the employee's insubordination *did* amount to gross misconduct, that did not mean that she was unsuitable for any other job.

Dismissal after final warning

5.102
Ordinarily, an employee has no redress when dismissed for committing the same or a similar offence while subject to a final

written warning for an earlier offence. It would be inappropriate to review the sequence of events that prompted the employers to issue a final warning unless the final warning itself was manifestly inappropriate. If it had been issued for an oblique motive, eg to lay the groundwork for a dismissal on a minor matter, that sequence of events might be considered. It is of no consequence that the employee had chosen not to appeal against the final warning (*Stein v Associated Dairies Ltd* [1982] IRLR 447, EAT; and *Co-Operative Retail Services Ltd v Lucas*, 15 November 1993, EAT).

Mitigation

5.103

Care should be taken not to confuse 'mitigation' with 'fairness' in a dismissal for dishonesty case. Length of good service, the amount of money or value of goods involved, the loss of pension or other rights, and the circumstances of the appropriation are all relevant. But where the theft destroys the trust that must exist between employee and employer, a dismissal will not be unfair. Although another employer might well have responded differently in the light of any mitigating circumstances, the dismissal does not thereby become unfair (*ECC International Ltd v McKenna & Another*, 14 July 1987, EAT).

'Blanket' dismissals

5.104

Sometimes, an employer will suspect that two or more employees in a group are involved in theft or some other dishonest activity. It might be impossible for him to 'pin down' which of the group is responsible or to establish how many employees are involved. If the matter is serious, and provided the employer has carried out reasonable investigations, his decision to dismiss every employee in the group will not be unfair even if one or more innocent employees are included amongst the dismissals. The suspects must be given the opportunity to state their cases. If any of their number advances an explanation consistent with innocence, he (or she) should not be dismissed. Otherwise, the dismissal is likely to be unfair (*Monie v Coral Racing Ltd* [1981] ICR 109, CA; and *Molloy & Mundell v Kemps Contact Lenses Ltd*, 30 July 1986, EAT).

5.105

Where the reason for dismissal relates to capability (eg stock losses caused by negligence or stupidity), the employer should not carry out a 'blanket' dismissal unless:

- satisfied on solid and sensible grounds that the action, if committed by an individual, would warrant dismissal; and

- a full investigation and proper procedures have been carried out, and he believes on reasonable evidence that more than one person could have been responsible; and

- the act was capable of being done by the applicant as well as by those within the identified group.

If those checks have been carried out, the possible innocence of one of the suspect group would not render that employee's dismissal unfair (*Whitbread & Co plc v Thomas & Others* [1988] ICR 135, EAT; and *Parr v Whitbread plc t/a Threshers Wine Merchants* [1990] ICR 427, EAT).

5.106

An employer may have strong and cogent reasons for believing that one member of a suspect group is incapable of negligence or dishonesty. If he retains that employee, but dismisses his colleagues, the dismissal of the latter would not necessarily be unfair. The case of each employee has to be considered separately (*Frames Snooker Centre v Boyce* [1992] IRLR 472, EAT).

Employee facing criminal charges

5.107

Difficulties often arise in cases where the trial of an employee, charged with a criminal offence relating to his (or her) employment, is unlikely to take place for several months. Interviews with witnesses might be construed as interference with the course of natural justice thereby limiting an employer's powers of investigation. It may be possible to suspend an employee pending the outcome of his trial. But the suspension would have to be on full pay, unless the employee's contract specifies otherwise. If, however, the case against the employee is very strong, and the employer has been able to make a reasonable investigation, the dismissal may be fair. The employee must first be given an opportunity to answer the allegations. If the evidence against the employee is very strong and the matter serious, the dismissal is unlikely to be held unfair. However, the employer will need to satisfy an employment tribunal that he had carried out a reasonable investigation of the circumstances before taking the decision to dismiss. A suspension ought nonetheless be considered. There is a large 'grey' area in this field.

5.108
In determining whether a dismissal is fair, an employment tribunal will not be influenced by the fact that the employee had been prosecuted for an offence connected with his (or her) work and had subsequently been acquitted (*Saeed v Greater London Council (ILEA)* [1986] IRLR 23, QBD). It is not the function of an employment tribunal to determine whether the employee was guilty or innocent of the alleged crime, but to consider the behaviour of the employer. In short, had the employer shown that he had acted reasonably in treating the employee's involvement in the alleged offences as a sufficient reason for dismissing him? (per Phillips J, *Harris (Ipswich) Ltd v Harrison* [1978] IRLR 382, EAT.)

Criminal convictions

5.109
If, on the other hand, an employee has pleaded guilty in court to theft from his (or her) employer, that fact, coupled with conduct known to the employer that is consistent with dishonesty, will be sufficient grounds for dismissal. It does not matter if the employee later protests his innocence, alleging that he pleaded guilty to avoid a possible sentence of imprisonment (*British Gas plc v McCarrick* [1991] IRLR 305, CA). If an employee pleaded 'Not Guilty' to the charges laid against him, but was nonetheless convicted, an employer would be entitled to rely on the conviction as legitimate grounds for dismissal – even if the employee later claims that he had been the victim of a miscarriage of justice. But it would be wise for an employer to have supporting evidence to confirm that there was a solid basis upon which the court returned a verdict of 'Guilty'.

5.110
So where money that was in the possession of a prison officer went missing, and no credible explanation was given for its

disappearance, a dismissal was held to be fair. If the offence is trivial or not relevant to the employment, a dismissal may not be reasonable (*Secretary of State for Scotland v Campbell* [1992] IRLR 263, EAT).

Dishonesty

5.111
Allegations of dishonesty will not necessarily involve the police or criminal prosecution. An employee found stealing from the till may often simply be summarily dismissed. Before taking the decision to dismiss, an employer must investigate the circumstances, listen to what the employee has to say and have *reasonable grounds* for believing that the employee is guilty (*British Home Stores Ltd v Burchell* [1980] ICR 303, EAT).

Incompetent representatives

5.112
If an employee entrusts his (or her) case to a representative, who fails to put the case adequately at a disciplinary hearing, or at the subsequent appeal hearing, a tribunal cannot reverse the decision unless the spokesperson was so incompetent that no reasonable employer would have relied on his assertions (*Al-Mehdaw v Secretary of State for the Home Department* [1990] AC 876, HL). Where the representative is a trade union-nominated official, the employer's ability to intervene may be more limited. In procedural matters, any failures by the representative will usually deemed to be those of the employee (see Chapter 2, paras 2.72 to 2.75).

Criminal offences outside employment

5.113
Where an employee is convicted of an offence committed outside his (or her) employment but the offence is relevant to the type of work he is employed to do, an employer should generally consider the possibility of an alternative post before dismissing that employee. A groundsman at a girls' school pleaded guilty to indecently assaulting his daughter and admitted to committing similar offences with two elder daughters. It was held that it was incumbent on the school to see whether there was work where there would be little risk to other

girls (*P v Nottingham County Council* [1992] ICR 706, CA). When a branch manager of a firm of estate agents was charged with gross indecency, he made it known that he intended to plead guilty to the offence in court. He was dismissed. It was held that the tribunal could not intervene. The employer was entitled to consider the effect on his work colleagues and the adverse publicity. There was no alternative work for him to do (*Royal Life Estates (South) Ltd t/a Fox & Sons v Campbell*, 1 October 1993, EAT).

Selection for redundancy

5.114
One of the greatest sources of dispute lies in cases involving selection for redundancy, especially where there is no laid-down selection procedure. If someone has to be made redundant, the employer has the invidious task of deciding who that person should be. How to proceed? The most important thing to do is to reflect, weigh up the options and give everyone, so far as is possible (through their elected representatives, if there are any), an opportunity to air their views. If an employee is dismissed without any form of consultation, a tribunal will very likely find that the dismissal was unfair – even though it is shown that consultation would very likely have made no difference to the outcome. It has to be proved, based on facts known to the employer at the time, that any consultation would have been 'utterly useless' or 'futile' (*Polkey v A E Dayton Services Ltd* [1988] ICR 142, HL).

5.115
An instance of this defence being successful occurred when employers restructured their organisation in secrecy and within strict time limits as a result of pressure from those who provided their sole source of revenue. The job performed by a director was lost and he was selected for redundancy without any consultation. The evidence established that there was no alternative position available for him. It was held that, in the exceptional circumstances, the dismissal was fair (*Leese v Food From Britain*, 4 March 1991, EAT).

5.116
An employer running a small business is not absolved from the duty to consult. But the consultation process may be very informal or indeed perfunctory. The important thing is that the would-be

redundant employee is given an opportunity to put forward his (or her) views (*De Grasse v Stockwell Tools Ltd* [1992] IRLR 269, EAT). Where an employer is contemplating making an employee redundant, he is duty-bound to provide a trade union, which he recognises for bargaining purposes, with written reasons for making the person redundant. But breach of this requirement does not, of itself, make a dismissal unfair.

5.117

The best starting-off point is to ask for voluntary redundancies. But, if this does not produce sufficient candidates, there must be compliance with any agreed formula for redundancy selection. If there is no formula, the employer must decide who is to be made redundant, weighing up the 'pros' and 'cons' in each case. Many employees will find reasons why someone else should have been selected for redundancy in preference to themselves. The criterion applied by the tribunals is whether the person selected is one of a number of candidates for redundancy whom the employer, in his (or her) discretion, might reasonably have selected. Whether the tribunal would have selected someone else is immaterial. When an employer uses vague and subjective selection criteria, such as an employee's attitude to his work, consultation is most important. The fact that, on an earlier occasion, the workforce expressed the view that they would prefer not to be consulted about proposed redundancies, does not absolve the employer from having to consult employees who have not waived their right to put forward their own views (*Graham v ABF Ltd* [1986] IRLR 90, EAT).

5.118

Every employee who is a candidate for redundancy should normally be spoken to individually, and be given an opportunity to suggest ways in which he (or she) might be kept in employment. This 'rule of thumb' applies even though the employer is adhering to a formula agreed with the employee's trade union – unless the numbers involved are so large that it would be impractical to carry out individual consultations (*Walls Meat Co Ltd v Selby* [1989] ICR 601, CA; and *Duncan v Marconi Command & Control Systems Ltd (Case B],* 14 October 1988, EAT).

5.119

Where a redundancy selection is made on the basis of a poor attendance record, an employer does not have to consider whether an employee's absences were due to an industrial injury sustained at work or mere malingering. Often it would not be practical to try to find out the reason. But the criteria for selection must be fair (*Dooley v Leyland Vehicles Ltd*, 17 June 1986, Ct.S).

5.120
Difficulties are likely to arise when questions of sex, marital status, race or disability are taken into consideration. For instance, a married Asian woman is selected for redundancy ahead of a single white widower with three children and a heavy mortgage. If the decision is taken on personal circumstances, or for humanitarian reasons, and not based on competence, experience, reliability and so forth, the dismissal is not only likely to be unfair but will also be in breach of the Sex Discrimination and Race Relations Acts 1975 & 1976, or of the Disability Discrimination Act 1995 (see Chapters 11, 12 & 13).

Suitable alternative employment

5.121
There is always a need to try to relocate an otherwise redundant worker. Failure to do so could result in a finding of unfair dismissal. It must be shown that the point had been considered at the time and there was no suitable alternate work available. The employer should not assume that the employee would not accept work at a more junior level. The employee might be prepared to 'lower his (or her) sights'. This duty usually extends to making enquiries of any 'associated employer' (see Chapter 3, paras 3.108 to 3.110), but a failure to do so may not be fatal (*Thomas & Betts Manufacturing Ltd v Harding* [1980] IRLR 255, CA; *MDH Ltd v Sussex* [1986] IRLR 123, EAT; and *Dick v Boots The Chemist Ltd*, 25 June 1991, EAT).

Breach of duty of fidelity

5.122
There is an implied duty of fidelity in every contract of employment. That is to say, an employee may not act in a way which is contrary to his (or her) employer's legitimate interests (see Chapter 8, paras 8.16 to 8.19). An intention to set up in competition in the future will not in itself amount to a breach, unless the person has abused his position as an employee, eg by making lists of his employer's customers (*Golden Cross Hire Co Ltd v Lovell* [1979] IRLR 267, EAT; and *Laughton & Hawley v Bapp Industrial Supplies Ltd* [1986] ICR 634, EAT). Where

there is a serious breach of the duty of fidelity, a dismissal will usually be fair always provided that there has been a full investigation of the circumstances and proper procedures have been followed. An employee who leaks important confidential information and trade secrets to a third party will be without any redress for his dismissal (*Berts Brewery Co Ltd & Others v Hogan* [1945] 2 AER 570, HC). A managing director colluded with a senior manager in attempting to persuade a colleague to join him in another company with a view to depriving their employers of their best client. He was dismissed. It was held to be fair (*Marshall v Industrial Systems & Control Ltd* [1992] IRLR 294, EAT).

Divided loyalties

5.123

Sometimes a husband and wife are employed in the same business and one leaves to join a competitor. If the one who remains has access to confidential information that would damage the employer's business interests if disclosed to a rival, and provided the risk of disclosure is unacceptably high, it would be not unfair to dismiss (*Dyer v Inverclyde Ltd*, 25 November 1987, EAT). If, on the other hand, a woman is dismissed because she has married a man employed by a rival firm – on the grounds that she might relay confidential information to her husband – her employer's reasons were held to be no defence to a claim of sex discrimination (see Chapter 11). The dismissal was based on the assumption that a man was more likely to be the primary supporter of his wife and children (*Coleman v Skyrail Oceanic Ltd t/a Goodman Tours* [1981] ICR 864, CA).

Internal appeals

5.124

It is not intended that a disciplinary panel within an employing organisation should follow the procedures of ordinary courts of law. All that is required is that the members of the panel should act fairly, and should give the appearance of doing so. This is particularly important when considering the final stages of an appeal process, where there is often the risk of error through a breach of natural justice (see paras 5.135 to 5.139 below). For an appeal to be able to cure procedural defects, the appellate process must 'be able to stand on its merits as conferring upon the employee all the rights that the contract of employment is intended to protect, notably proper notice of the complaint, and a full opportunity of stating the employee's case' (*Byrne v BOC Ltd* [1992] IRLR 505, EAT).

5.125
A distribution manager dismissed an employee following an admission of forgery, for which various explanations were given. But as the distribution manager was present at the appeal hearing conducted by a line manager and remained behind while the line manager deliberated, the dismissal was held to have been unfair. His presence gave the impression of bias and undue influence (*Rumbelows Ltd v Ellis*, 15 June 1988, EAT).

5.126
Often, a procedural defect in the disciplinary process will result in a dismissal being ruled unfair. But, if an employee appeals against the dismissal and there is a proper investigation of the facts and a full hearing at which the employee is allowed to state his (or her) case, that appeal can 'cure' the procedural defect. It can turn what might otherwise have been an unfair dismissal into a fair one. A mere review of the original decision to dismiss would not be sufficient (*Whitbread & Co plc v Mills* [1988] ICR 766, EAT; and *Clark v Civil Aviation Authority* [1991] IRLR 412, EAT).

5.127
An employer's disciplinary procedure contained detailed provisions for an appeal at each stage in the procedure. Breach of one of those stages turned an otherwise fair dismissal into one that was unfair. The employee had been denied his contractual rights. However, compensation was dealt with on the merits of the case (*Stoker v Lancashire County Council* [1992] IRLR 75, CA).

Illness and injury as grounds for dismissal

5.128
Dismissals for sickness are fraught with difficulties. Although employers cannot guarantee the continued good health of their employees, they have a common law and statutory duty to do all that they reasonably can to protect and preserve the health and safety at work of their employees eg by taking steps to ensure that employees do not come into contact with injurious substances.

5.129

The dismissal of a genuinely sick or injured employee is generally characterised as a 'capability' dismissal. Where it is for malingering or similar reasons (such as abuse of an employer's sick pay scheme), it is a 'conduct' dismissal. In rare circumstances, the dismissal can be for 'some other substantial reason', eg where the employee occupies a key position and is persistently absent for a series of unrelated illnesses (*Wharfedale Loudspeakers Ltd v Poynton*, 18 May 1993, EAT).

5.130

The distinction between lack of capability and conduct is narrow and blurred. But it may affect the procedures to be used. In the latter case, the ordinary disciplinary procedure should be followed. This also applies where the dismissal is based on a mixture of both grounds. But before dismissing an employee with a poor attendance record occasioned by genuine ill health, the employer should:

- consult the employee about his (or her) concerns, and the effect such absences are having on the employee's work and – although not essential – should forewarn him of the likely consequences if those absences continue (*A Links & Co Ltd v Rose* [1991] IRLR 353, CS);

- review the employee's situation, obtaining independent medical advice where necessary; and

- discuss the position with the employee, especially concerning any medical opinion obtained, to see whether there is any chance of improvement. (*Scott v Secretary of State for Scotland*, 14 July 1988, EAT.)

If the employer's need for the work to be done outweighs the employee's need to have still more time off work to recover, the dismissal will generally be held to be fair.

5.131

In exceptional circumstances there may be no need to consult. An employer, who urgently needed to replace a long-term sick employee, learned from the woman's doctor that her condition was more serious than she appeared to realise. If the employee visited her and told her the truth about her condition, it might cause great harm. Her dismissal was held to have been fair (*Eclipse Blinds Ltd v Wright* [1992] IRLR 133, Ct S).

5.132

An employer suspended an employee who had returned to work late, after the midday break, heavily intoxicated. The employer learnt that the employee had an underlying medical problem and made some perfunctory enquiries of the employee's doctor. He dismissed him for gross misconduct. The dismissal was held to have been unfair. It was unreasonable of the employer to have reached a conclusion without obtaining proper medical reports (*Forth Ports Authority v Lorimer*, 8 March 1991, EAT).

5.133

If an employee is frequently absent from work for a series of minor and unrelated illnesses – some supported by medical certificates – his (or her) employer does not generally need an independent medical opinion before taking the decision to dismiss. But he must warn the employee of the likely consequences should those absences persist (*International Sports Co Ltd v Thomson* [1980] IRLR 340, EAT). Under normal circumstances, an employer should not dismiss a sick employee without first seeking up-to-date medical advice. The employee should also be given an opportunity to discuss his situation with his employer. If, despite everything, there is little prospect of an improvement in the employee's health, the employer should consider his obligations under the Disability Discrimination Act 1995 (Is the employee covered?) before taking the decision to dismiss. The employer should also consider the possibility (or practicability) of transferring the employee to less onerous duties within the organisation.

5.134

Employers should remember that they may not approach an employee's doctor without first obtaining the employee's written consent. The employee must also be informed of his (or her) legal rights under the Access to Medical Reports Act 1988. The employee's consent is not required if he is to be examined by a company doctor or other specialist nominated by his employer.

Natural justice

5.135

In nearly every case, there are two sides to a story. Except in the most hopeless of cases, the employee should be allowed to state his (or her) case before any decision is taken to dismiss (*Clarke v Trimoco*

Group Ltd & Another [1993] ICR 237, EAT). Further, an employer must carry out a reasonable investigation to try to find out the truth before he reaches his final decision. If he was misled over the position because the employee failed to inform him of an important fact, that would not be fatal. The 'reasonableness' test will continue to apply from the moment the employee is notified of his dismissal until the time he actually leaves (*Morton v City of Glasgow District Council*, 20 March 1989, EAT; and *Stacey v Babcock Power Ltd* [1986] ICR 221, EAT).

5.136

If an employee has been summarily dismissed (that is to say, 'on the spot'), the decision to dismiss will be adjudged on the facts known to the employer at that time, unless further information is presented on appeal (*Monie v Coral Racing Ltd* [1981] ICR 109, CA).

5.137

If a decision to dismiss was patently correct on the information available when the employee was dismissed, but fresh evidence produced on appeal suggested that the decision to dismiss was wrong, the employer would be liable because 'the right of appeal... is a necessary element in the overall process of terminating the employment' (per Lord Bridge in *West Midlands Co-operative Society v Tipton* [1986] ICR 192, HL).

5.138

The same principle applies where an employee has been denied his (or her) contractual right to appeal or if the agreed procedure for hearing appeals has not been adhered to (*National Coal Board v Nash*, *The Times*, 7 May 1986, EAT). The fact that the worker is appealing against one or more previous warnings, on which the employer partly relies in deciding to dismiss for a subsequent offence, does not make a dismissal unfair. What is relevant is that the employee had been warned and was under that warning when he committed the subsequent offence. The fact that his appeal had not yet been heard would also have to be taken into consideration. If the appeal was due to be heard shortly after the disciplinary hearing, the latter should be delayed (*Tower Hamlets Health Authority v Anthony* [1989] IRLR 394, CA). In the case of a dismissal for redundancy, there is an exception to the rule that there should normally be a right of appeal. The absence of an appeals procedure in such a situation does not make the dismissal unfair (*Robinson & Others v Ulster Carpet Mills Ltd* [1991]

IRLR 348, CA, Northern Ireland). If an employer decides to switch to outside contractors for economic or cost reasons, he does not have to justify those grounds or even show that they were beneficial (*Hodgkins v CJB Developments Ltd*, 30 July 1984, EAT).

5.139
A person was dismissed for a valid reason but the dismissal was held to be unfair because of a breach of procedure. The compensation was reduced to 'Nil' for contributory fault. It was the employee who had caused the dismissal. An employer's irregularities, although unfortunate, did not bring about the dismissal (*Smith v Lodge Bros (Funerals) Ltd*, 19 October 1989, EAT).

Parity of treatment and penalties

5.140
There is an implied term in every contract of employment that an employer will *not* treat his employees arbitrarily, capriciously or inequitably. Failing to give an employee an annual pay rise to which she had become accustomed and which was given to other staff, did not amount to a fundamental breach of contract. It mattered not that the employer had behaved heartlessly: he had dealt with her case on its merits (*Murco Petroleum Ltd v Forge* [1987] ICR 282, EAT).

5.141
In deciding the appropriate remedy for misconduct, the punishment awarded to other employees for similar offences in the same circumstances is a relevant factor. It is always necessary to consider each case separately. If there are important distinguishing features, then failure to take them into account could be fatal (*Post Office v Fennel* [1981] IRLR 221, CA; and *Cowton v British Railways Board*, 28 November 1989, EAT). A disparity in treatment may be justified on the grounds that one person was young and led astray by a more senior employee, or one person had received several warnings whereas another had not. Where there had been a considerable increase in some particular type of trouble and employees had been warned to expect more severe punishment, then only those cases that occurred after that caution should be compared (*Whitbread & Co plc v Allen & Bishop*, 17 January 1989, EAT; and *Procter v British Gypsum Ltd* [1991] IRLR 7, EAT).

5.142

But, after making reasonable enquiries, an employer is entitled to come to a decision based on facts known to him at the time. This includes any findings and conclusions made by an appeal panel. If the dismissal was within the band of reasonable responses, it would not be unfair (*Securicor Ltd v Smith* [1989] IRLR 356, CA; and *Heald & Others v National Coal Board*, 27 January 1988, CA).

The duty of the tribunal

5.143

A tribunal does not apply a critical, or take a meticulous, approach to decisions taken by employers (*Iredale v Huddersfield Health Authority*, 20 April 1993, EAT). Nor does it apply its own views on what course it would have taken. It generally hears the evidence that was previously before the employer and asks itself: 'Have the employers made adequate enquiries into the incident and was there credible evidence on which they might reasonably have come to view that they took? Was it within the band of reasonable responses for the employee to have been dismissed?' (*Scottish Midland Co-operative Society Ltd v Cullion* [1991] IRLR 261, Ct.S). The validity of the 'band of reasonable responses' test, enunciated by the Court of Appeal in *British Leyland UK Ltd v Smith* [1981] IRLR 91, and since reinstated by the Court of Appeal in *HSBC Bank plc v Madden* (see paragraph 5.77 above) was called into question by the EAT in *Haddon v Van den Burgh Foods Limited* [1999] IRLR 672 (see next paragraph), giving renewed credence to the decision of the Court of Appeal in *Gilham & Others v Kent County Council (No. 2)* [1985] IRLR 18. There, the Court emphasised that the question as to whether a dismissal was fair was a pure question of fact for the industrial tribunal. 'The wording of section 98(4)', said Griffiths LJ, 'is straightforward and easy to understand, and I do not myself think that it helps to try and analyse it further, save only this, that a tribunal in applying the section must not ask themselves what they would have done, but must ask themselves how a reasonable employer would have acted'.

5.144

In *Haddon (qv)* the retiring President of the EAT, Mr Justice Morison, characterised the mantra: 'the tribunal must not substitute their own decision for that of the employer' as simply another way of saying that the tribunal must apply the reasonableness test by going somewhat further than simply asking what they themselves would have done. 'It is likely, however, that what the tribunal would themselves have done will often coincide with their judgment as to what a reasonable employer would have done'. And again, 'providing [the tribunal] apply the test of reasonableness, it is their duty both to determine their own judgment and to substitute it where appropriate'. That is a point of view, said the EAT in *Midland Bank plc v Madden* [2000] IRLR 288. But it is not for the EAT to outlaw the 'band of reasonable responses' test, thereby presuming to invalidate a decision of the Court of Appeal. While the members of an employment tribunal cannot help but apply their own judgements, it is not open to them to substitute their own views for those of the reasonable employer.

5.145

A tribunal must not substitute its own views on the credibility of witnesses for those of the employer. At a disciplinary hearing, the employer preferred the story given by one employee in preference to that advanced by another. The tribunal, having heard the witnesses, took the opposite view. The Court of Appeal held that the tribunal's views were irrelevant unless no reasonable employer could have taken the same view as the employer (*Linfood Cash & Carry Ltd v Thomson* [1989] ICR 518, EAT; and *Morgan v Electrolux Ltd* [1991] ICR 369, CA).

5.146

Although a tribunal will make a finding as to the *actual* reason for a dismissal, it is important that it should identify the precise basis upon which the decision was made, eg drunkenness in a hospital operating theatre. The 'reasonableness' test has to be applied to that ground (if within one of the seven 'permitted' reasons for dismissal) (see para 5.13 above) (*British Railway Board v Jackson* [1984] IRLR 235, CA). A tribunal does not apply the criteria of what they would have done in all the circumstances (*Moon & Others v Homeworthy Furniture (Northern) Ltd* [1977] ICR 117, EAT). A tribunal cannot tell an employer how to run his business and it is not its function to take into account policy decisions even if they had brought about a redundancy situation. Lord McDonald put it in this way: 'It may be, as the tribunal suggests, that the [employer] entered into the contract unreasonably, if not recklessly. Many employees have to be dismissed as a result of incompetent business management, but that does not make the dismissals unfair' (*Meikle v McPhail (Charleston Arms)* [1983] IRLR 351, EAT).

CONTRIBUTORY FAULT

5.147

The Acts provide that each of the basic and compensatory awards of compensation for unfair dismissal (see later) may be reduced by such amount as is 'just and equitable' if, in the opinion of the tribunal, the employee contributed to or was wholly or partly to blame for his (or her) dismissal.

The basic award of compensation may also be cut if the evidence shows that the employee had unreasonably refused an offer by his employer which (if accepted) would have had the effect of reinstating him in his employment in all respects as if he had not been dismissed (*Courtaulds Northern Spinning Ltd v Moosa* [1984] ICR 218, EAT; *Nelson v British Broadcasting Corporation (No. 2)* [1980] ICR 110, CA; and *TNT Express (UK) Ltd v Rigby & Others* [1994] ICR 1, EAT).

5.148

In assessing the amount of the reduction when a employee was dismissed while on strike, it is necessary to consider (a) the reason for the dismissal, (b) whether any conduct of the employee was blameworthy and (c) whether that conduct contributed to his (or her) dismissal. The merits of the strike or other industrial action on the part of a trade union considered in isolation have no bearing on the tribunal's decision (*Crossville Wales Ltd v Tracey & Another*, 14 March 1994, EAT). If a striking worker had incited others to take unconstitutional action, that might be one reason for reducing the award (*Gosling v Ford Motor Co Ltd*, 29 June 1992, EAT).

5.149

If a worker is habitually late for work, and his (or her) manager 'sees red' one day and sacks him without warning, the dismissal would probably be unfair. The employee might be two-thirds to blame for his dismissal; in which event, he would recover only one-third of the total compensation awarded. In some circumstances, a tribunal will find that an employee was 100 percent to blame for his dismissal, and the employee will recover nothing (*Sulemanji v Toughened Glass Ltd* [1979] ICR 499, EAT).

5.150

An employee's failure to make use of his (or her) employer's grievance or disciplinary procedures (including his right of appeal) does not amount to contributory fault; but it could be characterised as a breach of his duty to mitigate his loss, which would have the same effect (*W Muir Ltd v Lamb* [1985] IRLR 95, EAT). In appropriate circumstances, the performance of an employee caused by a lack of competence or his mental approach can be taken into account in determining contributory fault. A reduction in compensation would be warranted, for instance, if an employee is lazy or makes no attempt to improve (*Finnie v Top Hat Frozen Food* [1985] ICR 433, EAT).

Note: Under section 127A of the 1996 Act, an employment tribunal is empowered to reduce the amount of the compensatory award for unfair dismissal (see para 5.173 below) by the equivalent of up to two weeks' pay – if the evidence shows that the employee had failed to exercise his (or her) contractual right to appeal against his dismissal. If, on the other hand, it is clear that the employer had denied the employee his right of appeal, the amount of the compensatory award would be *increased* by up to two weeks' pay.

5.151
If a person is dismissed for one reason that turns out to be misconceived, but there were valid other grounds for doing so, the dismissal would be unfair. The compensation could be reduced to 'Nil' where this would be just, based on contributory fault relating to those other grounds. Where the employer took the view that it would not be right to dismiss for those other grounds, there could be no reduction in the compensation (*Trico Folberth Ltd v Devonshire* [1989] IRLR 396, CA).

Constructive dismissal cases

5.152
Even in constructive dismissal cases, an employment tribunal may reduce an award where no reason for the dismissal has been advanced. There does not have to be a direct causal link between the dismissal and contributory fault – only whether the action or record of the employee to any extent contributed to the dismissal. Further, there do not have to be exceptional circumstances (*Morrison v Amalgamated Transport & General Workers Union* [1989] IRLR 361, CA; *Holroyd v Gravure Cylinder Ltd* [1984] IRLR 259, EAT; and *Polentarutti v Autocraft Ltd* [1991] ICR 757, EAT).

5.153
In deciding on the degree of fault, the tribunals employ a 'broad brush' approach to the whole employment record, avoiding legalism

as much as possible. They consider whether there was any blameworthy, including 'bloody-minded', conduct by the employee that was causative of his (or her) dismissal (*Brown v Rolls Royce (1971) Ltd* [1977] ITR 382, EAT; *Warrilow v Robert Walker Ltd* [1984] IRLR 304, EAT; and *Cullen v Austin Rover Group Ltd*, 24 April 1986, EAT).

'Just and equitable'

5.154
Compensation may also be reduced under the 'just and equitable' provisions where, for example, the employer relies on conduct that was not known to him at the time of dismissal. This could occur where he dismisses an employee (unfairly) for incompetence, but discovers during the notice period that the employee had also been stealing from him (*Tele-Trading Ltd v Jenkins* [1990] IRLR 430, CA; and *Polkey v A E Dayton Services Ltd* [1988] ICR 142, HL).

5.155
If an employer has not followed his own procedural rules, including a failure to give an employee an opportunity to explain his (or her) conduct, and is accordingly adjudged to have dismissed the employee unfairly, the compensation may similarly be reduced in appropriate cases under the 'just and equitable' provisions. This would apply where all the information on misconduct was known to the employer at the time. The compensation can be reduced to 'Nil' or to a nominal amount (*Chaplin v H J Rawlinson Ltd* [1991] ICR 553, EAT). Compensation might also be reduced when a tribunal, in a 'breach of procedure' case, decides the degree of likelihood that the employee might still have been dismissed even if the proper procedure had been followed (*Rao v Civil Aviation Authority* [1994] IRLR 240, CA). However, in *King v Eaton (No. 2)* [1998] IRLR 686, the Court of Session allowed that an employment tribunal could refuse to allow an employer to advance additional evidence, that an employee would have been dismissed even if fair procedures had been followed, if admitting such evidence would be unrealistic or impracticable, or would place the tribunal in the invidious position of having to speculate on what might or might not have happened.

DISMISSAL OF REPLACEMENT EMPLOYEES

5.156

Section 106 of the Employment Rights Act 1996 allows that employees who have been specifically recruited to replace permanent employees who are absent from work on maternity leave (or for any other reason connected with pregnancy or childbirth) may be dismissed with (relative) impunity once the latter have returned to work and taken up their normal duties. Their dismissals will be treated in law as having been 'for a substantial reason of a kind such as to justify the dismissal of an employee holding the position which the employee held'. Provided the employer has acted 'reasonably' in such cases, the dismissals will be characterised as 'fair'.

5.157

That same rule applies to people hired on a purely temporary basis to provide cover for employees who have been suspended from work, either on medical or maternity grounds, in accordance with ss 64 and 66 of the 1996 Act. However, every such temporary employee must be given to understand, in writing, before accepting an offer of employment on such terms, that his (or her) employment *will* be terminated when the person he is replacing returns to work (*ibid* s. 106(2) & (3)).

REMEDIES FOR UNFAIR DISMISSAL

5.158

There are two options open to a dismissed employee:

(a) to seek reinstatement or re-engagement; or

(b) to claim compensation for unfair dismissal.

(*Source*: ERA 1996, s. 113.)

5.159

An employment tribunal's power to order the reinstatement or re-engagement of a dismissed employee is entirely discretionary. Indeed, it is rarely used – if only because the relationship between an employee and his (or her) former employer may well have become soured, given the circumstances that prompted the dismissal in the first place. Nonetheless, it is a tribunal's first duty to look to the practicability of making an order for reinstatement or re-engagement; and, in doing so, to consider the views of both parties (*Source*: ERA 1996, s. 116).

5.160
An order for reinstatement means that the dismissed employee should be returned to his (or her) old job on the same terms as before and with the same seniority etc, whereas re-engagement means being taken back on slightly different terms. An order for re-engagement must specify the identity of the employer, the remuneration, arrears of pay and benefits, rights and privileges (including seniority and pension rights) and the date for compliance. The employer must be allowed a reasonable time to rearrange his affairs (*Stena Houlder Ltd v Keenan*, 13 December 1993, EAT).

5.161
If an employer has established and genuinely believes that the relationship of trust and confidence has been irretrievably lost, that of itself would be enough to give a tribunal pause for thought. What a tribunal cannot do is substitute its own commercial judgment for that of the employer. Nor (generally) can a tribunal make an order that would have the effect of disrupting the employer's workforce, or that would result in another employee being made redundant in order to avoid overstaffing (*Mabirizi v National Hospital for Nervous Diseases* [1990] IRLR 133, EAT; *Port of London Authority v Payne & Others* [1993] ICR 447, CA; and *Cold Drawn Tubes Ltd v Middleton* [1992] ICR 318, EAT).

5.162
There must be strict compliance with the basic terms of an order for reinstatement. Where an employer, who purported to do so, but in fact gave two employees less favourable terms, it was held that that constituted a failure to reinstate in accordance with the law. It resulted in his having to pay the employees compensation that amounted in all to £38,147 (*Artisan Press v Srawley & Parker* [1986] ICR 328, EAT).

5.163
When minded to make an order for reinstatement or re-engagement, a tribunal must not be swayed or influenced by the employer's plea

that he had already recruited someone to take the place of the dismissed employee – unless he can demonstrate either

- that it was not reasonably practicable for the employee's work to have been done by anyone other than a permanent replacement; or

- that a reasonable time had elapsed before the employee indicated his wish to have his (or her) job back, and that he had no option but to take on a permanent replacement.

(*Source*: ERA 1996, s. 116(6).)

An employer who recruited a permanent replacement before a tribunal order for reinstatement was made, can escape liability by proving that he had made genuine efforts to find alternative employment but none was available. There is no duty to dismiss another employee to create a vacancy (*Freeman plc v Flynn* [1984] ICR 874, EAT).

5.164
An order directing an employer to reinstate or re-engage an unfairly dismissed employee will specify any benefit, including loss of earnings, that must be reimbursed to the employee when the employee returns to work. As there is no upper limit on the amount to be reimbursed in such circumstances, it is advantageous for a highly-paid employee to seek such an order, especially so if there has been a long delay between dismissal and the tribunal hearing and he (or she) has been unable to find employment elsewhere (*Source*: ERA 1996, ss 117(2) and 124(3)). In making an award concerning back-pay following an order of re-engagement, the tribunal may take into account any contributory fault, but not a failure to mitigate (*City & Hackney HA v Crisp* [1990] ICR 95, EAT).

5.165
An employer cannot be compelled to comply with an order for reinstatement or re-engagement. But if he (or she) refuses to comply, or fails to comply fully with the terms of any such order, the tribunal will order him to pay an *additional* award of compensation over and above any basic or compensatory award of compensation for unfair dismissal.

WHO PAYS THE COMPENSATION?

5.166

As a rule, it is up to the employer to pay the full amount of any award of compensation for unfair dismissal. But, if the proceedings were brought not only against the employer but also against a trade union or other person which/who used the threat of industrial action to pressurise the employer into dismissing the employee, the union or person concerned may (at the request of either the employer or the employee) be joined or sisted as a party to the proceedings. Indeed, that other party might well be ordered to pay the whole or part of any such award of compensation. It should be borne in mind that an order for compensation can only be made against a party who appears or is represented before a tribunal. An employer may claim that he dismissed an employee (the complainant) because of pressure brought to bear by a trade union or some other person, but unless the union or other person had been joined or sisted as a party to the proceedings, the employer will have 'to carry the can' himself (*Source*: TULRA 1992, s. 160).

HOW COMPENSATION IS CALCULATED

5.167

There are three heads of compensation for unfair dismissal. These are:

- the basic award;
- the compensatory award;
- the additional award.

Basic award

5.168

The basic award is calculated in very must the same way as the statutory redundancy payment (as to which, see Chapter 4, paras 4.33 to 4.37) – except that service before the age of 18 is *not* excluded from calculations. The award is subject to the same pro-rata reduction as occurs in redundancy payments if the employee was over the age of 64 at the effective date of termination of his (or her) contract of employment. Contributory fault is taken into account except (a) in redundancy cases, and (b) where the employee had unreasonably refused an offer of full reinstatement, which latter is deemed to be a failure to mitigate (as to which, see Chapter 2, paras 2.61 to 2.68) (*Source*: ERA 1996, ss 119 & 122).

From 1 February 2001 the maximum basic award of compensation for unfair dismissal is £7,200.

Minimum basic award in certain circumstances

5.169
But the basic award of compensation will be a minimum £3,300 if the employee in question was dismissed (or selected for redundancy) for an inadmissible reason, that is to say:

- for carrying out (or proposing to carry out) his (or her) duties as a *trade-union-appointed safety representative*, or as an elected *representative of employee safety*, or as a member of a safety committee, or as a person designated by the employer to carry out health and safety-related activities; or

- for performing (or proposing to perform) any functions or activities as a *workforce representative* for the purposes of Schedule 1 to the Working Time Regulations 1998 (SI 1998/1833), or as a candidate for election as such a representative; or

- for performing (or proposing to perform) his functions as a *trustee of a relevant occupational pension scheme*; or

- for performing (or proposing to perform) any functions or activities connected with his role as (or as a candidate for election as) an *employee representative*, that is to say, as a person elected to represent the interests of fellow employees in a situation involving collective redundancies or a transfer under the Transfer of Undertakings (Protection of Employment) Regulations 1981.

But that minimum award of £3,300 (2001/02) may also be reduced if the employee contributed to an extent to his own dismissal. But not so if the employee was unlawfully selected for redundancy on grounds related to his trade union membership or activities. In such a case, the reduction can only be made to the difference (if any) between the normal basic award and that £3,300 (*Source*: TULRA 1992, s. 156; ERA 1996, s. 120).

Basic award of two weeks' pay in certain cases

5.170

A redundant employee held to have been unfairly dismissed for having unreasonably refused an offer of suitable alternative employment (and who does not otherwise qualify for a redundancy payment) will nonetheless receive a basic award of compensation equivalent to two weeks' pay (ERA 1996, ss 121, 138 & 141).

Compensatory award

5.171

The compensatory award for unfair dismissal is such amount as an employment tribunal considers to be 'just and equitable' having regard to the loss sustained by the complainant', subject to a 2001/02 upper limit of £51,700. However, that upper limit may be exceeded to the extent necessary to enable the award fully to reflect the losses (including arrears of pay) sustained by the employee for the period between the date on which his (or her) employment ended and the date on which he was reinstated or re-engaged. If an employee has not been reinstated or re-engaged in compliance with a tribunal order to that effect, the upper limit on the amount of the compensatory award may likewise be exceeded to the extent necessary to enable the aggregate of the compensatory and additional awards fully to reflect those same losses (*Source*: ERA 1996, ss 117(1) & (2) and 124(3)).

Note: There is no upper limit on the amount of compensation (or the amount of the compensatory award) that may be awarded by an employment tribunal when an employee is found to have been unfairly dismissed or unfairly selected for redundancy for having taken action in a health and safety case (either as a designated 'competent person', safety representative, representative of employee safety, member of a safety committee, or as an employee) or if dismissed or unfairly selected for redundancy for having made a 'protected disclosure' (as defined by section 43A of the Employment Rights Act 1996).

5.172

The compensatory award includes:

- the estimated loss of wages (net of tax and other deductions) up to the time the employee secured employment elsewhere; or, if the employee's new job pays less than he (or she) was earning in his previous job, up to the date of the tribunal hearing. As a rule, the employee will not be given credit for income received during the notice period, but any money paid in lieu of notice will be taken into account (*Fentiman v Fluid Engineering Products Ltd* [1991] ICR 570, EAT) (*Source*: ERA 1996, ss 134 & 124).

- the estimated future loss of earnings, based on the employee's age, personal circumstances, qualifications and skills, state of health, likelihood of obtaining work elsewhere within a 'reasonable' time; and so on. But the award will not be assessed by reference either to the degree of unfairness of the dismissal itself or to the mental distress occasioned by the dismissal (*Fougere v Phoenix Motor Co Ltd* [1976] IRLR 259, EAT; *Ging v Ellward Lancs Ltd* [1991] ICR 222, EAT; and *Morris v Accro Co Ltd* [1985] ICR 306, EAT; *Addis v Gramophone Co* [1909] AC 488, HL; and *Re BCCI SA* [1994] IRLR 282, Ch D);

- the loss of any benefits, including pension rights, and expenses. Pensions can form a big item, raising the total award to well above the maximum. It is extremely complicated, and where necessary, actuarial advice should be sought;

- the loss of statutory rights (of usually about £100 – £200) (*S H Muffett Ltd v Head* [1987] ICR 1, EAT); and

- any expenses reasonably incurred in consequence of the dismissal, eg costs incurred in seeking a new job, but not legal expenses.

All of the above are subject to a pro-rata reduction for contributory fault together with a reduction for any failure on the part of the employee to mitigate his or her loss. This would include a person removing himself from the labour market by taking a training course for 12 months (see Chapter 2, paras 2.61 to 2.68), although if for a short period with little prospect of getting a job during that period, it may not apply (*Holroyd v Gravure Cylinder Ltd* [1984] IRLR 259, EAT).

5.173
The amount of the compensatory award may be reduced or increased by the equivalent of up to two weeks' pay if the employee declined his (or her) employer's invitation to appeal against his dismissal (in accordance with his employer's internal appeal procedures) or if his employer refused to allow such an appeal (*ibid* section 127A).

5.174

If, following an employee's dismissal, the firm for which he (or she) worked closed down, the compensatory award cannot run beyond the date of closure. It is of no consequence that it would have been economically viable for the business to have continued (*James W Cook & Co (Wivenhoe) Ltd v Tipper & Others* [1990] ICR 716, CA).

5.175

If an employee was initially dismissed on the basis of incorrect information, but his (or her) employer subsequently uncovered misconduct on which the employee could validly have been dismissed, then although the dismissal itself might have been technically unfair, the compensation can be reduced to 'Nil' on the basis of that new information – on the basis of the 'just and equitable' provision (*W Devis Sons Ltd v Atkins* [1977] ICR 662, HL).

In arriving at the net amount, account will (generally) be taken of money paid in lieu of notice and/or of any *ex gratia* payments (see Chapter 2, paras 2.58 to 2.60) and of any earnings after the expiry of the notice period (see Chapter 3, paras 3.9 & 3.10) (*TBA Industrial Products Ltd v Locke* [1984] ICR 228, EAT).

Additional award

5.176

If an employer refuses or fails to comply *fully* with an order for reinstatement or re-engagement, the tribunal in question will order him to pay such amount of compensation as it thinks fit, having regard to the loss sustained by the employee in consequence of his (or her) employer's failure to comply fully with the terms of the order.

5.177

But if the employee is not reinstated or re-engaged in compliance with the order, the tribunal will not only order the payment of basic and compensatory awards for unfair dismissal (as described above), but will also order the employer to pay an *additional award* of not less than 26 nor more than 52 weeks' pay – unless the employer satisfies the tribunal that it was not practicable to comply with that order. However, it is no defence for an employer to argue that he had already engaged a permanent replacement for the dismissed employee, unless he can demonstrate that it was not practicable for him to arrange for the dismissed employee's work to be done without engaging a permanent replacement (*Source*: ERA 1996, s. 117).

Note: For these purposes, the current (2001/02) upper limit on the amount of a week's pay is £240.

5.178

In deciding the amount of the additional award, the tribunal has to consider (i) the employer's conduct and (ii) the employee's loss. A deliberate refusal to take an employee back without any justification would warrant a figure at the top of the range. If, on the other hand, there is evidence that the employee would have been away sick for much of the period or was not prepared to consider any offer of alternative employment, it would be appropriate for a tribunal to adopt an amount at the lower end of the scale (*Morganite Electrical Carbon Ltd v Donne* [1987] IRLR 363, EAT).

RECOUPMENT OF SOCIAL SECURITY BENEFITS

5.179

An employer ordered by an employment tribunal to pay an award of compensation for unfair dismissal will be served with a *recoupment notice* by the Department of Social Security if the employee in question had received a jobseeker's allowance or income support pending the hearing of his (or her) complaint. The recoupment notice (which must be served within 21 days of the tribunal's decision) effectively requires the employer to deduct from the award an amount equal to the amount of any jobseeker's allowance or income support received by the employee between the date of his dismissal and the date on which the tribunal hearing took place (*Source*: Employment Protection (Recoupment of Jobseeker's Allowance & Income Support) Regulations 1996 (SI 1996/2349)).

5.180

In short, an award of compensation for unfair dismissal (or rather the prescribed element of that award) must not be paid to the employee in question until the employer has received a recoupment notice from the DSS. The 'prescribed element' is that portion of the award that relates to loss of income between the date on which the employee was dismissed and the date on which the tribunal reached its decision. When making an award of compensation, a tribunal will (where appropriate) remind the employer of his obligations under the 1996 Regulations.

If the parties to a dispute agree upon the figure for compensation, the recoupment regulations do not apply – which works to the advantage of the employee. The regulations do not apply to Social Security invalidity benefits, as these are classed as insurance benefits (*Hilton International Hotels (UK) Ltd v Faraji* [1994] ICR 259, EAT).

TIME LIMITS FOR 'PRESENTING' A COMPLAINT

5.181
A complaint of unfair dismissal must be 'presented' to the Secretary to the Tribunals (in practice, to the nearest Regional Office) within three months of the 'effective date of termination' of the employee's contract of employment (see Chapter 3, paras 3.15 to 3.21), or within six months if the employee was dismissed in the circumstances described in paras 5.9 to 5.11 above. An employment tribunal will not consider a complaint presented 'out of time' unless satisfied that it was not reasonably practicable for the complaint to have been presented sooner (*Source*: TULRA 1992, s. 239; ERA 1996, ss 111).

CASE LAW

Examples of successful unfair dismissal complaints

5.182
Employers had been 'keeping a quiet eye' on a meat-handler who they suspected of dishonesty, resolving to dismiss him unless he could offer a satisfactory explanation for his conduct. When asked whether he had anything to say regarding the allegations that he was handling meat in an improper manner, he replied he had done nothing wrong. He was dismissed.

Held: Failure to afford the employee a reasonable chance to clear his name was unfair and resulted in an unfair dismissal (*W Weddel & Co. Ltd v Tepper* [1980] ICR 286, CA).

5.183
Two employees were summarily dismissed on the grounds of breach of their implied duty of trust and fidelity when the employers learnt that they intended to leave and set up a rival company.

Held: As there was no evidence of a misuse of trade secrets or other confidential information, there had been no breach of duty and the dismissals were unfair (*Laughton & Hawley v BAPP Industrial Supplies Ltd* [1986] ICR 634, EAT).

5.184
An employee's contract was terminated on grounds of ill-health. The employers relied on a statement from their medical officer saying he was unfit to carry out his duties and should be retired. No full medical report was obtained.

Held: Although a full medical report was not essential, it was incumbent on the employer to obtain *adequate* information. He must then discuss that information with the employee so that he can have an opportunity to deal with any counter-proposals or comments put to him by the employee. The dismissal was unfair (*East Lindsay District Council v Daubney* [1977] ITR 359, EAT).

5.185
An electrician's work was satisfactory for four years, and then deteriorated. The employers found that this was affecting their business. While the man was on holiday, they dismissed him – without giving him the opportunity to explain his poor performance.

Held: Unless completely incapable, an employee should be warned that he is (or she) likely to be dismissed if he does not measure up to the job. Failure to do so in this case resulted in the dismissal being unfair (*Sutton & Gates (Luton) Ltd v Boxall* [1979] ICR 67, EAT).

Examples of unsuccessful unfair dismissal complaints

5.186
A Tunisian national was dismissed when his employer had been wrongly informed by the Department of Employment that the man needed a work permit, which he did not have. The error did not afford the employer a defence on the grounds of statutory prohibition, because none existed.

Held: The employer could rely upon 'some other substantial reason' and the dismissal was fair and equitable in the circumstances (*Bouchaala v Trusthouse Forte Hotels* [1980] ICR 721, EAT).

5.187
An employee certified himself sick in order to take a holiday in Majorca, but was seen there by an assistant engineer. Disciplinary procedures leading to a dismissal were put in hand. The employers, in breach of an agreement, unwittingly neglected to notify the employee's union representative about their intentions.

Held: The employer's breach of procedure was only one of a number of factors to be taken into account. The dismissal was fair (*Bailey v BP Oil (Kent Refinery) Ltd* [1980] ICR 642, CA).

5.188
A supervisor's outspoken views on morality and sexual matters distressed some of her younger subordinates. This created tension in the workplace. As a supervisor, she should have known better and was dismissed without benefit of the six weeks' notice to which she was entitled under her contract.

Held: Her dismissal for 'some other substantial reason' was fair. It was irrelevant that her employers had dismissed her without proper notice. That had nothing to do with the reason for the dismissal. She could recover damages for breach of contract in the county court (*Treganowan v Robert Knee & Co Ltd* [1975] ITR 121, QB).

Note: The employment tribunals may now hear certain breach of contract claims arising out of or outstanding on the termination of an employee's contract of employment.

5.189
A pilot damaged an aircraft very badly when landing. Fortunately, none of the passengers was injured. A Board of Inquiry set up by his employers concluded that the accident was due to pilot error and lack of judgement. The Board lacked independence but it was a fact-finding body carried out within the principles of natural justice. The pilot was dismissed on the basis of the Board's report.

Held: the dismissal was fair as the potential consequences of even the smallest departure from accepted standards of skill could be disastrous (*Alidair Ltd v Taylor* [1978] ICR 445, CA).

5.190

Employers requested employees to work overtime to complete an urgent order. Despite a threat of dismissal, three employees refused to cooperate in order to pressurise the employers into conceding a pay rise. Although their contracts did not provide for compulsory overtime, they were dismissed.

Held: At the time of their dismissals, the employees were taking part in unofficial 'industrial action'. Whether or not their employers' insistence on their working overtime was in breach of their contracts of employment was irrelevant. The tribunal had no jurisdiction to adjudicate (*Power Packing Casemakers Ltd v Faust* [1983] ICR 292, CA).

6

Action short of dismissal and victimisation

GENERAL INFORMATION

6.1
Nowadays, employees have the statutory right:

- not to have 'action short of dismissal' taken against them on trade union grounds (eg because they are, or are not, members of a trade union, or because of their involvement in trade union activities);

- not to be discriminated against (or subjected to any detriment) on grounds of sex, marital status, gender reassignment, race or disability;

- not to be victimised, harassed or subjected to any detriment for exercising (or proposing to exercise) certain of their statutory rights in employment.

These provisions are to be found, respectively, in:

- the Trade Union & Labour Relations (Consolidation) Act 1992 (s. 146);

- the Sex Discrimination Act 1975 (s. 4);

- the Race Relations Act 1976 (s. 2);

- the Disability Discrimination Act 1995 (s. 55);

- the Employment Rights Act 1996 (ss 44 to 47); and

- the National Minimum Wage Act 1998;

- the Tax Credits Act 1999;

- the Working Time Regulations 1998 (see para 18.33);

- the Part-time Workers (Prevention of Less Favourable Treatment) Regulations 2000 (see paras 24.13 to 24.14).

Any employer who abuses an employee's right not to be disciplined, harassed, victimised or subjected to any detriment, for any of the reasons summarised above, is liable to very heavy penalties indeed. Furthermore, it should be pointed out that an employee in such circumstances has no need to resign from his (or her) job in order to obtain redress from an employment tribunal.

An employee who is dismissed (or selected for redundancy) for bringing proceedings against his (or her) employer to enforce a relevant statutory right, or for simply alleging that such a right has been infringed, may complain to a tribunal regardless or his age or length of service at the material time. If such a complaint is upheld, the employer is liable to pay a substantial amount of compensation (as to which, see Chapter 5) (*Source*: ERA 1996, s. 104).

Trade Union & Labour Relations (Consolidation) Act 1992

6.2
An employee has the legal right not to have 'action short of dismissal' taken against him (or her) as an individual by an employer for the purpose of:

- preventing or deterring him from, or penalising him for, becoming a member of an independent trade union or taking part in its activities at 'an appropriate time'; or

- compelling him to be or become a member of any trade union, or of a particular trade union; or of a number of particular trade unions.

Nor may an employee be penalised for refusing either to have money deducted from his (or her) pay or to make a payment to charity (or whatever) as an alternative to paying trade union dues (*Source*: TULRA 1992 ss 146 & 151).

Note: The expression 'at an appropriate time' means a time, within the employee's normal working hours, at which, in accordance with arrangements previously agreed with, or consent given by his employer, it is permissible for him to take part in the activities of a trade union.

Complaint to an employment tribunal

6.3

An employee may complain to an employment tribunal that he (or she) has been subjected to 'action short of dismissal' contrary to section 146 of the 1992 Act. The complaint must be presented within three months of the date on which the action complained of relates; or, if that action was part of a series of similar actions, within three months of the last of those actions. A complaint presented 'out of time' will not normally be heard unless the tribunal is satisfied that it was not reasonably practicable for it to have been presented sooner.

6.4

If the complaint is upheld, the tribunal will make a declaration to that effect and will order the employer to pay compensation to the employee of such amount as the tribunal considers 'just and equitable' – having regard to the infringement complained of and to any loss sustained by the employee (loss of benefit, expenses reasonably incurred, etc) as a result of the employer's unlawful actions. A trade union or other person that pressurised the employer into acting in the way he did may be joined or sisted to the tribunal proceedings and may be ordered to pay the whole or part of any award of compensation payable to the employee. There may be a reduction in the amount of compensation awarded if the evidence shows that the employee caused or contributed to a greater or lesser extent to his employer's unlawful conduct (*Source*: TULRA 1992, ss 147 to 150).

What is 'action short of dismissal'?

6.5

'Action short of dismissal' (in the context of an employee's statutory right to be, or not to be, a member of a trade union) means any 'penalty' imposed by an employer (often characterised by the not-so-subtle bullying tactics of managers, supervisors, foremen, shop stewards and the like) that falls short of dismissal but is designed to force an employee either to quit his (or her) job (which resignation might well amount to a 'constructive dismissal) or to resign from or join a particular trade union. Using spurious reasons to deny a person promotion or opportunities for training, withholding an expected pay rise, submitting dishonest or ambiguous reports about the employee's capabilities, refusing to allow overtime working, overloading the employee with work and threatening disciplinary action if he is unable to meet impossibly high targets, or simply sending him 'to Coventry' – all are examples of the tactics sometimes employed by unscrupulous employers to 'persuade' a reluctant employee to do, or not to do, something that he has every legal right not to do or to do. It should be pointed out that if an employer's actions are in any way attributable to pressure tactics (such as the threat of industrial action) brought to bear by a trade union or other person (eg a shop steward), the latter may be joined (or sisted) as a party to proceedings before an employment tribunal; and may, in the event, be ordered to pay the whole or part of any award of compensation payable to the employee.

6.6
It is the object that the employer desires or seeks to achieve that has to be considered. The fact that his (or her) actions offended against the 1992 Act is irrelevant. An employee, who performed full-time union duties, had been frustrated in his attempts to gain promotion. However, he could not show that his managerial abilities were adequate. It was held that although the effect of the requirement was to prevent advancement, there was never any intention to hinder his union activities. His claim failed (*Gallagher v Department of Transport* [1994] IRLR 231, CA).

6.7
The statutory provisions also cover job applicants who are refused employment on the grounds of their trade union membership or activities. In one case, a man was denied employment because he was considered to be a political activist. The employer was concerned that the man might prove to be a disruptive influence because of his alleged predilection for trade union activities. The Court of Appeal held that a job applicant should not be turned away

simply because of his reputation (*Fitzpatrick v British Railways Board* [1982] ICR 221, CA) (*Source*: TULRA 1992, s. 137).

6.8

Where a tribunal finds that the employer had two or more purposes, one of which was to further a change in the relationship with all or any class of his employees, and another one fell within para 6.2 above, then it must disregard the latter unless they consider that no reasonable employer would have taken that action (*Source*: TULRA 1992, s. 148). The action must be directed at deterring a person individually from being a member, or not being a member, of a union. It would seem that where a union is de-recognised and it has the effect of altering an employee's conditions of service, it does not offend against the Act even where the effect is to reduce the power of the union, or it deters employees from being members of it. If the detriment were extreme it might be caught by the 1992 Act (*Source*: ERA 1996, s. 104).

6.9

The provisions in para 6.2 above may enable a person to rely on the Act where there is an inter-union dispute and the employer treats one group of workers differently from another. The trade union, of which the employee bringing the complaint is a member, must, however, be independent.

6.10

Members of the United Democratic Mineworkers' Union (UDM) were paid more than the National Union of Mineworkers (NUM), who alleged a breach of section 146 of the 1992 Act. It was held that as the employer's intention was to penalise the NUM, his action breached that section. The Act was designed to prevent an employee from being victimised for being a member of a particular (independent) union. Furthermore, the employer's actions were directed against the employees as 'individuals' even though primarily directed against the union (*National Coal Board v Ridgway & Another* [1987] ICR 641, CA).

6.11

Certain recognised unions had the right to distribute parking tickets to those of their members who worked in the employers' telephone exchange. An employee was refused a parking permit because he was not a member of one or other of the unions in question. The EAT held that the action complained of was capable of being 'action short of dismissal', so long as the action had been taken against him as an individual and he had accordingly been subjected to a detriment for not being a member of a recognised independent trade union (*Carlson v The Post Office* [1981] IRLR 479, EAT).

6.12
A lecturer, who was also a trade union official, was passed over for promotion. The job was offered to a less-qualified candidate. The lecturer complained that she had been passed over because of her trade union activities and her strong views about one of the training courses run by her employers. The tribunal held that the lecturer's failure to be promoted was due to her deeply held views which were inconsistent with a whole hearted commitment towards the course in question (*McCarthy v Somerset CC*, 29 February 1981, EAT).

Sex Discrimination Act 1975

6.13
An employer will be held to have unlawfully victimised an employee (or job applicant) on grounds of sex, marital status or gender reassignment if he treated the employee in question less favourably than he treated (or would treat) other persons (ie, single persons or persons of the opposite sex) in similar circumstances, and did so because the employee in question:

- brought proceedings before an employment tribunal; or

- gave (supporting) evidence or information to a tribunal in connection with any such complaint; or

- alleged that the employer (or would-be employer) had committed an unlawful act

contrary to the provisions of the Sex Discrimination Act 1975, the Equal Pay Act 1970, or sections 62 to 65 (implied 'equal treatment rule' in occupational pension schemes) of the Pensions Act 1995 (*Source*: SDA 1975, s. 4). See also Chapter 11.

Complaint to an employment tribunal

6.14
A complaint of unlawful victimisation under the enactments referred to in the preceding paragraph must be presented to an employment tribunal within three months of the alleged discriminatory act, or within such further period as the tribunal considers reasonable in the circumstances. If the tribunal finds that the employee's complaint is well-founded, it will make an order declaring the rights of the complainant and respondent employer in relation to the act complained of and/or will order the employer to pay the employee compensation of an amount corresponding to any damages the employer might have been ordered to pay by a county court or by a sheriff court – which damages may include an element of compensation for injury to feelings. The tribunal might also recommend that the offending employer 'puts his (or her) house in order' by changing his policies and practices to ensure that there is no recurrence of the type of victimisation that prompted the employee's complaint in the first place. If the employer chooses to ignore any such recommendation (compliance with which may be 'policed' by the Equal Opportunities Commission), the tribunal may increase the award of compensation by such amount as it considers to be 'just and equitable' in the circumstances, in the light of the employer's justification for doing so (*Source*: SDA 1975, ss 63 to 65).

Race Relations Act 1976

6.15
Similar provisions are to be found in the Race Relations Act 1976 (see Chapter 12), section 2 of which reminds employers that an employee will be treated as having been unlawfully victimised if he or she is treated less favourably (eg by being denied access to promotion, training, benefits, pay rises, transfers, etc) than other persons within the employing organisation on grounds of colour, race, nationality or ethnic or national origins (*Source*: RRA 1976, s. 2).

6.16
Complaints to, and the penalties imposed by, an employment tribunal for a breach of the 'non-victimisation' provisions of the Race Relations Act 1976, are the same as described in para 6.14 above).

Disability Discrimination Act 1995

6.17
The Disability Discrimination Act 1995 came into force on 2 December 1996 and repealed the largely ineffective (and, to an extent, outdated) Disabled Persons (Employment) Acts 1994 & 1958.

Under the new Act, it is unlawful for an employer to discriminate against disabled persons in his employ by paying them lower wages or salaries (or associated benefits) solely because they are disabled, or by offering other less favourable terms and conditions of employment. To refuse to promote or transfer a disabled person or to deny that person opportunities to improve his (or her) skills, is likewise unlawful.

6.18
An employee who is discriminated against in this way has every right to challenge the employer's actions before an employment tribunal and is under no obligation to terminate his (or her) employment in order to do so. If the employer responds to any such challenge (or to an allegation of unlawful discrimination) by victimising or dismissing the employee, that too is unlawful and will inevitably lead to a further complaint to a tribunal and an award of compensation. See also Chapter 13.

Complaint to an employment tribunal

6.19
A complaint of unlawful discrimination under the 1995 Act must be presented to an employment tribunal within three months of the act complained of (or within such further period as the tribunal considers reasonable in the circumstances. Should the complaint be upheld, the powers of the tribunal are as described in para 6.14 above (*Source*: DDA 1995, ss 8 & 55, and Schedule 3, Part I, paras 3 & 4).

Employment Rights Act 1996

6.20
Sections 44 to 47C of the Employment Rights Act 1996 state that an employee, (and, in some situations, a worker who is not an

'employee'), has the right not be subjected to any detriment by any act (or deliberate failure to act), by his (or her) employer done on the ground that:

- the employee – in his capacity as a 'competent person', safety representative, representative of employee safety, member of a safety committee, or as a person designated by the employer to carry out activities in connection with preventing or reducing risks to health and safety – brought to his employer's attention, by reasonable means, circumstances connected with his work which he reasonably believed were harmful or potentially harmful to health or safety (*ibid* s. 44);

- the employee – as a protected or opted-out shop worker or betting worker – had refused (or proposed to refuse) to do shop work or betting work on Sunday or on a particular Sunday (*ibid* s. 45);

- the worker (as an employee or otherwise) had refused to comply with a requirement that his employer imposed (or proposed to impose) in contravention of the employer's duties under the Working Time Regulations 1998; or had refused either to sign a 'workforce agreement' or to forego his rights under those Regulations; or, being a representative of the workforce or as a candidate for election as such a representative, had performed (or proposed to perform) his functions as such a representative or candidate (*ibid* s. 45A);

- the employee – being a trustee of a relevant occupational pension scheme – performed (or proposed to perform) any of his functions as such a trustee (*ibid* s. 46);

- the employee – being an employee representative for the purposes of Chapter II of Part IV of the Trade Union & Labour Relations (Consolidation) Act 1992 (consultations over collective redundancies) or Regulations 10 & 11 of the Transfer of Undertakings (Protection of Employment) Regulations 1981 (consultations over a proposed TUPE sale or transfer), or a candidate seeking election as an employee representative – had performed (or proposed to perform) any of his functions or activities as such a representative or candidate (*ibid* s. 47);

- the employee (as a young person aged 16, 17 or 18) had exercised (or proposed to exercise) his statutory right, under sections 63A and 63B of the 1996 Act, to take time off during his normal working hours in order to undertake study or training leading to a relevant qualification (*ibid* s. 47A);

- the employee (or worker) had made a 'protected disclosure' (as defined in *ibid* section 43A) (*ibid* s. 47B) (as to which, see Chapter 23);

- the employee is (or was) pregnant or had given birth to a child; or had been suspended from work on maternity grounds; or had availed herself of the benefits of ordinary maternity leave (or had sought to do so); or had exercised (or sought to exercise) her right to ordinary or additional maternity leave; or (whether male or female) had sought to exercise (or had exercised) his or her right to parental leave, or to time off for dependants; or had declined to sign a workforce agreement for the purposes of the Maternity & Parental Leave etc Regulations 1999 (SI 1999/3312) (*ibid* s. 47C).

Complaint to an employment tribunal

6.21

An employee may present a complaint to an employment tribunal that he (or she) has been subjected to a detriment in contravention of sections 44, 45, 45A, 46, 47, 47A, 47B or 47C of the 1996 Act. The complaint must be presented within three months beginning with the date of the act or failure to act or, where the act or failure to act was part of a series of similar acts or failures, the last of them. A complaint presented 'out of time' will not be heard unless the tribunal is satisfied that it was not reasonably practicable for it to have been presented sooner.

6.22

If the employee's complaint is upheld, the tribunal will make a declaration to that effect and may make an award of compensation (payable by the employer to the complainant) of such amount as it considers 'just and equitable' having regard to the infringement to which the complaint related and any loss attributable to the employer's actions. The award would include compensation for any expenses reasonably incurred by the complainant and any loss of benefit that the employee might reasonably be expected to have had but for his (or her) employer's act or failure to act. The compensation may be reduced by an appropriate amount if the evidence showed that the employee had been partly responsible for the employer's infringement of his statutory rights (*Source*: ERA 1996, ss 48 & 49).

National Minimum Wage Act 1998

6.23
Section 23 of the National Minimum Wage Act 1998 (see Chapter 19), cautions that workers have the right not to be punished, victimised or subjected to any detriment (by any act, or by any deliberate failure to act) by their employers, for enforcing (or attempting to enforce) their statutory right to be paid no less than the appropriate national minimum wage (NMW).

6.24
In short, workers cannot legally be punished (or dismissed) for qualifying (or for being about to qualify) for the NMW, for challenging or questioning their employer's refusal or failure to pay the appropriate NMW rate, for demanding sight of their payroll records, for reporting their employer's conduct to an Inland Revenue enforcement officer, or for bringing proceedings before an employment tribunal or court. A worker may pursue his (or her) rights under the 1998 Act regardless of his age or length of service at the material time. Nor need a worker resign in order to do so.

6.25
On a successful complaint to an employment tribunal, the worker's employer will be ordered to pay the worker such compensation as the tribunal considers 'just and equitable' in the circumstances, having regard to the infringement to which the complaint related and to any loss sustained by the worker which was attributable to the employer's actions. A worker who is not an employee, in the sense that he (or she) is not employed under a contract of employment, whose contract has been terminated in the circumstances described above, nonetheless has the right (as has an employee who has been dismissed) to challenge the fairness of that detrimental treatment before an employment tribunal, and will be

awarded compensation if his complaint is upheld (as to which, please turn to Chapter 5).

Tax Credits Act 1999

6.26
An employer ordered by the Tax Credits Office to pay tax credits to an employee 'through the payroll' may not legitimately victimise that employee (or subject him or her to any other penalty or detriment) for that reason. An employee in those circumstances may complain to an employment tribunal (without having to resign in order to do so) and will be awarded compensation if his or her complaint is upheld.

Other 'no detrimental treatment' provisions

6.27
See also Chapters 18 (para 18.33) and 24 (paras 24.13 & 24.14) for similar provisions under the Working Time Regulations 1998 and the Part-Time Workers (Prevention of Less Favourable Treatment) Regulations 2000 respectively.

Liability of trade unions and their officials for torts

BACKGROUND

7.1

Over the past 20 years or so, the law has vacillated over the liabilities of unions for the loss and damage caused to others by the civil wrongdoing or unlawful acts of their officials and members. In the field of employment, the problem generally manifests itself in the 'torts' of inducing or procuring a breach of an employment or commercial contract. It will usually occur during the course of industrial action when a trade union unlawfully interferes with a trade or business or uses intimidation to cause loss and damage to an employer.

7.2

If a union or one of its representatives (eg a shop steward) persuades employees in an unrelated company to stop providing services to the company with which the union is in dispute, it will have committed an actionable wrong. The employees in the first company would have broken their contracts of employment with *their* employer, which would have the 'knock-on' effect of blocking the supply of goods or services to the company in dispute with the union in breach of its (commercial) contract with the latter (*Lumley v Gye* [1853] 118 ER 740, HL). On the other hand an action directed at strangers to the contract, where the effect on the contracting party is indirect, is not actionable unless unlawful means have been used. So the distribution of leaflets to persuade shoppers not to buy mushrooms at a supermarket because of a dispute between the pickers and their employers was not actionable. It was too remote (*Middlebrook Mushroom Ltd v Transport and General Workers Union & Others* [1993] ICR 612, CA).

7.3

Before liability can be established, it has to be shown that the action is unlawful. To bring about a breach of a commercial contract, there must have been some pressure on employees to break their contracts (eg, by physically preventing them entering their own place of work or using similar tactics to halt the delivery of goods to the customer's premises). Further, it would need to be shown that the person inducing or procuring the breach knew (whether directly or inferentially) of the existence of such a commercial contract, and that the breach would be a necessary consequence of his (or her) action. Further, it must be shown that loss was sustained as a result (*Stratford & Son Ltd v Lindley* [1966] AC 269, HL; *Cornellia Tankers Ltd v ITWF* [1976] ICR 274, CA; and *Read v FSOS* [1902] 2 KB 732, CA).

7.4

Unlawful interference with a trade or business can occur where there are commercial expectations. Thus even where there is no firm contract to supply services, but they are reasonably expected and the action is intended to frustrate these hopes, the unlawfulness is complete (*Hadmore Productions Ltd v Hamilton* [1982] ICR 114, HL).

7.5

Intimidation could occur where, with a view to causing damage to the employer or a third party, a person threatens violence or a union threatens employees with loss of union membership if they fail to comply with an unlawful union instruction. Usually a person would be caught under the 'procuring or inducing breach of contract' provisions (above) as well as for conspiracy to unlawfully cause loss and damage to the employer or any third party affected by such action.

7.6

The immunity from actions in tort enjoyed by the trade unions before 1971 and, to a lesser extent, between 1971 and 1974, has now been largely eroded. The Trade Union & Labour Relations Act 1974 (long since repealed) restored the protection for economic torts, but not for other types of tort. The current position, incorporated in the Trade Union & Labour Relations (Consolidation) Act 1992, is more in line with that in other major industrialised nations. As the subject has strong political overtones, there is likely to be a further see-sawing in the position – but to what extent is a matter of conjecture.

7.7

Trade union officials and rank-and-file members of unions have never enjoyed the same measure of protection as the unions themselves. But few employers were prepared to take them to court. Doing so could be counter-productive (especially when very heavy losses were being sustained) and would very likely inflame an already overheated situation. Obtaining an injunction against a union would not have been worthwhile unless an employer had access also to the union's funds.

7.8

If a party (a 'tort-feasor') is liable for damages to another arising out of a 'tort', even though others were responsible for part of the loss, the party would be liable to pay the whole amount to the victim. He (or she) could seek a contribution from his fellow 'tort-feasors' to the extent to which they were responsible. The loss and damage recoverable are that which would normally flow from the 'tortious act'. Thus, if a person negligently injures another person thereby preventing that other from performing a lucrative three-month contract to sing in the USA, the singer would be entitled to compensation not only for the injuries he has sustained, but also for his net financial loss.

THE CURRENT POSITION

7.9

The law has been described as a 'legislative maze'. It is extremely complicated. As mentioned earlier, it has since been consolidated into the 1992 Consolidation Act, which makes it easier to find the relevant parts (*Dimbleby & Sons v National Union of Journalists* [1984] ICR 386, HL).

7.10

A union is 'vicariously' liable for the acts of its officials and (in certain circumstances) union members under both the 'common law' and the relevant statutory provisions.

When liability arises

7.11

The position at 'common law' lacks certainty and depends on the law of agency. This in turn requires consideration of the rule book of the union, and of any express or implied authority that a union official or member may have for taking any action. The current position may not be properly recorded (*Heaton's Transport Ltd v TGWU* [1972] ICR 308, HL; and *General Aviation Services (UK) Ltd v TGWU* [1985] ICR 615, HL).

7.12

Under the 1992 Act, it is provided that a tort shall be taken to have been done by a union *if authorised or endorsed by the union.* Furthermore, 'an act shall be taken to have been authorised or endorsed by a trade union if it was done, or was authorised or endorsed:

- by any person empowered..., or

- by the principal executive committee or the president or general secretary, or

- by any other committee of the union or any other official... (whether employed or not)' including any other group of persons constituted in accordance with the rules of the union or by a member of that group, the purpose of which included organising or co-ordinating industrial action.

(*Source*: TULRA 1992, s. 20.)

7.13

A committee or any other person, such as a shop steward, will be *prima facie* liable for their actions if they/he/she decide to call a strike without reference to executive members of the union – whether or not that group or individual has authority to take such action. An official of a union was authorised by an 'authorised person' to go ahead with a strike after negotiations with an employer had broken down. The official had acted within that delegated power. It was held that immunity was not lost because there was a close relationship between the two (*Tanks & Drums Ltd v TGWU* [1992] ICR 1, CA). The only way for a union to avoid liability for the actions of its officials is to publicly disavow those actions. The disavowal must be communicated in writing not only to the victim of the unlawful action but also to each member of the group or to the official concerned, using the following words:

'Your union has repudiated the call (or calls) for industrial action to which this notice relates and will give no support to unofficial industrial action taken in response to it (or them). If you are dismissed while taking unofficial industrial action, you will have no right to complain of unfair dismissal.'

(*Source*: TULRA 1992, s. 21(3).)

7.14
A union which fails to repudiate unofficial industrial action will be vicariously liable for damages flowing from the 'tort' committed by the group or individual. However, there will be no loss of immunity if the industrial action:

- relates to interferences with contracts of employment;

- is done 'in contemplation or furtherance of a trade dispute';

- does not involve certain types of *primary* or *secondary* action (or unlawful picketing);

- has the support of the members under a secret ballot;

- does not induce a breach of statutory duty, and is not designed to bring about union membership.

(*Source*: TULRA 1992, ss 220, 222, 224, & 226 to 234.)

Interference with contracts of employment

7.15
The nub of the immunity relates to an indirect attack upon an employer by means of breaches of the contract of employment. This is usually done by taking part in strikes, part withdrawal of labour, 'blacking' of goods, and other forms of industrial action, thereby preventing or hindering the employer from meeting his obligations under business or commercial contracts with his clients. Immense damage can be done on such occasions.

7.16

Employees may take industrial action of their own initiative, or be persuaded by others to do so, and may do so for a variety of purposes. What is lawful now is very limited. There are elaborate formulae for determining which types of industrial action enjoy immunity and which do not.

'In contemplation or furtherance of a trade dispute'

7.17

The expression 'in furtherance of a trade dispute' means a dispute between a worker and his (or her) employer relating wholly or mainly to one or more of the following:

- terms and conditions of employment;

- engagement or non-engagement, termination or suspension of employment;

- allocation of work;

- discipline;

- membership or non-membership of a union;

- facilities for officials of unions;

- machinery for negotiation or consultations, including recognition issues.

(*Mercury Communications Ltd v Scott-Garner* [1984] ICR 74, CA.)
(*Source*: TULRA 1992, s. 244.)

7.18

Industrial action in support of a dispute with a company outside the United Kingdom is action 'in contemplation or furtherance of a trade dispute' if its purpose (or intended outcome) is to improve terms and conditions or to secure bargaining rights, etc for the company's employees *within* the United Kingdom. For example, industrial action by UK employees in support of similar action by workers in the USA (eg for a shorter working week) would be lawful if both groups of employees work for the same international company and the success of the strike in the USA would lead to an improvement in the terms and conditions of employment of their colleagues in the UK. Industrial action prompted by fear of job losses can also be characterised as action 'in contemplation or furtherance of a trade dispute' because it relates to 'the termination of employment', but it must be genuinely based on 'something definite and of real substance' (*General Aviation Services (UK) Ltd v TGWU* [1985] ICR 615, HL; and *Conway v Wade [1909] AC 506, HL*).

7.19

However, the immunity is lost if there is interference with a contract by unlawful means, eg by nuisance, violence, or intimidation (*News Group Newspapers Ltd & Others v SOGAT '82 & Others* [1987] ICR 181, QBD; and *Associated British Ports & Others v TGWU, CA* (but overturned by the House of Lords on another point) [1989] ICR 557).

'Primary' and 'secondary' action

7.20

Primary action occurs when employees take direct industrial action against their employer, eg by going on strike or operating a 'go slow' in support of a claim for higher wages. *Secondary* action occurs when a person induces another to break or interfere with his (or her) contract of employment, or threatens that his own or another's contract will be broken or interfered with, where the employer in question is not involved in the dispute (*Source*: TULRA 1992, s. 224(2)). Except where there is lawful picketing (see paras 7.37 to 7.42 below), *all* forms of secondary actions are unlawful. Striking workers manning a picket line outside their employer's premises may use peaceful means to attempt to persuade drivers working for a supplier not to deliver goods to their employer. But if they succeed in turning drivers away or use violent or intimidatory tactics, they (or their union) may be sued for damages by the supplier whose commercial and employment contracts have been interfered with. Criminal prosecutions might also ensue (*Source*: TULRA 1992, s. 224).

'Support under a secret ballot'

7.21

Immunity from actions for tort will also be lost unless the industrial action has the support of a properly conducted secret ballot. A majority of those voting must vote in favour of the proposed action. Every person entitled to vote in the ballot must be sent a voting paper by post to his (or her) home address and be given a convenient and cost-free opportunity to vote by post. Each voting paper must contain the following unqualified statement:

'If you take part in a strike or other industrial action, you may be in breach of your contract of employment.

However, if you are dismissed for taking part in strike or other industrial action which is called officially and is otherwise lawful, the dismissal will be unfair if it takes place fewer than eight weeks after you started taking part in the action and, depending on the circumstances, may be unfair if it takes place later.'

(*Source: TULRA* 1992, ss 226 & 230, as amended by s. 4 and Schedule 3 to the Employment Relations Act 1999 brought into force on 24 April 2000.)

7.22
Separate ballots have to be conducted at each place of work unless (a) at least one of the members at each (or some) of those workplaces is affected by the same dispute; or (b) the union in question reasonably believes that it is ballotting all its members in a particular occupational category (or categories) who are employed by one or more of the employers with whom the union is in dispute; or (c) the union reasonably believes that it is balloting all its members who are employed by one or more employers with whom the union is in dispute. All members who are entitled to vote must be allowed to participate and there must be a majority in favour of action at that workplace before it is taken (*Source*: TULRA 1992, ss 228 & 228A).

7.23
These requirements apply to industrial action as well as to strikes, and there must be a specific unequivocal question relating to each. The instructions to take the action must be issued within four weeks of the ballot, otherwise it will be unlawful. It does not matter that the action is taken beyond the period provided it relates to those instructions (*Monsanto plc v TGWU* [1987] ICR 269, CA; and *Secretary*

of State for Scotland v Scottish Prison Officers Association & Others [1991] IRLR 371, Ct S). A temporary suspension of action while negotiations take place would not affect the validity of the ballot. But if the industrial action ceases because the union decide to change tactics, say, by mounting a public relations campaign, then a fresh mandate must be obtained before industrial action is resumed (*Post Office v Union of Communications Workers* [1990] ICR 258, CA).

7.24

If during the four-week period a court prohibits the industrial action and the order subsequently either lapses or is discharged, an application can then be made to the same court within eight weeks of the ballot for a direction that the time lost under the order should be disregarded when adding up the four weeks (*Source*: TULRA 1992, s. 234).

7.25

A union put four matters to its members and asked whether they were prepared to take strike action. It was held that the ballot was invalid. There was no 'trade dispute' in respect of three of them (see para 7.17 above). If there had been one concerning all, it would have been lawful (*London Underground Ltd v National Union of Railwaymen* [1989] IRLR 341, QBD).

7.26

Those union members who '... it is reasonable at the time of the ballot for the union to believe will be induced to take part, or... to continue to take part in the industrial action in question...' must be allowed to vote, and no others. The exclusion extends to those union members who are indirectly interested in the outcome of the dispute (*Presho v DHSS* [1984] ICR 463, HL) (*Source*: TULRA 1992, s. 227). Those eligible to vote must be sent a voting paper by post and, so far as is reasonably practicable, be allowed to return their votes by post without interference or constraint, in secret and without direct cost. The results must be fairly and accurately counted and the results made known to those entitled to vote. A complaint by an employer that a union had not given all of its members an opportunity to vote did not invalidate the ballot. The union was able to prove that they had taken all reasonably practicable steps to circulate all of its members. Furthermore, what failure there was would not have affected the result. The ballot would be unlawful if a person called on to strike is denied the right to vote, in the sense of being wrongly disqualified (*British Railways Board v National Union of Railwaymen* [1989] ICR 678, CA) (*Source*: TULRA 1992, s. 227).

Reporting the results of a ballot

7.27
Once the votes cast in a ballot have been counted, the trade union must, as soon as is reasonably practicable, inform every relevant employer *and* every person entitled to vote in the ballot of:

(a) the number of votes cast in the ballot;

(b) the number of individuals who answered 'Yes' to the question or, as the case may be, to each of the questions on the voting paper;

(c) the number of individuals who answered 'No' to the question or, as the case may be, to each of the questions in the voting paper; and

(d) the number of spoiled voting papers (if any)(*ibid* sections 231 and 231B).

A failure to notify all relevant employers of the outcome of the ballot (where there have been separate workplace ballots) would make it unlawful for the union to call out those of its members whose employers had not been correctly informed of the outcome of the ballot (*ibid* sections 231 & 231A).

Majority vote in favour of industrial action

7.28
If there has been a majority vote in favour of a strike and/or industrial action short of a strike (such as an overtime ban or a call-out ban), and the union decides to go ahead with that action, it must inform the affected employer (or employers), at least seven days beforehand (but not before it has informed the employer of the outcome of the ballot), of the date on which it intends to call its members out on strike or to take industrial action short of a strike. However, the seven-day notice period may be suspended for an

agreed period so as to enable the parties to the dispute to attempt to negotiate a settlement. In other words, it will no longer be necessary for the trade union to issue a fresh seven-day notice if such negotiations prove unsuccessful (ss 231A & 234A, as amended by the Employment Relations Act 1999).

7.29

The notice of strike action (or of industrial action short of a strike) must contain such information in the union's possession as would help the employer to make plans and bring information to the attention of those of his (or her) employees whom the union intends to induce (or has induced) to take part (or continue to take part) in that action. If the union possesses information as to the number, category or workplace of the employees concerned, the notice must contain that information (at least); but the union is under no statutory obligation to name the employees in question (thereby putting paid to the decision of the Court of Appeal in *Blackpool and The Fylde College v NATFHE* [1994] ICR 648, CA) (*Source*: TULRA 1992 s. 234A(5A)).

7.30

Furthermore, the notice given to the employer must state whether the industrial action is to be 'continuous' or 'discontinuous' (eg, an uninterrupted strike or a series of one-day strikes). If the industrial action is to be 'discontinuous', the union must specify the dates or days on which that action is to take place. The notice of intended industrial action given by the trade union in the circumstances described in this paragraph must also state that it is given for the purposes of section 234A(7) (*ibid*).

7.31

A trade union's call for industrial action, following a majority vote in favour, must be made by the person or persons specified on the voting paper within four weeks of the date (or the last of the dates) on which the ballot took place. However, that four-week period may be extended by up to a further four weeks if, but only if, both the trade union and the employer in question agree to such an extension (eg, with a view to achieving a settlement of the dispute between them). Where there have been separate workplace ballots, an agreement to extend would apply to those workplaces only in which such an agreement has been reached. If it is not, the proposed industrial action will be 'unprotected' and 'unofficial' and (if proceeded with) will expose the trade union to the risk of civil actions for damages from all affected quarters (*ibid* ss 233(3)(b) & 234).

7.32
The industrial action may also be deferred beyond the four-week period if, for one reason or another, there is a court order prohibiting the union from calling for industrial action during the whole or part of that period or if the union has itself given an undertaking to the court not to proceed with such action. When the injunction or undertaking lapses or is set aside, the union may immediately apply to the court for an order extending that four-week period. The court may refuse to do so if, following submissions by interested parties, it is persuaded that the result of the ballot no longer represents the views of the union members concerned, or something else has happened (or seems about to happen) which would prompt those members to vote against industrial action if offered another chance to vote in a ballot (*ibid*).

7.33
Trade unions must give notice to employers of the various stages involved in calling a strike, including describing the employees likely to be involved and must provide them with detailed results of the ballot. A further delay is caused while various formalities are complied with relating to the necessity to serve notices of the intended action on the employer. Failure to follow these requirements nullifies the procedure and will result in the union losing its immunity. So where a union told the employers that its 'members employed at a college' would be called out on a one-day strike, it was held that the notice did not comply with the rules. The employers were unable to identify the individual employees involved. It mattered not that as between the union and its members, disclosure of the latters' names might be a breach of their right to privacy.

7.34
A union instructed its members to take industrial action without a prior ballot. This resulted in expense to a ticket holder who was

prevented from travelling home by rail. The union was ordered to indemnify the commuter for his loss because they had unlawfully induced a breach of contract between British Rail and the traveller (*Falconer v NUR & ASLEF* [1986] IRLR 331, County Court).

7.35
A person may apply to the High Court (or the Court of Session) for an injunction if a trade union or other person has acted unlawfully, or is likely to do so, with a view to inducing a person to take part in industrial action, the effect (or likely effect) of which will be to prevent or delay the supply of goods or services or to reduce the quality of goods and services supplied to the individual. It would appear that the consequence will be that a person may intervene where he (or she) has suffered no harm. It will be sufficient that the proposed passenger was deprived of the opportunity of travelling (*ibid* s. 235A).

7.36
Every voting paper must state the names of the individuals authorised by the union to call industrial action in the event of a majority vote in favour of such action. Immunity will be lost if an unauthorised person, eg a shop steward, instructs members to take industrial action (*ibid* s. 229).

LAWFUL PICKETING

7.37
Picketing is lawful if, but only if, it is done by a person in contemplation or furtherance of a trade dispute *at or near his (or her) own place of work* (or, if dismissed, his former place of work). Picketing must be for the purpose of peacefully obtaining or communicating information or peacefully persuading another person to abstain from working. A trade union official may take part in a picket if he (or she) does so in a lawful manner and is representing his members at the time (*ibid* s. 220).

7.38
Several employees were made redundant when their employer lost a cleaning contract for a building. They picketed the building. The picket was held to be unlawful because there was no 'trade dispute'

between the employer (the owner/occupier of the building) and those picketing. Their picketing was directed at the company that was awarded the new contract, not their former employer (*J & R Kenny Cleaning Services (a firm) v Transport & General Workers Union, The Times*, 15 June 1989, CA).

Harassment on the public highway

7.39
Unreasonable harassment of employees on the public highway as they enter and leave their place of work constitutes a 'tort'. It matters not whether it is done by weight of numbers, intimidatory conduct or even physical obstruction. The union, which had encouraged large numbers to attend, were held vicariously liable for the consequences (*Thomas v NUM (South Wales Area)* [1985] IRLR 136, ChD).

Code of Practice

7.40
The *Code of Practice on Picketing* produced by the Secretary of State recommends that the number of pickets on a picket line should be *limited to six* at each of the entrances to their employer's premises. The police should be consulted before a picket line is mounted, and there must be no interference with essential services. A member of a union may not be disciplined for crossing an unauthorised picket line, or one manned by member(s) not at their place of work.

Inducing a breach of statutory duty

7.41
If an employer is duty-bound to carry out certain statutory duties, any attempt to persuade the employees to stop work can constitute action that is outside the protection of any immunity. But it must be shown that the action actually prevented compliance with those statutory duties and not merely that the action made compliance more difficult (*Meade v Haringey LBC* [1979] ICR 494, CA; and *Barretts & Baird (Wholesale) Ltd v Institute of Professional Civil Servants* [1987] IRLR 3, QBD).

Action designed to bring about union membership

7.42

Immunity is lost if one of the reasons for taking industrial action is that the employer has hired (or intends to employ) non-union labour or persons who are not members of a particular trade union. The result is the same, if the purpose of the industrial action is to pressurise employers into treating non-union members less favourably (*ibid* s. 222).

STRICT COMPLIANCE ESSENTIAL

7.43

A union will be liable if there is a failure to comply at any stage with any of the technical requirements of the 1992 Act. It must disassociate itself from unofficial action, especially if taken contrary to the rules or directions. Even if a union does disassociate itself, it may still be caught on occasions by factors outside its knowledge (*Shipping Company Uniform Inc v International Transport Federation & Another* [1985] ICR 245, QB; and *Metropolitan Borough of Solihull v NUT* [1985] IRLR 211, ChD).

Political and sympathy strikes

7.44

Political and sympathy strikes are no longer immune, nor are 'wildcat' strikes or those called by a union official out of spite. Furthermore, any grievance must be communicated to the employer first. Demarcation strikes are also no longer immune because they are not between an employee and his (or her) employer (*Conway v Lindley* [1965] AC 269, HL; *Torquay Hotels Co Ltd v Cousins* [1969] 2 Ch. 106, ChD; and *Norbrook Laboratories Ltd v King* [1984] IRLR 200, CA). But motive, eg hatred of an employer, does not remove the immunity, provided the purpose of industrial action falls within the statutory provisions. However, the person taking the action must honestly and genuinely believe that his objective is likely to be achieved by such action (*Express Newspapers Ltd v McShane* [1980] ICR 42, HL).

7.45

A newspaper group in dispute with its printers switched its work to a non-union printer. The National Union of Journalists, which was itself in dispute with an 'associated employer' of the non-union printer, instructed its members to 'black' all work sent to the non-union printer. The instruction was held to be unlawful (*Dimbleby & Sons v National Union of Journalists* [1984] ICR 386, HL). The union also failed in its attempt to create a *primary* dispute over terms and conditions of employment by demanding the insertion of a clause in the contracts of its members – to the effect that they would not be required to produce work for printing by a non-union printer. It did not come within the strict definition, ie, the dispute was not 'wholly or mainly' related to it (see para 7.17).

LIMITS ON DAMAGES

7.46

The maximum amount of damages that may be awarded against a union depends on its size. The figures below apply in respect of all actions against a union except for personal injury or a breach of duty arising out of a property dispute. The maximum applies to *each* case against a union (*Source*: TULRA 1992, s. 22(2)).

Total Membership	Maximum Damages
less than 5,000	£10,000
5,000 to 24,999	£50,000
25,000 to 99,999	£125,000
100,000 or more	£250,000

TIME LIMITS

7.47

Proceedings must be begun within six years of the breach complained of; otherwise they will be 'statute barred'.

8

A contract under the 'common law'

GENERAL INFORMATION

8.1

The 'common law' has evolved over the centuries from the decisions of the judiciary in a variety of cases. The great body of 'case law' created in this way remains the cornerstone of contemporary UK law. Up to 1963, the law governing contracts of employment was almost exclusively derived from this source. Nowadays, the employment tribunals have (limited) jurisdictions to entertain claims for breach of contract arising out of (or outstanding) on the termination of employment (see Chapter 1, paras 1.35 & 1.36) (*Source*: Employment tribunals Extension of Jurisdiction (England & Wales) Order 1994 and the Employment tribunals Extension of Jurisdiction (Scotland) Order 1994).

8.2

Under contemporary employment legislation, employees and their employers have a great many rights and obligations. However, many common law concepts still apply. The problem that generally arises is the meaning to be attached to various words and phrases, which frequently leads to litigation.

8.3

A contract of employment comes into being when an offer of employment is made and accepted on terms that are either mutually agreed or stipulated by the putative employer when inviting job applicants to come forward. A contract of employment will contain terms that are express (eg job title, rate of pay, working hours; and so on). It will also contain implied terms, such as the employer's implied duty of care, and the implied mutual duty of trust, confidence and fidelity. It would be otiose to suggest that an employee has an implied common law and contractual duty not to divulge his (or her) employer's trade secrets, chemical formulations, production processes, marketing strategies, pricing policies, etc to unauthorised persons; although that duty would (sensibly) appear as an express term in the contracts of employment of those who have routine access to such information. Implied terms are necessary to give business efficacy to the contract. The relationship in a particular case is such that it could not really work without them. The 'reasonableness' test is not applied (*Morley v Heritage plc* [1993] IRLR 400, CA).

8.4

So it was held that teachers had a professional and implied common law (or contractual) obligation to cooperate in the running of a school during school hours – in accordance with the timetable and other administrative arrangements. They were also duty-bound to carry out all reasonable instructions given to them from time to time (*Liverpool CC v Irwin* [1977] AC 239, HL; and *Sim & Others v Rotherham Metropolitan BC & Others* [1986] ICR 897, ChD).

8.5

Terms had been negotiated with a representative body, which conferred valuable rights on employees. But before an employee could benefit from them, he (or she) had to follow certain procedures. He knew nothing about them and could not reasonably be expected to be aware of them. It was held that the employer had an implied contractual duty to take reasonable steps to draw such terms to the employee's attention. Failure to do so entitled the employee to compensation for the loss that followed (*Scally & Others v Southern Health & Social Services Board & Another* [1991] ICR 771, HL).

8.6

When a contract of employment is silent on the question of mobility of employment, it has been held that an employer has an implied contractual right to move an employee from one site to another, for any reason, provided that the employee continues to work within reasonable daily reach of his (or her) home (*Courtaulds Northern Spinning Ltd v Sibson & Another* [1988] ICR 451, CA).

Conflict between express and implied terms

8.7
Sometimes an express term in an employment contract appears to conflict with an implied term. The general rule is that the express term prevails. But courts have ruled otherwise where justice demands it. An express term gave an employer discretion to order an employee to work overtime. The employee was required to work long hours that were clearly affecting his health. It was held that, notwithstanding the express term, an employer has an implied contractual duty to take reasonable care for the health and safety of his employees (*Johnstone v Bloomsbury Health Authority* [1991] ICR 269, CA).

WRITTEN STATEMENT OF EMPLOYMENT PARTICULARS

8.8
Nowadays, every employee has a legal right to receive written particulars of the terms and conditions of his (or her) employment – including precise information about rates of pay, working hours, holidays, sickness benefits; and so on (explained in more detail in Chapter 9). This clearly narrows the areas of dispute.

8.9
It should be borne in mind that people's memories are notoriously fickle when recollecting verbally-agreed terms. Although a handshake at the factory gate is just as enforceable as a contract reduced to writing, there is the inevitable risk of a misunderstanding between the parties (as to what was actually said and agreed). A written contract is always preferable.

WHAT IS A BREACH OF CONTRACT?

8.10
There is a 'breach of contract' when one or other of the parties fails to comply with his (or her) contractual obligations. For instance, an employer cannot impose a pay cut without the employee's express permission. If he does so, he is in breach of contract and must either reinstate the employee's rate of pay immediately or face the consequences. A 'breach of contract' gives rise to a 'common law'

cause of action that entitles the aggrieved party to claim various rights including recovery of any damage sustained by him. In assessing the amount, payments from an occupational pension scheme must be disregarded (*Hopkins v Norcross plc* [1994] ICE 18, CA). Nowadays, the employment tribunals also have (limited) jurisdiction to entertain 'breach of employment contract' claims.

CONSEQUENCE OF A BREACH

8.11

The precise terms of a contract of employment are important because the nature of the remedy depends on the extent and seriousness of the breach. If the breach is so fundamental as to go to the very root of the contract, the innocent party is entitled to treat the contract as at an end (see Chapter 2, paras 2.40 to 2.44) and sue for any loss suffered. But he (or she) is obliged to do all that he reasonably can mitigate his losses (see *ibid* paras 2.61 to 2.68). An employee who resigns (with or without notice) in circumstances in which he is entitled to resign without notice – by reason of his employer's repudiatory conduct – is treated in law as having been 'constructively' dismissed. Such an employee can seek redress by presenting a complaint of unfair constructive dismissal to an employment tribunal. In some circumstances (notably if he is claiming damages in excess of £25,000) the employee might prefer to have the issues resolved by a civil court.

8.12

It is not necessary for the conduct of a party to be culpable. For instance, an employer might be under a misapprehension that an employee could be required to spend nights away from home, whereas the employee's contract might stipulate otherwise. An attempt to force that employee to make an overnight trip could amount to a fundamental breach entitling him (or her) to quit his job and sue for breach of contract. In such a situation, neither the circumstances inducing the breach nor the circumstances that led the employee to accept such a repudiation, are relevant (*Wadham Stringer Commercials (London) Ltd. & Another v Brown* [1983] IRLR 46, EAT).

8.13

The disreputable conduct of a manager who, for instance, sexually assaulted his secretary would be a breach so fundamental as to entitle the secretary to resign and sue for damages. An employee who secretly sets up a competitive business, or who makes use of confidential information to undermine the employer's business, is guilty of gross misconduct and may be summarily dismissed (that is to say, without notice). One act of disobedience or misconduct can justify a summary dismissal where it is of such a nature as to show that the employee is repudiating the contract or one of its essential conditions. The secretary of a club, which was about to be closed down, refused to attend two committee meetings – in the mistaken belief that he was no longer obliged to attend such meetings. It was held that his employer was entitled to dismiss him 'on the spot' because he had deliberately chosen not to carry out an important duty (*Laws v London Chronicle (Indicator Newspapers) Ltd* [1959] 1 WLR 698, CA; and *Blythe v Scottish Liberal Club* [1983] IRLR 245, Ct S).

8.14

If the breach of contract is not serious, the contract continues and the aggrieved can only sue for damages. In practice, the worker (if he (or she) is the victim) will not begin proceedings against his employer if he wishes to retain his job. It is uncommon also and almost certainly counter-productive for an employer to sue an employee who, for instance, has quit his job without giving the notice of termination required by his contract of employment.

8.15

When an employee refused to perform the full range of his duties, his employers told him that he would not be required to work and would not be paid until he agreed to comply fully with his contractual obligations. The Court of Appeal held that the employers were entitled to withhold the whole of the employee's remuneration, even though he voluntarily attended for work and carried out a substantial part of his work (*Wilusznskiv v Tower Hamlets London Borough Council* [1989] ICR 493, CA). Likewise, an employee in a managerial position would be in breach of his (or her) implied obligation to perform his duties faithfully if he participates in a withdrawal of goodwill and/or takes part in half-day strikes. Accordingly, a claim for payment by the manager for a period when she was laid off, because of her refusal to give an undertaking to work normally, failed. The employer was entitled to refuse to accept part performance of her contract (*British Telecommunications plc v Ticehurst & Another* [1992] ICR 383, CA).

ACTING IN GOOD FAITH

8.16

An important implied term requires employees to carry out their duties in 'good faith'. But that same implied term does not require an employee to disclose his (or her) own misconduct, whether it occurred before the contract or during it. But there is an obligation 'to inform against other fellow servants [even] if by so doing so you inevitably incriminate yourself... [but this] depends on the contract and on the terms of employment of the particular servant. He may be so placed in the hierarchy as to have a duty to report either the misconduct of his superior as in *Swain v West (Butchers) Ltd* [1936] 3 AER 261 or the misconduct of his inferiors, as in this case' (per Stephenson, LJ, *Sybron Corporation v Rochem Ltd* [1983] ICR 801, CA).

8.17

A person who has a 'fiduciary' relationship with his (or her) employers, the nature of whose job requires him to act in the utmost good faith, must disclose any breaches of contract made by himself when negotiating a further agreement. This might apply where he was settling the terms of a 'golden handshake' package (*Horcal Ltd v Gatland* [1984] IRLR 288, CA).

8.18

A betting shop manager, who wished to place a bet at another betting shop, borrowed £15 from the till, replacing it with an IOU. He returned the money to the till before his employers found out about it. It was held that, although the manager had not necessarily acted dishonestly, he knew full well that his employers would not have approved of his actions. What he had done was inconsistent with the implied mutual duty of trust and confidence which is a necessary feature of every such contractual relationship. The employers were entitled to dismiss him summarily. (*Sinclair v Neighbour* [1966] 3 AER 988, CA). There is also an implied duty of fidelity in every contract of employment. An employee may not work for a competitor during the continuance of the contract, or secretly set up a private business that runs in conflict with his (or her) employer's interests (*Provident Financial Group plc & Another v Hayward* [1989] ICR 160, CA).

8.19

An employee is not duty-bound to disclose information to his (or her) employer about his own affairs that affect his employer's business interests – always provided that he had obtained that information outside the course of his employment. So when an employee was summoned to appear before a liquidator and to answer questions, the transcript of the exchange between the two men need not be disclosed, even though the questions were of great interest to the employer (*Macmilland inc v Bishopsgate Investment Trust plc & Others* [1993] ICR 385, Ch D).

Implied duty of confidentiality

8.20

As was indicated earlier, there is also an implied duty of confidentiality in every contract of employment. Employees must not reveal their employers' trade secrets or other confidential information to unauthorised third parties. Those in breach may be injuncted from doing so. Employers are similarly bound not to disclose to third parties information given to them in confidence by their employees. This would include names and addresses of employees given solely in the course of the employer/employee relationship (*Dalgleish & Others v Lothian & Borders Police Board* [1991] IRLR 422, Ct S).

WRONGFUL DISMISSAL

8.21

A wrongful dismissal usually occurs when a person is dismissed with insufficient notice or when the employer has been in breach of certain procedural requirements laid down in the contract of employment (*Jones v Lee & Another* [1980] ICR 310, CA). A local authority dismissed a social worker without a disciplinary hearing on the grounds that an independent panel of enquiry had stated, in a report, that she had been 'grossly negligent' in the supervision of a child under her care. It was held that she had been wrongfully dismissed. Under her contract of employment, she was entitled to a pre-dismissal hearing. By not holding such a hearing, her employers had denied her her contractual right to explain her conduct and to put forward any mitigating factors (*Dietman v Brent LBC* [1988] IRLR

299, CA). So too, when an employer presumed to sack a prison officer without following the statutory procedures relating to dismissal laid down in the Code of Discipline, the court held that the purported dismissal was void (*R v Secretary of State, ex parte Benwell* [1984] ICR 723, DC).

8.22

In considering whether a dismissal is wrongful, an employer is entitled (contrary to the position under the statutory law) to rely on any facts he discovers after the dismissal so as to justify it (*Boston Deep Sea Fishing & Ice Co v Ansell* [1888] 39 ChD 339, CA). It is not necessary that a party should intend to breach the contract of employment. Suffice that he does. So if a contract is silent on what notice (at common law) should be given to an employee, and the latter is dismissed with, say, three months' notice, but a court finds that a more reasonable period would have been six months, the employer will be liable (*Wadham Stringer Commercials (London) Ltd & Another v Brown* [1983] IRLR 46, EAT).

8.23

Where there has been a wrongful dismissal, the employee can choose whether to accept the repudiation or not. If he (or she) declines to do so, and is able to carry on working, the contract subsists, but he is only entitled to his salary while he works (*Decro-Wall International SA v Practitioners in Marketing Ltd* [1971] 2 AER 216, CA). If the employee is prevented from doing so, he is duty-bound to 'mitigate' his loss (see Chapter 2, paras 2.61 to 2.68). In practice, this means looking for work elsewhere. Once the employee enters other employment, he puts it out of his power to perform his duties under the original contract, and consequently will be 'taken to have accepted his wrongful dismissal as a repudiatory breach leading to a determination of the contract of service' (per Buckley LJ, *Gunton v Richmond-upon-Thames BC* [1980] ICR 755, CA).

8.24

Damages can be very high on occasions. Under his contract of employment, the Chairman of a company was entitled to 30 months' notice. His summary dismissal was held to be wrongful and he was awarded £84,300 as compensation for loss of salary and other benefits – after the court had taken account of his duty to mitigate his loss (*Shove v Downs Surgical plc* [1984] ICR 32, QB).

8.25

Some contracts come to an end by operation of law, eg by a winding-up order or by an Act of Parliament. On such occasions, employees are not entitled to notice, or money in lieu of notice. So when the Greater Manchester Council was abolished by the Local Government Act 1985, the council employees were debarred from relying on their contractual severance scheme that provided for a payment in lieu of notice (*R v Greater Manchester CC ex parte Greater Manchester Residuary Body*, 14 July 1987, CA).

THE EMPLOYER'S RIGHT TO DISMISS

8.26

Under the common law, an employer can 'hire and fire' whom he chooses (see para 8.35 below). He has no need to justify his conduct or give a reason for dismissing an employee. He is (generally) immune from any claim for damages so long as he gives the required length of notice and complies with any express or implied disciplinary or dismissal procedures laid down in the contract of employment. Thus, when a Chief Education Officer (with the approval of the local authority Education Committee) decided to dismiss a number of employees and offer them new contracts, the court held that the decision was void. The Education Officer had no power to dismiss, and the error was not put right by the Committee confirming the decision (*R v Birmingham CC ex parte NUPE & Others, The Times*, 24 April 1984, DC).

8.27

Public sector employers are likely to be in a different position to those in the private sector. When making a decision, they must consider all pertinent matters, omitting all irrelevant collateral considerations. It must be a decision to which a reasonable employer would also come (*R v Hertfordshire CC ex parte NUPE & Others* [1985] IRLR 258, CA).

8.28

An employee guilty of gross misconduct may be dismissed without notice. He (or she) is not entitled to money in lieu. Although there is no statutory definition of 'gross misconduct' it will usually include grave acts of fraud or dishonesty, physical violence, sexual or racial harassment, other forms of assault, drunkenness or drug taking, working for a competitor, or otherwise seriously damaging the employer's business interests. It also extends to gross incompetence by an allegedly skilled man (or woman), and to instances where an employee's conduct is seriously insulting or insubordinate (*Jilley v Transfleet Services Ltd*, 16 January 1981, EAT; and *Wilson v Racher* [1974] ICR 428, CA).

THE RIGHT TO SUSPEND

8.29
Sometimes a contract expressly or impliedly empowers an employer to suspend an employee in prescribed circumstances. For example, an employee will normally be suspended on full pay pending the outcome of an investigation into allegations of gross misconduct. In less serious circumstances, an employee might be suspended without pay (for a limited period) as an alternative to dismissal. Any period of suspension without pay, which persists for longer than two or three working days, could amount to a repudiation of contract.

8.30
As a general rule, an employee must be paid his (or her) normal wages or salary while suspended from work, unless his contract of employment makes provision to the contrary. An employer must comply with any procedural requirements, unless those requirements are non-contractual. So an Education Authority, which had a statutory power to suspend staff who were deemed medically unfit, were not entitled to suspend a teacher on half pay. The Authority had failed to adhere strictly to the formal requirements laid down in the Conditions of Service for Schoolteachers (*Whitley v Harrow London Borough Council, The Times*, 29 March 1988, QB).

INJUNCTIONS RESTRAINING DISMISSAL

8.31
The High Court has power to make an order of 'specific performance' of contracts or of 'prohibition' in certain employment cases. Such an order would not be made if it would have the effect of requiring an employer to continue to employ someone against his will. A failure to comply would amount to contempt of court,

leading on occasions to dire consequences. If there is still mutual trust and confidence, or the applicant employee can be relied upon to carry out his (or her) duties properly, and there is a 'workable situation', a court may injunct an employer not to terminate an employee's contract of employment pending the full trial. In rare instances, a court may grant an injunction, even where trust and confidence are lost. An employer was in breach of contract when he dismissed a senior employee who was suspended on full pay at the time. A court order restoring the position enabled the employee to pursue rights that he would otherwise have lost (*Robb v London Borough of Hammersmith & Fulham* [1991] ICR 514, QBD).

8.32

An employer reluctantly dismissed an employee with insufficient notice after bowing to trade union pressure. It was held that, as the employer was willing to reinstate the employee and it was practicable for him to do so, a declaration could be made nullifying the effect of the notice. The employee remained in employment until there was a full trial on the issues (*Hill v C A Parsons & Co Ltd* [1971] 3 AER 1345 CA).

8.33

If a contract is underpinned by statutory disciplinary procedures, a court is more likely to intervene in an employee's favour. A dispute arose between an ophthalmologist and a consultant in charge of a health clinic. To resolve the problem, the Health Authority dismissed the ophthalmologist in clear breach of a statutory disputes procedure. Had the injunction not been granted, the doctor would have become unemployable within the National Health Service and would have been unable to use its facilities for his private patients. The court held that a refusal to intervene would have allowed the Authority to 'snap its fingers' at the employee's contractual rights (*Irani v Southampton South Western Health Authority* [1985] IRLR 203, HC).

8.34

An offer of employment 'subject to satisfactory references' usually means references that are adequate in the eyes of the employer in question, not in those of a reasonable employer. The job applicant would never become an employee until accepted by the employer to whom he had applied for work, so no question of an injunction arose (*Wishart v National Association of Citizens Advice Bureaux Ltd* [1990] IRLR 393, CA).

8.35

A tribunal may order an employer to reinstate or re-engage a particular employee (see Chapter 5, paras 5.158 to 5.165), but has no power to enforce compliance with any such order. A refusal to comply will only lead to additional financial penalties. As Lord Davey famously remarked in the House of Lords in *Allen v Flood* [1898] AC 1, 'An employer may refuse to employ [a workman] for the most mistaken, capricious, malicious or morally reprehensible motives that can be conceived, but the workman has no right of action against him... A man has no right to be employed by any particular employer, and has no right to any particular employment if it depends on the will of another.'

VARIATION IN TERMS OF EMPLOYMENT

8.36

If an employer wishes to vary an employee's terms and conditions of employment, against the employee's wishes, he can do so at common law without exposing himself to an action for damages – provided he acts in a proper manner. If a manager is entitled to six months' notice, his (or her) employer can give him notice of dismissal to come into effect six months later. He might then offer to re-engage the same employee at half his (or her) former salary. Although the dismissal would not be wrongful, it might well be unfair (see Chapter 5).

8.37

Unless an employer has an express or (less likely) an implied contractual right to reduce an employee's rate of pay (or to vary any other condition of employment), his decision to do so would entitle the employee to resign and pursue a complaint of unfair constructive dismissal and/or to seek damages for any loss sustained by him (or her) as a result of the employer's actions (*Miller v Hamworthy Engineering Ltd* [1986] ICR 846, CA). What an employer cannot do is give notice to 'vary' a contract. He can only give the appropriate notice to dismiss the employee and offer new terms to come into effect after the notice period. The employee has the option either to accept the new terms or to terminate the employment (*Rigby v Ferodo Ltd* [1988] ICR 29, HL).

8.38

A local authority tried to substitute essential 'car user allowances' given to two employees under their contracts of employment.

Instead of driving their own cars on official business they were told that they had to use pool cars instead. The Court of Appeal declared the move unlawful under the contract. It was of no effect (*Heir & Williams v Hereford & Worcester CC* [1985] IRLR 505, CA).

8.39

If a contract of employment provides scope for contractual variations, the employer who imposes such variations is immune from any subsequent claim for damages. Tax men refused to use computers for collecting PAYE. It was held that, although they needed to acquire new skills in order to operate the machines, the requirement was not beyond the scope of their existing contracts of employment. In short, their consent to the new working methods was not necessary. 'It can hardly be considered that to ask an employee to acquire basic skills... is something the slightest bit esoteric or even nowadays unusual' (per Walton J, *Cresswell v Board of Inland Revenue* [1984] ICR 508, Ch D). It was further held that the employers were entitled to suspend without pay those who refused to operate the computers. The legal principle of 'no work, no pay' applied when the tax men refused to carry out a lawful requirement.

8.40

Employers retained the right in the contracts of employment with their staff to amend their rules 'from time to time'. Having introduced a non-contributory life scheme, they subsequently revoked it. It was held that the employers' decision fell within the powers conferred on them under the contracts and so was immune from interference by the courts (*Cadoux v Central Regional Council* [1986] IRLR 131, Ct S).

8.41

If an employer is in breach of contract by unilaterally varying the terms of a contract, it is for the employee to decide how to respond to that breach. He can leave the employment and claim damages for wrongful dismissal, and/or compensation for unfair 'constructive dismissal'. Or he can seek a declaration (from the courts) that the purported variations were unlawful and unenforceable against him. Alternatively, he can claim damages for any loss sustained because of the employer's breach (*Rigby v Ferodo Ltd* [1988] ICR 29, HL; and *Miller v Hamworthy Engineering Ltd* [1986] ICR 846, CA).

8.42

If an employee's response to a breach of contract is to do nothing and to carry on working as normal, he (or she) will, in time, be deemed to have 'affirmed' the contract, and will be bound by the new terms. The acceptance of a reduction in salary may be evidence of an affirmation. That assumption can be rebutted by evidence that the variation was accepted 'without prejudice' to the employee's other rights (see Chapter 2, paras 2.51 to 2.54) or where he has indicated that he objects to the variation and takes some action to assert his rights. In all such cases, the employee must act promptly (*Bliss v SE Thames Regional Health Authority* [1987] ICR 700, CA).

8.43

Sometimes an employee's contract of employment will incorporate terms contained in a collective agreement made with a 'recognised' trade union (see Chapter 9, para 9.5). If that recognition is subsequently withdrawn (either voluntarily or by the CAC – as to which, see Chapter 25) the terms of the collective agreement will still bind both the employer and the employee (*Robertson v British Gas Corporation* [1983] ICR 351, CA; and *Gibbons v Associated British Ports* [1985] IRLR 376, QBD).

COMPENSATION FOR BREACH OF CONTRACT

8.44

As was indicated earlier in this chapter, a wrongful dismissal will ordinarily give rise to a claim for damages (see para 8.11) before a tribunal or court. Damages are assessed on the basis of the difference between what the employee would have earned had he (or she) not been prematurely deprived of his job and what he earned (or might have expected to earn). The amount of damages is always subject to a duty on the employee to mitigate his loss by seeking alternative employment (see Chapter 2, paras 2.61 to 2.68).

8.45

If money is paid 'in lieu of notice', it may be paid either gross or net of tax and National Insurance contributions — at the whim of the employer. Although it may be expressed as a payment based on what the employee would have earned had he (or she) been permitted to work out his notice, it is nevertheless a payment intended to ward off a claim for breach of contract. In other words, it is a settlement figure. It is only where judgment is given for a breach of contract that it has to be net of tax. Perhaps surprisingly, the employer does not have to account to the Revenue for the notional tax deducted (*Gothard v Mirror Group Newspapers Ltd* [1988] ICR 729, CA).

8.46
The measure of damages is not generally affected by the employer's motives, except where there was an intention to avoid making a payment in breach of his statutory obligations. The fact that an employee was dismissed in a harsh and humiliating manner does not entitle him (or her) to compensation for 'injury to feelings'. Nor is it relevant that the manner of the employee's dismissal made finding alternative employment more difficult, although this would be taken into account by the court or tribunal when considering whether he had taken adequate steps to mitigate the loss (*Addis v Gramophone Co* [1909] AC 488, HL). A person who has been deprived of publicity, which would have enhanced his (or her) reputation, is entitled to damages in respect of that deprivation. Thus, the Court of Appeal held that an actor was entitled to recover damages when he was wrongfully prevented from appearing at a music hall. But he could recover nothing for his injured feelings (*Withers v General Theatre Corporation* [1933] 2 KB 536, CA).

TIME LIMITS

8.47
Claims for damages arising out of a breach of contract will be heard either by the civil courts or (within limits) by the employment tribunals. Claims before the civil courts will become 'statute-barred' if not brought within six years of the alleged breach, although an extension can be obtained in limited circumstances. Claims intended to be heard by the employment tribunals must be 'presented' within three months of the effective date of termination of the claimant's contract of employment. A claim presented 'out of time' will not be heard unless a tribunal is persuaded that it was not reasonably practicable for it to have been presented within the prescribed three-month period.

8.48
The employment tribunals have jurisdiction to hear most breach of employment contract disputes that arise or remain unresolved on the

termination of employment. However, they have no jurisdiction to deal with claims in respect of personal injury, or relating to intellectual property, tied accommodation, obligations of confidence, or covenants in restraint of trade. Nor can a tribunal order the payment of an amount exceeding £25,000. Claims for damages in excess of that figure must be referred to the civil courts (*Source*: Employment Tribunals Extension of Jurisdiction (England & Wales) Order 1994 and the Employment Tribunals Extension of Jurisdiction (Scotland) Order 1994).

Contracts of employment

MINIMUM NOTICE PERIODS

9.1
On completion of one month's service, every employee (part-time as well as full-time) has the legal right to be given a minimum of one week's notice to terminate his (or her) contract of employment. The notice period increases to two weeks on completion of two years' service, three weeks on completion of three years' service; and so on, at the rate of one week's notice for each complete year of service – subject to a statutory upper limit of 12 weeks' notice on completion of 12 years' service (*Source*: ERA 1996, ss 86 to 91).

Note: In computing when the notice period begins and ends, the day on which notice was actually given must be disregarded (*West v Kneels Ltd* [1987] ICR 146, EAT; and *Misset v Council of the European Communities*, *The Times*, 23 March 1987, ECJ). In other words, the notice period begins to run from the day following the day on which notice was given.

9.2
For their part, employees must give their employer a minimum of one week's notice to terminate their contracts of employment. These statutory minimum periods of notice may, of course, be overridden by more generous contractual rights and obligations (*Source*: Employment Rights Act 1996, ss 86 to 91). Nowadays, it is commonplace for senior employees and employees with specialist skills, who cannot be readily replaced, to be required/entitled under their contracts to give/receive at least six months' notice.

WRITTEN STATEMENT OF EMPLOYMENT PARTICULARS

9.3
The Employment Rights Act 1996, also requires employers to issue *each* of their employees (part-time, full-time, permanent or

temporary) with an accurate and up-to-date *written* statement of employment particulars. Furthermore, the employer must issue that written statement within two months of the date on which the employee's employment began, or – in the case of an employee who is required to work outside the UK within a month of being recruited – before the employee actually leaves the UK to take up his (or her) duties overseas. Any change in the particulars to be included in the written statement must be notified to the employee (again in writing) within four weeks of the effective date of change (see also para 9.37 below) (*Source*: ERA 1996, ss 1 to 7).

9.4
The written statement may be issued, either as:

- a single document that contains *all* of the prescribed particulars listed in the next paragraph; or

- a so-called 'principal statement' (containing the particulars listed in para 9.6 below) supplemented by two or more instalments containing the rest of those prescribed particulars.

Particulars to be included in the written statement

9.5
The written statement (whether presented in instalments or otherwise) must contain the following particulars:

(a) the names of the employer and the employee;

(b) either the place of work or, where the employee is required or permitted to work at various places, an indication of that and of the address of the employer;

(c) the date on which the employment began;

(d) the date on which the employee's period of continuous employment began (which may differ from the date in (c) above) – taking into account any employment with a previous employer that counts towards that period;

(e) the title of the job that the employee is employed to do or a brief description of the work which the employee has been employed to do;

(f) the scale or rate of remuneration (wages, salary, etc) expressed as an hourly, weekly, monthly or annual figure, or the method to be used for calculating remuneration;

(g) the intervals at which wages or salary are to be paid (eg weekly or monthly);

(h) any terms and conditions relating to hours of work (including any terms and conditions relating to normal working hours);

(i) any terms and conditions relating to the employee's entitlement (if any) to holidays, including public holidays and holiday pay (the particulars given being sufficient to enable the employee's entitlement, including any entitlement to accrued holiday pay on the termination of employment, to be *precisely* calculated);

(j) any terms and conditions relating to incapacity for work due to sickness or injury, including any provision for sick pay;

(k) any terms and conditions relating to pensions and pension schemes, plus a note stating whether there is in force a contracting-out certificate (issued in accordance with Chapter 1 of Part III of the Pension Schemes Act 1993) stating that the employment is contracted-out employment (for the purposes of that Part of the 1993 Act);

(l) the length of notice that the employee is required to give and entitled to receive to terminate his (or her) contract of employment;

(m) where the employment is not intended to be permanent, the period for which it is expected to continue or, if it is for a fixed term, the date when it is to end; and

(n) particulars of any collective agreement that directly affects the terms and conditions of the employment, including (where the employer is not a party to such an agreement) the names of the parties by whom the agreement was made;

(o) where the employee is required to work outside the UK for a period of more than one month:

(i)   the period for which he (or she) is to work outside the UK;

(ii)   the currency in which remuneration is to be paid while he (or she) is working outside the UK;

(iii)   any additional remuneration payable to the employee;

(iv)   and any benefits to be provided to or in respect of him (or her) by reason of his being required to work outside the UK; and

(v)   any terms and conditions relating to the employee's return to the UK.

As was indicated earlier, the written statement of employment particulars (whether given in instalments of otherwise) must contain all of the particulars (a) to (n) summarised above. If there are no particulars to be entered in the statement under any of those heads, the statement *must* say so. A 'Nil' return (or the omission of any reference to any one or other of those particulars) is *not* acceptable. If, for instance, an employer has no occupational sick pay scheme, the statement must say as much ('You will not be paid any part of your wages or salary if you are incapacitated for work because of illness or injury') – although the employer would do well to remind the employee that he (or she) nonetheless has the legal right (subject to the usual qualifying conditions) to be paid statutory sick pay (SSP) in respect of any such period of incapacity for work.

The same applies if an employee has no contractual right to annual holidays, paid or otherwise. That fact *must* be mentioned in the written statement. Again, silence on the subject is unacceptable and may lead to a reference to an employment tribunal.

Note: Under the Working Time Regulations 1998, which came into force on 1 October 1998, every worker (part-time as well as full-time), who has worked for his (or her) employer for 13 or more weeks, is entitled to a minimum of four weeks' paid annual holiday in every 'holiday year'. Furthermore, those four weeks must be taken in the 'holiday year' in which they fall due. Unused holidays may not be carried forward into the next holiday year; nor is a worker entitled to money in lieu of unused holidays other than when his or her employment ends (*ibid* Regs 12 to 15).

Particulars to be included in the 'principal statement'

9.6
As was mentioned in para 9.4 above, the written statement of terms of employment may be issued either as a single statement (incorporating *all* of particulars (a) to (n) listed in para 9.5 above) *or* it can be issued in instalments. However, one of those instalments (the so-called 'principal statement') *must* contain all of the particulars (a) to (i) repeated hereunder, that is to say:

(a) the names of both the employer and the employee;

(b) either the employee's place of work or, where the employee is required or permitted to work at various places, an indication of that and of the address of the employer;

(c) the date on which the employee's employment began;

(d) the date on which the employee's period of continuous employment began (including any period of employment with a previous employer that counts towards that period);

(e) the title of the job that the employee is employed to do or a brief description of the work that the employee has been employed to do;

(f) the scale or rate of remuneration (wages, salary, etc) expressed as an hourly, weekly, monthly or annual figure, or the method to be used for calculating remuneration;

(g) the intervals at which wages or salary are to be paid (eg weekly or monthly);

(h) any terms and conditions relating to hours of work (including any terms and conditions relating to normal working hours);

(i) any terms and conditions relating to the employee's entitlement (if any) to holidays, including public holidays and holiday pay (the particulars given being sufficient to enable the employee's entitlement, including any entitlement to accrued holiday pay on the termination of employment, to be *precisely* calculated).

The 'principal' statement and its accompanying instalments must, nonetheless, be issued to each employee within two months of the date on which his (or her) employment began. It should be pointed out that an employer has nothing to gain by withholding the written statement until the employee in question has completed two months' service (a not uncommon, if pointless, practice). An employee can still rely on the particulars to be included in the statement, whether or not he has actually received the statement.

Supplementary instalments

9.7

All of the remaining particulars (namely (j) to (n), (and (o), where appropriate, in para 9.5) may be included in a single document (eg a staff or works handbook) or in two or more separate documents or instalments. However, each of those documents or separate instalments must collectively give all of the information the employee is likely to need in relation to those particulars. Referring the employee to the existence and accessibility of other documents is *not* acceptable – *except* in the case of documents that explain terms and conditions relating to sickness or injury (sub-para (j)) and terms and conditions relating to pensions and pension schemes (sub-para (k)).

Disciplinary rules and procedures

9.8

The written statement must also include a note specifying any disciplinary rules applicable to the employee or referring the employee to the provisions of a document that the employee will have a reasonable opportunity to read or that will be readily accessible to the employee in some other way and that explains those rules. The note must also specify (by name or job title) a person to whom the employee can apply if he (or she) is dissatisfied with any disciplinary decision taken against him (and what needs to be done in order to register dissatisfaction). If there are further steps in the procedure, the note must either explain those steps or refer the employee to some other reasonably accessible document that explains them in some detail (*ibid* section 3(1)(a), 3(1)(b)(i) & 3(1)(c)). See also para 9.33 and the *Note* appended to para 9.9 below.

The requirement to include a note in the written statement explaining the employer's disciplinary rules and procedures does *not* apply to organisations in which the number of persons employed (including persons employed at other branches of the same organisation or by any associated employer) is less than 20 (*ibid* section 3(3)).

Grievances and procedure

9.9
In addition to information about disciplinary rules and procedures, the written statement must also include a note specifying, by description or otherwise, a person to whom the employee can apply for the purpose of seeking redress of any grievance relating to his (or her) employment, and the manner in which any such application should be made.

Note: Section 10 of the Employment Relations Act 1999 allows that a worker who is required or invited by his (or her) employer to attend a disciplinary or grievance hearing has the right to be accompanied at that hearing by a single companion of his own choosing. That companion may be a fellow employee, a shop steward or a (suitably qualified and experienced) full-time trade union official. The companion has the right to make representations but not to answer questions on the worker's behalf. Should the chosen companion be unavailable to attend on the date appointed for the hearing, the employer must postpone the hearing for up to five working days. The companion (if a fellow worker) must be allowed paid time off work to attend the hearing. It should be noted that section 10 of the 1999 Act (which came into force on 4 September 2000) does not impose any duty on trade union officials or other workers to accompany a colleague at a disciplinary or grievance hearing. But, any worker who does agree to accompany a colleague at such a hearing may not lawfully be dismissed or disciplined for doing so.

If there are further steps in the grievance procedure (eg appeals to progressively higher levels of management), the note must either explain those steps or refer the employee to some other document that explains them – so long as the employee has reasonable opportunities to read that document in the course of his (or her) employment or it is made reasonably accessible in some other way (*ibid* section 3(1)(b)(ii) & 3(1)(c)). See also para 9.35 below.

COMMENTARY

9.10
Although the written statement (often, although not entirely accurately, described as the 'contract of employment') is not expected to have the same precision and clarity as a lease or a will,

care ought nonetheless be taken when writing it. This is especially true of a contract given under seal (which will ordinarily include the particulars required to be given in the written statement). Quite expensive consequences can follow if an employee's contractual rights are expressed in terms that are imprecise or unambiguous.

For example, before a tribunal or court can determine the rights and wrongs of an alleged 'wrongful dismissal', the obligations of the parties to the contract must be ascertainable. This depends on what was agreed and written into the contract. Was the steel erector's work restricted to a radius of 100 miles of Birmingham, or could he (or she) be sent to work on a job anywhere in the British Isles? If he was sacked for refusing to work on a project in Bodmin, the question of what he could and could not be required to do would be crucial in deciding whether his refusal was in breach of his contract of employment, or whether his resultant dismissal was fair or unfair.

9.11

Not every term or condition of employment is suitable for incorporation in a contract of employment. So a recommended minimum period of notice in a redundancy situation was held to be for guidance only and was not contractually binding. In any event, the recommendation was contained in an Appendix that was directed primarily at procedural matters. It was too imprecise (*Griffiths v Buckinghamshire County Council* [1994] ICR 265, QBD).

9.12

The Employment Rights Act 1996 does not require an employee to sign his (or her) copy of the written statement; but he will nonetheless be bound by its terms. If the employee disputes any of the terms and conditions, he should make his objections known from the very outset (*W E Cox Toner (International) Ltd v Crook* [1981] ICR 823, EAT; and *System Floors (UK) Ltd v Daniel* [1982] ICR 54, EAT). The same principle applies where there is a variation of the terms. But, where the variation has no immediate practical effect, it is less likely that the employee will be taken to have affirmed it (*Jones v Associated Tunnelling Co Ltd* [1981] IRLR 477, EAT).

9.13

The fact that the principal terms of a contract are set out in writing does not necessarily mean that they are conclusive. If there is a dispute about any of those terms, those set down in writing in the document are likely to be very persuasive. In the absence of strong evidence to the contrary, a term will usually be held to be binding (*Gascol Conversions Ltd v Mercer* [1974] IRLR 155, CA).

9.14
Some terms are implied by law. Various regulations were incorporated into the contract of employment of a medical practitioner. Unknown to him, his employers amended his contract following negotiations with his trade union. The new terms conferred valuable rights on him. But, he failed to take the required procedural steps to gain access to those rights. It was held that the man's employer was under an implied duty to inform staff about the new scheme. His failure to do so resulted in damages being award to the practitioner of an amount equal to his loss (*Scally & Others v Southern Health & Social Services Board & Another* [1991] ICR 771, HL).

The names of the employer and employee

9.15
The requirement to include the names of both the employer and the employee in the written statement is not just a formality – a lot can depend on it. It identifies the employer, so that, if the need arises, the proper party can be sued. For instance, if the employer is stated to be HG Jones, then Mr Jones will be personally liable for any claim or debt. If it is stated to be H G Jones Ltd, then only the limited company will be held responsible, not the individual directors. A former employer (to the immediate past one) can also be liable in certain circumstances.

Date on which employment began

9.16
This is a very important insertion in the 'contract of employment' as it might well be critical in determining the employee's statutory employment rights, including his (or her) right not to be unfairly dismissed or his right to be paid a statutory redundancy payment. In giving the date on which the employee's period of continuous employment began, the written statement must state whether any period of employment with a previous employer counts towards that

period. This might be the case if the employee worked for an associated employer or for a company (firm or organisation) sold or transferred to his (or her) current employer in circumstances covered by Chapter I, Part XIV of the Employment Rights Act 1996 ('Continuous Employment') or by the Transfer of Undertakings (Protection of Employment) Regulations 1981 (see Chapter 17). Other statutory rights, such as the right to statutory maternity pay (SMP), extended maternity leave, a guarantee payment, and so on, are also dependent on an employee having been continuously employed for a prescribed minimum period.

9.17

If an employee had taken part in strike action on one or more occasions during his (or her) period of employment, the date on which that period of employment began will be held to have been postponed by the number of days lost on account of such action. This approach must be adopted to establish the total period of continuous employment when determining an employee's entitlement to a statutory redundancy payment, the amount of the basic award of compensation for unfair dismissal; and so on (*Source*: ERA 1996, s. 216).

The title of the job

9.18

The written statement must state the employee's job title or give a brief description of the work for which he (or she) is employed. If a degree of job flexibility is required, the statement should say as much or be accompanied by some other document, such as a job description, which emphasises the importance of flexible working arrangements. This is especially important in the case of production-line workers (eg in a food factory) where changing production requirements may require workers to transfer from one department to another. The scope of an employee's duties under his contract of employment will also be important in equal pay, discrimination and redundancy cases. A 'mobility clause' should also be inserted at this point.

9.19

A divisional contract surveyor, whose contract required him to carry out any duties consistent with his qualifications and experience, was made redundant when the job of 'divisional contract surveyor' ceased to exist. It was held that his dismissal was unfair because there were other jobs available which he was 'capable' of doing (*Cowen v Haden Ltd* [1983] ICR 1, CA).

Scale of remuneration and intervals when paid

9.20
An employee clearly has the right to know how much he (or she) is to be paid and at what intervals. The statement should anticipate and provide the answers to the following questions. Is overtime working compulsory? If so, how many hours a week? What are the overtime premium rates? What will I be paid if I work (or agree to work) on bank and public holidays? How is my pay is calculated? Am I entitled to a bonus or commission? How are they calculated? Is the bonus discretionary or payable as of right?

Note: With the coming into force on 1 April 1999 of the National Minimum Wage Regulations 1999 (SI 1999/584), every adult worker aged 22 and over must be paid a minimum of £3.70 per hour for all hours worked (or a minimum of £3.20 per hour if taking part in 'accredited training' for at least 26 days in the first six months of his or her employment). The prescribed national minimum wage (NMW) for workers aged 18 to 21, inclusive, is £3.20 an hour. At present, there is no prescribed NMW for workers aged 16 or 17. The written statement of employment particulars issued to every employee must acknowledge the employee's right to be paid no less than the appropriate NMW. Any term in a contract of employment (or written statement) which purports to override or undermine a worker's right to be paid the NMW is null and void. The 1999 Regulations are 'policed' by Inland Revenue enforcement officers. Paying a worker less than the appropriate NMW is an offence under the National Minimum Wage Act 1998, for which the penalty on summary conviction is a fine of up to £5,000 (for each offence). See para 19.2, Note (1).

If there are to be deductions from pay (or demands for payment) in respect of poor workmanship, spoiled or damaged goods, cash shortages or stock deficiencies, the contract (or written statement) must be very specific as to the exact circumstances in which any such deduction (or payment) will be made (or will be required to be paid) – while at the same time acknowledging the employee's statutory rights under Part II of the Employment Rights Act 1996 ('Protection of Wages'). The employer would also be well-advised to secure the employee's written agreement (by asking the employee to sign the written statement) to the making of any such deduction (or demand for payment).

Working hours

9.21
The hours that an employee is required to work are important, not only from the point of view of the employee's contractual right not to be required to work longer hours than those spelt out in the written statement, but also as a means of calculating his (or her) weekly pay. If overtime is to be compulsory, that fact should be stated. If voluntary, that too should be made clear. The employee should also be left in no doubt as to the possibility of his being transferred from day work to night work (or to shiftwork) and the circumstances in which such a change might be imposed.

Are meal breaks (and coffee or tea breaks) paid or unpaid? Can an employee be required to work at weekends or on bank and public holidays? If so, is the employee entitled to be paid at premium rates for such work; and is there provision for time off work in lieu of work carried out on such days?

Note: Under the Working Time Regulations 1998 (SI 1998/1833) a worker cannot be required to work more than an average 48 hours a week calculated over a reference period of 17 consecutive weeks. Individual workers may agree to work more than that average 48 hours, so long as they do so individually, voluntarily and in writing, and are reminded of their right to change their minds (without penalty). Any term in a collective or workforce agreement that purports to override an individual worker's right of choice is void and unenforceable. The Regulations also impose limits in relation to night work and shiftwork, and make provision for daily rest breaks, weekly rest periods, and paid annual leave. For further information, please turn to Chapter 18.

Holidays and holiday pay

9.22
An employee's entitlement to holidays and holiday pay must be clearly spelled out in the written statement, as must his (or her) entitlement to accrued holiday pay on the termination of employment. Indeed, the information to be included under this head in the written statement must be sufficient to enable the employee to calculate *precisely* his residual entitlement on termination.

Under the Working Time Regulations 1998, every worker (a term encompassing individuals who are not 'employees' in the strict legal sense), who has worked for his employer for 13 or more weeks, is entitled to a minimum of four weeks' paid holidays in every holiday year. Workers must take their full four-week holiday entitlement in the holiday year in which it falls due. Workers have no legal right to carry forward unused holidays into the next holiday year, nor to be paid money in lieu of unused holidays (unless their contracts terminate part-way through a holiday year). Any contract of employment (or otherwise), that purports to override a worker's statutory rights under the 1998 Regulations, is void and unenforceable.

9.23

Employers in some industries require their employees (notably those in production) departments to take their annual holidays to coincide with the annual factory shutdown (for essential maintenance). Although custom and practice in this respect over the years will usually be imported into the contract of employment, employers would be well-advised to include this requirement in the written statement or in an accompanying staff or works handbook, so long as the principal particulars appear in the statement itself. The same applies to holidays over the Christmas and New Year periods.

9.24

It remains to be seen whether an employee can be expected to 'nibble away' at his (or her) entitlement to annual holidays when asking for time off for dental visits or to deal with any domestic problems (death of a member of the family; and so on). With the coming into force on 15 December 1999 of the 'time off for dependants' provisions of the Employment Relations Act 1999 (now section 57A of the Employment Rights Act 1996), employees have the legal right to take a reasonable amount of *unpaid* time off work:

- to provide assistance when a dependant falls ill, gives birth, or is injured or assaulted;

- to make arrangements for the care of a dependant who is ill or injured;

- when a dependant dies (eg, to make funeral arrangements and/or to attend at the funeral);

- to make emergency arrangements for the care of a dependant (when current arrangements are unexpectedly disrupted or terminated); or

- to deal with an unexpected incident involving one or other of the employee's children while at school (eg, a playground accident, a disciplinary matter, or whatever).

Note: For these purposes, the term 'dependant' in relation to an employee means the employee's husband or wife, child, parent, or a person (other than a tenant, lodger or boarder) who lives in the same household as the employee, who reasonably relies on the employee either for assistance when injured, assaulted or taken ill or to make arrangements for the provision of care in the event of illness or injury. For further particulars, please turn to Chapter 14, paras 14.84 to 14.94.

Given that an employee has no statutory right to be paid when exercising his or her rights under the 'time off dependants' provisions of the 1996 Act, the written statement (or accompanying staff or works handbook) issued to that employee may make provision either for a short period of *paid* time off on compassionate grounds or afford employees the opportunity to use some of their annual holiday entitlement for that purpose.

Temporary employment and fixed-term contracts

9.25
If an employee is hired to do a specific job of work, which is expected to be completed within a few weeks or months (or whatever), the written statement must indicate the period for which the employment is expected to continue. If the contract is for a fixed term, the statement must indicate when that term is to end.

Under current legislation, a fixed-term contract for a period of two years or longer may include a clause effectively waiving the employee's right to a statutory redundancy payment on the expiry and non-renewal of the contract. However, the insertion of an 'unfair dismissal' waiver clause in a contract for a fixed term of one year or more, is no longer permissible, in the sense that it does not (and cannot) operate to deny an employee his or her statutory right to pursue a complaint of unfair dismissal on the expiry and non-renewal of that contract (*Source*: ERA 1996, s. 197, as amended by s. 18 of the Employment Relations Act 1999).

Information about pensions and pension schemes

9.26
The full particulars of such a complex subject are not easily incorporated into the written contract. It will usually suffice to deal with it in general terms, referring to other documents that will set out the relevant terms in greater detail. If there are no pension rights, the statement must say as much. It would also be helpful to explain other options available to employees (contracting out of the State Earnings-Related Pension Scheme, portable pension plans, etc).

Terms relating to incapacity for work due to sickness or injury

9.27
If an employee has no contractual right to be paid the whole or any part of his (or her) wages or salary during absences from work occasioned by illness or injury, the written statement should say as much. Silence on the subject is not acceptable. Indeed, should the employer's silence on this issue be referred to an employment tribunal, the latter might well import terms relating to sickness benefits into the employee's contract (with which the employer will be left with no choice but to comply).

Employers should not lose sight of the fact that employees generally (subject to certain *qualifying conditions*) have the legal right to be paid statutory sick pay (SSP) for a period of up to 28 weeks in any single period (or series of linked periods) of incapacity for work (PIWs). Any term in a contract (or written statement) that purports to override an employee's right to SSP, or to impose more stringent conditions, is void and unenforceable (*Source*: Social Security Contributions & Benefits Act 1992, Part XI).

9.28
If an employer chooses to make *discretionary* payments (in addition to any entitlement to SSP) to employees who are absent from work on grounds of sickness or injury, he should make it clear – either in the written statement or some other document – that such payments *are* discretionary. Any contractual entitlement to benefits under an occupational sick pay scheme could pose problems if a sick or

injured employee is dismissed *before* that entitlement is exhausted. Indeed, in such a situation, the employee could pursue a claim for damages (either in the civil court or before an employment tribunal) arising out of his (or her) employer's breach of his contractual rights.

9.29
Any employee who is unable to attend for work because of illness or injury should be aware of his (or her) employer's rules about the time limits for informing the relevant manager or supervisor (or the Personnel Department) about his non-availability for work. The rules about self-certificates for illness and the eventual production of a doctor's sick note should also be made clear, preferably in the written statement. It should be pointed out here that the notification and evidential rules, in the context of an employee's entitlement (if any) to SSP, are not as stringent as those necessarily laid down by an employer left to deal with the (sudden and unexpected) absence of a key employee.

9.30
Finally, SSP is payable to employees who are 'deemed' to be incapacitated for work in circumstances not ordinarily encompassed by an occupational sick pay scheme. For example, an employee who takes time off work for a breast-enhancement operation or for a vasectomy, or who is injured on a skiing holiday (or while taking part in an exceptionally hazardous sport), will be 'deemed' to be incapacitated for work under the Employer's SSP Scheme, but will not necessarily be entitled to payment under the terms of his (or her) employer's occupational sick pay scheme.

The employer's rules should state whether an employee can expect to be credited with additional days of holiday if he (or she) falls ill or is injured during his annual holidays (thereby foreshortening or interrupting those holidays).

Notice periods

9.31
The notice that an employee is required to give (or is entitled to receive) to terminate his (or her) contract of employment should not be less than the minimum statutory notice periods prescribed by

ERA 1996 (as to which, see Chapter 3 (paras 3.9 to 3.14) and para 9.1 above). If the notice to termintae given by an employer is less than that prescribed by statute, the 'effective date of termination' of the employee's contract of employment will (for the purposes of establishing his right to present a complaint of unfair dismissal, or to claim a redundancy payment) be the date on which the statutory period of notice would have expired had it been duly given by the employer on the date on which the notice to terminate was actually given.

9.32

An employee who is not given the notice to which he (or she) is entitled under the relevant contract of employment, or the notice prescribed by the Employment Rights Act 1996 (at section 86), whichever is the longer, may pursue a claim (or present a complaint) for damages arising out of that breach of contract. The employee is nonetheless under a common law duty to mitigate his loss, eg by actively looking for work elsewhere (see Chapter 2, paras 2.61 to 2.68) (*Robert Cort v Charman & Sons* [1981] ICR 816, EAT).

Disciplinary rules and procedure

9.33

An employer's disciplinary rules should make it clear to employees that he (or she) expects (indeed, insists upon) certain standards of conduct amongst employees, both in their relationships with one another and their immediate superiors, *and* in their dealings with customers, clients and members of the public. They should also be given to understand that socially unacceptable conduct (fighting, physical assault, sexual harassment, licentiousness, racial abuse, obscene language, drunkenness, drug taking, etc) will not be tolerated and will, in prescribed cases, lead to the summary dismissal of the offender. Failure to obey safety rules (eg by removing machine guards or indulging in dangerous 'horseplay') should also be added to the list.

The employer's disciplinary rules (some of which will be peculiar to the trade or industry in which the employer is engaged) must not only specify which offences will lead to summary dismissal, but must also describe the procedure to be followed in the event of a breach of those rules, the number of stages in that procedure, and the person or persons to whom an employee can appeal if dissatisfied with any disciplinary decision (including dismissal) taken against him. Those rules and their accompanying procedures should also acknowledge the now statutory right of workers to be accompanied at the formal stages of a disciplinary (or grievance) procedure by a single companion of their own choosing (fellow employee, shop steward or full-time trade union official) (as to which, see the *Note* to para. 9.9 above).

9.34

The dismissal of an employee contrary to the employer's clearly laid-down rules for dealing with breaches of discipline will invariably (but not always) lead to a finding of unfair dismissal. Much will depend on whether the breach was serious or merely a technicality and whether the result would inevitably have been the same based on the information available to the employer at the material time (see Chapter 5, paras 5.94 to 5.100, and 5.187) (*Polkey v A E Dayton Services Ltd* [1988] ICR 142, HL).

Grievances and procedure

9.35

An employee who is concerned about aspects of his (or her) work (pay, working hours, other terms and conditions, a poor performance appraisal, denial of an opportunity for promotion or transfer, etc) has the right to refer such concerns to an immediate superior, and (if the contract so provides) to progressively higher levels of management, until they are resolved (whether or not to the satisfaction of the employee in question). The written statement must include (or be accompanied by) a note identifying a person (by name or job title) with whom the employee can register his complaints and any ensuing steps in the procedure (including some indication as to how long the employee can expect to wait for a solution or answer to the problems (eg Stage 1 within seven working days; Stage 2 within five days, etc). As to the now statutory right of a worker to be accompanied (by a workmate, shop steward or full-time trade union official) at each of the formal stages of a grievance (or disciplinary) procedure, please see the *Note* to para 9.9 above.

Work outside the UK

9.36

A new recruit, who is to be posted overseas within one month of starting work, must be issued with the written statement of employment particulars before he (or she) leaves the UK. Furthermore, if the employee is to work outside the UK for more than one month, the statement must also contain particulars of:

- the period for which he is to work outside the UK;

- the currency in which remuneration is to be paid while the employee is working outside the UK;

- any additional remuneration payable to the employee, and any benefits to be provided to or in respect of him by reason of his being required to work outside the UK; and

- any terms and conditions relating to the employee's return to the UK.

(*Source*: ERA 1996, s. 1(4)(k).)

STATEMENT OF CHANGES

9.37

If, after the initial statement is issued, there is any change in any of the particulars included in the statement, the employer must supply each of the employees concerned with a further written statement containing particulars of the change – and must do so not later than one month after the change in question (*Source*: ERA 1996, s. 4)

Where only the name of the employer changes, no fresh statements have to be served. If the identity changes but nothing else, then it is sufficient for the employer to notify the employee in writing of the change in identity and restate the date on which the period of continuous employment began.

EXCLUDED CLASSES

9.38

A written statement of employment particulars need not be issued:

- to an employee who resigns or is dismissed within one month of starting work, but must be issued to an employee whose employment comes to an end (for whatever reason) after one month but before the end of the period of two months beginning with the date on which his (or her) employment began (*ibid* ss 2(6) and 198); or

- to a person employed as a seaman in a ship registered in the United Kingdom under a crew agreement the provisions and form of which are of a kind approved by the Secretary of State for Education & Employment (*ibid* s. 199(1));

REMEDIES FOR FAILURE TO SUPPLY A WRITTEN STATEMENT OF EMPLOYMENT PARTICULARS

9.39
If an employer fails to supply an employee with a written statement, or issues a statement that is incomplete, the employee can refer the matter for determination by an employment tribunal. The tribunal has power to determine what particulars should have been included in the statement. Where the particulars have been supplied but are alleged to be wrong, the tribunal can confirm, amend or substitute other terms. A tribunal is entitled to hear oral evidence from both sides as to what they understood the correct position to be, and, if necessary, what they intended (*Boothferry BC v Boyle*, 19 December 1984, EAT).

9.40
An employer is likewise entitled to refer a written statement to a tribunal where there is a dispute over its accuracy. The particulars as found by the tribunal will bind each party as if they had been included in the statement. A tribunal is now empowered to interpret the meaning of an agreement if the parties disagree as to what a term means. Thus if an employer fails to state what length of notice is required to terminate the employment and the tribunal finds on the evidence it should be the common law 'reasonable notice', it may go on to decide what is 'reasonable' (*Source*: Employment Tribunals Extension of Jurisdiction (England & Wales) Order 1994; and the Employment Tribunals Extension of Jurisdiction (Scotland) order 1994).

In exercising its statutory powers, a tribunal will not re-write or amend a binding contract. It will merely direct an amendment to or substitution for the particulars in dispute where there is an error or omission. It cannot make any monetary award.

9.41
The first task of an employment tribunal on a reference to it under section 11 of the 1996 Act (*References to employment tribunals*), is to:

- ascertain whether there are any express written or oral terms in the employee's contract;

- if there are none, then it must decide whether a term can be implied in all the circumstances that may include anything to be deduced from the conduct of the parties. If that fails to provide the answer, and there are factors pointing both ways, the term most favourable to the employee will usually be adopted;

- in the last resort, in a case where there is a mandatory requirement to provide particulars, eg notice periods or remuneration, a tribunal will need to determine what is 'reasonable' in the circumstances

(*Eagland v British Telecommunications plc* [1992] IRLR 323, CA.)

9.42
A tribunal may not invent terms in respect of non-mandatory requirements. For instance, if an employee claims sick pay during a lengthy absence, and there is nothing about it in the contract, and nothing can be deduced from the surrounding circumstances, a tribunal cannot decide that the employee should have been paid sick pay during his (or her) absence.

Effect of a declaration

9.43
Once a tribunal has made a declaration it becomes *res judicata* (see Chapter 27, paras 27.76 & 27.77) and all other courts and tribunals are bound by it. If the declaration is in favour of the employee, the new terms can be enforced by an employment tribunal or by a civil court. If other employees within the same organisation are affected by the declaration, the employer's final liability may be substantial.

Indeed, the employer can be ordered to repay any sum properly payable to the employee, without limit as to the amount.

AMENDING THE EMPLOYMENT CONTRACT

9.44
An employer can amend an employee's contract of employment provided the employee is agreeable. Although an increase in an employee's annual holiday entitlement or the granting of more generous sickness benefits is unlikely to be challenged, an employee will be more than a little upset if his (or her) employer decides to cut his annual salary from, say, £20,000 to £15,000. Any such unilateral variation would be tantamount to a repudiation of the employee's contract and actionable as such.

9.45
Under the common law, an employer can achieve the same end by dismissing the employee with notice and re-employing him (or her) on terms that suit the employer (as to which, see Chapter 8, paras 8.36 to 8.43). However, under statute law, the employee would be within his rights to resign (with or without notice) by virtue of his employer's repudiatory conduct and present a complaint of unfair 'constructive dismissal' – if the variation is serious and the employee objects to it (*Robertson v British Gas Corporation* 1983] ICR 351, CA). The dismissal will be unfair unless it is for one or other of the 'permitted' reasons (listed in Chapter 5 at para. 5.13). A variation of contract can be defended as being for 'some other substantial reason', if the change has been made for sound business reasons. It will nonetheless be necessary to demonstrate that there had been adequate consultation with the employee and every effort made to accommodate his objections (*Berriman v Delabole Slate Ltd* [1985] ICR 546, CA; *Ellis v Brighton Cooperative Society Ltd* [1976] IRLR 419, EAT; and *Evans v Elemeta Holdings Ltd* [1982] ICR 323, EAT).

TIME LIMITS

9.46
A complaint of an employer's refusal or failure to provide a written statement of employment particulars must be presented to the

Secretary to the Tribunals within three months of that refusal or failure or, where appropriate, within three months of the 'effective date of termination' of the employee's contract of employment. A tribunal will not consider a reference or complaint presented 'out of time' unless satisfied that it was not reasonably practicable for the reference or complaint to have been presented sooner (see Chapter 3, paras 3.68 to 3.78).

9.47

If an employer has become insolvent or is adjudged bankrupt, his employees may recover some, but not all, of any monies owed to them at that time from the Secretary of State for Education & Employment (in practice, the Department of Employment). If the latter refuse or fail to pay, the matter may be referred to an employment tribunal for a declaration as to what the Secretary of State should have paid and must pay (*Source*: ERA 1996, s. 183).

Restrictive covenants

GENERAL INFORMATION

10.1
During their employment, it is inevitable that directors, senior managers, chemists, engineers, research staff, and others occupying strategic positions within an organisation, will have access to trade secrets, product formulations, development plans, marketing and pricing strategies, and other confidential matters relating to the employer's business. An employee who resigns or is dismissed could do serious damage to his (or her) (former) employer's business should he allow that information to fall into the wrong hands. To protect his position, the employer will often incorporate so-called restrictive covenants in the contracts of employment of all key personnel. Such a covenant will put the employee on notice that he must not divulge any such confidential information to unauthorised third parties and, in many cases, will impose a duty on the employee not to compete with his (former) employer after his employment ends and not to accept employment with another employer in the same trade or industry.

10.2
A restrictive covenant will usually be for a limited period and will restrict the employee's post-employment activities within a clearly defined geographical area. A covenant in 'restraint of trade' will only be enforceable if it is shown to be reasonable as between the parties, and that it is in the public interest. It is for the employer to demonstrate that it is reasonable in area and time in order to reasonably protect his business. A claim that such a restriction is not in the public interest must be proved by the employee (*Spencer v Marchington* [1988] IRLR 392, HC).

10.3
The principle was enunciated by Lord MacNaughten in this way: 'The public have an interest in every person's carrying on his trade freely: so has the individual. All interferences with the individual

liberty of action in trading, and all restraints of trade of themselves, if there is nothing more, are contrary to public policy, and therefore void. That is the general rule. But there are exceptions... It is sufficient justification... if the restriction is reasonable... in reference to the interests of the parties concerned, and reasonable in reference to the interests of the public, so... as to afford adequate protection to the party in whose favour it is imposed, while at the same time it is in no way injurious to the public' (*Maxim-Nordenfelt Gun Co v Nordenfelt* [1894] AC 535, HL).

THE GRANTING OF AN INJUNCTION

10.4

In considering the interests of the parties, the covenant must be necessary to protect some trade secret or to prevent some personal influence being exercised over customers to entice them away. It must be for no longer than is necessary to prevent the employee from enjoying the unfair advantage that he (or she) had obtained from the acquisition of the information (*Herbert Morris Ltd v Saxelby* [1916] 1 AC 688, HL; and *Roger Bullivant Ltd & Others v Ellis & Others* [1987] ICR 464, CA). Once it is established that the restraint in favour of a firm is reasonable, an injunction will be granted (subject to judicial discretion). It matters not that the customer has indicated that he (or she) no longer wishes to trade with the company but intends to deal with the ex-employee instead (*John Michael Design plc v Cooke & Foley* [1987] ICR 445, CA).

10.5

If an employer has been wrongfully dismissed, the employer will be unable to enforce a restrictive covenant, because he cannot take advantage of his own wrong. But the employee who brings about his (or her) own (premature) dismissal will still be bound by such a covenant (*Rex Stewart Jeffries Parker Ginsberg Ltd v Parker* [1988] IRLR 483, CA). But if an employee is entitled to, and does, resign because of his employer's repudiatory conduct (ie, 'constructive dismissal': see Chapter 2, paras 2.40 to 2.44), the employer loses the right to enforce any restrictive covenant against that employee. This principle was applied where an employer was in breach of his implied contractual duty of mutual trust and confidence, and the employee resigned (*General Bill Posting v Atkinson* [1909] AC 118, HL; and *Dairy Crest Ltd v Wise*, 24 September 1993, QBD).

The 'blue pencil' test

10.6

The general rule is that where a covenant is too wide, any attempt to enforce it in the courts will fail. But where it is possible to apply the 'blue pencil' test, eg by deleting parts, leaving the rest intact without the necessity of rewriting it, and the remaining part is separate and not part of a single covenant, it will be enforced (*Attwood v Lamont* [1920] 3 KB 571, CA). The severed parts must usually be of trivial importance, or merely be of a technical nature. They must not go to the main import or substance of the restraint. There has been a tendency in some cases, where justice demands it, for courts to ascertain the true intention of the parties and give effect to it, even though it involved some redrafting (*Mason v Provident Clothing & Supply Co Ltd* [1913] AC 724, HL; and *GFI Group Inc v Eaglestone* [1994] IRLR 119, QBD).

10.7

If a covenant is capable of being construed as giving a wider protection than is necessary or was intended, it will fail entirely. The 'blue pencil' cannot be applied (*Office Angels Ltd v Rainer-Thomas & Another* [1991] IRLR 214, CA). So where an employee covenanted not to engage in several different businesses, it was held not to be severable into parts that could be enforced and parts that could be ignored. To do so would require some of the terms to be rewritten. But where an outgoing partner covenanted not to engage in similar work or to compete with the partnership, it was held that the covenant was severable. The latter term was effective; the former was not (*Attwood v Lamont* [1920] 3 KB 571, CA; and *Ronbar Enterprises Ltd v Green* [1954] 2 AER 266, CA).

10.8

Sometimes the principle can act very harshly where the harm is likely to be great. An interior designer with five years' experience in the furniture business covenanted not to work in a similar job in the UK for 12 months after she left the company. 'Untold damage' could be done to the employer by disclosure of confidential pricing and certain other information if she joined a competitor. It was held to be an appropriate case to injunct her from doing so (*A & D Bedrooms Ltd v Michael & Hyphen Fitted Furniture Ltd*, 8 March 1983, CA).

10.9

Each case has to be considered on its own particular facts. Previous authorities are usually of little help in deciding what is 'reasonable'. They do not bind the judge (*Dairy Crest Ltd v Pigott* [1989] ICR 92, CA).

WHERE THE COVENANTOR IS VENDOR OR SHAREHOLDER

10.10

Where a business is acquired on terms that the former owners or shareholders (whatever the size of their holding or whether they are also employees) agree to a restriction on their future activities to protect the goodwill of the undertaking, different considerations apply (*Systems Reliability Holdings plc v Smith* [1990] IRLR 377, Ch D).

10.11

A wider restrictive covenant will be upheld provided:

- it is legitimate for the purchaser to protect those interests; and
- the protection is no more than necessary.

Generally, the parties are the best judges of what is reasonable between them, and what price, in particular, should be paid for the restrictions. The court will shy away from trying to apply any sort of doctrine of 'proportionality', eg to establish whether the price is too low for the restriction (*Allied Dunbar (Frank Weisinger) Ltd v Weisinger (Case B)* [1988] IRLR 60, Ch D).

APPLICATION OF THE PRINCIPLES

10.12

A solicitor's articled clerk agreed with his employers not to practise as a solicitor within seven miles of a stated place for an unlimited period. It was held that the covenant was reasonable. Any person who had served in such a position must have acquired information about the affairs and clients of the business. That puts him (or her) in a position of being able to impair gravely the goodwill of his employer's practice (*Fitch v Dewes* [1921] 2 AC 158, HL).

10.13

A distinction has to be drawn between two categories of employees. There are those who have direct dealings with clients and enhance the goodwill of the business through their skills and personalities. In such a case, the employer has an identifiable proprietary interest in that goodwill and has the right to protect it. And then there are employees who operate on a highly personalised basis and who have acquired a reputation for efficiency, integrity and trustworthiness. Those qualities attach themselves to the employee, not to the business. In the latter instance, the employer would have no proprietary interest that could be made the subject matter of the restrictive covenant (*Marion White v Francis* [1972] 1 WLR 1423, CA; and *Cantor Fitzgerald (UK) Ltd v Wallace & Others* [1992] IRLR 215, QBD). It has been held that although the goodwill of a business might vest to a large degree in its staff, that did not make them an asset which could not be poached by competitors. So where four former employees set up in competition, a restriction, which sought to prevent then soliciting former colleagues to join them, was not enforceable (*Hanover Insurance Brokers Ltd & Another v Schapiro & Others, The Times*, 17 November 1993, CA).

10.14

Careful wording of a restrictive covenant is vital. In one case, a term sought to prohibit a company's shareholders from carrying on in business in competition with that firm for two years after they ceased to hold any shares. It was held that a former shareholder could not be restrained from becoming an employee of a company in competition. The covenant would apply only where he (or she) was setting up or operating his own firm (*WAC Ltd & Others v Whitlock* [1990] IRLR 22, CS).

INDIRECT RESTRAINTS OF TRADE

10.15

The same general principles apply to indirect restraints. An employee was required by his employers to join a pension scheme, a rule of which provided that, should he become employed in any activity in competition with or detrimental to the employers' interests, he would forfeit his rights under the scheme. It was held that the doctrine of restraint extended to those affected by indirect means. On the facts, the prohibition was unreasonable and therefore void (*Bull v Pitney-Bowes Ltd* [1966] 3 AER 384, QBD).

10.16

Two companies manufacturing similar products were situated close to each other. They got together and agreed that neither of them would employ a person who had been employed by the other company within the previous five years. The restraint was held to be void as it extended to all employees whether they possessed confidential information or not. Furthermore, the restraint was not limited to the period when the companies were situated near to each other. Although an employee would not be a party to such an agreement, he (or she) could apply for a declaration that the agreement was void, on the grounds that it interfered with his right to seek and obtain employment (*Kores Manufacturing Co Ltd v Kolok Manufacturing Co Ltd* [1958] 2 AER 65, CA; and *Eastham v Newcastle United Football Club Ltd* [1963] 2 AER 139, Ch D).

EQUITABLE RESTRAINTS

While employment subsists

10.17

It is an implied term in every contract of employment that an employee must serve his (or her) employer faithfully. Often, there is an express term to that same effect in the individual contract of employment. Before resigning, an employee may not make out a list of clients, or memorise their names for use at a later date. Doing so would amount to a breach of the duty of fidelity and would expose the employee to an action for damages (*Wessex Dairies Ltd v Smith* [1935] 2 KB 80, CA). So long as the employer/employee relationship persists, a worker can be restrained from setting up his own firm or working for a competitor. If what he is doing is harmful to his employer's legitimate interests, it does not matter that it is carried out in the employee's spare time. But an order will generally not be made where the effect would be to force the employee to continue working for the employer as an alternative to starving (*Hivac Ltd v Park Royal Scientific Instruments Ltd* [1946] 1 Ch 169, CA).

10.18

The production manager of a newspaper resigned with just one month's notice instead of the 12 months required by his contract. He planned to start work with a competitor. The Court of Appeal held that the employers were entitled to an order restraining the manager from joining the other firm until the full 12 months had run their course. They had refused (as was their right) to accept the ineffective notice and were prepared to pay him his salary for the 12 months, although not requiring him to work (*Evening Standard Co Ltd v Henderson* [1987] ICR 588, CA).

10.19
But where no work was to be provided ('Garden Leave') and the employee joined or proposed to join a competitor during the notice period, it was held that the employer could rely on the employee's breach of obligation of good faith to restrain him. It had to be proved that the period was not excessive and that some harm would be sustained by the employer if his trade secrets or other confidential were relayed to the rival employer. The remedy of damages for breach of contract was always open to the employer (*Provident Financial Group plc & Another v Hayward* [1989] ICR 160, CA). Although an employee can be restrained during (and after) employment from disclosing confidential information, he (or she) will not be injuncted from informing statutory bodies or the Inland Revenue of any irregularities discovered in the course of his employment. It would be against public policy to do so and it matters not whether the employee had acted out of malice (*In re A Company* [1989] ICR 449, Ch D).

Note: Since the coming into force on 2 July 1999 of the Public Interest Disclosure Act 1999 (the 'Whistleblowers' Act'), workers who make so-called 'protected disclosures' (alleging lawbreaking or wrongdoing by their employers) have the legal right not to be dismissed, selected for redundancy, or subjected to any other detriment for doing so. For further particulars, please turn to Chapter 23).

After employment ends

10.20
Occasionally, because of an administrative error or otherwise, an employer will not have secured a covenant from an employee purportedly restricting that employee's post-employment activities. Even without such a covenant, an employee can nonetheless be restrained from setting up in competition (or using information) in appropriate circumstances. There is an implied term in every contract of employment that, after the employment ends, an employee will not use or disclose information about his (or her)

former employer's business activities that is of such a high degree of confidentiality as to amount to a trade secret. But an employee *is* entitled to approach freely and canvas his former employer's customers, suppliers, or other contacts, as their names and addresses do not amount to a 'trade secret' (*Faced Chicken Ltd v Fouler & Another* [1986] IC 297, CA).

HOW ENFORCEABLE?

10.21
These rights and duties are only enforceable in the ordinary courts. Usually proceedings take the form of an application for an interlocutory injunction, ie for an order for a temporary ban until the full trial takes place. This generally has the effect of disposing of the action, as there is usually a delay of a year or two before the trial takes place – by which time, the problem will probably have resolved itself.

10.22
In deciding whether to grant an injunction, the court applies the 'balance of convenience' test, eg:

- whether there is a serious issue to be decided;

- whether damages would provide an adequate remedy to the employer; and

- whether the employer would be in an adequate position to compensate the employee for any damages should he (or she) lose at the full trial (*American Cyanamid v Ethic Ltd* [1975] AC 396, HL);

but it does not decide upon the relative strength of the cases unless 'the action cannot be tried before the period of restraint has expired, or [it] has run a large part of its course, that the grant of the interlocutory injunction will effectively dispose of the action...' (per Balcombe LJ, *Lawrence David Ltd v Ashton* [1989] ICR 123, CA).

10.23
Where it is necessary to assess the likely outcome of proceedings it is nevertheless undesirable that there should be a prolonged preliminary battle, effectively proving the case at the interlocutory stage (*Lansing Linde Ltd v Kerr* [1991] ICR 428, CA).

Search orders

10.24

A useful means of obtaining the necessary evidence to establish whether there has been a breach of a restrictive covenant is to obtain a search order (previously known as an 'Anton Piller' order) from the court. A search order is defined in Rule 25.1(1)(h) of the Civil Procedure Rules as an order under Section 7 of the Civil Procedure Act 1997. Under such an order, the plaintiff (employer), accompanied by a supervising solicitor (unless the order allows otherwise), is permitted to enter the defendant's (employee's) premises to search for, copy and/or retain, any and all documents belonging to the employer's business. The employer may then apply to the court for an order preventing the employee (or former employee), or any third party, from using or benefiting from the information contained in those documents – provided they are of a sufficiently high degree of confidentiality as to amount to a trade secret (*PSM International plc & Another v Whitehouse & Another* [1992] IRLR 279, CA).

TIME LIMITS

10.25

Claims must be brought before the ordinary courts within six years, after which they become 'statute barred'.

11

Equal pay and sex discrimination

GENERAL INFORMATION

11.1

The Equal Pay Act 1970, as amended, together with the Sex Discrimination Acts 1975 and 1986, and the Equal Pay (Amendment) Regulations 1983, were enacted to render unlawful unreasonable and unjustified discrimination on grounds of sex or marital status. Behind the legislation lies Article 199 (formerly Article 199) of the Treaty of Rome, and Regulations and Directives made under that Treaty (see Chapter 1, paras 1.19 to 1.30). As a result, this subject has become increasingly complicated and uncertain. The draftsmen of UK legislation, in following EC Directives, are 'required to patch new Flemish broadcloth upon the fine weave of our domestic law... (doing) the minimum damage to either fabric' (per Waite J, *McGrath v Rank Leisure Ltd* [1985] ICR 527, EAT).

11.2

European Union law is drawn in very wide and sweeping terms, and the European Court of Justice (see Chapter 1, paras 1.66 to 1.68) has to decide whether there has been a transgression of the Treaty on the facts of each case. The result is that there is now evolving a 'case law' similar to our own common law (see Chapter 8). As European law takes precedence over our own, it is always necessary to consider not only our own statutes and case law, but also the Treaty and decisions made under it. But the relevant European legislation must be clear before an English statute should be construed to conform to it (*Shields v E Coombes (Holdings) Ltd* [1978] ITR 473, CA; and *Roberts v Tate & Lyle Food & Distribution Ltd* [1983] ICR 521, EAT). The European Court has emphasised that there is a duty laid on national courts not to follow domestic legislation where it conflicts with European law. It is not necessary to wait until the law has been changed by legislative or constitutional means (*Nimz v Freie und Hansestadt Hamburg* [1991] IRLR 222, ECJ).

11.3

An added complication is that European law does not draw a line between equal pay and sex discrimination quite as explicitly as is done by the two UK statutes. A claim under Article 141 of the Treaty of Rome may be brought directly, where there is nothing in UK legislation that covers the relief sought by a litigant. Further, a worker employed in an 'organ of the State' (public servants, local authority employees, etc can rely on certain Directives (see Chapter 1, paras 1.23 to 1.31) (*Secretary of State for Scotland & Greater Glasgow Health Board v Wright & Hannah* [1991] IRLR 187, EAT).

EQUAL PAY ACT 1970

11.4

So far as the Equal Pay and Sex Discrimination Acts are concerned, there is no overlapping of the rights and duties arising out of them. The distinction between them, which is very important when considering which Act applies in a particular case, is that the Equal Pay Act is concerned with instances where an employee:

- of one sex receives less favourable treatment than one of the opposite sex in respect of pay received under a contract with the same or an 'associated employer' (see Chapter 3, paras 3.110 to 3.112); or
- is treated less favourably than an employee of the opposite sex regarding a term in the contract of either. This would arise, for instance, where a man's contract entitled him to the benefit of a company car for his own use, whereas a woman's contract precluded such a right, or omitted any reference to such an entitlement;

always provided that

- they are performing 'like work' (or work of a broadly similar nature – the differences between them being of no practical importance) in relation to terms and conditions of employment; work of equal value; or work rated as equivalent under a 'job evaluation scheme'.

(*Source*: EPA 1970, s. 1(2).)

A 'job evaluation scheme' is a study undertaken to evaluate a job in terms of the demands made on a worker under various headings (for instance, effort, skill, decision) and to compare that job with others in an undertaking or group of undertakings (*Bromley & Others v H & J Quick Ltd* [1988] ICR 623, CA) (*Source*: EPA 1970, s. 1(5)). The scheme itself must be prepared in an analytical way and must exclude any unfavourable treatment of either sex, that is to say, it 'must be based on the same criteria for both men and women and so drawn up so as to exclude any discrimination on grounds of sex' (*Bromley & Others v H & J Quick Ltd* [1988] ICR 623, CA EEC Directive 75/117) (*Source*: EPA 1970, s. 2A(3)).

11.5
Under a job evaluation scheme, the values accorded to each element were converted into 'bands'. It was held that a tribunal was entitled to take the final position into account. It mattered not that the original values assigned to the two persons being compared under the scheme were different (*Springboard Sunderland Trust v Robson* [1992] ICR 554, EAT).

11.6
If no members of the opposite sex are employed on similar work, and/or no job evaluation study has been carried out, or if there is a non-discriminatory scheme in existence that does not show that the applicant's job has been rated as equal to a named comparator, the employee may apply to the tribunal for an independent expert – drawn from a panel of independent experts designated by the Advisory, Conciliation & Arbitration Service (ACAS) – to be appointed to carry out an evaluation study (*Pickstone & Others v Freemans plc* [1988] ICR 697, HL; and *Avon County Council v Foxall & Others* [1989] ICR 407, EAT) (*Source*: EPA 1970, s. 2A(1)(a)).

11.7
The procedure is quite elaborate. A tribunal follows a number of steps, deciding:

* whether there are 'no reasonable grounds for determining that' a woman's work is of equal value to that of the male comparator (or vice versa), eg Is it a hopeless case? If the claim is certain to fail, it will be dismissed at this point (*Leverton v Clywd County Council* [1989] ICR 33, HL). If not, and

- the employer raises the defence of 'genuine material difference', that defence will be considered at a preliminary hearing. If it succeeds, the case will stop (*Reed Packaging Ltd v Boozer & Another* [1988] ICR 391, EAT). If not,

- the tribunal must refer the claim to an independent expert for a report. After the expert has gone through several formalities, his (or her) report is filed in the tribunal.

- When accepted by the tribunal, the findings of fact set out in the report are binding on the parties, in the sense that no new evidence may be introduced to contradict them. It does not prevent the parties from making submissions on them (*Sheffield Metropolitan District Council v Siberry & Another* [1989] ICR 208, EAT).

- A full hearing will take place at which the parties may present their experts' reports. The recommendations made by an independent expert have no special status and are not binding. They will be considered by the tribunal that may accept or reject them (*Tennants Textile Colours Ltd v Todd* [1989] IRLR 3, CA (Northern Ireland); and *Aldridge v British Telecom Ltd* [1989] ICR 720, EAT).

It should be borne in mind that, as the law now stands, the burden of proof (see Chapter 2, paras 2.16 to 2.20) vests in the applicant throughout. An independent expert's report which is favourable to the employee does not shift the burden of proof on to the employers (*London Borough of Barking & Dagenham v Camara* [1988] ICR 865, EAT).

Note: When Council Directive 97/80/EEC of 15 December 1997, 'on the burden of proof in cases of discrimination based on sex' is imported into UK domestic legislation – as it must be by 22 July 2001 – the burden of proof in such cases will shift from employees to employers.

11.8
When preparing his (or her) report, an independent expert must consider all the information supplied, including any representations by affected parties. Each party is then entitled to comment on the report. The expert must summarise those comments and give his conclusions, but must act fairly and take no account of the difference of sex. He should follow an analytical approach, in the sense of

describing the process of dividing a physical or abstract whole into its constituent parts (*Bromley & Others v H & J Quick Ltd* [1988] ICR 623, CA). Each side is fully entitled to obtain its own expert's report and to present evidence to the tribunal. In the end, it will be for the tribunal to decide, in the light of all the evidence submitted, whether or not the employee's claim is substantiated.

11.9
Even if a person of the opposite sex is employed in the same capacity and place as the complainant and earns the same, the latter may nevertheless make a complaint that another worker of the opposite sex is performing work of equal value in another area of operations and is paid more. It matters not how the disparity arises, whether for historical reasons or otherwise (*Pickstone & Others v Freemans plc* [1988] ICR 697, HL) (*Source*: EPA 1970, s. 1(2)(C)).

European law

11.10
Article 141 of the Treaty of Rome provides that 'men and women should receive equal pay for equal work', pay being described as 'the ordinary basic... wage and any other consideration, whether in cash or in kind, which the worker receives, whether directly or indirectly, in respect of his employment... [and] pay for the same work at piece rates shall be calculated on the basis of the same unit of measurement [and]... that pay for work at the time rates shall be the same for the same job'.

The meaning is amplified by Directive 75/117/EEC 'on the approximation of the laws of the Member States relating to the application of the principle of equal pay for men and women', Article 1 of which states that the 'principle of equal pay' means, for the same work or for work to which equal value is attributed, the elimination of all discrimination on grounds of sex with regard to all aspects and conditions of remuneration. In particular, where a job classification system is used for determining pay, it must be based on the same criteria for both men and women and so drawn up as to exclude any discrimination on grounds of sex. The Directive's provisions relating to pay have been interpreted as including any consideration, whether in cash or kind, whether immediate or future, provided that the worker received it, albeit indirectly, in respect of his (or her) employment. The fact that certain benefits were paid after the end of the employment relationship did not prevent them from being 'pay' within the meaning of Article 141 (*David Neath v Hugh Steeper Ltd* [1944] IRLR 91, ECJ).

11.11

But where actuarial tables are used to determine an employer's contribution to a pension scheme then, although the result is that payments made in respect of women are higher (because they live longer), it is not a breach of Article 141. The criteria to be applied is whether the formula used to establish the pension entitlement is the same. But it matters not that women can get a bigger lump sum on a conversion from a periodic pension (in consequence of them normally living longer) (*David Neath v Hugh Steeper Ltd* [1944] IRLR 91, ECJ).

11.12

Many arguments turn on whether a difference in pay is justified, and the extent to which such extraneous matters such as market forces, 'red circling', business efficiency, union pressure, shift working, etc. provide a defence. The European Court of Justice (see Chapter 28, paras 28.41 to 28.43), in general, tends to take a more robust view, sweeping aside historical circumstances as providing a valid defence. Our own courts are more cautious, although they *will* intervene where there is a perpetuation of past discrimination, often unintentional. Where there is underlying discrimination, the effect of which can clearly be seen, they will generally ensure that there is a remedy (*Sun Alliance & London Insurance Ltd v Dudman* [1978] ICR 551, EAT).

11.13

Indirect discrimination affecting women's pay is an area that is likely to be a fertile ground upon which claims can be successfully brought. This is especially so if there is a considerable disparity between the earnings of men and women in industry. If there is a substantial difference in the pay of two groups of workers, one predominantly male and the other female, both doing work of equal value and where there is the same access to both jobs, that of itself is sufficient to establish a *prima facie* case of discrimination (*Enderby v Frenchay*

Health Authority & Another [1993] IRLR 591, ECJ). It has been held that where there is a difference of pay, it is irrelevant that it was brought about by historical events untainted by gender discrimination. The sole criterion to be applied is whether the differential is due to any material factors, eg matters such as length of service, or working unsociable hours. Where market forces have resulted in the difference, eg the higher pay is due to difficulties in recruiting skilled operatives, or a group of employees has agreed to flexibility or adaptability, then that is a valid defence (*Barber & Others v NCR (Manufacturing) Ltd* [1993] IRLR 95, EAT).

11.14

The European court has ruled that where, under the terms of a collective agreement, part-timers (predominantly women) receive substantially less than full-timers (mainly men) as a result of increments relating to weekly working hours, then that is discriminatory. Such an arrangement has to be justified objectively. There must be pay parity if there is no solid justification for the difference, (*Nimz v Freie und Hansestadt Hamburg* [1991] IRLR 222, ECJ).

Note: With the coming into force on 1 July 2000 of the Part-time Workers (Prevention of Less Favourable Treatment) Regulations 2000, implementing (a little tardily) Council Directive 97/81/EC of 15 December 1997 'concerning the Framework Agreement on part-time work concluded by UNICE, CEEP and the ETUC', part-time workers must not be treated less favourably than comparable full-time workers in the same establishment. In short, they must be paid the same hourly rates of pay (unless a lower hourly rate is justifiable on objective grounds); the same overtime premium payments; the same sick and maternity pay; equal access to their employer's pension scheme; the same opportunities for training; the same contractual holiday entitlements, contractual maternity and parental leave; and the same career breaks; and (if redundancy looms) be subjected to the same redundancy selection criteria as those of their full-time colleagues who are employed under the same types of contract.

11.15

A private severance payment for a woman, aged 61, was calculated, *inter alia*, by reference to the statutory retirement age. It was held to be discriminatory. A man in identical circumstances would have received more (*McKechnie v UBM Building Supplies (Southern) Ltd* [1991] ICR 710, EAT).

The effect of EU law

11.16

The matter is complicated for the reasons explained in Chapter 1, paras 1.19 to 1.30. As the relevant European legislation is particularly concerned with discrimination in relation to both pay and conditions, it is always necessary to consider that law in respect of any employment problem. The European Court has held that Article 141 of the Treaty of Rome may be directly relied upon by any employee (*Defrenne v Sabena* [1976] ICR 549, ECJ). The prohibition on discrimination under that Article applies where a person of one sex does work of greater value than that undertaken by a person of the opposite sex, but is paid less. The work has to be carried on in the same establishment or service, and it may be either in the public or private sector (*Murphy & Others v Bord Telecom Eirann* [1988] ICR 445, ECJ). It follows that if women are doing work of greater value to that done by men, but are paid the same, there would still be discrimination. There would have to be some difference to reflect the higher value of their work. It would seem that the extent of the differential, could be subject to the doctrine of proportionality under European law (*Enderby v Frenchay Health Authority & Another* [1993] IRLR 591, ECJ).

11.17

Where a job classification system is used, it is permissible to take into account (objectively) the degree of strength or physical hardship required by a job, although this might adversely affect women as a whole. But the scheme, taken in the round, must be evenly balanced by taking into account all aptitudes that normally favour women as well, and so be fair to both sexes (*Rummler v Dato-Druck GmbH* [1987] ICR 774, ECJ).

11.18

Different terms, some more favourable and some less, applied to a female canteen worker, whose work had been adjudged to be of equal value to that of a male painter, a thermal engineer and a joiner. It was held that she could rely on UK domestic legislation giving her greater rights than under Article 141 of the Treaty of Rome. Each of the 'terms' applicable to one sex (within the meaning of the 1970 Equal Pay Act) had to be compared with similar terms applicable to the opposite sex. It mattered not that the value of the complete package was the same in each case (*Hayward v Cammell Laird Shipbuilders Ltd* [1988] ICR 464, HL). But it would be open to an employer to argue that the better 'perks' enjoyed by a woman constituted a genuine material factor justifying a pay differential. But the defence must be raised at the outset of the proceedings (*Leverton v Clwyd CC* [1989] ICR 33, HL) (*Source*: EPA 1970, s. 1(3))

Essence of the Equal Pay Act 1970

11.19
The basic concept of the 1970 Act is that it requires that every term in a woman's (or man's) contract of employment must not be less favourable than that in a man's (or woman's) contract. This is achieved by importing 'an equality clause' into every contract of employment. Any term in a contract of employment that is inconsistent with that implied 'equality clause' has no effect and any favourable term that is omitted will be deemed to be included (*Source*: EPA 1970, s. 1(1))

11.20
In deciding whether any term is less favourable, a comparison must be made with a member of the opposite sex who is employed by the same or any 'associated employer' (as defined in Chapter 3, paras 3.108 to 3.110). It does not matter that the two employees... who are being compared, work on the same premises or even in different parts of the country. But where a woman seeks to compare her pay with a male worker who works at different premises, the 1970 Act provides that it is necessary for 'common terms and conditions of employment [to be] observed either generally or for employees of the relevant classes' (*Source*: EPA 1970, s 1(6)). The effect of the provision is to remove from consideration any special local conditions (eg a higher cost of living) or those that relate to geographical circumstances. What needs to be done is to pose the question: 'If a man was employed on the female's premises, doing work of equal value, would he be paid the same as the female, or the same as the comparator at the other premises?' (*British Coal Corporation v Smith & Others* [1994] IRLR 342, CA).

11.21
But where the two employees under comparison work at different establishments, three tests have to be applied:

- the applicant and her comparator must be typical of their groups and have no personal factors (such as 'red circling' or 'marking time');

- common terms and conditions must be observed within each establishment;

- there must be no difference caused by geographical influences where the derivation or historic basis for any variations results in different employment regimes at each place (*British Coal Corporation v Smith & Others* [1993] ICR 529, EAT).

(*Source*: EPA 1970, s. 1(2)(c) & (6).)

11.22

A qualified nursery nurse sought to compare her worth with that of 11 male comparators doing work ranging from caretakers to clerks. They were employed at other establishments for the same employer, but under different contractual terms. It was held that she could bring herself within the section. She and her comparators were bound by the same 'Purple Book' terms of employment that set out the relevant scales (*Leverton v Clwyd County Council* [1989] ICR 33, HL). But the claim was defeated because the difference in the annual pay was due to a 'genuine material factor', namely, she worked for fewer hours each week and had longer holidays. In deciding whether a woman is entitled to equal pay with a man at another establishment, it is necessary to prove that, if a man were employed at her place of employment, he would be on the same terms and conditions as the man at the other premises, and that her work is of equal value (*British Coal Corporation v Smith & Others* [1994] IRLR 342, CA).

11.23

Under European Community law, a comparison may be made not only with a fellow employee of the opposite sex employed in the same undertaking, but also with a predecessor in the same job. The tribunal will have to take into account the time that had elapsed between the resignation (or dismissal) of the one and the appointment or recruitment of the other, and whether there had been any change in economic circumstances during that period (*McCarthys v Smith (No 2)* [1980] ICR 672, CA).

11.24

In order to come within the provisions of the 1970 Act, it is not necessary to show that the employer intended to discriminate, merely that the effect was discriminatory. The equality clause 'operates to counteract all discrimination whether direct or indirect... it looks at the effect... not whether they are expressed in overtly discriminatory words or with any particular intention' (per Browne-Wilkinson J, *Jenkins v Kingsgate Ltd* [1981] ICR 715, EAT).

11.25

An 'indirect' discriminatory effect concerning pay arose where a provision in a collective agreement had the effect of favouring men. They were mainly full-time workers as opposed to women who were mostly part-time. Only full-time workers were entitled to a severance payment on retirement. The European Court ruled that the provision had to be justified objectively on grounds other than sex (*Kowalska v Freie und Hansestadt Hamburg* [1992] ICR 29, ECJ). The European Court has further ruled that, as a party can rely on Article 141 directly, national legislation will not provide protection for any breach, where a provision has a more adverse effect against women (or men). It would have to be proved that the requirement was justified on objective grounds unrelated to sex (*Barber v Guardian Royal Exchange Assurance Group* [1990] ICR 616, ECJ). Statistical evidence that *prima facie* indicates that there is discrimination in pay between men and women in an organisation generally (and not just between a particular man or woman) will satisfy the burden of proof. The European Court has ruled that it is for the employer to show that the disparity is attributable to factors such as better job performance, and not to irrelevant factors such as the level of training received by an employee which has little relevance to the employee's ability to do the job in question (*Handels-og Kontorfunktionaerernes Forbund i Danmark v Dansk Arbejdsgiverforening* [1992] ICR 332, ECJ).

11.26

The mere fact that an employer is complying with a statutory regulation and has no power to depart from it, is not enough of itself to raise a defence where a requirement in that regulation is in breach of the Community law. The provisions and those that have come about as a result of consultations or agreements between various interested parties must have been screened to eliminate discrimination (*R v Secretary of State for Social Services & Others ex parte Clarke & Others* [1988] IRLR 22, QBD).

Defence of 'genuine material difference'

11.27
Once an employee has established a *prima facie* case of discrimination concerning pay or any other term in the contract, the employer can only escape liability if he can prove that the variation is due to a genuine material factor, which is not a difference of sex (*Rainey v Greater Glasgow Health Board* [1987] ICR 129, HL) (*Source*: EPA 1970, s. 1(3)). In an ordinary equal pay claim, the employer must prove that the genuine material difference applies, but in an equal value allegation, he need only show that it may be a defence (*McGregor v GMBATU* [1987] ICR 505, EAT). It may be shown, for instance, that the higher pay reflects longer service, which applies equally to both sexes and that it is not affected by past discrimination. It could be that the employee's pay has been 'red circled' for a legitimate reason (unrelated to sex). It would have to be shown that the lower salary would be paid to any successor employee, irrespective of sex.

11.28
Two women did work of equal value to that of a male comparator, but were paid less. All worked unsociable hours, with the women working the 'twilight' shift and the men on a system of rotating shifts. The Court of Appeal held that the defence of 'genuine material difference' succeeded. The men were paid extra for the additional inconvenience of working rotating shifts (*Calder & Another v Rowntree Mackintosh Confectionery Ltd* [1993] ICR 811, CA). Market forces, provided they are 'gender neutral', can also provide a 'material difference' defence. This was successfully raised where dinner ladies had established equal pay with some male council employees. When the work went out to competitive tender, it was necessary to reduce their pay in order to be competitive. Their claims for equal pay were rejected. If, on the other hand, a union were to negotiate a better deal for male employees at one establishment, who were performing work of equal value to women working at another, the defence would be likely to fail (*British Coal Corporation v Smith & Others* [1994] IRLR 342, CA; and *North Yorkshire CC v Ratcliffe & Others*, *The Times*, 11 May 1994, CA).

11.29

A tribunal is entitled to look beyond the 'personal equation'. It may consider economic factors connected with the efficient running of the business, provided they are objectively justified. The European Court of Justice has put it this way. It is up to the employer to show that 'the means chosen for achieving that objective correspond to a real need on the part of the undertaking, [and] are appropriate with a view to achieving the objective in question and are necessary to that end' (*Rainey v Greater Glasgow Health Board* [1987] ICR 129, HL; and *Bilka-Kaufhaus GmbH v Weber von Hartz* [1987] ICR 110, ECJ). This defence was not open to an employer who, having set salary levels which he later discovered were discriminatory, continued to pay at those rates. He did so without any justification apart from being advised to do so. It seems that if the comparator occupies a key position and it would cause immense harm should he leave, the employer could have relied on that fact (*McPherson v Rathgael Centre and Northern Ireland Office* [1991] IRLR 206, CA (Northern Ireland)). But where the fixed rates of pay within an organisation were not discriminatory, but an administrative error resulted in a male comparator being paid more than a female employee, that oversight was held not to be actionable. It was not gender-tainted (*Yorkshire Blood Transfusion Service v Plaskitt*, *The Times*, 17 August 1993, EAT).

To whom does equal pay legislation apply?

11.30

The 1970 Act applies to any worker, whether an employee or one who works under a contract to execute personally any service or labour (full or part-time), including serving members of the naval, military or air forces of the Crown, those serving a Minister of the Crown or employed in a government department (or in statutory bodies) and office holders (regardless of age or length of service). However, an equality clause does not operate in relation to terms:

- affected by compliance with any legislation regulating the employment of women; or

- affording special treatment to women in connection with pregnancy or childbirth.

Nor does it operate in relation to terms relating to a person's membership of (or rights under) an occupational pension scheme, being terms in relation to which (by reason only of any provision made by or under section 62 or 64 of the Pensions Act 1995) an equal treatment rule would not operate if the terms were included in the scheme.

(*Source*: EPA 1970, ss 1 & 6; SDA 1975, ss 7, 8 & 10.)

11.31

Article 141 of the Treaty of Rome has been held by the European Court of Justice to cover benefits made under a contractual scheme supplementing the State pension. The exclusion of part-timers from such benefits, which mostly affected women, was indirectly discriminatory, and breached the Article. To escape liability it was necessary to show that the scheme was based on objectively justified factors unrelated to any discrimination on the grounds of sex (*Bilka-Kaufhaus GmbH v Weber von Hartz* [1987] ICR 110, ECJ). The European Court of Justice has also held that benefits, including a (private) pension and redundancy pay, received by a prematurely dismissed man, were 'pay' within the meaning of Article 141. If the value of those benefits depended on different ages for men and women, that would be discriminatory. It has also been decreed that the German equivalent of statutory sick pay is 'pay' within the meaning of the Article (*Barber v Guardian Royal Exchange Assurance Group* [1990] ICR 616, ECJ; and *Rinner-Kuhn v FWW Spezial-Gebaudereinigung* [1989] IRLR 493, ECJ).

11.32

An employer contracted out a private occupational scheme under which a person's statutory old age pension was deducted from the sum. The rate was otherwise the same for each sex. It was held not to be discriminatory against women. The situations were not identical. Article 141 cannot be interpreted to give women a twofold benefit. That would be discriminatory against men (*Roberts v Birds Eye Walls Ltd* [1994] IRLR 29, ECJ).

CASE LAW

Complaints upheld

11.33
A waitress did identical work to that carried out by a waiter. He was paid more than her because he had the job title of 'banqueting supervisor'.

Held: The waitress was entitled to equal pay because the 'equality clause' applied. She did essentially the same work as the male comparator in spite of his having a different job title (*Sorbie v Trust House Forte Hotels Ltd* [1977] ITR 85, EAT).

11.34
A female's job as a catering supervisor was classed as Grade 2 under a job evaluation study. A man's job as a vending supervisor was also classed as Grade 2. Management and unions agreed the boundaries of the grades, but there were substantial objections from the staff to the scheme.

Held: As the job evaluation scheme had been accepted by both sides, although not implemented, her job had been rated as equivalent to the man's. Consequently she was entitled to a declaration in her favour (*Arnold v Beecham Group Ltd* [1982] ICR 744, EAT).

Complaints dismissed

11.35
A woman sought equality with a man who did the same clerking job as she did, although he was paid more. The man's employers showed that he had been transferred to lighter duties because of his age and deteriorating health. They had decided not to cut his pay or benefits.

Held: The reason was due to a material difference. The protection of the man's income and position had nothing to do with sex (*Methven v Cow Industrial Ltd* [1980] ICR 463, CA).

11.36
A female canteen worker sought equality with a male worker. He was required to work shifts (for which he received extra pay) and

was responsible for stock control and handling money. He was also largely unsupervised.

Held: The man, who received a productivity payment denied to the female canteen worker, was not employed on 'like work' for the purposes of the Equal Pay Act (*Capper Pass Ltd v Allan* [1980] ICR 194, EAT).

SEX DISCRIMINATION ACT 1975

11.37
There are two parallel provisions affecting the issue of sex discrimination in employment. These are the law as laid down in EC Directives, and UK domestic legislation (*Garland v British Rail Engineering Ltd* [1982] ICR 434, HL). This can lead to complications. It is always necessary to look at the provisions of European legislation where there is a doubt whether UK law covers the situation or is overridden by European law (*Pickstone & Others v Freemans plc* [1987] ICR 867, CA – upheld by HL on different grounds). What may *not* be done is to distort the wording of the Sex Discrimination Act so as to have it accord with European law. So where the European Court of Justice ruled in an indirect discrimination case that 'attention should be directed less to the existence of a requirement... and more to the discriminatory result', it was held that it was still necessary to apply the express provision of a 'requirement or condition' in the definition of indirect discrimination in the 1975 Act (*Bhudi & Others v IMI Refiners Ltd* [1994] ICR 307, EAT).

European law

11.38
Article 2(1) of Council Directive 76/207/EEC 'on the implementation of the principle of equal treatment for men and women as regards access to employment, vocational training and promotion, and working conditions' states that '... the principle of equal treatment shall mean that there shall be no discrimination whatsoever on the grounds of sex either directly or indirectly by reference in particular to marital or family status'. This is amplified by Article 5: 'Application of the principle of equal treatment with regard to working conditions,

including the conditions governing dismissal, means that men and women shall be guaranteed the same conditions without discrimination on the grounds of sex'. Article 3(1) adds that the 'application of the principle of equal treatment means that there shall be no discrimination whatsoever on grounds of sex in the conditions, including selection criteria, for access to all jobs or posts...'.

11.39
Where a Directive requires a Member State to import the legislation into its domestic legislation, the Directive itself cannot be directly relied upon by an employee in the private sector. Only those employed in organs (or emanations) of the State can sue on it (see Chapter 1, paras 1.23 to 1.26) (*Burton v BRB* [1982] 3 WLR 387, ECJ).

11.40
Where a measure adversely affects one sex (mostly women) compared to the opposite sex (mostly men) this would amount to indirect discrimination. But it would not be a violation of European law if it was shown:

- that the scheme was intended to achieve an appropriate policy;

- the means adopted were likely to achieve that objective; and

- the discriminatory effect was unavoidable.

(*Commission of the European Community v Kingdom of Belgium* [1993] IRLR 393, ECJ.)

11.41
It is not permissible to duplicate claims. An employee claimed discrimination under the Sex Discrimination Act 1986 but the case failed on its merits. It was held that it was not possible to launch further proceedings relying on the same facts but based on Equal Treatment Directive No 76/207 (*Blaik v Post Office* [1994] IRLR 280, EAT).

Part-time employees

11.42
It is acknowledged that many more women than men work part-time. If there is any resultant discriminatory effect, that effect must

be justified by factors other than a difference of sex. So when a group of part-time employees accompanied their full-time colleagues on a series of day-long training course organised by their employer, they were paid only their standard rate of pay in spite of having put in longer hours than usual. One of their number complained of unlawful discrimination. The European Court of Justice held that her allegation was well founded. The employers could only escape liability if it could be shown that the difference between the amount paid to her and that received by the full-timers was justifiable on grounds other than sex (*Arbeiterwohlfahrt der Stadt Berlin e v Botel* [1992] IRLR 423, ECJ).

11.43

There was a similar ruling in *Gerster v Freistaat Bayern*, 2 October 1997, ECJ. The Bavarian State Civil Service operated a rule that required part-time employees to complete a longer period of service than their full-time colleagues before they could be considered for promotion. Given that 87 per cent of part-timers in the German Civil Service were women, the ECJ observed that the 'longer service' rule amounted to indirect discrimination unless it could be justified on grounds unrelated to sex. The Civil Service argued that, by definition, it would take longer for part-timers to acquire the skills and capabilities needed to qualify them for promotion. While accepting that this might be so, the ECJ held that unless a national court identified a special correlation between working hours, length of service and the acquisition of specified skills, a rule such as that imposed by the Bavarian State Civil Service would be in breach of the Equal Treatment Directive (76/207/EEC).

TYPES OF DISCRIMINATION

11.44

The Sex Discrimination Act 1975 (as amended) identifies three types of discrimination. These are: 'direct discrimination', 'indirect discrimination' and 'victimisation'. The 1975 Act, with certain exceptions, applies equally to men and women. It not only forbids discrimination on grounds of sex or gender reassignment (see *Note* below) but discrimination also against married persons in the employment field (see paras 11.64 to 11.68 below). The 1975 Act is, of course, primarily directed towards the protection of women (*Source*: SDA 1975, ss 1, 2, 3 & 4).

Note: The Sex Discrimination (Gender Reassignment) Regulations 1999 (SI 1999/1102), which came into force on 1 May 1999, extended the Sex Discrimination Act 1975 to cover discrimination on grounds of gender reassignment in employment and vocational training. Accordingly, it is nowadays unlawful for an employer to treat an employee (or job applicant) less favourably than he (or she) would treat other employees on the ground that the person in question intends to undergo, is undergoing or has undergone gender reassignment. It is similarly unlawful to deny such a person access to contractual sickness or injury benefits if absent from work while undergoing gender reassignment. The term 'gender reassignment' means a process that is undertaken under medical supervision for the purpose of reassigning a person's sex by changing physiological or other characteristics of sex, and includes any part of such a process.

Direct discrimination

11.45
Unlawful direct discrimination occurs when an employer or would-be employer treats a woman (or man) less favourably on the ground of her (or his) sex – by denying that person access to employment, promotion, transfer or opportunities for training, or by dismissing or selecting that person for redundancy simply because she is a woman (or he is a man). Direct discrimination can be established by what is said or can be inferred from all the circumstances (*Source*: SDA 1975, s. 1(1)(a)). In determining whether there is direct discrimination, eg whether there is, in truth, any difference in the treatment of a woman compared to that of a man, it may be necessary in certain cases to discover the underlying reason for such treatment. An unmarried matron at a girl's school became pregnant and was dismissed because she declined either to marry the putative father or to leave voluntarily. It was held that the matron's subsequent dismissal did not amount to unlawful discrimination. It was the continuing and potentially damaging evidence of extramarital activity that was the reason for her dismissal. The same treatment would have been accorded whatever the sex of the 'offender' (*Berrisford v Woodward Schools (Midland Division) Ltd* [1991] ICR 564, EAT).

As was pointed out earlier, it is also directly discriminatory and, therefore, unlawful to discriminate against a person for no other reason than that the person in question (employee or job applicant) intends to undergo, is undergoing or has undergone gender reassignment (*ibid* s. 2A).

11.46

In deciding how an employer would treat a person of the opposite sex in identical circumstances, in the absence of direct evidence of past behaviour, a tribunal has to deal with a hypothetical situation. It has to draw inferences from the primary facts and reach a decision based on the balance of probabilities – bearing in mind that (for the time being at least – see *Note* below), the burden of proof in sex discrimination cases rest squarely on the shoulders of the applicant employee. A comparison may not normally be made between the treatment respectively accorded to a pregnant woman and a sick man, except, perhaps, for very short-term employment (*Webb v EMO Air Cargo (UK) Ltd* [1993] ICR, HL 1994, (1994) IRLR 482, ECJ).

Note: When Council Directive 97/80/EEC of 15 December 1997, 'on the burden of proof in cases of discrimination based on sex' is imported into UK domestic legislation – as it must be by 22 July 2001 – the burden of proof in such cases will shift from employees to employers.

11.47

A tribunal did not believe an employer who claimed that he was unaware that an employee was pregnant when he dismissed her. It was held that the tribunal was entitled to assume that the employer would have treated a male employee more favourably in similar circumstances, despite his protestations that he would have treated both equally (*Leeds Private Hospital Ltd v Parkin* [1992] ICR 571, EAT). There is a wide, grey dividing line between what is conceived to be the hypothetical treatment of the other sex. The mere fact that a woman dislikes an offensive display of female pictures in the workplace may not be enough in itself. A tribunal has to apply the norms of society at large and decide whether the woman has received less favourable treatment (*Stewart v Cleveland Guest (Engineering) Ltd, The Times*, 6 July 1994, EAT).

Indirect discrimination

11.48

Indirect discrimination occurs where the same requirement or condition is applied to both sexes, but:

- one sex is less likely to be able to comply with that requirement or condition than the other;

- it is not justified irrespective of sex;

- that it is a detriment to the person complaining because she (or he) cannot comply with it.

(*Source*: SDA 1975, s. 1(1)(b).)

See also Chapter 12, paras 12.9 to 12.13, for the correlation with racial discrimination.

11.49

The distinction between direct and indirect discrimination can sometimes be difficult to discern. The test for the former propounded by Lord Goff in *James v Eastleigh Borough Council* [1990] ICR 554, HL is: '... [W]ould the complainant have received the same treatment from the [employer] but for his or her sex'; for example, where there is not necessarily an intention to discriminate but that is the effect of the action, or inaction, taken or not taken, by an employer. But there can be indirect discrimination which does not offend against the law because, for instance, it is justified (*R v Birmingham City Council ex parte Equal Opportunities Commission* [1989] IRLR 173, HL).

11.50

It would seem that where a condition or requirement is imposed with the express intention of, say, excluding women from a job, then that would be direct discrimination. The defence of justification could not then be put forward. Furthermore, in both types of discrimination, like must be compared with like, where it is appropriate. A single woman's position must be compared with that of a single man or a group of women (of which an employee forms part) with a similar group of men (*Source*: EPA 1970, s. 5(3)). This provision may not be relied upon where an employer fears that the consequence of not taking discriminatory action might be very serious, eg the possibility of young women being sexually harassed. That there would be little risk were women to have contact with boys, was not a legitimate comparison (*Bain v Bowles & Others* [1991] IRLR 356, CA).

Ingredients of indirect discrimination

11.51

If a job specification contains a requirement or condition that can be complied with by most men, but not so by most women, it will be for the employer to justify that requirement or condition on grounds that have nothing to do with sex. For example, it is unlikely that as many women as men could comply with a requirement that they be at least 1.75 metres tall, or that they be able to lift and carry a sack weighing 50 kilograms or more. If lifting and carrying heavy weights is a routine feature of the job in question, well and good. But if it is only an occasional feature, an employer would have some difficulty in persuading an employment tribunal that his automatic exclusion of women from such work was justifiable.

11.52

In determining whether there is indirect discrimination it is necessary to establish the 'pool' from which the comparison is to be made. Generally the 'pool' must consist of members of both sexes who have the necessary qualifications and/or experience. It is permissible to restrict the pool to those with specialist qualifications or skills essential for the job in question (*Jones v University of Manchester* [1993] IRLR 218, CA). The imposition of a condition or requirement would be discriminatory if it is responsible for causing a considerable disparity in the proportions between the sexes. It is the proportion of the two sexes compared with each other that must be taken into account. So if 15 per cent of women only can comply with a particular job specification compared to, say, 40 per cent of men, the women have a far less chance of securing the job. An employer could escape liability for an apparently discriminatory requirement (eg all candidates must be at least 1.65 metres tall) if he could prove that it was justified (*Pearse v City of Bradford Metropolitan Council* [1988] IRLR 379, EAT; and *McCausland v Dungannon DC* [1993] IRLR 583, CA (Northern Ireland)).

11.53

Like must be compared with like. A school required its domestic staff (mostly women) to retire at 60. Gardeners and maintenance staff, on the other hand (mostly men) were permitted to stay on until 65. It was held that the employers had not discriminated, either directly or indirectly, against a female cleaner who was compulsorily retired at 60. Her position could not be compared to that of a gardener. In any event, the gardeners were kept on until 65 because of the difficulty in replacing them (*Bullock v Alice Ottley School* [1993] ICR 138, CA).

11.54

An employer seeking to rely on the defence of justification is entitled to show that there are 'objectively justified grounds which are other than economic, such as administrative efficiency, in a organisation which is not engaged in commerce or business' (per Lord Keith in *Rainey v Greater Glasgow Health Board* [1987] ICR 129, HL). There must be a real need for the measures adopted and they must be both appropriate and necessary. It has been held that, if the method of carrying out a scheme allows for the most economic and efficient use of available resources, being targeted at those most in need within a priority group, then although the effect might be discriminatory, this would be 'justifiable' (*Bilka-Kaufhaus GmbH v Weber von Hertz* [1987] ICR 110, ECJ; and *Cobb & Others v Secretary of State for Employment & Another* [1989] ICR 506, EAT).

11.55

A female teacher was required under her contract to coach badminton after school hours. When she adopted a child she was unable to continue with this duty, and her pay was reduced accordingly. Her complaint of unlawful sex discrimination failed because her employers established that the requirement was objectively justifiable when the discriminatory effect of the duty was balanced against their reasonable needs *Briggs v North Eastern Education & Library Board* [1990] IRLR 181, CA (Northern Ireland)) (*Source*: SDA 1975 s. 1(1)(b)(iii)).

11.56

What is *not* permissible is to take a decision based on wider social issues, however commendable or reasonable they may be. Only those necessary for the business of the employer are protected. A Member State is entitled to make legislative provisions that have a discriminatory effect on one sex, where the social and economic policies behind them justify such a course (*Greater Manchester Police Authority v Lea* [1990] IRLR 372, EAT; and *R v Secretary of State for*

Employment, ex parte Equal Opportunities Commission & Another [1992] ICR 341, Div Ct).

11.57

'Detriment' is a very wide term and can encompass such acts as a supervisor subjecting an employee to discriminatory abuse if such abuse puts the person abused 'at a disadvantage'. Generally it is limited to matters about which a reasonable employee could justifiably complain. An employer should have regard to the feelings of an employee whom he knows to be particularly sensitive (*Ministry of Defence v Jeremiah* [1980] ICR 13, CA; and *Wileman v Minilec Engineering Ltd* [1988] IRLR 144, EAT). What a person cannot do, in seeking to prove that he (or she) has suffered 'a detriment', is to try to obtain enhanced rights where they are not available to anyone of either sex in his grade. A claim that the refusal to provide them is discriminatory, because of his personal circumstances, will fail (*Clymo v Wandsworth London Borough* [1989] ICR 250, EAT).

Pregnancy and childbirth

11.58

It is now established that a pregnant woman in long-term employment who is absent from work on maternity leave may *not* be compared with a hypothetical man absent from work because of ill health. As the European Court put it: 'The protection afforded by Community law to a woman during pregnancy and after childbirth could not be dependent on whether her presence at work during maternity was essential to the proper functioning of the undertaking in which she was employed' (*Webb v EMO Air Cargo (UK)* [1994] IRLR 482, ECJ). The European Court of Justice has also ruled that there would be a breach of the principle of equality of treatment under the Equal Treatment Directive if a female was refused employment on economic grounds because of her pregnancy. That there was no male candidate for the job was irrelevant. The main reason for the decision not to employ her related to a factor that applied exclusively to women (eg pregnancy). Reliance on that fact was direct discrimination (*Dekker v Stichting Vormingscentrum voor Jong Volwassenen Plus* [1992] ICR 325, ECJ). The logic behind the decision is that men and women are equally liable to become ill, but women have the additional impediment of being unable to do their jobs through pregnancy. It would therefore be unfair to compare them with the hypothetical 'sick' man. Special protection has to be given so that they are not put at a disadvantage by reason of their condition. The ruling would probably not apply if an employer were to refuse to employ a heavily pregnant women to replace a woman absent from work on maternity leave if she too would be absent on maternity leave within weeks of taking up her temporary appointment (*Habermann-Beltermann v Arbriterwohlfahrt, Bezirksverband Ndb/Opfer* [1994] IRLR 364, ECJ; and *Webb v EMO Air Cargo (UK)* [1994] IRLR 482, ECJ).

11.59
A discretion is left to Member States as to the measures to be adopted to ensure the protection of women in connection with pregnancy and maternity to offset the disadvantages that women suffer in employment compared to men (*Habermann-Beltermann v Arbriterwohlfahrt, Bezirksverband Ndb/Opf er* [1994] IRLR 364, ECJ; *Webb v EMO Air Cargo (UK)* [1994] IRLR 482, ECJ; and *Hoffmann v Barmer Ersatzkasse* [1985] ICR 731, ECJ).

11.60
The European Court of Justice has also ruled that it was not discriminatory to dismiss a female who, having returned to work after maternity leave, was repeatedly absent through sickness, the origin of which lay in the childbirth. It was proved that the employers would have dealt in the same way with men who were similarly absent from work through sickness (*Handels-og Kontorfunktionaerernes Forbund i Danmark v Dansk Arbeijdsgiverforening* [1992] ICR 332, ECJ).

11.61
In *Brown v Rentokil* (Case C-394/96), the ECJ held that the dismissal of a *pregnant* woman – whose pregnancy-related illness incapacitated her for work for more than 26 weeks – was unlawful discrimination, notwithstanding a term in her contract of employment that stated that *any* employee absent from work because of sickness for more than 26 weeks, would be dismissed. Pregnancy, said the Court, was not comparable to a pathological condition. But it *was* a period during which there could arise 'disorders and complications' that were a specific feature of pregnancy. These could cause incapacity

for work. So the dismissal of a *pregnant* employee due to such incapacity must be regarded as essentially based on the fact of her pregnancy and would, therefore, be unlawful direct discrimination on the grounds of sex. Had the woman been incapacitated for work *after* her maternity leave (for reasons connected with her having been pregnant or given birth), the fairness or otherwise of her dismissal would be determined by the general rules applicable to a dismissal on the grounds of illness or injury – so long as 'female and male workers' absences caused by incapacity for work were treated in the same way. It they were, there was no discrimination'.

Sexual orientation

11.62
In the well-publicised case of *Grant v South West Trains Limited* [1998] IRLR 206, brought under Article 141 (formerly Article 119) of the Treaty of Rome ('equal pay for equal work'), the ECJ held that discrimination on grounds of sexual orientation is not unlawful discrimination on grounds of sex. However, with the coming into force on 2 October 2000 of the Human Rights Act 1998, that position will be increasingly untenable (see Chapter 26). Furthermore, under Council Directive 2000/78/EC of 27 November 2000, the Member States have until 2 December 2003 within which to introduce and implement domestic legislation outlawing discrimination on grounds *inter alia* of sexual orientation.

Victimisation

11.63
Discrimination can also occur by way of victimisation. This arises where an employee is treated less favourably for bringing or threatening to bring proceedings in respect of an alleged infringement of his (or her) rights under the 1975 Act, or the Equal Pay Act 1970, or sections 62 to 65 of the Pensions Act 1995 ('equal treatment rule' in occupational pensions schemes). This does not apply where the allegations are false and not made in good faith. Nor does it apply where there were other genuine factors that caused the person to treat the other less favourably, eg he was guilty of misconduct (*Source*: SDA 1975 s. 4).

Discrimination against married persons

11.64
An employer discriminates against a married person of either sex:

(a) if he treats that person less favourably than he would do an unmarried person; or

(b) if he applies to that person a requirement or condition that he applies or would apply equally to an unmarried person but the proportion of married persons who can comply with that requirement is considerably smaller than the proportion of unmarried persons of the same sex who *can* comply with it; and

(c) which he cannot show to be justifiable irrespective of the marital status of the person to whom it is applied; and

(d) which is to that person's detriment because he (or she) cannot comply with it.

Note that the comparison is such cases must be made between persons of the same sex, that is to say between single women and married women, and single men and married men. It is not possible to cross the sexual divide by making a comparison between a married man and a single woman or a married woman and a single man (*Source*: SDA 1975, ss 3 & 5).

11.65
In deciding whether there is discrimination, a distinction has to be drawn between whether the decision was taken because the person was married or whether somebody else was a better candidate for a job, or for promotion, or whatever the complaint is. In the case of a married woman, no consideration must be given to the fact that she has small children or might become pregnant and leave work to have children.

11.66
A married woman with several young children applied for a job as a waitress, but was rejected because the proprietor thought there was a strong risk that she might want to take too much time off work to attend to their needs. Her children might fall ill or there might be

difficulty with babysitters. Her dismissal on those grounds was held to constitute unlawful discrimination under the 1975 Act. The employer was equating this one person with all women with young children. He should have reached a decision bases on the woman's previous employment record. Had he made enquiries of former employers to establish whether they had found her to be unreliable? (*Hurley v Mustoe* [1981] ICR 490, EAT).

11.67
Part-time workers in a factory were selected for redundancy ahead of full-time workers. It was alleged that this indirectly discriminated against married women. They were more likely to have children to look after, and so be prevented from working full time. It was held that for proportional purposes their position should be compared with single women with children. There was no statistical evidence to support the proposition that their position was more adversely affected (*Kidd v DRG (UK) Ltd* [1985] ICR 405, EAT).

11.68
The same defences are available to an employer as in straightforward sex discrimination cases, including the defence that being single is a 'genuine occupation qualification' for the employment in question, although it is not easy to think of examples (but see paras 11.77 to 11.80 below). A married man applying for work in the UK or elsewhere within the EU (eg at an isolated construction site, where the workers are housed in temporary dormitory-style accommodation) might reject an offer of employment if informed that he would not be permitted to take his wife with him. But the imposition of such a rule would not normally amount to discrimination against married persons contrary to section 3 of the 1975 Act as the rule would apply equally to single men unhappy about being separated from their girlfriends or partners (although it should be emphasised that any such case would be decided on its merits) (*Source*: SDA 1975, ss 6(3)(a)&(b) & 48).

WHEN DISCRIMINATION IS UNLAWFUL

11.69
It is unlawful for an employer, in relation to employment by him at an establishment in Great Britain, to discriminate against a woman (or man):

- in the arrangements made for determining who should be offered that employment. This might occur where a woman is 'filtered out' by a junior manager at an early stage in the interviewing process, even if the final selection of the most suitable candidate is made by someone at a more senior level – whether or not anyone was actually appointed to the vacancy in question (*Brennan v Dewhurst* [1984] ICR 52, EAT);

- in the terms on which an offer of employment is made, eg offering a male bookkeeper a salary of, say, £20,000 a year; and a female, £18,000 a year (unless the difference in salary is justifiable on grounds other than sex);

- by refusing or deliberately omitting to offer him (or her) that employment.

It is likewise unlawful for an employer, in the case of a woman already employed by that employer at an establishment in Great Britain, to discriminate against her:

- in the way he affords her access to opportunities for promotion, transfer or training, or to any other benefits, facilities or services, or by refusing or deliberately omitting to afford her access to them; or

- by dismissing her, or subjecting her to any other detriment.

(*Source*: SDA 1975, s. 6.)

11.70
Problems will often arise over questions put to candidates at interviews. If such questions are gender-stereotyped and have a demoralizing effect on the job applicant so that his (or her) performance is undermined, that in itself can be a detriment amounting to discrimination. But there is nothing to prevent a prospective employer from exploring difficulties in the job to assess whether the interviewee will be able to cope with them (*Simon v Brimham Associates* [1987] ICR 596, CA; *Woodhouse v Chief Constable of West Yorkshire Police*, 27 July 1990, EAT).

11.71

The ramifications of the expression 'subjecting a person to a detriment' are extensive. It was held to apply when an employer refused to allow a woman with small children to work part-time. She could have been accommodated at no great expense and without any significant disruption (*Home Office v Holmes* [1984] ICR 678, EAT).

Sexual harassment

11.72

The 1975 Act contains no definition of the expression 'sexual harassment'. The concept has evolved from two sources, (i) as a 'detriment' under the Sex Discrimination Act 1975; and (ii) from a Recommendation of the European Commission on measures for the protection of the dignity of women and men at work. The Recommendation (which does not have the force of law) states that there should be no unwanted conduct of a sexual nature, whether physical, verbal or non-verbal (*Wadham v Carpenter Farrer Partnership* [1993] IRLR 374, EAT).

11.73

If a woman complains of unwanted sexual advances by a male colleague and the latter contends that the woman had consented to such advances, it will be for the tribunal to decide whether the employee's complaint was justified. Given that the public airing of such matters may cause embarrassment, the tribunals are empowered to hear evidence in private should the circumstances so warrant. There is power to make a so-called *restricted reporting order*, which forbids the identification of the parties until the tribunal's decision is promulgated (*Source*: Employment Tribunals (Constitution & Rules of Procedure) Regulations 1993, Schedule 1, para 14[1]). The issue of acceptance or consent was raised in *Snowball v Gardner Merchant Ltd* [1987] IRLR 397. In that case, the EAT held that a complainant's attitude to matters of sexual behaviour was relevant and admissible for the purposes of determining the degree of injury to feelings she suffered (and hence the amount of compensation payable) as a consequence of her having been sexually harassed.

11.74

It would seem that a woman has the right to decide what causes her offence and what she finds unacceptable conduct in order to establish a harassment. The test of the objective 'reasonable employee' does not apply. In *Wileman v Minilec Engineering Ltd* [1988] IRLR 144, the EAT held that, in determining whether sexual harassment constituted a job, health or career-threatening detriment, an employment tribunal was entitled to take into account the fact that, on occasion, the complainant wore scanty and provocative clothes. In a more prominent case, a female teacher brought proceedings under the Sex Discrimination Act 1975 when she felt obliged to move to another school because of unremitting sexual harassment by two male colleagues. It was held that their conduct amounted to a 'detriment' and *was* actionable (*Porcelli v Strathclyde DC* [1986] ICR 564, Ct S).

11.75

A male employee was alleged by two women cleaners working in the same department to have sexually harassed them. He was suspended. At a disciplinary hearing, the allegation was unproved and he was returned to his old job. An allegation was made that it was discrimination to allow him back. A tribunal found that the claim of the earlier sexual harassment was substantiated (although unknown to the employers). But it ruled that it was not discrimination to permit the employee to return. The Act made it necessary to look at the treatment and not at the consequence of that treatment. The man would have been allowed back whether the fellow employees were women or a man complaining of homosexual advances by a male employee (*Balgobin & Another v London Borough of Tower Hamlets* [1987] ICR 829, EAT).

Retirement age

11.76

The state is entitled to fix difference ages at which men and women may draw their state pensions, but not the age at which they may be compulsorily retired (*Beets-Proper v F Van Lanschot Bankiers NV* [1986] ICR 706, ECJ). An employer provided redundancy terms, under which men and women could both receive a cash payment or an early retirement pension at the age of 55. This meant that the women received theirs five years earlier, and the men ten years earlier, than their state pensions. It was held that this was not discrimination. Both sexes were entitled to the same rights, and as the state was entitled to discriminate in fixing the age of retirement for each sex, that had to be disregarded (*Roberts v Tate & Lyle Industries Ltd* [1986] ICR 371, ECJ).

'Genuine occupational qualification'

11.77
Denying a person a job (or access to opportunities for promotion, transfer or training, or to any related benefits, facilities or services) on the grounds of sex is permissible in law if being of a particular sex is a 'genuine occupational qualification' for the vacancy or job in question (*Timex Corporation v Hodgson* [1982] ICR 63, EAT). For example, being a man might well be a genuine occupational qualification for a job involving work in certain Middle Eastern countries whose laws, customs or cultural inclinations preclude any business dealings with women. Toilet and changing-room attendants is another example (*Source*: SDA 1975, s. 7).

11.78
Although a job might require a measure of physical strength, it would be unlawful to deny that job to a woman simply because she is a woman. If physical strength or stamina is an important consideration, the only way to avoid a complaint of unlawful discrimination would be to apply the same aptitude tests to all job candidates, male as well as female. If lifting and carrying heavy weights is only an occasional feature of the work, there is no reason why a woman should not be capable of doing that work (even if that meant calling upon the help of one or other of her workmates when such an occasion arose). In *Etam plc v Rowan* [1089] IRLR 150, the EAT held that being a woman was not a 'genuine occupational qualification' for employment as a sales assistant in a women's clothes shop. A man could quite happily carry out the bulk of the work without causing any inconvenience or embarrassment to customers. In a delicate situation, he could easily call upon one of his female colleagues for assistance. The same approach was adopted in an earlier case, that of *Wylie v Dee & Co* [1978] IRLR 103. There, a woman was refused a job as a sales assistant in a menswear shop

because sales assistants were required, on occasion, to take a tape measure to a customer's inside trouser leg. The tribunal held that, should any customer be unhappy about being ministered to by a woman in that way, the assistant could always call for assistance from one of her male colleagues.

11.79

If a job involves working or living in a private house where there is likely to be a degree of physical or social contact with a person of the opposite sex living in the same house, or knowledge of intimate details of such a person's life, and where there might be reasonable objection, then discrimination on grounds of sex is permissible. The same applies where the nature of the job requires the holder to live in communal accommodation, which includes dormitories or other shared sleeping accommodation (including sanitary facilities) which, for reasons of privacy or decency should be used by men only, or by women only. However, a tribunal would need to be satisfied that the accommodation in question could not be altered or extended to overcome the difficulty and that the employer had acted reasonably in denying employment on such grounds (*Sisley v Britannia Security Systems Ltd* [1983] ICR 628, EAT) (*Source*: SDA 1975, s. 7(2)).

11.80

There are corresponding and supplementary exceptions relating to gender reassignment. Accordingly, it is not *prima facie* unlawful to discriminate against a job applicant or existing employee on grounds of gender reassignment if a particular job involves the holder of the job being liable to be called upon to perform intimate physical searches pursuant to statutory powers (eg, immigration officials, customs officers, and the like); or if the job involves working or living in a private house where a person living in that house might reasonably object to the degree of physical or social contact (or knowledge of intimate details of such a person's life) that is a likely or inevitable feature of that job; or if the nature of the job requires a person undergoing gender reassignment to live in communal accommodation, which includes dormitories or other shared sleeping accommodation (including sanitary facilities) that, for reasons of privacy or decency should be used by men only, or by women only; or if the holder of the job provides vulnerable individuals with personal services promoting their welfare (or similar personal services) and, in the reasonable view of the employer, those services cannot be effectively provided by a person while that person is undergoing gender reassignment.

Discrimination on health and safety grounds

11.81
Section 51 of the 1975 Act allows that discrimination on grounds of sex is also permissible where the employment of women in certain activities and processes is prohibited by regulations made under (or saved by) the Health & Safety at Work, etc Act 1974. For example, pregnant women and women of 'reproductive capacity' must *not* be employed (or be allowed to continue working) in work that exposes them to lead or ionising radiations. However, reliance on Section 51 has recently been challenged, and challenged successfully, before the European Court of Justice (ECJ). In *Mahlburg v Land Mecklenburg–Vorpommern* (2 February 2000), and in *Habermann-Beltermann v Arbeiterwohlfahrt, Bezirksverband Ndb/Obf e V* (No. c-421/92). In those cases, the ECJ rules that it is not permissible to refuse to employ a new or expectant mother in work otherwise prohibited to her on health and safety grounds if the employment in question is intended to be *permanent* and she is the best candidate for the job. In short, such a candidate must be appointed to the vacancy for which she has applied and either be offered suitable alternative employment until she begins her maternity leave period or be suspended from work on full pay until the risks associated with what is essentially a temporary indisposition have passed and she is in a position (legally) to take up her duties.

Other exceptions

11.82
In certain limited instances, positive discrimination is allowed by a training body. It may limit one sex access to facilities for training, to redress any imbalance that existed during the previous 12 months (*Source*: SDA 1975, s. 48).

11.83
The 1975 Act does not apply to the armed forces or to the various cadet corps. Nor does it apply to ministers of religion, to charitable

organisations conferring benefits on persons of one sex only; to any sport, game or activity of a competitive nature where the physical strength, stamina or physique of the average woman puts her at a disadvantage to the average man; to the treatment of a person in relation to an annuity, life assurance policy, accident insurance policy or similar matter involving the assessment of risk, where the treatment was effected by reference to actuarial or other data from a source on which it was reasonable to rely; or to acts done for the purpose of ensuring the combat effectiveness of the naval, military of air forces of the Crown (*Source*: SDA 1975, ss 19, 43–45, 52 & 85).

PERSONS TO WHOM THE 1975 ACT APPLIES

11.84
The 1975 Act applies to a person of any age, whether an employee, an applicant for a job, or a person under a contract personally to execute any work or labour. Nor is length of service a limiting factor. For the current position relating to persons employed wholly or mainly outside Great Britain, please turn to Chapter 3, paras 3.84 & 3.85 (*Source*: RRA 1976).

11.85
The Act also applies to contract labour, eg to persons supplied by employment agencies, to partnerships, to trade unions and employers' organisations, to professional and trade bodies, to qualifying and vocational training bodies, to the Employment Service Agency and the Training Service Agency. It also applies to the police (but with some limited exceptions) and to the prison service. Midwifery is included (*Source*: SDA 1975, ss 9, 11, 12, 14 to 16, 17, 18 & 20).

11.86
Those who unlawfully instruct others to discriminate are caught by the Act, as well as those who carry out such instructions, even in good faith. So too are those who pressurise others to discriminate (*Simon v Brimham Associates* [1987] ICR 596, CA). Employers and principals are (vicariously) liable for the unlawful acts of discrimination committed by their staff and agents during the employment. It matters not whether it is to their knowledge or not, unless they can prove that they have taken such steps as were reasonably practical to avoid such incidents occurring (*Source*: SDA 1975, ss 39–41).

Discrimination by barristers and advocates

11.87
Sections 35A and 35B of the 1975 (inserted by the Court & Legal Services Act 1990) point out that it is unlawful, in relation to any offer of pupillage or tenancy, for a barrister or barrister's clerk to discriminate against a woman in the arrangements that are made for the purpose of determining to whom it should be offered; in respect of any terms on which it is offered; or by refusing or deliberately omitting to offer it to her. The same rule applies to discrimination by an advocate in relation to taking on any person as his (or her) pupil.

Discriminatory advertisements

11.88
It is unlawful to publish or cause to be published an advertisement that indicates, or might reasonably be construed as indicating, an intention by a person to do an act that is (or might be) unlawful under the 1975 Act. It is also a form of indirect discrimination to advertise job vacancies in any journal or magazine the clear majority of whose readers are female or male – unless being of a particular sex is a 'genuine occupational qualification' for the vacancy in question (*Source*: SDA 1975, ss 37 & 38). An advertisement that uses job titles such as (or is accompanied by an illustration depicting a) barmaid, waitress, chambermaid, flight stewardess, sales girl, etc might also be taken to indicate an intention to discriminate against men unless the accompanying copy contains a clear indication to the contrary. Publishers will also be liable under the Act if they allow such advertisements to be published in their newspapers or magazines. If illustrations are used in job advertisements, they should depict persons of both sexes.

CASE LAW

Complaints upheld

11.89
A young girl applied for a job with an organisation aimed at alleviating unemployment among juveniles. She was not allowed to join a particular activity because she would be the only girl in a group of men and certain emotional problems were anticipated.

Held: Even though the employers' motives were honourable, it was still discrimination (*Grieg v Community Industry* [1979] ICR 356, EAT).

11.90
After the 1975 Act became law, women were allowed to become full-time postal workers. Before that, they could never be more than 'temporary full-time' workers. The allocation of 'walks and rounds' nonetheless continued to be based on service as a full-time postal worker' (while prior service as a temporary full-time worker was discounted).

Held: Because the allocation of work was based on length of service it was unlawful discrimination under the 1975 Act. Women were still not being given an equal chance. The title given to the length of service was irrelevant (*Steel v Union of Post Office Workers* [1978] ICR 181, EAT).

Complaints dismissed

11.91
Women did the lighter work in their employer's warehouse, handling books and magazines. The heavier work was done by men. The women themselves made it clear that the heavier work was too much for them. When the lighter work fell off, three of the women were made redundant.

Held: The work of the men and women was different. There was no discrimination; nor were the women who left entitled to equal pay (*Noble v David Gold & Sons (Holdings) Ltd* [1980] ICR 543, CA).

11.92
Taxis were owned and maintained by the driver but run by a firm to whom the owner paid a weekly sum in return for business. The driver obtained permission to employ a relief driver for his night shift but, when the firm learned it was a woman, they told him to dismiss her, which he did.

Held: The driver did not supply contract labour nor provide services for the purpose of finding employment for women; consequently the Act did not apply (*Rice v Fon-A-Car* [1980] ICR 133, EAT).

QUESTIONS AND REPLIES

11.93

An employee (or job applicant) who believes that she (or he) has been discriminated against in contravention of the Sex Discrimination Act 1975, whether by her present employer or by a would-be employer, may question the person concerned asking him to explain why he has contravened her rights under the 1975 Act. The procedure is explained in the Sex Discrimination (Questions & Replies) Order 1975 (SI 1975/2048). The form prescribed by the Regulations is Form SD74, copies of which are available from the Equal Opportunities Commission or from any Job Centre or unemployment benefit office of the Department for Education & Employment) (*Source*: SDA 1975, s. 74(2)(b)).

Note: Form SD74 is an eight-page document that not only provides space for preparing the questionnaire to be submitted, but also gives a great deal of practical advice both to the person aggrieved and to the person to whom the questions are directed. The document points out that an employer cannot be compelled to respond to the allegations made against him. However, the employer is cautioned that an employment tribunal may draw any such inference as is just and equitable from a failure, without reasonable excuse, to reply within a reasonable period, or from an evasive or equivocal reply, including an inference that the employer had unlawfully discriminated against the employee (or the rejected job applicant).

The questionnaire must be served within three months of the alleged act of discrimination, or, within 21 days of an Originating Application (Form IT1) being sent to the Secretary to the Tribunals (see Chapter 26, paras 26.10 to 26.16). A Chairman (or a tribunal) has power to extend the 21 days, and this will generally be granted where a reasonable explanation for the delay is given (*Williams v Greater London Citizens' Advice Bureaux* [1989] ICR 545, EAT). In appropriate circumstances, a further questionnaire may be served with leave. This will normally be given where the information sought is not available in existing documents, so that an order for Discovery or Inspection would not be apt (*Carrington v Helix Lighting Ltd* [1990] ICR 125, EAT).

THE EQUAL OPPORTUNITIES COMMISSION

11.94

The Equal Opportunities Commission (EOC) is charged with the duty of eliminating unlawful discrimination, and is armed with several powers to enable it to carry out that duty. *First,* it may conduct formal investigations into cases where it believes that an employer's conduct contravenes the Sex Discrimination and Equal Pay legislation. If it does find a default it may issue a 'non-discrimination notice' requiring the employer to cease the discrimination or the alleged discriminatory practice. An employer who is served with a Non-Discrimination Notice must either comply with its terms or appeal to an employment tribunal within the next six weeks. An employer can also apply to the High Court for a Judicial Review (see Chapter 1, paras 1.48 to 1.63) (*Source*: SDA 1975, ss 53, 57, 67 & 68).

Note: If the tribunal finds that any of the requirements of a Non-Discrimination Notice are unreasonable (perhaps because they are based on incorrect findings of fact or for any other reason), it may quash the Notice or part of it. It may also substitute any other requirement (*Source*: SDA 1975, s. 68(2)&(3)).

11.95

Second, the EOC may seek a declaration from an employment tribunal that an employer is engaging (or has engaged) in discriminatory practices, or has published a discriminatory advertisement, or has instructed another (eg an employment agency) to discriminate against job applicants on grounds of sex (or marital status) (*Source*: SDA 1975, s. 73).

11.96

Third, the EOC may offer its services to any individual (employee, job applicant, or otherwise) who is preparing or planning to present a complaint of unlawful sex discrimination to an employment tribunal. It will do so where a question of principle is involved, or where it would be unreasonable to expect that person to act on her (or his) own behalf – bearing in mind the complexities that attend many such cases (*Source*: SDA 1975, s. 75).

EOC Code of Practice

11.97

The Equal Opportunities Commission has produced a *Code of Practice for the Elimination of Discrimination on the Grounds of Sex and Marriage and the Promotion of Equality of Opportunity in Employment*, copies of which are available from The Stationery Office.

REMEDIES

11.98

An employee (or aggrieved job applicant) may complain to an employment tribunal that her (or his) employer, or a particular employer, has discriminated against her on grounds of sex or marital status or that he has breached her rights under the Equal Pay Act 1970. If the complaint is upheld, the tribunal will make an order:

- declaring the rights of the complainant and the respondent (the employer) in relation to the act to which the complaint relates;

- requiring the respondent employer to pay to the complainant compensation of an amount corresponding to any damages he could have been ordered by a county court or by a sheriff court to pay to the complainant.

The tribunal may also make a recommendation that the respondent take within a specified period action designed to obviate or reduce the adverse effect on the complainant of any act of discrimination to which the complaint relates. Failure to comply with a recommendation without reasonable justification can lead to a further award of compensation or an increase in the existing award (Source: SDA 1975, s. 65).

Note: In sex discrimination cases, a tribunal can award compensation for injury to feelings. Interest can also be awarded in the appropriate circumstances. The amount has to be kept moderate and calculated on the same basis as in defamation cases. A sum between £500 and £5,000 would be appropriate although the figure tends to rise yearly (*Bradford City Metropolitan Council v Arora* [1991] ICR 226, CA). Exemplary damages may not be awarded (*Deane v Ealing Borough Council & Another* [1993] ICR 329, EAT). But the power to award compensation does not arise if the discrimination is indirect and there was no intention to discriminate (*Source*: EPA 1970, ss 2(1A) & 2(5); SDA 1975 ss 65(a), (b) & (c), and 66(3)).

11.99

There is no upper limit on the amount of compensation that may be awarded in sex (race and disability) discrimination cases or in 'protected disclosures' and certain health and safety cases. Damages for loss of earnings, prospective loss of earnings and injured feelings and other losses are included in the compensation. The measure for damages is based on the principle that, as best as money could do it, the employee should be put into the position in which she would have been but for the employer's unlawful conduct. This is subject to the usual tests of evaluation of the loss of a chance, causation, remoteness of damage and a duty to mitigate (see Chapter 2, paras 2.61 to 2.68) (*Ministry of Defence v Cannock & Others, The Times,* 2 August 1994, EAT).

TIME LIMITS FOR COMPLAINTS

Complaints under the Equal Pay Act 1970

11.100
In 'equal pay' cases, an Originating Application (Form IT1) must be sent to the Secretary to the Tribunals (in practice, the nearest Regional Office of the Tribunals) within six months of the alleged breach of the implied 'equality clause' or within six months of the effective date of termination of the employee's contract of employment.

11.101
Contrary to s. 2(5) of the EPA 1970, which limits an award of arrears of pay and damages to the period of two years immediately preceding the date on which a complaint under the EPA is brought, the EAT, in *British Railways Board v Paul* [1988] IRLR 20, held that the two-year limit was incompatible with European law and ruled that claims could be lodged in respect of losses sustained over a period of up to six years preceding the commencement of proceedings.

11.102
Only one application concerning the same complaint may be made, unless a later application refers to different matters (*British Railways Board v Paul (qv)*). If proceedings are initially taken in the county court and the question of the operation of the 'equality clause' arises, the case can be stopped and referred to an employment tribunal for a decision. The Secretary of State is also empowered to refer a case to the tribunal. There is no time limit on such referrals (*Source*: EPA 1970, s. 2(3) & (4)).

Complaints under the Sex Discrimination Act 1975

11.103
A complaint under the 1975 Act must be 'presented' within three months of the matter complained of, or, if there is continuing discrimination, at any time. If the employee has (allegedly) been unlawfully dismissed, the complaint must be presented within three months of the effective date of termination of her (or his) contract of employment (*Lupetti v Wren's Old House Ltd* [1984] ICR 348 EAT; and *Barclays Bank plc v Kapur & Others* [1991] ICR 208, HL) (*Source*: SDA 1975, s. 76(1)). If a complaint is presented 'out of time', a tribunal has power to adjudicate if, in all the circumstances, it is 'just and equitable' to do so (*Source*: SDA 1975, s. 76(5)).

Where a person has been denied a promotion on grounds of sex (marital status or (now) gender reassignment) – although the effect of that denial continues – proceedings must be initiated within three months of the denial (*Amies v Inner London Education Authority* [1977] ICR 308, EAT; and *Sougrin v Haringey Health Authority* [1992] IRLR 416, CA).

12

Racial discrimination

GENERAL INFORMATION

12.1

The Race Relations Act 1976 is almost identical in scope to the Sex Discrimination Act (see Chapter 11). Indeed, many of its provisions are worded similarly except for the substitution of the word 'race' or 'racial' for 'sex'.

12.2

Discrimination on 'racial grounds' means discrimination based on a person's colour, race, nationality, national or ethnic origins. 'Racial group' means any group of persons defined by reference to colour, race, nationality or ethnic or national origins. It has been held that Sikhs are covered by the 1976 Act but not Rastafarians. The former had a long history whereas the latter had existed for only 60 years (*Mandla & Another v Lee & Others* [1983] 2 AC 548, HL; and *Dawkins v Crown Supplies (PSA) Ltd* [1993] IRLR 284, CA) (*Source*: RRA 1976, s. 3).

12.3

This Act also deals with various criminal offences that are rarely invoked; and provides for various civil causes of action. The latter are dealt with in the County Court (in England) or Sheriff's Court (in Scotland) (*Source*: RRA 1976, ss 43 to 52).

12.4

European law contains provisions against discrimination but, curiously, they are limited to discrimination on grounds of nationality as laid down in Article 7 of the Treaty of Rome. If another Article specifically prohibits discrimination, the wording of that other Article must be considered alone (*Ingetraut Scholz v Opera Universitaria di Cagliari & Another The Times*, 29 March 1994, ECJ).

12.5

The Commission for Racial Equality (CRE) was set up by the 1976 Act. Like the Equal Opportunities Commission (EOC), the CRE is charged with the duty of eliminating discrimination at all levels and in every field. For these purposes, it has a variety of powers (see para 12.41).

WHAT IS RACIAL DISCRIMINATION?

There are three types of racial discrimination rendered unlawful by the 1976 Act: 'direct' discrimination, 'indirect' discrimination and victimisation.

Direct discrimination

12.6

Direct discrimination arises where an employer (or other person), on racial grounds, treats a person (and this includes a company) less favourably than he treats or would treat other persons (including a company) (*Source*: RRA 1976, s. 1(1)(a)).

12.7

But it is always necessary to compare like with like. So where two Indian nationals were refused employment when they declined to produce evidence of a right to work (which they had), it was not discriminatory. The same requirements were put to all non-British and non-EU subjects (*Dhatt & Another v McDonald's Hamburger Ltd* [1991] ICR 238, CA) (*Source*: RRA 1976 s. 3(4)). Furthermore, it is essential to allege and prove that the treatment received was less favourable on the grounds of race or colour than would be the case with others not of the claimant's group. It is not sufficient to establish that the treatment was poor or deplorable. The alleged discriminator may dislike the claimant as a person, or he might treat all deplorably, irrespective of background (*Chapman & Another v Simon* [1994] IRLR 124, CA).

12.8

It is necessary to see whether there is any departure from the requirement of equality of treatment and not that the effect of the treatment produces different results. Some employers failed to follow their own equal opportunities policy when they refused to allow a complainant to see his references when considering him for promotion. It was held that there was no evidence to show he had been treated unfavourably in comparison to other applicants (*Quereshi v London Borough of Newham* [1991] IRLR 264, CA).

Indirect discrimination

12.9
Indirect racial discrimination occurs when an employer imposes a condition or requirement that acts as an absolute bar to selection if a job applicant (or candidate for promotion, transfer or training) is unable to satisfy that requirement or condition; and if:

* the number of persons in the racial group to which the applicant belongs who can comply with that requirement or condition is considerably smaller than that of others not of that group; and

* the requirement or condition is not justified on non-racial grounds;

* it is to the applicant's detriment because he (or she) cannot comply with it;

but, where there is discrimination affecting a racial group, only the Commission for Racial Equality (see para 12.43 below) can bring proceedings (*Perera v Civil Service Commission* [1983] ICR 428, CA) (*Source:* RRA 1976, s. 1(1)(b)).

12.10
To establish whether a condition or requirement has a discriminatory effect on an applicant, it is necessary:

* to identify the ethnic group to which the applicant belongs;

* to consider the extent of the geographic area to be taken into account when considering the relative proportions; and

* to establish what was the condition or requirement which that group in that area could not comply with (*Tower Hamlets LBC v Qayyum, The Times*, 2 May 1988, EAT).

If there are several conditions or requirements to be satisfied, the importance attached to each by an employer (or prospective employer), will also be relevant in deciding whether there has been discrimination (*Meer v London Borough of Tower Hamlets* [1988] IRLR 399, CA). A company can escape liability for a discriminatory condition or requirement by proving 'on the balance of probabilities' (see Chapter 2, paras 2.16 to 2.20) that it was justifiable for non-racial reasons, eg that it is necessary for reasons of health or safety, or for some other non-racial reason (*Gurmit Singh Kambo v Vaulkhard, The Times*, 7 December 1984, CA). A company that insisted on its production-line employees having short hair in compliance with food hygiene regulations was held not to have discriminated against a Sikh who was refused employment because of his insistence (for cultural and religious reasons) on wearing his hair long (*Panesar v Nestlé Co Ltd* [1980] ICR 144, CA).

12.11
However, a genuine belief in the justification of a particular condition or requirement is not enough. An objective test must be applied and a balance struck between the reasonable needs of the party applying the condition or requirement and the discriminatory effect it had on the complainant. It has to be 'capable of being justified... 'without regard to' the colour, race, etc of the applicant' (*Orphanos v Queen Mary College* [1985] IRLR 349, HL) (and see Chapter 11, paras 11.79 to 11.83 for analogous provisions in the Sex Discrimination Act 1975). Thus, the governors of a Church of England school were held to be justified in imposing a requirement that candidates for the post of head teacher had to be committed communicants, even though that requirement effectively ruled out most Asians. The person appointed would quite often be required to administer the sacrament at communion. (*Board of Governors of St Matthias Church of England School v Crizzle* [1993] ICR 401, EAT).

12.12
The phrase 'cannot comply' means that an applicant must prove that, in practice, persons of his (or her) racial group cannot accept a requirement that is inconsistent with their customs and cultural traditions (*Mandla & Another v Lee & Others* [1983] IRLR 209, HL). So a Sikh whose religion requires him to wear a turban was prevented from taking a job as a bus conductor by a company rule that all conductors must wear the regulation uniform cap. As there was no *prima facie* justification for the rule (eg on grounds of health, safety or hygiene), the rule was tantamount to unlawful indirect

discrimination. There must be a comparison with persons where the relevant circumstances are the same, or are not materially different. It does not matter whether there is no intention to discriminate; it is unlawful if the effect is to discriminate (*R v Birmingham City Council ex parte EOC* [1989] IRLR 173, HL) (*Source*: RRA 1976, s. 3(4)).

12.13
An employer in Italy refused to take into account the previous employment in public service in Germany of a former German citizen. It was held by the European Court of Justice that this was unjustified indirect discrimination under Article 48 of the Treaty of Rome that reads as follows: '1. Freedom of movement for workers shall be secured within the Community...' and again: '2. Such freedom shall entail the abolition of any discrimination based on nationality between workers of the Member States as regards employment, remuneration, and other conditions of work and employment' (*Ingetraut Scholz v Opera Universitaria di Cagliari & Another, The Times*, 29 March 1994, ECJ). See also the *Note* to para 12.16 below.

Victimisation

12.14
There can also be discrimination by way of victimisation. This arises where a person is treated less favourably because he (or she) has brought proceedings or given evidence or information under the Race Relations Act 1976, or has alleged an infringement of his rights under that Act. However, this does not apply where the alleged victim makes a false allegation or one not made in good faith (see also Chapter 11, para 11.63) (*Source*: RRA 1976, s. 2(1), s. 2(2)).

12.15
To prove victimisation it is necessary to consider the reasons behind the act or omission complained of, and to decide whether those reasons were justified on non-racial grounds. Consequently, it is important to identify the person who took the relevant decision and to question him (or her) about his motives (*Aziz v Trinity Street Taxis Ltd & Others* [1988] ICR 534, CA; and *Subasinghe-Sharpe v London Borough of Brent*, 5 December 1991, EAT).

DISCRIMINATION AGAINST JOB APPLICANTS AND EMPLOYEES

12.16

It is unlawful for a person, in relation to employment by him at an establishment in Great Britain (but see *Note* below) to discriminate against a job applicant on racial grounds:

- in the arrangements made for the purposes of determining who should be offered that employment; or

- in the terms on which that employment is offered; or

- by refusing or deliberately omitting to offer that employment.

It is likewise unlawful for an employer, in the case of a person employed by him at an establishment in Great Britain, to discriminate against that employee on racial grounds:

- by denying the same terms and conditions of employment to that employee as are available to other employees doing the same or equivalent work;

- by withholding (or denying access to) opportunities for promotion, transfer or training, or any other benefits, facilities or services; or by refusing or deliberately omitting to afford the employee access to them; or

- by dismissing or subjecting the employee to any other detriment.

(*Source*: RRA 1976, s. 4(1) & (2).) See also paragraph 12.22 below.

Note: In a recent case, the EAT held that sections 4 and 8 of the 1976 Act – which only permit complaints under the Act to be brought by persons employed at (or seeking employment at) an establishment in Great Britain (and Northern Ireland) – conflict with Article 48 of the Treaty of Rome ('freedom of movement of workers'). In the case in question, a Mr Bossa, an Italian national living in the UK, answered an advertisement in the British press placed by Alitalia, the Italian airline. The airline was seeking to recruit flight attendants to be based in Italy. During his interview at Gatwick airport, Nordstress Limited (the company contracted by Alitalia to interview candidates on their behalf) informed Mr Bossa that they were forbidden by the Italian authorities to recruit Italian nationals living outside Italy and to take them back to Italy. The EAT held that Article 48 of the Treaty applies to all citizens of the European Economic Area (ie the EU plus Iceland, Norway and Liechtenstein) and has both 'horizontal' and 'vertical' direct effect. It could therefore be relied on by both public and private sector employees and job applicants discriminated against on the grounds of their nationality or national origins. In short, Article 48 overrides any conflicting provisions in UK domestic legislation. The EAT upheld Mr Bossa's appeal and referred his case back to the employment tribunal (*Bossa v Nordstress Limited*, EAT 571/96).

12.17

In *de Souza v Automobile Association* [1986] ICR 514, CA) a coloured employee overheard two other employees discussing him in a racially derogatory way. The Court of Appeal held that that was not of itself actionable. It is the effect of such conduct that has to be considered. The complainant would need to show that he had been subjected to a detriment, eg that what he had overhead had adversely affected his health and general well-being or his ability to carry out his duties efficiently.

Note: Under section 4A of the Public Order Act 1986, it is a criminal offence, punishable by a fine of up £5,000 and/or imprisonment for a term not exceeding six months, for any person, with intent to cause a person harassment, alarm or distress, to use threatening, abusive or insulting words or disorderly behaviour, or to write or display graffiti which is threatening, abusive or insulting. The 1986 Act (amended in this instance by the Criminal Justice & Public Order Act 1994) applies equally to offences committed within the workplace.

GENUINE OCCUPATIONAL QUALIFICATION

12.18

There are circumstances in which discrimination on racial grounds is lawful where being of a particular racial group is a 'genuine occupational qualification' for a particular job or occupation. Thus, in the interests of authenticity, it is permissible for the proprietors or managers of a Chinese restaurant to restrict their recruitment of waiters to persons who are either themselves Chinese or of Chinese appearance.

The same applies where a job involves participation in a dramatic performance or some other form of entertainment, or as a model, or where personal services promoting the welfare of people of a particular racial group are provided. See also Chapter 11, paras 11.77 to 11.79A (*Source*: RRA 1976 s. 5).

12.19

A local authority sought to restrict two appointments to Afro-Caribbean or Asian applicants to perform functions of an essentially managerial and administrative nature. The Court of Appeal held that being Afro-Caribbean or Asian was not a genuine occupational qualification for either job, as the persons doing those jobs would not be dealing directly with the client base and would not therefore be providing 'personal services'. In short, they would not be working at a level where language and cultural understanding were important (*London Borough of Lambeth v Commission for Racial Equality* [1990] IRLR 231, CA).

12.20

A person was required for the post of nursery worker to deal with children of primarily Afro-Caribbean origin. A white man was rejected because it was thought that a person from the same ethnic background as the children would be more suitable. It was held that as the work *did* involve the provision of 'personal services', the employers were not in breach of the 1976 Act. They *were* entitled to take in account the type of person who would most effectively provide the services required (*Greenwich Homeworkers Project v Marroll (Case A)*, 19 October 1990, EAT).

TO WHOM DOES THE 1976 ACT APPLY?

12.21

The Act applies to a person of any age, whether an employee, an applicant for a job, or a person under a contract personally to execute any work or labour. Nor is length of service a limiting factor. For the current position relating to persons employed wholly or mainly outside Great Britain, please turn to Chapter 3, paras 3.84 & 3.85 (*Source*: RRA 1976).

12.22

For the purposes of the 1976 Act, a person is deemed to be employed at an establishment in Great Britain provided that he (or she) does at least part of his work within Great Britain. This rule applies even where the work is done mainly elsewhere. Thus, an employee who ordinarily works outside Great Britain (eg, in another EEA Member State), who is sent (albeit temporarily) to work in Great Britain, enjoys the same protection under the 1976 Act as persons who ordinarily work inside Great Britain (*ibid* s. 5, as amended by the Equal Opportunities (Employment Legislation) (Territorial Limits) Regulations 1999 (SI 1999/3163).

Note: Article 3(1)(g) of Council Directive 96/71/EC of 16 December 1996 'concerning the posting of workers in the framework of the provision of services' (the 'Posted Workers' Directive), which came into force in the UK on 16 December 1999, requires every Member State to ensure that employment legislation concerning equality of treatment between men and women and other provisions on non-discrimination are extended to 'posted workers', that is to say, workers who, for a limited period, carry out their work in the territory of that state, having been posted there in certain circumstances by an undertaking established in another Member State. For further particulars, please turn to Chapter 22.

Persons employed on ships registered in Great Britain, or on aircraft or hovercraft registered in the United Kingdom and operated from Great Britain, are also protected unless their work is wholly outside the territorial waters (*Wood v Cunard Line Ltd* [1990] IRLR 281, CA). In determining whether a person works 'wholly outside Great Britain', it is necessary to consider what was contemplated by the parties at the time of making the contract of employment. Subsequent unforeseen events are not relevant (*Deria v General Council of British Shipping* [1986] ICR 172, CA). But see the *Note* to para 12.17.

12.23
The Act also applies to contract labour, eg to those who are supplied by some third party, to partnerships where there are six or more partners, to trade unions and employers' organisations, to professional and trade bodies, to vocational training bodies, to the Employment Service Agency, the Training Service Agency and to the police. It also applies to barristers (or barristers' clerks) and to advocates minded to offer pupillages or tenancies. An employment tribunal has the power to adjudicate where there is a complaint of discrimination by a qualifying body relating to a decision by that body, except where there is a right of 'appeal or proceedings in the nature of an appeal' from such a decision. The essential feature of such an appeal is the independence of the appellate body, the ability of an aggrieved to make oral representations to it, and the fairness of the proceedings (*Khan v General Medical Council* [1993] ICR 627, EAT) (*Source*: RRA 1976 ss 7, 10, 11, 12, 13 to 16, 26A, 26B, and 54(2)).

12.24
Those who give instructions to discriminate unlawfully on racial grounds are also caught by the 1976 Act, as are those who put pressure on others (such as an Employment Agency) to do likewise. Employers and principals are vicariously liable for the unlawful acts

of their employees or agents in the course of their employment unless they can prove that they took such steps as were reasonably practicable to avoid the discrimination. Employers should make their 'equal opportunity policies' known to their staff, complemented by adequate supervision and training (*Balgobin & Another v LB of Tower Hamlets* [1987] ICR 829, EAT) (see Chapter 11, para 11.86) (*Source*: RRA 1976 ss 30, 31 & 32).

12.25

A post office worker had written racist comments on an envelope addressed to his neighbours. It was held that it was not done in the course of his employment. This was a personal act of his, unrelated to his work (*Irving & Another v Post Office* [1988] IRLR 144, CA).

12.26

Those who help others to breach the 1976 Act are also liable provided they do so knowingly. But it is a defence, for example, for an employment agency or newspaper publisher to show that they had acted on an assurance given by an employer, or whomever, that there would be no breach of the 1976 Act and that it was reasonable for them to have relied on that assurance (*Source*: RRA 1976, s. 33).

12.27

It is unlawful to impose a requirement or condition that results in an act of unlawful racial discrimination, or to publish an advertisement that clearly indicates an intention to discriminate. Acts done by a Minister of the Crown, or a government department, or on behalf of the Crown, by a statutory body or a person holding a statutory office, are all within the scope of the Act (*Source*: RRA 1976 ss 28, 29 & 75).

12.28

The provisions do not apply to the armed services. Disputes within the services can only be dealt with by their own internal disciplinary bodies. Discriminatory provisions in charitable instruments are void but acts done to safeguard national security are exempt (*Source*: RRA 1976, ss 34, 39, 42, & 75(2)(c), (8)&(9)). Any act done pursuant to a condition or requirement contained in a statutory instrument is immune except in respect of indirect discrimination. To escape liability for indirect discrimination, it must be shown that, in the exercise of discretion in the performance of public duties, a non-discriminatory approach had been adopted where reasonably possible (*Hampson v Department of Education & Science* [1990] ICR 511, HL) (*Source*: RRA 1976 s. 41).

European Union law

12.29
There is some overlap between the European law and that of our domestic legislation. Article 48 of the Treaty of Rome prohibits discrimination on the grounds of nationality in employment. In one respect the effect of Article 48 may be nullified by Article 223 that states that no Member State can be obliged to supply information, the disclosure of which would be contrary to its essential security interests. So documents in the possession of the state need not be supplied to an aggrieved person to enable him (or her) to mount a case against any organ or emanation of the state (*R v Secretary of State for Transport & Civil Aviation Authority ex parte Evans & Commission for Racial Equality*, 2 December 1991, Div Ct). But see the *Note* to para 12.16 above.

Positive discrimination

12.30
In certain limited instances, positive discrimination is allowed by a training body in affording a racial group access to facilities for training. But this can only be done to redress an imbalance that has existed throughout the previous 12 months. The same rules apply to employers and trade unions in respect of access to training. However, it was held that this duty does not extend to an obligation to provide English lessons to a Thai croupier to enable him to qualify as a manager (*Mecca Leisure Group plc v Chatprachong* [1993] ICR 688, EAT) (*Source*: RRA 1976, ss 37 & 38).

CASE LAW

Complaints upheld

12.31
A senior police officer claimed that the Northern Joint Police Board had not shortlisted him for the vacant post of Chief Constable, Northern Constabulary, because he was English and not Scottish. He

had therefore been discriminated against on the grounds of his nationality or national origins.

Held: Although the English and Scots have more or less the same ethnic origins, they are of different national origins. The claimant had every legal right to pursue his complaint on those grounds.

12.32

A white barmaid was instructed by the licensee of a public house not to serve any coloured people. When she objected, she was dismissed.

Held: By dismissing her for these reasons, the employer had treated the barmaid less favourably on racial grounds. That was an act of unlawful discrimination (*Zarczynske v Levy* [1979] ICR 184, EAT).

12.33

An Afro-Caribbean man applied for a job and was told that he would be informed of the outcome within a day or two. Having heard nothing further, he telephoned the employers in question, only to be told that the vacancy had been filled. A week later, the man spotted another job advertisement by the same firm. He again applied for the vacancy, but received the same answer.

Held: Discrimination on grounds of race was proved (*Johnson v Timber Taylors (Midlands)* [1978] IRLR 146 IT).

12.34

A requirement was made that a student would have to undergo a 21-month course, as opposed to a one-year diploma, to complete the academic stage of the Bar, because he did not have a UK or Irish Republic university degree.

Held: It was discriminatory. The proportion of persons not from the UK or Irish Republic who could comply was considerably smaller than those from other countries who could, and it was not otherwise justifiable (*Bohon-Mitchell v Council of Legal Education* [1978] IRLR 525, IT).

12.35

A Job Centre put forward a man with a foreign name for a job as a driver, but was told by prospective employers that it would be no use sending him round.

Held: Even though there were other grounds for properly rejecting him, eg his bad driving record, it was still discrimination (*Kirszak v Swinnerton & Son Ltd* [1979] COIT 851, IT).

Complaints dismissed

12.36
An Asian was one of a group of taxi drivers who operated as an association to promote their interests. He brought a claim against the association in the tribunal alleging discrimination but it was dismissed. During the hearing he disclosed that he had made secret tape recordings of conversations with some members but the contents were never revealed. Later, the association expelled him on the grounds that his underhand activities amounted to a breach of trust (*Aziz v Trinity Street Taxis Ltd & Others* [1988] ICR 534, CA).

Held: That he *had* received less favourable treatment contrary to the Act but it was not that which caused the association to expel him.

12.37
An orthodox Sikh, wearing a beard as required by his religion, sought a job in a chocolate factory. He was refused because the prospective employer applied a strict rule of no beards or excessively long hair, on the grounds of hygiene (supported by food safety regulations). On a complaint of indirect discrimination, it was asserted that the rule was justified.

Held: As there was scientific evidence to support the employer's contention, there was no unlawful discrimination (*Panesar v Nestlé Co Ltd* [1980] ICR 144, CA).

12.38
Workers employed in the paint shop of a firm were all African Asians who had gone there as a result of introductions from those already working there. This resulted in a *de facto* segregation. It was not the intention of the employers that this would be so.

Held: There was no evidence that the employers (or union) treated them less favourably merely by reason of the fact that they were concentrated in a unit and had the worst jobs (*Pel v Modgill: FTATU v Modgill* [1980] IRLR 142, EAT).

12.39

A 45-year-old Indian complained of direct and indirect discrimination. The latter was on the grounds of an upper age limit in respect of the post of lecturer in a college. Although his qualifications were suitable, he was not shortlisted. An upper age limit of 35 years was applied, although with some exceptions. It was claimed that the proportion of immigrants who could comply with this limit was smaller than native-born lecturers.

Held: Both allegations failed. There was nothing to show the person selected was less well qualified. The number of immigrants who could not comply was not so much lower as to amount to a 'detriment' (*Bains v Avon County Council*, 7 June 1978, EAT).

QUESTIONS AND REPLIES

12.40

An employee (or job applicant) who believes that he (or she) has been discriminated against in contravention of the Race Relations Act 1976, whether by his own employer or by a would-be employer, may question the person concerned asking him to explain why he has contravened his rights under the 1976 Act. The procedure is explained in the Race Relations (Questions & Replies) Order 1977 (SI 1977/842). The form prescribed by the Regulations is Form RR65, copies of which are available from any Job Centre or unemployment benefit office of the Department for Education & Employment, or from the Commission for Racial Equality (CRE) (*Source*: RRA 1976, s. 65).

Note: Form RR65 is an eight-page document that not only provides space for preparing the questionnaire to be submitted, but also gives a great deal of practical advice both to the person aggrieved and to the person to whom the questions are directed. The document points out that an employer cannot be compelled to respond to the allegations made against him. However, the employer is cautioned that an employment tribunal may draw any such inference as is 'just and equitable' from his failure, without reasonable excuse, to reply within a reasonable period, or from an evasive or equivocal reply, including an inference that the employer had unlawfully discriminated against the employee (or the rejected job applicant).

The questionnaire must be served within three months of the alleged act of discrimination, or, within 21 days of an Originating Application (Form IT1) being sent to the Secretary to the Tribunals (see Chapter 26, paras 26.10 to 26.16)). A Chairman (or a tribunal) has power to extend the 21 days, and this will generally be granted where a reasonable explanation for the delay is given (*Williams v Greater London Citizens' Advice Bureaux* [1989] ICR 545, EAT). In appropriate circumstances, a further questionnaire may be served with leave. This will normally be given where the information sought is not available in existing documents, so that an order for Discovery or Inspection would not be apt (*Carrington v Helix Lighting Ltd* [1990] ICR 125, EAT).

THE COMMISSION FOR RACIAL EQUALITY (CRE)

12.41
The Commission for Racial Equality (CRE) has identical duties and powers to the Equal Opportunities Commission. These are explained in Chapter 11, at paras 11.94 to 11.97) (*Source*: RRA 1976 ss 43–52 & 58–65).

Code of Practice

12.42
The CRE has issued a *Code of Practice for the Elimination of Racial Discrimination and the Promotion of Equal Opportunity in Employment*, copies of which can be purchased from the Stationery Office. The code recommends (*inter alia*) that employers should declare their commitment to equal opportunities within their organisations and nominate a senior manager with responsibility for ensuring that the policy is carried out. There should be discussions with employees about the implementation of the policy, together with training, and guidance on the legal implications. The criteria used to select staff should be reviewed to ensure that the selection process is not discriminatory. The composition of the staff should be analysed according to ethnic origins and positive steps taken to encourage racial groups to train for work in areas in which they are under-represented. The Code suggests also that deliberate acts of discrimination be treated as disciplinary offences.

REMEDIES AND TIME LIMITS

12.43
The remedies available for a breach of the 1976 Act are the same as those for discrimination on grounds of sex, marital status or gender

reassignment (see Chapter 11, paras 11.98 & 11.99). With the coming into force, on 3 July 1994, of the Race Relations (Remedies) Act 1994, there is no longer an upper limit on the amount of compensation that may be awarded in such cases.

A complaint of unlawful racial discrimination must be presented to an employment tribunal with three months of the alleged discriminatory act or, as appropriate, within three months of the 'effective date of termination' of the complainant's contract of employment (*Source*: RRA 1976 ss 56 & 68).

Disability discrimination

GENERAL INFORMATION

13.1
The Disability Discrimination Act 1995, which came into force on 2 December 1996, contains provisions very similar to those in the Sex Discrimination and Race Relations Acts 1975 and 1976. The new statute, which (for the time being at least) does *not* apply to firms or businesses with fewer than 15 people on the payroll, makes it unlawful for an employer to discriminate against job applicants and employees because they are disabled. The 1995 Act is 'policed' and (where appropriate) enforced by the Disability Discrimination Commission established under the Disability Rights Commission Act 1999.

13.2
There is no upper limit on the amount of compensation that may be awarded by an employment tribunal for an infringement of an employee's (or job applicant's) rights under the 1995 Act (as to which, see *'Complaint to an employment tribunal'* below (at para 13.16).

MEANING OF 'DISABILITY' AND 'DISABLED PERSON'

13.3
For the purposes of the 1995 Act, a person is disabled (or has a disability) if he (or she) has a physical or mental impairment that has a substantial and long-term effect on his ability to carry out normal day-to-day activities.

The expression 'mental impairment' includes an impairment resulting from, or consisting of, a mental illness, but only if the illness is a clinically well-recognised illness. The effect of an impairment (physical or mental) is a long-term effect if:

- it has lasted at least 12 months;

- the period for which it lasts is likely to be at least 12 months; or

- it is likely to last for the rest of the life of the person affected.

If an impairment ceases to have a substantial adverse effect on a person's ability to carry out normal day-to-day activities, it is to be treated as continuing to have that effect if that effect is likely to recur. Furthermore, an impairment is to be taken to affect the ability of the person concerned to carry out normal day-to-day activities only if it affects one of the following:

- mobility;

- manual dexterity;

- physical coordination;

- continence;

- ability to lift, carry or otherwise move everyday objects;

- speech, hearing or eyesight;

- memory or ability to concentrate, learn or understand; or

- perception of the risk of physical danger.

The Act and the accompanying code of practice (see *'Codes of Practice'* below) point out that a person who has a progressive condition, which is likely to change and develop over time (such as cancer, multiple sclerosis, muscular dystrophy, and the HIV infection) will be taken to have an impairment that has a substantial adverse effect on his (or her) ability to carry out normal day-to-day activities if the condition is likely to result in his having such an impairment (*ibid* Schedule 1).

Severe disfigurement

13.4
A severe disfigurement (facial or otherwise) falls within the meaning of 'disability' unless it consists either of a tattoo (which has not been removed) or a piercing of the body for decorative and other non-medical purposes, including any object attached through the piercing for such purposes (*ibid* Schedule 1, para 3, as modified by

the Disability Discrimination (Meaning of Disability) Regulations 1996 [SI 1996/1445] referred to in the following paragraphs as 'the 1996 Regulations').

Addictions and other conditions excluded

13.5
A person who is addicted to alcohol, nicotine or any other substance is not thereby a disabled person within the meaning of the 1995 Act – unless the addiction in question (in the case of an addiction to drugs) was originally the result the result of the administration (or mal-administration) of medically prescribed drugs or other medical treatment (1996 Regulations, Reg 3).

Also excluded from the scope of the Act are the following personality disorders:

(a) a tendency to set fires;

(b) a tendency to physical or sexual abuse of other persons;

(c) exhibitionism; and

(d) voyeurism.

Seasonal allergic rhinitis (hay fever) does not amount to a disability unless the condition aggravates the effect of another condition.

Status of registered disabled persons

13.6
Persons hitherto registered as disabled, under the (now repealed) Disabled Persons (Employment) Act 1944 & 1958, will be deemed to have disabilities, and hence to be disabled persons for the purposes of the 1995 Act, for an initial period of three years from 2 December 1996. After that period has elapsed, any such person will be deemed to have had a disability and to have been disabled during those three years. A certificate of registration (issued under regulations made under section 6 of the 1944 Act) will be conclusive evidence that the person to whom it was issued is (or was) a disabled person.

UNLAWFUL DISCRIMINATION

Discrimination in recruitment

13.7
It is unlawful for an employer to discriminate against a disabled job applicant by taking steps (whether overt or covert) to ensure that no disabled person is interviewed or shortlisted for employment within the organisation (however well-qualified that person may be for the vacancy under consideration). If an employer is prepared to recruit disabled persons, it is nonetheless unlawful for him to do so on terms and conditions that are less favourable than those that would otherwise be offered (or have been offered) to able-bodied persons appointed to (or occupying) the same or similar positions.

13.8
An employer has, of course, every right to refuse to employ a person with a particular disability, if the nature of the work to be done (or the associated risks to health and safety) would make it impossible or highly dangerous for the job applicant to do that work. The same would apply if there is no possible way to modify the work equipment or to adapt it for use by a person with that particular disability, or to make that work equipment more accessible to the employee (without incurring enormous and unacceptable costs). Should an employer's refusal to employ a particular disabled person be referred to an employment tribunal, it will be for the employer to show that the job applicant's disability militated against his (or her) being offered the job in question.

13.9
Use of expressions, such as 'dynamic', 'energetic', 'alert', 'pleasant appearance', etc – in advertisements lodged in newspapers and magazines or in cards posted in the windows of employment agencies, and the like – could be interpreted as showing an intention to discriminate on grounds of disability and might well be submitted in evidence before an employment tribunal. The same would apply to advertisements, job specifications etc that call for unnecessary qualifications or skills that bear little relation to the duties of the jobs in question. Any newspaper proprietor or manager of an employment agency or business who knowingly publishes or publicises a patently discriminatory advertisement is guilty of an

offence under the 1995 Act. The penalty on summary conviction is a fine of up to £5,000 (*ibid* section 57).

Discrimination in employment

13.10
It is unlawful for an employer to discriminate against any disabled person in his employ by paying that person a lower wage or salary than that paid to an able-bodied person doing the same or similar work or by offering other less favourable terms and conditions of employment. To deny a disabled person the same opportunities for promotion, transfer and further training as are available to able-bodied persons is also discriminatory and unlawful.

An employee who believes that he (or she) has been discriminated against in this way has no need to resign in order to obtain redress from an employment tribunal. It would be a foolhardy employer indeed who would respond to such a challenge to his authority by victimising or disciplining the employee. That too is unlawful and could lead to a further hearing before a tribunal and an award of a substantial award of compensation (as to which, please turn to Chapter 6, notably paras 6.17 to 6.19).

Dismissing the disabled employee

13.11
It should be stressed that a disabled person is not immune from dismissal. But, it *is* inadmissible in law and automatically unfair to dismiss a disabled person (or select him or her for redundancy, ahead of more suitable candidates – able-bodied or otherwise) because the employee in question is disabled, and for no other reason. If the employee is dismissed for a permitted reason, including redundancy (eg misconduct, incompetence, etc), an employment tribunal is nonetheless likely to scrutinise the reasons for dismissal very carefully. A disabled person's inability to match the performance of able-bodied persons doing the same or similar work will not necessarily be indicative of 'incompetence' if the quality of the work produced is not in dispute.

13.12

Employers should be cautious about dismissing an absentee employee on grounds of ill health, even if that employee has exhausted his (or her) entitlement to occupational sick pay, without first obtaining an up-to-date medical opinion on the nature of the employee's illness, and the likelihood of his returning to work in the medium or long-term future. A decision to dismiss should be based on the need for the work to be done (and the disruption and cost associated with the employee's continued absence) and may be justifiable on those grounds alone. As was mentioned earlier, a disabled employee has no immunity from dismissal. As always, the ultimate test will be that of 'reasonableness'.

EMPLOYER'S DUTY TO MAKE ADJUSTMENTS

13.13

An employer is duty-bound to make whatever 'adjustments' are reasonable and appropriate so as to ensure that job specifications, working hours, starting and finishing times, and his policies in relation to performance assessment, recruitment, promotion, transfer or access to training, do not needlessly put disabled persons at a disadvantage relative to their able-bodied colleagues.

13.14

The same general rules apply to any physical features of the employer's premises that inhibit access to an employee's workbench or desk or which make it difficult for a disabled person to move freely about those premises. Chairs and desks may need to be modified or adapted. The On/Off buttons on a machine may likewise need to be relocated. Telephones may have to be fitted with a voice-enhancing device for use by an employee who is deaf or partially deaf; and so on. If some of the work a disabled person is employed to do is relatively insignificant but, nonetheless, beyond the employee's capabilities, the employer will need to consider assigning that part of the employee's work to another employee. In some situations, the code of practice alluded to earlier (see also para 13.16 below) suggests that it might well be appropriate to provide a reader or interpreter.

13.15

Although an employer cannot be expected to go to inordinate lengths to accommodate a disabled employee, or to invest large sums of money in modifying his premises or work equipment, he may well be required to satisfy an employment tribunal (in response to a complaint of unlawful discrimination) that he had done all that he reasonably could in the circumstances.

CODES OF PRACTICE AND GUIDANCE

13.16

The reader is referred to the following codes of practice and guidance, both of which are available from The Stationery Office. These are:

- *A Code of Practice for the Elimination of Discrimination in the Field of Employment Against Disabled Persons or Persons Who Have Had a Disability* (ISBN 0 11 270954 0), which came into force on 2 December 1996; and

- a booklet titled *Guidance on matters to be taken into account in determining questions relating to the definition of disability* (ISBN 0 11 270955 9).

A list of associated (and free) publications, leaflets, etc produced by *Disability on the Agenda* will be provided by telephoning **0345 622 633**. These include *A brief guide to the Disability Discrimination Act 1995* (DL 40) and a *Disability Discrimination Act Information Pack* (DL 50).

OBTAINING REDRESS

Questions and replies

13.17

An employee (or job applicant) who believes that he (or she) has been discriminated against in contravention of the Disability Discrimination Act 1995, whether by his own employer or by a would-be employer, may question the person concerned asking him to explain why he has contravened his rights under the Act. The procedure is explained in the Disability Discrimination (Questions & Replies) Order 1996 (SI 1996/2793). The form prescribed for this purpose, with its accompanying Notes, is Form DL56, copies of which will be supplied free of charge by telephoning the Disability on the Agenda line on 0345 622 633 (or textphone 0345 622 644), from any Job Centre or unemployment benefit office of the Department for Education & Employment, or from the Commission for Racial Equality (CRE)(*Source*: DDA 1995, s. 67).

Note: Form DL56 not only provides space for preparing the questionnaire to be submitted, but also gives a great deal of practical advice both to the person aggrieved and to the person to whom the questions are directed. The document points out that an employer cannot be compelled to respond to the allegations made against him. However, the employer is cautioned that an employment tribunal may draw any such inference as is 'just and equitable' from his failure, without reasonable excuse, to reply within a reasonable period, or from an evasive or equivocal reply, including an inference that the employer had unlawfully discriminated against the employee (or the rejected job applicant).

The questionnaire must be served within three months of the alleged act of discrimination, or, within 21 days of an Originating Application (Form IT1) being sent to the Secretary to the Tribunals. A Chairman (or a tribunal) has power to extend the 21 days, and this will generally be granted where a reasonable explanation for the delay is given (*Williams v Greater London Citizens' Advice Bureaux* [1989] ICR 545, EAT).

Complaint to an employment tribunal

13.18
An employee (or would-be) employee who believes that he (or she) has been unlawfully discriminated against on grounds of disability may complain to an employment tribunal. Such a complaint must be presented within three months of the alleged unlawful act or (if the employee has been dismissed) within three months of the effective date of termination of his contract of employment.

13.19
If the complaint is upheld, the tribunal will make a declaration to that effect and will order the employer to pay compensation to the complainant (which may include compensation for injury to feelings), the amount of which will be calculated by applying the principles applicable to the calculation of damages in claims in tort or (in Scotland) in reparation for a breach of statutory duty. The

tribunal may also recommend to the employer that he take appropriate steps to remedy the situation which initiated the complaint in the first place (bearing in mind that the employee who brought the complaint may be still in the employer's employment). In short, the tribunal may recommend to the offending employer that he adapt, modify or adjust certain features of the workplace to review any discriminatory effect. If an employer fails to comply with any such recommendation, the tribunal may increase the amount of compensation payable to the employee (*ibid* section 8).

RELATED PROVISIONS AND LEGISLATION

Occupational pension schemes

13.20
Under section 6 of the 1995 Act, every occupational pension scheme will be taken to include a 'non-discrimination rule' relating to the terms of admission to (or membership of) such a scheme. The rule effectively requires the trustees (or managers) of the scheme to refrain from doing (or omitting to do) any act which, if done by an employer, would amount to unlawful discrimination under the 1995 Act.

Companies Act 1985

13.21
Paragraph 9 of Schedule 7 to the Companies Act 1985, requires every company that employs an average of more than 250 people per week (including part-timers, but excluding persons employed wholly or mainly outside the UK) to include in the directors' report attached to its annual accounts a statement outlining its policy in relation to the employment, training, career development and promotion of registered disabled persons.

Chronically Sick & Disabled Persons Act 1970

13.22
Section 8A of the Chronically Sick & Disabled Persons Act 1970 (as amended) imposes a duty on the owners and developers of proposed

new offices, shops, factories, retail parks, and the like, to consider the needs of disabled persons when designing the means of access to (and within) such premises, including the means of access to (and the provision of) suitable parking facilities, toilets, cloakrooms and washrooms. Section 76 of the Town & Country Planning Act 1990 requires local authorities to draw the attention of persons seeking planning permission for such developments to the relevant provisions of the 1970 Act and to the *Code of Practice for Access for the Disabled to Buildings*. Any person injured as a direct consequence of a builder or developer's failure to comply with the 1970 Act may face a claim for damages in the ordinary courts.

CASE LAW

13.23
To date, the tribunals have identified asthma, epilepsy, post traumatic stress disorder, ureteric colic, clinical depression and, more recently, dyslexia, as conditions capable of amounting to a 'disability' within the meaning of the 1995 Act. But, as was pointed out by the EAT in *O'Neill v Symm & Co Ltd* [1998] IRLR 933, this does not mean that such conditions will always amount to a disability. The acid test is whether the condition in question has a long-term adverse effect on an employee's (or would-be employee's) ability to carry out normal day-to-day activities. In each case, it is for a tribunal to determine whether that test is satisfied. The fact that an employee is taking medication or controlling his (or her) condition through the use of inhalers (as is the case with asthmatics) does not mean that the employee is not disabled (*Jones v Cadstart Ltd*, COIT 2101363/96). Furthermore, as the 1995 Act itself points out, a progressive condition (such as cancer, multiple sclerosis or muscular dystrophy, or infection by the human immunodeficiency virus (HIV)), which has an effect (but not a substantial adverse effect) on a person's ability to carry out normal day-to-day activities, will be deemed to have such a substantial adverse effect if that is the likely end result (*ibid* Schedule 1, para 8(1)).

13.24
It is as yet uncertain whether a stress-induced illness falls within the definition of 'disability' under the 1995 Act (see para 13.3 above). In *Walker v Northumberland County Council* [1995] IRLR 35 (brought before the 1995 Act came into force) an employee who had suffered

two nervous breakdowns, as a direct consequence of being subjected to a health-endangering workload, accepted an out of court settlement from his employers. It was held that he might well have claimed unfair constructive dismissal on the grounds that his employers had breached their common law and implied contractual duty of care. In *O'Neill v Symm & Co Ltd* (*qv*), an employment tribunal held that ME (or myalgic encephalomyelitis) – a condition capable of being caused or exacerbated by stress – could be characterised as a 'disability', but the decision of the tribunal was by no means conclusive.

13.25

Case law confirms that an employer's refusal to employ disabled persons in certain hazardous jobs is justifiable if there is no practicable or cost effective way of making any adjustments or arrangements to eliminate or minimise the risks associated with the work in question, or to eliminate risks that are likely to compound or aggravate the disabilities in question. Thus, the London Underground Limited was held to have been justified in refusing to employ a job applicant suffering from depression because of the possible side effects from the medication he was receiving and the risks to the safety of the travelling public (*Toffel v London Underground Ltd*, IDS Brief 609).

13.26

A employee who had been absent from work for 18 months with a work related back injury was dismissed when medical evidence confirmed that he would be unlikely to return to work within the foreseeable future. The man complained that he had been unlawfully discriminated against on the grounds of his disability. An employment tribunal (and the EAT that heard his appeal) disagreed. They found that he had been no less favourably treated than would any other sick or injured employee who had been absent from work for a similar period. The Court of Appeal rejected that line of reasoning. 'In deciding whether the reason for less favourable treatment does not (or would not) apply to others, it is simply a case of identifying others to whom the reason does not (or would not) apply. The test of less favourable treatment is based on the reason for the treatment of the disabled person and not on the fact of his disability'. It does not, said the Court, turn on a like-for-like comparison of the treatment of the disabled person and of others in similar circumstances. Thus, it is not appropriate to make a comparison of the cases in the same way as in the Sex Discrimination and Race Relations Acts. There is no express provision in the Disability Discrimination Act, said the Court, which requires a comparison of the cases of different persons in the same or not materially different circumstances. In short, the questions to be asked are these: Why was the employee dismissed? Was it for a reason related to his disability? If so, could the employer justify dismissing the employee for that reason? If 'No', the employer's actions amounted to unlawful discrimination under section 5(1) of the 1995 Act (*Clark v TDG Limited t/a Novacold* [1999] IRLR 318, CA).

13.27
But there can be no discrimination under the 1995 Act if an employer had no prior knowledge of an employee's disability. A woman suffering from chronic fatigue syndrome (ME) was dismissed because of her poor health and attendance record. On her self-certificates for illness, she claimed to be suffering from an (unspecified) viral illness. As her employers were unaware of the true nature of her illness, they could not be held to have treated her less favourably for a reason related to her disability (*O'Neill v Symm & Co Ltd* [1998] IRLR 933, EAT).

13.28
There was a similar outcome in *Ridout v TC Group* [1998] IRLR 628. There, a woman suffering from photosensitive epilepsy (and who had previously disclosed that fact in her job application) was interviewed by her prospective employer under fluorescent lighting. She later complained that the employer had failed to make reasonable adjustments to the lighting in the room in order to accommodate her disability. The EAT upheld the employment tribunal's decision that the employer had not been in breach of his duty to make reasonable adjustments to the lighting in the interview room. No reasonable employer, said the EAT, could be expected to know of the deleterious effects of fluorescent lighting unless the woman had taken the trouble to forewarn him of those effects.

13.29
In *Kenny v Hampshire Constabulary* [1999] IRLR 76, a man suffering from cerebral palsy needed help when using the toilet. He complained that his employers had failed to comply with their

statutory duty under section 6 of the Disability Discrimination Act to make such arrangements or adjustments as were necessary or appropriate to enable him to use the toilet during working hours. In evidence, it was revealed that, in spite of their best efforts, his employers had been unable to find sufficient volunteers from amongst the employee's workmates and had been unable to find funds sufficient to secure the services of a carer. The EAT pointed out that an employer's duty under section 6 of the 1995 Act was to provide job-related assistance and to make such structural alterations to the premises as would enable a disabled employee to move freely about the employer's premises. That duty did not extend to providing toilet assistance or transport to and from work.

Maternity, parental and family leave

GENERAL INFORMATION

14.1

Legislation governing the rights of female employees before and after childbirth is currently to be found in Part VIII of the Employment Rights Act 1996, as substituted by section 7 and Schedule 4 (Part I) of the Employment Relations Act 1999 and 'fleshed out' by the Maternity & Parental Leave etc. Regulations 1999 (SI 1999/3312), which latter came into force on 15 December 1999. The law regulating an employee's entitlement or otherwise to statutory maternity pay (SMP) or the State Maternity Allowance (MA) is to be found in Parts II and XII of the Social Security Contributions & Benefits Act 1992, and in Regulations made under (or saved by) that Act. The 1992 and 1996 Acts apply to persons employed in England, Scotland and Wales. Cognate legislation covers persons employed in Northern Ireland.

Other legislation referred to in this chapter includes the Workplace (Health, Safety & Welfare) Regulations 1992 (SI 1992/3004); the Control of Lead at Work Regulations 1998 (SI 1998/543); the Ionising Radiations Regulations 1999 (SI 1999/3232); and the Management of Health & Safety at Work Regulations 1999 (SI 1999/3242).

STATUTORY RIGHTS SUMMARISED

14.2

This chapter summarises the rights of pregnant employees and new mothers to:

- ordinary maternity leave;
- additional maternity leave;
- statutory maternity pay (SMP);

and the duty of an employer to ensure that no woman in his employ is permitted to return to work within two weeks of giving birth (or, if she is a factory worker, within four weeks of that date) – which period is referred to as the 'compulsory leave period' (per s. 72, ERA 1996 and s. 205, Public Health Act 1936).

It also deals with the rights of parents, adoptive parents and others to:

- parental leave (see paras 14.57 to 14.83 below; and

- time off for dependants (see paras 14.84 to 14.94).

Other statutory rights

14.3

Other statutory rights discussed in this chapter include the right of a pregnant employee, or a new or breastfeeding mother (where appropriate):

- to be permitted a reasonable amount of paid time off work for antenatal care (see paras 14.43 to 14.44 below);

- to be paid her normal wage or salary if suspended from work on maternity grounds (subject to the conditions described in paras 14.45 to 14.50 below);

- to be transferred from night work to day work (if her doctor certifies that such a move is advisable on medical grounds) (see para 14.51 below);

- to 'put her feet up' during normal working hours in rest facilities necessarily provided by her employer (see para 14.52 below); and

- to be provided with written reasons for her dismissal if dismissed (or selected for redundancy) while pregnant or during either of her ordinary or additional maternity leave periods (paras 14.53 to 14.55).

Note: The rights to maternity leave explained in this chapter do *not* extend to women employed as the masters or crew members of fishing vessels (who are paid only by a share in the profits or gross earnings of their vessels), or to women employed under a contract of employment in police service or to women engaged in such employment (sections 199(2) and 200(1), Employment Rights Act 1996).

Protection from dismissal or detriment

14.4

It is as well to point out that it is automatically unfair to dismiss a woman, select her for redundancy, or subject her to any other detriment (demotion, transfer, or the denial of a promised pay rise, promotion, training etc) for exercising or presuming to exercise her statutory rights in pregnancy, childbirth or maternity (including her right to parental leave and time off for dependants – which latter are discussed elsewhere in this book). The awards of compensation in such cases are likely to be substantial (per s. 99, ERA 1996, reinforced by the Maternity & Parental Leave etc Regulations 1999 (SI 1999/3312)).

PART 1:
RIGHTS IN PREGNANCY AND MATERNITY

ORDINARY MATERNITY LEAVE

14.5

Every pregnant employee has the legal right to take up to 18 weeks' ordinary maternity leave, whether she is in full-time or part-time employment and regardless of her length of service at the material time. If she is healthily pregnant, she has the right also to decide when her ordinary maternity leave period is to begin (subject to the proviso that, unless she gives birth prematurely, she may not start her leave before the Sunday of the 11th week before her expected week of childbirth (EWC) nor later than the date on which childbirth actually occurs).

Note: The rules relating to the dismissal of an employee who has been recruited specifically to replace an employee who is absent from work on maternity leave are explained in para 14.56 below.

Meaning of 'childbirth'

14.6

Section 235(1) of the 1996 Act defines *childbirth* as meaning the birth of a living child or the birth of a child whether living or dead after 24 weeks of pregnancy. The *expected week of childbirth* (or EWC) is the period of seven calendar days (from Sunday to the following Saturday, inclusive) during which childbirth is expected to occur. The word *confinement* no longer appears in the 1996 Act. However, it is still used in social security legislation (and means exactly the same as *childbirth*).

Contractual vis-à-vis statutory rights

14.7

An employee who has a contractual as well as a statutory right to maternity leave may take advantage of whichever of those rights is the more favourable to her (not both). The same applies if she has a contractual right to be paid the whole or part of her normal wages or salary during her ordinary maternity leave period. In that event, her employer may offset SMP (if any) paid to that employee against the amount paid under her contract (and vice versa) – but only in respect of weeks in which both the contractual and statutory amounts are due. For example, an employee may be entitled under her contract to 26 weeks' paid maternity leave, but her employer cannot insist that she delay her return to work until the end of that 26-week period, as that would deny her her legal right to return to work (on full pay) at the end of her 18-week ordinary maternity leave period

Change of employer

14.8

If there has been a change of employer (for example, in circumstances in which there is no break in a mother-to-be or new mother's period of continuous employment), the new employer (who may be an associated employer of her previous employer) inherits her contractual and statutory rights in employment. The same applies if part or whole of the business or undertaking in which she is employed is transferred or sold as a going concern to another employer (*Source*: Regulation 14 Statutory Maternity Pay (General) Regulations 1986). If her former employer or the previous owner had started paying her SMP before the changeover or before the business was sold or transferred, the new employer must continue paying SMP; and so on. In short, when determining an employee's statutory rights in connection with pregnancy or confinement (including her right, if any, to SMP), the new employer must treat her employment with the former owner of the business as one (ie, seamless) with her period of employment with him.

Notification procedure

14.9
Once she has made up her mind, the pregnant employee must inform her employer of the date on which she intends to begin her ordinary maternity leave. She must do so at least 21 days before the date in question (and in writing, but only if her employer insists). At the same time, she must confirm that she is pregnant and must specify her EWC. If her employer asks her to produce a certificate of expected confinement (signed by her doctor or registered midwife), she must do so. The standard form of certificate is Form Mat B1, although any form of certificate will do, so long as it contains the necessary information and is signed by her doctor or midwife. If for one reason or another, she is unable to give the requisite 21 days' advance notice, she must do so as soon as is reasonably practicable. The employee's maternity leave period begins on the notified date, unless she gives birth or is taken ill with a pregnancy-related illness before that notified date, as to which see *Premature birth* and *Pregnancy-related illnesses* below.

Note: A doctor or midwife will not normally issue Form Mat B1 until the beginning of the 14th week before the expected week of childbirth. Form Mat B1 is in two parts. Part A nominates the week in which childbirth is expected to occur; while Part B (Mat B2) certifies the date on which childbirth actually occurred.

14.10
An employee who neglects (or wilfully refuses) to give the prescribed minimum 21 days' advance notice, or to provide the necessary supporting documentation (other than in circumstances in which it was not reasonably practicable for her to do so) runs the risk of having to defer her maternity leave maternity leave and may forfeit her right to SMP. An employee who is unhappy about her employer's refusal to pay SMP may refer the matter for a decision by an adjudication officer (or 'Decision Maker') at her local Inland Revenue National Insurance Contributions office.

Premature birth

14.11

If an employee gives birth prematurely (that is to say, before her EWC and before the date on which she intended to begin her maternity leave, whether or not she had already notified her employer of that intended date), her ordinary maternity leave period begins with the day on which childbirth occurs. But she risks forfeiting her entitlement to ordinary maternity leave (and, where appropriate, SMP) unless she informs her employer as soon as is reasonably practicable that she gave birth on such-and-such a date.

14.12

If she had not done so already, she must also inform her employer of her EWC (supported by a Form Mat B1, if her employer asks her to produce that document or its equivalent) – bearing in mind that it is her EWC, not the actual date of birth, which determines her entitlement, if any, to SMP and the start date of her additional maternity leave period. It is useful to note (as was pointed out earlier) that one side of Form Mat B1 is a 'Certificate of Expected Confinement'; the other, a 'Certificate of Confinement'. If an employee gives birth prematurely, she should ask her doctor or midwife to sign both sides of the form before sending it off to her employer.

Note: An employee whose baby is stillborn within the first 24 weeks of pregnancy has no legal right to maternity leave (but will usually qualify for statutory sick pay (SSP) and, very likely, occupational sick pay, for so long as it takes for her to recover and return to work). But, if the stillbirth occurs *after* 24 weeks of pregnancy, she retains her right to ordinary maternity leave and, if she qualifies, to additional maternity leave also.

Pregnancy-related illnesses

14.13

If a pregnant employee falls ill (or is still ill) with a pregnancy-related illness at any time on or after the beginning of the 6th week before her EWC, her ordinary maternity leave period must begin immediately (regardless of the date on which she had otherwise intended to start her maternity leave). If she has been receiving SSP in respect of her illness, those payments must cease – to be replaced by SMP (but only if she qualifies for SMP). No further payments of

SSP are permissible during the maternity leave period, even if the employee does not qualify for SMP during that period. In these circumstances also, she must notify her employer as soon as is reasonably practicable that she is absent from work wholly or partly because of pregnancy and, if she has not already informed her employer of her EWC, must do so as soon as possible (supported, if her employer asks to see it, by a certificate of expected confinement or equivalent document signed by her doctor or midwife). As was indicated earlier, a failure to provide such information will, at best, delay her right to maternity leave and, where appropriate, SMP.

Note: A pregnant employee who is on sick leave (because of an illness or injury that has nothing to do with her being pregnant) may continue to draw statutory sick pay or invalidity benefit until her *notified leave date* (ie, the date on which she intended her maternity leave period to begin) or until her baby is born, whichever occurs sooner.

Contractual rights during ordinary maternity leave

14.14
An employee who is absent from work on ordinary maternity leave is *not* entitled to be paid her normal wages or salary during her absence (unless her contract of employment says otherwise), but she *is* entitled to the benefit of the terms and conditions of employment that would have been applicable to her if she had not been absent (and had not been pregnant or given birth to a child).

14.15
If, for example, her entitlement to paid annual holidays or sick leave (or, indeed, a pay rise) is calculated by reference to her length of service, the number of weeks she is away on maternity leave must count as part of her period of continuous service. If her employer pays pension contributions while she is at work, he must continue to pay those contributions at the same level while she is on maternity leave (that is to say, based on her normal wages or salary). However, her own contributions must be based only on the amount of any contractual remuneration or SMP actually paid to her during her maternity leave (*per* section 23 and Schedule 5 to the Social Security Act 1989). The point is that, save for the suspension of her right to be paid her normal wages or salary, an absentee employee's remaining terms and conditions of employment prevail throughout her ordinary maternity leave period. When she returns to work after her

ordinary maternity leave, she must be permitted to do so in the job she was doing before her absence began, in much the same way as if she had simply been absent from work on her annual holidays (*ibid* section 71).

Return to work after ordinary maternity leave

14.16

A woman returning to work during or at the end of her ordinary maternity leave period is entitled to do so in the job in which she was employed immediately before that period of leave began. Unless she wishes to return to work early (see para 14.18 below), she has no need to forewarn her employer of her intention to return to work, no more than she would be expected to send him a postcard reminding him that she will be returning to work after her annual holidays. All she has to do is turn up for work on the appointed day and get on with the job she was doing before her maternity leave period began. While it would be sensible for an absentee employee to keep in touch with her supervisor or head of department to ensure that everything is in readiness for her return to work, this is by no means a legal requirement.

Note: A woman's right to return to work in her original job could be put at risk if she takes *more than four weeks' parental leave* immediately after the end of her ordinary maternity leave period. In short, she may be moved to a similar job if her employer can demonstrate that it was not reasonably practicable to permit her to return to work in the job she held immediately before her ordinary maternity leave period began. For further information on **Parental Leave**, please turn to paras 14.57 to 14.83.

14.17

A woman's ordinary maternity leave period will usually end after 18 weeks (unless she has a contractual right to a longer period of leave, see para 14.7 above), but must continue for so long as may be necessary to accommodate the 'compulsory maternity leave period' (see *Note* below). If illness or injury prevents her returning to work at the end of her ordinary maternity leave, she must nonetheless comply with such procedures for notifying sickness absence as are laid down in her contract of employment or in any associated document. An employer does not have the right to postpone an employee's return to work after the end of her ordinary (or, indeed, her additional) maternity leave period (*ibid* regulation 11).

Note: As was indicated earlier, an employee must not be permitted to return to work within two weeks of giving birth (or within four weeks of doing so, if she is in factory employment), even if this means extending her ordinary maternity leave period beyond the regulation 18 weeks. An employer who ignores this requirement is guilty of an offence and liable on summary conviction to a fine of up to £500 (ERA 1996, s. 72).

An early return to work?

14.18

But if an employee plans to return to work early – bearing in mind that she may not lawfully do so within the compulsory maternity leave period referred to in para 14.17 above) – she must give her employer at least 21 days' notice of her intentions, although there is no need for her to do so in writing. If she returns to work unannounced and earlier than the due date, or after having given less than 21 days' notice, her employer has every right to send her home and to insist that she delay her return until those 21 days have elapsed or until the end of her ordinary maternity leave period, whichever occurs sooner. An employer has no right to delay an employee's return to work beyond the end of her ordinary maternity leave period. An employee who is denied her right to return to work after her ordinary maternity leave is treated in law as having been dismissed and may pursue a complaint of unfair or unlawful dismissal before an employment tribunal.

Dismissal during ordinary maternity leave

14.19

Section 99 of the 1996 Act (supported by Regulation 20 of the Maternity & Parental Leave etc Regulations 1999 (*qv*) cautions employers that it is unlawful and automatically unfair to dismiss an employee (or select her for redundancy) during her ordinary (or additional) maternity leave period if the reason (or, if more than one, the principal reason) for her dismissal or selection is that she is (or was) pregnant or had given birth to a child, or because she had exercised her statutory rights in relation to pregnancy and childbirth.

Redundancy during ordinary maternity leave

14.20

If an employee is made genuinely redundant during her ordinary maternity leave, her employer is nonetheless duty-bound to offer her suitable alternative employment before her employment under her old contract comes to an end. The alternative employment must begin on the day following the day on which her previous employment ended and, to be 'suitable', must involve work that is both suitable and appropriate for her to do in the circumstances (given her qualifications, experience and skills) and on terms and conditions of employment not substantially less favourable to her than those that would have applied had she continued to be employed in her original job. In short, she should enjoy the same or equivalent status or seniority under the new contract, work in the same location (if not in the same department or section), receive the same or a comparable rate of pay, and be entitled to the same annual holidays, the same sickness benefits; and so on (*ibid* regulation 10).

14.21
If an employee is made redundant during her ordinary maternity leave period without being offered suitable alternative employment, or without being consulted about the suitability of any available vacancies, her dismissal will be held to have been unfair. If she believes that she has been unfairly treated, she has the right to pursue her case before an employment tribunal. If the tribunal finds in her favour or believes that she was selected for redundancy principally because she was pregnant or because she had given birth to a child (or for a connected reason), it will order her employer to pay a substantial award of compensation – the more so if she elects to pursue her complaint under the Sex Discrimination Act 1975.

14.22
If the employer's defence is that there was no suitable alternative employment to offer the employee, or that she had unreasonably refused an offer of what would ordinarily be considered to be suitable alternative employment, or that there was nothing untoward about the employer's motives in selecting her for redundancy, the case will be decided on its merits.

14.23
An employer should be extremely cautious about dismissing an employee (for a reason other than redundancy) during her ordinary (or additional) maternity leave period – bearing in mind that her contract of employment subsists during her absence and that she is accordingly entitled to the same consideration as any person who is

absent from work on holidays or sick leave. To dismiss an employee *in absentia* will usually be held unfair – the more so if the evidence shows that she was not told about the reasons for her dismissal, had not been forewarned of the likelihood of her being dismissed, and not been afforded an opportunity either to put her side of the case or to appeal against her employer's decision to dismiss her – issues of procedural fairness re-emphasised by the House of Lords in *Polkey v Dayton Services Limited* [1987] IRLR 503.

Note: Unless dismissed for an unlawful or inadmissible reason (or for a reason connected with her having been pregnant or given birth to a child), an employee dismissed during her maternity leave period for a reason other than redundancy (eg, misconduct) will not normally qualify to bring a complaint of unfair dismissal unless employed by her employer for a continuous period of at least one year ending with the effective date of termination of her contract of employment. However, there is nothing to prevent her pursuing her complaint (regardless of her length of service) if she is convinced that the real reason for her dismissal was an unlawful or inadmissible reason.

ADDITIONAL MATERNITY LEAVE

14.24
In addition to her right to a minimum of 18 weeks' ordinary maternity leave, a woman who has been continuously employed for one year or more at the beginning of the 11th week before her expected week of childbirth (EWC), is entitled to 29 weeks' additional maternity leave beginning with the Sunday of the week in which her child was born. Furthermore, she has the (qualified) right to return to work, after her additional maternity leave period, in the job in which she was employed at the beginning of her ordinary maternity leave period, and on terms and conditions no less favourable to her than those that would have applied but for her absence (see also para 14.31).

Note: The rules relating to the dismissal of an employee who has been recruited specifically to replace an employee who is absent from work on maternity leave are explained in para 14.56.

Notification procedure

14.25
An employee who has the right to take additional maternity leave has no need to inform her employer in advance that she intends to

take advantage of that right; nor need she inform her employer (as was the case under the previous regime) that she intends to exercise her right to return to work after her additional maternity leave period. Her additional maternity leave period commences automatically following the end of her ordinary maternity leave period. The only advance notification an employee is required to give her employer is the 21 days' advance notification of the date on which she intends to begin her ordinary maternity leave (as described earlier in this section).

Contractual rights during additional maternity leave

14.26
The Maternity & Parental Leave etc Regulations 1999 make it clear that an employee's contract of employment continues during her additional maternity leave period although not necessarily to the same extent as her contractual rights during her ordinary maternity leave period.

14.27
Regulation 17 of the 1999 Regulations states that, during her additional maternity leave, an employee is entitled to the benefit of her employer's implied obligation to her of trust and confidence and to any terms and conditions relating to:

(a) notice to terminate her employment;

(b) compensation in the event of redundancy; or

(c) disciplinary and grievance procedures.

In short, if she is dismissed during her additional maternity leave, she must be paid her normal wages or salary during the notice period (or money in lieu of notice). If she is made redundant, she must be paid any entitlement to statutory redundancy pay, plus any 'top up' payment by way of severance pay (to which she would otherwise be entitled but for her absence). If she is to be dismissed, or has a grievance against her employer, she is entitled to be treated in the same way as any other employee facing dismissal or intent upon pursuing any such grievance.

Dismissal during additional maternity leave

14.28
Section 99 of the 1996 Act (supported by Regulation 20 of the Maternity & Parental Leave etc Regulations 1999 (*qv*)) cautions employers that it is unlawful and automatically unfair to dismiss an employee (or select her for redundancy) during her additional (or ordinary) maternity leave period if the reason (or, if more than one, the principal reason) for her dismissal or selection is that she had given birth to a child, or because she had exercised any of her statutory rights in relation to pregnancy and childbirth (including her right to ordinary or additional maternity leave).

14.29
If an employee is dismissed during her additional maternity leave period (for a reason other than redundancy), it will be for an employment tribunal to decide whether her dismissal was fair – bearing in mind that the tribunal is likely to question her employer's motives in dismissing her *in absentia* and his failure to follow the correct procedure when doing so. If the tribunal finds that the employee was dismissed for an unlawful or inadmissible reason, it will make a declaration to that effect and will order the employer either to reinstate or re-engage the employee in her old job or pay her an additional award of compensation (over and above the amount of the basic and compensatory awards of compensation for unfair dismissal).

Redundancy during additional maternity leave

14.30
An employee made redundant during her additional maternity leave is entitled to the same consideration as an employee made redundant during her ordinary maternity leave period. In short, she is entitled to be offered suitable alternative employment beginning on the day following the day on which her previous employment ended on terms and conditions of employment not substantially less favourable to her than those that would have applied had she continued to be employed in her original job – as to which, please return to para 14.20 above.

Return to work after additional maternity leave

14.31

A woman returning to work at the end of her additional maternity leave period need do no more than turn up for work on the due date. In short, she no longer needs to forewarn her employer of her intentions (but see next paragraph). Furthermore, she is entitled to return to work in the job in which she was employed before her ordinary maternity leave period began – unless it is not reasonably practicable for her employer to permit her to return to work in that job, in which case she is entitled to return to work in another job that is both suitable for her and appropriate for her to do in the circumstances. Whether she returns to work in her original job or in a 'suitable and appropriate' alternative job, she must be permitted to do so:

(a) on a salary or wage (or rate of pay) not less favourable to her than the remuneration that would have been applicable to her had she not been absent from work at any time since the commencement of her ordinary maternity leave period;

(b) with her seniority, pension rights and similar rights as they would have been if the period (or periods) of her employment prior to her additional maternity leave period were continuous with her employment following her return to work; and

(c) otherwise on terms and conditions no less favourable than those that would have applied to her had she not been absent from work after the end of her ordinary maternity leave period (*ibid* regulation 18).

Note: A woman who takes parental leave lasting for no longer than four weeks, immediately after her additional maternity leave period, retains her right to return to work in the job she held before her ordinary maternity leave period began *unless* it would not have been reasonably practicable for her to have returned to that same job after her additional maternity leave period and it is still not reasonably practicable for her to do so at the end of that period of parental leave. A woman who takes more than four weeks' parental leave immediately following the end of her additional maternity leave period is entitled to return to her original job or, if that is not reasonably practicable, to a similar job. For further information about **Parental Leave**, please turn to paras 14.57 to 14.83.

14.32

A woman, whose return to work after additional maternity leave is delayed by illness or injury, need do no more than inform her employer of that fact (in accordance with her employer's rules in relation to the notification of sickness absence).

Note: Employers should note that they no longer have the statutory right to delay an employee's return to work after childbirth (for whatever reason); nor do would-be-returning employees forfeit their right to return to work if illness or injury intervenes to prevent them doing so within four weeks of the notified date. Those provisions of the Employment Rights Act 1996 have now been repealed.

An early return to work?

14.33
An employee who wishes to return to work early, that is to say, *before* the end of her additional maternity leave period, must notify her employer (at least 21 days beforehand) that she intends to return to work on that earlier date. If she returns to work early and unannounced, without having given the prescribed 21 days' advance notice, her employer has every right to send her home and to insist that she delay her return until those 21 days have elapsed, or until the end of her additional maternity leave period, whichever occurs sooner. She has no right to be paid if she ignores her employer's instructions and remains at work during the notice period.

Seeking confirmation of employee's intention to return

14.34
If concerned that an employee may not be returning to work after her additional maternity leave period (or that she may change her mind about doing so), her employer may write to her – after she has given birth, but not earlier than 21 days before the end of her 18 weeks' ordinary maternity leave period – asking her to confirm in writing the date on which childbirth actually occurred and whether or not she intends to return to work at the end of her additional maternity leave period. To be valid, the employer's letter must:

(a) include a statement explaining how the employee may calculate the date on which her additional maternity leave period ends; and

(b) warn her that she is liable to be dismissed or subjected to some other detriment (eg, demotion or transfer) if she fails to respond within 21 days of receiving the letter.

An employee who is dismissed, demoted, transferred or otherwise disciplined for not responding to her employer's letter (or for failing to do so within the prescribed 21 days) thereby forfeits her right to the protection otherwise extended to employees who are dismissed or subjected to a detriment for exercising their rights in pregnancy and maternity. However, she may question the 'reasonableness' of her employer's actions before an employment tribunal, if she considers that she has been treated too harshly (as to which, see next paragraph).

14.35
Clearly, it would be unwise of an employer to assume without more that an employee's failure to respond to his letter within the prescribed 21 days, gives him carte blanche either to dismiss her (and recruit a replacement) or to demote or transfer her to some other job within his organisation. The employee might well have been hospitalised or moved to another address, or be overseas or visiting relations. In the interests of judicial fairness (given that the employer's actions might well be the subject of a complaint to an employment tribunal), her employer would be expected to make reasonable enquiries about her whereabouts (eg, by telephoning her home or asking amongst her workmates and friends) before taking her failure to reply at face value.

Unfortunately, an employer has no legal redress against an employee who changes her mind about returning to work after childbirth after having confirmed her intention to do so.

Failure to permit a return to work

14.36
An employee who is denied her statutory right to return to work after either of her ordinary or additional maternity leave periods will be treated in law as having been unfairly dismissed if her dismissal is solely or mainly attributable to the fact that she exercised her right to maternity leave or took advantage of the benefits of the terms and conditions of employment to which she was entitled during that leave. In short, her employer will need to satisfy an employment tribunal that he had a legitimate reason for dismissing the employee (unconnected with her having taken advantage of statutory maternity rights) and had acted fairly and reasonably in doing so.

14.37

If an employer can satisfy an employment tribunal that the employee's original job was no longer available because of redundancy and that he had acted fairly and lawfully in selecting her for redundancy – there being no suitable available vacancy to offer her, or that she had been offered suitable alternative employment by an associated employer which she had either accepted or unreasonably refused – her dismissal will be held to have been fair (*ibid* section 81).

Note: If the evidence before an employment tribunal shows that the employee was selected for redundancy for an inadmissible reason (eg, because of her sex or for reasons connected with her having taken advantage of her statutory rights in connection with pregnancy or childbirth, including her right to maternity leave), her dismissal will be held to have been inadmissible and unfair (*ibid* regulation 20(2)).

14.38

Finally, an employee who has been denied her right to return to work after additional maternity leave will not be held to have been unfairly dismissed:

(a) if, immediately before the end of her additional maternity leave period (or immediately before her dismissal, if her additional maternity leave ended with her dismissal) the number of persons employed by her employer (including the employee herself), added to the number employed by any associated employer, did not exceed five; and

(b) her employer (who may be the same employer or a successor) can satisfy the tribunal that it was not reasonably practicable either to permit her to return to work in her original job or to offer her suitable alternative employment, or for an associated employer to offer her a job of that kind (s. 96(2), ERA 1996).

As was indicated earlier, the alternative employment (or job) offered to an employee who has been denied her right to return to work in her original job, must involve work that is both suitable and appropriate for her to do (given her qualifications, experience and skills) and must be on terms and conditions of employment not substantially less favourable to her than those that would have applied had she been permitted to return to work in her original job. In short, she should enjoy the same or equivalent status or seniority, be employed in the same place (if not in the same department or section), receive the same or a comparable rate of pay, and be entitled to the same annual holidays, the same sickness benefits; and so on.

STATUTORY MATERNITY PAY (SMP)

14.39

To qualify for statutory maternity pay (SMP) during her ordinary maternity leave period, a pregnant employee must have worked for her employer for a continuous period of at least 26 weeks at the beginning of the 14th week before her expected week of childbirth (EWC). Furthermore, she must at that time have average gross earnings of £72 or more per week (or £312 or more per month) (the figures for 2001/02) calculated over the eight-week period ending with the last payday before the beginning of that 14th week. If she satisfies both these requirements, she is entitled to be paid SMP for up to 18 weeks during her ordinary maternity leave period. If she returns to work before the end of her ordinary maternity leave period, payments of SMP must cease at the end of the week immediately preceding the day on which she returned to work.

Note: A woman who does not qualify for SMP may nonetheless be entitled to the State Maternity Allowance (MA) or a payment from the Social Fund.

14.40

There are two rates of SMP: the higher rate and the lower rate. The higher rate, which is equivalent to 90 per cent of the employee's average weekly earnings, is payable for each of the first six weeks of the maternity pay period. The lower rate is payable for the remaining 12 (or fewer) weeks. The current (2001/02) lower rate of SMP is £62.20 per week.

14.41

SMP is payable in weekly tranches only (a 'week' being the period of seven calendar days from Sunday to Saturday, inclusive). There is no equivalent daily rate of SMP. It follows that a woman who chooses to (or has no choice but to) begin her ordinary maternity leave part-way through a week will not be entitled to receive any SMP in respect of the remainder of that same week, Likewise, if she chooses to return to work part-way through a week (eg, before the end of her ordinary maternity leave period), her SMP must cease on the Saturday of the previous week. A woman who is recalled to work (albeit briefly), during her ordinary maternity leave period, thereby forfeits her right to SMP in respect of each and every week during which she carries out such work.

Note: As is indicated elsewhere in this chapter, the maternity leave period for a woman who gives birth prematurely starts on the day on which childbirth occurred. The same applies if she is taken ill with a pregnancy related illness at any time on or after the beginning of the sixth week before her EWC. In the latter instance, her ordinary maternity leave period begins on the day on which she is first absent from work for that reason.

Recovery of SMP

14.42

An employer who has lawfully paid SMP to an employee can recover 92 per cent of the gross amount paid by deducting that amount from the total amount of employees' and employers' National Insurance contributions payable (together with income tax) to the Collector of Taxes within 14 days of the end of each income tax month. An employer who qualifies for Small Employer's Relief can recover 100 per cent of the gross amount of SMP payments made, plus an additional five per cent as compensation for National Insurance contributions paid on SMP (*vide* the Statutory Maternity Pay (Compensation of Employers) Amendment Regulations 1999 (SI 1999/363).

Note: An in-depth review of the rules relating to the payment of SMP is beyond the scope of a book of this size. For further particulars, the reader is commended to DSS Manual CA29 (*Statutory Maternity Pay Manual for Employers*), copies of which are freely available from the Employer's Orderline on 0845 7646646. Employers can also contact the **Employer's Helpline** on 0845 7143143.

TIME OFF FOR ANTENATAL CARE

14.43

A pregnant employee who has, on the advice of her doctor (or registered midwife) made one or more appointments to attend at any place for the purpose of receiving antenatal care, is entitled to be permitted by her employer to take paid time off during her normal working hours to enable her to keep those appointments. Before allowing time off for such purposes, her employer has the right to require the employee to produce for his inspection a Certificate of Expected Confinement (Form Mat B1), signed by her doctor or registered midwife, as well as evidence in the form of an appointment card (or similar) confirming that she has made one or more appointments to attend at an antenatal clinic. However, the employer cannot insist on inspecting either document until after the employee has made her first visit to the clinic (*Source*: ss 55 & 56, ERA 1976).

14.44

A pregnant employee, who has been denied her statutory right to paid time off work in the circumstances described above, may complain to an employment tribunal, but must do so within three months of the date of the appointment concerned, or within such further period as the tribunal considers reasonable. If her complaint is upheld, the tribunal will order the employer to pay the employee a sum equivalent to her loss or the value of her time during the period when she was refused time off. If the tribunal finds that the employer had failed to pay the employee the whole or part of any wages or salary to which she was entitled in respect of any such time off, it will also order the employer to pay the amount which it finds due to her. (*Source*: ERA 1996, s. 57).

SUSPENSION ON MATERNITY GROUNDS

14.45

An employee is suspended from work on maternity grounds if, in consequence of any relevant health and safety legislation or a recommendation contained in a code of practice issued and approved under section 16 of the Health & Safety at Work etc Act

1974, she is suspended from work by her employer because she is pregnant, or has recently given birth or is breastfeeding a child.

14.46

Before being suspended from work in the circumstances described above, the employee has the right to be offered suitable alternative work by her employer (if such is available). To be suitable, the alternative work must be both suitable and appropriate (in the light of the employee's qualifications, skills and experience) and on terms and conditions that are no less favourable to her than the corresponding terms and conditions of her usual job.

14.47
If there is no suitable alternative work for the employee to do (or she has not unreasonably refused an offer of suitable alternative work), she must be suspended from work on full pay until such time as it is safe for her to resume her normal duties. If there is any disagreement, the employee may refer the matter for determination by an employment tribunal. Any such reference or complaint must be presented within three months of the day in respect of which payment was denied or, in the case of an employer's failure to offer suitable alternative employment, within the period of three months beginning with the first day of the suspension period. A complaint presented 'out of time' will not normally be heard unless the tribunal is satisfied that it was not reasonably practicable for the complaint to be presented within the prescribed three-month period.

14.48
If an employment tribunal finds that the employer had failed to pay the remuneration to which the employee was entitled during the period of her suspension on maternity grounds, it will order the employer to pay the employee the amount which it finds is due to her. If the finding is that the employer had failed to provide the employee with suitable alternative work, the tribunal will make an award of compensation to be paid by the employer to the employee – the amount of which shall be such as the tribunal considers 'just and equitable'.

14.49
Restrictions on the employment (or continued employment) of pregnant women are to be found in the code of practice accompanying the Control of Lead at Work Regulations 1998 (*qv*), and in Schedule IV to the Ionising Radiations Regulations 1999 (*qv*). Furthermore, regulations 16 & 18 of the Management of Health & Safety at Work Regulations 1999 (*qv*) state that the risk assessment necessarily carried out by every employer must include an assessment of the risks facing pregnant employees, new mothers and employees who are breastfeeding. If there are any significant risks arising out of their working conditions or from the products or

processes to which they are exposed, they must either be transferred to more suitable work or, if that is not possible, be suspended from work on full pay for so long as is necessary. The risks in question may be related to the physical, biological or chemical agents to which any such employee is, or may be, exposed (including those specified in Annexes I and II of Council Directive 92/85/EEC 'on the introduction of measures to encourage improvements in safety and health at work of pregnant workers and workers who have recently given birth or are breastfeeding'). An employer who fails to comply with his duties under the regulations referred to above is guilty of an offence and liable to prosecution and a heavy fine.

Replacement employees

14.50
A person employed specifically to replace an employee who has been suspended from work on maternity grounds may be dismissed (for 'some other substantial reason') once the person he (or she) has been employed to replace returns to normal working – subject to the proviso that the replacement employee must be made aware of the nature of his employment at the very outset (in writing) and must be informed in clear and unequivocal terms that dismissal will take place once the permanent employee returns to work. However, the test of 'reasonableness' will nonetheless apply (*Source*: ERA 1996, s. 106(3) & (4)).

RESTRICTIONS ON NIGHT WORK

14.51
If a new or expectant mother works at night and produces a certificate signed by her doctor (or registered midwife) to the effect that working at night could be detrimental to her health and safety (or, in the case of a pregnant employee, to that of her unborn child), her employer must either transfer her to daytime work (without loss of pay) or suspend her on full pay for the period specified in the certificate. Non-compliance with this requirement is an offence under the Health & Safety at Work etc Act 1974 (*Source*: Regulation 17, Management of Health & Safety at Work Regulations 1999).

REST FACILITIES – PREGNANT EMPLOYEES AND NURSING MOTHERS

14.52
Regulation 25(4) of the Workplace (Health, Safety & Welfare) Regulations 1992 (*qv*) requires every employer to provide suitable rest facilities for the use of employees who are pregnant or breastfeeding, or who have given birth within the previous six months. In a large establishment, the facilities may consist of a small well-ventilated room equipped with (or adjacent to) a toilet and washbasin and be furnished with one or two daybeds. In the smaller business, a clean and comfortable reclining chair in a curtained-off area may suffice, so long as any employee making use of the facility is assured of a measure of privacy. Wherever possible, the rest area or facility set aside for these purposes should be situated as near as possible to the washrooms and toilets used by other (female) employees. A failure to provide this facility is an offence under the Health & Safety at Work etc. Act 1974, which could lead to prosecution and the imposition of a fine.

WRITTEN REASONS FOR DISMISSAL

Pregnancy or maternity leave dismissals

14.53
An employee who is dismissed (for whatever reason), either while pregnant or after having given birth (in circumstances in which her ordinary or additional maternity leave period ends by reason of the dismissal) must be provided by her employer with a written statement explaining the reasons for her dismissal – regardless of her working hours or length of service at the relevant time and regardless of whether she has asked to be issued with such a statement. Furthermore, the statement must be given or sent to the employee within 14 days of the date on which her dismissal took place (*Source:* s. 92(4), ERA 1996).

14.54
On a complaint to an employment tribunal, an employer who has refused or failed to provide the written statement, or has failed to do so within the prescribed 14 days, or provides a statement containing

information that is inadequate or untrue, will be ordered by the tribunal to pay the employee a sum equivalent to two weeks' pay without limit as to the amount (*Ladbroke Entertainments Ltd v Clark* [1987] ICR 585, EAT) (*Source*: s. 93, ERA 1996). Where appropriate, the tribunal will also make a declaration as to what it finds the employer's real reasons were for dismissing the employee – bearing in mind that a complaint arising out of an employer's failure to provide a written statement will very likely be heard at the same time as a complaint of unfair or unlawful dismissal (*ibid*).

14.55
A complaint that an employer has refused or failed to provide written reasons for dismissal must be presented to the Secretary to the Tribunals within three months of the effective date of termination of the employee's contract of employment. A complaint presented 'out of time' will not normally be heard unless the tribunal is satisfied that it was not reasonably practicable for the complainant to have acted sooner (see Chapter 3, paras 3.68 to 3.83) (*ibid* s. 93(3)).

The written statement of reasons for dismissal referred to in the previous paragraph is admissible in evidence in proceedings before a tribunal or court (*ibid* s. 92(5)).

DISMISSING A MATERNITY LEAVE REPLACEMENT

14.56
Dismissing a replacement employee, recruited to replace an employee who is absent from work on maternity leave, will not present a problem so long as the replacement had been informed in writing, when first recruited, that he or she would be dismissed on the return to work of the permanent incumbent. In short, the dismissal of a replacement employee in those circumstances would be treated in law as a dismissal 'for a substantial reason of a kind such as to justify the dismissal of an employee holding the position which the replacement employee held'. However, the test of 'reasonableness' will nonetheless apply (*ibid* s. 106(1), (2) & (4)).

PART 2:
PARENTAL LEAVE

14.57

The right of certain employees (in their capacities as parents or adoptive parents) to be granted up to 13 weeks' *unpaid* parental leave is to be found in Part III of the Maternity & Parental Leave etc Regulations 1999 (SI 1999/3312) that came into force on 15 December 1999 – implementing Council Directive 96/34/EC of 3 June 1996 'on the framework agreement on parental leave concluded by UNICE, CEEP and the ETUC'.

14.58

The right to parental leave is available to those employees only who have been continuously employed with their respective employers for a period of one year or more and who are either the parents of a child born on or after 15 December 1999 or who adopted a child on or after that date.

NATURE OF RIGHT

14.59

The natural parents of a child born on or after 15 December 1999 may each take up to 13 weeks' unpaid leave during the first five years of the child's life. If the mother gives birth to twins, the entitlement applies to each child during those first five years.

14.60

The parents of a child placed for adoption with them on or after 15 December 1999, may likewise each take up to 13 weeks' unpaid parental leave during the first five years following the adoption or until the child turns 18, whichever occurs sooner.

14.61

The parents of a disabled child (that is to say, a child who has been awarded a disability living allowance) may each take up to 13 weeks' unpaid parental leave until the child's 18th birthday.

14.62

A week's leave, for these purposes, is a period of absence from work that is equal in duration to the period for which an employee is normally required to work in any week. For an employee whose working hours (under his or her contract) vary from week to week, a week's parental leave is a period of absence from work that is equal in duration to the total of the employee's contractual working hours in any one year divided by 52. An employee who takes parental leave for a day or two at a time, will have taken a full week's parental leave when the aggregate of those days equates to the number (or average number) of days in a week in which he or she is normally required to work. Overtime hours should not be included in calculations unless an employee is required under his or her contract to work a specified number of overtime hours each week.

14.63

When dealing with a first request for parental leave, an employer has the right to ask for documentary evidence of parental responsibilities in the form of a birth certificate or adoption papers, or (in the case of a disabled child) evidence that a child has been awarded a disability living allowance. An employer may decline a request for parental leave until such time as that evidence is produced for his inspection.

How much leave can be taken at a time?

14.64

The amount of parental leave that can be taken at any one time is a matter for negotiation and agreement between employees and their employers. If there is nothing in an employee's contract of employment (eg, in the written statement of employment particulars, a staff or works handbook, a company policy document) concerning an employee's right to parental leave – including the amount of parental leave that may be take at any one time, the procedures attendant upon requests for parental leave, or the employer's right to postpone parental leave in specified circumstances – the default (or fallback) provisions outlined in Schedule 2 to the 1999 Regulations will apply (see **Fallback Scheme** below).

14.65

Collective and workforce agreements can also be used to determine procedures for dealing with requests for parental leave, the amount of leave that may be taken at any one time; and so on. If an employee's terms and conditions of employment are determined by a collective agreement between the employer and a recognised independent trade union (and those terms are imported into each employee's contract of employment), that same forum may be used to give practical effect to an employee's statutory right to parental leave. A workforce agreement may be used for parental leave purposes if the terms and conditions of employees (or certain identifiable groups of employees) are not otherwise determined by agreement with a recognised independent trade union.

14.66
An employer wishing to conclude a workforce agreement on parental leave must oversee the conduct of a secret ballot for the election of an appropriate number of employee representatives to negotiate the agreement with him. The number of representatives to be elected is a matter for the employer, depending on the size of the workforce or of the group of employees to be covered by the agreement. The employer must see to it that every employee is afforded an opportunity to vote in the ballot and to put his or her name forward as a candidate for election as an employee representative. The employer must provide the necessary facilities and must ensure that votes are counted fairly and accurately.

14.67
To be valid, the resultant workforce agreement must be in writing; must be signed by the negotiating parties; must be shown to all affected employees (together with a guide explaining what the agreement means); and must last for no longer than five years. The agreement should (advisedly) lay down procedures for applying for parental leave, indicate how much leave may be taken at any one time; and, where appropriate, explain the circumstances in which the employer may postpone a request for parental leave (including the employee's right to take that postponed leave at a later date). If negotiations fail to produce a workforce agreement, the fallback parental leave scheme explained below automatically applies

14.68
Any term in a contract of employment (or in a collective or workforce agreement) that purports to override or undermine an employee's statutory right to parental leave is null and void. That said, there is nothing to prevent an employer providing more generous parental leave provisions, including a period of paid parental leave.

Contractual and statutory rights during parental leave

14.69
Although the continuity of a period of employment is not broken by periods of unpaid parental leave, the only contractual rights that prevail during such absences are those relating to notice periods, severance payments (that is to say, payments in excess of statutory redundancy pay), and access to the employer's disciplinary or grievance procedures. Both parties to the employment contract are bound by their mutual and implied contractual duty of trust and confidence. From the employee's standpoint, this means that, during any period of parental leave, the employee must not work for any other employer and must not disclose to any unauthorised person confidential information relating to his (or her) employer's trade secrets, business activities, etc (as to which, please turn to Chapter 5, para 5.122).

14.70
Apart from the express and implied contractual rights referred to in the previous paragraph, all other terms and conditions of employment (eg, the right to be paid, accrual of occupational sickness benefits, holidays in excess of the statutory minimum, occupational pension rights, etc) are held in suspense when an employee is absent from work on parental leave. An employer may, of course, choose to override these statutory limitations and may, for example, continue to allow an employee the use of a company car or mobile phone during his or her absence on parental leave.

14.71
An employee's statutory rights remain undisturbed during parental leave, including the right not to be unfairly or unlawfully dismissed, the right to be paid a statutory minimum redundancy payment if dismissed for redundancy, and the entitlement to accrue paid annual leave under the provisions of the Working Time Regulations 1998.

Returning to work after parental leave

14.72
An employee who takes parental leave for a period of four weeks or less (other than immediately after taking *additional* maternity leave)

is entitled to return from leave to the exact same job that he (or she) held before that period of leave began. That same rule applies if (having completed a minimum of one year's service) a woman takes parental leave for a period of four weeks or less immediately after the end of her *ordinary* maternity leave period.

14.73

An employee who takes parental leave for a period of more than four weeks is likewise entitled to return from leave to the job in which he (or she) was employed before that period of absence began – unless it was not reasonably practicable for his employer to permit him to return to that job; in which case, the employee has the right to return to another job which is both suitable for him and appropriate for him to do in the circumstances. That same rule applies if (having completed one year's service with her employer), a woman takes more than four weeks' parental leave immediately after her *ordinary* maternity leave period.

14.74

A woman who takes parental leave for a period of four weeks or less immediately after her *additional* maternity leave period is entitled to return from leave to the job in which she was employed before her maternity absence began – unless it would not have been reasonably practicable for her to return to that job if she had returned at the end of her additional maternity leave period, and it is still not reasonably practicable to permit her to do so at the end of that period of parental leave.

Note: As was demonstrated earlier in this Chapter, an employee who is made redundant during her ordinary or additional maternity leave periods has the right to be offered suitable alternative employment under a contract that takes effect on the day following the day on which her original contract came to an end. Should she accept such an offer, her right to return to work after her ordinary or additional maternity leave is a right to return to work in that alternative job (not the job she held before her absence began). If the same employee takes parental leave immediately after either of her maternity leave periods, it is the alternative job (not her original job) to which she has the qualified right to return.

The 'fallback' scheme

14.75

In the absence of any alternative arrangements (negotiated individually or under the terms of a collective or workforce agreement), the fallback scheme outlined in Schedule 2 to the 1999 Regulations comes into play. There is anecdotal evidence that most small to medium-sized firms have adopted the fallback scheme.

14.76

Under the fallback scheme, an employee may take parental leave in blocks (or tranches) of one week or more, unless the child in question is entitled to a Disability Living Allowance, in which case the leave may be taken in single days or periods of less than one week. No more than four weeks' parental leave may be taken in any one year. For these purposes, a year is the period of 12 months that begins on the date on which the employee first became entitled to take parental leave in respect of the child in question (that is to say, either the day following the date on which the employee completed 12 months' continuous service with his (or her) employer, or the date on which the child was born or placed for adoption, whichever occurs later).

14.77

Employees seeking parental leave under the fallback scheme must (if asked to do so) provide their respective employers with evidence of parental responsibility (in the form of a birth certificate, adoption papers or evidence that a child has been awarded a Social Security Disability Living Allowance). Such evidence need only be produced on the first occasion that a parent submits a request for parental leave in respect of a child born or placed for adoption on or after 15 December 1999 (although, strictly speaking, an employer has the right to demand such evidence each time the same employee seeks further tranches of parental leave). The procedure may, of course, be repeated in the case of a second or subsequent child.

14.78

As a rule, a request for parental leave must specify the dates on which the period of leave is to begin and end, and must be submitted to the employer at least 21 days before the date on which the requested period of leave is to begin. If the applicant is a father-to-be, the request for leave must be made at least 21 days before the beginning of the expected week of childbirth (EWC), and must specify that EWC and the duration of the intended period of leave. If a period of parental leave is to begin on the date on which a child is to be placed for adoption with an employee, the request for leave must be submitted at least 21 days before the beginning of the week in which the placement is to occur, and must specify the week in question and the duration of the intended period of leave. An employer's unreasonable refusal to agree to a request for parental leave will very likely be scrutinised by an employment tribunal, the more so if an employee's child was born prematurely or the intended adoption date was unexpectedly brought forward.

14.79

The fallback scheme allows that an employer may postpone the intended start date of a requested period of parental leave for a period of up to six months. This is permissible if the employee's absence from work during that period is likely to cause undue harm to the employer's business. Such a situation might arise if a key worker has asked for parental leave at a very busy time of the year or if a number of employees have asked for overlapping periods of parental leave, leaving the employer seriously understaffed. However, postponement is not permissible if the requested period of parental leave is intended to begin on the day of a child's birth or on the day on which a child is to be placed with an employee for adoption.

14.80

Within seven days of receiving a request for a period of parental leave, an employer intending to postpone that leave must write to the employee explaining his reasons for the postponement and setting out alternative dates for the beginning and end of that leave. Before doing so, the employer must discuss the postponement with the employee and agree alternative start and finishing dates. A postponed period of parental leave must be of the same duration as the period of leave originally requested. An employee may take the postponed period of leave, even if the revised start date occurs after the child's 5th birthday (or after the 5th anniversary of the date on which the child was placed with the employee for adoption; or, in the case of a child entitled to a Disability Living Allowance, after the child's 18th birthday).

Unfair dismissal

14.81

An employee will be treated in law as having been unfairly dismissed if the reason (or principal reason) for the dismissal or selection for redundancy was that the employee had taken (or sought to take) parental leave. The same rule applies if the employee was dismissed or selected for redundancy for refusing to sign a workforce agreement or (as appropriate) for performing or proposing to perform or carry out his (or her) legitimate functions or activities as a workforce representative or as a candidate for election as such a representative. For further particulars, please turn to Chapter 5.

Detrimental treatment

14.82
An employee has the right also not to be punished, victimised or subjected to any other detriment (demotion, transfer, loss of promotion prospects, forfeiture of opportunities for training, etc) for exercising or proposing to exercise his or her statutory right to parental leave, or for refusing to sign a workforce agreement, or (where appropriate) for performing or proposing to perform his (or her) functions or activities as a workforce representative or as a candidate for election as such a representative. For further particulars, please turn to Chapter 6 and to the **Index** entries under 'victimisation'.

Further information

14.83
The Department of Trade & Industry has published a booklet titled *Parental Leave: A guide for employers and employees* (Ref. URN 99/1193) copies of which may be obtained (free of charge) from:

DTI Publications Orderline
ADMAIL 528
London
SW1W 8YT

Telephone:	0870 1502 500
Fax:	0870 1502 333
E-mail:	dtipubs@echristian.co.uk

PART 3:
TIME OFF FOR DEPENDANTS

14.84
Every employee (regardless of his or her age, length of service or working hours) has the right to be permitted a reasonable amount of *unpaid* time off work to care for dependants (per section 57A, Employment Rights Act 1996, as inserted by section 8, Schedule 4, Part II, Employment Relations Act 1999).

This statutory right, which came into effect on 15 December 1999, applies to a situation in which an employee needs time off work to take action which is necessary:

(a) to provide assistance on an occasion when a dependant falls ill, gives birth, or is injured or assaulted;

(b) to make arrangements for the provision of care for a dependant who is ill or injured;

(c) in consequence of the death of a dependant;

(d) because of the unexpected disruption (or termination) of existing arrangements for the care of a dependant;

(e) to deal with an incident at school involving one of the employee's children.

14.85
For obvious reason, an employee cannot be expected to give his (or her) employer advance warning of his need to take time off work in the circumstances described above. However, he must inform his employer of the situation as soon as is reasonably practicable (either by telephoning from home as soon as possible or, if suddenly called away from work, by notifying his supervisor or immediate manager of the situation before leaving the premises).

14.86
It should be pointed out that, in the absence of any contractual arrangement to the contrary, an employee's right to take time off for dependants does not extend to dealing with other types of domestic emergency, such as a boiler explosion or gas leak, although

employers would undoubtedly be prepared to be reasonable in such cases.

Meaning of 'dependant'

14.87

For these purposes, a 'dependant' is an employee's wife, husband, partner, child, parent, or some other person living in the same household as the employee (other than as a tenant, lodger or boarder) who reasonably relies on the employee for assistance if he or she falls ill or is injured or assaulted, or to make arrangements for the provision of care in the event of illness or injury. The definition would also include a parent, grandparent, aged aunt or other close relative (whether or not living in the same household as the employee, but nearby) who is dependant on the employee for routine care and assistance.

14.88

A live-in nanny or 'au pair' would also qualify (especially if living at a considerable distance from home), as would an elderly neighbour living alone who has no immediate family to call upon in an emergency. It is not yet clear whether a person sharing accommodation with an employee and one or two others (either as a live-in partner or friend) would fall within this category. In such circumstances, it is up to the employer to exercise a degree or judgement when asked to make a decision in the matter.

14.89

It would be open to an employer to take disciplinary action against any employee who breaches his (or her) implied contractual duty of trust and confidence by abusing the right to time off in circumstances that do not warrant such time off.

How much time off is reasonable?

14.90

Section 57A of the 1996 Act makes the point that an employee has the right to take a reasonable amount of unpaid time off work *to provide assistance* in a genuine emergency, *to make arrangements* for the care of a dependant, or *to collect a child from school* if he (or she) has had an accident or has been involved in some other incident. That right does not include taking extended leave of absence to care for an injured dependant or sick child or to wind-up a deceased relative's affairs. Should there be any dispute as to what and what does not constitute a reasonable amount of time off (given the circumstances), the matter should be dealt with through the usual 'grievance' channels (or, if need be, will be resolved by an employment tribunal). In some circumstances, it would not be unreasonable to require an employee to 'dip into' his or her annual holiday entitlement.

Complaint to an employment tribunal

14.91
A complaint of an employer's refusal or failure to permit an employee to take time off for dependants must be lodged with an employment tribunal within three months of the date on which that refusal or failure occurred. Should the employee's complaint be upheld, the tribunal will make a declaration to that effect and will order the employer to pay the employee such compensation as it considers to be 'just and equitable' in the circumstances.

Protection from detriment

14.92
Section 47C of the 1996 Act (supplemented by regulation 19 of the Maternity & Parental Leave etc Regulations 1999) cautions that an employee has the right not to be subjected to any detriment by any act, or by any deliberate failure to act, by his (or her) employer, done because the employee took or sought to take time off for dependants under section 57A of that Act. On a successful complaint to an employment tribunal, the employer would be ordered to pay the disadvantaged employee an appropriate amount of compensation, including compensation for the loss of any benefit that would otherwise have been available to the employee but for the employer's actions (or failure to act). See also **Index** entries under 'victimisation'.

Unfair dismissal

14.93

An employee who is dismissed or selected for redundancy will be held to have been unfairly dismissed if the reason (or, if more than one, the principal reason) for his (or her) dismissal or selection was that he had taken or sought to take time off for dependants under section 57A of the 1996 Act. A complaint of unfair dismissal in such circumstances (if upheld) would result in the employer being ordered to pay the employee a substantial amount of compensation (comprising a basic award of a maximum £7,200, a compensatory award of up to £51,700 and, where applicable, an additional award of between 26 and 52 weeks' pay). A complaint of unfair dismissal in such circumstances may be presented regardless of the employee's age or length of service at the material time. For further particulars, please turn to Chapter 5.

Further information

14.94

For further information, the reader is commended to DTI publication: *Time Off for Dependants: A guide for employers and employees* (Ref URN 99/1186), copies of which are available, free of charge, from:

DTI Publications Orderline
ADMAIL 528
London
SW1W 8YT

Telephone:	0870 1502 600
Fax:	0870 1502 333
E-mail:	dtipubs@echristian.co.uk

Miscellaneous statutory rights

SUSPENSION ON MEDICAL GROUNDS

15.1
Current health and safety legislation empowers Employment Medical Advisers (EMAs) and appointed factory doctors to suspend any employee from work on medical grounds if the employee's exposure to certain hazardous substances at the workplace poses a particular risk to his health. An employee suspended from work on medical grounds is entitled to be paid his normal wage or salary during the suspension period for a maximum of 26 weeks or until such time as the EMA or factory doctor declares that it is safe for that employee to return to work (whichever occurs sooner). To qualify for payment during a period of suspension on medical grounds, the employee must:

- have been continuously employed for a minimum period of one month ending with the day immediately preceding the day on which the suspension begins (but see *Note* below);

- not otherwise be incapable of work by reason of disease or bodily or mental disablement;

- remain 'on standby' (that is to say, must be readily contactable and available to return to work at short notice) in case his employer finds other work for him to do; and

- not have unreasonably refused any such offer of suitable alternative work – whether or not the work in question is of a kind that he is normally required to do under the contract of employment.

(*Source*: ERA 1996, s. 65.)

Note: The right to payment during a period of suspension on medical grounds does not apply to any employee engaged under a fixed-term contract of three months or less unless, at the end of the day immediately preceding the date on which the suspension period begins, he had already worked under that contract for *more than* three months.

15.2

The Regulations under which employment medical advisers and factory doctors have the right to suspend employees are:

- the Control of Lead at Work Regulations 1998 (SI 1998/532) – exposure to lead (including lead alloys, any compounds of lead, and lead as a constituent of any substance or material);

- the Control of Substances Hazardous to Health Regulations 1999 (SI 1999/437) – exposure to one or other of the substances listed in Schedule 5 to the Regulations;

- the Ionising Radiations Regulations 1999 (SI 1999/3232) – exposure to electromagnetic or corpuscular radiation capable of producing ions and emitted from a radioactive substance or from a machine or apparatus that is intended to produce ionising radiation or in which charged particles are accelerated by a voltage of not less than five kilovolts; and

- the Management of Health & Safety at Work Regulations 1999 (SI 1999/3242) – exposure to processes or working conditions, or to physical, biological or chemical agents, which could involve risk, by reason of her condition, to the health and safety of a new or expectant mother, or to that of her baby.

Note: A woman suspended from work on maternity grounds (as distinct from medical grounds) has no need of a qualifying period of employment and has the qualified right to be paid her normal wages or salary so long as the suspension period continues. For further particulars, please turn to Chapter 14, paras 14.45 to 14.49).

People suspended from work in the circumstances summarised above will not necessarily be ill when suspended, but may be showing symptoms (headaches, fatigue, etc) commonly associated with exposure to the hazardous substances in question.

Excluded classes

15.3

The 'medical suspension' provisions of the Employment Rights Act 1996 do not apply to share fishermen, or to police officers (*Source*: ERA 1996, ss 199 & 200).

Dismissal of a replacement employee

15.4
A person employed specifically to replace an employee who has been suspended from work on medical grounds may be fairly dismissed (for 'some other substantial reason') once the person he (or she) has been employed to replace returns to normal working – always provided that the replacement employee is made aware at the very outset (preferably in writing) of the circumstances of his employment and is informed that dismissal will take place once the permanent employee returns to work. However, the test of 'reasonableness' will nonetheless apply (*Source*: ERA 1996, s. 106(3) & (4)).

Complaints

15.5
An employee who has been suspended from work on medical grounds may complain to an employment tribunal that his (or her) employer has refused or failed to pay him the whole or part of his normal wages during the period of suspension. Such a complaint must be presented within three months of the alleged refusal or failure (or within such further period as the tribunal considers reasonable in a case where it is satisfied that it was not reasonably practicable for the complaint to have been presented within that period of three months).

If such a complaint is upheld, the employer will be ordered to pay the employee the amount of remuneration that it finds is due to him (*Source*: ERA 1996, s. 70).

See also **Suspension on maternity grounds** (Chapter 14, paras 14.45 to 14.50).

TIME OFF WORK

15.6
The rights of employees to be allowed a reasonable amount of paid or unpaid time off work during normal working hours are to be found in the Trade Union & Labour Relations (Consolidation) Act

1992, the Employment Rights Act 1996, and in regulation 25 of the Transnational Information & Consultation of Employees Regulations 1999 (SI 1999/3323). The right to paid (or unpaid) time off work is available in prescribed circumstances to:

- trade union officials;

- trade union members;

- officials or members of prescribed public bodies;

- redundant employees (to look for work or arrange training);

- safety representatives (trade-union appointed or otherwise);

- pregnant employees needing antenatal care;

- employees attending to the needs of dependants;

- pension scheme trustees;

- employee representatives (collective redundancy and TUPE consultations);

- young persons aged 16, 17 or 18 who are undertaking study or training leading to a 'relevant qualification';

- member of 'special negotiating bodies' (SNBs) and European Works Councils (EWCs) and 'information and consultation representatives'; and

- a worker ('employee' or otherwise) accompanying another worker at any formal stage of a disciplinary or grievance procedure.

With one exception (namely, the employee under notice of redundancy, who must have 'notched up' two years' continuous service), the right to time off work is available to all relevant employees, regardless of their age, length of service or working hours at the material time.

15.7

The right to be *paid* during time off work is available to all but two of the categories listed above. Trade union members given time off during working hours to attend trade union-organised meetings (or whatever) are *not* entitled to be paid while absent from their work stations or desks. The same applies to employees who are justices of the peace or members of certain public bodies.

The amount of time off to be allowed (in the circumstances summarised above) must be 'reasonable'. A dispute over whether the amount of time off allowed was reasonable or unreasonable may well lead to proceedings before an employment tribunal.

Excluded classes

15.8
Merchant seamen do not have the right to time off for public duties or (if under notice of redundancy) to time off to look for work or arrange for retraining. However, none of these exclusions applies to the trustees of relevant occupational pension schemes unless they are relevant members of the House of Lords or the House of Commons staff (*Source*: ERA 1996, ss 194, 195, 199 & 200; and TULRA 1992, ss 281 & 285).

Time off for trade union duties

15.9
Trade union officials (shop stewards, works convenors, and the like) must be paid their normal wages or salary when granted time off to carry out their official duties or when undergoing approved training in relevant aspects of industrial relations. To qualify, the official in question must be an official of an independent trade union recognised by the employer for the purposes of collective bargaining.

15.10
The statute provides that 'the amount of time off which an employee is to be permitted to take... and the purposes for which, the occasions on which and any conditions subject to which time off may be so taken are those that are reasonable in all the circumstances having regard to [paragraph 8-20 of the] Code of Practice issued by ACAS...' (*Source*: TULRA 1992, s. 170(3)). The phrase 'reasonable in the circumstances' covers the nature, extent and purposes of the time already being taken off (*Wignall v British Gas Corporation* [1984] IRLR 493, EAT).

15.11
The way that the tribunals approach these provisions was summarised by Slynn J in *Sood v GEC Elliott Process Automation Ltd* [1980] ICR 1, EAT: 'It seems to us that when questions involving

industrial relations arise, a union official may well be entitled, as part of his duties, to take part in the planning of strategy and in discussing with other workers who are at the time negotiating with their employers, so long as the latter employers are associated with a particular trade union official's own employees. Nor do we accept the argument that a trade union official is only entitled to take time off for the purpose of negotiating where the employers have laid down the particular industrial relations structure... the test is whether the time off is required to enable the official to carry out his duties in relation to a matter which arises in relations between employees and management. We do not consider that the mere exchange of information between the trade union officials themselves necessarily qualifies, even if those officials represent workers in a particular group of companies'. See also *London Ambulance Service v Charlton & Another* [1992] IRLR 510, EAT.

15.12
Trade union officials who work shifts are not entitled to be paid when carrying out those of their official duties that occur outside normal shift working hours; nor have they any legal right to take time off work in lieu of the time spent carrying out those duties. But if they work nights and their official duties occur during the day, it probably would be reasonable to give them the night off and pay them, to enable them to carry out those duties (*Hairsine v Kingston-upon-Hull City Council* [1992] ICR 18, EAT).

15.13
An employee minded to complain about his (or her) employer's refusal to allow him time off work to carry out his duties as a trade union official (or about his employer's failure to pay him during such time off) must do so within three months of the alleged refusal or failure (or, if that is not reasonably practicable, as soon as possible). If the complaint is upheld, the tribunal will make a declaration to that effect, and will order the employer to pay to the employee such amount of compensation as it considers 'just and equitable in all the circumstances' (*Source*: TULRA 1992, ss 168, 171 & 172).

15.14
The award of compensation will comprise:

- the wages that have been wrongly withheld; and

- compensation for any other injury sustained (eg hurt feelings).

But a tribunal cannot order an employer to allow time off for a special occasion or at a specified level, nor can it impose conditions. But any observations made of what it considers to be reasonable time off are likely to be taken into consideration at a later complaint (*Corner v Buckinghamshire County Council* [1978] IRLR 320, EAT).

15.15
In assessing the amount of lost wages, the tribunal will include premiums for duties that the employee was contractually bound to perform, eg for shift work. But any extra payment for non-compulsory overtime, even if regularly undertaken, would not be recoverable (see Chapter 3, para 3.89) (*McCormack v Shell Chemical UK Ltd* [1979] IRLR 40, EAT; and *Davies & Alderton v Head Wrightson Teesdale Ltd* [1979] IRLR 170, EAT).

Time off for trade union activities

15.16
The right to a reasonable amount of time off work to participate in the activities of an independent trade union extends to any member (as opposed to an official) of such a union, so long as that union is recognised by the employer as having bargaining rights in relation to terms and conditions of employment, etc. The trade union activities must not of themselves comprise industrial action and may only take place at 'an appropriate time', that is to say, at a time during normal working hours in accordance with arrangements agreed with or consent given by the employer. However, an employer is *not* duty-bound to pay trade union members who have asked for (and been granted) time off to participate in such activities. See also Chapter 5, para 5.26) (*Source*: TULRA 1992, s. 170).

15.17
The ACAS *Code of Practice: Tine off for trade union duties and activities* states (at paragraph 21) that the type of trade union activities for which a reasonable amount of (unpaid) time off work should be permitted during working hours are:

- 'attending workplace meetings to discuss and vote on the outcome of negotiations with the employer;

- meeting full-time officials to discuss issues relevant to the workplace;

- voting in properly conducted ballots on industrial action;

- voting in union elections'.

And again, at paragraph 25: 'The amount and frequency of time off should be reasonable in all the circumstances. Although the statutory provisions apply to all employers without exception as to size and type of business or service, trade unions should be aware of the wide variety of difficulties and operational requirements to be taken into account when seeking or agreeing arrangements for time off, for example:

- 'the size of the organisation and the number of workers;

- the production process;

- the need to maintain a service to the public;

- the need for safety and security at all times.'

15.18

The refusal by an employer must be unreasonable before a member has a remedy. Thus, if the purpose of the time off is to plan industrial action, or foment unrest, then an employer can refuse to allow it. Indeed, he may be able to dismiss without it being held to be unfair (see paras 5.9 to 5.11) (*Oxford & County Newspapers & Another v McIntyre & Shipton*, 29 July 1986, EAT) (*Source*: TULRA 1992, s. 170(2)).

15.19

An employee who has been denied his (or her) statutory right to time off work (or, if qualified, who has not been paid in respect of such time off) may complain to an employment tribunal. The complaint must be presented within three months of the employer's refusal (or failure to pay) or, if this is not reasonably practicable, within such further period as is reasonable in the circumstances. If the complaint is upheld, the tribunal will:

- make a declaration to this effect; and

- award compensation for any injury sustained, eg hurt feelings.

(*Source*: TULRA 1992, ss 170(4), 171 & 172.)

Time off for public duties

15.20
Employers must allow those of their employees who are justices of the peace or members of certain public bodies a reasonable amount of time off work to enable them to carry out their official duties. Although an employee has no legal right to be paid at such times, an employer's refusal to pay could be construed as a refusal to allow time off, the more so if an employee simply cannot afford to take time off without pay. This view was endorsed by Slynn J in *Corner v Buckingham County Council* [1978] ICR 836. There, he remarked that 'in considering where there has been refusal to grant time off, the [employment] tribunal can look at the conditions subject to which an employer is prepared to grant time off (including conditions relating to pay) and could say that they really amounted to a refusal to allow time to be taken'.

15.21
In deciding whether the time off is reasonable, the following factors must be taken into account:

- how much time off is needed to enable an employee to carry out his (or her) public duties;

- how much time off is required to carry out a particular duty;

- how much time off has already been permitted (eg time off for trade union duties and activities); and

- the circumstances of the employer's business and the effect the employee's absence (or further absence) would have on it.

(*Source*: ERA 1996, s. 50(4).)

15.22
A balancing act has to be carried out, and each case has to be decided on its own particular facts. However, there is no obligation on the

employer to rearrange the duties of an employee to enable him (or her) to make up for the time lost (*Ratcliffe v Dorset CC* (1978) IRLR 191, EAT).

15.23
A complaint relating to an employer's refusal or failure to allow time off work for public duties must be presented to an employment tribunal within the time limits described in para. 15.19 above. If the complaint is upheld, the tribunal will make a declaration to that effect and may make an award of compensation to be paid by the employer to the employee. The amount of compensation will be such as the tribunal considers 'just and equitable' in the circumstances, having regard to the employer's default in failing to permit the employee to take time off, and any loss sustained by the employee that is attributable to the matters to which the complaint relates (*Source*: ERA 1996, s. 51).

Time off during redundancy notice

15.24
To qualify for the right to paid time off work during his (or her) notice period, a redundant employee must have been continuously employed for at least two years at the (projected) effective date of termination of his contract of employment. If the employee has been given less than the *statutory* notice period, his (projected) length of service must be calculated to the end of that longer notice period. The purpose of the time off is to enable the employee to look for work elsewhere or to make arrangements for re-training after the employment comes to an end. As the penalty for refusing paid time off work in these circumstances is a maximum 40 per cent of a week's pay, it follows that an employer should allow up to two days' time off work (consecutive or in the aggregate) during the employee's notice period (*Source*: ERA 1996, ss 52 & 53).

15.25
A complaint of an employer's failure to allow time off in the circumstances described, or to pay the employee his (or her) normal wages or salary at such times, must be presented to an employment tribunal within three months of the alleged refusal or failure to pay (or within such further period as the tribunal considers reasonable). If the complaint is upheld, the tribunal will make a declaration to

that effect and may order the employer to pay the employee the amount which it finds is due to him, subject to a maximum of two day's pay (*Source*: ERA 1996, s. 54).

Time off for safety representatives and representatives of employee safety

15.26

The subject of health and safety at work (and the eponymous 1974 Act) is considered in Chapter 16. Trade-union-appointed safety representatives and elected representatives of employee safety, have certain statutory functions to perform. Their employer must permit them to take such time off work (with pay) as is reasonable and necessary to enable them to carry out those functions – and paid time off also for the purposes of undergoing such training in aspects of those functions as may be reasonable in all the circumstances (*Source*: Safety Representatives & Safety Committees Regulations 1977 (Reg 4(2)) & Health & Safety (Consultation with Employees) Regulations 1996 (SI 1996/1513) (Reg 7(2)).

15.27

According to the Health and Safety Commission's *Approved Code of Practice: Safety representatives & safety committees*, the functions of safety representative's include encouraging cooperation between their employer and the workforce in promoting and developing essential measures to ensure the health and safety of employees; and bringing to the employer's notice any unsafe or unhealthy conditions or working practices, or unsatisfactory arrangements for welfare at work, which come to their attention whether on an inspection or day to day observation. Copies of the code (ISBN 0 7176 1220 1) are available from HSE Books.

Note: The code of practice (or *Brown Book*) referred to above relates to the role and functions of trade-union-appointed representatives, although there can be little difference between those and the functions of employee-elected representatives.

15.28

A complaint of an employer's refusal or failure to permit time off work in the circumstances described (or to pay an employee his (or her) normal wages or salary during such time off) must be presented to an employment tribunal within three months of the alleged refusal or failure (or within such further period as the tribunal considers reasonable in a case where it is satisfied that it was not reasonably practicable for the complaint to be presented within the prescribed three-month period) (*Source*: Safety Representatives & Safety Committees Regs 1977, Reg 11; and Health & Safety (Consultations with Employees Regs 1996, Sch 2).

If such a complaint is upheld, the tribunal will make a declaration to that effect and will order the employer to pay compensation to the complainant of such amount as it considers just and equitable, having regard to the employer's default in failing to permit time off and to any loss sustained by the employee that is attributable to that failure. In the case of a failure to pay a representative his normal wages or salary during such time off, the tribunal will order the employer to pay the employee the amount that it finds is due to him.

Time off for antenatal care

15.29
The right of a pregnant employee to be permitted a reasonable amount of paid time off work to enable her to keep one or more appointments at an antenatal clinic (or similar establishment), on the recommendation of her doctor or registered midwife, is discussed earlier in this handbook (see Chapter 14, paras 14.25 & 14.26).

Time off work – pension scheme trustees

15.30
Under section 16 of the Pensions Act 1995 an employee may be nominated and appointed by his (or her) colleagues to represent their interests as members of a relevant occupational pension scheme (that is to say, a scheme established under a trust by their employer). Every such *pension scheme trustee* has the legal right to be permitted a reasonable amount of paid time off work to enable him to perform his duties as such a trustee or to undergo training relevant to the performance of those duties. Just how much time off is reasonable is a matter of common sense and judgement. When considering a request for time (eg to attend a meeting of the trustees of the pension scheme) an employer is entitled to consider the effect the employee's absence from his desk or workbench is likely to have on the business, but must be mindful also that an employee-elected trustee should not be too circumscribed in the exercise of his legitimate functions.

15.31
A pension scheme trustee who believes that he (or she) is not being reasonably treated in the matter of time off work, or who is aggrieved at his employer's refusal or failure to pay him his normal wages or salary at such times, may present a complaint to an employment tribunal. The complaint must be presented within three months of the alleged refusal of failure (or, if the employee has resigned or been dismissed) within three months of the effective date of termination of the employee's contract of employment. If the complaint is upheld, the tribunal will make a declaration to that effect and will order the employer to pay to the employee such compensation as is considered appropriate in the circumstances (*Source*: ERA 1996, ss 58, 59 & 60).

Time off work – employee representatives

15.32
Under the Collective Redundancies & Transfer of Undertakings (Protection of Employment) (Amendment) Regulations 1995 (SI 1995/2587), trade-union-appointed and/or employee-elected *employee representatives* have the right to be consulted by their employers when 20 or more redundancies are mooted (collective redundancies) or when proposals are afoot for the sale or transfer of the whole or part of the employer's business or for the acquisition of the whole or part of another employer's business (as to which, see Chapter 4, paras 4.41 to 4.47, and (in relation to transfers of undertakings) Chapter 17, paras 17.21 to 17.26.

15.33
Employee representatives in the circumstances described above have the legal right to be permitted a reasonable amount of paid time off work to enable them to carry out their functions efficiently. An employer who denies them that right (or who refuses or fails to pay them their normal wages or salary during such time off as is granted) will be called upon to explain his intransigence before an employment tribunal. If the complaint against him is upheld, he will be ordered to pay an appropriate amount of compensation. It must be emphasised that an employee attempting to exercise his (or her) statutory rights in this context has no need to resign in order to obtain redress for an alleged breach of those rights. A complaint must nonetheless be presented to the Secretary to the Tribunals

within three months of the alleged failure to allow time off or within three months of the employer's refusal or failure to pay. If the employee has resigned (or been dismissed), the three-month period begins to run from the effective date of termination of the employee's contract of employment (as to which, see Chapter 3, paras 3.68 to 3.83).

Time off for young persons for study or training

15.34

An employee aged 16 or 17, who is not receiving full-time secondary or further education, and who has not achieved (inter alia) grades A* to C in at least five GCSE subjects, has the right to be permitted by his (or her) employer to take a reasonable amount of paid time off work in order to undertake study or training leading to an academic or vocational qualification likely to enhance the employee's employment prospects. That same right extends to any 18-year-old employee who began his studies before his 18th birthday (*Source*: ERA 1996, s. 63A, as inserted, with effect from 1 September 1999, by the Teaching & Higher Education Act 1998).

Note: For a full list of the standards of achievement encompassed by section 63A of the 1996 Act (unfortunately, too numerous to reproduce here), the reader is commended to the Right to Time Off for Study or Training Regulations 1999 (SI 1999/986), copies of which are available from The Stationery Office (Telephone 0870 600 5522). The text of the Regulations may be freely downloaded from the Stationery Office's Web site: www.hmso.gov.uk.

15.35

The amount of time off to be permitted in the circumstances described in the preceding paragraph, and the occasions on which and any conditions subject to which time off may be so taken, are those that are reasonable given the requirements of the employee's study or training balanced against the employer's business circumstances and the effect that the employee's absences would have on the efficient running of the business (*ibid*).

15.36

An employer's refusal or failure to allow a young person in his employ to take time off for study or training (or a refusal to pay the employee for such time off) may be referred to an employment tribunal. If such a complaint is upheld, the tribunal will make a declaration to that effect and will order the employer to pay the employee an amount equivalent to the amount he (or she) would have been paid had he been permitted to take time off or, if the employee had been granted time off, but without pay, the amount that the tribunal finds is due to the employee in respect of that time off.

Time off – members of SNBs and EWCs

15.37

Since the coming into force on 1 February 2000 of the Transnational Information & Consultation of Employees Regulations 1999 (*qv*) – implementing Council Directive 94/45/EC of 22 September 1994 'on the establishment of a European Works Council or a procedure in Community-scale undertakings, etc' – employees who are members of a 'special negotiating body' (SNB) or of a European Works Council (EWC), or who are 'information and consultation representatives' now have the right to be permitted such time off work (with pay) as is necessary to enable them to carry out their functions as such members or representatives. That same right extends to employees canvassing for election as such a member or representative.

15.38

An employee (*qua* member, representative or candidate), who is refused paid time off work in the circumstances described in the previous paragraph, may complain to an employment tribunal. If his (or her) complaint is upheld, the employer in question will be ordered to pay an appropriate amount of compensation. For further information about European Works Councils, please turn to Chapter 22.

ITEMISED PAY STATEMENT

15.39

Every employee (part-time, full-time, seasonal or casual) is entitled to receive an itemised pay statement on every occasion that he (or she) receives a pay packet or pay statement (weekly, fortnightly, monthly, or whatever). The statement must itemise:

- the gross amount;

- the amount of each fixed deduction authorised by the employee (SAYE schemes, trade union dues, mortgage payments, etc);

- the amount of any variable deductions and what each is for (PAYE, National Insurance and pension contributions, etc);

- the net amount paid (after deductions);

- details of how the net amount is paid (by cash or cheque, or by credit transfer to one or more named banks or building societies).

(*Source*: ERA 1996, ss 8 to 10.) See also Chapter 5, para 5.49 concerning the payment of 'tax credits'.

15.40
Separate particulars of each fixed deduction need not be shown in a pay statement if, but only if, the aggregate amount is shown *and* the employer has already provided the employee with a so-called 'standing statement of fixed deductions'. The latter statement must be amended or updated as often as may be necessary and re-issued to the employee (if not amended or updated in the meantime) at least once every 12 months.

15.41
An employee, regardless of his (or her) age or length of service at the material time, may refer the matter to an employment tribunal if his employer fails to provide an itemised pay statement (or issues a pay statement that does not comply with the statutory requirements). Any deductions from an employee's wages or salary, which are not explained in an accompanying pay statement, will be treated by the tribunal as 'unnotified deductions'. In short, the tribunal may order the employer to refund any and all such deductions from the employee's pay over the period of up to 13 weeks immediately preceding the date on which the employee's Originating Application (Form IT1) was received by the Secretary to the Tribunals.

15.42
It is important to note that an employee has no need to resign from his (or her) employment in order to obtain redress from an employment tribunal. An employer who reacts to any such challenge to his authority by dismissing the employee in question, runs the risk of being

summoned before a tribunal yet again and of being ordered to pay the employee a very substantial amount of compensation indeed, as to which see Chapter 5, paras 5.44 to 5.45 (*Source*: ERA 1996, s. 104).

15.43

References or complaints to an employment tribunal in the circumstances described above must be presented with three months of the employer's refusal or failure to provide an itemised pay statement (or one that is incomplete). If the employee has been dismissed or is no longer employed, the complaint must be presented within three months of the effective date of termination of the employee's contract of employment. A complaint presented 'out of time' will not be heard unless a tribunal is satisfied that it was not reasonably practicable for it to have been presented sooner.

'GUARANTEE PAYMENTS'

15.44

An employee who is not provided with work by his (or her) employer, throughout a day on which he is ordinarily required to work, has the legal right to be paid a 'guarantee payment' in respect of that and any subsequent 'workless days' – subject to a maximum of five 'workless days' in any period of three consecutive months. From 1 February 2001, the maximum guarantee payment is £16.70 a day (which figure is adjusted each year in line with the September on September change in the retail price index). If an employee earns less than an average £16.70 a day, the employer need only pay the lower amount (*Source*: ERA 1996, ss 28 to 35).

15.45

An employer's failure or inability to provide work must have been prompted by:

- a diminution in the requirements of the employer's business for work of the kind which the employee is employed to do (eg a dramatic downturn in orders); or

- some other occurrence (such as a power failure, fire, flood, non-delivery of raw materials, etc) affecting the normal working of the employer's business in relation to work of the kind that the employee is employed to do.

However, an employer is not obliged to make guarantee payments to any of his employees if his inability to provide them with work is due to a strike, lock-out or other industrial action prompted by other employees (or by persons employed by an 'associated employer') – even if the employees seeking guarantee payments are not directly involved in the dispute in question.

Cautionary note

15.46

It is as well to point out that an employer has no automatic right to lay off any employee without pay when business is slack (or for any other reason) unless that right has already been conceded by employees in their contracts of employment. In the absence of any such contractual right (express or otherwise), laying off an employee without pay is a breach of contract that could lead to a claim for damages before a court or tribunal or to enforced resignation and a complaint of unfair constructive dismissal. If an employee has a contractual right to be paid the whole or part of his (or her) normal wages or salary when laid off, any guarantee payment in respect of a 'workless day' may be offset against any payment of wages or salary in respect of that same day, and vice versa.

Qualifying conditions

15.47

To qualify for a guarantee payment in respect of a workless day, an employee must have worked for his (or her) employer for a period of at least one month ending with the day immediately preceding the day in question. Furthermore, if asked to do so, the employee must keep himself available for work (ie must remain 'on standby') on the off-chance that his employer may have suitable alternative work for him to do. An employee who does not remain on standby or who reasonably refuses an offer of alternative work (even if the work in question is not of the type he is ordinarily required to do under his contract of employment) will forfeit his right to a guarantee payment.

15.48

If a shift or night worker's working hours begin and end before and after midnight, the 'workless day' will be the day on which the major portion of the shift falls. If the hours on either side of midnight are the same, the workless day will be the day on which the shift ends.

15.49
The following do not qualify for guarantee payments:

- any employee with less than one month's service at the end of the day preceding the relevant 'workless day';

- a person employed on a fixed-term contract for a period of three months or less (or contracted to carry out a specific task that is expected to be completed within three months) – unless (contrary to expectations) he (or she) has been continuously employed for a period of more than three months ending with the day before the relevant 'workless day'.

Employees (such as salesmen) who do not have normal working hours, employees who ordinarily work outside Great Britain, masters and crew engaged in share fishing, and members of the police and armed forces are also excluded (*Source*: ERA 1996, ss 29, 192, 199 & 200).

DAMAGES FOR BREACH OF CONTRACT

15.50
Nowadays, employment tribunals share jurisdiction with the county courts to entertain claims for damages arising out of a breach of contract that arises or remains on the termination of an employee's contract of employment – eg dismissal without the appropriate notice ('wrongful dismissal') or dismissal in breach of an employer's own contractual procedures for terminating employment.

15.51
Damages can generally be divided into three types:

- ordinary damages to compensate the aggrieved for the loss he (or she) has sustained, eg the amount of wages, holiday entitlement and so forth;

- aggravated damages for injury to feelings that are compensatory in nature, although difficult to evaluate;

- exemplary damages that are punitive – intended to deter a defendant rather than compensate a plaintiff.

(*Duffy v Eastern Health & Social Services Board* [1992] IRLR 251, Fair Employment Tribunal (Northern Ireland).)

15.52
It matters not that the defendant's behaviour was high-handed, malicious, insulting or oppressive. Exemplary damages may only be awarded where:

- the defendant was motivated by a search for profit; or

- they are specifically authorised by statute; or

- the defendants are exercising some form of governmental function – extending, in appropriate circumstances, to the acts of local, authorities.

(*Broome v Cassel & Co* [1972] AC 1029, HL; and *Bradford City Metropolitan Council v Arora* [1991] ICR 226, CA.)

15.53
Where a statute directs that an award should be made, *inter alia*, for injury to feelings – such as in claims relating to unjustified disciplinary action – generally the amount should be modest. If the statute specifies a minimum award, that would be an appropriate amount provided there are no other aggravating features. Damages should be akin to those in claims for defamation (*Bradley & Others v National & Local Government Officers' Association* [1991] ICR 359, EAT).

15.54
Except in well-defined circumstances, there is a general principle that, when assessing damages, credit must be given for benefits received. It has been held that this precept does not apply in wrongful dismissal claims, where the benefit is an accelerated pension (*Hopkins v Norcross plc* [1994] IRLR 11, CA). Where money is paid in lieu of notice, it may be net or gross at the employer's discretion. However, whatever the basis of the calculation, it is in fact a sum tendered to avoid a claim being pursued in the courts or in a tribunal. Similarly, if compensation for future loss of

income is offered to avoid litigation, it may be gross or net (see Chapter 8, paras 8.44 to 8.46) (*Dietman v Brent LBC* [1988] IRLR 299, CA).

Interest on Awards

15.55
Except for awards under the Equal Pay and Sex Discrimination Acts (see next paragraph), a respondent employer, who fails to pay an award of compensation to a former employee within 42 days of promulgation of the tribunal's decision, must pay interest on that award. The rate is the same as in the civil courts (*Source*: Employment Tribunals (Constitution & Rules of Procedure Regs 1993 (SIs 1993/2687 & 1993/2688)).

15.56
Interest on awards under the Sex Discrimination and Equal Pay Acts accrue from the day after promulgation of the tribunal or court's decision. But interest is not payable if the full amount of the award is paid within 14 days of promulgation. Further a tribunal is entitled at its discretion to make an order for the payment of interest from the date when it finds that the act of discrimination occurred, or from the midway point of the period in respect of which a financial award is calculated (*Source*: Sex Discrimination & Equal Pay (Remedies) Regulations 1993 (SI 1993/2798)).

INSOLVENCY OF EMPLOYER

15.57
An employer's insolvency will usually result in the automatic (possibly formal) dismissal of some or all of his workforce – given that the company or organisation in question must then cease trading and go into liquidation. In such circumstances, Part XII of the Employment Rights Act 1996 allows that an employee may recover the following amounts from the Secretary of State for Employment:

- up to eight weeks' arrears of pay;
- payment for any statutory period of notice to which the employee was entitled to at the time of his (or her) dismissal;

- payment in respect of up to six weeks' holiday that accrued due to the employee during the period of 12 months immediately preceding the dismissal or insolvency;

- any 'basic award' of compensation for unfair dismissal awarded by an employment tribunal, which remains unpaid;

- any reasonable sum by way of reimbursement of a fee or premium paid by an apprentice or articled clerk.

For these purposes, the current (2001/02) upper limit on the amount of a week's pay is £240. Subject to that upper limit, the sum payable must represent the actual loss to the employee during the weeks in question, after deduction of tax and National Insurance contributions (*Westwood v Secretary of State for Employment* [1985] ICR 209, HL). The Secretary of State will pay the amount due to an employee out of the National Insurance Fund; but is entitled to make a deduction in respect of any social security benefits received by the employee during the relevant period (*Westwood v Secretary of State for Employment* [1985] ICR 209, HL).

(*Source*: ERA 1996, Part XII.)

Excluded classes

15.58
Part XII of the 1996 Act does not apply to: employees of the Crown; members of the armed services; House of Lords or House of Commons staff; the masters or crew of fishing vessels paid by a share in the profits or gross earnings of those vessels; employees who normally work outside the territory of the Member States of the European Economic Area (EEA); or to merchant seamen (*Source*: ERA 1996, ss 191, 192, 194, 195, & 199).

Complaints to an employment tribunal

15.59
A former employee may complain to an employment tribunal if the Secretary of State has refused to make a payment under the 'insolvency provisions' of the 1996 Act or has paid a smaller sum than was allegedly due. Such a complaint must be presented within three months of the refusal or underpayment. If the complaint is

upheld, the tribunal will make a declaration that the Secretary of State is in default and will determine what amount ought to have been paid. A complaint presented 'out of time' will not be entertained unless the tribunal is satisfied that it was not reasonably practicable for it to have been presented within the prescribed three-month period (*Source*: ERA 1996, s. 188).

WRITTEN REASONS FOR DISMISSAL

15.60

An employee who has been dismissed by his (or her) employer, and who had been continuously employed for one or more years ending with the effective date of termination of his contract of employment (as to which, see Chapter 3, paras 3.15 to 3.21), is entitled to ask his former employer to be provided with a written statement of reasons for his dismissal. The employer must supply (or send) those written reasons within 14 days of receiving the employee's request. The written statement is admissible in evidence in any proceedings before an employment tribunal or court (*Source*: ERA 1996, s. 92).

Note: A woman who is dismissed (for whatever reason) while pregnant or on maternity leave, must be provided with written reasons for her dismissal, whether or not she has asked for such reasons. For further particulars, please turn to Chapter 14, paras 14.53 to 14.55.

15.61

It does not matter that the employee knew perfectly well why he (or she) had been dismissed: he has the right to have documentary proof of the reasons for his dismissal – which can be relied on should the employee decide to present a complaint of unfair dismissal to an employment tribunal (*McBrearty v Thompson t/a Highfield Mini-Market*, 9 April 1991, EAT).

15.62

Although a request for written reasons may be made orally, an employee would be best advised to do so in writing (preferably by 'recorded delivery' post). In the event of a dispute (eg an employer denying having received any such request), a letter sent by recorded delivery will provide documentary proof that the request was indeed made and received.

15.63

The employer should explain to a former employee, in broad terms, what were the true reasons for the latter's dismissal. An employer, who wishes to rely on the contents of a letter previously sent to the employee setting out those reasons, is entitled to do so, provided he encloses a copy of that earlier letter with the written statement. There will be a technical breach if he fails to do so. It matters not that the reason for dismissal was good or wholly misconceived – provided it was the true reason operating on the employer's mind (*Gilham v Kent County Council* [1985] ICR 233, CA; and *Harvard Securities plc v Younghusband* [1990] IRLR 16, EAT).

15.64

If an employer tells a former employee that the reason for his (or her) dismissal was redundancy, when, in truth, the employee was dismissed for being a troublemaker (and might well have been validly dismissed for that reason), the employee will be entitled to be compensated. Although not obliged to provide detailed reasons, an employer must provide information sufficient to enable the employee to understand what prompted the dismissal. Particular events on which reliance is placed should be identified, eg 'You were dismissed for misconduct arising out of the events of March 3, when you punched such-and-such a manager on the nose' (*Walls v The City Bakeries*, 24 February 1987, EAT).

15.65

Where there is a genuine dispute over whether an employee had been dismissed or resigned, and the employer reasonably believes that there had been no dismissal, a failure to supply written reasons will generally not attract any remedy (*Broomsgrove v Eagle Alexander Ltd* [1981] IRLR 127, EAT; and *Banks v Lavin*, 20 October 1989, EAT).

Complaint to an employment tribunal

15.66

An employer who unreasonably refuses or fails to provide a written statement of reasons for dismissal (eg there being evidence of a deliberate or intentional withholding of the information), will be ordered to pay the employee two weeks' gross pay, without limit as to the amount (*Ladbroke Entertainments Ltd v Clark* [1987] ICR 585, EAT) (*Source*: ERA 1996, s. 93).

15.67

A complaint that an employer has refused or failed to provide written reasons for dismissal must be presented to the Secretary to the Tribunals within three months of the 'effective date of termination' of the employee's contract of employment (as to which, see Chapter 3, paras 3.15 to 3.21). A complaint presented 'out of time' will not normally be heard unless the tribunal is satisfied that it was not reasonably practicable for the complainant to have acted sooner (*Source*: ERA 1996, s. 93).

RIGHTS TO TRADE UNION MEMBERSHIP

15.68

A trade union may not lawfully deny membership to an individual, or expel an existing member – *unless* that individual or member does not belong (or no longer belongs) to the particular trade, industry or profession or occupation that the union represents. But an applicant or member may be excluded or expelled if he (or she) does not live (or no longer lives) in that part of Great Britain in which the trade union operates or does not work for (or no longer works for) the only employer with whom the union has dealings. Conduct is another factor that may justify the exclusion or expulsion of a would-be or existing member – so long as that conduct does *not* relate to membership or non-membership of another trade union, or to employment with a particular employer (or at a particular place), or to his or her membership or non-membership of a particular political party.

15.69

Nor can an individual or existing member be excluded or expelled from membership for failing to support (or for voicing opposition to) a strike organised by the union itself or by another trade union, or for doing (or refusing to do) something for which he (or she) could not lawfully be disciplined by any other trade union (as to which, see paras 15.89 to 15.91 below) (*Source*: TULRA 1992, ss 174 to 177).

Time limits and penalties

15.70

A person who believes that he (or she) has been unlawfully excluded or expelled from a trade union may present a complaint to the

Secretary to the Tribunals within six months of the exclusion or expulsion or, if that is not reasonably practicable, within such further period as is reasonable (*Source*: TULRA 1992, s. 175).

15.71
If an employment tribunal finds such a complaint to be well-founded, it will make a declaration to that effect. The complainant then has six months within which to apply for an award of compensation to be paid to him (or her) by the union (but must not apply until four weeks have elapsed from the date of the tribunal's declaration). If the trade union admits or re-admits the complainant to membership within those four weeks, the union will be ordered to pay the complainant such compensation as it considers to be just and equitable in the circumstances, subject to a minimum of £5,500. If the trade union has not admitted or re-admitted the complainant within those four weeks, the complainant may apply directly to the Employment Appeal Tribunal (EAT). In such circumstances, the EAT will order the trade union to pay compensation of between £5,500 and £58,900 (being the aggregate of the maximum basic and compensatory awards for unfair dismissal). Either award of compensation may be reduced to the extent that the complainant caused or contributed to his exclusion or expulsion but *not* so as to reduce the award to below £5,500 (*Source*: TULRA 1992, s. 176).

UNJUSTIFIED DISCIPLINARY ACTION BY UNION

15.72
Akin to the right of a member not to be unjustifiably expelled from membership of his (or her) trade union is his right under sections 64 and 65 of the Trade Union & Labour Relations (Consolidation) Act 1992 not to be unjustifiably disciplined by that same trade union (eg by withdrawal of benefits, suspension, imposition of a fine, or whatever):

- for failing to participate in or support (or for voicing opposition to) a strike or other industrial action (whether by members of the union or by others); or

- for refusing to contravene, for a purpose connected with such a strike or other industrial action, a requirement imposed by or under the contract of employment; or

- for making a bona fide assertion (whether before a court or tribunal, or otherwise) that his union (including any official or representative or a trustee of its property) has contravened, or is proposing to contravene a requirement which is, or is thought to be, imposed by or under the rules of the union or any other agreement or by or under an Act of Parliament (whenever passed) or any rule of law; or

- for encouraging or assisting a person to comply with his (or her) contract of employment; or

- for contravening a requirement imposed by (or in consequence of) a determination that infringes his or another individual's right not to be unjustifiably disciplined; or

- for failing to agree, or for withdrawing agreement, to a deduction from his wages (under a check-off arrangement) in respect of his trade union dues; or

- for resigning (or proposing to resign) from the union or from another union, or for becoming or proposing to become (or for refusing to become or for being) a member of another union; or

- for working with (or proposing to work with) individuals who are not members of the union, or who are (or are not) members of another union; or

- for working with, or proposing to work with, an employer who employs (or has employed) individuals who are not members of the union or who are (or are not) members of another union; or

- for requiring the union to do anything that the member in question is entitled to require the union to do by or under any provision of the Trade Union & Labour Relations (Consolidation) Act 1992.

(*Source*: TULRA 1992, ss 64 & 65.)

A recommendation from a branch to the central committee that a member should be expelled from a union does not fall within the meaning of unjustifiable discipline. There must be a final decision to expel the member (*Transport & General Workers Union v Webber* [1990] ICR 711, EAT).

Time limits and remedies

15.73

A claim must be presented to the Secretary to the Tribunals within three months of the matter complained about, or if that is not reasonably practicable, within such further period as is considered reasonable in the circumstances. An attempt to pursue an internal appeal or otherwise attempt to have the union decision reversed or reconsidered might be treated as a valid ground for delay (*Source*: TULRA 1992, ss 66 & 67).

15.74

The tribunal will make a declaration that there has been unlawful disciplinary action, and:

- provided the union agrees to withdraw the disciplinary action, will make an award of compensation up to a maximum of £58,900 on the basis of what is 'just and equitable';

- where the union refuses to withdraw the disciplinary action, or fails to take all steps necessary for the reversal of anything done for the purpose of giving effect to the unlawful action, then the matter must go to the Employment Appeals Tribunal (EAT). Compensation is the same as above, subject to a minimum basic award of £3,300 (2001/02) (eg the same as for a dismissal held to have been automatically unfair – as to which, see Chapter 5);

but, in both instances, it will be subject to reduction for contributory fault (see Chapter 5, paras 5.147 to 5.155) or for a failure to mitigate loss (see Chapter 2, paras 2.61 to 2.68) (*Source*: TULRA 1992, s. 176).

15.75

There must be full compliance with these requirements. A union wrote to the applicant's employers notifying them that he had been expelled and that no further deductions in respect of union dues were to be taken from his pay or sent to them. The expulsion of the applicant was reversed, but no action was taken on the notification. This resulted in an award of compensation by the EAT (*Leese v Food From Britain*, 4 March 1991, EAT).

15.76

A union expelled some of its members who had refused to take part in industrial action. Thereafter, members of the local branch had written objectionable articles about them to frighten them. It was held that £2,250 (the minimum at that time) was the appropriate measure of damages for injury to feelings. The remedy had to relate to the expulsion itself – not to any subsequent conduct on the part of others (*Bradley & Others v National & Local Government Officers Association* [1991] ICR 359, EAT).

15.77
An appeal from a decision of an employment tribunal lies to the EAT, but on a point of law only (see Chapter 27, para 27.1).

UNLAWFUL REFUSAL OF ACCESS TO EMPLOYMENT

15.78
It is unlawful for a prospective employer (whether under pressure from a trade union or otherwise) to refuse to employ a person either because that person is, or is not, a member of a trade union or because he (or she) has refused to accept a requirement to become or remain a member of a particular union, or of any union. It also unlawful to require a job applicant (or new recruit) to accept a deduction from his pay or to demand a payment from any such person as an alternative to trade union membership (*Source*: TULRA 1992, s. 137).

15.79
It is similarly unlawful for an employment agency to refuse to provide its services to people who are (or are not) members of a trade union or to accept instructions from an employer not to supply job applicants who fall within either category. It is also unlawful to publish an advertisement (or notice circulated privately) that indicates, or might reasonably be understood as indicating, an intention to discriminate on trade union grounds. A subsequent refusal to interview (or advance the name of a job applicant) who responds to such an advertisement will be deemed without more to be unlawful discrimination on trade union grounds (*Source*: TULRA 1992, s. 138).

15.80
These provisions do not apply to employment (or access to employment) in relation to the police service; to service as a member of the naval, military or air forces of the Crown; to employment as

master or as a member of the crew of a fishing vessel where the employee is remunerated only by a share in the profits or gross earnings of the vessel; to employment wholly outside Great Britain; to employment on a ship registered at a port outside Great Britain; or to employment in respect of which a Minister of the Crown has issued a certificate exempting that employment for the purpose of safeguarding national security (*Source*: TULRA 1992, ss 274, 275, 280, 284 & 285).

15.81
A person denied access to employment because of his (or her) membership or non-membership of a trade union may present a complaint to an employment tribunal, but must do so within three months of the alleged unlawful act (or, if that is not reasonably practicable, within such further period as the tribunal considers reasonable). If the complaint is upheld, the offending employer and/or employment agency (and/or a person or trade union joined or sisted to the proceedings) will be ordered to pay compensation of up to £50,000. An employment tribunal may also recommend that the respondents do what needs to be done to put matters to rights for the complainant. If that recommendation is ignored, the tribunal may increase the amount of compensation payable (*Source*: TULRA 1992, ss 139 to 142).

Access to employment denied on grounds of sex, race or disability

15.82
It is unlawful for an employer to discriminate against a job applicant – on grounds of sex, marital status, gender reassignment, race, colour, national or ethnic origins, nationality or disability – by refusing to interview, shortlist or employ any such person regardless of that person's qualifications, experience or evident suitability for the vacancy in question. It is also unlawful to discriminate against such a person by offering less favourable terms and conditions of employment or by withholding opportunities for promotion, transfer or training. For further particulars, please turn to Chapters 11, 12 & 13.

REHABILITATION OF OFFENDERS

15.83

People who break the law, and who are convicted and sentenced by the courts, will often have difficulty securing employment. Some offences (eg speeding offences) will not necessarily stand in the way of a person who is looking for work; others (street crimes, shoplifting, etc) will undoubtedly have a more serious effect. A man with three serious convictions for fraud is unlikely to be offered employment as a cashier in a bank or financial institution. A woman with a string of convictions for shoplifting would probably have some difficulty securing employment as a floorwalker or shop assistant in a department store.

15.84

The Rehabilitation of Offenders Act 1974 (ROOA 1974) acknowledges that it would be unfair for a convicted person to be forever precluded from obtaining employment in the field of his (or her) choice. The Act provides for the rehabilitation of persons who have been convicted of certain crimes, so long as they do not commit further offences during a specified 'rehabilitation period'. At the end of that period, their convictions become 'spent'. This means that, at the end of the 'rehabilitation period' (five, seven or ten years, as appropriate – see *Note* below) such a person need not disclose details of the conviction in question when applying for work, filling out job applications or answering questions at an employment interview. In short, a person with a 'spent' conviction may effectively lie at an employment interview if asked the question: 'Have you been convicted of any offences?' (*Source*: ROOA 1974, s. 4).

Note: Details of the rehabilitation periods for particular sentences, and for certain sentences confined to young persons, are to be found in s. 5, Tables A and B, of the 1974 Act.

15.85

It is unfair of an employer to dismiss an employee on discovery that the employee in question had refused to reveal details of a 'spent' conviction when first recruited – unless the employee falls within one of the *Exceptions* listed below. An employer who uses fraud, dishonesty or a bribe, to uncover details of an employee's previous convictions, is guilty of an offence and liable on summary conviction to a fine of up to £5,000 and/or imprisonment for a term not exceeding six months (*Source*: ROOA 1974, s. 9).

Sentences excluded from rehabilitation

15.86
Sentences excluded from rehabilitation under the 1974 Act are:

- a sentence of imprisonment for life;

- a sentence of imprisonment, youth custody, detention in a young offender institution, or corrective training, for a term exceeding thirty months;

- a sentence of preventive detention;

- a sentence of detention during Her Majesty's pleasure, or for life, or under section 205(2) or (3) of the Criminal Procedure (Scotland) Act 1975, or for a term exceeding 30 months, passed under section 53 of the Children & Young Persons Act 1933 (young offenders convicted of grave crimes) or under section 206 of the said Act of 1975 (detention of children convicted on indictment) or a corresponding court-martial punishment;

- a sentence of custody for life.

Exceptions

15.87
But there are exceptions to the general rule. The right to conceal details of 'spent' convictions does *not* apply to solicitors, barristers, advocates, chartered (or certified) accountants, teachers in higher education, dentists, dental hygienists (or dental auxiliaries), veterinary surgeons, nurses, midwives, ophthalmic opticians, dispensing opticians, pharmaceutical chemists, registered teachers (in Scotland), persons in professions to which the Professions Supplementary to Medicine Act 1960 apply, registered osteopaths or registered chiropractors. The same applies to any office or employment concerned with the provision to persons aged under 18 of accommodation, care, leisure and recreational facilities, schooling, social services, supervision or training, being an office or employment of such a kind as to enable the holder to have access, in the course of his (or her) normal duties to such persons, and any other office or employment the normal duties of which are carried out wholly or partly on the premises where such provision takes place.

15.88

'Spent' convictions must also be disclosed in relation to judicial appointments, appointments in the police force (or as a traffic warden), the ownership of an independent school, dealerships in securities, and to the managers (and trustees) of unit trust schemes. The same applies to regulated employments (eg to persons dealing in firearms), and to any person applying to the police or to a court of summary jurisdiction for a licence to keep explosives. A person seeking a Gaming Board Licence must also reveal details of any and all convictions, 'spent' or otherwise (*Sources*: ROOA 1974; Rehabilitation of Offenders (Exceptions) Order 1975 (SI 1975/1023); and the Rehabilitation of Offenders (Exceptions) (Amendment) Order 1986 (SI 1986/1249)).

TRADE UNION RECOGNITION

15.89

If an employer recognises an independent trade union to any extent, for the purpose of collective bargaining, the union acquires certain rights, such as the right to be consulted on redundancy dismissals. The officials and members of that union likewise acquire the right to paid/unpaid time off work for trade union duties and activities, discussed earlier in this chapter. Collective bargaining means negotiations relating to or connected with one or more of the matters specified in Chapter 7 (at para 7.17). A recognition agreement union does not need to be in writing or be formally agreed (*Source*: TULRA 1992, ss 168, 178, 188 & 196).

15.90

It is a question of fact and degree whether there is 'recognition'. It requires 'mutuality, that is to say, that the employer acknowledges the role of union' that 'may be... express or implied'. The course of conduct must be 'clear and unequivocal... over a period', and 'there may be partial recognition, that is to say, recognition in certain respects but not in others' (*NUGSAT v Albury Brothers Ltd* [1978] ICR 62, EAT (affirmed on appeal, [1979] ICR 86, CA). Mere discussion with a union over matters specified in Chapter 7, para 7.17 is not sufficient; it must be established that an employer is willing to negotiate with a view to reaching agreement in one of those areas.

15.91

An employer was a member of a trade association. The latter had effected agreements with a trade union relating to the terms and conditions for those working in the trade. The employer used it as the basis of an agreement with his own workforce. It was held that that alone was insufficient to establish 'recognition' (*Peart & Co Ltd v TASS Craft Section*, 16 December 1988, EAT).

15.92

Recognition cannot be imposed on an employer by a third party or by an extraneous event where it is against the employer's will. Only the acts of the employer are relevant for the purposes of deciding whether he has (intentionally or otherwise) recognised a union (*Cleveland CC v Springett & Others* [1985] IRLR 131, EAT).

15.93

At the present time, a trade union has no legal right to be 'recognised' by a particular employer, nor any right to complain to an employment tribunal should an employer decide to withdraw recognition. However since the coming into force on 6 June 2000 of s. 1 and Schedule A to the Employment Relations Act 1999, any employer with 21 or more people on the payroll must now respond to a 'valid request' for trade union recognition. The new legislation is summarised in Chapter 25.

TRANSFER OF AN UNDERTAKING

15.94

Under the Transfer of Undertakings (Protection of Employment) Regulations 1981 (SI 1981/1794, as amended), an employer proposing the sale or transfer or his business (or part of that business), or the acquisition of another business, is duty-bound to consult representatives of a recognised independent trade union and/or employee-elected representatives about his proposals and the effect the relevant transfer is likely to have on affected employees. Long enough before the transfer, to enable purposeful consultations to take place, the employer must inform those representatives of:

- the fact that the relevant transfer is to take place;
- when, approximately, it is to take place, and the reasons for it;

- the legal, economic and social implications of the transfer for the affected employees;

- the measures that he envisages he will, in connection with the transfer, take in relation to those employees or, if he envisages that no measures will be so taken, that fact; and

- if the employer is the transferor, the measures that the transferee envisages he (or she) will, in connection with the transfer, take in relation to such of those employees as become employees of the transferee after the transfer or, if he envisages that no measures will be so taken, that fact.

15.95
The defence of 'not reasonably practicable' is available to an employer who fails to forewarn and consult the relevant employee representatives. For a breach, the 'appropriate compensation' is a maximum of 13 weeks' pay for every affected employee (*Source*: TUPE Regs 1981, Reg 10(11)). For further particulars, please turn to Chapter 17.

TRADE UNION DUES AND THE 'CHECK-OFF' SYSTEM

15.96
An employer must not deduct trade union dues (ie, membership subscriptions) from a worker's pay (in accordance with check-off arrangements previously agreed with a trade union) unless he has received written authorisation from each of the workers concerned (*per* section 68, Trade Union & Labour Relations (Consolidation) Act 1992, as amended by the Deregulation (Deduction from Pay of Union Subscriptions) Order 1998).

Note: Itemised pay statements necessarily issued to employees must identify deductions in respect of trade union dues (as to which, please turn to the section titled **Itemised pay statement** elsewhere in this handbook).

15.97
Before 23 June 1998, when the Deregulation Order referred to in the previous paragraph came into force), a written notice authorising the deduction of union dues from a worker's pay had to be renewed once every three years. This is no longer necessary. Any written authorisation given before 23 July 1998 (a so-called 'preserved

authorisation') that has not yet expired remains valid for a period of three years from the date on which it was given (unless withdrawn in the meantime). But any renewal of that authorisation will be subject to the new arrangements.

15.98
An employer may write in the following terms to any worker of his who has signed a preserved authorisation (as outlined in the Schedule to the 1998 Order):

DEDUCTION OF TRADE UNION SUBSCRIPTIONS FROM PAY

Following the coming into force of the Deregulation (Deduction from Pay of Union Subscriptions) Order 1998, you no longer need to re-authorise payments of trade union subscriptions by 'check-off' (deduction from pay by your employer) every three years and your employer need not give you advance written notice of any increase in the rate of deductions. The law continues to require your written authorisation before check off can start and you continue to have the right to stop paying by check off at any time, by giving notice in writing to your employer.

This notice affects you if you pay your union subscription by check off and you gave your authorisation before the date on which the Order came into force.

If you are content for the new arrangements to apply to you, <u>you need do nothing</u>.

If, however, you wish the previous arrangements to continue to apply to you, you must give notice to that effect in writing to your employer at [*name and address of employer*] within 14 days of receiving this notice.

If you do so, your current authorisation will expire three years after you gave it, but any subsequent authorisation will be subject to the new arrangements.

15.99
If a worker writes to his (or her) employer asking him to stop deducting union dues from his wages or salary, the employer must

act on that request on the worker's next pay day or (if the request was not received in time) as soon as 'reasonably practicable' after that pay day (*ibid*).

15.100
Under section 68A of TULRA 1992, a worker may complain to an employment tribunal that his (or her) employer has deducted union dues from his pay in contravention of these requirements. The complaint must be presented within the period of three months beginning with the date on which the unauthorised deduction was made or (if there have been a number of such deductions) the date on which the last of those deductions was made. If the complaint is upheld, the tribunal will make a declaration to that effect and will order the employer to make restitution.

Political fund contributions

15.101
Although content to have his (or her) membership subscription (or union dues) deducted from his pay packet under a check-off arrangement, a worker may be less than happy about contributing to the union's political fund. To ensure that no such contributions are deducted from his pay, the worker must first write to his trade union in the following terms (*ibid* section 84):

To: (Name of Trade Union)

POLITICAL FUND (EXEMPTION NOTICE)

I give notice that I object to contributing to the Political Fund of the Union, and am in consequence exempt, in manner provided by Chapter VI of Part I of the Trade Union & Labour Relations (Consolidation) Act 1992, from contributing to that fund.

Signature of Member:

Address: ....Date: ....

The next step is to write to his employer confirming that he has written to his trade union in the terms outlined above and certifying that he is exempt from any obligation to contribute to his trade union's political fund. The employer must respond on the first payday on which it is reasonably practicable for him to do so – by seeing to it that no amount representing any such contribution is deducted from the worker's pay (*ibid* section 86).

15.102

A worker, who has instructed his (or her) employer to cease deducting political fund contributions from his pay, may complain to an employment tribunal if his employer has ignored his instructions or has responded by refusing to deduct *any* union dues from the worker's pay (while continuing to operate a check-off arrangement for other members of the same trade union). If the complaint is upheld, the tribunal will make a declaration to that effect and will order the employer to repay the amount wrongly deducted from the worker's pay. Non-compliance with the terms of such an order (within the next four weeks) will prompt a further complaint to a tribunal and an order directing the employer to pay the worker the equivalent of two weeks' pay (*ibid* section 87, as substituted by section 6 of the Employment Rights (Dispute Resolution) Act 1998).

15.103

Breach of these provisions entitles an employee to apply to an employment tribunal for restitution. The application (or complaint) must be 'presented' within three months of the relevant unlawful deduction, or within such further period as the tribunal considers reasonable. If the tribunal finds the complaint to be well-founded, it will order the employer to repay the amount in question.

DEDUCTIONS FROM PAY

15.104

As a rule, an employer has no right to deduct money from the wages or salary of an employee (or to demand a payment in respect of breakages, cash shortages, damaged goods, or whatever) without that employee's express permission. There are, of course, exceptions to this rule, which are explained below.

15.105

Any such deduction (or demand for payment) will be void and unenforceable (and the monies recoverable) unless:

- the employer's right to make that deduction (or demand for payment), and the circumstances in which such a deduction (or demand) might be made, are clearly laid down in writing in the employee's contract of employment (either the written statement of terms of employment issued in accordance with sections 1 to 7 of the Employment Rights Act 1996 or in some associated document, signed and dated), a copy of which must have been supplied to the employee in advance of any such deduction (or demand); or

- the employee had previously given his (or her) consent in writing to the making of that deduction (or demand).

Any term in a contract of employment (or related document) that authorises the employer to make deductions (or demands for payment) will apply only to incidents or events that occurred *after* the employee's authorisation or agreement was given or obtained. In short, an employer cannot require an employee to give retrospective consent to the deduction of money from his or her pay (or to make a payment) in respect of an incident (such as a breakage or cash shortage) that occurred before that consent was given.

The provisions are to be found in Part II of the Employment Rights Act 1996 ('*Protection of Wages*').

Exceptions

15.106
The obvious exceptions are deductions from pay authorised or demanded by statute. An employer does not need an employee's prior written consent before deducting PAYE income tax or National Insurance contributions from the employee's wages or salary.

Furthermore, the rule restricting the right of an employer to deduct money from an employee's pay (or to make a demand for payment) does not apply:

- to the recovery or reimbursement of overpaid wages or salary, or to any over-payment in respect of business expenses incurred by the employee in the course of his (or her) employment;

- to third party requests for deductions (eg pension contributions, etc) in accordance with any relevant provision in the employee's contract of employment;

- to attachment of earnings (or garnishee) orders made by a court under the Attachment of Earnings Act 1971 or related legislation;

- to deductions (or payments) made (or required) in respect of an employee's participation in a strike or other form of industrial action;

- to deductions or demands for payment in response to a court or tribunal order requiring the payment of a specified amount to the employee's employer.

(*Source*: ERA 1996, ss 13 & 14.)

15.107
The expression 'wages' (or, for that matter 'salary') applies to all emoluments, however classified, including shift allowances, overtime payments, bonuses, commission, sickness and holiday pay, etc – but not to advances, loans, expenses, pensions or redundancy payments or any other payments made other than in the employee's capacity as a employee. It also covers sums 'whether payable under the employee's contract or otherwise'. It has been held to embrace discretionary but legitimately expected commission payments, unless there is evidence that the agreement to make such payments has been withdrawn (*Kent Management Services Ltd v Butterfield* [1992] ICR 272, EAT).

15.108
The correct way to assess deductions from pay in respect of absences from work due to industrial action is to approach the problem on a 'breach of contract' basis. For how many days' work annually did the employers pay the employee his (or her) salary? If the employee was contracted to work 200 days a year, but was absent on strike for ten of those 200 days, the appropriate deduction would be one-twentieth (or five per cent) of the employee's annual salary (*Smith & Others v London Borough of Bromley*, 5 April 1991, Cty Ct).

15.109
The non-payment of any sum due and payable to an employee, would be deemed to be an unauthorised deduction and, therefore, recoverable under Part II of the Employment Rights Act 1996. To escape liability the employer would have to satisfy an employment tribunal that the deduction fell within the category of lawful

deductions listed in para. 15.97 above (*Delaney v Staples (t/a De Montfort Recruitment)* [1992] ICR 483, HL).

15.110

Further, where there is a dispute over the justification of a deduction made within the Act, a tribunal will have to decide whether it is sustainable. For instance, if an employer deducts the cost of repairs to a motor car, for which an employee is liable, the sum must be justified and reasonable. Any figure above that sum is irrecoverable (*Fairfield Ltd v Skinner* [1992] ICR 836, EAT).

15.111

An employment tribunal has jurisdiction to entertain complaints under Part II of the Employment Rights Act 1996. Where it finds a complaint to be well-founded it will make a declaration to that effect and will order the employer to repay the unlawful deduction. Such a complaint must be 'presented' to a tribunal within three months of the alleged unlawful deduction or (if the deduction is one of a series of such deductions) within three months of the last of those deductions; or, if that is not reasonably practicable, within a reasonable period thereafter.

15.112

An employment tribunal also has jurisdiction to deal with 'breach of employment contract' claims, including claims arising out of an employer's failure to give the correct notice of termination ('wrongful dismissal'). That jurisdiction is shared with the County court, although claims for damages in excess of £25,000 are still the exclusive preserve of the County court.

15.113

The wording of Part II of the 1996 Act (which has replaced similar provisions in the now-repealed Wages Act 1986) can lead to curious results. If a tribunal has ruled that an employer had unlawfully made an deduction in respect of a loan made to an employee, because he had not obtained the employee's prior written authorisation to the making of that deduction, the employer will not only be ordered to repay the money deducted but will also be debarred from recovering the deducted amount in any other proceedings before a civil courts (*Delaney v Staples (t/a De Montfort Recruitment)* [1992] ICR 483, HL).

15.114

An employee may refuse to accept any unilateral variation in the terms and conditions of his (or her) employment, eg a cut in the rate of pay. Because an employer can impose such a variation, an employee has the choice either to accept the repudiation (by resigning and pursuing a complaint of unfair constructive dismissal) or by continuing to work under protest. This happened to an employee who was shortly afterwards made redundant. The EAT held that he could recover the amount that had been unlawfully 'deducted' from his wages. By protesting about the cut in his pay, the employee had not 'affirmed' the variation in his contract (*MacRuary v Washington Irvine Ltd*, 17 March 1994, EAT).

15.115

If an employee has certified to his (or her) employer that he has resigned his membership of a trade union, the employer must cease deducting union dues from the employee wages on the next pay day after notification, or as soon as reasonably practicable thereafter. An employer's failure to respond will be deemed to be a contravention of the employee's rights under Part II of the Employment Rights Act 1996, thereby entitling the employee to apply to the tribunal for reimbursement of the amount (or amounts) unlawfully deducted (*Source*: TULRA 1992, s. 68).

Cash shortages and stock deficiencies

15.116

As is the case with other types of deductions or demands for payment, an employer cannot legitimately deduct money (or demand a payment) in respect of cash shortages or stock deficiencies unless his right to do so and the circumstances in which he can exercise that right are clearly and unequivocally laid down in the employee's contract of employment. Alternatively, the employee must have agreed in writing to the making of any such deduction or demand *before* any incident or event that would otherwise prompt the employer to make such a deduction or demand for payment. In other words, any consent given after the event is void and unenforceable (*Source*: ERA 1996, ss 17 to 21).

15.117

The amount deducted from an employee's pay packet on a particular pay day must not exceed one-tenth of the *gross* wages or salary due to the employee on that pay day. The same rule applies whatever the amount of money owed, even if the employer has deducted a number of cash shortages or stock shortages directly attributable to the same employee. In short, the total amount recoverable may have to be recovered by a series of deductions from the employee's pay packet (none of which may exceed the prescribed maximum 10 per cent on any one pay day).

15.118

A *demand for payment* in respect of a particular cash shortage or stock deficiency must be preceded by a letter or memorandum addressed to the employee in question informing him (or her) of the total amount payable in respect of that cash shortage or stock deficiency and of the pay day (or sequence of pay days) on which such payments are to be made. Second and subsequent demands for payment must also be made in writing and must be given on the pay day on which payment is required. Any demand for payment on a day other than a pay day will be null and void. As with deductions from pay, the amount payable by an employee on any one pay day must not exceed one-tenth of the employee's gross pay on that pay day (*Source*: ERA 1996, s. 18).

15.119

Furthermore, an employer is debarred from making any deduction (or demand from payment) in respect of a cash shortage or stock deficiency that has remained undetected for 12 or more months. In other words, an employer has 12 months within which to recover (or begin to recover) the amount of any previously undetected cash shortage or stock deficiency. Any deductions (or demands) made 'out of time' will be unlawful and recoverable before an employment tribunal (*Source*: ERA 1996, ss 18(2) & (3) and 20(2) & (3)).

Monies outstanding on the termination of employment

15.120

Should a person in retail employment resign or be dismissed before he (or she) has repaid the full amount of any monies owed to the employer in respect of cash shortages or stock deficiencies, the employer may (in accordance with a previously agreed arrangement, *but not otherwise*) either deduct all or part of the amount outstanding from any final payment of wages or salary due to the employee, or demand repayment of that outstanding amount. In the event of a refusal or failure to pay, the employee may have no option but to sue for recovery in the ordinary courts (*Source*: ERA 1996, s. 22).

Complaints to tribunals

15.121

If an employer has made an unauthorised deduction from an employee's wages or salary, the employee may present a claim for reimbursement to an employment tribunal. The complaint or claim must be 'presented' within three months of the date on which the relevant unauthorised deduction or payment was made. The time limit may be extended where it was not reasonably practicable for the employee to present his (or her) complaint within the prescribed three months, and it was done as soon as reasonably practicable thereafter (*Source*: ERA 1996, ss 23 to 26). If the employee's complaint is upheld, the tribunal will make a declaration to that effect and will order the employer to reimburse the full disputed amount. In certain cases, the tribunal will direct that any amount owed to the employee in respect of a cash deficiency or stock shortage is to be reduced by the amount of any unauthorised deduction or payment, in spite of the fact that the employer had already been ordered by the tribunal to reimburse that same amount to the employee (*Source*: ERA 1996, s. 23).

15.122

As with a number of other statutory rights in employment, an employee, who believes that one or other of his (or her) statutory rights have been infringed, may complain to an employment tribunal without having to resign his job in order to do so. If the employer responds to any such challenge to his authority by dismissing that employee (or selecting him for redundancy), the dismissal will be automatically unfair (regardless of the age or length of service of the employee in question) and will almost certainly result in the employer being ordered to pay a substantial amount of compensation (*Source*: ERA 1996, s. 104). For further particulars, please turn to Chapter 5 (paras 5.44 & 5.45).

REFERENCES FOR FORMER EMPLOYEES

15.123

An employer is under no legal obligation to provide an employee with a reference. If he (or she) does so, care should be taken not to provide a reference that is patently untrue. Indeed, it might be highly damaging to an employee's prospects if the reference is given out of vindictiveness or malice, or out of sheer incompetence. It is essential to provide a 'careful reference'. An employer is in a unique position to know the character, skill and diligence of a former employee.

15.124

A former employer provided an untrue reference for a former employee 'so strikingly bad as to amount to... a "kiss of death" to his career in insurance'. It was held that there was a failure to exercise due care and skill in the preparation of the reference. This entitled the employee to compensation for the loss he had sustained (*Spring v Guardian Assurance plc & Others* [1994] ICR 596, HL).

15.125

Employers are duty-bound to provide written reasons for dismissal in certain circumstances (see paras 15.50 to 15.67 above). Problems could arise if a sympathetic reference contradicts the information provided in a written statement of reasons for dismissal. In *Castledine v Rothwell Engineering Ltd* [1973] IRLR 99, a dismissed employee produced a reference supplied by his former employer that stated that he 'had carried out his duties satisfactorily, often under difficult conditions'. The written statement of reasons for dismissal, supplied by the same employer, claimed that the employee had been dismissed on grounds of incompetence. When confronted with such conflicting evidence, the employment tribunal had no difficulty in concluding that the employee's dismissal had been unfair.

15.126

In a relatively recent case (*The Daily Telegraph*, 7 February 2000), a woman who had been denied a reference by her former employers (seemingly as a punishment for taking proceedings against them for alleged sex discrimination – which later prompted an out of court settlement) was awarded some £190,000 in damages because of her resultant inability to find work. The House of Lords held that her former employer's actions (even after she had left their employment) amounted to unlawful victimisation under the Sex Discrimination Act 1975.

15.127

With the coming into force on 1 March 2000 of the Data Protection Act 1998, employers will (from 24 October 2001) be duty-bound to disclose the contents of references (whether given in confidence or otherwise) issued by former employers, if and when asked to do so by an employee to whom any such reference relates. That duty does not, however, extend to references issued by the employer himself. For further particulars, please turn to Chapter 21, paras 21.18 and 21.19.

Health and safety at work

EMPLOYER'S DUTY OF CARE

16.1
An employer has a common law, as well as statutory, duty to take reasonable care for the health and safety of his workforce. He must provide them with a safe working environment (including safe means of access to and from his premises), safe tools, appliances and equipment, and protection against any hazards associated with their employment.

16.2
An employee who is injured in the course of his (or her) employment may sue his employer for damages. To succeed in such an action, he will need to prove negligence on the part of his employer and that he was injured as a direct result of that negligence.

16.3
An employer cannot deny negligence on grounds only that he was not in breach of a statutory duty (eg that he was under no obligation in law to guard a particular machine, or to provide an employee with this or that item of protective clothing or equipment). Liability at common law will still exist if the employer should have known of a particular hazard and did nothing to protect his employees from the possible consequences.

16.4
If, on the other hand, an employer has complied with a statutory duty to guard a particular machine (indeed, any duty under a particular statute or set of regulations), he may be able to claim in his defence that he had fulfilled his common law duty of care to an injured worker. But, if a worker is injured in the course of his (or her)

employment, in consequence of a defect in any machine or appliance provided by his employer, and the defect is attributable wholly or partly to the fault of a third party (usually the manufacturer or supplier of the machine or appliance in question), the employer will nonetheless be held liable for the employee's injuries and may face a civil action for damages in the ordinary courts. The expression 'injury' includes loss of life, any impairment of a person's physical or mental condition, and any disease. Any term in a worker's contract, which purports to exclude or restrict the employer's liability in such circumstances, is null and void. In short, an injured worker may sue his (or her) employer for damages regardless of the existence or his acceptance of any such contract term (*Source*: Employer's Liability (Defective Equipment) Act 1969).

16.5
An injured employee may sue his (or her) employer on two counts: (a) that he was negligent and in breach of his common law duty of care, and (b) that he was in breach of a duty imposed by statute. Under the provisions of the Employer's Liability (Compulsory Insurance) Act 1969, an employer must insure against civil liability for damages arising out of personal injury sustained by his employees.

Duty to customers, clients, etc

16.6
In addition to his duty of care towards his own workforce, the occupier of premises owes a like duty to persons invited or permitted to be on those premises (such as guests, customers, patrons, clients, tradesmen, etc). This 'common duty of care' has been codified by the Occupiers' Liability Act 1957. In short, the owner or occupier of business premises may well be sued for damages if a member of the public is injured as a direct consequence of his negligence. Furthermore, he runs the risk of being prosecuted under the 1974 Act for failing to take all reasonably practicable steps to safeguard the interests of those members of the general public who have a valid or legitimate reason for being on or near his premises (*Source*: HASAWA 1974, s. 3). If a customer, client, tradesperson (or whomever) is killed or seriously injured while visiting or present in a shop, factory, warehouse, restaurant, office

block, department store or wherever and the accident is (or appears to be) directly attributable to the manner in which that business was conducted, the owner or occupier must notify the 'relevant enforcing authority' immediately (in compliance with the Reporting of Injuries, Diseases & Dangerous Occurences Regulations 1995, not otherwise discussed in this book).

HEALTH & SAFETY AT WORK ETC ACT 1974

16.7
In addition to their common law duty of care, employers have a statutory duty, under section 2 of the Health & Safety at Work, etc Act 1974 (HASAWA), to ensure, so far as is reasonably practicable, the health, safety and welfare at work of their employees. To that end, every employer must:

- provide and maintain plant, machinery, equipment, tools, appliances and systems of work which are, so far as is reasonably practicable, safe and without risk to health;

- arrange, so far as is reasonably practicable, that employees are not put at risk (or exposed to risk) in connection with the use, handling, storage or transport of dangerous articles and substances (such as chemicals, dusts, noxious fumes or vapours, etc);

- provide as much information, instruction, training and supervision as is necessary to ensure, so far as is reasonably practicable, the health and safety at work of his employees;

- ensure, so far as is reasonably practicable, that the buildings, offices, workshops, and other areas or places in which people are employed to work, are safe and without risks to health;

- provide and maintain safe means of access to (and egress from) all parts of the premises;

- provide and maintain a working environment (including facilities such as toilets, washrooms, cloakrooms, rest areas and the like) which, so far as is reasonably practicable, is not only safe and without risks to health, but also adequate in terms of heating, lighting, ventilation, and seating, etc.

(*Source*: HASAWA 1974, s. 2.)

16.8

It is an employer's duty also to conduct his undertaking in such a way as to ensure, so far as is reasonably practicable, that persons not in his employment (contractors, tradesmen, etc) who may be affected thereby are not needlessly exposed to risks to their health or safety. That same general duty extends to other persons (members of the public, customers, guests, clients, etc) on the employer's premises who may be affected by the way in which he conducts his business (*Source:* HASAWA 1974, s. 3).

16.9

An employer's duties under the 1974 Act are reinforced and supplemented by a variety of statutes and regulations – the latter now in the ascendancy as older statutes (such as the Factories Act 1961) are replaced by more up-to-date legislation, prominent amongst which are:

- the Electricity at Work Regulations (SI 1989/635);

- the Workplace (Health, Safety & Welfare) Regulations 1992 (SI 1992/304);

- the Health & Safety (Display Screen Equipment) Regulations 1992 (SI 1992/2792);

- the Personal Protective Equipment at Work Regulations 1992 (SI 1992/2966) (as amended);

- the Manual Handling Operations Regulations 1992 (SI 1992/2793);

- the Chemicals (Hazard Information & Packaging for Supply) Regulations 1996 (SI 1996/1092);

- the Construction (Health, Safety & Welfare) Regulations 1996 (SI 1996/1592);

- the Fire Precautions (Workplace) Regulations 1997 (SI 1997/1840);

- the Provision & Use of Work Equipment Regulations 1998 (SI 1998/2306);

- the Management of Health & Safety at Work Regulations 1999 (SI 1999/3242); and

- the Control of Substances Hazardous to Health Regulations (SI 1999/437) (as amended).

Note: A list of current health and safety legislation (including a computer diskette) is available from HSE Books at the address given at the end of para 16.14 below.

Risk assessment

16.10
Regulation 3 of the Management of Health & Safety at Work Regulations 1999 (*qv*) imposes a duty on *every* employer (and on every self-employed person) to make a 'suitable and sufficient assessment' of the risks to which his employees are exposed while they are at work and of any risks to members of the public (customers, clients, visitors, guests, passers-by) who may be affected by the way in which he conducts his business or undertaking – the purpose being to identify the measures the employer needs to take to comply with the restrictions and prohibitions imposed upon him by or under contemporary health and safety legislation. That duty extends to assessing the risks associated with an outbreak of fire (per Part II of the Fire Precautions (Workplace) Regulations 1997); the risks confronting new and expectant mothers and women of child-bearing age; and the risks to inexperienced and immature young persons. Risk assessment is also mandatory under each of the Regulations listed above.

Meaning of 'risk assessment'

16.11
Risk assessment is nothing more or less than a systematic general examination of workplace activities, environmental factors and working conditions that will enable the employer (or self-employed person) to identify the risks posed not only by working methods, machines, tools, and equipment, processes, noise, electricity, ionising radiation, flammable liquids and gases, dusts, fumes and vapours, and a seemingly endless list of prescribed hazardous substances (including lead and asbestors), but also by factors such as temperature, humidity, poor lighting and ventilation, the inadequacy of the means of access to (and egress from) premises, obstructions in corridors and walkways, the condition of floors, floor coverings and so on. It is only when he has assessed the hazards and determined the degree of risk that an employer can hope to take the steps he is required to take in law to eliminate or minimise those risks. Indeed, the whole tenor of the 1999 Regulations (and of the hazard-specific

regulations listed above) is that employers (and self-employed persons) cannot realistically expect to comply with their general duties (to employees and members of the public) under the Health & Safety at Work, etc Act 1974) unless they *do* carry out a risk assessment and make a genuine effort to eliminate the risks uncovered by that assessment.

HEALTH AND SAFETY COMMISSION AND EXECUTIVE

16.12
The 1974 Act also established the Health and Safety Commission (HSC) and the Health and Safety Executive (HSE). The former is responsible for monitoring matters relating to health and safety, and the latter for enforcement (through the health and safety inspectorate).

16.13
Subordinate legislation provides for the appointment of one or more trade-union-nominated *safety representatives* or (where is no recognised trade union) the election of *representatives of employee safety*, whose functions include responsibility for monitoring health and safety issues at the workplace (*Cleveland CC v Springett & Others* [1985] IRLR 131, EAT) (*Source*: Safety Representatives & Safety Committees Regulations 1977 (SI 1977/500) and the Health & Safety (Consultation with Employees) Regulations 1996 (SI 1996/1513)).

Codes of practice

16.14
Section 16 of the 1974 Act empowers the Health & Safety Commission (HSC) to issue approved codes of practice 'for the purposes of providing practical guidance with respect to the requirements of any provisions of sections 2 to 7' [of the 1974 Act] or of any of the *existing statutory provisions* – which latter expressions encompasses all current and related health and safety legislation.

A failure to comply with any provision of a code of practice is not an offence per se; but, as is the case with a breach of the Highway Code, is admissible in evidence before a tribunal or court.

To date, the HSC has issued some 50 plus codes of practice, a complete list of which is to be found in the current HSE Catalogue available from:

HSE Books
PO Box 1999
Sudbury
Suffolk
CO10 6FS
Telephone: 01787 881165
Fax: 01787 881165

For further information about HSE publications, readers can now access HSE's online catalogue: www.hsebooks.co.uk

HEALTH AND SAFETY INSPECTORS

16.15
Health and safety inspectors, many of whom are local authority environmental health officers, are duty-bound to investigate and, where appropriate, enforce adherence to health and safety legislation in their separate areas of responsibility. They visit factories, offices, shops, roadworks, construction sites, hotels, restaurants, leisure complexes, schools, hospitals, etc (indeed, any premises in which people are employed to work) as often as may be appropriate (the more so if they have been formally notified of an accident or dangerous occurrence involving injury – or any serious risk of injury – to persons or property).

16.16
If an inspector discovers a contravention of the Act, he (or she) can either:

- verbally (and informally) advise the relevant employer of the contravention and caution him to set matters to right before his next visit (eg inadequate ventilation, faulty power points, loose guard rails, slippery floors, etc); or

- serve the employer with an Improvement Notice or (if there is a serious infringement) a Prohibition Notice formally advising the employer to take appropriate action either immediately or within prescribed time limits (usually 21 days); or

- institute criminal proceedings before a magistrates' court.

An inspector will not institute criminal proceedings unless satisfied that the employer in question has deliberately and persistently flouted the law or that the contravention was so serious (eg a dust explosion) as to warrant prosecution (*Source*: HASAWA 1974, s. 33).

Improvement notices

16.17
An Improvement Notice is a document cautioning an employer that, in the inspector's opinion, he or she is contravening one or other of the *existing statutory provisions* (see paras 16.3 & 16.6 above), or has done so and is likely to do so again. The inspector must give reasons, and will require the employer to remedy the contravention within a period of not less than 21 days or within some other specified period (*Source*: HASAWA 1974, s. 21).

16.18
The notice may be withdrawn by an inspector at any time before the end of the period specified. The period may be extended more than once, provided no appeal against it has been lodged. An employer can appeal to an employment tribunal on the grounds that it is not 'reasonably practicable' to comply with the notice, but must do so within 21 days of the service of the notice on him, or within such further period as is reasonable in the circumstances. The lodging of an appeal has the effect of suspending the operation of the notice until the appeal is finally disposed of. It may be by way of a hearing or a withdrawal of the appeal. (*Source*: HASAWA 1974, ss 23 & 24. See also Schedule 4, Rule 2 to the Employment Tribunals (Constitution & Rules of Procedure) Regulations 1993 (SI 1993/2687, as amended by SIs 1994/536 & 1996/1757).

Prohibition notices

16.19
An inspector may service a Prohibition Notice on an employer if, in his (or her) opinion, the activities carried on by the employer involve, or are likely to involve, a risk of serious personal injury. The notice must state that the inspector is of that opinion, specifying the matters giving rise to that risk, and identifying the relevant statutory provisions that are, or would be, contravened. It will also state that the activities must cease within the time specified in the notice and until the matters specified in the notice have been remedied. Where

the inspector states in the notice that he believes that the risk of serious personal injury is imminent, those activities must cease immediately (*Source*: HASAWA 1974, s. 22).

16.20
If a prohibition notice is not intended to have immediate effect, the inspector may withdraw it at any time before the end of the period specified in the notice. He (or she) may extend, or further extend the period provided no appeal has been lodged.

16.21
An appeal to an employment tribunal, against the service of a prohibition notice, must be lodged within 21 days of the date of service of the notice, although the tribunal may extend the time limit where it is satisfied, on an application made in writing to the Secretary to the Tribunals, that it is not or was not reasonably practicable for an appeal to be brought within that time. However, the lodging of an appeal does not automatically suspend the operation of the notice. A separate application to do so has to be made to the tribunal (*Source*: HASAWA 1974, s. 24(3)(b)).

Defence of 'not reasonably practicable'

16.22
In deciding whether it is 'reasonably practicable' to comply, it is necessary that 'a computation must be made by the owner, in which the quantum of risk is placed on one scale and the sacrifice involved in the measure necessary for averting the risk (whether in money, time or trouble) is placed on the other: and that if it be shown that there is a gross disproportion between them – the risk being insignificant in relation to the sacrifice - the [employers] discharge the onus on them' (per Asquith LJ in *Edwards v National Coal Board* [1949] 1 KB 704, CA).

16.23
Thus, an employer would have to show that the risks were small compared to the cost of carrying out the remedial work. For instance, an inspector might serve a notice on an employer requiring him to fit appropriate banisters to an otherwise dangerous or steep staircase. These might cost £10,000. If evidence is advanced to show that the

staircase was very rarely used or that the risk of injury is small, the tribunal might well cancel the notice or approve a less expensive alternative (*West Bromwich Building Society v Townsend* [1983] ICR 257, DC).

Procedure on appeal

16.24
The manner in which proceedings are conducted is dealt with in Chapter 26. The onus is on the employer to show that it is not reasonably practicable to comply with the terms of an improvement or prohibition notice. The tribunal may either cancel or affirm the notice. If the notice is affirmed, the tribunal may modify the notice to the extend that it deems fit (*Source*: HASAWA 1974, s. 24(2)).

Costs

16.25
The tribunal may make an order that a party to the proceedings shall pay to the other party either a specified sum in respect of the costs incurred by that other party or, in default of agreement, the taxed amount of those costs. A tribunal will not generally exercise that power against a health and safety inspector unless satisfied that the improvement or prohibition notice should never have been issued on the information available to the inspector at the material time. But, it is likely to make an order against an employer who brings an appeal that is lacking in merit or is otherwise hopeless (*Source*: Employment Tribunals (Constitution & Rules of Procedure) Regulations 1993 [*qv*] Sch. 4, Rule 12).

Proceedings in a magistrates' court

16.26
Employers served with an improvement or prohibition notice must either appeal to an employment tribunal, and avail themselves of the defence of not 'reasonably practicable', or comply with the notice. The offence lies in their failing to comply (*Dearey v Mansion Hide Upholstery Ltd* [1983] ICR 610, DC).

16.27
If proceedings are brought against an employer in the magistrates' court on the grounds that he has failed to comply with an improvement or prohibition notice, or with a notice that has been modified on appeal by the tribunal, the employer cannot raise the defence of not 'reasonably practicable', whether or not there are valid grounds for resisting the allegation. However, if proceedings are brought for a breach of a relevant statutory provision, the defence of not 'reasonably practicable' *is* available, but the employer must prove it, on a balance of probabilities (*Source*: HASAWA, ss 33(1) & 40).

Appeal to the High Court

16.28
An appeal from the decision of an employment tribunal, or from that handed down in a magistrates' court, lies to the divisional court of the High Court, which has powers very similar to those of the Employment Appeal Tribunal (see Chapters 27 and 28).

Penalties

16.29
The penalty for a failure to comply with the terms of an improvement or prohibition notice (including any such notice as modified on appeal) is a fine, on summary conviction, of up £20,000 and/or imprisonment for a term not exceeding six months. On conviction on indictment, the penalty is a fine of an unlimited amount and/or imprisonment for a term not exceeding two years (*Source*: HASAWA 1974, s. 33(2A).

16.30
The penalty for a contravention of an employer's statutory duties under sections 2 to 6 of the 1974 Act is a fine, on summary conviction, of a maximum £20,000 or, if the offender is convicted on indictment, a fine of an unlimited amount. For a breach of health and safety regulations, the penalty is a fine of up £5,000 or, if the offender is convicted on indictment, an unlimited fine.

Transfer of undertakings

GENERAL INFORMATION

17.1

Far and away the most controversial legislation to appear in the UK in recent years has been the Transfer of Undertakings (Protection of Employment) Regulations 1981. The TUPE Regulations (so-called) – which came into force on 1 May 1982, implementing Council Directive 77/187/EEC of 14 February 1977 (the 'Acquired Rights' Directive) – protect the rights of employees when the undertaking (company, firm, trade or business) for which they work (or part of that undertaking) is sold or transferred as a 'going concern' to another employer.

17.2

The Regulations apply to the transfer of a UK-based undertaking (or part of such an undertaking) from one person to another – whether effected by sale or by some other disposition (other than by the sale of shares), or by operation of law. Such a transfer (which may be effected by a series of two or more transactions, and may take place whether or not any property is transferred) is referred to in the Regulations as a 'relevant transfer', and it is the meaning of this expression that has produced so many confusing and contradictory decisions in the courts (see *Meaning of 'relevant transfer'*, paras 17.30 to 17.41 below). The expression 'undertaking' includes any trade or business (regulation 2).

The person selling or disposing of his (or her) business (the seller) is referred to as the 'transferor', while the person to whom the business is sold (the purchaser) is known as the 'transferee'.

Note: If the receiver, administrator or liquidator of a company that has gone into receivership or liquidation (or that is voluntarily wound up by its creditors) transfers the company's undertaking, or part of the company's undertaking, to a wholly-owned subsidiary of the company, the 'relevant transfer' will be deemed not to have been effected until immediately before the transferee company ceases (otherwise than by reason of its being wound up) to be a wholly-owned subsidiary of the transferor company, or until immediately before the relevant undertaking is transferred by the transferee company to another person, whichever occurs first. For the purposes of the TUPE Regulations, the transfer of the relevant undertaking will be taken to have been effected immediately before that date by one transaction only (regulation 4).

TUPE REGULATIONS SUMMARISED

17.3

When a TUPE transfer occurs, the transferee (buyer) inherits the contracts of employment of the persons employed by the transferor (seller) immediately before the transfer took place. In short, those contracts of employment do not come to an end (as they might otherwise have done under the common law) but are treated in law as if they had originally been made between the affected employees and the transferee. So, if food manufacturer A sells one of his factories to food manufacturer B, as a going concern, food manufacturer B inherits the contracts of employment of every person employed in that factory (and their rights under those contracts) (*ibid* regulation 5).

17.4

A transferee who inherits the contracts of employment of persons employed in the undertaking immediately before the 'relevant transfer' (see paras 17.30 to 17.41 below) also inherits the transferor's rights, powers, duties and liabilities (including liability for redundancy payments, money in lieu of notice, compensation for unfair dismissal, subsisting allegations of sex discrimination, monies owed to employees, etc, but *not* any criminal liabilities) under, or in connection with, those contracts. Furthermore, anything done by the transferor *before* the transfer takes place, in or in relation to any such contract (or to a person employed in the undertaking in question), is deemed in law to have been done by the transferee.

17.5

Once a 'relevant transfer' has taken place it is not open to the transferee to presume to vary the contracts of employment of the transferred employees with a view to harmonising their working hours, rates of pay, holiday entitlement, etc with those of his existing workforce. Nor may the transferee insert fresh terms, such as a restrictive covenant, in the transferred employees' contracts (*Credit*

Suisse First Boston (Europe) Limited v Padiachy [1998] IRLR 504, QBD; *Credit Suisse First Boston (Europe) Limited v Lister* [1998] IRLR 700, CA). This rule applies even if the employees in question are happy to accept any such variation in their terms and conditions of employment and are no worse off as a result of that variation (*Foreningen af Arbejdsledere i Danmark v Daddy's Dance Hall A/S* [1988] IRLR 315; *Rask v ISS Kantineservice A/S* [1993] IRLR 133). In the *Wilson/Bexendale* case (see next paragraph) Lord Slynn of Hadley opined (*obiter*) that any variation of the terms of an employee's contract that is due to a TUPE transfer and for no other reason is invalid. There can, however, be a valid variation, he said, for reasons that are not due to the transfer. 'It may be difficult,' he concluded, 'to decide whether the variation is due to the transfer or attributable to some separate cause, but there may come a time when the link with the transfer is broken or can be treated as no longer effective.'

17.6

In *Wilson v St Helen's Borough Council/BFL v Baxendale & Meade* [1998] IRLR 706), the House of Lords held that a dismissal for a reason connected with a TUPE transfer (whether by the transferor or the transferee), while automatically unfair (unless for an ETO reason), is nonetheless legally effective and not a nullity – thereby overruling the Court of Appeal on that same point ([1997] IRLR 505). An employee dismissed by a transferor cannot compel the transferee to employ him (or her). Under English domestic law, said their Lordships, the dismissal of an employee by an employer brings to an end the working relationship between them. As a general rule, the English courts will not specifically enforce contracts of employment. If a dismissal is in breach of contract, the employee can claim damages for wrongful dismissal. If it is unfair, the employee may seek redress from an employment tribunal; in which event, the employer will be ordered either to reinstate or re-engage the dismissed employee and/or pay a substantial amount of compensation. But, save for the purpose of enforcing rights under it, the contract of employment is gone. As was indicated earlier, a transferee who does not take on the transferor's employees – because they have already been dismissed by the transferor or by the transferee himself – must, nonetheless, meet all the transferor's contractual and statutory obligations in relation to those employees, including a liability to pay damages for wrongful dismissal and/or compensation for unfair dismissal.

17.7

All of which suggests that the only way a transferee can legitimately vary the terms of conditions of incoming TUPE-transferred employees is to dismiss them all (which dismissals will be automatically unfair if not for an ETO reason involving changes in the workforce) and then offer to re-engage some or all of them on a terms and conditions that they may or may not find acceptable. By any measure, this 'take it or leave it' option (and a willingness to pay compensation for unfair dismissal) cannot be in the interest of good industrial relations practice, nor preferable to a negotiated and consensual variation in the terms and conditions of incoming employees.

17.8

In the joined cases of *Bernadone v Pall Mall Services Group & Others* and *Martin v Lancashire County Council* ([2000] IRLR 487), the Court of Appeal held that the liabilities inherited by a transferee under TUPE include any and all liabilities of the transferor in tort. Although tortious liabilities do not arise 'under' the contract of employment, they do arise 'in connection with' the contract, given that the employer's common law duty of care arises out of the relationship of employer and employee. In short, an employee injured in the course of his (or her) employment with the transferor (his former employer) may nonetheless sue the transferee (his new employer) for damages in negligence. However, the former employer's right to an indemnity under his employer's liability insurance policy also transfers to the new employer. In other words, it is the transferor's insurers, not the transferee's, who must pay any damages awarded by the court in such circumstances.

17.9

A transferee does *not*, however, inherit any term in an employee's contract of employment that relates to an occupational pension scheme as defined in Section 1 of the Pension Schemes Act 1993 (although moves are afoot to remove this exception).

17.10

The phrase 'immediately before the transfer' is given a wide interpretation. It covers any person in the employ of the vendor who is dismissed in consequence of the proposed sale, whether or not negotiations for the sale had been completed or a buyer identified. It could apply where a liquidator trims the workforce before seeking purchasers to make a business more attractive, but not where he has run out of work and there is a true redundancy situation (*P Bork International A/S v Foreningen af Arbejdsledere i Danmark* [1989] IRLR 41, ECJ; *Litster v Forth Estuary Engineering Ltd* [1989] ICR 341, HL; and *Wendleboe v L J Music Aps* [1985] ECR 457, ECJ).

An employee's refusal to transfer

17.11
There is no transfer of a contract of employment (or of the rights, powers, duties and liabilities under, or in connection with, that contract) if the employee in question informs the transferor (or the transferee) that he (or she) objects to becoming employed by the transferee (*ibid* regulation 5(4A)).

17.12
An employee who refuses to work for the new owner of his (or her) former employer's business, for whatever reason, effectively brings his contract of employment to an end. In short, the termination of his employment does not amount to a dismissal in law and the employee has no right to complain of unfair dismissal, regardless of his length of service at the material time (*ibid* regulation 5(4B)) (*Katsikas v Konstantinidis* [1993] IRLR 179, ECJ).

17.13
However, a substantial and detrimental change in the employee's working conditions immediately before the transfer might well amount to so serious a repudiation of his contract as to entitle him to resign (with or without notice) and pursue a complaint of unfair constructive dismissal (*ibid* regulation 5(5)). That right would nonetheless be denied him if he had not been continuously employed for at least one year and was under normal retiring age at the effective date of termination of his contract of employment.

17.14
In *Hay v George Hanson (Building Contractors) Ltd* ([1996] IRLR 427), the Employment Appeal Tribunal said that an employee who had expressed unhappiness about the prospect of working for the transferee could not be said to have objected to (or refused) the transfer. Although the TUPE Regulations are not specific on this

point, an employee who refuses outright to transfer should inform his (or her) employer in clear and unequivocal terms (whether by word or deed, or by a combination of the two) that he refuses to work for the transferor.

Effect of transfer on collective agreements

17.15
If, at the time of the 'relevant transfer', the transferor has a collective agreement with a recognised trade union in respect of any employee whose contract is inherited by the transferee, the transferee inherits that collective agreement in respect of that same employee (and the rights and obligations that go with it) as if it had been made between himself and the trade union in question (*ibid* regulation 6).

17.16
The transferee does *not*, however, inherit any term in a collective agreement as relates to an occupational pension scheme as defined in Section 1 of the Pensions Act 1993.

Dismissal of employee because of 'relevant transfer'

17.17
If, either before or after the 'relevant transfer', the transferor (or the transferee) dismisses any employee of the transferor (or of the transferee) for a reason in any way linked to the transfer itself, the employee in question will be treated in law as having been unfairly dismissed. The only justification for such a dismissal would be an 'economic, technical or organisational reason entailing changes in the workforce' – often referred to as an 'ETO' reason – which, if genuine, will be treated by an employment tribunal as having been for 'some other substantial reason' of a kind to justify the dismissal of an employee holding the position which that employee held (*ibid* regulation 8).

17.18
In short, an employer (transferor or transferee) will need to justify his decision to dismiss one or more of the employees affected by the transfer on grounds that have nothing whatsoever to do with the transfer (eg misconduct) or for a genuine ETO reason involving changes in the workforce. For example, it is arguably absurd (in a

situation in which an undertaking or part of an undertaking is absorbed within the transferee's organisation) for the transferee to be left with a duplicated management team (two marketing managers, two chief accountants, two personnel managers, etc), and (say) 100 or more production workers (when he only needs 60) without being able to make the appropriate organisational changes. If he has a highly sophisticated production process requiring far fewer workers, logic dictates that a number of workers will have to be made redundant. If the transferee can justify those redundancies (and the redundancy selection process) on purely business grounds (ie an ETO reason), the dismissals are likely to be held fair.

17.19

Curiously, an employee dismissed in consequence of a 'relevant transfer' does not qualify to present a complaint of unfair dismissal unless continuously employed for a minimum period of one or more years ending with the effective date of termination of his (or her) contract of employment and under 'normal retiring age' at that time (*ibid* regulation 8(5)).

Effect of 'relevant transfer' on trade union recognition

17.20

If, after a 'relevant transfer', the undertaking (or part of the undertaking) transferred maintains an identity distinct from the remainder of the transferee's undertaking, any independent trade union recognised to any extent (or for any purpose) by the transferor shall be deemed to be recognised to that same extent (or purpose) by the transferee. If the transferred undertaking does *not* maintain an identity distinct from the remainder of the transferee's undertaking, but is simply absorbed within the latter undertaking, the recognition agreement no longer applies.

Duty for inform and consult representatives

17.21

A 'relevant transfer' will inevitably impact on persons employed by both the transferor and transferee. Many will simply be concerned to know what effect the transfer is likely to have on their jobs, prospects or continued employment. To allay such concerns, the Regulations advise both the transferor *and* the transferee, first, to inform the 'appropriate representatives' about the transfer and, second, consult them and listen to their representations.

First, the representatives must be informed of:

(a)   the fact that the relevant transfer is to take place, when, approximately, it is to take place, and the reasons for it;

(b)   the legal, economic and social implications of the transfer for all affected employees;

(c)   the measures that the employer envisages will, in connection with the transfer, be taken in relation to those employees or, if it is envisaged that no measures will be so taken, that fact; and

(d)   if the employer is the transferor, the measures which the transferee envisages he will, in connection with the transfer, take in relation to such of those employees whose contracts of employment he will inherit after the transfer or, if he envisages that no measures will be taken, that fact.

The information in (a) to (d) must be conveyed to the 'appropriate representatives' long enough before the relevant transfer to enable them to take an active part in the subsequent consultations. To that same end, the transferee must likewise give the transferor advance information about his own intentions under (d) above.

17.22

The term 'appropriate representatives' means employee representatives elected by the employees themselves or, if the employees are of a description in respect of which an independent trade union is recognised by the employer, representatives of that trade union (eg shop stewards). In an undertaking in which there are both employee-elected and trade-union appointed representatives, the employee must deal with those trade union representatives. If there is no trade union representing the interests of the affected employees (that is to say, the employees who may be affected by the transfer or may be affected by measures taken in connection with it), the employer must consult either with existing employee-elected representatives (who may have been elected for other purposes) or invite the affected employees to elect one or more of their number to represent their interests in consultations relating to the proposed transfer. If there are no elected employee representatives, the employers on both sides must invite the affected employees to elect one or more of their number to be representatives and give them sufficient time to carry out the election and to complete it *before* the information and consultation process takes place (*ibid* regulation 10 and 10A).

Note: When overseeing the election of employee representatives, the employer must do whatever is necessary to ensure that the election is fair. Although the employer has the right to decide on the appropriate number of representatives, he cannot presume to dictate which employees can put their names forward as candidates and which cannot. The employer must also allow the affected employees sufficient time to cast their votes *in secret*, and must see to it that the votes given at the election are accurately counted (*ibid* regulation 10A)).

17.23

Second, if either the transferor or transferee envisages taking (unspecified) measures in relation to any employees affected by the transfer, he must consult with the appropriate representatives with a view to seeking their agreement to those measures. During the consultation process, the transferor or transferee must (a) consider any representations made by those representatives, (b) reply to those representations, and (c), if he rejects any of those representations, give his reasons for doing so. Before, during and after such consultations, the employer in question must allow those representatives access to the affected employees and provide whatever accommodation and facilities they may need in that respect (eg an office, tables and chairs and, perhaps, use of a telephone).

Penalties for failure to inform or consult

17.24

An appropriate representative (or in the case of a trade-union-appointed representative, the union in question) or one or more of the affected employees may complain to an employment tribunal that their employer had refused or failed to inform or consult them about the 'relevant transfer'. Such a complaint must be presented within the period of three months beginning with the date on which the relevant transfer took place. If the complaint is upheld, the tribunal will order the respondent employer to pay the complainant/s an appropriate amount of compensation; in short, a sum not exceeding 13 weeks' pay as the tribunal considers just and equitable having regard to the seriousness of the employer's failure to inform or consult. A complaint presented 'out of time' will not be entertained unless the tribunal is satisfied that it was not reasonably practicable for the applicant to have done so within that prescribed three-month period.

17.25
A failure to pay the compensation referred to in the preceding paragraph will lead to a further complaint to a tribunal and to an order directing the employer to pay the relevant amount (*ibid* regulation 11, as amended by the Collective Redundancies & Transfer of Undertakings (Protection of Employment) (Amendment) Regulations 1999 (SI 1999/1925)).

17.26
An employer may defend his failure to comply with the duty to inform and consult if he can satisfy a tribunal that there were special circumstances which rendered it not reasonably practicable for him to do so, but that he took all such steps towards the performance of that duty as were reasonably practicable in those circumstances. However, it is no defence for the employer to argue (as transferor) that he was prevented from complying fully with his duty to inform the appropriate representatives because of the transferee's refusal or failure to provide the information referred to earlier in this section. If, on the other hand, the transferor has given notice to the transferee that he intends show that fact, the giving of that notice will make the transferee a party to the proceedings, and liable in his turn to pay the whole or part of any award of compensation.

Restriction on contracting out

17.27
Any provision of any agreement (whether a contract of employment or otherwise) will be void in so far as it purports to exclude or limit the operation of the TUPE Regulations or to preclude any person from presenting a complaint to an employment tribunal arising out of an employer's failure to inform or consult the appropriate representatives about the transfer (*ibid* regulation 12).

17.28
In *Thompson & Others v (1) Walon Car Delivery, (2) BRS Automotive Ltd*, EAT/256/96, the EAT held that a 'compromise agreement' concluded with the transferor several days after a 'relevant transfer',

and purporting to exclude the right of an employee to bring proceedings under TUPE, could not be relied upon by the transferee.

Excluded classes

17.29
Regulations 8, 10 and 11 of the TUPE Regulations do not apply to employees who, under their contracts of employment, ordinarily work outside the United Kingdom. A person employed to work on board a UK-registered ship is regarded as a person who ordinarily works in the UK unless the employment is wholly outside the UK or he (or she) is not ordinarily a resident in the UK.

Note: Regulation 8 relates to the dismissal of an employee because of a relevant transfer; regulation 10, to an employer's duty to inform and consult the appropriate representatives; and regulation 11, to the consequences of an employer's failure to inform and consult.

MEANING OF 'RELEVANT TRANSFER'

17.30
There has to be a 'transfer from one person to another'. The European Court of Justice (ECJ) has held that the Acquired Rights Directive provides protection where there is a change in the natural or legal person responsible for the running of an undertaking (*Landorganisationen i Danmark v Ny Molle Kro* [1989] ICR 330, ECJ), a view endorsed by the ECJ in (amongst others) *Dr Sophie Redmond Stichting v Bartol & Others* [1992] IRLR 366 and *Rask & Christensen v ISS Kantineservice A/S* [1993] IRLR 133.

17.31
There has to be a transfer of a 'going concern' or an economic entity so that the purchaser can carry on the business without interruption. It does not matter that there are modifications. Goodwill is often included but is not essential. Where there was a change of tenants at a public house owned by a brewery it was held that continuity was preserved for an employee who worked there. The new tenant had been put in possession of a going concern and was running the same business as that run by his predecessor (See *JMA Spijkers v Gebroers Benedik Abbatoir CV & Another* [1986] 2 CMLR 296 ECJ; *Kenny & Another v South Manchester College* [1993] IRLR 265, QBD; *McLellan v*

Cody & Cody, 7 October 1986, EAT Oct. 7, 1986, EAT; and *Safebid Ltd v Ramiro & Others*, 3 May 1990, EAT).

17.32
But where a firm holding a catering concession prematurely stopped running the business, which was then carried on temporarily with a different sort of catering facility by the company that had granted the concession, the EAT held that this was not a 'relevant transfer' within the meaning of the 1981 Regulations (*Caterleisure Ltd v TGWU & Others*, 14 October 1991, EAT).

17.33
Where it is shown, on the other hand, that, shortly after the sale, the employees were re-engaged by the transferee, the Regulations would probably bite. A business was put out to tender. The company that previously ran it lost the contract to a competitor. That other company engaged nearly all the former employees who were previously engaged in the business. It was held that the 1981 Regulations applied (*Harrison Bowden Ltd v Bowden* [1994] ICR 186, EAT; *Dines & Others v Initial Health Care Services Ltd & Another* [1994] IRLR 336, CA).

17.34
The possible permutations are endless, but there have been several important rulings on what is meant by and what are the consequences of the TUPE Regulations. The tribunals and courts must apply a purposive construction to the relevant provisions so as to achieve what they are manifestly intended to achieve (*Marleasing SA v La Comercial Internacional de Alimentacion* [1990] ECR 4153, ECJ).

17.35
It matters not how many transfers take place or between whom, provided that there is an economic entity in existence that the final employer carries on in some capacity, eg as purchaser of the business, or as franchisee or licensee (*Foreningen af Arbejdsledere i Danmark v Daddy's Dance Hall A/S* [1988] IRLR 315, ECJ; *LMS Drains Ltd & Metro-Rod Services Ltd v Waugh*, 6 June 1991, EAT).

The 'Spijkers' test

17.36

In *Spijkers v Gebroeders Benedik Abbatoir CV* ([1986] 2 CMLR 486), the ECJ held that the decisive criterion for establishing the existence or otherwise of a TUPE transfer (or 'relevant transfer') is whether the undertaking (or part of the undertaking) transferred retains its identity after the change of ownership. In other words, whether the activities or the nature of the trade or business carried on (or resumed) by the transferee are essentially or identifiably the same as those carried on by the transferor before the transfer took place. The ECJ in *Spijkers* listed a number of factors to be taken into account in deciding whether these conditions are fulfilled:

- the type of undertaking (trade or business) in question and the activities carried on by that business;

- whether or not tangible assets (including furniture and equipment, raw materials, stock in hand, finished products and the like) were transferred to the new owner of the business;

- the value of intangible assets (such as 'goodwill') at the time of the alleged transfer;

- whether or not the majority of persons working in the business were taken over by the new employer;

- whether the new owner continued to do business with the same customers or clientele after the alleged transfer took place;

- the degree of similarity between the activities carried on before and after the transfer, and the period (if any) for which those activities are suspended.

Finally, it is for the national court to make the necessary factual appraisal, in order to establish where or not a TUPE transfer has occurred.

17.37

The fact that an activity (i) was only ancillary, (ii) the business transferred only involved one person and (iii) there was no transfer of any tangible assets could not deprive an employee from the protection of the Regulations (*Christel Schmidt v Spar-undLeihkasse der früheren Amter Bordesholm, Kiel und Cronshagen, The Times*, 25 May 1994, ECJ).

The 'Süzen' and related cases

17.38

In *Rygaard v Stro Molle Akustik* ([1996] IRLR 151), the ECJ held that a transfer must involve the transfer of a 'stable economic entity'. But the 'cat was set amongst the pigeons' (so to speak) in *Ayse Süzen v Zehnacker Gebäudereinguing GmbH Krankenhausservice & Lefarth GmbH* ([1997] IRLR 255), when the ECJ ruled that, in the case of a 'second generation transfer', an activity does not of itself constitute such an entity. There would, it said, have to be a significant transfer of assets and a transfer of the majority of skilled workers from one contractor to the next before such a transfer could be held to be a 'relevant transfer' within the meaning of the 1981 Regulations. In the *Süzen* case, a cleaner who worked at a school in Germany was dismissed (along with seven of her colleagues) by the cleaning company by whom she was employed when it lost its cleaning contract at the school. The contract was awarded to another cleaning company. The ECJ held (following the opinion of the Advocate-General) that a change of contractors does not qualify as a 'relevant transfer' unless significant tangible or intangible assets (or a majority of the workforce in terms of numbers and skills) also transfers to the second (or new) contractor. In labour-intensive undertakings (such as contract catering or cleaning), where there are no significant assets, there will not be a transfer within the meaning of the TUPE Regulations unless a majority of the former contractor's workforce is taken on by the new contractor.

17.39

Following swiftly on the heels of the *Süzen* decision came the decision on 26 March 1997 of the Court of Appeal in *Betts v Brintel Helicopters Limited and KLM Era Helicopters* ([1997] IRLR 361). In the *Betts* case, Brintel Helicopters had a contract to 'ferry' men and equipment to and from a number of North Sea oil rigs owned by Shell. When Brintel's contract expired, the contract was awarded to KLM Era Helicopters who did not (nor needed to) take on any of Brintel's staff or equipment. The Court agreed with *Süzen* and held that the changeover of contractors did not constitute a 'relevant transfer'.

17.40

Süzen was applied by the ECJ in *Francisco Hernández Vidal v Gomez Perez & Others* ([1999] IRLR 132) and, again, in *Sanchez Hidalgo &*

Others v Asociación de Servicios Aser & Sociedad Cooperativa Minerva ([1999] IRLR 136). In the *Hernández Vidal* case, the ECJ held that a situation in which an organisation terminates its contract with a cleaning firm and decides to do its own cleaning would be covered by the 'Acquired Rights' Directive, so long as the operation is accompanied by the transfer of an economic entity between the last two undertakings. However, 'the mere fact that the maintenance work carried out, first, by the cleaning firm and then by the undertaking owning the premises, is similar, does not justify the conclusion that a transfer of such an entity has occurred'. And again: 'In certain sectors such as cleaning, the activity is essentially based on manpower. Thus, an organised grouping of wage earners, who are specifically and permanently assigned to a common task, may, in the absence of other factors of production, amount to an economic entity' – a view repeated by the ECJ in the *Sanchez Hidalgo* case, which was decided on a similar set of circumstances. In short, it is for the national court to determine whether the maintenance of the premises that awarded the contract was organised in the form of an economic activity within the outside cleaning firm before the firm awarding the contract decided to carry out the work itself.

17.41
However, in *ECM Vehicle Delivery Service Limited v Cox* ([1999] IRLR 416), the Court of Appeal (while distinguishing *Süzen* and cases like it, for reasons which are far from clear, given their similarity) held that an employer could not prevent the 1981 Regulations applying simply by refusing to take on the putative transferee's employees. Indeed, said the Court, an employment tribunal had every right to challenge those motives before deciding whether a TUPE transfer had in fact occurred.

Comment

17.42
Over the years, the tribunals and courts have delivered a number of seemingly inconsistent (it not wholly contradictory) decisions on the interpretation of the 1981 Regulations. The old adage holds true: that each case must be decided on its particular merits – which is, of course, of little comfort to employers who (short of seeking an opinion from a tribunal or court) are left to decide for themselves whether their activities (notably the termination or non-renewal of

cleaning, maintenance and related contracts, or the outsourcing of some of their operations, eg payroll services) fall within the scope of the TUPE Regulations.

For further references in this book to the TUPE Regulations (and there are many), please consult the **Index**.

Recent developments

17.43
A consultation document published by the Department of Trade & Industry on 12 January 1998 invited 'the business community, employees and other interested parties' to put forward their views on the European Commission's proposals to amend Council Directive EC 77/187/EEC (the 'Acquired Rights' Directive) 'on the approximation of the laws of the Member States relating to the safeguarding of employees' rights in the event of transfers of undertakings, businesses or parts of businesses'.

17.44
The European Commission's proposals (not all of which are supported by the UK Government) included proposals for redefining (or clarifying) the term 'relevant transfer' and for bringing takeovers by share transfer within the Directive's coverage. The Commission has also proposed ending the current exclusion of certain occupational pension schemes from the terms and conditions inherited by transferees. It also suggests an amendment that would allow transfer-related variations to terms and conditions of employment of affected employees if made by agreement between the relevant employers and the 'appropriate employee representatives'.

17.45
In a consultative document issued in mid-2000, the Department of Trade & Industry set out its proposals for enabling employers contemplating the sale or purchase of a business to obtain fast-track access to the employment tribunals for guidance on whether the intended purchase or sale is likely to constitute a 'relevant transfer' within the meaning of the TUPE Regulations. The consultative document also seeks the views of interested parties on the transfer of pension rights. Amending legislation is expected by July 2001.

Working Time Regulations 1998

GENERAL INFORMATION

18.1

The Working Time Regulations 1998 (which came into force on 1 October 1998) implement Council Directive 93/104/EC of 23 November 1993 ('concerning certain aspects of the organisation of working time') and Council Directive 94/33/EC of 22 June 1994 ('on the protection of young people at work').

SUMMARY

18.2

The 1998 Regulations apply to all workers over compulsory school age who are employed under contracts of employment. They also apply to agency workers, freelancers, 'agency temps', and the like (but not self-employed persons) who carry out work for (but are not employed by) an employer who is in a position to regulate their working hours, rest breaks and periods of employment.

The Regulations prescribe:

- an *average* working week of no more than 48 hours (calculated over a reference period of 17 weeks – which reference period may be increased to 26 weeks by the employer (but only in prescribed circumstances), or to up to 52 weeks under a collective or workforce agreement;

- an upper limit on night time working of an average eight hours in each 24-hour period; or, for night workers engaged in hazardous activities, an absolute maximum of eight hours in that same 24-hour period;

- initial and follow-up health assessments (or, in the case of workers under the age of 18, initial and follow-up health and capacities assessments) for workers required to work at night;

- a weekly rest period of a minimum 24 hours (or 48 hours in any fortnight); and for adolescent workers, a minimum weekly rest period of 48 hours;

- a daily rest period of a minimum 11 consecutive hours between shifts for adult workers; and for adolescent workers (see below), a minimum of 12 consecutive hours;

- a minimum 20-minute rest break each day for adult workers during a working day or shift exceeding (or likely to exceed) six hours; and, for adolescent workers, a minimum 30-minute rest break during a shift lasting or expected to last more than four-and-a-half hours;

- four weeks' paid annual holidays – once a worker has completed 13 weeks' service with his or her employer.

For these purposes, an 'adolescent worker' is a worker who has lawfully left school (that is to say, is over compulsory school age) but has not yet had his or her 18th birthday. It follows that an 'adult worker' is a worker aged 18 years and over.

18.3
The Regulations will be enforced both by the employment tribunals (in relation to an employee's statutory rights to rest breaks, paid annual holidays, etc); and by the Health & Safety Executive (in relation to the limits on weekly working time, night work, etc) (as to which, see paras 18.30 to 18.34 below).

Excluded categories

18.4
The Regulations do not apply to managing executives or to other persons with autonomous decision-making powers (including workers, such as travelling sales representatives whose working hours comprise a mix of standard and voluntary hours); or to family workers, or to persons officiating at religious ceremonies in churches and religious communities. The latter are nonetheless entitled to a minimum of four weeks' paid holidays each year.

18.5
Nor do they apply to workers employed in air, rail, road, sea, inland waterway and lake transport; or to doctors in training; or to specific

activities of the armed forces, the police, fire brigades, ambulance services, customs and immigration officers, the prison service, the coast guard, or to lifeguard crews and other voluntary rescue services (although some of these exceptions are currently being challenged through the courts by representative trade unions). See also para 18.36 below.

Average working week

18.6

Unless a worker has agreed with his (or her) employer (in writing) to work longer hours, his average working week, including overtime, must not exceed 48 hours. For these purposes, a week is the period of seven consecutive days from Sunday to Monday, inclusive (regulation 4). It must be emphasised that a worker's right to refuse to work more than an average 48-hour week cannot be overridden by a collective or workforce agreement or by any contrary provision in his contract of employment. A worker who agrees with his employer to opt out of that maximum average 48-hour week must do so voluntarily and in writing, as to which, see para 18.35 below. Furthermore, the opt-out agreement itself must advise the worker in question of his statutory right to change his mind by giving an agreed period of notice (of not less than seven days nor more than three months).

18.7

Following amendments introduced by the Working Time Regulations 1999 (SI 1999/3372), employers no longer need to keep detailed records of the weekly hours worked by people who have opted out of the maximum average 48-hour week. However, they must keep records sufficient to satisfy an Health and Safety Inspector (or local authority Environmental Health Officer) that the working hours of all other workers do not exceed the statutory maximum. See also para 18.29 below.

18.8

An employee's average weekly working hours are to be calculated over a reference period of 17 weeks or, in special circumstances, 26 weeks. The standard reference period of 17 weeks may be extended to 26 weeks in the case of workers sent to distant locations whose patterns of work vary from location to location and who may need to work long hours to complete a given task in the shortest possible time. The same extended reference period may be appropriate in the case of dock workers, security guards, postal workers, hospital and care workers, workers in the media, gas, water and electricity industries, farm workers, and so on. Calculations must not include those working days during which an employee is absent from work because of sickness, annual holidays or maternity leave). See also para 18.27, which allows for the further extension of the 17-week reference period to one of up to 52 weeks under the terms of a workforce or collective agreement.

Length of night work

18.9
A night worker (see below) should not be required to work at night for more than an average eight hours in any period of 24 consecutive hours – which 'average' is to be calculated over a reference period of 17 weeks. If, on the other hand, a night worker is engaged in especially hazardous work, or in work involving heavy physical or mental strain, it is the employer's responsibility to ensure that the worker does not work more than eight hours in *any* 24-hour period during which he (or she) performs night work (Reg 5).

18.10
Night work will be regarded as involving special hazards (or heavy physical or mental strain) if it is identified as such in a collective agreement, a workforce agreement (see paras 18.27 & 18.28 below), or in the risk assessment exercise necessarily carried out by every employer in accordance with Regulation 3 of the Management of Health & Safety at Work Regulations 1999 (SI 1999/3242).

18.11
A 'night worker' is a worker who normally works three or more hours of his (or her) daily working time during night time, or who is likely during night time to work such proportion of his annual working time as may be specified in a collective agreement or workforce agreement. For these purposes, the expression 'night time' means a period of not less than seven hours that includes the period between midnight and 5.00 am, as determined by either of a collective agreement or workforce agreement or, in default of any such determination, the period between 11.00 pm and 6.00 am.

Health assessment and transfer of night workers to day work

18.12

An employer must not assign an adult worker to night work without first providing that worker with the opportunity of a free health assessment (unless the worker has already had a health assessment prior to being assigned to night work on an earlier occasion and the employer has no reason to believe that the previous assessment is no longer valid). Further opportunities for free health assessments must be provided at regular intervals so long as the night worker continues to work at night (Reg 6).

18.13

A young person under the age of 18 *must not* be assigned to work during the period between 10.00 pm and 6.00 am (the 'restricted period') without being afforded an opportunity for a free 'health and capacities' assessment, and for repeat assessments at regular intervals thereafter.

Transfer to day work

18.14

If a night worker is (or appears to be) suffering from health problems recognisably associated with night work, the employer should, whenever possible, transfer that worker to more amenable work during the day.

Note: If a new or expectant mother works at night and produces a certificate signed by her doctor (or registered midwife) to the effect that working at night could be detrimental to her health and safety (or, in the case of a pregnant employee, to that of her unborn child), her employer must either transfer her to daytime work (without loss of pay) or suspend her on full pay for the period specified in the certificate. Non-compliance with this requirement is an offence under the Health & Safety at Work etc Act 1974 (*Source*: Regulation 17, Management of Health & Safety at Work Regulations 1999).

Pattern of work

18.15

Employees engaged in monotonous work (or in work that is carried out at a pre-determined rate) must be given adequate rest breaks if the work they do is such as to pose a risk to their health and safety. Production-line workers could well fall into this category (Reg 7).

Daily rest

18.16
Adult workers (that is to say, workers aged 18 and over) are entitled to a rest period of at least 11 consecutive hours in each period of 24 consecutive hours. However, this does not apply to a situation in which a shift worker changes shift and cannot take a daily rest period between the end of one shift and the start of the next one. Nor does it apply to a worker engaged in work (such as catering or cleaning) that occurs at different times of the day and is split up over the day. In such circumstances, the employer must nonetheless allow that shift worker to take an equivalent period of compensatory rest or, if that is not possible, 'appropriate protection' (Regs 9(1), 20 & 22).

18.17
For a young person under the age of 18, the prescribed minimum daily rest period is 12 consecutive hours – although that minimum period may be interrupted if the young person is engaged in activities involving periods of activity that are split up over the day or of short duration. In exceptional circumstances, a worker under the age of 18 may be required to do work otherwise done by an adult during his (or her) rest period if the need for him to do so is prompted by unusual or unforeseeable circumstances – so long as that work is of a temporary nature and must be performed immediately. In such a situation, the employer must nonetheless allow that young worker to take an equivalent period of compensatory rest within the following three weeks (Regs 9(2) & 23).

Weekly rest period

18.18
In addition to his (or her) right to a minimum rest period of at least 11 hours in every period of 24 consecutive hours, an adult worker must be afforded at least one full day off work (that is to say, 24 consecutive and uninterrupted hours) in every period of seven consecutive days. Alternatively, an adult worker must be permitted two such days off work – separate or consecutive – in every period of 14 consecutive days, if the employer prefers the latter alternative approach. This provision does not, however, apply to an adult shift

worker when he changes shift and cannot take a weekly rest period between the end of one of one shift and the start of the next one. The employer must nonetheless allow that worker to take an equivalent period of compensatory rest or, at the very least, afford him 'appropriate protection' (Regs 10(1) & (2), 20 and 22).

18.19

A young worker under the age of 18 is entitled to two days off work (preferably consecutive) in each seven-day period during which he (or she) works for his employer (Reg 10(3)).

The beginning of any such period of seven or 14 consecutive days will either be as laid down in any collective or workforce agreement applicable to the workers in question or, in the absence of any such agreement, midnight between Sunday and Monday.

Rest breaks

18.20

Adults who work more than six hours a day are entitled to a rest break during the working day of at least 20 uninterrupted minutes. Workers under the age of 18, who work more than four-and-a-half hours a day, are entitled to a rest break of at least 30 minutes (preferably consecutive). Workers have the legal right to spend their rest breaks away from their desks or workstations (already a requirement under current health and safety legislation for persons employed in prescribed hazardous activities or processes) (Reg 11).

18.21

In exceptional circumstances, a worker under the age of 18 may be required to do work otherwise done by an adult during his (or her) rest break if the need to do so is prompted by unusual or unforeseeable circumstances – so long as that work is of a temporary nature and must be performed immediately. In such a situation, the employer must nonetheless see to it that the young worker in question is allowed, and takes, an equivalent period of compensatory rest within the following three weeks (Regs 11(4) & 23).

18.22

The terms and conditions under which rest breaks are to be provided and granted may be contained in any related provision in either or both of a collective agreement or a workforce agreement (as to which, see paras 18.27 & 18.28 below).

Paid annual leave

18.23
Every worker with 13 or more weeks' service is entitled to a minimum of four weeks' paid annual holidays. Those four weeks must be taken in full in the holiday year in which they fall due. They may not be replaced by a payment in lieu under any circumstances (except on the termination of the employee's contract of employment) nor may unused holidays be carried forward or 'rolled-over' into the next holiday year (Regs 12, 13 & 14).

18.24
The 'holiday year' is the period of 12 consecutive months that begins on such date during the calendar year as may be provided for in a collective agreement or a workforce agreement, or as may be specified in the written statement of terms and conditions of employment necessarily issued to employees in accordance with sections 1 to 7 of the Employment Rights Act 1996. In the absence of any such agreement or alternative provision, the holiday year will either be the period of 12 consecutive months that begins on 1 October 1998 (and each subsequent anniversary of that date) or, if the employee's employment begins after 1 October 1998, on the date on which his (or her) employment begins (and each subsequent anniversary of that date).

18.25
Public and bank holidays may be incorporated into the four weeks' paid holiday entitlement unless the contract stipulates (or has always stipulated) otherwise. In short, an employer may not presume to include public and bank holidays in an employee's holiday entitlement if that employee has previously enjoyed the contractual (or implied contractual) right to paid annual holidays *in addition to* bank and public holidays.

Entitlements under other provisions

18.26
If an employee is already entitled to minimum rest periods, rest breaks or annual holidays under his (or her) contract of employment, those terms

will prevail – so long as they accord with the employee's minimum statutory rights under the Working Time Regulations 1998. If one or other (or all) of those terms are less beneficial to the employee, the 1998 Regulations will take precedence in respect of that term (or those terms) and will be 'deemed' to be imported into the employee's contract of employment. In short, an employee may take advantage of whichever right is, in any particular respect, the more favourable (Reg 15).

COLLECTIVE AND WORKFORCE AGREEMENTS

18.27
The rights of workers (or an identifiable group of workers) under the Working Time Regulations 1998 – in relation to night work, daily and weekly rest periods, and rest breaks – may be modified or excluded by a collective agreement or by a workforce agreement. Either type of agreement may also (for objective or technical reasons, or for reasons concerning the organisation of work) modify the reference period for determining the length of the average working week by substituting for the prescribed period of 17 weeks, a period not exceeding 52 weeks (Reg 21).

Meaning of 'workforce agreement'

18.28
An agreement is a 'workforce agreement' for the purposes of the 1998 Regulations if:

(a) it is in writing;

(b) it specifies the date on which it is to take effect;

(c) it has been signed either by a majority of the workforce (by excluding those whose terms and conditions of employment have otherwise been agreed in a collective agreement) or by their elected representatives;

(d) before the agreement was made available for signature, copies – together with any notes for guidance – had been distributed to all affected employees for their consideration;

(e) in the case of an agreement signed by the majority of affected employees, it specifies a date, no later than five years after the date in (b) above, in which it will cease to have effect.

Records

18.29

An employer must maintain adequate records of the working hours and periods of employment of day workers, shift workers and night workers so as to satisfy health and safety inspectors that there has been no abuse of an employee's rights under the Working Time Regulations 1998. Details of opportunities for health assessments (and/or of 'health and capacities' assessments) must also be committed to writing. All such records must be maintained for at least two years (Reg 8).

ENFORCEMENT BY HEALTH AND SAFETY EXECUTIVE

18.30

Responsibility for enforcing those provisions of the 1998 Regulations which relate to maximum weekly working hours, the upper limits on night time working, health assessments, patterns of work and the maintenance of adequate records, rests with the Health & Safety Executive. Inspectors will have the right to enter and inspect an employer's premises, to talk to employees and take statements, and to examine records. If there is evidence of non-compliance, a friendly warning may be followed by an improvement or prohibition notice and, ultimately, prosecution. The penalty for non-compliance (in the appropriate circumstances) is a fine of up to £20,000 or, if a conviction is obtained on indictment, a fine of an unlimited amount (Regs 26 & 27).

COMPLAINTS TO AN EMPLOYMENT TRIBUNAL

18.31

Workers denied their statutory rights to minimum daily and/or weekly rest periods, rest breaks during the day, or paid annual holidays may complain to an employment tribunal. Any such complaint must be 'presented' to the Secretary to the Tribunals (in practice, the nearest regional office of the employment tribunals) within three months of the date of the employer's refusal or failure to comply, or within such further period as the tribunal considers reasonable, in the light of the worker's explanation for the delay (Reg 28A).

18.32

If the worker's complaint is upheld, the tribunal will make a declaration to that effect and will order the employer to pay compensation to the worker of such amount as it considers 'just and equitable' in the circumstances. If the complaint arose out of the employer's failure to pay the worker in respect of his (or her) entitlement to four weeks' annual holidays, the tribunal will also order the employer to pay the worker the amount which it finds to be due.

Right not to suffer detriment

18.33

Section 45A of the Employment Rights Act 1996 (as inserted by regulations 2(1) and 31(1) of the 1998 Regulations) cautions employers that a worker has the right *not to be disciplined or subjected to any detriment* at the hands of his (or her) employer:

- for refusing (or proposing to refuse) to comply with a requirement imposed (by the employer) in contravention of the Working Time Regulations 1998; or

- for refusing to forgo a right conferred by those Regulations; or

- for failing to sign a workforce agreement for the purposes of those Regulations; or

- for bringing proceedings against his employer to enforce a right conferred on him by those Regulations; or

- for alleging that the employer had infringed such a right.

For further particulars, please turn to Chapter 6.

Dismissal for asserting a statutory right

18.34

A worker who is dismissed (or selected for redundancy) for asserting his (or her) statutory rights under the Working Time Regulations 1998, or for challenging his employer's refusal or failure to acknowledge those rights, may present a complaint of unfair dismissal to an employment tribunal regardless of his age or length of service at the material time. For further details, please turn to Chapter 5, paras 5.37 to 5.39.

CASE LAW

18.35

In *Sindicato de Médicos de Asistencia Pública (Simap) v Conselleria de Sanidad y Consumo de la Generalidad Valenciana* (C-303/98), the ECJ held that workers (such as doctors) who are required to be 'on call' (that is to say, readily contactable) during certain hours of the day or night, are not to be regarded as 'working' unless they are actually called out and at their place of work. The Court also held that consent to work more than an average 48-hour week must be given individually and in writing, and *not* by trade union representatives under the terms of a collective agreement.

18.36

In *Bowden & Others v Tufnells Parcels Express Limited* (Case No. 1102254/98), the employment tribunal held that the 1998 Regulations did *not* apply to office workers employed by a road transport business. Proposals to correct this and related anomalies affecting 'non-mobile workers' have since been adopted by the European Commission, although amendments to Working Time Directive 93/104/EC have yet to put in an appearance.

18.37

In *Barber v R J B Mining UK Limited* ([1999] IRLR 308) the High Court held that there was an implied term in every contract of employment that, in the absence of a voluntary 'opt-out', a worker cannot lawfully be required to work more than an average 48 hours a week. This contractual right enabled the employees in question to bring their breach of contract case before the High Court. As the employees in question had already worked more than that average number of hours during the rolling 17-week reference period, the High Court declared that they had every right to reduce their weekly hours or, if need be, stop work for a time until the average fell within the 48-hour limit.

18.38

In *Clark v Oxfordshire Health Authority* ([1988] IRLR 125), the contract under which a 'bank nurse' was engaged imposed no duty on her employers to provide her with work. Nor did it impose any duty on her to accept any offer of work that was forthcoming. She was nonetheless a 'worker' and was entitled to the protection afforded by the 1998 Regulations (working hours, rest breaks and rest periods, etc) when she was at work. However, because of the nature of her contract, she was unlikely to build up an entitlement to paid annual holidays unless employed for 13 or more consecutive weeks.

19

National minimum wage

GENERAL INFORMATION

19.1
With the coming into force on 1 April 1999 of the National Minimum Wage Regulations 1998 (SI 1998/584) every UK worker aged 18 and over now has the statutory right to be paid no less than the national minimum wage (NMW) appropriate to his (or her) age.

19.2
From 1 October 2000, the national minimum wage (NMW) for workers aged 22 and over is £3.70 an hour – or £3.20 an hour, during their first six months of employment, if in receipt of 'accredited training' for 26 days or more during those first six months. For workers aged 18 to 21, inclusive, the appropriate NMW is £3.20 an hour. At present, there is no NMW for workers aged 16 or 17. Certain payments made to workers (such as overtime premium payments, shift allowances, cost of living allowances, 'weighting' allowances and the like) do not count towards the NMW, nor do most benefits in kind. See also paras 19.12 to 19.18 below.

Note (1): At the time of going to press, the Government has accepted the Low Pay Commission's recommendation to increase the adult NMW rate from £3.70 to £4.10 with effect from 1 October 2001 (subject to the then prevailing economic conditions). The increase for workers aged 18 to 21 will be announced in May 2001.

Note (2): The term 'accredited training' means training undertaken with a *new* employer during normal working hours (at or away from the workplace) that leads to a vocational qualification approved by the Secretary of State for Education. It does *not* apply to in-house training devised and provided by employers. (See also *Excluded categories* below.)

19.3
A refusal or failure to pay the appropriate NMW is an offence, the penalty for which, on summary conviction, is a fine of up to £5,000 – for each offence. Inland Revenue enforcement officers have the right to enter an employer's premises and to inspect wage records.

19.4

Workers who are dismissed, selected for redundancy, or subjected to any other detriment, for questioning or challenging their employer's refusal or failure to pay the NMW, or for bringing proceedings before a tribunal or court, will likewise be entitled to compensation (see also Chapter 5, paras 5.46 & 5.47). Indeed, a worker who suspects that he or she is being paid less than the NMW may write to his or her employer demanding to see the relevant wage records, and must be supplied with those records within the next 14 days. An employer who fails to comply with such a request will be ordered to pay the worker in question the sum of £288 (that is to say, 80 times the level of the NMW), as well as compensation for the shortfall in pay.

PRACTICAL GUIDANCE

Meaning of 'worker'

19.5

A 'worker' is a person who does work for an employer, either under a contract of employment or under a contract *sui generis* (that is to say, of its own kind). In short, the term encompasses employees, seasonal and casual workers, freelancers, agency 'temps', pieceworkers (or output workers), workers paid entirely on commission, and homeworkers. All such workers must be paid no less than the appropriate NMW rate. See also para 19.11 below. As a 'rule of thumb' a worker's employer is the person (or organisation) who (or which) pays a worker's wages or salary, and deducts payments in respect of PAYE Tax and NI contributions. It is important to stress that workers over normal retiring age or the State Pension Age (60 or 65, as the case may be) must be paid the appropriate NMW rate if they are workers.

19.6

The only category of person who is not a 'worker' in this sense, and who does not qualify for the NMW, is the self-employed person. The genuinely self-employed person is engaged under a contract *for* services to carry out a specific task or activity in return for an agreed fee. The self-employed person prepares his (or her) own annual accounts for submission to the Inland Revenue, pays his own taxes and National Insurance contributions, submits his own invoices (preferably on a pre-printed form), is (where appropriate) registered for VAT, provides his own tools and equipment, and is not under the direction or control of any other person. An employer would be well advised to demand proof of 'self-employed' status from any person who holds himself out to be self-employed.

19.7
Employers who choose to categorise some or all of their workers as 'self-employed', in order to avoid paying the appropriate NMW rate, are liable to prosecution and heavy fines – unless they are in a position to convince Inland Revenue enforcement officers that the workers in question are indeed self-employed.

19.8
Agency 'temps' are usually employed by the employment business that hires them out to client employers. It is the employment business (not the client employer) that is responsible both for paying a 'temp's' wages (within clearly defined time limits) and for ensuring that their workers are paid the appropriate NMW rate.

Excluded categories

19.9
The NMW need not be paid until their 19th birthdays to 18-year-old apprentices who began their apprenticeships at 16 or 17. Nor need it be paid to apprentices age 19 and over during the first 12 months of their apprenticeships or until their 26th birthdays, whichever occurs sooner. An 'apprentice', for these purposes, is a person who is either employed under a contract of apprenticeship or who is taking part in the Government's Modern Apprenticeship programme.

19.10
Also excluded from the NMW during their placements with employers are 'sandwich course' students, students obtaining work experience, teacher trainees, and trainees on government-funded schemes (such as the 'New Deal', 'Work-based learning for adults', and so on).

Note: Also excluded are members of the armed forces, share fishermen, voluntary workers (who receive no pay for their time apart from genuine expenses), and prisoners.

19.11

But, those exclusions do *not* apply to students taking a 'gap year' between school (or college) and university. Nor do they apply to students undertaking postgraduate studies (whether taking up employment independently or as an adjunct to their studies). All such people must be paid no less than the appropriate NMW rate during their employment.

DEDUCTIONS AND PAYMENTS THAT DO OR DO NOT COUNT TOWARDS THE NMW

19.12

As was mentioned in the preamble above, there are some payments included in a worker's gross wages or salary (such as overtime premium payments and shift allowances) that do *not* count towards the NMW; and there are others that do. Likewise, there are certain benefits in kind and deductions from pay (or payments made to an employer) that must be excluded from calculations. There is, for example, no upper limit on the amount of rent that an employer may charge a worker for 'live-in' accommodation (a not uncommon feature of employment in the hotel and leisure industries). However, as is explained in paras 19.16 to 19.18 below, that portion of the rent paid by a worker, which exceeds a specified hourly, daily or weekly amount, does not count towards the NMW. In short, the excess amount must be deducted from the worker's gross wages or salary in order to establish whether the worker in question is being paid the appropriate NMW rate.

19.13

Other deductions (or payments by a worker) that do *not* count include deductions in respect of meals compulsorily purchased by a worker from his or her employer; and deductions in respect of uniforms or protective clothing and equipment. The object of the exercise here is to ensure that employers do not use deductions from pay (or demands for certain payments from workers) as a means of 'clawing back' (or reducing the effect of) the NMW.

Deductions and payments that do not count

19.14

The following components of a worker's gross wages or salary in a particular pay reference period (week, fortnight or month) do *not* count as part of the NMW:

- overtime premium payments;

- shift allowances;

- premium payments for work carried out on a bank or public holiday;

- unsociable hours payments;

- 'danger money';

- 'standby' or 'on call' allowances;

- travel allowances;

- 'cost of living' allowances (eg, 'London weighting' payments);

- payments carried forward from a previous pay reference period.

Benefits in kind provided by an employer (whether taxable or not) do *not* count towards the NMW. These include:

- a company car;

- petrol, oil and lubricants;

- meals (or the notional value of such meals) if, as is unlikely, a worker is required by his (or her) contract to take his meals in a staff or works canteen;

- luncheon vouchers (or the notional value of such vouchers);

- the employer's contributions to an occupational pension plan;

- relocation expenses;

- free health insurance; and

- that part of the rent charged by an employer for live-in accommodation that exceeds a specified hourly, daily or weekly amount (see paras 19.16 to 19.18 below).

Furthermore, tips paid directly to a worker (or distributed amongst fellow workers), which are not paid through the payroll, do not count towards the NMW. The same applies to deductions from pay (or payments made to an employer) in respect of protective clothing and equipment, uniforms, dry cleaning or laundry costs, tools, etc.

Deductions and payments that count

19.15
Deductions or payments that *do* count towards the NMW include:

- incentive payments, bonuses, commission;

- tips, gratuities and service charges collected centrally by the employer and distributed to a worker through the payroll (but not otherwise);

- deductions in respect of PAYE tax and NI contributions;

- a worker's pension contributions;

- a fine imposed in accordance with a worker's contract for misconduct (including authorised deductions in respect of cash shortages or stock deficiencies);

- deductions in respect of overpaid wages or salary (or overpaid expenses);

- deductions (or payments) in respect of live-in accommodation up to a prescribed maximum (explained more fully in paras 19.16 to 19.18 below);

- voluntary deductions in respect of trade union dues, private health insurance, membership of a social club;

- deductions or payments in respect of meals voluntarily purchased by a worker from a staff or works canteen; and

- deductions in respect of goods and services *voluntarily* purchased by a worker from his or her employer.

Live-in accommodation

19.16
Live-in accommodation is a common feature of employment in the hotel and leisure industry, both for the convenience of employers and that of workers. Although technically there is no upper limit on the amount of rent that a worker may be required to pay for live-in accommodation, the 1998 Regulations make it clear that employers will not lessen the effect of the NMW Regulations by charging more than a prescribed amount for such accommodation.

19.17

The most that an employer may offset against the NMW by way of accommodation charges is 50 pence for each hour of a worker's contractual weekly hours or £19.95 a week, whichever is the lower of those two amounts. In short, the *maximum* that may be offset against the NMW is £19.95 a week. If a worker works a 35-hour week, the maximum that may be offset against his or her NMW is £17.50 a week. If a 30-hour week, £15; and so on.

19.18

If a worker occupies live-in accommodation for less than a whole week (eg, five days a week), the maximum daily amount that may be offset against the NMW is whichever is the lower of 50p per hour for each of the worker's contracted (or average) daily hours or £2.85. A day for these purposes is the period from midnight to midnight.

CATEGORIES OF WORKER

19.19

Most workers in industry and commerce can be categorised as salaried or hourly paid. Other categories include seasonal workers, casual workers, workers paid wholly or mainly by commission, agency 'temps', and homeworkers.

Salaried workers

19.20

The ranks of salaried workers traditionally include senior executives, managers, accountants, clerks, secretaries, etc, most of whom are paid at regular monthly intervals by cheque or credit transfer to their bank accounts. A salaried worker's pay usually remains the same month after month (unless absent from work because of illness or injury or on maternity or parental leave, or on approved leave of absence without pay). A salaried worker's pay will also encompass meal and rest breaks, and annual holidays.

19.21

Many salaried workers (especially those in the middle and higher echelons of management) are not paid for overtime working, it being a feature of their contracts that they work such additional hours as may be necessary for the more efficient performance of their duties. Given that salaried jobs are no longer the exclusive preserve of 'white-collar' workers, there will, of course, be salaried workers who are relatively lowly paid (eg, in the region of £7,500 to £10,000 per annum), whose hourly rate of pay in a particular pay reference period may dip below the appropriate NMW rate – the more so if the worker in question regularly works overtime hours (paid or otherwise) or is paying more than £19.95 a week in rent for 'live-in' accommodation provided by his or her employer. As was explained earlier (see paras 19.12 to 19.14 above), there are a number of payments or deductions from pay that do not count towards the NMW.

EXAMPLE
24-year-old Sally Brown works as an Assistant Manager at a small London hotel. She earns a salary of £8,250 per annum, and is contracted to work a 5-day, 40-hour week (including meal and rest breaks). She is paid monthly, receives all her meals free of charge, but occupies 'live-in' accommodation provided by her employer, for which she pays rent of £200 a month. Mary often works more than 40 hours a week when the hotel is busy or there are staff shortages. She is paid time-and-a-half for all hours worked in excess of 173 hours a month.

Mary's gross salary for January 2001 (before the deduction of PAYE tax and NI contributions) was made up as follows:

Monthly pay (£8,250, divided by 12):	£687.50
Overtime pay (23 hours @ £5.97/hour):	£137.31
Gross pay:	£824.81
LESS rent of £200	

Was Mary paid less than the NMW for January 2001? To answer that question, Mary's overtime premium payments (£45.77) must be disregarded, as must all rental payments in excess of £19.95 a week (or £69.16 a month), ie £130.84. These 'specified reductions' effectively reduce Mary's gross pay for January 2001 from £824.81 to £648.20. As Mary worked a total of 196 hours during January her hourly rate of pay for that month was £3.31; that is to say, £0.39 per hour less than the NMW of £3.70 for her age. It follows that Mary's employer must pay her an additional £76.44 for January 2001.

19.22

All things being equal, determining whether or not a salaried worker has been paid the appropriate NMW in respect of a particular pay reference period is a relatively simple matter. For example, the hourly rate of pay for a woman earning £15,000 a year, who is paid monthly and is required to work a 35-hour week (or 152 hours a month), is £8.24 – clearly well above the appropriate NMW rate for her age. If she is entitled to be paid a premium rate of £10.30 an hour (time-and-a-quarter) for all hours worked in excess of 152 a month, she would need to work some 185 and more overtime hours in a particular month before her effective hourly rate of pay for that month reduces to less than £3.70 an hour.

Note: The term 'pay reference period' means the period (not exceeding one month) in respect of which wages or salary are normally paid (monthly, weekly, fortnightly, or whatever). Workers who are paid weekly have a pay reference period of one week. Those who are paid monthly have a pay reference period of one month. Some workers, notably casual workers, will have a pay reference period of one day. Workers who are paid less frequently than once every month (eg, every three months) nonetheless have a pay reference period of one month. In short, the maximum pay reference period for any worker (under the 1999 Regulations) is one month.

Hourly paid workers

19.23
As the term implies, hourly paid workers are paid for the number of hours they work each week or month (whatever the pay reference period). They are traditionally paid overtime for all hours worked in excess of their standard (or contractual) working hours, but are not normally paid for meal and rest breaks. If they work a system of shifts, they may be paid a shift allowance. If they work normally on a bank or public holiday (or on a rest day), they may be paid at a higher hourly rate for such work or they may have a contractual right to an equivalent amount of paid time off work to be taken at an agreed later date. If employed under a contract of employment, their terms and conditions of employment (including working hours, rate of pay, shift allowances, overtime premium payments, and the like) must be explained in the written statement of employment particulars necessarily issued to each of them within two months of the date on which their employment began.

19.24
Hourly paid workers must be paid no less than the appropriate NMW rate for all hours worked in the standard pay reference period. Working hours do not include recognised meal and rest breaks (even if the worker is paid during such breaks, or works throughout a recognised meal or rest-break), absences from work occasioned by

annual holidays, sick leave, maternity leave, parental leave, time off for dependants, and so on. Nor do they include time when a worker is engaged in a strike or other form of industrial action (including a 'go slow' or 'work to rule'). Whether or not a worker is entitled to be paid all or part of his (or her) wages when sick or injured will depend on the terms of his contract (although he will have the qualified right to be paid statutory sick pay at such times). Payments in respect of maternity leave and annual holidays are regulated by statute (notably the Employment Rights Act 1996 and the Working Time Regulations 1998, discussed elsewhere in this book).

19.25
An hourly paid worker who is on standby or 'on-call', at or near his (or her) workplace (or who is at work, as required, but is not actually provided with work, or is unable to work because of a machine or plant breakdown) must be paid no less than the NMW for that time. The same applies when a worker is travelling between jobs, but not when he is travelling from and to his home and place of work.

Pieceworkers and 'output' workers

19.26
There are workers who do not receive a basic wage, but are paid entirely on the basis of the work they do, the sales (or number of telephone calls) they make or the goods they produce. Such people may work from home or in premises provided by their employer. Unless (as is unlikely), they are genuinely self-employed, every such worker must be paid no less than appropriate NMW wage rate for every hour worked (based on what their employer agrees is a fair estimate of the hours they work). The NMW rules for pieceworkers, output workers, and the like, are complicated. Interested employers are advised to acquire a copy of the DTI's Detailed Guide to the National Minimum Wage (Ref URN 99/662), copies of which are available from the address given at the end of this chapter.

RECORDS

19.27
Regulation 38 of the 1998 Regulations imposes a duty on employers to keep records 'sufficient to establish that he is remunerating

[workers] at a rate at least equal to the national minimum wage'. Those records must be kept in a form that enables the information about a worker in respect of any one reference period to be produced in a single document. Furthermore, the employer must keep those records (either in paper form or on a computer or computer disk) for a rolling three-year period and must make those records available either to a worker (on request) or an Inland Revenue enforcement officer (on demand). An employer who fails to keep such records, or who keeps or produces false or inaccurate records, is guilty of an offence and liable on summary conviction to a fine of up to £5,000 – for each and every such offence.

ENFORCEMENT AND PENALTIES FOR NON-COMPLIANCE

19.28

As was mentioned in the preamble, the National Minimum Wage Act 1998 and its accompanying regulations are policed and enforced by Inland Revenue enforcement officers. Section 14 of the 1998 Act cautions employers that enforcement officers have the power to enter an employer's premises (at reasonable times), to inspect and take copies of pay records, to require an explanation of any such records, to ask questions, and to talk to workers. Enforcement officer can also issue enforcement notices requiring an employer to pay the appropriate rate of NMW to identified workers or to make up the shortfall between the NMW and the wages actually paid to those workers (backdated as appropriate). A failure to comply with the terms of an enforcement notice will prompt the issue of a penalty notice requiring the recalcitrant employer to pay £7.20 a day to each affected worker for every day of continued non-compliance.

19.29

There are a number of criminal offences under the 1998 Act, each of which attracts a penalty of up to £5,000 – for each offence. These are:

- a refusal or wilful neglect to pay the appropriate NMW rate;

- a failure to maintain adequate and accurate payroll records and time sheets;

- keeping false or inaccurate records;

- intentionally obstructing an Inland Revenue enforcement officer in the exercise of his or her authority; and

- refusing or neglecting to give information to an Inland Revenue enforcement officer.

Complaints by workers

19.30

Workers who know (or suspect) that they are not being paid the appropriate NMW rate have the right to ask to see their payroll records. Any such request must be made in writing. An employer who fails or refuses to produce those records within 14 days, or who prevaricates or refuses to make those records available, will be ordered by an employment tribunal to pay the worker in question an amount equal to 80 times the appropriate NMW rate. A worker may also apply to a tribunal or county court for the recovery of any amount of wages or salary that fell short of the NMW. Any such application must be lodged with the Secretary to the Tribunals on Form IT1 within three months of the employer's alleged refusal or failure.

19.31

Workers have no need to resign in order to pursue their statutory rights before an employment tribunal. If denied their right to be paid no less than the appropriate NMW rate, they may complain to an employment tribunal and/or invoke the assistance of an Inland Revenue enforcement officer. An employer who dismisses such a worker, or selects him (or her) for redundancy, or subjects him to some other detriment (eg, by demoting or transferring him, withholding a promised pay rise, or by denying opportunities for overtime, etc) – for challenging or questioning the employer's refusal or failure to pay the NMW (before a tribunal or court, or otherwise), or for asserting his statutory rights – will be ordered to pay the worker a substantial amount of compensation. See also Chapter 5, paras 5.46 & 5.47.

FURTHER INFORMATION

19.32

The Department of Trade & Industry (DTI) has published a *A Detailed Guide to the National Minimum Wage* (Ref URN / 662), copies of which may be obtained without charge from:

DTI Publication Orderline
ADMAIL 528
London
SW1W 8YT
Tel: 0870 1502 500
Fax: 0870 1502 333
E-mail: dtipubs@echristian.co.uk

19.33
For further assistance on the national minimum wage, employers may call **NMW Enquiries** on **0845 6000 678** or write to the following address:

NMW Enquiries
Freepost PHQ1
Newcastle upon Tyne
NE98 1ZH

20

European Works Councils

20.1

UK-based multinational companies with 1,000 or more employees 'on the payroll' (of whom 150 or more are employed in each of at least two EEA Member States) must respond positively to a valid request for the establishment of a European Works Council (EWC) or for a European-level 'information and consultation procedure'. This requirement is to be found in the Transnational Information & Consultation of Employees Regulations 1999 (SI 1999/3323), implementing Council Directive 94/45/EC 'on the establishment of a European Works Council or a procedure in Community-scale undertakings and Community-scale groups of undertakings for the purposes of informing and consulting employees'. For convenience, the Regulations are referred to throughout this section as 'the 2000 Regulations' or by their acronym 'TICER'.

Note: Directive 94/45/EC was adopted by all other EU Member States on 22 September 1994 under Article 2(2) of the so-called Social Chapter, and was later extended to cover Norway, Liechtenstein and Iceland (which latter, together with the EU Member States, comprise the European Economic Area, or EEA). The deadline for national implementation within the EEA was 22 September 1996. Originally rejected by the then UK government when it opted out of the Social Chapter, the original directive was formally extended to the UK by EU Directive 97/74/EC of 15 December 1997. Strictly speaking, the deadline for implementation within the UK was 15 December 1999, although TICER did not officially come into force until a month later, on 15 January 2000.

20.2

Multinational companies in the UK, which had voluntarily established their own EWCs or European-level information and consultation procedures – either before 22 September 1996 (under Article 13 of Directive 94/45/EC) or before 15 December 1999 (under Article 3 of Directive 97/74/EC) are not bound by TICER so long as the EWCs and procedures in question cover the entire workforce in each case. Nor do the Regulations apply to the UK-based subsidiaries of a multinational company established elsewhere in the

EEA that had already been voluntarily included in EWC arrangements established by the company's central management.

20.3

Council Directive 94/45/EC (or, as appropriate, extending Directive 97/74/EC) applies equally to any foreign-owned multinational company whose head office or central management is outside the EEA (eg, in Japan or the USA) – so long as the company in question employs 1,000 or more people within the EEA, and has at least 150 personnel in each of at least two EEA Member States. In short, the company's 'designated EEA representative' (or, if the company has not designated any such representative, the central management of its largest EEA-based undertaking) must respond to a valid employee or employee-sponsored request for the establishment of an EWC (or information and consultation procedure) for its EEA workforce.

Information about employee numbers

20.4

Any UK-based employees of a multinational company (or their appointed or elected representatives), who are minded to submit a request to their employer for the establishment of an EWC (or European-level information and consultation procedure), have the legal right under TICER to seek and obtain data from local or central management about the number of persons employed by the company both within the UK and in every other EEA member state in which the company has operations.

20.5

Should the company refuse or fail to provide those data within one month of receiving such a request (or provide information suspected of being false or incomplete), the matter may be referred to the Central Arbitration Committee (CAC) which, if it upholds the employees' complaint, will order the company either to provide that information by a specified date or face an action for contempt of court. The CAC may decide, on the other hand, from the evidence before it, that the company in question is, or is part of, a multinational company employing 1000 or more employees within the EEA (with 150 or more employees in each of at least two EEA Member States), and will make a declaration to that effect. In the latter instance, the employees may rely on that declaration when submitting a request for the establishment of an EWC or European-level information and consultation procedure.

Calculating the number of people employed

20.6
Each EEA Member State has its own rules for calculating the number of people employed by a multinational company within its territory. For UK-based employees, the total number of persons employed by the company in the UK are to be ascertained by adding together the numbers employed in each of the 24 months immediately preceding the date on which the request to establish an EWC (or alternative procedure) was received (whether the employees in question were employed throughout the month or not), and by dividing the resultant figure by 24. Part-time employees working, or contracted to work, fewer than 75 hours a month (excluding overtime hours), may be counted as half-units, if the company so chooses.

Meaning of valid request

20.7
A request for the establishment of an EWC (or some other form of European-level information and consultation procedure) is valid for the purposes of TICER if it comprises:

(a)   a single request *in writing* by 100 or more employees (or by their elected or appointed representatives) in at least two undertakings or establishments in at least two EEA Member States; or

(b)   one or more separate requests *in writing*, on the same or different days, by employees or their representatives, which, when taken together, mean that at least 100 or more employees in at least two undertakings or establishments in at least two different Member States have made requests.

Each request must be sent to the undertaking's central or local management and must specify the date on which it was sent.

20.8
A UK-based multinational company contesting the validity of a request for the establishment of an EWC (or a European-level

information and consultation procedure) may apply to the Central Arbitration Committee (CAC) for a declaration on the matter. It cannot reject the request out of hand and must put its case to the CAC within three months of the date on which the request was made (or within three months of the last request, if that is the one that brings the numbers up to 100). If the CAC upholds the validity of the employees' request (or requests), the company's central management must begin negotiations for the establishment of an EWC (or alternative information and consultation procedure).

Negotiations for the establishment of an EWC

20.9
Once it has received a valid request for the establishment of an EWC (or alternative information and consultation procedure), the company in question has six months within which to begin negotiations with employees or their representatives. This entails setting up a 'special negotiating body' (SNB) comprising employee elected or appointed representatives drawn from each of the EEA Member States in which the company has operations. If the company fails or refuses to begin negotiations within that six-month period, it will have no choice but to accept the statutory or fallback EWC set out in the Schedule to TICER (see *The Statutory EWC* below).

Note: The central managements of multinational companies, which fall within the scope of TICER, are under no statutory obligation to initiate negotiations for the establishment of an EWC or a European-level information and consultation procedure.

Composition of the SNB

20.10
The SNB must comprise at least one, but no more than four, representatives from each of the relevant EEA Member States. If between 25 and 50 per cent of the company's total workforce works in a particular Member State, one additional member must be elected or appointed to the SNB, if 50 per cent or more, but less than 75 per cent, two additional members; and, if 75 per cent or more, three additional members.

20.11

The UK members of the SNB must be elected by a secret ballot of the entire UK workforce, unless there is already a standing consultative committee in existence whose members were themselves elected by a ballot of the entire UK workforce. In the latter case, it will be for the committee itself to nominate one or more of its members to represent the interests of employees on the SNB. What *is* important is that the persons elected or appointed to the SNB represent the interests of all employees, not just a particular group or sector of employees.

20.12

If there is to be a ballot of the entire workforce, every UK employee must be afforded the right and opportunity to vote, and must be permitted, without hindrance, to put his or her name forward as a candidate for election as an SNB member. The company's UK central management must discuss its arrangements for the conduct of the ballot with existing employee representatives and must appoint one or more 'independent ballot supervisors' to ensure that workplace ballots are conducted in secret and that the votes cast are counted fairly and accurately.

20.13

Similar procedures apply for the election or appointment of SNB members from each of the other EEA Member States in which the company has operations. Those procedures will be as laid down in the national legislation of the Member States in question.

Negotiations with the SNB

20.14

Once an SNB has been established, it is up to the company's central management to begin negotiations with the SNB for the establishment of an EWC or information and consultation procedure, and to inform local managements accordingly. The 2000 Regulations stress that the central management of a multinational company and the SNB are 'duty-bound to negotiate in a spirit of cooperation with a view to reaching a written agreement on the detailed arrangements for the information and consultation of employees' throughout the organisation. During negotiations, the SNB will take decisions by a majority of the votes cast by its members (with each member being entitled to one vote).

20.15
The role of the SNB is to determine, with central management, by written agreement, the scope, composition, functions and term of office of an EWC. The parties may agree to adopt the statutory or fall-back EWC (outlined in the Schedule to TICER) or one tailored to their own needs (see *The Statutory EWC* below) They may decide, on the other hand, in writing, to establish an information and consultation procedure instead of an EWC.

20.16
If the parties decide to proceed with the establishment of an EWC, the agreement establishing it must:

(a)   identify each of the company's EEA operations covered by the agreement;

(b)   specify the number of members to be elected or appointed to the EWC (by whatever means), the allocation of seats, and the terms of office of the members;

(c)   explain the EWC's functions, and the procedures for information and consultation;

(d)   specify the location, frequency and duration of EWC meetings; and what funding and other resources are to be allocated to the EWC to enable it to carry out its functions; and

(e)   determine the duration of the agreement and the procedure for its renegotiation.

The parties to the agreement must decide on the method to be employed for the election or appointment of EWC members from each of the EEA Member States in which the company has operations. Those members may be elected by a workforce ballot in each of the Member States in question or be appointed by a standing consultative committee from amongst its own members.

20.17
If the parties decide to establish an information and consultation procedure instead of an EWC, the agreement establishing the procedure must specify a method by which the information and consultation representatives are to enjoy the right to meet and discuss the information conveyed to them; which latter must relate

in particular to questions that significantly affect the interests of employees throughout the EEA. The information and consultation representatives may be either elected or appointed in accordance with the terms of the agreement.

20.18

Central management must pay for (or reimburse) all legitimate expenses incurred by the members of the SNB (travelling, accommodation, meals, etc) during negotiations for the establishment of an EWC or an information and consultation procedure.

20.19

Once agreement has been reached on the establishment of an EWC (or an information and consultation procedure), it is up to the central management of the company in question to implement that agreement. If it fails to do so, it will be ordered by the EAT to take such steps as are necessary to establish the EWC (or procedure) or face proceedings for contempt of court. The central management will also be ordered to pay the Secretary of State for Trade & Industry a penalty of up to £75,000.

Subsidiary requirements

20.20

A company's central management that refuses (within six months of receiving a valid request) to commence negotiations for the establishment of an EWC (or for an information and consultation procedure) will be ordered by the EAT tribunal to adopt the fall-back or statutory EWC outlined in the Schedule to the 2000 Regulations (see *The Statutory EWC* below) or face an action for contempt of court. When making that order, the EAT will also order the central management to pay a penalty of up to £75,000.

20.21

If the negotiating parties fail to agree on the establishment of an EWC (or alternative information and consultation procedure) within three years of the date on which a valid request for the establishment of such an EWC or procedure was made, the parties will have no choice but to adopt the fall-back or statutory EWC outlined in the Schedule to TICER.

FUNCTIONS OF AN EWC

20.22
Neither TICER nor the originating EC Directive offer any advice as to the information that must be, or need not be, relayed to the members of an EWC (or to information and consultation representatives) by the central management of a multinational company. That is a matter for negotiation and agreement. However, the fall-back or statutory EWC described in the Schedule to Directive 94/45/EC provides several clues. The statutory EWC (which may be imposed on the central management of any multinational company that refuses or fails to negotiate for the establishment of an EWC or a European-level information and consultation procedure) states that an EWC has 'the right to meet with the central management once a year, to be informed and consulted, on the basis of a report drawn up by the central management, on the progress of the business... '.

20.23
Furthermore, 'the meeting shall relate in particular to the structure, economic and financial situation, the probable development of the business and of production and sales, the situation and probable trend of employment, investments, and substantial changes concerning organisation, introduction of new working methods or production processes, transfers of production, mergers, cut-backs or closures of undertakings, establishments or important parts thereof, and collective redundancies'. See also *Compliance and enforcement* below.

Confidential information

20.24
Both the originating Directive and TICER acknowledge that the central management of a multinational company has the right to withhold from the members of an EWC (or from information and consultation representatives) any information or document that would, if disclosed, do serious harm or be prejudicial to the company's legitimate business interests. Central management has the right also to insist that certain documents or information entrusted to an EWC (or to information and consultation representatives) be held by them in confidence – although the

members or representatives in question may apply to the CAC for a declaration as to whether it was reasonable for the central management to impose such a requirement.

20.25

If the CAC considers that the release or disclosure of allegedly confidential information is unlikely to prejudice or cause serious harm to the company's business interests, it will make a declaration to that effect. In short, the CAC will either order the central management to disclose documents or information previously withheld from an EWC (or from information and consultation representatives) or will release members of the EWC (or the representatives in question) from any obligation imposed on them by central management to hold certain information or documents in confidence – subject to any conditions which the CAC considers appropriate in the circumstances.

Protection for members of an EWC, etc

20.26

Under the original Directive and TICER, any employee of a qualifying multinational company who is:

(a) a member of an SNB or EWC;

(b) an information and consultation representative; or

(c) a candidate for election as a member of an SNB or EWC, or as an information and consultation representative;

has the right to be permitted by his (or her) employer to take a reasonable amount of paid time off during normal working hours in order to perform his functions as such a member, representative or candidate.

20.27

An employer who refuses to allow time off in the circumstances described above, or who fails to pay the employee his (or her) normal wages or salary during such time off, will be ordered by an employment tribunal to pay the employee an amount equal to the remuneration to which he would have been entitled but for the employer's refusal or failure.

Victimisation or dismissal

20.28
An employee who is a member of an EWC or SNB (or an information and consultation representative) or a candidate for election as such a member or representative, has the right also not to be disciplined, dismissed, selected for redundancy or subjected to any other detriment (eg, denial of a promotion, transfer, opportunities for training, a promised pay rise, or whatever) for exercising his (or her) statutory rights under TICER or for performing his functions as such a member, representative or candidate.

20.29
That same protection extends to employees who have challenged their employer's refusal or failure to acknowledge their statutory rights under TICER or who have brought proceedings before the CAC, the Employment Appeal Tribunal (EAT) or an employment tribunal to enforce or secure any entitlement conferred on them by TICER. Employees have the right also not to be victimised, disciplined, dismissed or selected for redundancy for seeking information about the number of persons employed by their employer, or for influencing or seeking to influence the voting intentions of other employees (in a ballot for the election of SNB or EWC members or for information and consultation representatives), or for voting in such a ballot, or for expressing doubts about the conduct or outcome of the ballot.

Complaint to an employment tribunal

20.30
An employee who is dismissed or selected for redundancy for exercising his (or her) statutory rights under TICER (whether before an employment tribunal or otherwise) may complain to an employment tribunal regardless of his age or length of service at the material time. The amount of compensation that may be awarded in such cases is substantial. An employee who is victimised, disciplined or subject to any other form of detriment for presuming to assert those same statutory rights has no need to resign in order to seek redress before an employment tribunal, and will be awarded such compensation as the tribunal considers 'just and equitable' in the circumstances.

Disclosure of confidential information

20.31
Any member of an SNB or EWC (or an information and consultation representative) who is dismissed, selected for redundancy or otherwise disciplined for unlawfully disclosing information or the contents of any document entrusted to him (or her) in confidence thereby forfeits the protection otherwise available to such employees under TICER – unless the disclosure amounts to a 'protected disclosure' as defined by section 43A of the Employment Rights Act 1996 (as to which, please turn to Chapter 23).

COMPLIANCE AND ENFORCEMENT

20.32
Complaints about the failure of a company's central management to respond positively to a valid request for, or to implement an agreement for, the establishment of an EWC (or an information and consultation procedure), may be presented to the Employment Appeal Tribunal by an employee, employee representative or member (or former member) of an SNB. If such a complaint is upheld, the EAT will order the central management of the company in question to take such steps as are necessary to establish the EWC or procedure in accordance with the terms of the agreement concluded with the SNB or, if there is no such agreement, to establish an EWC in accordance with the Schedule to TICER. When making such an order, the EAT will also issue a written penalty notice to the central management of the multinational company in question requiring it to pay to the Secretary of State for Trade & Industry a penalty of up to £75,000 in respect of that failure.

In determining the amount of the penalty payable by a defaulting company's central management, the EAT will take into account the gravity of the failure, the period of time over which the failure occurred; the reason for that failure; the number of employees affected by the failure; and the number of persons employed by the company throughout the EEA.

THE STATUTORY EWC

20.33

The statutory (or fall-back) EWC, referred to in the text above will be imposed by the EAT on the central management of a company that has disregarded a valid request for the establishment of an EWC (or information or consultation procedure) and has refused to commence negotiations within six months of the date on which that request was made. The statutory EWC is also likely to be imposed if the negotiating parties are deadlocked and fail to reach agreement within three years of that date. It is as well to add that the negotiating parties are free to adopt the statutory EWC, if that is what they have agreed to do.

Composition of the statutory EWC

20.34

The statutory EWC must comprise a minimum of three and a maximum of 30 members, with at least one member from each of the EEA Member States in which the company has operations. If between 25 and 50 per cent of the company's total EEA workforce works in a particular Member State, one additional member must be elected or appointed to represent the interests of employees in that Member State – rising to two additional members from a Member State in which 50 per cent or more but less than 75 per cent of the workforce is employed; and three additional members from a Member State in which the numbers employed account for 75 per cent or more of the company's total EEA workforce.

Appointment or election of UK members of the statutory EWC

20.35

The UK members of the statutory EWC may be elected or appointed by the members of an existing negotiating committee (representing the interests of the entire UK workforce for the purposes of collective bargaining) or, if there is no such committee, by a secret ballot of the entire UK workforce (similar to the balloting procedures described earlier in this section). Every employee must be afforded an opportunity to vote in the ballot and to put his or her name forward as a candidate for election as a member of the EWC.

Information and consultation meetings

20.36
The statutory EWC has the right to meet with central management once a year in an information and consultation meeting, on the basis of a report drawn up by the central management on the progress of the business and its prospects. Additional meetings should take place if there are exceptional circumstances directly affecting the employees' interests (eg, collective redundancies, the closure of certain establishments, etc).

20.37
Furthermore, EWC meetings must relate in particular to issues such as the company's structure, economic and financial situation; its probable future development (including production and sales plans); employment trends; likely future investments; proposed organisational changes; the planned introduction of new working methods or production processes; transfers of production; mergers, cutbacks or closures of undertakings or establishments; collective redundancies; and so on.

Procedures

20.38
The statutory EWC may adopt its own rules of procedure. It has the right also to conduct its own meeting before joining central management at the formal information and consultation meeting; and may be assisted in its deliberations by one or more experts of its own choosing. Once discussions with management have ended, the EWC must take steps to inform the workforce (or their representatives) of the content and outcome of the information and consultation procedure.

20.39
Central management is duty-bound to pay the EWC's travel and accommodation costs, as well as any cost involved in organising meetings and arranging for interpretation facilities (although it need not pay the pay the expenses of more than one expert appointed by the EWC to assist it in carrying out its tasks). Central management must see to it that EWC members have whatever financial and material support they may need to enable them to carry out their duties in an appropriate manner.

Data protection

21.1

With the coming into force on 1 March 2000 of the Data Protection Act 1998 (which repeals and replaces the eponymous 1984 Act), the contents of traditional paper-based personnel files (with their ragbag collections of application forms, written 'contracts', CVs, references, holiday chits and requests for time off, sick notes, accident and injury reports, health assessments, training memos, transfer and promotion documents, disciplinary warnings, evaluations, performance-related assessments, and so on – whether in chronological order or otherwise) now fall within the definition of *personal data* recorded as part of a 'relevant filing system'. The same applies to card-index or 'rollerdex' systems, wage records, and other personal data stored manually.

21.2

Under the 1998 Act, a 'relevant filing system' is any non-automated or manual system that is structured either by reference to individuals or by reference to criteria relating to individuals, and which is assembled in such a way that specific information relating to a particular individual is readily accessible. Arguably, the contents of the typical personnel file, as described in the previous paragraph, are neither 'structured' nor 'readily accessible'. Indeed, some commentators have expressed the view that, because they are unstructured, such files fall outside the scope of the 1998 Act.

21.3

Others have argued, equally cogently, that they do not. Wiser counsel urges employers to err on the side of caution by applying the new Act's 'data protection principles' (see below) to all personal data that relates to individual employees. In short, the right of employees to be informed about (and to scrutinise) personal data kept on them by their employers is no longer restricted to information processed by computer (as was the case under the now repealed 1984 Act).

21.4

In future, employees will have the right also to examine the contents of paper-based files relating to them, to take copies of any documents on those files (although there are exceptions), and to demand that inaccurate, irrelevant or sensitive information be corrected, deleted or removed. If any inaccurate or incorrect information has been relayed to third parties, the employer must also see to it that those third parties are promptly apprised of the true situation. The 1998 Act not only extends the right of employees to access all forms of personal data, but also places a greater emphasis than previously on an individual's right to privacy (as to which, see *Sensitive personal data* below).

Note: 'Processing', in relation to information or data, whether done manually or by computer, means obtaining, recording, or holding the information or data; or carrying out any operation or set of operations on that information or data, including organising, adapting, altering, retrieving, disclosing, erasing or destroying it.

21.5

It is as well to point out that processing personal data on a computer in a coded format may be appropriate from the point of view of security, but it does not relieve an employer of his statutory duty to disclose that data when an employee asks to see it. Coded data must, of course, be translated into plain English (and a hard copy produced) before it is made available to the employee.

Meaning of 'personal data'

21.6

'Personal data' means data relating to an individual (in this context, an employee or worker, job applicant or former employee) who can be identified from that data (or from other data or information held by or likely to come into the possession of the *data controller* (the individual's employer, would-be employer or former employer)) and includes any expression of opinion about that individual. Furthermore, and this was not the case under the 1984 Act, the term personal data also includes any indication of the intentions of the data controller (or any other person) in respect of the individual in question. But see *Information that need not be disclosed* below.

COMPUTERISED RECORDS

21.7

Under the 1984 Act, UK employers (and other data users) who kept computerised personnel records (or who used the services of computer bureaux to store such records on their behalf) had to be registered 'data users' – unless the records in question were kept solely for the purposes of calculating and paying wages, salaries and pension monies. Even though registration was not required in the latter situation, the data stored on computer could not (and still cannot) legally be used for any other purpose. Nor may it be disclosed to any person except for the purpose of obtaining actuarial advice on pension issues or for use in medical research into the health and accident records of persons employed in particular occupations. Those same rules continue to apply during the 'first transitional period' (see later in this section) to all computer-based personal data where the processing of such data began or was already under way before 24 October 1998.

Note: 24 October 1998 is the date by which Council Directive 95/46/EC of 24 October 1995 should have been implemented in the UK (as in all other EU Member States). Although the 1998 Act did not come into force until 1 March 2000, 24 October 1998 is the key date for the determing the completion of the first and second transitional periods (see **Transitional provisions** below).

21.8

Auditors retain the right to inspect computerised personnel records, but only for the purposes of preparing accounts or for giving information about the data user's financial affairs. Apart from these exceptions, none of the information stored on computer (or on disk) may be disclosed to any other party or organisation (other than in an emergency, eg, for preventing injury or for forestalling any risk to the health or safety of the individual/s concerned) without the express permission of the person to whom that information relates (*ibid* sections 32 and 34).

1984 Act 'data protection principles'

21.9

Under the 1984 Act (whose provisions prevail during the first transitional period for computer-based records in existence before 24

October 1998), employers (formerly *data users*, now *data controllers*), who maintain computerised personnel records for any purpose, other than the payment of wages, salaries and pensions, must also be registered data users (but see *Note* below) and must see to it that the information so stored complies with certain data protection principles. In short, under the 1984 Act, all *personal data* relating to employees (or former employees) that is stored on computer:

(a) must be secure – and programmed so as to be incapable of being accessed, altered, lost, destroyed or disclosed to any unauthorised person;

(b) must have been obtained fairly and lawfully (and not by doubtful means, eg, from unauthorised or unreliable sources);

(c) must be used or processed only for the purposes specified in the data registration certificate;

(d) must not be used or disclosed other than to a person of a description covered by the registration certificate;

(e) must be adequate and relevant and contain no more information than is strictly necessary in relation to the purpose (or purposes) for which the data is held;

(f) must be accurate and updated regularly; and

(g) must not be kept for longer than is necessary for the purpose/s for which it is kept – unless held for statistical, historical or research purposes, in which case it can be held indefinitely.

Note: The system of registration under the 1984 Act is to be replaced by a new notification system (discussed later in this Chapter).

21.10
An employee has the right (at reasonable intervals and without undue delay) to be informed about any computer-based or computer-generated personal data relating to him (or her). He has the right also to examine that data and to have inaccurate or unnecessary information corrected, updated or erased. What constitutes *reasonable* access will depend on the particular circumstances. But three or four times a year would not be unreasonable.

Note: Unfortunately, there is little if any case law on the subject. The fact that an employer is entitled to charge a fee of up to £10 each time an employee asks for access to personal data would undoubtedly be a deterrent to some employees.

21.11

Finally, an employee should not expect to be given access to personal data at a moment's notice. He (or she) may have to wait up to 40 days (the maximum under the Act), before that information is supplied. However, refusing to supply such data (or needlessly delaying issuing that data) is an offence under the Act for which the penalty is a fine of up to £5,000.

THE NEW REGIME

21.12

With the repeal of the Data Protection Act 1984, and its replacement by the eponymous 1998 Act, employees now have the right to enquire about and to be supplied with copies of *all* personal data relating to them, whether that data is kept on computer or in a manual (or paper-based) filing system. The Act will be enforced, as always, by the Data Protection Registrar (since renamed the 'Data Protection Commissioner').

21.13

Under the 1998 Act, the procedure for gaining access to personal data is essentially unchanged. An employee may write asking his (or her) employer about the type of information held on his personnel file (or elsewhere), the source of that information, the purpose(s) for which it is being held or processed, and the names or job titles of the people who routinely have access to that information. An employer may legitimately charge a fee (of up to £10) for providing the requested information but must not keep the employee waiting for longer than 40 days.

Note: If revealing the source of contentious information on an employee's file means disclosing the identity of the person who provided that information in the first place, the employer must first obtain the permission of that person before doing so. If that permission is withheld, the employer must edit the information in such a way as to omit that person's name or other identifying particulars.

21.14

Subect to the transitional provisions summarised below, an employee also has the right to be supplied with a copy (or a hard copy in the case of computerised data) of any personal data on his (or her) personnel or related file, and may insist on the removal or correction of any information that he considers to be false or inaccurate. As was the case under the 1984 Act, an employer has the right to charge a fee (currently up to £10) for supplying a particular employee with copies of any personal data relating to him (*ibid* section 7).

Evaluating an employee's capabilities

21.15
Information held on computer or (now) on an employee's personnel file, which expresses an opinion about that employee's capabilities, character, attitudes, conduct, performance, etc must be disclosed to that employee on request. This is also the case under the new regime.

21.16
However, an employee now has the additional right to challenge his (or her) employer's *sole* reliance on the computerised processing of his personal data to evaluate his work performance, capabilities, reliability, conduct, etc – the more so if decisions stemming from that automated evaluation are likely to have a significant impact on the employee's prospects for advancement or career development within the employing organisation. In short, the employee will have the right to demand an intelligible explanation of the logic involved in such decision taking and may write to his employer requiring him to ensure that no such decision is to be taken based solely on a computerised evaluation of his personal data.

Information that need not be disclosed

21.17
The definition of *personal data* in the 1998 Act differs slightly from that given in the 1984 Act, to the extent that it now includes any indication of an employer's intentions with respect to an individual employee, which suggests that an employee will be entitled to know in advance whether he (or she) is to receive a pay rise or is about to be transferred, promoted, disciplined or dismissed. However, this does not appear to be the case. Schedule 7 to the Act (*Miscellaneous Exemptions*) makes it clear that employees have no statutory right to demand to see (or to be provided with copies of documents whose contents comprise information processed for the purpose of

management forecasting or planning – the more so if the premature disclosure of such information is likely to prejudice the conduct of the employer's business (*ibid* Schedule 7, para 6).

21.18
Nor need an employer reveal the contents of a reference relating to an existing or former employee that he has written in confidence to a prospective new employer. Nor need he reveal the contents of a reference sent to some other body or institution that is considering an employee for further education or training, or that relates to the appointment (or prospective appointment) of an employee to any public office; or that is given in respect of any service the employee hopes or intends to provide to another person or organisation (*ibid* Schedule 7, paragraph 1).

21.19
Although not obliged to supply a copy of a confidential reference that he has written in respect of an existing or former employee, an employer must (when asked to do so) supply copies of confidential references received from former employers of that employee – without revealing the names or identities of third parties referred to in those references.

Sensitive personal data

21.20
The 1998 Act introduces new rules relating to the processing of 'sensitive personal data' – that is to say, data that consists of information relating to a person's racial or ethnic origins, or to his (or her) religious beliefs, political opinions, trade union membership, physical or mental health, sexual life, or criminal convictions.

21.21
In future, an employer may not process sensitive personal data (or reveal such data to a third party) without the employee's express consent, preferably in writing, unless the data in question is needed for legal reasons or in compliance with an employer's statutory duties. In some circumstances, an employee will need to be persuaded that certain sensitive data (eg, concerning an employee's racial or ethnic origins) is processed so as to enable the employer to monitor the effectiveness of his equal opportunities policy.

21.22

Job application forms that require a would-be employee to reveal sensitive data should explain why that information is needed. For example, in certain trades and industries involving exposure to specified hazardous substances, health and safety legislation effectively requires women of 'reproductive capacity' to disclose whether they are pregnant or are breastfeeding or have recently given birth. Such information will need to be kept on file for obvious reasons (at least for so long as it remains relevant). Job applicants who have a liability to epileptic seizures, or who are insulin treated diabetics, or who have a alcohol or continuing drug dependency, or who have suffered from a psychotic illness within the previous three years, may not be employed to drive large vehicles; and so on. The Rehabilitation of Offenders Act 1974 also requires job applicants (and, in some cases, existing employees) who are applying for appointment or transfer to particular occupations to disclose details of any and all criminal convictions (including 'spent' convictions).

The eight 'data protection principles' (1998)

21.23

The 1998 Act contains eight data protection principles that differ slightly in subject matter and content from the seven principles laid down in the 1984 Act. Once the 1998 Act is fully in force, personal data (whether 'processed' by automated or non-automated means):

1. must be processed fairly and lawfully;

2. must be obtained for one or more specified lawful purposes;

3. must be adequate, relevant and not excessive in relation to the purposes for which it is processed;

4. must be accurate and, where necessary, kept up to date;

5. must not be kept longer than is necessary;

6. must be processed in accordance with the rights of employees (or former employees);

7. must be safeguarded by appropriate technical or organisational measures against unauthorised or unlawful processing, and against accidental loss, damage or destruction; and

8. must not be transferred to a country or territory outside the European Economic Area unless that country or territory ensures an adequate level of protection for the rights and freedoms of data subjects.

21.24
In brief, an employer should only process personal data if the information kept on file is necessary or justifiable:

- for the purposes of entering into a contract of employment (employee's name, address, age, sex, address, marital status, number of dependants, schooling, academic qualifications, employment history, etc); or

- in the context of an employee's (or employer's) statutory or contractual rights, duties or obligations (eg, doctor's sick notes, attendance records , performance appraisals, disciplinary records and warnings, health assessments, information about accidents, injuries or diseases); or

- for PAYE tax, National Insurance, or occupational pension scheme purposes).

Certain information should only be kept on file for so long as is strictly necessary. Files should be 'laundered' at regular intervals to remove extraneous, invalid, irrelevant or out of date information (particularly important in the case of former employees). If an employee asks for inaccurate, false or irrelevant material to be removed from his (or her) personal file, the employer should comply, unless of course he disagrees with the employee's assessment of that information (in which event, the matter may be referred to the High Court or a county court for determination).

21.25
Finally, and most importantly, an employer must see to it that appropriate security measures are in place to prevent personal data held on computer or in paper form falling into the wrong hands. As was indicated earlier, sensitive personal data should not be kept on file without the express permission of the individual(s) unless there is an overriding legal requirement for the retention of such data.

TRANSITIONAL PROVISIONS

21.26

In the following paragraphs, the term 'first transitional period' means the period that began on 1 March 2000 and ends on 23 October 2001. The 'second transitional period' is the period that begins on 24 October 2001 and ends on 23 October 2007.

Computerised or automated data

21.27

Computerised or automated systems containing personal data processed *before* 23 October 1998 need not comply with the new data protection principles during the first transitional period. However, during that period, the employer (the *data controller*) must nonetheless continue to process and provide access to that personal data under the old rules, that is to say, in all respects as if the 1984 Act had not been repealed. After that first transitional period, the provisions of the 1998 Act must be complied with in full.

21.28

Computerised systems set up to process (and processing) personal data on or after 24 October 1998, must comply fully with the 1998 Act from 1 March 2000 (when the Act came into force).

Manual records in existence before 24 October 1998

21.29

During the first transitional period (which ends on 23 October 2001), a relevant filing system (that is to say, manual or paper-based files set up before 24 October 1988 and structured either by reference to individuals or by reference to criteria relating to individuals, in such a way that specific information relating to a particular individual is readily accessible) are exempt from the eight data protection principles and Parts II and III of the 1998 Act ('Rights of Data Subjects & Others' and 'Notification by Data Controllers'). Nor need they comply fully with the substantive provisions of the Act until the end of the second transitional period – except that during that second transitional period, employers must see to it that personal data held in those manual files is processed in accordance with the right of their employees (the *data subjects*) and that each employee is:

(a) given a description of the personal data held in his (or her) personnel file (and in any related paper-based systems or files), informed of the purposes for which that data is held, and of the names or job titles of the persons (externally or internally) to whom that data is (or may be) disclosed;

(b) advised of his qualified right at any time to submit a request in writing asking his employer to cease processing personal data which (for specified reasons) is likely to cause him or another person substantial and unwarranted damage or distress.

During that second transitional period also, the employer must comply with the seventh and eighth principles.

21.30
In short, employers processing personal data held in manual files (set up before 24 October 1998) have some seven years in all in which to 'put their houses in order' – by auditing and sanitising those files and putting the necessary compliance procedures in place.

21.31
What is not yet clear (and this has been the subject of some speculation) is whether personal data added to those files on or after 24 October 1998 'enjoy' the benefit of the same seven-year transitional period or whether such data must comply with the 1998 Act from 1 March 2000. In her *Introduction to the Data Protection Act 1998*, the Data Protection Registrar (now Commissioner) states that personal data on existing employees added to files in existence before 24 October 1998 is 'unlikely' to alter the character of those files unless that additional material 'produces a different effect on the overall processing operation'. Further guidance may be obtained by telephoning the Data Protection Commissioner's Information Line on 01625 545745.

Manual records set up on or after 24 October 1998

21.32
During the first transitional period, manual and other paper-based files set up on or after 24 October 1998, must comply immediately with all provisions of the 1998 Act – *unless* the data held on those

files is no different to the data kept on manual files set up before 24 October 1998 and there is nothing different about the way in which that data is processed. The same applies if the processing does not produce a new effect or result, and if the categories of employees to whom that data relates are the same.

Register of data controllers

21.33

The system of registration with the Data Protection Registrar (now Commissioner) under the now-repealed Data Protection Act 1984 has been (or is about to be) replaced by a so-called 'system of notification' under the 1998 Act. This will result in a register of *data controllers* (effectively, in the context of employment, employers or employing organisations) replacing the former Register. Employers registered as data users prior to the commencement of the notification regime are exempt from the prohibition against processing without notification until such time as their registrations expire or until 24 October 2001, whichever occurs sooner. New notification regulations are expected shortly. A failure to register (or 'notify') is an offence for which the penalty on summary conviction is a fine of up to £5,000 or, if a conviction is obtained on indictment, a fine of an unlimited amount. The information (or the 'registerable particulars') to be provided by a data controller (the employer) when complying with the prescribed registration or notification procedures is:

(a) his (or her) name and address;

(b) the name and address of the representative, if the data controller has nominated a representative;

(c) a description of the personal data being (or to be) processed and of the categories of data subject (eg, job applicant, employee or former employee) to which it relates;

(d) a description of the purpose (or purposes) for which personal data is to be processed;

(e) the name or description of any countries or territories outside the European Economic Area to which the data controller transfers, intends to transfer or may wish to transfer, the data; and

(f) where the personal data is of a type which is exempt from the prohibition against processing without notification (ie, personal data processed in a non-automated or manual filing system), and where notification does not extend to such data, a statement of that fact.

The notification made by a data controller must provide, in addition to particulars (a) to (f) above, a general description of the security measures taken to protect the personal data (although that information will not appear on the register).

Comment

21.34

It is important to stress that the above is little more than a summary of the principal provisions of the 1998 Act and should not, repeat not, be relied upon by any employer or would-be employer as his primary source of information. Many of the Act's provisions are and will be supported by supplementary regulations. The Data Protection Registrar (now Commissioner) has already published an *Introduction to the Data Protection Act 1998,* and, more recently, a draft Code of Practice titled *The Use of Personal Data in Employer/Employee Relationships* (the 'Employment Code'). Copies of the draft code may be obtained by telephoning the Office of the Data Protection Commissioner on 01625 545700. Alternatively, it (and related guidance notice notes and publications) may be downloaded from either of the following Web sites:

> www.dataprotection.gov.uk
> http://wood.ccta.gov.uk/dpr/dpdoc.nsf
> (Click on 'Guidance and other Publications'.)

22

Posted workers

22.1
The term 'posted worker' is used to describe a worker who is sent from one EU Member State to another to carry out work (albeit for a limited period) in that other Member State. The relevance of the term is to be found in European Parliament & Council Directive 97/71/EC of 16 December 1996 'concerning the posting of workers in the framework of the provision of services'. The purpose of the Directive, which came into force in the UK on 16 December 1999, is to ensure that employers sending workers on temporary assignments to other EU countries, or tendering for contract work in another Member State, do not acquire a competitive edge by paying their workers less, or by offering terms and conditions below the legal minimum in that other Member State. A 'limited period', for these purposes, is a period of up to one year from the beginning of the posting (including any previous periods for which the post in question was filled by a posted worker).

22.2
Implementation of the 'Posted Workers' Directive in the UK does not require specific legislation. However, the Directive has prompted minor amendments to the Sex Discrimination Act 1975, the Race Relations Act 1976, the Trade Union & Labour Relations (Consolidation) Act 1992, the Disability Discrimination Act 1995, and the Employment Rights Act 1996, each of which previously limited the application of certain employment rights to persons who ordinarily work in Great Britain. Those limitations have now been removed.

Note: The territorial limits in the enactments referred to above were repealed by section 32 of the Employment Relations Act (which came into force on 25 October 1999) and by the Equal Opportunities (Employment Legislation) (Territorial Limits) Regulations 1999 (which came into force on 16 December 1999).

Duties of employers

22.3
UK employers sending one or more of their workers to carry out work for a limited period in another EU Member State must familiarise themselves with the laws, regulations and administrative provisions of that Member State, and/or (so far as building work is concerned) with any collective agreements or mandatory arbitration awards in that Member State that relate to:

(a) minimum paid annual holidays;

(b) minimum rates of pay (including overtime rates);

(c) conditions for hiring out workers, notably workers supplied by temporary employment businesses (or 'employment agencies', as they are often, if incorrectly, referred to in the UK);

(d) health, safety and hygiene at work;

(e) protective measures with regard to the terms and conditions of employment of children, young persons, and new or expectant mothers; and

(f) equality of treatment between men and women, and other provisions prohibiting discriminatory treatment on specified grounds;

and must guarantee that the workers posted to that Member State enjoy no less favourable terms and conditions during their periods of posting.

22.4
It is, of course, open to employers to apply more favourable terms and conditions to those of their workers who are posted to other EU Member States for a limited period. If they are entitled (in any respect) to more favourable terms under their existing contracts of employment (whether imported by statute or otherwise), those more favourable terms must, of course, prevail.

22.5
Article 4 of the Directive acknowledges that employers may have some difficulty 'tracking down' the employment laws and health

and safety legislation of other Member States. To that end, Article 4 imposes a duty on each of the Member States to designate one or more liaison offices or one or more competent national bodies to provide that information. Furthermore, they must cooperate with one another to ensure that that information is disseminated and freely available. Until such time as the network, so to speak, is complete, interested readers should direct their enquiries to the labour attaches at the relevant embassies. See also, **Further information** below.

22.6

Employers in other EU Member States who post their workers to the UK for a limited period will, of course, need to familarise themselves with (in chronological order):

(a) the Employment of Women, Young Persons & Children Act 1920;

(b) the Children & Young Persons Act 1933;

(c) the Children & Young Persons (Scotland) Act 1937;

(d) the Equal Pay Act 1970;

(e) the Health & Safety at Work, etc Act 1974;

(f) the Sex Discrimination Act 1975;

(g) the Race Relations Act 1976;

(h) the Workplace (Health, Safety & Welfare) Regulations 1992;

(i) the Disability Discrimination Act 1995;

(j) the Employment Rights Act 1996;

(k) the Working Time Regulations 1998;

(l) the National Minimum Wage Regulations 1999;

(m) the Maternity & Parental Leave etc Regulations 1999; and

(n) the Management of Health & Safety at Work Regulations 1999;

and health and safety regulations (such as the Diving at Work Regulations 1997, the Control of Lead at Work Regulations 1998, the Control of Substances Hazardous to Health Regulations 1999, etc) that contain measures for the protection of workers engaged in prescribed hazardous activities.

Categories of workers

22.7
The Directive identifies three categories of workers. These are:

1) workers sent by their employers to another EU Member State to carry out work for customers or clients in that other Member State;

2) workers sent by their employer to work in a subsidiary or associated company established in that other Member State; and

3) temporary workers employed by an employment business (or placement agency) who are hired out on agreed terms to a client employer in another EU Member State.

Category (1) workers

22.8
Typical of 'Category (1)' workers are people sent by their employers to carry out building work (see *Note* below) in another Member State (for a limited period) or to install plant and equipment (eg, a ventilation system or a refrigeration unit) purchased by a client or customer in that other Member State (where the installation of such equipment is an integral part of the contract for the supply of such equipment).

Note: The expression 'building work' includes all work relating to the construction, repair, upkeep, alteration or demolition of buildings, and, in particular: excavation, earthmoving, actual building work, assembly and dismantling of prefabricated elements, fitting out or installation, alterations, renovations, repairs, dismantling, demolition, maintenance (including upkeep, painting and cleaning work), and improvements.

22.9
However, the terms of the Directive do not apply to skilled or specialist workers sent by their employer (the supplier) to install plant and equipment in a customer or client's premises in another EU Member State (so long as the work in question does not amount to building work) if their posting to that other Member State does not last for more than eight days.

22.10

Although it is uncommon nowadays for UK building workers to be sent by their employers to work on a construction site in another Member State, UK employers planning to do so should be alert to the existence (and complexity) of a variety of collective agreements and mandatory arbitration awards (peculiar to several EU Member States, notably Germany) that might well reduce the cost effectiveness of such postings. It is more usual for UK workers to travel independently to other EU Member States looking for work on a building or construction site (as they have every right to do).

Note: Article 3(3) of the Directive allows that a Member State may ('after consulting employers and labour') legislate for a derogation from the Directive's provisions relating to minimum rates of pay and overtime rates for workers in Categories (1) and (2) who are posted to another EU Member State for a period of one month or less. The UK government has decided (for the time being at least) not to exercise that option.

Category (2) workers

22.11

The 'Category (2)' worker is a worker temporarily transferred by his (or her) UK employer to another branch of the organisation, or to a subsidiary or associated employer situated in another EU Member State, and who remains in the employ of his or her UK employer during the period of posting. Such workers must be treated no less favourably than resident workers during their stay in that Member State in terms of minimum pay rates, maximum working hours, minimum rest breaks and rest periods, annual holidays, equal treatment regardless of gender, race or disability; and health and safety protection.

Category (3) workers

22.12

The third category of worker is the 'temp' or agency worker, who is employed under a contract of employment with an employment business (or placement agency) in one Member State, and who is hired-out for a limited period to a 'user undertaking' in another EU Member State. So long as he or she remains in the employ of that business or agency throughout the period of posting, the hired-out worker must be paid no less than the minimum rates of pay and overtime rates applicable to comparable workers in the Member State in question and enjoy the same statutory protection (in terms of working hours, period of employment, rest breaks, holidays, health and safety measures, etc).

22.13
Furthermore, Article 9 of the Directive allows that a Member State may take steps to ensure that employment businesses and placement agencies established in other Member States provide a guarantee that temporary workers posted to its territory are hired out on terms and conditions no less favourable than those that apply to its own temporary workers.

Enforcement

22.14
Any worker sent by his (or her) employer to work for a limited period in another EU Member State, whose wages or salary, working hours, holiday entitlement, etc are less favourable than those prescribed for workers normally resident in that Member State, may enforce his or her rights under the Posted Workers Directive by instituting proceedings before the appropriate tribunal or court in that Member State or in the Member State in which he normally works.

LIKELY IMPLICATIONS FOR UK EMPLOYERS

22.15
Nowadays, it is uncommon for relatively lowly paid workers in the UK or elsewhere to be sent by their employers to carry out short-term assignments in other EU Member States. Such postings are usually confined to businessmen and women, accountants, bankers, technicians, engineers, and the like (whose terms and conditions of employment are unlikely to fall below the minima prescribed for workers engaged in comparable activities in those other Member States). This will not necessarily be true of nurses, waiters, waitresses, secretaries, interpreters, bricklayers, carpenters, plumbers, etc, employed by employment businesses (or placement agencies) who are hired out to clients in other Member States for limited periods. In the latter case, the Posted Workers Directive 'comes into play' (so to speak) if, but only if, the workers in question

remain in the employ of the relevant business or agency throughout the period of their postings.

Free movement of workers

22.16

The nationals of one Member State who travel to another Member State in search of work (eg, as waiters, waitresses, builders, etc) usually do so independently – exercising their right under Article 39 (formerly Article 48) of the Treaty of Rome 'to move freely within the territory of Member States', 'to accept offers of employment actually made', 'to stay in a Member State for the purpose of employment', and 'to remain in the territory of a Member State after having been employed in that State'.

Further information

22.17

Readers seeking further information about the Directive may telephone the DTI's Helpline on 0645 555105 or (for more specific advice) contact Mike Lowell at the DTI on (020) 7215 5921.

The Directive itself may be viewed on Web site:

http://europa.eu.int/eur-lex/en/lif/dat/1996/en 396L0071.html

Public interest disclosures

23.1
Under the Public Interest Disclosure Act 1998, which came into force on 2 July 1999, any worker who makes a so-called protected disclosure has the right not to be dismissed, selected for redundancy or subjected to any other detriment (demotion, forfeiture of opportunities for promotion or training, etc) for having done so. Any term in a contract of employment or other document (such as a 'worker's contract') that purports to undermine or override a worker's right to make a protected disclosure is null and void.

Note: The relevant provisions of the 1998 Act (commonly referred to as 'the Whistleblower's Act') have been inserted as Part IVA (sections 43A to 43L) of the Employment Rights Act 1996. Those relating to a worker's right not to be dismissed, selected for redundancy or subjected to any detriment for making a protected disclosure are to be found in sections 47B, 103A and 105 of the 1996 Act. The latter Act is hereinafter referred to as 'the 1996 Act'.

Meaning of 'qualifying disclosure'

23.2
Section 43A of the 1996 Act defines 'protected disclosure' as meaning a qualifying disclosure, that is to say, any disclosure of information that, in the reasonable belief of the worker making the disclosure, tends to show one or more of the following:

(a) that a criminal offence has been, is being or is likely to be committed;

(b) that a person has failed, is failing or is likely to fail to comply with a legal obligation to which he (or she) is subject;

(c) that a miscarriage of justice has occurred, is occurring or is likely to occur;

(d) that the health and safety of an individual has been, is being or is likely to be endangered;

(e) that the environment has been, is being or is likely to be damaged; or

(f) that information tending to show any matter falling within any one of the preceding paragraphs has been, or is likely to be deliberately concealed.

It is important to note the use of the word 'worker', in this context. A worker is a person who is either an employee in the accepted sense (that is to say, a person employed under a contract of employment) or a person who works personally for another person under some other form of contractual arrangement (perhaps as a freelance operator, a trainee, a casual labourer, or agency worker). The term does not however apply to a person who is genuinely self-employed.

23.3
A worker prompted to make a disclosure about alleged wrongdoing by (or within) the organisation for which he (or she) works may do so:

(a) to his employer (either directly or in accordance with established procedures for dealing with such allegations) or to another person whom the worker reasonably believes to be solely or mainly responsible for the alleged unlawful or criminal conduct;

(b) to a legal adviser (if made in the course of obtaining legal advice);

(c) to a Minister of the Crown (if the disclosure is made in good faith, and the worker in question is employed by a Government-appointed person or public body);

(d) to the appropriate enforcing authorities (such as the Health & Safety Executive, the Commissioners of the Inland Revenue, the Environmental Agency, etc (see below));

(e) (subject to certain conditions) to some other person or agency, if the disclosure relates to an exceptionally serious failure on the part of the worker's employer or some other person; or

(f) (subject to certain conditions) to some other person or agency (eg, the media, or a professional body responsible for policing standards and conduct in a particular field).

Disclosure to employer or other responsible person

23.4
A worker may make a qualifying disclosure directly to his (or her) employer, or to some other person whom he reasonably believes to be solely or mainly responsible for the alleged wrongdoing, and will enjoy the protection available to him under Part IVA of the 1996 Act, so long as he acts in good faith (*ibid* section 43C).

23.5
If an employer has developed or authorised a simple and readily accessible procedure to encourage workers to air their concerns about alleged wrongdoing within his organisation (eg, breaches of health and safety legislation), then those procedures should be exhausted before a worker takes it upon himself (or herself) to air those concerns or allegations elsewhere (see *Disclosure in other cases* below). He may choose, on the other hand, to present his allegations of wrongdoing directly to the appropriate enforcing authorities (so long as he does so in good faith and reasonably believes those allegations to be substantially true).

23.6
An employer's in-house procedures for dealing with allegations of wrongdoing are unlikely to inspire confidence unless they involve other members of the workforce or workforce representatives elected or appointed by their peers to deal with such issues and make representations to their employer. A reasonable employer will, of course, respond positively to qualifying disclosures about supposed criminal activities or other wrongdoing within his organisation. So long as those disclosures were made in good faith, it would be wholly irresponsible (not to mention costly) for an employer to react by disciplining the worker or workers concerned, or by dismissing them or subjecting them to some other detriment.

Disclosure to the 'appropriate authorities'

23.7
A worker who makes a qualifying disclosure to a prescribed person or body – such as the Health & Safety Executive, the Inland Revenue, HM Customs & Excise, the Environment Agency, the Audit

Commission, the Director General of Fair Trading, and the like (see *Note* below) – will enjoy the protection afforded by the 1998 Act, so long as he (or she) does so in good faith and reasonably believes that the allegations of wrongdoing he is making are substantially true (*ibid* section 43F).

Note: A list of the persons and descriptions of persons prescribed for the purposes of section 43F of the 1996 Act is to be found in the Schedule to the Public Interest (Prescribed Persons) Order 1999 (SI 1999/1549) and is reproduced in DTI Booklet URN 99/511 (*Guide to the Public Interest Disclosure Act 1998*), copies of which are available free of charge from the DTI's Publications Orderline (Telephone: 0870 1502 500).

Disclosure in other cases

23.8
A worker who makes a qualifying disclosure to some other person or body (other than his (or her) employer or the appropriate enforcing authority) will enjoy the protection of the law, if he:

(a) made the disclosure in good faith;

(b) reasonably believed that the information disclosed, and any allegation contained in it, were substantially true;

(c) did not make the disclosure for purposes of personal gain;

(d) reasonably believed (at the time he made the disclosure) that he would have been punished, dismissed, selected for redundancy or subjected to some other detriment had he made the disclosure to his employer or to the appropriate enforcing authority;

(e) (in the absence of an appropriate enforcing authority), reasonably believed that his employer would have concealed or destroyed any incriminating evidence; or

(f) had previously made the same or a similar disclosure to his employer or the appropriate enforcing body without avail.

Whether or not it was reasonable for the worker to have made the qualifying disclosure to a person or body other than his immediate employer (or the appropriate enforcing authority) will depend in large part on the identity of the person or body to whom the disclosure was made. An employment tribunal will also consider the seriousness of the alleged wrongdoing (and the likelihood of its happening again), whether the disclosure in question contained information in breach of the employer's duty of confidentiality to another person (eg, a customer or client), the employer's or the prescribed enforcing authority's response (or failure to respond) to a previous disclosure of the same (or substantially similar information), and whether, in making the same or similar allegations to his employer on a previous occasion, the worker had complied with any procedure whose use by him was authorised by his employer (*ibid* section 43G).

23.9
Challenging an employer's failure to pay the appropriate national minimum wage, or to comply with his duties under the Working Time Regulations 1998, or to provide personal protective equipment, or for discharging toxic chemicals into the environment, or for defrauding the Inland Revenue etc, may not achieve the desired result if made directly to the person allegedly responsible for such breaches of the law, or if doing so is likely to prompt the concealment of any damaging documents or other evidence before the relevant authorities have had an opportunity to make their own assessments of the situation.

23.10
A worker might also be concerned about the risk to his (or her) livelihood, the more so if his previous allegations on the same or a similar theme have been dismissed out of hand or 'swept under the carpet', or he has been warned 'to keep his mouth shut'. Whether influenced by such considerations or otherwise, a worker has the right to make his disclosures about alleged wrongdoing to the body, person or authority responsible for investigating and enforcing the particular law which the worker reasonably believes has been (is being or is about to be) broken.

Disclosures about exceptionally serious failures

23.11
A worker who has made a qualifying disclosure (eg, to a newspaper) about an *exceptionally serious failure* (either by his (or her) employer or by some other person) will enjoy the protection afforded by the Employment Rights Act 1996 if, but only if, he:

(a) made the disclosure in good faith;

(b) reasonably believed that the information disclosed, and any allegations contained in it were substantially true;

(c) did not make the disclosure for purposes of personal gain; and if, given the circumstances;

(d) it was reasonable for him to have made the disclosure.

Whether or not the failure in question was exceptionally serious is a matter of fact, not of opinion. In other words, a worker's reasonable belief that a particular failure was exceptionally serious will not be enough. The failure must in fact have been exceptionally serious.

23.12

In determining whether or not it was reasonable for the worker to have made the disclosure in question, an employment tribunal will have regard in particular to the identity of the person or organisation to whom the disclosure was made (*ibid* section 43H). All of which suggests that a worker would be well advised to obtain legal advice before make a qualifying disclosure that, if aired in the public domain, could not only undermine his (or her) right not to be dismissed or subjected to a detriment for doing so but could also lead to his being sued in defamation.

Other forms of protection

23.13

It should be remembered that the Employment Rights Act 1996 offers considerable protection to employees who allege (in good faith) that their employer has infringed their statutory rights under that Act, the Trade Union & Labour Relations (Consolidation) Act 1992, or the Working Time Regulations 1998. Under the National Minimum Wage Act 1998, for example, Inland Revenue enforcement officers have the right to question workers and to act on any information supplied by those workers concerning their employer's alleged failure to pay the appropriate national minimum wage rate. There are any number of similar examples, all of which complement a worker's rights under the 'Protected Disclosures' provisions of the 1996 Act (eg, the right of employees under section 100 of that same Act to bring to their employer's attention (by reasonable means) circumstances connected with their work that they reasonably believe to be harmful or potentially harmful to health or safety).

Complaint to an employment tribunal

23.14
A worker may complain to an employment tribunal that he (or she) has been penalised, victimised or subjected to some other detriment for making a protected disclosure. Should the worker's complaint be upheld, his employer will be ordered to pay him such compensation as the tribunal considers appropriate in the circumstances (including compensation for the loss of any benefit that the worker might reasonably be expected to have enjoyed) but for his employer's conduct or failure to act.

23.15
A worker (as 'employee') who has been dismissed (or selected for redundancy) for making a protected disclosure may complain to an employment tribunal and will be awarded a substantial amount of compensation if his (or her) complaint is upheld. A worker who is not an employee in the strict legal sense, but whose detrimental treatment amounted to a termination of his contract, may likewise complain to an employment tribunal, and will also be awarded compensation if his complaint is upheld. It is as well to point out, that there is no upper limit on the amount of compensation that may be awarded in such cases.

23.16
Complaints to an employment tribunal, in the circumstances described above, must be presented within three months of the effective date of termination of an employee's contract of employment, or within three months of the alleged detrimental treatment (including, in the case of a worker who is not an employee, detrimental treatment amounting to a termination of the worker's contract). Such complaints may be presented regardless of the worker's age or length of service at the material time.

Part-time workers

Overview

24.1

With the coming into force on 7 April 2000 of the Part-time Workers (Prevention of Less Favourable Treatment) Regulations 2000 (SI 2000/1551), any part-time worker who is treated less favourably (or believes that he (or she) has been treated less favourably) than a comparable full-time worker, is entitled to demand and receive from his employer a written statement explaining the reasons for such treatment. If dissatisfied with his employer's explanations, the part-time worker may seek redress from an employment tribunal. A part-timer who is dismissed, selected for redundancy or subjected to any other detriment for exercising or asserting his statutory rights under the Regulations, or for bringing proceedings before an employment tribunal, may complain (yet again) to a tribunal and will be awarded such compensation as the tribunal considers to be 'just and equitable' in all the circumstances.

24.2

The 2000 Regulations implement EC Directive 97/81/EC of 15 December 1997 'concerning the Framework Agreement on part-time work concluded by UNICE, CEEP and the ETUC'. The purpose of the last is 'to provide for the removal of discrimination against part-time workers and to improve the quality of part-time work'. It is also designed 'to facilitate the development of part-time work on a voluntary basis and to contribute to the flexible organisation of working time in a manner which takes into account the needs of employers and workers'.

Previous legislation

24.3

Since 6 February 1995 (when the Employment Protection (Part-time Employees) Regulations 1995 (SI 1995/31) came into force), part-time employees (that is to say, individuals employed under contracts of employment) have enjoyed the same statutory rights as their full-time contemporaries. In short, the qualifying period for access to those statutory rights is the same for part-timers as it is for full-time employees. The 1995 Regulations were prompted in large part by the decision of the House of Lords in *R v Secretary of State for Employment, ex parte the Equal Opportunities Commission* ([1994] ICR 317). Their Lordships held that the provisions of the then Employment Protection (Consolidation) Act 1978, which differentiated between part-time and full-time employees, contravened Article 119 (now Article 141) of the Treaty of Rome.

The new Regulations

24.4
Unlike the 1995 Regulations (referred to in the previous paragraph), the 2000 Regulations apply to all 'workers'. In other words, they apply not only to persons employed under contracts of employment or apprenticeship but also to casual or seasonal workers, freelancers, agency 'temps', homeworkers and others who, while not 'employees' in the strict legal sense, undertake to do or perform personally any work or services for an employer – whether the contracts under which they are employed are express (that is to say, oral or in writing) or implied. Such a worker is usually said to be engaged under a contract *sui generis* (that is to say, 'of its own kind'). The Regulations do not, however, apply to individuals who are genuinely self-employed. Furthermore, they add a new dimension by requiring employers to review the terms and conditions on which part-time workers are employed, compare them with the terms and conditions and contractual benefits available to 'comparable full-time workers', and make the necessary adjustments, adopting (where appropriate) the principle of *pro rata temporis* .

Note: The principle of *pro rata temporis* means that where a comparable full-time worker receives (or is entitled to receive) pay or any other benefit, a part-time worker employed under the same type of contract must receive (or be entitled to receive) not less than the proportion of that pay or other benefit that the number of his (or her) weekly hours bears to the number of weekly hours worked by that full-time worker (*ibid* Reg 1(1)).

Meaning of 'full-time' and 'part-time' worker

24.5

Under the 2000 Regulations a 'full-time worker' is a person who is paid wholly or partly by reference to the time he (or she) works and, having regard to the custom and practice of the employer in relation to workers employed under the same type of contract, is identifiable as a full-time worker. A 'part-time worker', on the other hand, is a person who works under the same type of contract as a full-time worker, but works fewer hours than that full-time worker. On reflection, no more precise definition is possible. A person ('employee' or otherwise), who works (say) a 40-hour, five-day week in a particular organisation, will ordinarily be regarded as a full-time worker within that organisation. A worker in the same organisation, who is employed under the same type of contract as that full-time worker, but works fewer than 40 hours a week, is a part-time worker (*ibid* Reg 2).

Meaning of 'comparable full-time' worker

24.6

It follows that, for the purposes of the 2000 Regulations, a worker is a 'comparable full-time worker' in relation to a part-time worker if, at the time when the alleged less favourable treatment occurred, both of those workers were employed by the same employer at the same establishment, worked under the same type of contract, carried out the same or broadly similar work, and possessed (where relevant) the same or a broadly similar level of qualification, skills and experience.

If there is no comparable full-time worker at the establishment in question, a part-time worker may compare his (or her) treatment with that received by a 'comparable full-time worker', working at another establishment (branch office, factory, depot, warehouse, etc) situated elsewhere within the same organisation (*ibid*).

24.7

Workers employed under the following types of contract are *not* employed under the same types of contract:

(a)　employees working under a contract of employment that is neither a fixed-term contract nor a contract of apprenticeship;

(b)   employees working under a contract of employment for a fixed term that is not a contract of apprenticeship;

(c)   employees working under a contract of apprenticeship;

(d)   workers who are neither employees nor employed under a fixed-term contract;

(e)   workers who are not employees but are employed under a fixed-term contract;

(f)   any other description of worker that it is reasonable for the employer to treat differently from other workers on the ground that workers of that description have a different type of contract.

For example, (a) is not the same type of contract as (b); (c) not the same as (d); (e) not the same as (a); and so on.

LESS FAVOURABLE TREATMENT OF PART-TIME WORKERS

24.8
Part-time workers must not be treated less favourably than comparable full-time workers solely because they work part-time – unless different treatment is justified on objective grounds. This means that a part-time worker must be paid the same hourly rate of pay as a comparable full-time worker. A different hourly rate of pay may be justifiable on performance-related grounds, so long as a worker's performance is measured fairly and consistently under a performance appraisal scheme (*ibid* Regs 5 to 7).

Note: A full-time worker who becomes a part-time worker, following a termination or variation of his (or her) previous contract, whether of the same type or not, must be treated as if there were a comparable full-time worker employed under the terms that applied to him immediately before the variation or termination. The same applies if a former full-time worker returns to work part-time with his former employer in the same or a similar job within 12 months of the termination of his previous contract, whether or not the contract under which he is re-engaged is the same type of contract or a different or varied contract (*ibid* Regs 3 & 4).

Terms and conditions of employment

24.9
It is not uncommon for employer's occupational sick pay schemes to provide more generous benefits to full-time workers (eg full salary

or wages for a period of up to 3 months in every 12-month period). By the same token, it is not unusual for part-time workers to receive no more than their entitlement to statutory sick pay (SSP) when incapacitated for work on grounds of illness of injury. Such a sweeping differential is no longer acceptable, or justifiable. When calculating the rate of *occupational* sick pay (or maternity pay), or the length of service required to qualify for such payments, or the period over which such contractual payments are made, part-time workers must not be treated less favourably than comparable full-time workers in the same employment. Indeed, any differential treatment could give rise to allegations of unlawful sex discrimination, let alone a complaint to an employment tribunal under the 2000 Regulations. That same general prohibition applies to differential treatment in relation to occupational maternity and parental leave schemes, annual holiday entitlements (in excess of the statutory minimum entitlement), unpaid career breaks, access to occupational pension schemes, access to opportunities for training and promotion, redundancy selection criteria, and so on – unless that different treatment is justifiable on objective grounds (*ibid* Reg 3).

Other benefits

24.10
Other benefits available to comparable full-time workers, such as health insurance, subsidised mortgages and staff discounts, should be applied to part-time workers on a pro rata basis, unless their exclusion is justified on objective grounds. Some benefits, such as health insurance, company cars, luncheon vouchers and the like, are 'indivisible'. Although it may not be possible to provide such benefits pro rata, that is not of itself an objective justification for withholding them. However, the disproportionate cost to the employer of providing such benefits may prove to be objectively justifiable. One way of overcoming the problem of company cars is to calculate the financial value of the benefit to a comparable full-time worker and apply that value pro rata (eg in the form of a car allowance) to the part-time worker. See also **Further information** at the end of this chapter.

24.11
In future, employers will need to scrutinise the relative terms and conditions of their full-time and part-time workers and eliminate any

discrepancies or anomalies that cannot be justified on objective grounds. In determining whether a part-time worker has been treated less favourably than a comparable full-time worker, the principle of *pro rata temporis* (referred to earlier in this section) may be applied – unless it is inappropriate. It would be inappropriate, for example, to apply that principle to basic rates of pay, overtime payments (but see next paragraph), access to pension schemes, opportunities for training, transfer or promotion, career-break schemes, enhanced-maternity or parental-leave schemes, or redundancy selection criteria.

Exception in relation to overtime payments

24.12

The new Regulations acknowledge that part-time workers have no right to premium payments in respect of overtime work until such time as their working hours (including overtime hours) during a particular pay reference period exceed the number of hours ordinarily worked by comparable full-time workers in that same period. But, once that point is reached, premium payments for hours worked in excess of those full-time hours must be the same as those paid to comparable full-time workers (*ibid* Reg 3(4)).

Written statement of reasons for less favourable treatment

24.13

Any part-time worker who considers that he (or she) is being treated less favourably than a comparable full-time worker may ask his employer for a written statement explaining the reasons for that treatment. The employer must provide that statement within the following 21 days (*ibid* Reg 4).

24.14

A failure to provide that written statement, without reasonable excuse, is admissible in evidence before an employment tribunal. Furthermore, when entertaining a complaint of less favourable treatment, the tribunal may draw any inference from that failure as it considers just and equitable (including an inference that the employer has infringed the complainant's statutory rights). The same applies if the explanation given in the written statement is evasive or equivocal (*ibid*).

Note: There is no need for a separate written statement if a part-time 'employee' who has been dismissed has already requested and received a written statement of reasons for dismissal under Section 92 of the Employment Rights Act 1996 (as to which, please turn to Chapter 14, paras 14.53 to 14.55 and Chapter 15, paras 15.60 to 15.67, elsewhere in this book (*ibid* Reg 4(4)).

Unfair dismissal and detrimental treatment

24.15
A part-time worker (other than a worker who is not an 'employee') who is dismissed or selected for redundancy will be treated in law as having been unfairly dismissed or selected if the reason (or, if more than one, the principal reason) for his (or her) dismissal or selection was that he:

(a)   had complained to an employment tribunal about an alleged infringement of his rights under the 2000 Regulations;

(b)   had asked his employer for a written statement of the reasons for his less favourable treatment;

(c)   had given evidence or information in proceedings before an employment tribunal brought by another worker;

(d)   had alleged (in good faith) that his employer had infringed the 2000 Regulations;

(e)   had refused (or proposed to refuse) to forego a right conferred on him by the 2000 Regulations; or

(f)   that his employer believed or suspected that the worker had done (or intended to do) any of the things mentioned in (a) to (e) above

(*ibid* Reg 5(1), (3) & 4.)

24.16
A part-time worker who has been victimised, disciplined or subjected to any other detriment, including termination of his (or her) contract on any of the grounds (a) to (f) specified in the previous paragraph, has the right to refer the matter to an employment tribunal without having to resign in order to do so (*ibid* Reg 5(2), (3) & (4)).

Complaints to employment tribunals, etc

24.17

A part-time worker (regardless of his (or her) age or length of service at the material time) may complain to an employment tribunal that his employer has infringed his statutory rights under the 2000 Regulations – either by subjecting him to a detriment (including termination of his contract) or some other punishment, or (in the case of an employee) by dismissing him or selecting him for redundancy. Such a complaint must be presented within three months of the alleged detrimental treatment or, if the employee has been dismissed or made redundant, within three months of the effective date of termination of his contract of employment. A tribunal may consider a complaint that is out of time if, in all the circumstances of the case, it considers that it is just and equitable to do so.

24.18

If a complaint of unlawful detrimental treatment is upheld, the tribunal will make a declaration to that effect and may order the employer to pay compensation to the worker and/or recommend that the employer take appropriate corrective action (within a specified period) to obviate or reduce the adverse effect of any matter to which the worker's complaint relates. A failure to take such corrective action will prompt the tribunal either to increase the amount of compensation already awarded to the worker or (if no compensation had previously been awarded) order the employer to pay compensation to the worker. The amount of compensation awarded in such circumstances will be such amount as the tribunal considers just and equitable, and will include compensation for the loss of any benefit that the worker might reasonably be expected to have had but for his employer's infringement of his rights under the 2000 Regulations (or the employer's failure to take the recommended corrective action) (*ibid* Reg 6).

24.19

A worker (*qua* employee) who has been dismissed (or selected for redundancy), in contravention of the 2000 Regulations will be treated as having been unfairly dismissed (regardless of his (or her) age or length of service at the material time) and will awarded compensation comprising a basic and compensatory award (maximum £7,200 and £51,700, respectively) and, where appropriate, an additional award of compensation of between 26 and 52 weeks' pay (as to which, please turn to Chapter 5, paras 5.158 *et seq* elsewhere in this book (*ibid* Reg 5(1)).

Further information

24.20
The Department of Trade & Industry (DTI) has published a guide to the Part-time Workers Regulations 2000 titled *The Law & Best Practice: A detailed guide for employers and part-timers*, copies of which may be secured either by telephoning the DTI Publications Orderline on 0870 1502 500 or by accessing the Web site www.dti.gov.uk/er/pt-detail.htm. A copy of the Regulations themselves may be either purchased from The Stationary Office (telephone 0870 600 5522) or downloaded from the Web site www.legislation.hmso.gov.uk/si/si2000/20001551.htm.

25

Trade union recognition

25.1

Schedule A1 to the Trade Union & Labour Relations (Consolidation) Act 1992 (as inserted, with effect from 6 June 2000, by section 1(1) & (3) and Schedule 1 to the Employment Relations Act 1999) lays down the (somewhat complicated) procedures attendant upon a request by a trade union for recognition and collective bargaining rights. It also contains no less complicated procedures for derecognition.

The new provisions summarised

25.2

In brief, any employer with 21 or more workers 'on the payroll' may be presented with a valid request for trade union recognition. If the employer ignores or rejects such a request, or refuses to negotiate, the trade union may apply to the Central Arbitration Committee (CAC) for compulsory recognition. So long as the CAC is satisfied that the trade union's application is both valid and admissible, and accepts that more than 50 per cent of the workers in the proposed bargaining unit are members of that trade union, it will order the employer to recognise that trade union. If, on the other hand, the CAC is not entirely persuaded that a majority of the workers in the bargaining unit want the trade union to negotiate on their behalf, it will serve notice that it intends to arrange a secret ballot. If 40 per cent or more of the workers entitled to vote in the ballot, and a majority of those voting, vote in favour of recognition, the CAC will make a compulsory recognition order. A refusal to comply with such an order is a contempt of court, punishable by imprisonment or a fine.

Note: In the 1992 Act, the term 'worker' applies to any individual (other than a person who is genuinely self-employed) who works (or normally works) under a contract of employment or under any other contract whereby he (or she) undertakes to do or perform personally any work or services for another party to the contract.

In other words, the term not only applies to employees in the accepted sense, but also to casual workers, seasonal workers, homeworkers and freelancers engaged under some other contractual arrangement.

25.3
The new provisions also lay down procedures for derecognition (not discussed in any detail in this section). An application for derecognition may be made by either party to a recognition agreement, so long as the agreement in question was imposed by the CAC (in accordance with the procedures explained in this section). However, the CAC will not entertain an application for derecognition if made within three years of its original decision. If the numbers (or average numbers) employed in a particular organisation fall below 21, the employer may notify the union that his bargaining arrangements with the union are to end on a specified date (which must be not less than 35 working days after the date on which the employer notified the union of his decision). The union may challenge the validity of the employer's decision by making an application to the CAC. A voluntary recognition agreement may be terminated by either party at any time, without the need for a statutory procedure (so long as the CAC did not impose a method for collective bargaining in relation to that voluntary agreement).

Training

25.4
A trade union that has been accorded recognition rights by the CAC in respect of a particular bargaining unit (and has adopted a method specified by the CAC for the conduct of collective bargaining) has the right to consult with their employer about his plans for training the workers within that bargaining unit (see paras 25.30 to 25.33 below).

Earlier legislation

25.5
Before Schedule A1 to the 1992 Act came into force, there were no statutory provisions for compulsory trade union recognition. Earlier statutory provisions in the Employment Protection Act 1975 were repealed by the Employment Act 1980 on 15 August 1980. Since then, collective bargaining agreements have been concluded on an entirely

voluntary basis, with either party having the right to opt out on giving the appropriate or agreed period of notice.

25.6
A number of statutory employment rights (eg the right of trade union officials and members to a reasonable amount of paid or unpaid time off work, etc) hinge on their being officials or members of recognised independent trade unions. The same applies to a union's right to consult with employers concerning collective redundancies and 'relevant transfers' under the Transfer of Undertakings (Protection of Employment) Regulations 1981). Safety representatives, likewise, have no statutory right to perform their official functions unless the trade union that appointed them is a recognised independent trade union. An employer is not duty-bound to disclose information to a trade union for the purposes of collective bargaining unless the union is a recognised independent trade union; and so on. Those rights (discussed elsewhere in this book) remain unaffected by the new statutory provisions.

THE VALIDITY OF A REQUEST FOR RECOGNITION

25.7
Under the new statutory provisions, a trade union may submit a request for recognition to any employer in Great Britain who has 21 or more people on the payroll (including persons employed by an associated employer), or to any employer who has employed an average of 21 or more people over the previous 13 weeks. However, such a request will not be valid unless it:

(a)   is in writing (signed by one or more members (or an official) of the trade union in question);

Note: Paragraph 9 of Schedule A1 to the 1992 Act allows that the Secretary of State for Trade & Industry may make an order prescribing the form of requests for trade union recognition or the procedure for making them. Furthermore, the Schedule is silent as to whether a request for trade union recognition must be signed by a full-time trade union official or by the workers themselves. What is clear is that a request for recognition can only be made by workers who are themselves members of the union in question.

(b)   identifies the union making the request (which must be an 'independent' trade union);

Note: A trade union is 'independent' if it has a certificate of independence issued by the Certification Officer in accordance with sections 2 to 9 of the 1992 Act, and that certificate has not been cancelled or withdrawn.

(c) identifies the bargaining unit (or proposed bargaining unit) – that is to say, the group or groups of workers the union wishes to represent in collective bargaining with the employer; and

(d) states that the request is made under Schedule A1 to the Trade Union & Labour Relations (Consolidation) Act 1992.

To determine whether an employer has 21 or more workers 'on the payroll', workers employed by any associated employer incorporated outside Great Britain must be ignored, unless they ordinarily work in Great Britain. A worker employed on board a ship registered under section 8 of the Merchant Shipping Act 1995 is to be treated as ordinarily working in Great Britain unless the ship is registered as belonging to a port outside Great Britain; or the employment is wholly outside Great Britain; or the worker is not ordinarily resident in Great Britain (*ibid* paragraph 7(5)).

25.8
A request for trade union recognition may be submitted by two or more trade unions acting in unison (or separately) in respect of two or more proposed bargaining units within the same organisation. For simplicity's sake, the legislation discussed in this section is in the context of one trade union applying for recognition in respect of one or more groups of employees (the 'bargaining unit').

Meaning of 'bargaining unit' and 'collective bargaining'

25.9
Paragraphs 1 and 2 of the Schedule define the expression 'bargaining unit' (or 'proposed bargaining unit') as meaning the group or groups of workers on whose behalf a trade union is seeking recognition. 'Recognition' means recognition for the purposes of collective bargaining. In short, an independent trade union that is recognised by an employer (following a declaration to that effect by the CAC) has the statutory right to negotiate with that employer on matters relating to pay, working hours and holidays. It is, of course, open to

the parties to agree to negotiate on other matters (eg, guarantee payments, sickness benefits, enhanced parental leave; and so on) – whether the agreement is made before or after the Central Arbitration Committee (CAC) makes a declaration for trade union recognition (see below), or independently of any such declaration (*ibid* paragraphs 1 & 2).

Note: For the purposes of Part I of Schedule A1 to the 1992 Act, the term 'collective bargaining' is restricted to negotiations in respect of pay working hours and holidays. In short, the meaning of 'collective bargaining' given by section 178(1) of the 1992 Act does not apply to a declaration by the CAC that a trade union must be recognised by an employer for collective bargaining purposes. See also **Collective agreements** elsewhere in this handbook).

Voluntary or negotiated agreements

25.10
Upon receiving a valid request for trade union recognition, an employer has 10 working days within which to accept it, ignore it or reject it. That period of 10 working days begins with the day following that on which the employer received that request.

25.11
If the parties voluntarily agree a bargaining unit within those 10 working days and agree also that the union is to be recognised as entitled to conduct collective bargaining on behalf of that unit, the issue is settled. No further steps need be taken under Schedule A1 to the 1992 Act. This rule also applies if a trade union has made an application to the CAC for compulsory recognition but withdraws that application before the CAC has declared automatic recognition or has notified the parties of its intention to arrange for a ballot (see below).

25.12
If an employer does not accept a trade union's request for recognition, but is willing to negotiate, the parties have a further 20 working days (30 in all) within which to reach agreement. However, there is nothing to prevent the parties agreeing to conduct their negotiations over a longer period; the more so if the issues under discussion are likely to be complicated. If the parties reach agreement on recognition and on the composition of the bargaining unit within those further 20 working days (or within an agreed

longer period), the trade union will be treated as recognised and no further steps are necessary under Schedule A1. It is then up to the parties to decide the scope and method of collective bargaining. During negotiations, both parties may invite the assistance of the Advisory, Conciliation & Arbitration Service (ACAS).

25.13
If the negotiations fail, and there is no agreement before the end of the 20-day negotiating period (or within the longer agreed period), the union seeking recognition may apply to the Central Arbitration Committee (CAC) asking it to decide:

(a) whether the proposed bargaining unit (or some other bargaining unit) is appropriate; and

(b) whether the union has the support of a majority of the workers constituting the appropriate bargaining unit.

If, on the other hand, the parties have agreed an appropriate bargaining unit, but have failed to reach agreement on the issue of recognition, the union may apply to the CAC to decide the question whether the union has the support of a majority of the workers constituting that bargaining unit.

25.14
The CAC will decline to consider an application by a trade union in the circumstances described above if the evidence shows that the union had rejected (or failed to accept) a proposal by the employer that ACAS be invited to assist them with their negotiations – so long as the employer's proposal was made within the period of 10 working days beginning with the day following that on which the employer had indicated his willingness to negotiate.

Employer rejects request for trade union recognition

25.15
If an employer ignores or rejects a valid request for trade union recognition (and has made it plain that he is unwilling to negotiate under any circumstances), the trade union may apply to the CAC to decide whether the proposed bargaining unit (or some other bargaining unit) is the appropriate bargaining unit; and whether the

union in question has the support of a majority (more than 50 per cent) of the workers constituting the appropriate bargaining unit. The trade union must not submit its application to the CAC until 10 working days have elapsed (following the date on which the employer received their request for recognition).

'PRELIMINARY TESTS' BY THE CAC

25.16
Once the CAC has received and acknowledged a trade union's application for recognition (or for a decision concerning the appropriate bargaining unit) it must first decide (within the next 10 working days) whether the application is both valid and admissible. The 'validity test' was explained earlier in this section. To be admissible, the application must:

(a) be made in such form as the CAC specifies; and

(b) be supported by such documents as the CAC specifies.

Furthermore, the trade union must have informed the employer of its decision to apply to the CAC and must have supplied the employer with a copy of its application and any supporting documents.

25.17
Nor will the union's application be admissible unless the CAC is satisfied:

(c) that at least 10 per cent of the workers constituting the proposed (or agreed) bargaining unit are members of the union in question;

(d) that a majority of the workers constituting that proposed (or agreed) bargaining unit would be likely to favour recognition of the union as entitled to conduct collective bargaining on their behalf;

(e) that the application does not include any workers in the relevant bargaining unit in respect of whom the same union has already been recognised as being entitled to conduct collective bargaining (*unless* the matters in respect of which the union is entitled to conduct collective bargaining do not include pay, working hours or holidays);

(f) that the proposed bargaining unit does not overlap with another unit in respect of which the CAC has already accepted an application (ie, one or more workers apparently included in each of two or more bargaining units);

(g) that the application is not substantially the same as an application accepted by the CAC within the previous three years;

(h) that the application has not been made within three years of a previous declaration by the CAC that the union was *not* entitled to be recognised in respect of the same (or a substantially similar) bargaining unit; or

(i) that the application has not been made within three years of the same union (or group of unions) having been derecognised in respect of the same (or substantially the same) bargaining unit; or

(j) (if the application has been made by two or more unions) that the unions will not only cooperate with one another in a manner likely to secure and maintain stable and effective collective bargaining arrangements, and show that they would be prepared also (if requested by the employer) to act together on behalf of the workers constituting the relevant bargaining unit (ie, to engage in single-table bargaining).

If the CAC accepts the union's application as being both valid and admissible, it must then proceed with that application.

25.18
If the employer and the union have already agreed the bargaining unit, the CAC need do no more than determine the level of support for recognition. If the parties have not agreed a bargaining unit, the CAC must decide the appropriate bargaining unit before determining whether the majority of workers in that unit would be likely to favour recognition.

Acceptance of a trade union's application

25.19
If the CAC proceeds with an application for trade union recognition, and is satisfied that a majority of the workers in the bargaining unit

are members of the union in question, it *must* make a declaration that the union is recognised as entitled to conduct collective bargaining on behalf of the workers constituting the relevant bargaining unit, *unless*:

(a) satisfied that a secret ballot should nonetheless be held in the interests of good industrial relations; or

(b) a significant number of the union members within the bargaining unit inform the CAC that they do not want the union to conduct collective bargaining on their behalf; or

(c) evidence of trade union membership within the bargaining unit leads the CAC to conclude that there are doubts whether a significant number of the union members within that bargaining unit want the union to conduct collective bargaining on their behalf.

If none of conditions (a) to (c) in the preceding paragraph is met, the CAC must serve notice on the parties that it intends to hold a secret ballot of the workers in that bargaining unit. If, within the next 10 working days, the union asks the CAC not to conduct such a ballot (suspecting that it may not obtain a majority vote in favour of recognition) the CAC will take no further action and the union will *not* be recognised.

Conduct and outcome of a secret ballot for recognition

25.20
If a secret ballot is to take place, the CAC must appoint a qualified independent person (a scrutineer) to conduct the ballot (eg, a person nominated by the Electoral Reform Society or a designated solicitor or accountant), and must inform the parties of the name of the person appointed, the period within which the ballot is to take place, and whether the ballot is to be a workplace or postal ballot (or a combination of both).

25.21
The ballot must be conducted as quickly as possible, usually within 20 working days of the appointment of the independent scrutineer (or within such longer period as the CAC decides is appropriate, given

the number and distribution of workers in the relevant bargaining unit). As indicated in the previous paragraph, the ballot may be held either at the workplace or by post (or by a combination of both methods (eg, if the workers are scattered throughout Great Britain or are 'on the road' or at sea at the time the ballot is to be held).

25.22

Both the employer and the union (or unions) concerned must cooperate with the CAC in the conduct of the ballot and must share the costs. The employer must (within 10 working days) supply the CAC with a list of the names and home addresses of the workers in the agreed or declared bargaining unit (but must not give that same information to the union). It must nonetheless allow the union reasonable access to all of those workers in that unit in order to solicit votes and ascertain their opinions. If asked to do so by the union, the independent scrutineer appointed by the CAC must send any pamphlets or other material to the home addresses of the workers entitled to vote in the ballot, provided the union bears all postage and other costs associated with sending that information to those workers.

25.23

If the employer does not cooperate with the union(s) or with the independent scrutineer appointed to conduct the ballot, or denies the union reasonable access to the workers entitled to vote in the ballot, or is dilatory in supplying the CAC with the names and home addresses of the workers in the relevant bargaining unit, the CAC may order the employer to take the appropriate remedial steps within a specified period. Should the employer refuse or fail to comply with the order, the CAC may declare the union to be recognised; in which event it must take steps to cancel the ballot; or (if the ballot has already taken place) must ignore its outcome.

Ballot result

25.24

Once the ballot has been held and the votes counted, the CAC must inform the employer and the union of the outcome. The CAC must declare the union to be recognised if, but only if, recognition was supported by a majority of those who voted in the ballot *and* by at least 40 per cent of those entitled to vote.

25.25

To give an example: let us assume that the relevant bargaining unit comprises 100 workers, 60 of whom cast their votes in the ballot. If recognition is supported by 39 of those who voted, that would constitute a majority vote (65 per cent) in support of recognition – but only by the workers who actually voted. But that does not amount to the required 40 per cent support by the 100 workers who were entitled to vote. In such a case, the CAC must declare that the trade union has not been recognised. If just one more worker had voted in favour of recognition, the outcome would have been different.

25.26

If recognition *is* supported by a majority of those who voted in the ballot *and* by 40 per cent or more of those entitled to vote, the CAC must declare the trade union to be recognised as having collective bargaining rights in respect of the workers who comprise the relevant bargaining unit (limited to negotiations in relation to pay, working hours and holidays, although, as was indicated earlier in this section, there is nothing to prevent the parties agreeing to expand the scope of negotiations).

25.27

If, within the next 30 working days, the parties are unable to agree on a method for conducting collective bargaining, they may ask the CAC to intervene. If there is no agreement within the next 20 working days, the CAC must specify the method for collective bargaining (unless the parties jointly and expressly ask it not to do so); but, again, that method will apply only to negotiations over pay, working hours and holidays, although the parties may agree to vary it to cover other matters as well.

25.28

If the parties agree a method of collective bargaining (either with or without the assistance of the CAC), one of those parties may apply to CAC for help in brokering a second, more acceptable agreement. If the parties are still unable to agree, the CAC will impose a bargaining procedure.

Any method of collective bargaining imposed by the CAC is legally binding on both the employer and the union, and may be enforced by a court order. A failure to comply with such an order (by either of the parties) will ordinarily constitute a contempt of court, with all that that entails.

No further application within three years

25.29
Once an application for trade union recognition has been decided (eg, if there has been no CAC declaration for recognition), that decision may not be re-opened for another three years.

TRAINING

25.30
Once a trade union has been recognised by the CAC as having collective bargaining rights on behalf of a bargaining unit, and the CAC has specified a method for the conduct of such bargaining (unless the parties have varied or replaced that method or have agreed that the method is not to be legally enforceable), the employer must, from time to time, invite the trade union to send representatives to a meeting for the purpose of:

(a) consulting about the employer's policy on training the workers within the bargaining unit;

(b) consulting about his plans for training those workers within the period of six months following the date on which the meeting takes place; and

(c) reporting about the training provided for those workers since the previous meeting.

25.31
Training meetings must be called at six-monthly intervals, starting with the date on which the CAC declaration for recognition was made. At least two weeks before each scheduled meeting, the employer must provide the trade union with any information it needs to enable it to participate fully in the meeting, save for:

(a) information relating to a particular individual, unless the individual has consented to its being disclosed;

(b) information communicated to the employer in confidence;

(c) information whose disclosure would cause substantial injury to the employer's business interests (other than its effect on collective bargaining); or

(d) information whose disclosure would be against the interests of national security or that the employer may not disclose without breaking the law or that has been obtained by the employer for the purposes of bringing, prosecuting or defending any legal proceedings.

An employer must take account of any written representations about matters raised at a training meeting that he receives from the trade union within four weeks of the date on which the meeting took place (*ibid* section 70B).

Complaint to an employment tribunal

25.32
A trade union may present a complaint to an employment tribunal that an employer has failed to comply with his obligations (in relation to a bargaining unit) under section 70B of the 1992 Act. The complaint must be presented within three months of the employer's alleged failure.

25.33
Should the trade union's complaint be upheld, the tribunal will make a declaration to that effect and may order the employer to pay up to two weeks' pay to each person who, at the time when the employer's failure occurred, was a member of the bargaining unit in question. For these purposes, the amount of a week's pay is subject to a maximum of £240 (2001/2002) (*ibid* section 70C).

DETRIMENTAL TREATMENT OF WORKERS

25.34
Part VIII of Schedule A1 to the 1992 Act cautions employers that a worker has the right not to be subjected to any detriment by any act (or by any deliberate failure to act) by his (or her) employer if the act or failure to act takes place because the worker:

(a) sought to prevent or secure trade union recognition; or

(b) supported or did not support his employer's proposal to recognise a trade union; or

(c) acted to prevent or secure the ending of collective bargaining arrangements, or indicated that he did or did not support the ending of those arrangements; or

(d) influenced or sought to influence the way in which fellow workers cast their votes in a CAC ballot relating to trade union recognition; or influenced or sought to influence other workers to vote or to abstain from voting in the ballot; or

(e) voted in such a ballot; or

(f) failed or declined (or proposed to fail or decline) to do any of the things referred to in paragraphs (a) to (e).

In other words, a worker must not be disciplined or otherwise victimised or punished (eg, forfeiture of an expected pay rise, or denial of opportunities for overtime, transfer, promotion, training, etc) for doing anything he (or she) is lawfully entitled to do in the context of a valid request (or an application to the CAC) for trade union recognition.

25.35

On a successful complaint to an employment tribunal, the employer in question will be ordered to pay the worker such compensation as the tribunal considers 'just and equitable' in the circumstances, having regard to the infringement complained of and to any loss sustained by the complainant that is attributable to the employer's conduct or failure to act.

25.36

A worker has no need to resign (or to terminate the contract under which he or she has been employed or engaged) in order to pursue a complaint of unlawful detrimental treatment. Nor are there any qualifying requirements in terms of age or length of service. However, the complaint must be presented within three months of the alleged detrimental treatment.

25.37

A worker, who is not an employee, whose detrimental treatment effectively amounts to a dismissal, will be awarded compensation equivalent to the compensation he (or she) would have been awarded by an employment tribunal if, had he been an employee, he had successfully pursued a complaint of unfair dismissal against his former employer.

Dismissal of an employee

25.38

A worker who is an employee, who has been dismissed (or selected for redundancy) for doing any of the things referred to in the previous paragraphs (relative to a request, or application to the CAC, for trade union recognition), may complain to an employment tribunal regardless of his (or her) age or length of service at the material tribunal. If such a complaint is upheld, the employer in question will be ordered to pay a substantial amount of compensation (as to which, please turn to Chapter 5, paras 5.167 to 5.178). See also para 5.27.

Human Rights Act 1998

Overview

26.1

The Human Rights Act 1998, which came into force on 2 October 2000, gives 'further effect' to the rights and freedoms guaranteed to all citizens under the European Convention on Human Rights & Fundamental Freedoms made at Rome on 4 November 1950. The 1998 Act does not create any new statutory or common law rights. What it *does* do is impose a duty on 'public authorities' (government departments, local authorities, borough councils, the police, health authorities and the like) to act in a way that is compatible with a Convention right. It likewise imposes a duty on the tribunals and courts (as public authorities in their own right), when determining a question which has arisen in connection with a Convention right, to take into account any relevant judgment, decision, declaration or advisory opinion of the European Court of Human Rights (ECHR); any opinion or decision of the European Commission of Human Rights; and any decision of the Committee of Ministers under Article 46 (as to the jurisdiction of the ECHR). Furthermore, without affecting their validity, continuing operation or enforcement, UK primary and subordinate legislation (eg, statutes, regulations and orders) must be read and given effect in a way that is compatible with the Convention rights (*ibid* s. 3).

Practical guidance

26.2

It is important to bear in mind that the Human Rights Act 1998 has 'vertical direct effect' only. This means that while civil servants and public sector employees may sue their employers (government departments, local authorities, borough councils, the police and other public or quasi-public authorities) for damages arising out of an alleged breach of their Convention rights, that same option is not available to workers in the private sector. Private sector workers, who are pursuing complaints or claims against their employers before the tribunals or courts, alleging a breach of one or other of their statutory or contractual rights, may rely on (or pray in aid) a particular Convention right during the subsequent proceedings, but may not bring proceedings against their employer solely on the basis of an alleged breach of that right. They may, on the other hand, legitimately expect the tribunal or court entertaining their complaints or claims to interpret UK law in a way that is compatible with their Convention rights and to take account of any judgement or decision of the ECHR (and related Strasbourg-based institutions) that may have a bearing on the proceedings.

26.3
For example, an employee in the private sector, who has been dismissed for misusing his (or her) employer's facilities (eg by playing computer games during working hours or by making too many private phone calls, or by accessing or downloading inappropriate material from the Internet), or for turning into work scruffily dressed, or for questioning a supervisor's judgement in a particular situation, and so on, may be prompted to pursue a complaint of unfair dismissal before an employment tribunal. But that same employee cannot institute proceedings before a tribunal or court solely on the ground that his employer's actions infringed his Convention right to respect for his private and family life (Article 8), or his right to freedom of expression (Article 10), and so on.

THE CONVENTION RIGHTS

26.4
Widespread speculation about the likely impact of the Human Rights Act includes the suggestion that employers should undertake a wholesale review of their job application forms and reconsider the propriety of asking questions about a job applicant's age or date of birth, marital status, sex, current and recent health problems, attendance record with a previous employer or willingness to wear a uniform while on duty. There have been suggestions also that an employer's imposition of a dress code could infringe a worker's right to 'freedom of expression' under Article 10 of the Convention. Still others, that using CCTV surveillance and intercepting workers' telephone calls and e-mails without their knowledge, might also amount to an infringement of their Article 10 rights, unless wholly justified. What then are workers' rights under the Convention and how well-informed are such suggestions?

Many of the rights and freedoms guaranteed under the European Convention (listed in Schedule 1 to the 1998 Act), such as the right to life, the prohibition of torture (or of slavery and forced labour), have little relevance to the modern workplace. Those that are relevant or may have a bearing on the development of employment policies and procedures are Articles 8, 9, 10, 11 and 14.

Article 8: Right to respect for private and family life

26.5

In *Halford v United Kingdom* ([1997] IRLR 471), the ECHR held that telephone calls from business premises may be covered by notions of 'private life' and 'correspondence' within the meaning of Article 8 of the Convention. Article 8 states that 'everyone has the right to respect for his private and family life, his home and his correspondence'. The European Court rejected the UK Government's submission that employers should, in principle, be at liberty to monitor their employees' telephone calls without their prior knowledge. The Court ruled (an important point) that, as Ms Halford was unaware that the private and business calls she made from her office were liable to be intercepted, she was entitled to assume that her right to privacy would be respected.

26.6

Employers, nonetheless, have every right to expect their employees to carry out their duties efficiently and productively, and not spend their working hours making or receiving private phone calls, misusing fax and e-mail facilities, or 'surfing' (or downloading inappropriate or illegal material from) the Internet for their own purposes. Indeed, employees caught misusing or abusing their employer's facilities in this way can expect to be disciplined and, in serious cases, summarily dismissed (eg if caught emailing offensive, obscene, sexist, racist, libellous or defamatory messages or material to fellow employees or to clients, customers, friends or others outside the organisation).

26.7

The situation has since been regularised by the Telecommunications (Lawful Business Practice) (Interception of Communications) Regulations 2000 (SI 2000/2699), which came into force on 24 October 2000. The 2000 Regulations were made under Section 4(2) of the Regulation of Investigatory Powers Act 2000, which imports the

EU Telecoms Data Protection Directive (97/66/EC) into UK domestic legislation. Under these Regulations, employers may legitimately monitor or record all telecommunications transmitted over their systems, without the consent of the people using those systems, if that monitoring or recording is done to establish the existence of facts, or to ascertain compliance with regulatory or self-regulatory practices or procedures. They may do so also for quality control purposes, for the prevention or detection of crime, for investigating or detecting unauthorised use of the telecoms system, or for ensuring the effective operation of their telecommunications systems. Employers may also monitor (but not keep a record of) telephone calls or e-mail transmissions to check whether the communications in question are relevant to the employer's business.

26.8
Employers must nonetheless 'make all reasonable efforts' to inform employees that their phone calls, e-mail transmissions, etc may be intercepted. This can best be achieved by posting notices to the like effect on (or adjacent to) telephones and PCs cautioning employees that unauthorised use might well result in disciplinary action or dismissal. It is as well to add that employers are under no legal obligation to inform third parties (ie outside callers) that their calls or incoming e-mails may be monitored or recorded.

26.9
Employers should take appropriate steps to inform new recruits and existing employees that their telephone calls, e-mail transmissions and use of the Internet are likely to be monitored and/or recorded. So far as job applicants and new recruits are concerned, this is best done at the pre-employment interview and during induction training. The same applies to CCTV surveillance of sensitive work areas, body searches, sick visits, and random drug testing. Staff and works handbooks should clearly state the employer's policy on such matters, reinforced (especially when CCTV cameras are present) by suitable notices posted about the workplace.

26.10
In keeping with their Article 8 rights, employees should not be denied the opportunity to make and receive private phone calls when there is an urgent domestic crisis (eg a sick or injured relation, a death in the family, a gas explosion at home, a burst water pipe

and the like) that requires their immediate attention. Most reasonable employers will permit a limited number of private phone calls from the office or workshop (either with or without the prior permission of supervisors), while others provide payphones for the use of employees when an emergency arises. It is all a question of balance (balancing the legitimate interests of the employer against those of the workforce). An employee who is dismissed for abusing the right to make private phone calls may pursue a complaint of unfair dismissal before an employment tribunal and may rely on Article 8 of the Convention if convinced that his or her employer acted unreasonably in taking the decision to dismiss.

Other Article 8 issues

26.11

The notion advanced by some commentators that it is an infringement of an employee's (or would-be employee's) human rights to require a job applicant to complete a job application form stating his (or her) date of birth, marital status, ages of children, current and previous health and attendance records, criminal convictions, disabilities and the like is absurd. The need for such information can be justified on a variety or practical and legal grounds. For instance, an employer will need to know an employee's date of birth to ensure compliance with (amongst others) the National Minimum Wage Act 1998, the Management of Health & Safety at Work Regulations 1999 and legislation prohibiting or restricting the employment of young persons and school-age children in certain occupations. Such information is also necessary in order to calculate an employee's entitlement to a redundancy payment, and for pension and actuarial reasons. Information about an employee's disabilities or current and previous health record is necessary to enable the employer to make the 'appropriate adjustments' to the workplace and to ensure that the person in question is not unwittingly engaged in work involving exposure to dangerous chemicals, processes or substances, or in any work calculated to exacerbate an existing disease or medical condition.

26.12

In some industries, employers are liable to prosecution if they knowingly employ a new or expectant mother, or a woman who is breastfeeding, in work that is likely to pose a risk to her own health and safety or to that of her new or unborn child. There is a body of UK health and safety legislation that specifically prohibits the employment of such women (indeed, in some circumstances, any woman of child-bearing age) in work involving exposure to physical, biological or chemical agents that are either embryotoxic or regarded as agents causing foetal lesions or likely to disrupt placental attachment. Regulation 18 of the Management of Health & Safety at Work Regulations 1999 states that an employer need not alter the working conditions or hours of work of a woman (or suspend her from work on maternity grounds) if she has refused or neglected to inform him, when asked to do so, that she is pregnant or breastfeeding or has given birth within the previous six months. Given the possible ramifications, it is a nonsense to suggest that it is an invasion of a woman's Article 8 right to privacy to ask such questions.

26.13

An employer who refuses to permit a woman to return to work in a part-time or job-sharing capacity after she has given birth may be able to justify that decision on wholly objective grounds, notwithstanding the *prima facie* infringement of her Article 8 right to respect for her private and family life (see *Home Office v Holmes* [1984] IRLR 299). However, in all such cases, the burden of proof rests squarely on the shoulders of the employer (see also *Kidd v DRG (UK) Limited* [1985] IRLR 190 and *Clymo v Wandsworth London Borough Council* [1989] IRLR 241).

26.14

An employment tribunal will not willingly gainsay an employer's prerogative to reorganise the pattern of working hours (or to introduce a system of shifts) in the interests of greater business efficiency or profitability. However, when contemplating any such reorganisation, employers should nonetheless consult with the affected employees and take into account any attendant disruption to their family and domestic commitments. In short, they should act, and be seen to have acted, 'reasonably'. In *United Bank Limited v Akhtar* ([1989] IRLR), an employee with a sick wife and two small children was held to have been constructively dismissed (notwithstanding a mobility clause in his contract) when he found it impossible to comply with his employer's unreasonable request to transfer to another branch of the bank within the next six days.

Article 9: Freedom of thought, conscience and religion

26.15
Article 9 of the Convention allows that 'Everyone has the right to freedom of thought, conscience and religion. This right includes freedom to change his religion or belief and freedom, either alone or in community with others and in public or private, to manifest his religion or belief, in worship, teaching, practice and observance'.

26.16
In *Ahmad v ILEA* ([1981] EHRR CD 168), an employer refused to allow a Mr Ahmad, one of his employees and a devout Muslim, to take 45 minutes off work every Friday to attend prayers at his local mosque. Mr Ahmad, a primary-school teacher, resigned in protest and subsequently presented a complaint of unfair constructive dismissal to an employment tribunal. In evidence, it was revealed that his employer had offered to reduce Mr Ahmad's working hours from a five-day week to one of four-and-a-half days; but he had refused to accept that offer on the grounds that he would suffer a loss of pay and benefits. By a majority decision, the tribunal held that, notwithstanding Article 9 of the European Convention, Mr Ahmad had no legal or contractual right to take time off work for religious worship, whether paid or otherwise. Mr Ahmad's attempts to pursue the matter before the ECHR were ruled inadmissible by the European Commission on Human Rights. They held that Mr Ahmad's employers had properly considered his Article 9 rights by offering to reduce his working hours to enable him to attend the local mosque in his own time.

26.17
In a not dissimilar case, that of *Stedman v UK* ([1997] 23 EHRR CD 168), a Ms Stedman, who was contracted to work on Sundays, was dismissed when she refused to do so. Such work, she said, offended her religious sensibilities. The European Commission on Human Rights decided that it was Ms Stedman's refusal to comply with her contractual obligations, not her religious beliefs, that had led to her being dismissed. She was well aware, when she applied for the job, that she would be required to work on Sundays. If she did not wish to do so, she should not applied for the job in the first place.

26.18
Save for Northern Ireland, it is not yet unlawful in the UK to discriminate against job applicants or existing employees because of

their religious beliefs or affiliations. With the coming into force of the Human Rights Act 1998, any employee who is dismissed or forced to resign, either for observing or promoting his (or her) religious duties or beliefs or for persistent bullying or harassment at the hands of unsympathetic or bigoted colleagues and supervisors, may pray Convention Article 10 in aid of his contention that he had been unfairly dismissed – the more so if the evidence shows that the employer had done little or nothing to put an end to such treatment or abuse. The employee may also bring an action for damages arising out of his employee's breach of the duty of trust and confidence implicit in every contract of employment.

Article 10: Freedom of expression

26.19
'Everyone', says Convention Article 10, 'has the right to freedom of expression.' While employees undoubtedly have the right to propound their views on a variety of topics, they do not have the right (certainly not in the workplace) to create an unhealthy atmosphere or to disrupt the smooth and efficient running of their employer's business by making critical remarks to (or in the presence of) clients or customers. Nor can they expect to escape disciplinary action or dismissal if they make rude, offensive, racist or sexist remarks to fellow employees.

Standards of dress and appearance

26.20
In spite of suggestions to the contrary, the long-standing right of employers to prescribe minimum standards of dress and appearance amongst their employees is unlikely to be affected by the Human Rights Act 1998. Case law has long since endorsed (and will continue to endorse) the right of employers to dismiss or discipline workers who stubbornly refuse to dress smartly or decently, or who fail to comply with accepted standards of personal cleanliness and hygiene. There is legislation, for example, that prohibits eating, drinking or smoking (not to mention the use of cosmetics) on health and safety grounds (eg the Control of Substances Hazardous to Health Regulations 1999). Under the Food Safety (General Food Hygiene) Regulations 1995, 'food workers' must comply with certain hygiene standards when handling 'open food', and so on.

Uniforms and protective clothing

26.21

It is not open to the employment tribunals to undermine or challenge the right of employers to run their businesses efficiently and profitability (*Schmidt v Austicks Bookshops Limited* [1977] IRLR 360; *Boychuk v Symons Holdings Limited* [1977] IRLR 395). If employees are required by their contracts to wear uniforms or protective clothing while at work (in order to convey a corporate image, or in the interests of health, safety or hygiene), they can expect to be disciplined or dismissed for refusing to do so, and are unlikely to receive a great deal of sympathy when they allude to a supposed infringement of their Article 10 rights when pursuing complaints of unfair dismissal before the employment tribunals.

26.22

Flight attendants, waiters, chefs, ticket collectors, bus conductors, security guards, receptionists, cashiers, shop assistants, postal workers, housekeepers in hotels, etc are likewise unlikely to persuade a tribunal (let alone the European Court) that the uniforms they are required to wear under their contracts infringe their right to 'freedom of expression' under Article 10 of the Convention. Nor is a tribunal likely to accept the contention that wearing a uniform is unnecessary on the grounds that it has no effect whatsoever on an employee's ability to carry out his (or her) duties efficiently or safely (*Burrett v West Birmingham Health Authority* [1994] IRLR 7). In *Smith v Safeway plc* ([1996] IRLR 456), the Court of Appeal held that a male employee had been fairly dismissed for refusing to cut his long hair, even though the same requirement did not apply to female workers. In *Panesar v Nestlé* ([1980] ICR 144), a Sikh was held to have been justifiably rejected for employment as a food worker because of his refusal to shave off his beard on religious grounds.

26.23

However, notwithstanding *Schmidt* (*qv*), an employer's arbitrary refusal to allow a woman to wear tailored trousers to work, instead of a skirt, is nowadays likely to be challenged as amounting to unlawful discrimination under the Sex Discrimination Act 1975 (*Owen v The Professional Golfers Association* (1999), unreported).

Tattoos, body piercing, etc

26.24

An employer's rules relating to unsightly or offensive tattoos, facial and body piercing, outrageous hairstyles and the like, may, of course, be challenged before the tribunal courts in support of a complainant's contention that his (or her) dismissal for failing to comply with such rules was not only unfair but an infringement of his rights under Convention Article 10. Such a challenge would be unlikely to succeed if the employee's duties involved work with 'open food' or routine and face-to-face contact with members of the general public. However, a consistent approach is important. In *Harris v McDonalds* (COIT 1392/25), a female employee, with barely noticeable tattoos on her fingers and arms, and whose work brought her into direct contact with customers, was held to have been unlawfully discriminated against when it was revealed in evidence that her employers had not taken similar action against male employees with clearly-visible tattoos on *their* forearms.

Article 11: Freedom of assembly and association

26.25

Article 11 states that 'Everyone has the right to freedom of peaceful assembly and to freedom of association with others, including the right to form and to join trade unions for the protection of his interests.'

26.26

The right of a worker to be or not to be or to remain a member of, or to refuse to join, an independent trade union, or any trade union, and the concomitant right of such a worker not to be discriminated against, disciplined, dismissed or selected for redundancy for exercising that right (or for participating 'at an appropriate time' in the activities of an independent trade union), has long since been entrenched in UK domestic legislation (notably, the Trade Union & Labour Relations (Consolidation) Act 1992). Indeed, any employee who is dismissed or selected for redundancy (or otherwise discriminated against) because of his (or her) membership or non-membership of a trade union may complain to an employment tribunal and is likely to be awarded a substantial amount of compensation if his complaint is upheld (as to which, please turn to Chapter 5, para 5.26 and Chapter 6, paras 6.2 to 6.12).

Article 14: Prohibition of discrimination

26.27
Article 10 of the Convention cautions that 'The enjoyment of the rights and freedoms set forth in this Convention shall be secured without discrimination on any grounds such as sex, race, colour, language, religion, political or other opinion, national or social origin, association with a national minority, property, birth or other status.'

26.28
UK domestic legislation currently prohibits discrimination on grounds of sex, marital status, gender reassignment, race, colour, nationality, national or ethnic origins, disability and trade union membership or non-membership. In Northern Ireland only, it is unlawful to discriminate against job applicants and existing employees because of their political opinions or religious affiliations. Article 10's prohibition of discrimination on 'any grounds' suggests that the list is by no means exhaustive and could be said to encompass discrimination on grounds of age, religion and sexual orientation. Whether or not workers can pray Article 14 in aid of their contention that they had been unfairly or unlawfully dismissed (or discriminated against on such grounds) remains to be seen – the more so as Article 10 is not a free-standing right but merely provides that 'the enjoyment of the rights and freedoms set forth in [the] Convention shall be secured without discrimination on any ground...'. Regrettably, there is little, if any, relevant ECHR case law on the subject.

26.29
On 27 November 2000, the European Council adopted Council Directive 2000/78/EC, establishing 'a general framework for the respect of the principle of equal treatment between persons irrespective of race or ethnic origin, religion or belief, disability, age, or sexual orientation. The new Directive covers access to employment and occupation, promotion, vocational training, employment and working conditions, and membership of certain bodies'. The UK (along with other EU Member States) must import the Directive into its domestic legislation by 2 December 2003, at the latest, although legislation outlawing discrimination on grounds of age need not be introduced until 2 December 2006.

FURTHER INFORMATION

26.30
The Home Office has published an introductory guide to the Human Rights Act titled: *Human Rights Act: An introduction,* and a more detailed *Study Guide,* copies of which may be obtained by telephoning 0845 600 1151 or Minicom 0845 600 0347.

26.31
The reader is also commended to the Data Protection Commissioner's *CCTV Code of Practice* and a related document titled *Telecoms Guidance,* either or both of which will be supplied on request by telephoning the Commissioner's Office on 01625 545745. The documents may also be downloaded from the following Web site: www.dataprotection.gov.uk.

Tribunals and courts in action

GENERAL INFORMATION

27.1

Employment tribunals (formerly known as 'industrial tribunals'), of which scores sit each day in various parts of the country, are independent courts presided over by a legally qualified chairman who is usually accompanied by two lay members. The latter are specialists in the field of industrial relations, one being drawn from the employer's side of industry; the other from the trade unions. The chairman (and this includes female 'chairmen') is responsible for taking a note of the proceedings and of any argument. This is the only official record of the evidence. It will not be a verbatim account, but the essence of the evidence given and any submissions will be written down.

27.2

The members (and chairman) must have no connection with the case before them. This includes knowing any witnesses or being related to them or having a financial interest in a firm that is before the tribunal (*University of Swansea v Cornelius* [1988] ICR 735, EAT). If there is such a connection, it must be disclosed. Failure to do so will result in the findings of the tribunal being set aside and a retrial ordered. It matters not that there was no evidence of bias by the individual: justice must be seen to be done (*R v Mulvihill, The Times*, 13 July 1989, CA).

27.3

If there is alleged to be some misbehaviour or dereliction of duty by a chairman or a member, this must be raised at the hearing. The chairman should be asked to make a note of the complaint. Although justice has to be done, it cannot be done on an appeal unless there is some record of what was alleged to have happened. An allegation was made on an appeal that a member had fallen asleep during the proceedings. Enquiries were made of the member who refuted the charge. It was held that as no complaint had been lodged at the hearing itself, in the course of which there were a number of adjournments, an impartial observer would not have thought that any injustice had been caused. The appeal was dismissed (*Red Bank Manufacturing Co Ltd v Meadows* [1992] ICR 204, EAT).

27.4
The intention is that the proceedings should be as informal as possible. All the parties should feel at ease. Tribunals do follow, in substance, the ordinary procedure applicable in the courts in the presentation of evidence.

27.5
There is power, with the consent of both parties, for the tribunal to adjudicate with the chairman and one member only sitting. This might arise if one of the two members were to become ill shortly before a case was scheduled to commence. Where one party has failed to enter an appearance and consequently cannot take part in the proceedings, then only the consent of the other party need be obtained (*Comber v Harmony Inns Ltd* [1994] ICR 15, EAT) (*Source*: ETCRP Regs 1993, Reg 7(1)&(3)).

27.6
When all three are sitting, the majority view prevails but, where there are two, the chairman has a casting vote in the event of a disagreement. Surprisingly, there is unanimity in about 96 per cent of cases. This shows the degree of objectivity applied in this sensitive area (*Source*: ETCRP Regs 1993, Sch 1, Rule 10(1)).

27.7
Chairmen are empowered to hear the following claims sitting on their own:

- a complaint by an employee under section 68A of TULRA 1992 that his (or her) employer has made a deduction from his wages in contravention of section 68 (Right not to suffer deduction of unauthorised or excessive trade union subscriptions) (s. 68A);

- a complaint by an employee that his employer has failed (wholly or in part) to pay remuneration under a protective award (s. 192);

- an application for interim relief by an employee who has presented a complaint of unfair dismissal on grounds relating to trade union membership or activities (s. 161);

- an application by an employer (or by an employee) for the revocation or variation of an order for interim relief (s. 165);

- an application by an employee on the grounds that his employer has failed to comply with the terms of an order for interim relief (s. 166);

- a complaint by an employee under section 126 of the Pension Schemes Act 1993 that the Secretary of State has failed to pay the whole or part of his insolvent employer's unpaid contributions into an occupational (or personal) pension scheme (s. 126, Pension Schemes Act 1993);

- a reference by an employee concerning his employer's failure to provide (a) a written statement of employment particulars, or (b) a written statement of a change in any of the particulars to be included in the written statement, or (c) an itemised pay statement (ERA 1996, s. 11);

- a reference concerning (a) an employee's right (or otherwise) to a redundancy payment, or (b) the amount of a redundancy payment (ERA 1996, s. 163);

- a reference by an employee concerning the Secretary of State's refusal or failure to pay a redundancy payment (or to pay any substitute amount under the terms of an exemption order) that remains unpaid because of the employer's insolvency (ERA 1996, s. 170);

- a complaint by an employee that his employer has made an unlawful deduction from his wages or has demanded (and received) an unlawful payment in contravention of Part II of the Employment Rights Act 1996 (*Protection of Wages*) (ERA 1996, s. 23);

- a complaint by an employee that his employer has failed to pay the whole or any part of a guarantee payment to which the employee is entitled (ERA 1996, s. 34);

- a complaint by an employee that the Secretary of State has failed to pay out of the National Insurance Fund certain monies owed to the employee by his insolvent employer (ERA 1996, s. 188);

- a complaint by an employee that his employer has failed to pay the remuneration due to him in respect of a period of suspension on medical grounds (ERA 1996, s. 70(1) relating to s. 64);

- a complaint concerning the appointment by an employment tribunal of an 'appropriate person' to institute or continue proceedings under the Employment Rights Act 1996 on behalf of a deceased employee (ERA 1996, s. 206(4)); and

- a complaint concerning an employer's failure to pay the whole or part of an award of compensation (ordered by an employment tribunal to be paid) in respect of his failure to inform or consult *appropriate representatives* in advance about a proposed TUPE transfer (TUPE Regs 1981, Reg 11(5)).

Even if a tribunal chairman is entitled to hear a reference, complaint or application alone, he (or she) may nonetheless order that it be heard by a full tribunal if there is a likelihood of a dispute on the facts arising. In doing so, he would have regard to the views of the parties, and whether there are other proceedings taking place that cannot be heard by him acting alone.

A Minister of the Crown may direct, on grounds of national security, that specified proceedings should be heard and determined by the President of the Employment Tribunals sitting alone.

(*Source*: Employment Tribunals Act 1996, s. 4(2) & (5), as amended by the Employment Rights (Dispute Resolution) Act 1998, s. 3.)

27.8
The parties presenting and responding to a complaint before an employment tribunal hearing are not expected to know a great deal. It is for the chairman to distil the evidence and to apply the law. For example, an employee may have presented a complaint to the effect that he (or she) is entitled to compensation for unfair dismissal. The strict legal position may be that he is entitled only to a statutory redundancy payment (*Murphy v Epsom College* [1985] ICR 80, CA).

27.9
If one of the parties is unrepresented at the hearing and appears to have little understanding of the law, the chairman will elicit any pertinent information by asking questions of the parties. It is the

duty of the tribunal to establish the relevant facts and to seek out the truth. The two lay members will also ask questions, although this is usually done when a witness has finished giving his (or her) evidence. It is not incumbent on chairmen to raise points on behalf of a party, especially if the party is represented (albeit incompetently), although in practice they generally do. It is up to each side to ensure that they are aware of any technicalities that may be fatal or do serious damage to their cases (*Dimtsu v Westminster City Council* [1991] IRLR 450, EAT).

COMMENCEMENT OF A CASE

27.10
Proceedings before an employment tribunal will be instituted (that is to say, set in motion) when an applicant (usually an employee or trade union) completes Form IT1 (*Originating Application to an Employment Tribunal*) and 'presents' it to the address specified on the form itself or to:

> The Secretary to the Tribunals
> Central Office of the Employment Tribunals
> 7th Floor
> 19–29 Woburn Place
> London WC1H 0LU

(*Source*: Employment Tribunals [Constitution & Rules of Procedure] ('ETCRP') Regulations 1993 (SI 1993/2687) Sch 1, Rule 1.)

27.11
To be valid the Originating Application must identify:

- the name and address of the applicant;

- the names and addresses of the person or persons against whom relief is sought; and

- the grounds, with particulars thereof, on which relief is sought (unfair dismissal, race discrimination, etc) (*Dodd v British Telecommunications plc* [1988] ICR 116, EAT).

Once received by the Secretary to the Tribunals, Form IT1 is said to have been 'presented'. Although an originating application can be presented in the form of a letter, applicants are best-advised to complete Form IT1, copies of which are readily available (or should be) from local offices of the Department of Employment or from Citizens Advice Bureaux. Form IT1 provides guidance on completing the form and explains what particulars need to be included.

27.12
The employer ('the respondent') will be sent a copy of the Originating Application and a Notice of Appearance (Form IT3) which he should complete and return to the Secretary to the Tribunals (or to the address given on the form) within the next 21 days (*Source*: ETCRP Regs 1993, Sch 1 Rule 3). If the respondent employer has a valid reason for not returning Form IT3 on time, he may apply for an extension of time, which is usually granted. If refused, because the grounds for the delay are unacceptable, the only way to reverse that decision is by way of an appeal; but the employer may find that it cannot be overturned (*Ryan Plant International Ltd v Price* [1976] ICR 424, QBD; and *'7' Snooker Club v Shirley*, 28 April 1988, EAT).

27.13
There is no obligation on either party (applicant or respondent) to give a detailed explanation when lodging a complaint or a rebuttal in the Originating Application or Notice of Appearance. If an employer is relying on a particular ground (or reason), it is unlikely that he will be permitted to change that reason at the subsequent tribunal hearing. In one case, an employer originally resisted a complaint of unfair dismissal on the grounds that he had sacked the employee for being 'inefficient'. At the subsequent hearing, he was debarred from alleging that the real reason was suspected dishonesty. So too when an employer, who originally relied on 'redundancy' as the reason for dismissal, was refused permission at the tribunal hearing to change it to another ground (*Hotson v Wisbech Conservative Club* [1984] IRLR 422, EAT; and *Nelson v BBC* [1977] ITR 273, CA).

27.14
An employee alleged in her Originating Application that her employer had refused to permit her to return to work after maternity leave. She sought an order that she should be allowed to do so under her contract of employment. It was held that her 'pleadings' should be widely construed and so include, by inference, a claim for unfair dismissal (*Leffen v Bexley London BC, The Times*, 14 November 1985, EAT).

27.15
If an employment tribunal rejects an employer's stated reason for dismissal (eg lack of capability) – in spite of his having produced evidence to support that reason – and decides on the evidence that the real reason for the dismissal was misconduct, the employer's failure to apply the correct label will not necessarily result in a finding of unfair dismissal. But where the employer relies on a particular reason, but fails to prove it, the dismissal is likely to be held unfair (*William Muir (Bond 9) Ltd v Wood*, 21 August 1986, EAT; and *Smith v City of Glasgow DC* [1987] ICR 796, HL).

27.16
An application to amend either of the Originating Application or the Notice of Appearance can always be made during the course of proceedings to enable the tribunal to adjudicate on the point. This will generally be granted, so long as this does not prejudice the other party's case.

NOTICES

27.17
Any notice, or other document or letter posted to the address specified by the parties in the Originating Application or Notice of Appearance (or to any notified change of address) is deemed, without further proof, to have been properly served upon that party. If the latter claims not to have received it, then the onus of disproving receipt will be on the party in question. It is important to keep the tribunal informed of any changes of address. A case cannot proceed until a respondent has been served with his (or her) copy of the Originating Application and Notice of Appearance. It follows that it is essential for an applicant to provide his (or her) former employer's current address or, if that is not possible, his registered address, if any (*Source*: Interpretation Act 1978, s. 15).

27.18
Once a party has given an address for service, it would seem that documents sent to that address, but returned to the tribunal by the post office, would still constitute good service. This would enable a tribunal to strike out a claim where a case was not being pursued and the applicant had disappeared.

'FURTHER PARTICULARS'

27.19

Either party has the right to see the nature of the other's case in the pleadings. A party who needs to know more about the other party's case is entitled to ask for 'Further Particulars'. For example: 'What is the exact nature of the incompetence alleged?' 'Is it alleged that the discrimination was direct or indirect?' The tribunal of its own motion may also ask for further particulars in order to clarify the issues or assist in some other way (*International Computers Ltd v Whitley* [1978] IRLR 318, EAT). What a party cannot do is to use the 'further particulars' procedure in an attempt to find out the evidence to be adduced by the other side or the names of their witnesses. The procedure is only available to enable justice to be done, by identifying matters in issue, ie to know the case that has to be met (*Byrne & Others v The Financial Times Ltd* [1991] IRLR 417, EAT).

27.20

An applicant employee who had been dismissed for taking part in industrial action claimed that another person, who had also taken part, had not been sacked. If this was correct, the tribunal had power to adjudicate on the dismissal (see Chapter 5, paras 5.9 and 5.10). It was held that the former employers were entitled to know the identity of that other person so as to be able to challenge the employee's contention. It mattered not that revealing that other employee's name would enable the employers to dismiss that employee, thereby defeating the applicant's claim (*P & O European Ferries (Dover) Ltd v Byrne* [1989] IRLR 245, CA).

27.21

A party who refuses or fails to supply further particulars voluntarily may be ordered to do so, so long as those particulars:

- are relevant;
- are not oppressive; and
- will help in fairly disposing of the case or incurring costs.

But complicated pleading battles are discouraged by the tribunals. The line can sometimes be a fine one. Further particulars relating to damages are generally not ordered until liability has been determined in favour of an employee (*Colonial Mutual Life Assurance Society Ltd v Clinch* [1981] ICR 752, EAT).

27.22
If the applicant employee refuses or fails to comply with an order for further particulars, his (or her) Originating Application will be struck out. If it is the respondent employer who is in default, the Notice of Appearance (or the relevant part of it) will likewise be struck out and the employer will be debarred from defending. In either case, the party in question must be afforded an opportunity of showing cause why an order for disclosure should not be made. When an order against the respondent has been made, the applicant is not entitled to an automatic judgment in his favour. He will still have to prove his case before the tribunal (*Source*: ETCRP Regs 1993, Sch 1 Rule 4(7)).

Interrogatories

27.23
A tribunal or a party is empowered to require a litigant to furnish to the tribunal a written answer to any question if it may clarify any issue likely to arise or assist in the progress of the proceedings. Failure to reply can lead to the applicant's complaint being dismissed or a respondent being debarred from defending the action brought against him (*Source*: ETCRP Regs 1993, Sch 1 Rule 4(3)).

DISCOVERY AND INSPECTION OF DOCUMENTS

27.24
There is power vested in the tribunals to order Discovery and Inspection of Documents where this is necessary for 'fairly disposing of the proceedings or for saving costs'. An order must not be oppressive in the sense of being too demanding financially or physically (*West Midlands Passenger Transport Executive v Singh* [1988] ICR 614, CA) (*Source*: ETCRP Regs 1993, Sch 1 Rule 4(1)(b)).

27.25
In some circumstances, an employer may be reluctant either to produce a document that is highly confidential or to allow such a document to be seen and read by a third party. Before the case comes to a hearing, the document must nonetheless be shown to the

tribunal chairman, who, having seen it, will decide whether it should be disclosed. If the document must be disclosed, the chairman can rule that certain parts be covered up (*Leyland Cars (BL Cars) Ltd v Vyas* [1979] ICR 921, HL).

27.26
The test of whether a document should be disclosed is not its probative value, but whether it might be expected to lead to a line of enquiry that would be of assistance to the other party. The information sought can relate to details of other employees that would normally be protected from disclosure by the Data Protection Act 1984. That can be overridden by a Court or Tribunal Order (*The Captain Gregos*, *The Times*, 22 December 1990, EAT; and *Rowley v Liverpool City Council*, 24 October 1989, CA).

27.27
An order can be sought for the production of relevant statistics, but only if such statistics exists or can be readily produced without any great difficulty or expense. In one case, statistics that showed the relative success rates of white and black applicants for a senior post were ordered to be disclosed. They were 'logically probative' on the issue of discrimination. But where written statements had been obtained from fellow employees on a pledge of confidentiality, an order for disclosure was refused (*West Midlands PTE v Singh* [1988] ICR 614, CA; *Carrington v Helix Lighting Ltd* [1990] ICR 125, EAT; and *Demmel v YKK Fasteners (UK) Ltd*, 17 March 1987, EAT).

27.28
A party may not use the disclosure procedure as a 'fishing expedition' to find evidence upon which to mount a case. But he (or she) may seek an order to improve a *prima facie* case that would not, on its own, have been very strong (*Leverton v Clywd CC* [1989] ICR 33, HL). There is no general obligation on a party to disclose what relevant documents they have in their possession. A party who produces some documents is duty-bound not to withhold others which might mislead the other side to misconstrue the effect of those disclosed (*Birds Eye Walls Ltd v Harrison* [1985] ICR 278, EAT).

27.29
Not all documents have to be produced for inspection. Some may be 'privileged', that is to say, may form part of a special type of

document that came into existence for the purposes of litigation. Examples are briefs to counsel, opinions from counsel, solicitors' letters to clients, and matters of that kind. Such documents must nonetheless be disclosed so that the other side can, in appropriate cases, dispute whether 'privilege' should be attached to them. That privilege does not extend to confidential documents passing between non-professionally qualified advisers and the persons whom they are advising. This is because such advisers are not subject to the control of disciplinary bodies and do not owe a duty to the courts (*New Victoria Hospital v Ryan* [1993] ICR 201, EAT).

27.30

Other documents belonging to public bodies such as a Police Authority are subject to 'public interest immunity'. However, a chairman has power to order disclosure after inspection of them by himself/herself. The chairman has to balance the public interest in non-disclosure against that of justice to the other party, and the importance of any document to the issue to be decided. In short, he (or she) must ensure that there is no repugnance to natural justice (*Halford v Sharples* [1991] ICR 582, CA; and *R v Bromell Re Coventry Evening Newspapers Ltd, The Times*, 28 July 1992, Div Ct). So it was held that documents created as a result of using the grievance procedure were not covered, even though the procedure arose from a police order. Its purpose was to promote non-discriminatory practices and to punish offenders (*Commissioner of Police of the Metropolis v Locker* [1993] ICR 440, EAT).

27.31

Where appropriate, the chairman can order parts to be covered up where they are of little relevance to the issues to be decided, or give instructions that they may only be viewed by the other party's legal advisers.

27.32

If public interest immunity is claimed on the grounds that disclosure might endanger national security, it is generally not appropriate for a tribunal to weigh up the degree of danger involved in deciding whether to make an order that a document be produced. But a court or tribunal must be vigilant to ensure that immunity is only claimed in appropriate circumstances. The ultimate decision rests with the judiciary (*Balfour v Foreign & Commonwealth Office* [1993] ICR 663, EAT).

27.33
Where documents are in the possession of a third party, a tribunal can order that third party to attend the hearing in person and to bring with him (or her), and produce, any documents that are relevant and that will help to dispose fairly of the case or save costs. An order cannot be made for the third party to provide discovery and/or inspection of documents (*Source*: ETCRP Regs 1993, Sch 1 Rule 4(2)(b)).

APPLICATIONS TO AMEND PLEADINGS

27.34
Where a claim is made on one ground, but after the close of pleadings and when all the documents have been inspected, it is thought that the claim would be better placed on another basis, an application to add the additional ground should be made to the tribunal. If the time limit for proffering that other allegation is outside the usual time limits (see Chapter 3, paras 3.68 to 3.78), the tribunal has discretion to allow the amendment having 'regard to all the circumstances of the case. In particular, they should consider any injustice or hardship which may be caused to any of the parties...' (*British Newspapers Printing Corporation (North) Ltd v Kelly & Others* [1989] IRLR 222, CA; and *Clocking v Sandhurst Ltd* [1974] ICR 650, NIRC).

IMPORTANCE OF DOCUMENTS

27.35
A party who plans to use documents at a tribunal hearing, ought to supply copies to the other side *well before* the date set for the hearing. A failure to do so may result in the other side asking for an adjournment to study them, especially if they are bulky or complicated. Indeed, an order for costs 'thrown away' may be made against him (or her) (see paras 27.80 & 27.81 below). Documents are usually the most important part of any case. Often they are self-explanatory and usually provide very compelling evidence.

27.36
If an employer contends in evidence that the applicant employee was dismissed after receiving a number of customer complaints about the

quality of workmanship of the goods made by the employee, the tribunal's acceptance or otherwise of such an allegation may depend on the employer's demeanour in the witness box, which may be good or poor. But, if the employer produces several written complaints from customers in support of the contention, those documents will speak for themselves. Clearly, the applicant employee did produce defective goods. The only question remaining is: 'Why?'.

27.37
Both parties to a tribunal hearing should produce three bundles of documents, numbered consecutively, and bound or stapled in (reverse) chronological order. These should be sent to the tribunal at least one week in advance of the date set for the hearing. This will give the chairman and the lay members an opportunity to read and absorb ahead of the hearing.

COMBINED PROCEEDINGS

27.38
If two or more employees have common matters of fact or law to be decided against the same employer, or it is desirable to make an order, either side may apply for the cases to be heard together. Very often the tribunal of its own motion will raise the matter with the parties. There will be a saving of time and costs if the proceedings are heard together. Although both, or all, the cases will be heard together, the tribunal will nonetheless give its decision for each employee separately. Furthermore, each of the parties is entitled to be separately represented (*Source*: ETCRP 1993, Sch 1, Rule 18). If either party objects, then it is likely that no order will be made, unless the case for it is overwhelming. This latter position could arise where two employees have been dismissed for fighting. It would be undesirable to hear the cases separately. There may have to be a preliminary hearing to decide the point (see paras 27.50 to 27.53 below) (*Courage Ltd v Welsh & Others*, 18 March 1991, EAT).

Joinder and Representative Respondents

27.39
Apart from its powers to 'join' a trade union and/or any other person as a party to any proceedings (eg because that union or other

person is alleged to have used the threat of industrial action to pressurise the employer into dismissing the employee), a tribunal may direct that any person, against whom relief is sought, be also 'joined' as a respondent. However, if that person ceases to be directly interested in the subject of the proceedings, the tribunal may order him (or her) to be dismissed from the action (*Source*: ETCRP Regs 1993, Sch 1 Rule 17). As an application to 'join' is made *ex parte* (eg without notice to the other side), a tribunal has power to hear an application to set the order aside. This may be done by a different chairman (or tribunal, if it was made in the course of proceedings) to that which made the original order (*Reddington & Others v Park Communications Ltd & Others* [1994] ICR 172, EAT).

STRIKING OUT

27.40
A chairman of his (or her) own motion, or on an application being made, is empowered to strike out a pleading if it is found:

- that the contents of an Originating Application or a Notice of Appearance are 'scandalous, frivolous or vexatious'. 'Scandalous' relates to such matters as allegations of dishonesty, or degrading or outrageous conduct that is unrelated to the issues to be decided. 'Frivolous' applies where the claim is bound to fail; and 'vexatious' where the proceedings are brought for the wrong motives (*O'Keefe v Southampton City Council* [1988] ICR 419, EAT)

  The term 'frivolous and vexatious' generally connotes that the claim is unsustainable and constitutes an 'abuse of process'. This power to strike out does not extend to the conduct of a party, eg writing abusive letters to the other side or even to the staff of the tribunal; or

- at any stage, that the manner in which proceedings have been conducted by or on behalf of an applicant or a respondent have been 'scandalous, frivolous or vexatious';

- that there has been 'want of prosecution', eg where an applicant (or his (or her) representative) does not 'press home' his case, eg by failing to respond to letters from the tribunal;

but, before an order can be made, the defaulter must be given written notice of an intention to make the order. A time limit will be imposed on the defaulter to show cause why an order should not be made. If no representations are made that time limit, the claim or defence will be struck out (*Source*: ETCRP Regs 1993, Sch 1 Rule 13(2)(d), (e) & (f)).

27.41
Generally speaking, a 'striking-out' order for want of prosecution will not be made where:

- complex issues of law are involved and the public interest requires them to be resolved;
- the delay is not both inordinate and inexcusable;
- no serious prejudice is caused to the employer.

(*Evans, exec of & Another v Metropolitan Police Authority* [1992] IRLR 570, CA; and *Birkett v James* [1978] AC 297, HL.)

The object of the rule is to obtain compliance, not to punish. If there is no element of deliberate defiance, a striking out order is not appropriate (*National Grid Co plc v Virdee* [1992] IRLR 555, EAT). The fact that an employer has offered to pay the employee the maximum that a tribunal can award on a claim is not enough to obtain an order striking out the Originating Application. It would not be vexatious to allow the proceedings to continue. There would need to be an admission that the claim was well founded (*Telephone Information Services Ltd v Wilkinson* [1991] IRLR 148, EAT).

WITNESSES

27.42
Sometimes a witness is reluctant to appear for one side, and it may be essential that he or she attends. A party can apply for an order from the tribunal for the person to be directed to appear. Provided the tribunal is satisfied that efforts have been made to persuade the person to give evidence voluntarily but have failed and the evidence to be given is relevant, then an order will be made. A tribunal may make an order of its own motion where it thinks it appropriate

(*Source*: ETCRP Regs 1993, Sch 1 Rule 4(2)(a)). If a witness is, or is likely to be, hostile, no order will be issued. A party calling a witness cannot cross-examine that witness.

27.43

The full name and address of the witness must be provided. The order, when made, is generally sent by the tribunal to the person against whom it is drawn. There must be enough time to give him (or her) time not only to receive the order, but also to challenge the basis upon which attendance is required. If person in question claims that he (or she) cannot give any relevant evidence, or that if made to give evidence it would help the other side, it is probable that the order would be revoked.

ADJOURNMENTS

27.44

If proceedings on the same subject matter are taking place before both the High Court and an employment tribunal, a party to those proceedings may apply in writing to the tribunal for the case not to be listed for hearing before the decision in the High Court is given. If the other side does not oppose the application, the case will generally be adjourned *sine die*. A finding of fact in proceedings in either forum is binding on the other (*Jacobs v Norsalta Ltd* [1977] ICR 189, EAT).

27.45

There is generally a very long delay before proceedings are heard in the High Court, whereas they are heard and disposed of relatively quickly in the tribunals. It is sometimes in the interests of justice to proceed in the latter, where this is feasible. If an application to adjourn is resisted, a Hearing for Directions will normally be convened to decide what course to follow. Only a chairman will sit at such a hearing (*Mavity Gilmore Jaume Hill Brook FCA Ltd v Brooks*, 7 February 1991, EAT; and *First Castle Electronics Ltd v West* [1989] ICR 72, EAT).

27.46

In deciding whether to stay proceedings, the tribunal has to consider: 'In which court is this action most conveniently and appropriately to be tried bearing in mind all the surrounding circumstances (including the complexity of the issue), the amount involved, the technicality of the evidence, and the appropriateness of the procedures?' (*Bowater plc v Charlwood* [1991] ICR 798, EAT).

27.47
If an application for an adjournment is made at the commencement of a tribunal hearing, or during the hearing, but is opposed by the other party, then in the event of it being granted an order for costs (see paras 27.80 & 27.81) is likely to be made against the person obtaining the order. This could arise, for instance, if a witness fails to attend, through not having been told of the date set for the hearing (*Source*: ETCRP Regs 1993 Sch 1 Rule 12(4)).

27.48
An order *must* be made where the employer asks for the adjournment in a case where:

- the employee seeks reinstatement or re-engagement; or

- where the claim arises out of a failure to allow a woman to return to work following absence due to pregnancy or childbirth; and

- in each case the employer is unable to proceed because of his failure, without a special reason, to adduce evidence on the non-availability of the job.

(*Source*: ETCRP Regs 1993, Sch 1 Rule 12(5).)

27.49
Adjournments sought on the grounds that proceedings are currently taking place in the criminal courts will be granted if overall justice demands such a course. However, consideration will be given to the delay, the costs involved, the prejudice to the applicant and whether the same issue will have to be decided in both forums.

PRELIMINARY HEARING

27.50
Sometimes it is apparent from the information given in an Originating Application that the applicant employee's complaint will fail. For instance, it may appear that the applicant had not accrued

the necessary qualifying period of continuous employment to entitle him (or her) to present such a complaint. The tribunal will generally write to the applicant seeking further clarification. The employee may, for example, be able to show that his employment with a previous or 'associated' employer counts (or should count) towards his total period of continuous employment with his present (or former) employer; and that, in fact, he *has* accrued the necessary qualifying period of employment.

27.51
If the employer disputes any facts put forward by the employee, or he is able to show that there are other grounds that prevent an employee from pursuing his (or her) claim, then the tribunal would list the case for consideration on those preliminary points. The hearing would deal with that (or those) matter/s alone. If the applicant is successful, the case will proceed (probably later) to a hearing on its merits (*Source*: ETCRP Regs 1993, Sch 1 Rule 6(1)).

27.52
The procedure described above is very frequently used when an applicant has failed to present his (or her) Originating Application on time. The employee would have to prove, for example, on a complaint of unfair dismissal that it was not reasonably practicable to have presented the complaint within three months of the effective date of termination of the contract of employment but that it had been presented within a reasonable period thereafter. If the employee can satisfy the tribunal on the latter ground, the complaint will be heard (although it has to be said that complaints presented 'out of time' are not often accepted).

27.53
A preliminary hearing may take place to consider whether a claim for equal pay for work of equal value should be dismissed on the basis 'that there are no reasonable grounds for determining that the work *is* of equal value'. Or it may adjudicate on which persons should be included in a 'pool' for the purposes of comparing the sexes in considering whether there has been indirect discrimination (*Bromley & Others v H & J Quick Ltd* [1988] ICR 623, CA) (*Source*: EPA 1970, s. 2(A)(1)).

PRE-HEARING REVIEW

27.54

Some claims are *prima facie* bound to fail. For instance, a manager's complaint of unfair dismissal will almost certainly founder if he (or she) was sacked for secretly setting up a competitive company and using his employer's trade secrets. If the employee is determined to press ahead with the complaint – and he cannot normally be prevented from doing so – there would be an enormous waste of money, not only to the employer, but also to the public purse. To address this problem, the employment tribunals are empowered to conduct a 'pre-hearing review'. No evidence is called at such a hearing, but the parties may make submissions on their cases as presented in the documents, or on the agreed facts (*Source*: ETCRP Regs 1993, Sch 1 Rules 7 & 13(8)).

27.55

For instance, does the applicant accept that he (or she) *did* set up in business in direct competition with his employer using trade secrets or formulations obtained by him in the course of his employment. Does he not agree that he was sent to prison for stealing several thousand pounds from the office safe? What is it that he is disputing? What is the basis of his claim that his dismissal was unfair?

27.56

If the tribunal forms the view that an applicant employee's complaint has no reasonable prospect of success it may order the applicant to pay a deposit of up to £500 that would be forfeit if (as seems certain) he (or she) loses his case at the full tribunal hearing. However, in deciding the amount of any such deposit, the tribunal has to take reasonable steps to ascertain the ability of the party to pay that amount. The same rule applies to a hopeless defence, eg where an employee's dismissal has been manifestly unfair. The employer in that situation would similarly be required to put down a deposit. The deposit must be paid to the Central Office of the Employment Tribunals within 21 days, or within such further period as is allowed (following representations during that period) but not exceeding a further 14 days in all, eg 35 days. A failure to pay the deposit within the specified time limits will result in a striking out of the claim, or of all (or the relevant part) of a defence.

CONSENT ORDERS

27.57
Sometimes, in the course of a case, either at the interlocutory stage, or at a preliminary or full hearing, the parties will agree to 'settle out of court'. The claim will be formally dismissed on those agreed terms. Generally, a consent order, especially when made by a party who is (or has been) legally represented, cannot be later withdrawn and the complaint re-presented. It does not matter that, on further consideration of the agreed terms, one of the parties (usually the employee) feels aggrieved (*House of Fraser (Stores) Ltd v Davies*, 15 February 1990, EAT).

ACKNOWLEDGEMENT OF LIABILITY

27.58
Sometimes an employer realises that he is liable to pay at least some compensation to an employee, but the latter will not settle the claim. The employee either insists on having the matter disposed of at a full tribunal hearing, or alternatively makes wholly unreasonable demands. Unlike proceedings before the county court or High Court (see paras 27.93 & 27.97 below) there is no provision for a payment into court. The only procedure available in tribunal proceedings is for one of the parties (usually the employer) to make a 'without prejudice' offer in a letter (see Chapter 2, paras 2.51 to 2.54).

THE FULL TRIBUNAL HEARING

27.59
Ordinarily, the parties at a tribunal hearing are the employee (the 'applicant') and the employer (the 'respondent'). Where there are several employees pursuing claims against the same employer in respect of the same matter and the claims have been consolidated they all appear together, although each has the right to be heard separately. In practice, one person will usually speak for all.

27.60
The vast majority of employment tribunal hearings are (and must be) public hearings (anyone may attend, including the press). However, there are a number of exceptions to this rule. There is, for instance,

an exception if a Minister of the Crown has directed a tribunal to sit in private on grounds of national security or, if in the opinion of the tribunal itself, the evidence that it is about to hear relates to matters of such a nature that it would be against the interests of national security to allow that evidence to be given in public.

A tribunal hearing will also take place in private if the evidence to be presented is likely to consist of information that a person could not otherwise disclose without contravening a prohibition imposed by or under an enactment. The same applies if the evidence includes information communicated to a person in confidence or otherwise obtained in consequence of the confidence reposed in him (or her) by another person; or comprises information, the disclosure of which would cause substantial injury to the employer's business. For instance, the public disclosure of details about a diamond merchant's security arrangements would very likely have a most serious effect upon the employer's business (*CSO Valuations A G v Taylor*, EAT 105/93) (*Source*: ETCRP Regs 1993, Sch 1 Rule 8(2)).

27.61

An employment tribunal is empowered to conduct the proceedings with a view to the 'just handling' of the case. It can take some of the evidence in private and the rest in public. Further, being the master of its own procedure, it can take any reasonable course to enable the relevant facts to be elicited (*Kennedy v Commissioner of Police for the Metropolis, The Times*, 8 November 1990, EAT).

27.62

Each of the parties to the proceedings has the right to be represented by whomever he (or she) wishes. If represented by a lay person, it is as well to ensure that not only is that person familiar with the law and procedure but also knows how to conduct the case before the tribunal. Poor representation can prove to be a disaster (*Martin v British Railways Board* [1989] ICR 24, EAT).

27.63

It is permissible for either party not to be present at the hearing, but to make written representations instead. A copy of the statement (with exhibits attached) must be supplied to the other party, and to the tribunal, at least seven clear days before the hearing takes place. The tribunal does have power to abridge time in appropriate circumstances. Using this procedure is often fraught with danger because a tribunal can only come to a decision based on the evidence adduced. Some unforeseen point may have been overlooked (*Derrybaa Ltd t/a Le Mange Tout v Castro Blanco* [1986] ICR 546, EAT; and *Showmaster Ltd v Lawson*, 25 July 1990, EAT) (*Source*: ETCRP Regs 1993, Sch 1 Rules 8(5) & 13(2)(c)).

27.64

The person on whom the burden of proof lies (see Chapter 2, paras 2.16 to 2.20) has the right to present his (or her) case first. If he opens it, he should outline the principal events and their dates in summary form, going through the relevant exhibits where this is helpful. It must be borne in mind that the documents will generally speak for themselves. Opinions should be avoided as they tend to carry little weight. For instance, it is one thing to say: 'This applicant was very often late for work', which may mean different things to different people. It is a subjective point of view. Producing the relevant time sheets – showing the precise number of times the employee was late for work over a given period and how much working time was lost as a consequence of that late attendance – is much more potent. In short, those time sheets speak for themselves.

27.65

The litigant should call his (or her) witnesses, and get each to deal with the relevant events. It is best to obtain from each a 'proof of evidence'. This will enable a party to concentrate on the points that matter and remind him of what the witness should say. The other party to the proceedings will cross-examine the litigant's witnesses and should put to them any matters in dispute or elicit any other material facts. It is his (or her) duty to cross-examine 'a witness, on material parts of his evidence, if it is to be challenged,... so that not only the witness, [but also the other side may] have the chance to deal with it'. Failure to do so may result in a decision being overturned on appeal, and a rehearing ordered, perhaps at the expense of the party in default (*Batley plc v Jones*, 18 July 1988, EAT). When one party has finished calling all the evidence, the other side will call their witnesses in the same way and they too will be subject to cross-examination.

Restricted reporting orders

27.66

In any case that involves allegations of sexual misconduct (eg sexual harassment – as to which, see Chapter 11, paras 11.72 to 11.75), the employment tribunal may, at any time before promulgation of its decision in respect of an originating application, either on the application of a party (made by notice to the Secretary to the Tribunals, or of its own motion) make a *restricted reporting order*. A tribunal will not make a restricted reporting order unless it has given each party an opportunity to advance oral argument at a hearing.

A restricted reporting order may also be made in proceedings on a complaint under section 8 of the Disability Discrimination Act 1995, in which evidence of a personal nature is likely to be heard by the tribunal.

For so long as a restricted reporting order remains in force, the names (and addresses) of the persons specified in the order must not be made public (either by the media or by any other person). A copy of the order will be displayed on the notice board of the tribunal (with any list of the proceedings taking place before the tribunal) and on the door of the room in which the proceedings affected by the order are taking place (*Source*: ETCRP Regs 1993, Sch 1 Rule 14).

Bias

27.67

A party at a tribunal hearing, who believes that the tribunal is biased against him (or her), has the right to apply to the tribunal that it should disqualify itself from hearing the case further. If granted the tribunal would order that it be tried by another tribunal. Before such an order can be made, the other side must be given the opportunity to make representations. The test of bias is whether there is a real danger of injustice occurring as a result of the alleged prejudice, either conscious or unconscious. The mere appearance of bias is not enough (*R v Gough* [1993] AER 724, HL; and *Kennedy v Commissioner for the Metropolis, The Times*, 8 November 1990, EAT). It also matters not whether the alleged bias was for reasons unconnected with the merits of the issue. An objective test by the 'reasonable man' has to be applied. An appellate body has to consider all the evidence before coming to its own conclusions on the facts (*Reg. Inner West London Coroner, ex parte Dallaglio, The Times*, 16 June 1994, CA). A party who feels that there may be bias against him may be unaware that the way he is presenting a case is bound to cause annoyance, or that there is almost no basis upon which the action can succeed; hence the exasperation by the adjudicating body.

'Hearsay evidence'

27.68
When presenting evidence, it should be borne in mind that the strict rules about 'hearsay evidence' are not applied in the tribunals. Most of such evidence is admitted (except sometimes on a crucial point) and the tribunal will decide what weight to attach to it. It is obviously better to obtain as much 'primary evidence' as possible, ie the person who witnessed some event or overheard a conversation. It carries vastly more weight (*Coral Squash Clubs Ltd v Matthews & Arm* [1979] ICR 607, EAT) (*Source*: ETCRP Regs 1993, Sch 1 Rule 9(1)).

Summing-up

27.69
When all the evidence-giving is completed, each party is usually permitted to sum up its case before the tribunal – covering not only with the facts but also the relevant law. If case law is to be cited, it is best to provide the tribunal clerk with a list of the relevant cases ahead of the hearing. These can be obtained and considered in advance if necessary. The observations of Waite J (see also Chapter 28, para 28.21) should be borne in mind. In applying the law tribunals have to seek to 'penetrate [any] superficial disguise, to look to the form and not to the substance of the arrangements' in determining the true position between the parties. Unscrupulous persons should be discouraged from trying to circumvent the intention behind the legislation or express provisions contained in it (*Surrey CC v Lewis* [1986] ICR 404, EAT). This approach was approved by Lord Ackner on a final appeal to the House of Lords (*Surrey CC v Lewis* [1987] ICR 982, HL).

THE DECISION

27.70
After completion of the final speeches, the tribunal will retire to reflect on the matter and give its decision. If the tribunal is composed of three members, its decision may be taken by a majority. If a tribunal consists of two members only, the chairman will have a second or casting vote. Sometimes the tribunal will reserve its decision for further consideration – to be notified to the parties at a later date.

27.71
The decision of the tribunal (which may either be given verbally or reserved) will be recorded in a document signed by the chairman. The document will contain a statement as to whether the reasons are given in summary or extended form; and, where the tribunal has made an award of compensation or comes to any other determination, by virtue of which one party is required to pay a sum to the other (excluding an award of costs or allowances), the document will also contain a statement of the amount or of the sum required to be paid, followed by a table showing how the amount or sum was calculated or by a description of the way in which it was calculated.

27.72
Sometimes the decision will be given in full. But normally it will consist of a précis of the facts and the result. Later, the decision will be set out in a formal document. The reasons for the decision will be given in summary form except where:

- the proceedings involved the determination of an issue arising under (or relating to) the Equal Pay Act 1970, the Sex Discrimination Acts 1975 or 1986, the Race Relations Act 1976, or the Disability Discrimination Act 1995;

- one of the parties to the proceedings has made a verbal request (during the hearing itself) for the reasons to be given in extended form; or where such a request is made in writing after the hearing, either before any document recording the reasons in summary form is sent to the parties, or within 21 days of the date on which the document was sent to the parties; or

- the tribunal considers that reasons given in summary form would not sufficiently explain the grounds for its decision;

and in those circumstances, the reasons shall be given in extended form (*Source*: ETCRP Regs 1993, Sch 1 Rule 10(1) to (5)).

27.73

Once an oral decision has been given, or where a reserved decision has been sent to the parties, it is said to have been 'promulgated' and becomes binding on the parties. Any clerical mistake in the documents recording the decision or giving reasons for the decision (including errors arising from an accidental slip or omission) may be corrected at any time by the chairman who will sign and issue a 'certificate of correction', a copy of which will be sent to each of the parties and, if the proceedings had been referred to that tribunal by a court, to that court (*Spring Grove Service Group plc v Hickinbottom, The Times*, 25 October 1989, EAT) (*Source*: ETCRP Regs 1993, Sch 1 Rules 10(5), 10(9) & (11)).

27.74

The full decision of the tribunal does not have to be the product of fine legal draughtsmanship, but it must be sufficiently informative to enable the parties to know why they have won or lost. The decision will normally outline the facts leading up to the complaint and, where there is a conflict on a basic point, it will state which point of view it prefers. There is no duty on a tribunal to analyse all the facts and arguments, nor to state its reasons for accepting or rejecting every disputed fact, especially where the conclusions rest on credibility (*Meek v City of Birmingham DC* [1987] IRLR 250, CA; *Palmer v British Railways Board*, 14 December 1990, EAT; and *B v K & Another*, 17 March 1994, EAT) (*Source*: ETCRP Regs 1993 Sch 1 Rule 10(4)).

27.75

In coming to its decision, the tribunal is entitled to consider matters that it considers important, even though the parties had not placed much significance on them. It is also entitled to pay attention to the extent to which a point has or has not been relied on by a party during a hearing (*Neale v Hereford & Worcester CC* [1986] ICR 471, CA). But this is subject to the overriding consideration that each side must be given the opportunity to argue any point that may not have been raised, but which the tribunal considers to be important.

Effect of a decision

27.76

Generally, once a tribunal has decided an issue in the proceedings, eg that the applicant employee was indeed an employee, or that his (or her) summary dismissal was justified by reason of gross misconduct, that determination of fact is binding on every other tribunal and court. But the other proceedings must be between the same parties. It is said to be *res judicata* or that there is an 'issue estoppel'. It cannot be rescinded except on appeal (*Munir & Farooqi v Jang Publications Ltd* [1989] ICR 1, CA; and *Crawford & Crawford v Salveson*, 14 May 1990, EAT).

27.77

It does not matter that the tribunal was wrong in their interpretation of the law, or that an order made was improper in the circumstances. All other courts and tribunals are bound by that decision, except where there are special circumstances. This could arise, for instance, where a judge or chairman has made a mistake on the material at his (or her) disposal, eg if the date on a document vital to the proceedings had been misread (*O'Laoire v Jackel International Ltd (No.2)* [1991] ICR 718, CA; and *Arnold & Others v National Westminster Bank plc*, *The Times*, 26 April 1991, HL).

27.78

The recording of an agreement between the parties by a tribunal in a decision for a redundancy payment does not imply *per se* that it is a statutory redundancy payment (*Secretary of State for Employment v Cheltenham Computers Bureau Ltd* [1985] ICR 381, EAT). On the other hand a finding of fact, for instance, that an employee was late arriving for work on six occasions, not ten (as alleged by the other party), may be different. It will be based on the evidence laid before a tribunal. If there are further proceedings before another tribunal, other evidence may be produced that will irrefutably show that the finding was wrong.

27.79

A finding of fact made in a test case that the wages of a (comparator) employee had been 'red circled' (ie frozen) may be used in a related case to determine whether that case would be bound to fail. A decision to strike out such a claim on the basis that it was 'vexatious' (see para 27.40 above) was upheld on appeal (*Ashmore v British Coal Corporation* [1990] ICR 485, CA).

COSTS

27.80
This has been a ticklish subject for a long time because many undeserving claims are brought and some unmeritorious defences made. If it is shown that a party has acted 'frivolously, vexatiously, abusively, disruptively or otherwise unreasonably', an order for costs may be made (*Source*: ETCRP Regs 1993, Sch 1 Rule 12(1)). The order may be made in respect of the bringing or conducting of the proceedings. A party who is unduly prolix in the presentation of his (or her) case is at risk. If an adjournment is sought in the middle of proceedings because of some failure, that too would be likely to attract an order for costs. There is an upper limit of £500 where a tribunal makes a fixed order, unless the parties agree a higher figure. The tribunal may direct that the costs be taxed in the county court, in which case they are likely to exceed £500 (*Source*: ETCRP Regs 1993, Sch 1 Rule 12(1) & 12(3)).

27.81
The mere fact that a complaint has been dismissed does not of itself provide grounds for saying that it was brought unreasonably. There has to be some degree of 'pig-headedness' about prosecuting the case before an order for costs will be made. Even where an order *is* made, it has to be tailored to the ability of the party to comply with it (*Carr v Allen Bradley Electronics Ltd* [1980] ICR 603, EAT). Thus, if a former employee is out of work, has no capital and is living on social security, it would be unlikely that a tribunal would make an award of costs exceeding £100. If the amount remains unpaid, the other party can recover the amount in question through the County court. This may turn out to be more expensive than the sum ultimately recovered. An application for costs must be made either at the hearing, or within a reasonable time after it. If the tribunal's decision is reserved, the party seeking costs must do so reasonably promptly after received the reserved decision (*Colin Johnson v Baxter* [1985] IRLR 96, EAT).

EXPENSES

27.82
The tribunal pays litigants and witnesses an allowance for loss of earnings (up to a certain amount), as well as an attendance allowance (again within prescribed limits). A tribunal can order that payment be withheld against a party, if the complaint should not have been brought or for any related reason. Professional advisers, representatives of employers' organisations and trade union officials are not entitled to be paid for their attendance at the hearing (*Source*: ETCRP Regs 1993, Sch 1 Rule 12).

REVIEW OF A TRIBUNAL'S DECISION

27.83
A tribunal has the power, on the application of one or other of the parties, or of its own motion, to review any decision on the grounds that:

- the decision was wrongly made as a result of an error on the part of the tribunal staff;

- a party did not receive notice of the proceedings leading to the decision;

- the decision was made in the absence of a party;

- new evidence has become available since the conclusion of the hearing to which the decision relates, provided that its existence could not have been reasonably known of, or foreseen, at the time of the hearing; or

- the interests of justice require such a review.

A tribunal may not review a decision of its own motion unless it is the tribunal that issued the decision.

(*Source*: ETCRP Regs 1993, Sch 1 Rule 11(1) & (2).)

27.84
The chairman has power to refuse an application for a 'review' if he (or she) thinks that it has no reasonable chance of success. He must inform the parties (within 14 days after promulgation) that he is of

the opinion that the tribunal had made a mistake, inviting them (if they so wish) to show cause why there should not be a review (*Casella London Ltd v Banai* [1990] ICR 215, EAT) (*Source*: ETCRP Regs 1993, Sch 1 Rule 11(3)&(5)). What a disabused party cannot do is use the 'interests of justice' provision to re-litigate a case. The procedure can only be invoked to repair an error of jurisdiction or a defect of process or the technical correctness of a decision. If a party feels that there has otherwise been an error of law, the appropriate course would be to appeal (*Blockleys plc v Miller* [1992] ICR 749, EAT).

27.85
If a party claims that there is new evidence that he (or she) could not have known about at the time of the proceedings, or that the party could not have unearthed with reasonable diligence, or have reasonably foreseen to be important, he must send a copy of the written statement provided by the person who is to give further evidence to the tribunal. It is for the chairman to decide whether the full tribunal should be reconvened to consider the application for a review (*Borden (UK) Ltd v Potter* [1986] ICR 647, EAT; and *Vauxhall Motors Ltd v Henry* [1978] ITR 332, EAT).

27.86
Further, although the chairman has a wide power to order a review, it is one that has to be exercised cautiously. The interests of all parties must be considered. 'Failings of a party's representatives (professional or otherwise), will not generally constitute grounds for review. That is a dangerous path to follow. It involves the risk of encouraging a disappointed applicant to seek to re-argue his case by blaming his representative for the failure of his claim. That may involve the tribunal in inappropriate investigations into the competence of the representative... If there is a justified complaint... that may be the subject of other proceedings' (*Ironside Ray & Vials v Lindsay*, 20 January 1994, EAT).

27.87
A tribunal chairman has power to refuse an application for a review if he (or she) thinks that it has no reasonable chance of success. Where appropriate, he may cause the parties to be informed that he believes that the tribunal has made a mistake and enquire whether one or other of them wishes to apply for a review (*Casella London Ltd v Banai* [1990] ICR 215, EAT). An application for a review may be

made by one of the parties at the hearing itself or (if not then) within 14 days of the promulgation of the relevant decision, although there is power to extend time in the appropriate circumstances (*Source*: ETCRP Regs 1993, Sch 1 Rule 11(4)).

27.88

The rules allow a review of a declaration, a recommendation, and an order, including a striking-out order, but not, it would seem, of an interlocutory order. It matters not whether it is described as a 'Decision' (*Nikitas v Metropolitan Borough of Solihull* [1986] ICR 291, EAT). In determining whether a ruling is interlocutory, '... regard must be had to the nature of the application made... An order is not final unless it would have finally determined the proceedings whichever way the application... had been decided. Thus... an order striking out... is interlocutory, because, had the court below decided the matter the other way, the action would have continued' (*Salter Rex & Co v Ghosh* [1971] 2 QB 597, HC).

27.89

On reviewing its decision, a tribunal may confirm the decision, or vary or revoke the decision under the chairman's hand. If it revokes the decision, the tribunal will order a re-hearing before either the same or a differently constituted tribunal (*Source*: ETCRP Regs 1993, Sch 1 Rule 11(7)).

ENFORCEMENT OF AWARDS

27.90

All monetary awards from a tribunal are enforceable in the county court. If a party fails to make payment then a plaint may be taken out in the County court, lodging with it a copy of the decision. If the party still refuses (or fails) to pay, judgment can be obtained and, if necessary, bailiffs can be sent to seize assets to the appropriate value. Any other declaration or order cannot be enforced save as provided under the statutory provisions. An order for reinstatement or re-engagement cannot be specifically enforced. The only remedy open to an aggrieved employee who has not been reinstated or re-engaged is to apply to the tribunal for an additional award of compensation for breach of the order. If the award of compensation is not paid, the aggrieved party may bring proceedings for recovery in the county court.

THE COUNTY COURT

General information

27.91
The County court and its powers are derived from statute. The court is presided over by a circuit judge who sits on his (or her) own, although assessors can sit with the judge in special cases. A district judge also sits there and deals with smaller claims and with interlocutory work. All civil actions start there where the claim does not exceed £50,000, although some may be transferred to the High Court if they are particularly difficult.

27.92
Proceedings before the County court are conducted in a formal way, although there are many litigants who are (or choose not to be) represented. The judge has to try to unravel the relevant facts before applying the law. Unlike the conduct of proceedings before an employment tribunal, the rule concerning the admissibility of 'hearsay' evidence in the County court is strictly applied. The witnesses must be present in the court if the case is to be proved. There are also strict rules regarding discovery and inspection of documents. Also, unlike the tribunals, the loser in a County court action generally has to pay his (or her) own and the other party's costs, regardless of his ability to pay, unless protected by a legal aid certificate (in which case, the loser's liability will generally be limited to his maximum contribution to the legal aid certificate).

Payment into court

27.93
Sometimes a party acknowledges that he (or she) is liable to make some payment to the other side. A settlement cannot be reached because the other party is being unreasonable. There is a procedure by which he can make a payment into court up to the amount of the perceived liability. If such a payment is made, the other side have to make up their minds whether to accept or reject the money paid in. If the other side accept the money, they are entitled to their costs up to that point. If they decline and, in the subsequent action, recover less

than the amount paid in, they will have to pay all the costs incurred after the payment into court.

27.94
It is possible sometimes to make a 'without prejudice' offer to settle a case. This is dealt with in Chapter 2 (at paras 2.51 to 2.54).

Legal aid

27.95
Legal aid is available, not only for advice but also for representation in court. A party's means have to be assessed first. If they come within the approved range he (or she) will be granted a legal aid certificate, subject to a contribution that will be assessed.

27.96
The county court has no power to deal with claims over £50,000 unless both parties agree that the jurisdiction of the court should be enlarged. Otherwise, a party found to be entitled to a judgment over that amount will be unable to recover the difference. The court enforces its own judgments as well as those of the tribunals. It matters not that the amount being recovered in respect of an action before a tribunal exceeds its jurisdiction.

THE HIGH COURT

General information

27.97
The High Court is presided over by a High Court judge who sits alone. High Court rules regarding 'hearsay evidence', discovery of documents (and so forth) are strictly applied. They otherwise follow, in the main, those applicable in the county court. There is no restriction on the High Court's jurisdiction. Furthermore, unlike the County court, the powers of a High Court judge are derived not only from statutes but also from its 'inherent' jurisdiction, that is to say, from the Sovereign. The procedure for making payment into court is the same as in the county court (see para 27.93 above).

27.98

The High Court is not a place for the uninitiated. Litigants should obtain professional help. There are not only difficulties in conducting a case in the correct way but great risks regarding costs. Costs are awarded against the loser, and they can be extremely high on occasions.

Legal aid

27.99

Legal aid is available in High Court actions, not only for advice but also for representation. If a party loses, he (or she) will generally only have to pay costs limited to the amount of his legal aid contribution. It is strongly recommended that the legal aid facility be used.

28

Appeal courts and procedure

EMPLOYMENT APPEAL TRIBUNAL (EAT)

General information

28.1
An appeal lies to the Employment Appeal Tribunal (EAT) *on any question of law* arising from any decision of (or arising in any proceedings before) an employment tribunal under, or by virtue of:

- the Equal Pay Act 1970;

- the Sex Discrimination Act 1975;

- the Race Relations Act 1976;

- the Trade Union & Labour Relations (Consolidation) Act 1992;

- the Disability Discrimination Act 1995;

- the Employment Rights Act 1996;

- the National Minimum Wage Act 1998;

- the Tax Credits Act 1999;

- the Employment Tribunals Act 1996; or

- the Working Time Regulations 1998.

An appeal to the EAT also lies from a refusal of the Certification Officer to issue a trade union with a certificate of independence, or by a decision of his (or hers) to withdraw its certificate (*Source*: ETA 1996, s. 21; and TULRA 1992, s. 9).

The rules of procedure for the EAT are to be found in the Employment Appeal Tribunal Rules 1993 (SI 1993/2854) (hereinafter referred to as EAT Rules 1993).

28.2

This right extends to appeals against interlocutory orders (eg an order for the discovery of documents). But in such a case it must be shown that a tribunal (or chairman) has exercised its discretion on wrong principles (*Medallion Holidays Ltd v Birch* [1985] ICR 578, EAT).

Composition of EAT

28.3

Proceedings before the EAT are presided over by a High Court or Court of Appeal judge accompanied by two or four *appointed* members, 'so that in either case there is an equal number of persons whose knowledge or experience of industrial relations is as representatives of employers, and of persons whose knowledge or experience of industrial relations is as representatives of workers'.

With the consent of the parties to the appeal, proceedings before the EAT may be heard by a judge and one appointed member, or by a judge and three appointed members. However, appeal proceedings on a question arising from any decision of (or arising in any proceedings before) an employment tribunal – which consisted of a tribunal chairman sitting alone (see Chapter 27, para 27.7) – shall be heard by a judge sitting alone, unless a judge directs that the appeal proceedings should be heard by a judge and one or three appointed members. In matters affecting national security, a minister of the Crown may direct that the appeal be heard by the President of the Appeal Tribunal alone. (*Source*: ETA 1996, s. 28).

28.4

The definition of 'law' and 'fact', so as to enable an appeal court to intervene, has been the subject of much judicial debate. Lord Radcliffe put it this way: '... I think that it is a question of law what meaning is to be given to the words of the Income Tax Act: "trade, manufacture, adventure or concern in the nature of trade" and for that matter what constitutes "profits or gains" arising from it. Here we have a statutory phrase involving a charge of tax, and it is for the courts to interpret its meaning, having regard to the context in which it occurs and to the principles which they bring to bear upon the meaning of income... In effect it lays down the limits within which it would be permissible to say a "trade" as interpreted... does or does not exist. But the field so marked out is a wide one and there are many combinations of circumstances in which it could not be said to be wrong to arrive at a conclusion one way or the other'.

All these cases in which the facts warrant a determination either way can be described as questions of degree and therefore as questions of fact' (*Edwards [Inspector of Taxes] v Bairstow & Another* [1956] AC 14, HL).

28.5

The consequence is that, where there are two cases with very similar facts, then two differently constituted tribunals can reach different decisions, neither of which can be overturned on appeal. This type of situation frequently arises in disputes over whether a person is an 'employee' or a 'self-employed' person (*O'Kelly v Trusthouse Forte plc* [1983] ICR 708, CA; and *Four Seasons (Inns on the Park) Ltd v Hamaret*, 17 April 1985, EAT).

28.6

A 'point of law' generally arises in the following circumstances:

- where the tribunal has made an error in law. This could arise, for instance, where it has ruled that it has power to make a redundancy award when the applicant employee presented his (or her) claim some 12 months after the effective date of termination of the employment. There is no power to make an award where the claim is that length 'out of time';

- where there is no evidence to support an important finding of fact that appears to form the basis of the tribunal's decision. For instance, if a tribunal were to make a finding that an employee had been warned on five occasions about his (or her) conduct before being dismissed and that consequently the dismissal was fair in the circumstances, whereas the evidence given was that it was another worker who had received the warnings, and the employee who was dismissed had never received any warnings, let alone five, then a decision based on such erroneous facts would be palpably wrong;

- where there has been a failure to take a material factor into account. An example of this occurred in a case where a tribunal failed to follow an authority binding on it. It should have taken into account a previous written warning that had been given to an employee for another kind of misconduct. The weight to be attached to it depended on the circumstances (*Auguste Noel Ltd v Curtis* [1990] IRLR 326, EAT);

- where the decision was 'perverse', that is to say, one which no reasonable tribunal could have reached. In effect, the decision would raise the reaction 'My goodness, that was certainly wrong', because the agreed evidence pointed in the opposite direction (*Chiu v British Aerospace plc* [1982] IRLR 56, EAT; and *Neale v Hereford & Worcester CC* [1986] ICR 471, CA);

- where there is clear evidence of bias by the tribunal (or by any of its members). This is difficult to prove. An aggrieved party with a particularly bad or unmeritorious case is unlikely to get far on an appeal. But if a view has been expressed during the hearing indicative of bias, then a fresh hearing will be ordered (*Walker, Laird, Heron & Harper v Marshall*, 2 June 1989, EAT).

In deciding whether a decision is 'perverse', it is not sufficient that the EAT would certainly have come to a different conclusion. They must be left in the position of having to rule that no reasonable tribunal could have reached that decision. This is because there are many factors that affect the minds of those adjudicating (*Piggott Brother & Co Ltd v Jackson & Others* [1992] ICR 85, CA).

28.7
The lay (industrial) members of the EAT are expected to apply their expertise in industrial relations matters to determine what failures have been made by either of the parties to the appeal. They will consider what more might have been done by the parties, before deciding whether the decision of the tribunal that heard the case was perverse (*East Berkshire Health Authority v Matadeen* [1992] ICR 723, EAT).

28.8
If all the relevant information is derived from documents alone, the decision is purely one of law. The appeal court can intervene if the tribunal or a lower court have erred. But where it depends partly on documents and partly on evidence, then it is a mixed issue of law and fact. There can only be intervention if there has been some misdirection (*Clifford v Union of Democratic Workers* [1991] IRLR 518, CA).

28.9

It is in the matter of an alleged failure to take a material factor into account that most confusion generally occurs. Many litigants feel that their story is right, and they find it difficult to understand how a reasonable tribunal could have believed the other side.

28.10

If there was credible evidence to support the tribunal's findings then the EAT will (or should) not interfere. An appellate court must be able to identify a finding of fact made by the tribunal that was unsupported by any evidence or find that there has been a clear misdirection in law (*Piggott Brother & Co Ltd v Jackson & Others* [1992] ICR 85, CA).

28.11

The fact that a tribunal's evaluation of the relevant materials leads to a different conclusion to that of another tribunal on the same or similar facts is not in itself grounds for interfering. This point is particularly pertinent where, for instance, a tribunal has to decide whether a casual worker is an employee, or who is correctly the employer.

28.12

Except in very rare circumstances, an issue must have been raised before the employment tribunal before it can be re-argued on appeal. A complaint had been made before a tribunal that an employee had been unfairly selected for redundancy because of his work performance and experience. He was not allowed to argue on appeal that it was unfair because of a failure to consult him or warn him about the impending redundancy (*Duncan & Others v Wallacetown Engineering Ltd*, 6 May 1986, EAT; and *Jones v R M Douglas Construction Ltd* [1979] ICR 278, EAT).

28.13

It does not matter that a failure to put a conclusive point arose through the incompetence of an advocate. A litigant's remedy in such circumstances is against the representative himself (or herself) and not against the other party (*Lindsay v Ironside Ray & Vials* [1994] IRLR 318, EAT).

28.14

But a well known exception to the rule exists on the issue of jurisdiction. The latter can be raised at any stage in the proceedings.

Indeed an appellate court will not only take the point itself, but is bound to do so once brought to its attention. It will then act on that fact (*House v Emerson Electric Industrial Controls* [1980] ICR 795, EAT; and *Sheikh v Anderton*, 21 March 1989, CA). Where jurisdiction had not been raised in the tribunal below but there is a chance of establishing lack of jurisdiction before the EAT by calling fresh evidence (that had always been available), the position becomes more difficult. Generally, the EAT will *not* remit a case back to the same or a differently constituted tribunal in a situation in which an employer, who had failed to put his case on one basis, then wished to 'change tack' by alleging lack of jurisdiction (*Barber v Thames TV plc* [1992] ICR 661, CA).

A worker has no need to resign in order to pursue his (or her) statutory rights before an employment tribunal.

28.15
If an employment tribunal makes a finding of fact based on its assessment of the credibility of witnesses, eg if it said that it 'preferred' the evidence given by 'A' rather than that given by 'B', where the lay members had relied on their experience of industrial relations, it is extremely rare that the EAT will reverse the tribunal's decision. Stephenson, LJ in an appeal on a contributory fault point said: 'In a question which is obviously a matter of opinion and discretion, as is this kind of apportionment of responsibility, there must be either a plain error of law, or something like perversity, to entitle an appellate tribunal to interfere...' (*Hollier v Plysu Ltd* [1983] IRLR 260, CA).

28.16
Sir John Donaldson, MR, (as he was then) put it this way: 'It was very important to remember that where a right of appeal was confined to questions of law, the appellate tribunal has loyally to accept the findings of fact with which it was presented and, where it was convinced that it would have reached a different conclusion of fact, it has to resist the strong temptation to treat findings of fact as holdings of law or mixed findings of fact and law. The correct approach involved a recognition that Parliament had constituted the industrial tribunal the only tribunal of fact and that conclusions of fact had to be accepted unless it was apparent that, on the evidence,

no reasonable tribunal could have reached them' (*Martin v Glynwood Distributors Ltd* [1983] ICR 511, CA).

28.17
The appeal courts discourage litigants from searching around in a decision with a fine tooth comb to find grounds of appeal. A decision is not expected to record all the findings of fact or to contain a detailed analysis of the evidence but merely to give the findings in broad terms (*Retarded Children Aid Society v Day* [1978] ICR 437, CA; and *Kearney & Trecker Marwin Ltd v Varndell* [1983] IRLR 335, CA).

28.18
It is permissible for a tribunal in mid-hearing to give a preliminary view of the case. This must be for the purpose of saving time or promoting a settlement; but such a course has to be exercised with care. It should be made clear that no concluded view has or would be taken until all the evidence is heard and until the parties have made their submissions. A failure to do so is likely to result in the decision being set aside, on the grounds that justice must not only be done but seen to be done (*Ellis v Ministry of Defence* [1985] ICR 257, EAT).

28.19
In a case before the Court of Appeal, certain evidence was unchallenged and was crucial in that it provided a proper and adequate reason for the dismissal of a member of staff. A failure by the tribunal to record in their decision that the evidence in question *had* been considered before holding that the dismissal was unfair, was held to indicate that they had either overlooked that evidence or, if they had not done so, that their decision was perverse (*United Counties Omnibus Ltd v Amin*, 20 January 1986, CA).

28.20
If a tribunal has misdirected itself on the law but has nevertheless reached the correct decision, the EAT will not overturn the decision – provided it is satisfied that 'the verdict of the tribunal was plainly and unarguably right' (*Dobie v Burns International Security (UK) Ltd* [1984] ICR 812, CA).

28.21
The EAT is generally bound by precedent, even when a decision is given by another division of the EAT. There are several exceptions,

but usually it can find distinguishing features in an appeal to enable it to come to another view. Hence, it is unwise to rely on other cases too much. They may hold the day, but a party can come unstuck. Waite J succinctly put the point in this way: 'Sometimes the judgment in a particular case will be found to express in concise and helpful language some concept which was regularly found in this field of inquiry and it becomes of great illustrative value. But reference to such a case could never be a substitute for taking the explicit directions of the statute as the guiding principle' (*Anandaraja v Lord Chancellors Dept* [1984] IRLR 131, EAT).

Bias

28.22
Many a litigant whose complaint has been dismissed by an employment tribunal will feel that the tribunal was biased against him (or her). To overturn a decision on this ground, it is not sufficient to rely on perceptions. A person who is aggrieved by a decision that goes against him may seek a rehearing before a fresh tribunal. He could perhaps present his case in a better way. The test of bias is explained in Chapter 27, para 27.67; but is very difficult to prove on an appeal (*R v Gough, The Times*, 24 May 1993, HL; and *Kennedy v Commissioner of Police for the Metropolis, The Times*, 8 November 1991, EAT).

When further evidence may be given

28.23
The general rule is that on an appeal to the EAT, no further evidence may be advanced. An exception lies:

- where it was not known that additional evidence existed at the time of the tribunal hearing; and

- that it is credible and likely to have an important influence on the result; and

- that the evidence could not reasonably have been unearthed at the time.

(*Howard v NGA* [1985] ICR 101, CA; and *Ladd v Marshall* [1954] 1 WLR 1489, CA.)

28.24

But the EAT will not permit a disaffected party to take advantage of its discretion by allowing him (or her) to re-litigate his case again. The power is exercised in only the most exceptional circumstances (*Saunders v Bakers Food & Allied Workers Union* [1986] ICR 28, EAT).

28.25

An employee claimed that he had not worked since his dismissal and was awarded compensation on that basis. The employer later learnt that in fact he did have a job at the time of the hearing. It was held that further evidence on it could be adduced (*Bagga v Heavy Electricals (India) Ltd* [1972] ICR 118, NIRC). It should be borne in mind that, in the instance quoted (and in many like it), the employer could have applied to the tribunal for a review of its decision (see Chapter 27, paras 27.83 to 27.89). On those different facts, the tribunal might be persuaded to amend the previous award of compensation. In most cases, this would be a better and cheaper course to follow (*Trimble v Supertravel Ltd* [1982] ICR 240, EAT).

Desirability of representation

28.26

It should be borne in mind that legal representation before the EAT is likely to be essential if only because an appeal from the decision of an employment tribunal may be brought only on a point of law, which will almost certainly require a substantial knowledge of the law and the ability to research related case law. It is also important to be able to argue a legal point with conviction. The law is no longer simple, and the 'common law' (reviewed in Chapter 8) will often be brought to bear on a problem involving the interpretation of statute law.

28.27

Legal aid is available for representation before the EAT, as well as advice. Eligible litigants are strongly advised to make use of it. Alternatively, a lawyer should be instructed privately where possible. Only about 25 per cent of appeals to the EAT are wholly or partly successful. There is no point in embarking on an appeal, with all the consequent expense, unless there is a reasonable chance of success.

Costs

28.28

Costs can be, and are awarded, by the EAT where it finds that the proceedings before it were 'unnecessary, improper or vexatious, or... there has been... other unreasonable conduct...' (*Source*: EAT Rules 1993, Rule 34). Strong feelings in the justice of a litigant's case are not enough. There have to be valid grounds upon which the EAT can intervene. A suggestion that a tribunal was biased will not find a sympathetic ear if the evidence shows that their decision could be right.

28.29

An employer appealed against a tribunal decision that an employee had been unfairly dismissed. He also appealed against an order for costs. The tribunal had found that there was no evidence to support the employer's contentions. The EAT, in dismissing their appeal, made an order for a further £500 costs on the basis that the appeal raised issues of fact rather than law (*Rock plc v Fairbrother*, 11 February 1986, EAT).

Time limits

28.30

An appeal to the EAT against a decision of (or order by) an employment tribunal must be lodged within 42 days of promulgation of that decision (or order) (*Source*: EAT Rules 1993, Rule 3(2)). The time limits still apply where a party has applied to the tribunal for a review of its decision (see Chapter 27, paras 27.83 to 27.89). A party is entitled to appeal and apply for a review at the same time, and should do so if he (or she) wants to preserve his rights in respect of each. Although the EAT has power to extend the time for lodging an appeal, it is only rarely exercised (*Source*: EAT Rules 1993, Rule 37(1)).

THE HIGH COURT

General information

28.31

The High Court, when it sits as the 'Divisional Court' has an appellate jurisdiction. It hears appeals from the tribunals and magistrates' courts relating to decisions given on health and safety at work cases and also those concerning the imposition or amount of a training levy (not otherwise discussed in this handbook).

28.32
Like the EAT, the High Court can only interfere where the tribunal or inferior court has gone wrong on a point of law and not whether they would have taken a different view had they tried the case themselves.

THE COURT OF APPEAL

General information

28.33
A further appeal is possible from the EAT, to the Court of Appeal, on a 'point of law' only. This could arise in two ways. First, the EAT might have gone wrong in interpreting a section of an Act. Second, they might have reversed a tribunal on a 'point of law' that was in fact one of 'fact', and where they had no power to intervene.

28.34
The approach of the Court of Appeal is to consider, not so much whether the EAT went wrong, but whether the original tribunal decision was right (*Adlington & Others v British Bakeries (Northern) Ltd* [1989] IRLR 218, CA).

28.35
The Court of Appeal is generally composed of three Lord Justices of Appeal, although, occasionally only two will sit. Before the Court of Appeal will adjudicate in any case, leave to appeal must have been granted by the EAT. The Court of Appeal itself will sometimes give leave where this has been refused by the EAT.

Desirability of representation

28.36
Although strictly entitled to appear before the Court of Appeal on his (or her) own behalf, it is important that a litigant be represented by counsel and solicitors. An unqualified individual may not, in any

event, conduct an appeal on behalf of a company or others. A litigant appearing on his own behalf would need to be extremely knowledgeable and be able to present his case with great skill, otherwise his appearance is likely to be a disaster. Not only may he lose his case but he may also be ordered to pay the other side's costs. The Lord Justices are extremely busy and deal mostly with points of great principle. They do not suffer fools gladly.

Costs

28.37
Contrary to the position in the tribunals below, costs in the Court of Appeal are always awarded against the loser, except in very rare circumstances. If a litigant has a legal aid certificate, then his (or her) liability for an order for costs is generally limited to the maximum amount of his contribution to legal aid.

THE HOUSE OF LORDS

General information

28.38
A final appeal is possible from the Court of Appeal to the House of Lords in respect of any matter of great public importance. Only the Court of Appeal can certify that the matter is of such importance and grant leave to appeal. If it is refused, an application can be made to the Judicial Committee of the House of Lords who can decree that the case may proceed.

28.39
This is no place for amateurs in the House of Lords and great learning is required to present an appeal. A litigant may appear in person if acting on his (or her) own behalf, but is generally strongly discouraged unless he has considerable knowledge of the law and an expertise acquired over a great many years.

28.40
Legal aid *is* available for representation, but, as in the Court of Appeal, the loser pays the other party's costs.

THE EUROPEAN COURT OF JUSTICE (ECJ)

General information

28.41
The ECJ can only entertain claims referred to it by one of the UK's own judicial bodies, or where one Member State of the European Community takes proceedings against another. After certain formalities, the European Commission (see Chapter 1, para 1.68) may allow a claim by an individual to proceed there.

28.42
A reference to the ECJ may be made by a judge where it is considered that the interpretation of the Treaty of Rome is necessary to enable him (or her) to give a judgment in a case before him. The judge must refer it where a question is raised under Community law and there is no appeal against his decision under UK domestic legislation (Articles 177 & 177 (3)).

28.43
The procedure for presenting claims (which is elaborate), is laid down in the Treaty 'Protocols'. Written proceedings are followed by oral hearings, after which an 'Advocate General' will state his (or her) opinion. Months later, the court's verdict will be given, which will usually accord with the views expressed by the Advocate General. The ECJ will only adjudicate on the interpretation of the Treaty and gives general guidance, leaving it to a Member State's domestic courts to apply that interpretation to a particular case. The Court tends to follow its own previous decisions, although it is not bound to do so (*Worringham & Another v Lloyds Bank plc* [1981] ICR 558, ECJ; [1982] ICR 299, CA).

THE EUROPEAN COURT OF HUMAN RIGHTS (ECHR)

General information

28.44
The European Court of Human Rights Court (ECHR) (which is composed of judges from each of the EU Member States) sits in Strasbourg. The Court adjudicates in disputes between an individual

litigant and a country (such as the UK) that is a signatory to the *European Convention on Human Rights and Fundamental Freedoms* (which latter has since been given 'further effect' in the UK by the Human Rights Act 1998 – which came into force on 2 October 2000, as to which, please turn to Chapter 26).

28.45

A litigant does have direct access to the ECHR, but before any claim is accepted, it must be lodged with the Commission set up by the Council of Europe whose role is to vet the claim to ensure that it is admissible. A claim will be admissible if:

- all domestic remedies have been exhausted;

- the proceedings before it have been taken within six months of the final adjudication in a UK court;

- it relates to a right guaranteed by the Convention.

If the Commission finds that the complaint is admissible, it will try to bring about a 'friendly settlement' between the litigant and the Member State in question. If it fails to do so, it will draft a report setting out the facts and its opinion whether the Convention has been a violated.

28.46

The case will then be referred to the Committee of Ministers of the Council of Europe who will make a decision on it, unless the Commission or the State concerned refer it to the court. Unlike the European Court of Justice, the decisions of the ECHR are not enforceable in the signatory countries. However, they carry great moral force and there is a duty on a State to ensure that its laws conform to any rulings given.

28.47

It was a result of a judgment given in respect of the three railwaymen, who were denied employment in British Rail because they refused to continue their membership of a union, that the legislation relating to the closed shop was revoked. The ECHR had ruled that the existing provisions breached Article 11 of the Convention that guaranteed the freedom of association (*Young & Others v United Kingdom* [1981] IRLR 408, ECHR). The same principle was held to apply to a taxi-driver who was required to be a member of a specific organisation for taxicab operators. The effect of this ruling is likely to be far-reaching (*Sigurjonsson v Iceland, The Times,* 27 July 1993 ECHR).

Index